A Handbook for Travellers in Switzerland, the Alps of Savoy and Piedmont, the Italian Lakes, and Part of Dauphiné – Primary Source Edition

John Murray

HANDBOOK

FOR

TRAVELLERS IN SWITZERLAND,
THE ALPS OF SAVOY AND PIEDMONT,
THE ITALIAN LAKES,
AND PART OF DAUPHINÉ.

The Editor of the HANDBOOK for SWITZERLAND, PIEDMONT, and SAVOY, is very solicitous to be favoured with corrections of any mistakes and omissions which may be discovered by persons who have made use of the book. Those communications especially will be welcomed which are founded upon personal knowledge, and accompanied by the name of the writer to authenticate them. Travellers willing to make such communications are requested to have the kindness to address them to the Editor of the HANDBOOK, care of Mr. Murray, Albemarle Street.

*** Certificates in praise of Inns must be signed by respectable and well-known persons. No attention can be paid to letters from Hotel-keepers in praise of their own inns; but the Editor will be happy to receive from them local information as to new roads or other facilities for Travellers. Prepaid letters only are received.

CAUTION TO TRAVELLERS.—By Act of Parliament, the introduction into England of *foreign Editions* of works, in which a British copyright subsists, is *totally prohibited*. Travellers will therefore bear in mind that even a single copy is contraband, and is liable to seizure at the English Custom-house.

CAUTION TO INNKEEPERS AND OTHERS.—The Editor of the Handbooks has learned from various quarters that persons have of late been extorting money from innkeepers, tradespeople, artists, and others, on the Continent, under pretext of procuring recommendations and favourable notices of them or their establishments in the Handbooks for Travellers. The Editor therefore thinks it his duty to warn all whom it may concern, that recommendations in the Handbooks are not to be obtained by purchase, and that the persons alluded to are not only unauthorised by him, but are totally unknown to him. All those, therefore, who put confidence in such promises, may rest assured that they will be defrauded of their money without attaining their object.

LONDON: PRINTED BY WILLIAM CLOWES AND SONS, LIMITED, STAMFORD STREET
AND CHARING CROSS.

A

HANDBOOK

FOR

TRAVELLERS IN SWITZERLAND,

THE ALPS OF SAVOY AND PIEDMONT,
THE ITALIAN LAKES, AND PART OF DAUPHINÉ.

Seventeenth Edition, Revised.

WITH TRAVELLING MAPS, PLANS OF TOWNS, ETC.

LONDON:

JOHN MURRAY, ALBEMARLE STREET;
PARIS: GALIGNANI & CO.; BOYVEAU.
1886.

THE ENGLISH EDITIONS OF MURRAY'S HANDBOOKS MAY BE OBTAINED
OF THE FOLLOWING AGENTS.

Belgium, Holland, and Germany.

AIX-LA-CHAPELLE . } MAYER.	LEIPZIG . . BROCKHAUS.—TWIETMEYER.
AMSTERDAM . MULLER.—KIRBERGER.	MANNHEIM . . BENDER.—LOFFLER.
ANTWERP . MERTENS.	METZ . . . ALCAN.
BADEN-BADEN . MARX.	MUNICH . . MANZ. — ACKERMANN. — KAISER.
BERLIN . . ASHER.—MITSCHER & ROS-TELL.	NÜRNBERG . SCHRAG.—ZEISER.
BRUSSELS . KIESSLING.	PESTH . . HARTLEBEN.—G. HECKENAST. —OSTERLAMM.—RATH.
CARLSRUHE . A. BIELEFELD.	PRAGUE . . CALVE.
COLOGNE . GREVEN.—DUMONT.	ROTTERDAM . KRAMERS.—PETRI.—ROBBERS.
DRESDEN . BURDACH.—PIERSON.	STRASSBURG . TRÜBNER.
FRANKFURT . JÜGEL.	STUTTGART . METZLER.—NEFF.
GRATZ . LEUSCHNER & LUBENSKY.	TRIESTE . . COEN.—SCHIMPFF.
THE HAGUE . NIJHOFF.	VIENNA . . GEROLD.—BRAUMÜLLER.
HAMBURG . MAUKE SÖHNE.	WIESBADEN . KREIDEL.
HEIDELBERG . MOHR.	

Switzerland.

BÂLE . . GEORG.—AMBERGER.	NEUCHATEL . GERSTER.
BERNE . . DALP.—JENT & REINERT.	SCHAFFHAUSEN . HURTER.
COIRE . . GRUBENMANN.	SOLEURE . . JENT.
CONSTANCE . MECK.	ST. GALLEN . HUBER.
GENEVA . SANDOZ.—H. GEORG.	ZURICH . . ORELL FUESSLI & CO.—MEYER & ZELLER.—LEUTHOLD.
LAUSANNE . ROUSSY.	
LUCERNE . KAISER.	

Italy.

BOLOGNA . ZANICHELLI.	PARMA . . ZANGHIERI.
FLORENCE . GOODBAN.—LOESCHER.	PISA . . NISTRI.—JOS. VANNUOCHI.
GENOA . GRONDONA.—ANTOINE BEUF.	PERUGIA . VINCENZ.—BARTELLI.
LEGHORN . MAZZAJOLI.	ROME . . SPITHÖVER. — PIALE. — MO-NALDINI.—LOESCHER.
LUCCA . BARON.	
MANTUA . NEGRETTI.	SIENA . . ONORATO PORRI.
MILAN . SACCHI. — DUMOLARD. — HOEPLI.	TURIN . . MAGGI. — L. BEUF.— BOCCA FRÈRES. — LOESCHER. — BALFOUR.
MODENA . VINCENZI & ROSSI.	
NAPLES . BRITISH LIBRARY (DORANT). —HOEPLI.—FURCHHEIM.	VENICE . . ONGANIA.—COEN.—MEINERS. —QUERCI.
PALERMO . PEDONE.—LAURIEL & CO.	VERONA . MÜNSTER.—MEINERS.

France.

AMIENS . CARON.	LYONS . . H. GEORG.—MÉRA.
ANGERS . RARASSÉ.	MARSEILLES . CAMOIN FRÈRES.—MEUNIER.
AVIGNON . CLÉMENT ST. JUST.	NANTES . PETIPAS.—POIRIER LEGROS. —ANDRÉ.
AVRANCHES . ANFRAY.	
BORDEAUX . CHAUMAS.— MÜLLER.— SAU-VAT.—FERET.	NICE . . BARBERY FRÈRES.—JOUGLA. —GALIGNANI.
BOULOGNE . MERRIDEW.	ORLEANS . GATINEAU.—PESTY.
CAEN . BOISARD. — LEGOST. — CLE-RISSÉ.	PARIS . . GALIGNANI.—BOYVEAU.
	PAU . . LAFON.
CALAIS . RIGAUX CAUX.	RHEIMS . BRISSART BINET.—GEOFFROY. —GIRET.
CANNES . ROBAUDY.	
CHERBOURG . LECOUFFLET.	ROUEN . LEBRUMENT.—HAULARD.
DIEPPE . MARAIS.	ST. ÉTIENNE . DELARUE.
DINANT . COSTE.	ST. MALO . HUE.
DOUAI . JACQUART.—LEMÂLE.	ST. QUENTIN DOLOY.
GRENOBLE . VELLOT ET COMP.	TOULON . MONGE ET VILLAMUS.
HAVRE . BOURDIGNON. — FOUCHER. — BUYS.	TOULOUSE . GIMET ET COTELLE.
	TOURS . GEORGET.
LILLE . BÉGHIN.	TROYES . LALOY.—DUFEY ROBERT.

Spain and Portugal.

GIBRALTAR . ROWSWELL.	MADRID . DURAN.—BAILLIÈRE.
LISBON . LEWTAS.	MALAGA . DE MOYA.

Russia, Sweden, Denmark, and Norway.

ST. PETERSBURG . WATKINS.—WOLFF.	ODESSA . CAMOIN.
MOSCOW . GAUTIER. — DEUBNER. — LANG.	CHRISTIANIA . CAMMERMEYER.—BENNETT.
	STOCKHOLM . SAMSON & WALLIN.—FRITZE.

Malta.	Ionian Islands.	Constantinople.
CRITIEN.—WATSON.—CALLEJA.	CORFU . J. W. TAYLOR.	S. H. WEISS.

Greece.	At Cairo.
ATHENS—KARL WILBERG.	A. HANNA & CO.

India.

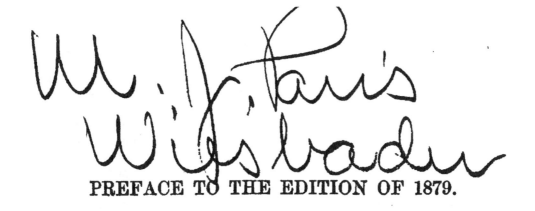

PREFACE TO THE EDITION OF 1879.

MURRAY's *Handbook for Switzerland, Savoy, and Piedmont* was the first systematic guide-book of English origin to those countries. It was based on the principle of personal knowledge of the routes described, and constructed for the use of a generation of travellers, among whose interests the beauties of nature or historical associations took the first place.

Since the publication of the first edition in 1838 two new classes of visitors have made Switzerland and the adjacent regions their summer resort. An eager band of *mountaineers* has explored the Alps in their most secret recesses, and conquered their proudest pinnacles. A much larger company of *tourists* circles yearly for a few weeks in autumn along a narrow and beaten track through two or three of the most beautiful districts on the northern side of the great chain. Their interests appear, in many cases at least, scarcely to extend beyond the practical details of travel— means of conveyance, inns, tariffs, bills,—and they have no desire to turn aside to see scenery which has not been already stamped with the approval of their fellows.

It has not been thought expedient to remodel this work so as to suit either class. It would be impossible to condense into one volume, in a form which would attract English readers, the minute details as to every byeway and glacier pass, or the interesting personal narratives of "first ascents," which distinguish the admirable 'Alpine Guide' of Mr. Ball. It seems, on the other hand, undesirable to limit the scope of these pages, and absurd to encumber them with long lists of tariffs and time-tables, which the next year, in many cases, must render inaccurate, and which could never be safely consulted without a further reference to the tables of the year, accessible in every hotel.

The present Editor has endeavoured, therefore, to maintain the Handbook in its original character as a practical *Traveller's* Guide. In it English travellers will find, in one volume, a comprehensive account of the whole Central and Western Alps, in which every route of importance is described in detail, while bypaths and glacier excursions are briefly indicated.

Plans of the principal towns are inserted, and a carefully-prepared route-map of Savoy and Piedmont. Besides the two route-maps, there will be found numerous district-maps. Of these, four are new, and two have been re-engraved for the present Edition.

An independent Index has been prepared for the Swiss section of the Handbook, as well as for the section relating to the Pennine Alps, Savoy and Piedmont; and as each is furnished with a map, the two parts may be bound up separately for convenience, without injuring the completeness of either.

The following are among the principal alterations and additions made in the text of this Edition. The Introduction has been re-arranged, and in great part re-written; several new routes have been added; others have been divided so as to make reference more easy; glacier passes, which require no apprenticeship in climbing, and have become frequented routes, are fully described; while the principal ascents are, as a rule, noted. The whole book has been thoroughly and carefully revised, amplified, and methodised. Among the sections most enlarged and amended are those relating to Davos and the Engadine, Zermatt, the Pennine Alps, the Graian Alps and Dauphiné, the Lombard and the Maritime Alps.

The Editor desires to acknowledge his special obligations to the Handbooks issued by M. Joanne, the 'Schweizerführer' of Herr Ivan von Tschudi, and to the numerous local Handbooks published under the auspices of the Italian Alpine Club, and referred to in the subsequent list of authorities. He also wishes to thank the many Alpine Clubmen, Swiss travellers and residents who have put at his service their intimate knowledge of particular districts, and thus enabled him, in spite of the enormous increase in the amount of the information to be gathered together since the book was first published, to maintain throughout its claim to be founded on the personal knowledge of the most competent travellers.

June, 1879.

The Seventeenth Edition has been brought up to date as far as possible with regard to railways, population of towns, inns, and general information from personal knowledge, the best Swiss authorities, and the notes with which the Editor has been favoured by travellers.

July, 1886.

SWITZERLAND.

(WITHOUT THE PENNINE ALPS.)

CONTENTS.

INTRODUCTORY INFORMATION.

LIST OF ROUTES.

⁎ The names of many places are necessarily repeated in several Routes; but to facilitate reference, they are printed in *Italics* only in those Routes under which they are fully described.

SECTION II.

THE ALPS OF SAVOY AND PIEDMONT.

(INCLUDING THE ITALIAN LAKES, THE PENNINE ALPS, AND PART OF DAUPHINÉ.)

PRELIMINARY INFORMATION AND SKELETON TOURS.—Page . 299

INTRODUCTORY INFORMATION.*

§ 1. GENERAL INFORMATION FOR TRAVELLERS.

Passports.—Passports are not at present (1886) required from English travellers in France, Switzerland, or Italy. In time of peace the tourist, who intends to keep to the beaten tracks of the Central Alps, will find a passport unnecessary. Should he propose, however, to extend his journey to remote districts on the Italo-French frontier, he will do well to provide himself with one, since the government officials have a right to demand from any stranger proof of his identity, and a passport, provided with a *visa*, is the simplest and most generally recognised form in which such proof can be presented. The passport should be carried on the person, as it will be wanted, if at all, at some unexpected moment. Travellers should not resent too impetuously any want of manners on the part of subordinate officials, with whom they may come into contact. The offer of a cigar will often have more effect than the most spirited remonstrance in bringing to a speedy close a difficulty arising from misapprehension of their character.

* The introductory information given here refers generally to the Alpine Districts described in this volume. Further information as to the Alps of Savoy and Piedmont, the Pennine Alps, and the Italian Lakes, is given at the commencement of the second portion of the work.

A passport can be procured at the Foreign-Office, Downing Street, by leaving or sending a letter of recommendation from any M.P., or London banker, magistrate, clergyman, solicitor, or surgeon, and calling or sending the next day for the passport, for which a fee of 2s. is charged.

Those who have not time or a servant at their disposal should forward their letters of recommendation to Dorrell and Son, 15, Charing Cross, Lee and Carter, 440, Strand, or one of the tourist agents, who for a small charge will procure the passports and visas, and will also mount the passport in a case, which some travellers prefer.

Customs.—The Swiss now levy import-dues only on a few bulky articles, and no examination of passengers' luggage is made on entering or leaving the country. Examinations are made on entering France, Italy, Austria, or the German States.

The officials, as a rule, are content with opening one article of each traveller's luggage. Cigars, lace, and unmade-up stuffs for clothing are almost the only articles charged for. There are strenuous regulations against the transport of cartridges through France.

In the Italian Lakes the traveller has constantly to cross the frontier. He will, however, be little troubled except at the railway douane of *Chiasso*, where the head officials have made themselves notorious for harshness in the execution of their duty and discourtesy towards travellers. Those *leaving* Italy with any purchases which may possibly be mistaken for " works of art prior to the present century " should be particularly careful to avoid Chiasso, as the custom-house officials will detain the goods, and refuse to answer any inquiries by letter as to the means by which they can be released, a course for which they are said to have the authority of their government.

Money.—By a decree of the Diet in 1850 the currency of Switzerland was reduced to conformity with that of France. Francs and centimes are the current money. The coinage is distinguished by the word HELVETIA on the obverse, and is among the best in Europe.

The silver coins consist of pieces of 5 francs, 2 francs, 1 franc, and ½ franc (50 centimes). The small coins consist of pieces of 5, 10, and 20 centimes, struck in *billon* (nickel and copper), and are much more convenient than French or English copper.

French twenty-franc pieces and francs, current all over Switzerland, are the best money the traveller can take with him; but English sovereigns and bank-notes are usually taken at inns throughout Switzerland and on the Italian lakes, at a value of 25 francs.

A safe and convenient method of carrying money is by circular notes issued by Coutts & Co., Herries & Co., the Union Bank, the London and Westminster Bank, and other banks, payable at all the large towns in Europe. They may be procured for any sum from 10l. upwards, and are changed free of charge by the bankers at all Swiss towns, and at the principal inns wherever English are well known. By going to the bankers the traveller secures any benefit there may be from the current rate of exchange. The security they ought to afford against loss is diminished by the frequent carelessness of innkeepers, in changing the notes without requiring to see the " Letter of Indication " the bearer is bound to present to prove his signature. English cheques are commonly changed by innkeepers in large towns.

The German gulden is exchanged in Switzerland at the rate of 2 francs 10 centimes: the Austrian florin at 2 francs 45 centimes. The Prussian thaler at 3 francs 70 centimes. The Reichs-Mark at 1 franc 25 centimes.

The coinage of Italy is the same as that of France. The paper currency is now at par, and is being gradually replaced by gold and silver coinage. Italian paper should be changed before crossing the frontier.

Measures.—On the Federal map of Switzerland (the Swiss Ordnance Map) the heights above the sea-level are indicated in mètres.

FRENCH MEASURES.

1 mètre	=	3·2809 Eng. feet	=	3 feet 3¾ inches, nearly.
1 kilomètre	=	0·628 Eng. mile	=	5-8ths of a mile, nearly.
1 Old French foot	=	1·066 Eng. foot	=	1 foot, 1 inch, nearly.
1 French league	=	2·485 Eng. miles	=	2½ miles, nearly.
1000 mètres	=	3280·9 Eng. feet	=	3281 feet, nearly.
8 kilomètres			=	5 miles, less 52 yards.
50 kilomètres			=	31 miles, 1 furlong, 57½ yards.
1 kilogramme	=	2·204 lbs. avoirdupois	=	2 lbs. 3¼ oz. nearly.
1 hectare	=	10,000 sq. mètres	=	2 acres, 1 rood, 35 perches, nearly.

TABLE A.—FRENCH MÈTRES REDUCED TO ENGLISH FEET.

Mètres.	English Feet and Decimal Parts.	Mètres.	English Feet and Decimal Parts.	Mètres.	English Feet and Decimal Parts.
1	3·281	20	65·618	300	984·270
2	6·562	30	98·427	400	1312·360
3	9·843	40	131·236	500	1640·450
4	13·123	50	164·045	600	1968·539
5	16·404	60	196·854	700	2296·629
6	19·685	70	229·663	800	2624·719
7	22·966	80	262·472	900	2952·809
8	26·247	90	295·281	1000	3280·899
9	29·528	100	328·090		
10	32·809	200	656·180		

To reduce mètres to English feet, multiply by 3, and to the product add a 12th of it, and an 8th of that 12th.

SWISS MEASURES.

1 Swiss foot	=	11 inches, 10 lines, nearly.		
1 Swiss league or Stunde }	=	2·983 Eng. miles	=	3 miles, less 92 feet.
1 Swiss Post	=	3·00 Swiss stunde	=	9 miles, less 92 yards.
1 Swiss arpent	=	0·89 Eng. acres	=	9-10ths of an acre, nearly.
1 Swiss pound	=	1·102 lb. avoird.	=	½ Fr. kilog. = 1 lb. 1½ oz., nearly.

ITALIAN MEASURES.

1 Piedmont mile	=	1·503 Eng. mile	=	1½ mile and 57 yards.
1 Italian mile	=	1 mile, 1 furlong, 45 yards.		
1 Italian Post	=	8 Italian miles	=	9 miles, 1 furlong, 142 yards.

Post.—The postage on an ordinary letter under ½ oz. is 10 centimes. If addressed to a direction within 5 miles, half-price. Postcards are 5 centimes throughout Switzerland and 10 centimes to other countries included in the Postal Union.   Unsealed packages containing no letters or articles of value pay 10 centimes up to 250 grammes.

Letters under ½ oz. to all countries included in the Postal Union and to the United States of America cost 25 centimes.

In addressing letters, the name, and particularly the initial letter, should be clearly written, and the addition "Esquire" avoided.   It is better when possible to have the letters addressed to an inn rather than Poste Restante. In many places of summer resort, particularly in the Engadine, the post-office staff is wholly unequal to the call on it, and letters are constantly delivered to the wrong person, or, having been placed under a wrong letter, refused when actually lying in the office.   It is well therefore, in country offices, when expected letters are not received, to request to be allowed to look for oneself.

When newspapers are expected they should be specially asked for, as they are often kept apart.

There is a parcel post between Great Britain and Switzerland.   Parcels under 3 lbs. cost 1s. 9d., between 3 and 7 lbs., 2s. 2d.

Telegraph.—The electric telegraph wires are now carried to almost every town and considerable village in Switzerland, and to many solitary inns.   Messages within the Swiss frontier are charged as follows: 35 centimes for two words, 40 centimes for 3 and 4, and so on, adding 5 centimes for every odd or two even words.   The name of the sender is put at the end of the message.

Circular Tours and Tickets.—Of late years two new systems have sprung into existence to meet the case of persons more or less incapable, from want of experience in travel or ignorance of foreign languages, of taking care of themselves while abroad.

The first is known as the "Personally-conducted Tour."   The tourist pays down a fixed sum, which, with very few extras, includes all his expenses.   For this he is entitled to be taken round a predetermined route, in company with some 20 to 60 chance companions, and in charge of an experienced agent, who fills, as far as possible, the place of courier to the party. He has no bills to pay, no conveyances to hire, no arrangements to make; in exchange for these advantages, he must of course surrender his freewill and make the best of his society.   This is an arrangement suited only for those who would otherwise be altogether excluded from the advantages of foreign travel, many of which, however, are necessarily lost by such a system.

The second arrangement is fit for more advanced tourists, and may occasionally be made use of with advantage even by old travellers, who are content to fix beforehand where they will go, and by what route they will come back.

Circular routes are arranged in great variety, and in return for a payment usually as nearly as possible equivalent to the ordinary fares, books are issued containing tickets not only for railways and steamers, but for coaches and horses, in the order in which they will be wanted on the tour, which as a rule is made reversible.

Books of slips (called coupons) are also issued.   Each coupon costs 8 shillings, and in return for it, at any of the hotels mentioned in the list given with the coupons, the traveller has a right to dinner, breakfast, and bed.   The hotels designated are, as a rule, good, and the system may be worked so as to effect a small saving in money. The tourist, however, must beware how he indulges in extras, such as cups of tea or foot-baths, as some innkeepers are quick to take an unfair advantage of such excesses.

The agents for Circular Tours and tickets are Messrs. Cook & Co., of Ludgate Hill Circus, E.C., by whom they were established, and Messrs. Gaze, of 142, Strand, W.C.; the railway companies also issue through or return-tickets to most of the principal foreign towns.

N.B.—In travelling with through-tickets made up of many leaves, the tourist should be careful to see that the guard collects only the right one. Mistakes are common, and redress is the contrary, in this matter.

Luggage.—There is a very convenient system in force in Switzerland, by which luggage can be forwarded from any post or railway station within the frontier to another, at a moderate expense. The traveller has only to leave his package, properly and clearly addressed, with the post-master, and in return he will receive a ticket, which he must keep.

In making application for the luggage, it is well to present a card with the name of the applicant clearly written, and sometimes to ask to look over the packages in the office, as post-masters have been known to declare that luggage had not arrived when it was under their eyes. Miscarriages, however, are very rare.

Luggage can also be sent across the frontier, but in this case the key of each piece must be sent with it, if it is to enter France or Italy. The Swiss custom-house is satisfied with a written declaration that the contents are traveller's luggage. Forms for this declaration are supplied at the offices.

§ 2. MODES OF TRAVELLING.

Railways.—Down to the year 1855 the only railway in Switzerland was a short line from Zürich to the Swiss Baden. The reason of this was not the extreme natural difficulty of the country, Switzerland being in fact, with the exception of the passes through the central mountains of the Alps and the Jura, not a very difficult country. The lowlands, or parts round Berne, Aarau, Neuchâtel, Lausanne, &c., do not offer to the engineer such serious obstacles as many parts of the south of England; and by means of the valleys of the Rhine and the Rhone, railways can penetrate deep into the Alps with remarkable ease. The real difficulty consisted in the extraordinary and incredible jealousies between not only the different cantons, but the different communes or parishes, and the legal difficulties in obtaining the land. A change in government, however, having taken place in 1848, a system of railways was planned by the Department of Public Works, and has been carried into execution; some of the lines being made by English engineers and with English capital.

Northern Switzerland is now traversed in every direction by lines of railroad, connecting the principal towns. The Central Alps have been pierced by the St. Gothard Tunnel, and the commerce of Germany thus obtains direct access to Milan and the Mediterranean at Genoa.

For further particulars as to the lines in operation and the train-service, readers are referred to the foreign 'Bradshaw,' and the 'Indicateur des

Chemins de Fer Suisses,' or the 'Reisebegleiter für die Schweiz,' published periodically, and costing a few centimes. In German Switzerland the carriages are on the American system with a passage down the middle. Here travellers, who do not object to occasional crowding, may travel with advantage second-class.

In French Switzerland the carriages are very inferior, and the second-class company, particularly in Canton Vaud, is apt to be noisy and disagreeable.

Excursion Tickets, and return-tickets, available for 2 or 3 days, may be procured in summer on many of the lines.

The regulations as to luggage differ on the various lines. As a rule, little luggage is allowed without extra payment, and as on most Continental railways, the traveller must pay for and see it labelled after he has taken his ticket. For this purpose it is necessary to be at the station at least ten minutes before the hour of starting. Swiss time is 27 minutes in advance of Paris, and 35 min. in advance of Greenwich time.

Steamboats.—Steamers now run on all the principal lakes. Those on the Lakes of Lucerne and Geneva and on the Italian lakes are spacious boats, with upper decks and good restaurants on board. For fares and times, see 'Bradshaw' or the local time-tables. Tickets are sold on board. Beware on some of the lakes of the touts for hotels or voituriers who infest the boats.

Diligences.—Well-appointed Diligences traverse almost every road in Switzerland where railways have not been laid down, and connect the chief railway stations with the places in their vicinity. They belong to the Federal Government, and are attached to the post-office as in Germany.

A list is to be bought at the offices and is also contained in the 'Indicateur des Chemins de Fer.' The regular diligences have a *coupé* in front with three seats, and a *banquette*, with the same number, on the roof behind the box. The *intérieur*, or second-class compartment, has six seats and occupies the body of the cumbrous vehicle. The conductor has an outside seat in the rear, which will often hold two, and may be secured for a consideration.

The fares are fixed by rules dated 1879. In the lowlands 15 centimes by kilomètre is charged for a seat in the *intérieur*, 20 centimes in the *coupé* or *banquette*. In the mountains, 25 centimes for the *intérieur*, 30 centimes for first-class places. Return-tickets available for three days are issued at a reduction of 10 per cent. Each traveller is allowed 40 lbs. of luggage free: overweight packages are charged according to a moderate tariff.

The pace along level ground seldom exceeds 6 miles an hour; at the smallest symptom of a hill the horses fall into a walk: down hill they occasionally go fast; and to those who have not become hardened by use it is rather a nervous thing to see the heavy diligence turn round the corners of the zigzags in the face of precipices, with the reins flying loose, and the horses apparently under no control. They, however, know the road, and accidents are seldom heard of.

The conductors are generally civil; the clerks, &c., at the diligence offices occasionally disobliging.

There is a very convenient plan adopted as to places. At the *Dépôts,* or principal stations, they book any number of passengers up to an hour before the departure. When the time for starting arrives, all the luggage and as many passengers as the vehicle will hold are put into the diligence, and the rest of the passengers are sent by other carriages, called "suppléments," or "beiwagen," of which there are often 3 or 4. A party of 4 can generally get a "supplément" to themselves, and travel very comfortably, seeing the scenery well. At the *Bureaux* of smaller places the booking is contingent on there being room, but on the frequented passes a practically unlimited number of "beiwagen" are put on to meet a demand. Unless at the place from which the diligence starts, it is useless to take places for the banquette or coupé, for at the intermediate stations they are generally full.

The advantages of diligences are economy and, in making a long journey, speed. The objection to them is that unless the traveller secures a place in the banquette or a "supplément" he sees little of the country. A solitary traveller may often avail himself of the diligence with advantage. A party of from 3 to 5 will find it better worth their while to travel post or in a hired carriage.

On some of the most frequented roads immense covered vans known as "Pavillon Postwagen" have been put on, which afford a free view.

Posting.—The Federal Government adopted in 1852 a general and uniform system of Posting (Extrapost), which has been introduced into all parts of the country, and the great roads are now supplied with post-horses, except where railways have been completed. Full information respecting the posting system may be obtained from the Official Swiss Post Book (*Tarif Suisse de la Poste aux Chevaux*), or the smaller *Extrapost Tarif*, to be obtained at every post-bureau.

The horses and harness are generally good; the drivers tolerably skilful, but they get over the ground very slowly. The *regulation pace* is 6 miles an hour, and is not often exceeded. Upon certain stages up-hill the tariff compels you to take an extra horse, or leader (*renfort*, German *Vorspann*), or to pay for it if not taken, sometimes with very little apparent reason. The chief objection to travelling post is the necessity of frequently changing carriages and repacking luggage.

Voituriers and Cars.—The Voiturier (German, *Lohnkutcher*, Italian, *Vetturino*) is a coachman who holds at the service of travellers his own carriage with 2, 3, or 4 horses. In former times he was a most important figure in Swiss travel. On the great roads and in the districts frequented by travellers he still exists; but, owing to the change in the mode of travel, he is rapidly changing in character. The "vetturino" of the old school, generally an Italian, was, as a rule, civil, obliging, and intelligent. He was in the habit of taking long engagements of several weeks for complete tours, and the preliminary bargain, in which he regarded himself at liberty to make the best terms he could, once concluded, he served his employer with much fidelity. The new school are, many of them, mere drivers, who are hired from day to day at a fixed rate, are careless alike of their horses and their travellers, and are sometimes even of doubtful honesty.

New Tariffs have been lately made in most of the cantons regulating the hire of carriages. The prices in many cases are far too high, so that for those who do not mind the trouble of changing carriages, it is cheaper to travel post. Bern, Graubünden, and Uri are among the cantons which have fixed tariffs, and they are in force on almost all the Alpine roads. Where no tariff exists, the price for a 2-horse vehicle varies from 30 to 50 francs for the day, but if taken for one or two days only, will be nearer the higher sum. A " pourboire" beyond the agreed price is always expected, but the amount may be settled beforehand.

The Railway termini are the head-quarters of the voituriers ; at all of them there are many persons who keep horses for hire, and will either conduct the traveller themselves, or send coachmen in their employ. *Return* horses and carriages are sometimes to be met with at cheaper rates.

Before making an engagement, it is prudent to ask the landlord of the hotel, or some other respectable inhabitant, to recommend a person of approved character. The landlord should be referred to apart, not in presence of the coachman, nor, indeed, with his cognizance. Besides ascertaining that the voiturier is a respectable man, that his horses are good, and his carriage clean and stout, it is desirable in many cases that he should speak French as well as German, and, in all, that he should be acquainted with the roads to be traversed. If the carriage is hired for a long tour, the engagement should, in the first instance, not be made for any specific time, at least not for a long period, until man and horses have been tried. It is better to take him on from day to day, holding out the prospect of his being continued if he behaves well. It should also be ascertained whether the well-mannered individual who addresses you as the proprietor of the carriage, and makes the bargain with you, will or will not be the driver.

It is advisable, before setting out on a long tour, to have an agreement in writing drawn up. (See Forms of Contract in Murray's *Handbook of Travel Talk.*) It will be important that the payment by the day, or for the journey, the time to be occupied on the road, the daily resting-places, the payment of the charge for leaders (Vorspann), and the question of back-fare, be all clearly understood and agreed to.

Despite some disadvantages, voiturier travelling is the most comfortable for a family or party of 4 or 5 members on the carriage-roads.

The usual speed is from 30 to 40 miles a-day, proceeding at the rate of about 6 miles an hour. Whilst on the road the voiturier goes nearly as fast as the diligence or post-horses, but it is necessary to halt in the middle of the day, about two hours, to rest. The distances which one pair of horses will achieve day after day, by means of walking up the smallest ascents, and using the break skilfully on all descents, are incredible.

Two travellers will find the pleasantest and most economical mode of conveyance in one of the one-horse *calèches,* or chaises, *Einspänner,* which are common in most parts of the Alps. They hold comfortably 2 persons, and are generally furnished with a hood affording shelter from sun and rain, while not shutting out the view. In front there is a seat for the driver, on which a guide will also find room. They go at a rate of 5 or 6 m. an hour, except on very hilly roads. The fare is about 1 franc an English mile ; and the driver receives 1 fr. trinkgeld for 8 or 10 miles. The luggage may be attached on a board behind.

The *char-à-banc,* once the national carriage of French Switzerland, is nearly obsolete. It may be described as the body of a gig, or a bench, as its name implies, placed sideways upon four wheels, surrounded by leather curtains made to draw, whence it has been compared to a four-post bed-stead on wheels.

Horses and Mules.—Previous to 1800, until Napoleon commenced the magnificent carriage-roads which will assist in immortalising his name, the usual mode of conveying either passengers or goods across the Alps was on the backs of men, or of horses or mules. Even now, upon the minor passes, the entire traffic is carried on by the same means. In other instances, where the beauties of the scenery attract an influx of strangers, mules are kept for their conveyance, even where they are not required for the transport of merchandise.

The hire of a horse or mule throughout Switzerland, generally fixed by a printed tariff, ranges from 10 to 15 fr. a-day, and 1 fr. or 2 fr. to the man who leads it; at Martigny and Chamonix it is 6 fr., but also 6 fr. for the man, and this often is not mentioned when you ask the charge for a mule. Back-fare must be paid if the animals are dismissed at a distance from home, and at so late an hour of the day that they cannot return before night.

The horses used in the Bernese Oberland, on the Rigi, and in other parts of Switzerland, are clever animals, which will carry you up and down ascents perfectly impracticable to horses unused to mountains; but they are perhaps excelled by the mules of Chamonix and other parts of Savoy. Of these the sagacity, strength, and sureness of foot are really wonderful. The paths which they ascend or descend with ease are steeper than any staircase, sometimes with rugged rocks instead of steps. Sometimes they are covered with broken fragments, between which the beasts must pick their way, at the risk of breaking their legs; at others they traverse a narrow ledge, with an abyss on one side and a granite cliff on the other. In such dangerous passes the caution of the animal is very remarkable; he needs no rein, but will find out the best track far better than his rider; and, in such circumstances, it is safer to trust entirely to his sagacity, than to attempt to guide him, for, by confusing the animal, there will be risk of his losing his footing, and perhaps tumbling head-long. The rider who mounts a mule or mountain horse must give up his preconceived notions, and let the reins hang comparatively loose. There are very few accidents from the falling of the animals; the only instance within the writer's knowledge happened to a gentleman who was a great horseman, and no doubt attempted to interfere with his mule. The chief danger in alpine riding consists in the risk of a traveller being placed on the back of an animal hitherto accus-tomed only to inanimate burdens. This naturally arises most commonly in unfrequented districts, and especially affects ladies. Descending the passes on horseback is· generally disagreeable, and sometimes dangerous, and the rider should always dismount when requested to do so by the guide. In fact, those who can walk fairly should, if they have not too much luggage, only hire the horses to the head of the pass, as they will be of comparatively little use on the descent. Each saddle has a flap or pil-lion attached, on which a knapsack or carpet-bag not weighing more than about 30 lbs. may be carried. In Switzerland horses are generally let out by their owners, who, in their own interest, refuse to allow their animals to be overloaded. Travellers may as a rule, however, accept the statements made as to the number of horses requisite, or the amount each can carry. This remark does not apply to the refusal of some horse-drivers in the height of the season to allow any package whatever to be attached to a riding-horse or mule. A portmanteau requires an extra mule. Side-saddles are now to be found in all frequented districts; in remote villages, and especially in the Italian Alps, ladies must take their own saddles, or be content with the best substitute that can be improvised.

A tariff of the prices to be paid for horses is in many places to be seen at the inn.

Chaises-à-porteurs.—Those who are unable to ride or walk may be carried over the mountains in a *chaise-à-porteurs* (Germ. *Tragsessel*; It. *Portantina*), which is nothing more than an arm-chair borne upon poles in the manner of a sedan. In the Bernese Oberland two bearers will sometimes undertake to carry a lady of light weight for many successive days over the ordinary passes; but, as a general rule, two, in some places four extra bearers must be taken to relieve by turns, and each man expects 6 fr. a-day, and 3 fr. for each day of return. This was the customary manner of conveying travellers across the Alps, down to the latter half of the eighteenth century.

§ 3. GUIDES.

Guides are, as a general rule, indispensable in ascending lofty mountains, in exploring glaciers, and in crossing the minor passes traversed by bridle- or foot-paths rarely used, and in many places not distinctly marked, or confounded with innumerable tracks of cattle. Nevertheless, travellers having a knowledge of the language of the country, in addition to some experience of mountain journeys, and provided with a good map, may cross many of these passes alone with impunity. In bad weather a guide may be required in situations where, under ordinary circumstances, his presence might be dispensed with, and the solitary traveller should always be very cautious in venturing alone on the hills where, far from human help, a sprain may have the most serious result. No one without thorough knowledge of the high Alps, should be foolish enough to trust himself over ice or snow without a guide. It is entirely a new world; and when the slightest check occurs, an inexperienced person is utterly at a loss. He does not know what ice will bear him, where the crevasses run, where avalanches fall, or where the safe track is likely to be, and, with the best ordinary judgment, is quite as likely to run into danger as to avoid it.

The "expeditions without guides," read of from time to time in the 'Times' or the 'Alpine Journal,' are made by parties consisting exclusively of men who have served a long apprenticeship in the Alps under the best guides.

Guides abound in Switzerland, and at Chamonix, and may also be found in the Piedmontese valleys, and in Dauphiné. They may be divided, roughly, into two classes, glacier guides and ordinary guides. The former are, or ought to be, competent to take travellers into the region of eternal snow, not only agile climbers, but also versed in the complicated rules of ice-craft. In former years, men of this class were mostly found in the great centres of alpine travel, Chamonix, Zermatt, and the Bernese Oberland. Lately, however, the number of travellers wishing to ascend some great peak, has led to the appearance in these districts of a set of men tempted to serve as glacier-guides by the high pay offered, but without the nerve, knowledge, or experience of the true guides. To avoid such companionship is one of the chief difficulties of the inexperienced traveller, who will do well to attend to the advice given below on this point. First-rate guides are still found in the Alpine centres, but these are seldom disengaged, being secured months beforehand by their habitual employers. Thoroughly capable men may, however, be discovered in Switzerland by careful inquiry, and in less crowded districts and villages, in Dauphiné, at Courmayeur, Breuil, Alagna, in many hamlets of the Pennine and eastern Swiss Alps there are now excellent glacier guides.

As a body, despite the occasional misconduct of individuals, the guides are intelligent, trustworthy, and hard-working men. All who have frequently employed them can bear witness to their coolness, courage, and skill in moments of danger, on the difficult ice-ridge, in the intricate maze of an ice-fall, or when overtaken by sudden storm and fog. In such situations the traveller fully appreciates their steadiness and knowledge, and the care with which, if they see need, they watch and guide his footsteps, and by judicious use of the rope render a slip impossible or harmless.

A traveller who contemplates frequent excursions into the snow regions, does best by securing a guide for the whole tour. Many guides have now a large knowledge of the alpine chain. But even if some part of the proposed route is unknown to the guide, his general experience, with the aid of a good map or the local knowledge of the porter, who in glacier expeditions can seldom be dispensed with, will suffice. He is also frequently useful as an interpreter, if the traveller is unacquainted with the language; he carries a knapsack, and will act generally as a courier, only at a far cheaper rate.

In engaging a guide the best plan is to apply, before leaving England, to an experienced friend, and write in advance to the guide recommended. When this has not been done, some alpine climber may generally be met abroad, to whom application can be made. Failing this, the traveller may safely apply to one of the famous guides, such as Christian Almer of Grindelwald, Melchior Anderegg of Meiringen, or François Devouassoud of Chamonix, to recommend him a suitable escort. There are a few innkeepers who may also be trusted. Every guide is bound to carry a certificate-book, which may be usefully referred to: the traveller should, however, be careful to notice by whom the certificates are signed, and only to give weight to the recommendations of experienced climbers. If these are present he may safely disregard the depreciatory remarks of unknown tourists, who, in their ignorance, will sometimes disparage a guide on account of his refusal to lead them into danger.

Glacier-guides are found in Dauphiné [at La Grave, St. Christophe and Ville Vallouise, Valgodemar and Val Jouffrey] at Balme in the Valli di Lanso, at Chamonix, Courmayeur, Breuil, St. Pierre and Arolla in the Pennine Alps; in the Zermatt valley; at Saas, Macugnaga and Alagna; at the Bel Alp and Eggischhorn, in the villages of the Bernese Oberland, in the Maderaner Thal, at Stachelberg, Klosters in the Prätigau, and at Pontresina.

"Ordinary guides" are peasants fitted by honesty, intelligence, and local knowledge, to take travellers over the mule- and foot-passes below the snow-level. Such men are found in most Alpine villages. They are, many of them, pleasant companions, from whom the traveller may obtain much interesting information on Swiss life. They will carry a heavy knapsack, or a light one, and the provision sack, where the latter is a necessity. When the traveller rides, the guide leads his horse and tells him where to dismount.

The established rate of hire per day for glacier guides is 8 to 10 francs; for ordinary guides 6 francs for ordinary excursions, for which no special tariff exists. The charges for glacier expeditions are frequently fixed by tariff. Guides employed for a length of time by competent mountaineers are, as a rule, content with 14 to 20 francs for a glacier pass, and 30 to 40 francs for a difficult ascent. Any higher demand is excessive. For single expeditions the tariff prices are much higher, *e.g.* Mont Blanc 100 francs Piz Bernina 80 francs, Matterhorn 100 francs. Such a distinction is fair. The risk and labour of dragging an inexperienced tourist up Mont Blanc or the Wetterhorn deserves a different rate of remuneration to the comparatively slight exertion involved in showing the way to a climber able, under ordinary circumstances, to take care of himself.

If the guide is dismissed at a distance from home, the employer must pay 8 francs a day for his return home and his railway and diligence fares, unless he procures him a fresh engagement. The guide is expected to find himself out of his pay while at inns, but when out for the day or bivouacking on the mountains the employer provides food and drink for the whole party. Guides when taken to E. Switzerland, Tyrol, the French Alps, or other remote places where no distinction is made in prices between guides and travellers at the inns, often stipulate beforehand for an allowance, which should be readily made by the traveller, who gains by not having his guide's expenses covered by increased charges in his own bill.

Those fortunate enough to secure a first-rate guide should remember that such men are accustomed to be treated as companions by their ordinary employers; and that, while willing to render any service asked of them, they are exceedingly sensitive to rudeness or random fault-finding, such as English tourists sometimes use towards those whom they consider their inferiors.

For many years the guides of Chamonix have formed a corporation, and similar unions have sprung up in other districts. The disadvantages of such restrictions on free trade are partly compensated for by a fixed tariff and a certain control. Where such unions have been managed solely by their own members, great abuses have sprung up; the incompetent majority have studied their own interests, and not those of their capable comrades, or of travellers. Latterly the Alpine Clubs have done their best to put these bodies on a sound footing, and to make them really useful by keeping out, or in a separate class, the inferior men. Their rules and tariffs have been in many instances revised by a commission of the Swiss Club under the presidency of Herr Ivan von Tschudi. The Chamonix corporation, however, is still full of abuses, and the " guide chef " is not always an individual to whom the traveller can profitably appeal either for advice or redress.

§ 4. ACCOMMODATION—INNS, PENSIONS, BATHS, ALPINE HUTS.

Inns are recommended in this book from the best information that the editor can procure, but it is obvious that the information must be eight or nine months old at the latest, and in many instances much older. In the interval the landlord may have been changed, or may have become more careful from adversity, or careless from prosperity, and the inn may be completely altered. In the following pages the inns believed to be the best in each town are mentioned first.

Two centuries ago, the most important men in Canton Valais were the innkeepers, and to the present day, in some parts of the country, they appear to be the only wealthy inhabitants. It is not uncommon to find an innkeeper who is a magistrate. Consequently, it is sometimes difficult to obtain redress against them for an injury or act of insolence, owing either to the interest they possess with the courts, or to their being themselves the justices. As a rule, however, they are respectable men, and difficulties seldom arise.

Switzerland is well provided with excellent hotels and inns. The great annual influx of strangers is of the same importance as some additional branch of industry or commerce would be.

Many of the largest hotels are now in the hands of Joint-stock Companies. There are three classes of Swiss hotels. The palaces which border the lakes, and injure the scenery of the Upper Engadine, inferior in luxury to no houses of their kind in Europe ; the comfortable but plain mountain hotels, found at such resorts as Chamonix, Zermatt, Grindelwald, or Pontresina ; and the mountain inns, rough, but generally clean, erected for the accommodation of mountaineers and lovers of Alpine byways.

It may be laid down as a general rule, that the wants, tastes, and habits of the English are more carefully and successfully studied in the Swiss hotels than in those of any other part of Europe. At most of the hotels, in addition to the 1 o'clock dinner, there is a *late table-d'hôte* at 6 or 7 o'clock ; and tea may generally be had tolerably good. Several innkeepers have gone so far as to build *English chapels* as an inducement to our travellers to pass the Sunday with them, and in many mountain inns an English clergyman is offered free lodging with the same object, and the guests of other nations are ejected from the public sitting-room while English service is performed. Cleanliness is to be met with almost everywhere, until you reach the S. slopes of the Alps, and even there of late years a great improvement has taken place. In Canton Berne, in particular, the inns, even in the small and remote villages, are patterns of neatness, such as even fastidious travellers may be contented with. In the Italian valleys of Monte Rosa, in Val Maggia and Val Bregaglia, the inns compare not unfavourably with those on the Swiss side of the mountains, and even in Dauphiné insects and starvation are no longer the rule.

The drainage in some of the larger houses has been badly reported of within the last few years. Any cases where such complaints continue, will be noted in future editions.

List of usual Charges of the first-class Swiss Hotels.

	Fr. fr. c.		Fr. fr. c.
Tea or coffee, morning or evening, with bread, butter, and honey (eggs, meat and fish are charged separately, *à la carte*, 2 or 3 portions are usually sufficient for 4 or 5 persons)	1 50	to	2 0

	Fr. fr. c.		Fr. fr. c.
Déjeuner à la fourchette (table-d'hôte) . . .	2 50	to	3 50
Table-d'hôte at 6	4 0	„	6 0
Dinner in private (ordered in advance in the public room)	6 0	„	10 0
Servants, board and lodging, 5 francs a day.			
Bougie	1 0		
Bain de pied, het or cold	0 50		
Servants (service de l'hôtel), by day per head . .	1 0		

With large families, who make some stay, special arrangements will generally be made.

The charges for *Rooms* vary, according to the floor and the views they command, from 2 50 to 6 francs. An apartment (that is, a suite of rooms with salon) varies in the same way from 10 to 50 francs.. The *Salles-à-manger* in the larger Swiss hotels are handsome, clean, and airy apartments.. Smoking is not allowed in them, and in consequence of this, and of a higher charge being made for meals in private rooms, most persons take breakfast, tea, and supper in them.

A party of 3 or 4 persons staying a week or more, even in a first-rate hotel, should not pay more than 10 or 12 fr. each, board and lodging, per diem. At Interlaken the charge in some hotels for good board and lodging is not more than 6 fr. a-day; and at some of the baths near Bex not more than 4½ fr. for those who remain some weeks. At some of the small inns in remote valleys the charges are extremely moderate.

English travellers halting at an *Inn* about mid-day to rest their horses, if there be no table-d'hôte at 12 or 1, should order a déjeuner à la fourchette (Gabelfrühstück), for which they will be charged 2 to 3 fr. 50 c. per head. If they order *dinner*, they will be charged 4 or 5 fr. for the same food.

French is almost invariably spoken at the inns on the high-roads, even in the German cantons, except in remote parts, as in the side valleys of the Grisons. Nevertheless, the German language or a French and German-speaking guide as interpreter is essential to the traveller's comfort. English is spoken in the large hotels.

All arrangements for the hire of carriages, horses, or guides, should be concluded over-night: he who waits till the morning will generally find either the conveyances engaged, or the price demanded for them increased, and, at all events, his departure delayed.

Among the mountains, the traveller may obtain, in perfection, the small alpine *Trout*, which are of great excellence; sometimes, also, chamois venison, which is far inferior to park venison, and generally badly cooked; wild strawberries are very abundant, and, with cream or red wine, by no means to be despised.

Tolerably good wine is made in the Cantons Neuchâtel, Vaud, and Valais; but the best is not often found at inns. French Beaujolais wine is found good in all first-class hotels. At many mountain inns there are in reality but two or three qualities of native wine; the colour of the bottle, the label, and the price, vary with the demands of the traveller. *Yvorne* is considered the best Swiss white wine; *Vin de Glacier* is a sound white wine of some strength. Some persons like *Swiss Champagne*, which is refreshing, and the *Vino d'Asti*, a sweetish Piedmontese wine that tastes like perry, but is rather more exciting than allaying to the thirst.

The following inns are recommended as good halting-places outside the large towns; but it must be borne in mind that, owing to the multiplication of hotels, no list can pretend to anything like completeness. AA are first-class hotels, A comfortable inns, B good mountain quarters.

Alagna	A	Ilanz	B
An der Lenk	A	Interlaken	AA
Aosta	A	Kandersteg	B
Arolla	B	Klosters	B
Axenstein (Brunnen)	AA	Lausanne	AA
Baveno	AA	Luc, St.	B
Bel Alp	A	Lucerne and Lake	AA
Bergtün	B	Lugano	AA
Bernina Hospice	B	Macugnaga	B
Bex	A	Maderaner Thal	B
Bignasco	A	Maggiore Lake (Pallanza, Baveno,	
Bürgenstock	AA	Stresa, Locarno)	AA
Chamonix	AA	Meiringen	A
Champéry	A	Mendrisio	A
Château d'Oex and Neighbour-		Mottarone, Monte	A
hood	A	Moritz, St.	AA
Ceresole	B	Mürren	A
Col d'Ollen	B	Orta	B
Como Lake (Bellagio, Cadenabbia,		Pesio	A
Como)	AA	Pontresina	A
Courmayeur	AA	Promontogno	A
Davos	AA	Le Prese	A
Diablerets	A	Ragatz	AA
Eggischhorn	A	Reichenbach	A
Engadine (Silvaplana Sils Maria)	A	Rhone Glacier Hotel	A
Engadine (St. Moritz Pontresina		Rigi Kaltbad and Staffel	AA
Samaden Maloja)	AA	Rosenlaui	B
Engadine Lower (Tarasp)	A	Seelisberg	AA
Engelberg	A	Simplon	B
Engstlen	B	Sixt	B
Evolena	B	Stachelberg	AA
Fée	A	St. Martin Lantosque	B
Geneva Lake, head of, hotels and		Tarasp Bad	AA
pensions	AA	Thusis	A
Generoso, Monte	A	Valdieri	A
Gervais, St.	A	Villard, near Bex	A
Giessbach	AA	Waldstätterhof (Brunnen)	AA
Glion	AA	Wesen	A
Gressoney	B	Weissbad	A
Grindelwald	A	Weissenstein (Soleure)	A
Heiden	A	Zermatt and Riffel Alp	AA
Hospenthal	A	Zinal	B

Pensions or Hôtel-Pensions are houses at which travellers who stay a week or more are lodged and boarded at a fixed sum per diem, varying between 4½ fr. in some of the pensions near Bex to 10 fr. at Grindelwald, and even higher sums at the great palaces on the lakes. Wine is generally an extra. This arrangement is very general, and of great advantage to families and travellers of regular habits; its only disadvantage is the necessity of being in to meals at fixed hours, not always those most agreeable to English habits.

Baths and Cures.—The Swiss baths have been celebrated since the middle ages. In the sixteenth century fifty treatises, dealing with twenty-one different resorts, were published. So famous at this period was the Swiss Baden, that Zürich ladies are said to have insisted on a covenant in their marriage-settlements, that they should be taken there at least once a year. St. Moritz, which had been brought into notoriety by Paracelsus about 1539, was already one of the most famous Baths. Scheuchzer, in his 'Itinera Alpina,' published with the "imprimatur" of Sir Isaac Newton, speaks of "Acidulas S. Mauritianas frequentatas admodum a Rhætis, Helvetis, Germanis, Italis." In 1501 a Bishop of Sion built "a magnificent hotel" at Leukerbad, to which the rich were carried up in panniers on the backs of mules. Brieg, Gurnigel near Berne, the baths of Masino, Tarasp, and Pfäffers, were also popular in early times. During the last twenty years, English doctors have awakened to the beneficial effects of the combination with mineral waters and a regular life of the pure air of high altitudes. The consequence has been a rush of patients to the Upper Engadine, comparable to the sudden fury for the seaside which seized our ancestors in the last century. Probably, as doctors acquire larger topographical knowledge of the Alps, and of the variety of climates they offer, and more experience of the different ways in which a high climate affects different constitutions, they will cease to direct all their patients to the same spot.

Many visitors find the Engadine air too stimulating, and suffer constantly, until removed, from sleeplessness and headache. For these there are many bathing establishments, within the alpine region, at a less elevation. In a descending scale may be mentioned Davos, Tarasp, Alveneu, Stachelberg, Ragatz, Seelisberg, and Axenstein above the Lake of Lucerne, Gurnigel near Berne, and Interlaken. This list is far from complete, and may be largely added to if the Italian side of the Alps is included. Those to whom iron-waters are an object, will, of course, have to limit their choice.

In the old-fashioned Swiss baths, which have not acquired any reputation outside the country, the arrangements are generally rough, and the charges extremely moderate. At the principal baths (such as St. Moritz, Tarasp, Ragatz) the visitor will find all the comforts, and most of the luxuries he has been accustomed to at the great German baths.

There are in Switzerland other cures, besides the water and air cure (Luftkur), in which faith is placed. In Canton Appenzell the patient is put upon a diet of the milk left after cheese has been made: this is called " Molken kur." Near Vevey the grape " kur " is popular. The white sorts only are used, and of these from six to seven pounds are not unfrequently consumed by the invalid in one day. The grapes are eaten in the morning and forenoon, the other diet being chiefly animal; neither vegetables, milk, coffee, nor wine are allowed. The grapes are supposed to improve the quality of the blood, and to act on the liver and mucous membranes. It might be imagined that the appetite would be palled by so large a quantity of fruit, but, on the contrary, it is said to be keenly excited: the " kur " is followed, during a fortnight or three weeks, under medical surveillance.

Mountain Huts.—For the convenience of mountain climbers, a considerable number of huts have been built in high situations among the glaciers. Those erected by the Swiss Alpine Club are solidly built and fairly furnished, and most of them offer a tolerable shelter against the weather. By their means, many high ascents are brought within the reach of travellers not prepared to undertake days of prolonged exertion, and the sublime effects of sunrise and sunset may be witnessed at leisure from such lofty standpoints as the Col du Géant or the Gleckstein. Hay-beds and rugs are generally found, but provisions must, of course, be taken. The traveller will in every case do well to ascertain from the local guides the condition of the hut he means to make use of.

§ 5. DIRECTIONS AND REQUISITES FOR TRAVELLERS.

The first and most indispensable requisites for the alpine traveller, are an observant disposition, a cheerful temper, and a determination not to be easily put out, or distracted from the admirable aspects of nature he has come to see, by personal trifles. In the words of Gibbon, "He should be endowed with an active, indefatigable vigour of mind and body, which can seize every mode of conveyance, and support, with a careless smile, every hardship of the road, the weather, or the inn." The tourist who, on his return home, can only dilate on the comparative merits of the hotels he has rested at, or on his disputes and misadventures on the road, has journeyed to very little purpose.

Owing to the very imperfect education in natural science the majority of the present generation of Englishmen have received, our fellow-countrymen do not, as a rule, succeed (as the Germans do) in interesting themselves in any of the special natural pursuits, such as geology or botany, for which the Alps offer a tempting field; and they show a singular indifference to the political institutions of the Swiss Republic, and the questions which agitate its citizens. They find, however, a sufficient excuse in the variety of the scenery, which in Switzerland is enough to occupy those who have any appreciation of natural beauty, during the few weeks usually allotted to a summer tour.

Season.—It is a common complaint that Switzerland is overcrowded. This is only true between the 1st of August and the 15th of September. The season for Swiss travel may be said to commence in June and to end in October. The carriage-passes are generally open for wheel traffic at some time between the middle of May and June, according to the weather; the Wengern Alp, Tête Noire, and similar passes are, as a rule, practicable for mules and tourists by the later date. Those who visit the Alps in early summer, find the Alpine flowers in full beauty, the effect of some of the middle ranges added to by snow; and, as the rush of travellers does not begin before the 1st of August, they obtain better accommodation and more civility, in inns and on the road. The weather, however, is apt to be variable. In August it generally settles for a few weeks; the snow-beds, which give trouble on the higher mule-passes, have disappeared, and the middle mountains, such as the Eggischhorn and Faulhorn, are easily accessible. September and October are often delightful months, and the latter is especially suited for tours in the Italian valleys. At this season the brilliant tones of the foliage, the long shadows, and the delicate mists, which, in fine weather, gather every night to disperse before the morning sun, afford a grateful change from the hard monotonous glare of midsummer. The pedestrian feels the heat less oppressive in the valleys; but the climber is liable to find himself cut off from his pursuit by a heavy snow-fall, which the sun has no longer power to remove.

Mountaineers frequent the Alps from June to September. Rock mountains, *e.g.*, the Matterhorn, Dent Blanche, Finsteraarhorn, Schreckhorn, are easiest in late summer, when the snow and ice have melted off the crags. An ascent, which will be comparatively easy six weeks later, is often excessively laborious and dangerous at the beginning of July. Snow mountains and many high passes, on the other hand, are often easiest in early summer. The crevasses are well bridged, "Bergschrunds" in some cases unopened, and snow takes the place of ice on many slopes and ridges.

These facilities are counterbalanced, however, by the increased danger from avalanches above the snow-level. One of the first English mountaineers (Mr. Tuckett), in climbing with the best guides at this season, has had several narrow escapes. The early traveller, therefore, should take the best guides, consult them beforehand on the prudence of any ascent he contemplates, and implicitly follow their advice.

Some enthusiastic lovers of the Alps have invented a new pleasure by visiting Chamonix or Zermatt at Christmas. The winter aspect of the Alps has other charms besides that of novelty. The want of colour in the landscape is relieved by wonderful depth and tenderness in the atmosphere; the waterfalls are converted into fantastic columns of ice, and the pine-forest in its snow mantle presents effects of singular beauty. Some of the loftiest summits (Mont Blanc, the Jungfrau, the Wetterhorn, the Schreckhorn) have also been attained at this season; but such feats, if not more dangerous, involve naturally far more exposure and hardship than in summer, and are never likely to become popular.

German doctors have discovered that, in some cases or stages of lung disease, a winter residence in mountain air has a most beneficial effect, and the discovery has been acknowledged and adopted by English physicians. Davos and Wiesen, in Canton Graubünden, are considered very favourable spots, and the comforts required by invalids can now be had there. Over 1000 patients, of whom 200 were English, spent the winter of 1878-79 at Davos, and the number annually increases. The Upper Engadine also claims to be a suitable winter residence for invalids.

The climate of the head of the Lake of Geneva is also considered favourable to patients. It resembles that of the Cornice, with less sunheat, and an absence of sea-air, and is therefore suitable to patients who cannot bear an atmosphere so stimulating as that of Cannes or Nice.

Plan of Journey.—In planning his journey, the inexperienced traveller may find some assistance in the Skeleton Routes subsequently given. In a first tour, he will probably yield to the natural temptation to see as much as possible in the time at his disposal; as he grows older in travel, he will learn that the most vivid and enduring impressions are those that are gained by a stay of some duration near one centre, and that the pressure and worry of constant moving-on more than counterbalance the pleasure of novelty.

Two or three days of comparative rest in the week should generally be allowed. It is wise to study a tour beforehand, so as to draw out a programme of the places to be visited, and the manner in which time may be distributed. But to treat such a self-imposed scheme as an unalterable law, to be adhered to despite weather, fatigue, or better information, is a serious, though common, mistake.

Alpine travellers may be divided into four classes: the *Infirm*, who are limited to such spots as can be reached in carriages or chaises-à-porteurs; *General Travellers*, the largest class, including many ladies who can enjoy a day's ride and from time to time a walk of several hours in Alpine air; *Pedestrians*, who habitually prefer their own legs to any animal's; and lastly, *Mountaineers*, whose first object is to seek adventure and explore the strange beauties of the world of snow and ice. It is obvious that little general advice can be given applying equally to all classes. The expenses of those who constantly employ carriages will be the heaviest. The unambitious pedestrian will spend least, while the mule-hire of the "general traveller" will be equalled if not exceeded by the sums the mountaineer must pay for guides and provisions.

For carriage or general travelling, four is a good party. Pedestrians and mountaineers generally travel in twos or threes; more than three travellers should not, as a rule, be on the same rope in glacier expeditions. Those who will start early in the morning are well rewarded. They enjoy the coolness and clearness of the first hours of the day, and, arriving in good time in the afternoon, have the first choice of rooms and time for an evening stroll. To walk along a high road in an alpine valley is generally an unprofitable expenditure of time and energy: this remark does not apply to the carriage-passes. Expense is diminished, and the irksomeness of a possibly unwelcome companion avoided, by carrying one's own knapsack. On the other hand, the additional strain of a burden diminishes the pedestrian's freedom of motion and power of enjoyment. A man with a knapsack unconsciously acquires the habit of plodding straight on, where, if unladen, he would turn aside to enjoy a view or secure a rare plant. On a frequented pass a pedestrian may often find an opportunity of sending on his traps with the luggage of another party. A good compromise, where this is impossible, is to engage a porter as far as the top of the hill.

Language.—A knowledge of the language of the country is, of course, of the greatest service to the traveller, doubling the profit and enjoyment of his tour. In the Central and Western Alps the languages spoken are French, Italian, German, and, in Canton Graubünden, Romansch, an independent Romance language. German or Italian is, however, generally understood at the inns in Romansch districts. The traveller who, being ignorant of German or Italian, proposes to leave the highroad, will do well to engage a courier or guide who can speak the language of the country he is about to visit, as well as French. All languages are impurely spoken in the Alpine regions; those who suffer from shyness need not, therefore, be under any fear as to their pronunciation. In venting his indignation, however, the imperfect linguist will be prudent in confining himself to words of the exact force and meaning of which he is assured. It is seldom necessary or expedient to resent an overcharge by such expressions as "voleur," or to swear at a foreign official.

Outfit.—Portmanteaus are best procured in England. The general traveller can take what he likes in a capacious carpet-bag on his mule's back. He should not omit a good bundle of cloaks in a mackintosh cover, and a luncheon-basket, not too cumbrous, may often prove serviceable.

Parchment, or adhesive labels, for writing directions for the baggage (the managers of public conveyances abroad often *insist* upon each package being addressed, before they will take charge of it); and one or two leather straps, to keep together books, coats, shawls, &c., or small parcels, will be found very useful.

The following hints are addressed chiefly to pedestrians.

The outfit described below is somewhat ample, but, with what is carried on the person, may be contained in an ordinary knapsack, such as are sold in London. This should be as light as possible, made of oilcloth, with broad shoulder-straps. Mr. White has invented an improved frame for carrying the knapsack (supplied by Price, 33, Marylebone Street, W.). It is not, however, suitable for rock-climbing. Those who carry their own traps often prefer a bag hung in the hollow of the back, after the pattern now adopted for the army.

The *clothes* should be a suit of woollen tweed, of medium thickness— better too thick than too thin, for the changes of temperature on the mountains are considerable, and it is easier to protect yourself against heat than cold. The pockets should be made to button up, one being expressly made to hold maps. The pedestrian who travels without a compass and the best map procurable of the district he proposes to explore, deserves any misadventure which may befall him. A light *mackintosh* or tweed waterproof can be strapped on the bag or knapsack.

2. A second pair of trousers (thin) to put on in the evening after rain.

3. Two flannel shirts, a few linen collars, and two pairs linen drawers.

4. Three pair of thick and soft woollen socks: the Scotch or Irish are the best; and 2 pairs thin silk socks for evening.

5. A night-shirt, not too bulky.

6. Pocket-handkerchiefs.

7. A pair of leather slippers, stout enough to stroll out in at evening.

The boots and socks are all-important. The boots should be laced shooting-boots, with low broad heels and projecting welt, strongly nailed. When in use, they should be greased every night. Extra laces should be carried.

Washing materials, brushes, razor, &c., are best carried in a small mackintosh roll. The hat should be a light felt (not black) broad-brimmed enough to protect the back of the head. The following small articles, or some of them, may be carried in the pockets or knapsack: guide-book, map, note-book, drinking-cup of leather or metal, flask, knife with corkscrew, needles and thread in a case, soap-cerate plaister, a field-glass, a compass; an umbrella, useful both for sun and rain, is added by some old travellers.

Diet and Precautions for Health.—Nothing is more conducive to health than the combination of exercise, pure air, and wholesome enjoyment which is found by a pedestrian in the Alps. Like most good things, however, an alpine tour may be abused. Dr. Clifford Allbutt has laid down ('Alpine Journal,' vol. viii. p. 32) some elementary rules.

If not already in training, be content to make very short journeys at first. After a fortnight's practice you will learn your powers. Never start on an empty stomach, however disinclined for food. Take, during the day's walk, frequent light meals, in preference to one or two heavy ones. Chocolate will often be found a useful substitute for meat, and cold tea or coffee, made with milk and sugar, for wine. Some ingenious and sensible climbers carry a large india-rubber bowl, a lemon and some sugar. By adding snow or ice-water to their wine, they can make, at a moment's notice, an excellent cup, less heating and more refreshing than pure wine. Beware how you drink of cold springs, when heated. Start at a slow, steady pace, and reserve any attempts at speed for the last hour or two. Arrange your tour so as to allow, as far as possible, intervals of rest between the hard days.

Immediately on your arrival, after a day's walk, take some light refreshment (a crust and a glass of lemonade), wash with soap and tepid water, and change your linen. If at all fatigued, or if the circulation be hurried, lie down after washing and dressing, and try to sleep for a few minutes before dinner. When over-fatigued, it is sometimes better to take a basin of soup and go to bed than to add a heavy meal to the fatigues of the wearied body; at such times weak tea is preferable to wine. A good restorative is egg-flip, made of brandy and egg; and a tumbler of lemon-juice, water, and sugar, if sipped (not gulped down), materially allays feverishness. Lemons can often be obtained at the inns.

For sickness and diarrhœa the most convenient and efficient medicine is chlorodyne; but ordinary mild diarrhœa is often beneficial, and should not be checked. A doctor prescribes " Carbonate of soda 20 grains, a teaspoonful each of syrup of ginger and tincture of rhubarb, to be taken three or four times a-day. If the diarrhœa continues, 15 grains of prepared chalk, bismuth, and charcoal, may be taken in water as often. To this, in obstinate cases, 20 to 30 grains of laudanum may be added. Incipient diarrhœa may sometimes be checked by a good pull of brandy." (*C. A.*)

Constipation should be met by the use of compound rhubarb pills. Seidlitz powders, divided into small doses, are a convenient and cooling draught. Quinine pills are often useful.

As a rule, the less medicine the traveller takes the better.

In a few spots on the Italian side, and in some on the Swiss, especially the valley of the Rhone, there is malaria in marshy places and about the embouchures of rivers, where they empty themselves into lakes, and travellers should avoid sleeping in such districts.

Care of the Feet.—Wash them at night, when heated, with soap and lukewarm water, in the morning with cold. If there is any tenderness, soap them before starting, leaving the soap on. Blisters, if they form, must be pricked gently at the edges. Broken blisters and abrasions are best treated with repeated paintings of collodion. If walking is a necessity, paint first with collodion, and then cover over with soap-cerate plaister (to be bought at Bell's, 338, Oxford Street), taking care to put on a piece sufficiently large fully to cover the wounded part. Bruises are best treated with calendula.

Expense.—The expenses of a tour naturally vary, according to the habits of the traveller, the means of conveyance he uses, and the amount of ground he passes over. In the mountains, his hotel bill may be kept down to 10 to 12 francs a-day: in the towns it will rise to about 15 or 16 francs. A traveller who takes a guide adds about 8 francs a-day to his expenses; those who use horses, 15 francs. A journey of a month to five weeks may be reckoned at between 30*l.* and 40*l.* a-head, without extravagance, for an ordinary tour. This sum includes railway fares out and home. The terms on which tourists can contract for circular tickets and coupons will be found in the agents' circulars.

§ 6. DIRECTIONS AND REQUISITES FOR MOUNTAINEERS.

Mountain-climbing has been treated as unjustifiable, on the ground that is dangerous. The danger is, as in yachting, doubtless real, but by care is reduced to a minimum, while the advantages are certain and lasting. Some critics occasionally ask " What is the good of it?" a question justly irritating to the intelligent lover of mountains. It has drawn many replies, but few better than the following, from a most distinguished mountaineer—Mr. Leslie Stephen. "People still sometimes ask (though they have often had it explained to them) What is the use of going up a mountain? What more do you see at the top than you would at the bottom? Putting out of question the glorious exercise and excitement of climbing a mountain, it would be well worth any trouble to see such views as those which can only be seen on the highest peaks. No doubt there are many views downstairs more capable of being made into pictures. The vast cloudy panorama stretched below your feet from an Alpine summit makes an impression on your mind which can be described neither on canvas nor in writing. It gives an exhilarating sense of unrivalled sublimity, which could no more be given in a painting than one of the scenes in 'Paradise Lost.' It is the constant presence before your eyes of such impressive though indescribable scenery which gives to Alpine exercise such absorbing interest.

" As for the theory that you ought to walk 10 m. a-day and meditate on the beauties of nature, it may do for poets and painters, but it is hard doctrine for a man with a stomach and legs. A man can no more feel the true mountain spirit without having been into the very heart and up to the very tops of the mountains than he can know what the sea is like by standing on the shore. It is just as easy to evolve the idea of a mountain top out of the depths of your moral consciousness as that of a camel. The small patch of glistening white, which you are told is a snow-slope, looks very pretty out of the valley to any one, but it will look very different to a man who has only studied it through an opera-glass, and to one who has had to cut his way up it step by step for hours together. The little knob which your guide-book says is the top of some unpronounceable 'Horn' will gain wonderfully in majesty when you have once stood upon it, and felt as if you were alone in the midst of the heavens, with the kingdoms of earth at your feet; and if you meditate till doomsday on the beautiful lights and shades, the graceful sweeps of the mountain ridges, you will not be a bit nearer to the sensation of standing on a knife-like ridge, with the toe of your boot over Italy, and the heel over Switzerland."

There are, it must be added, beauties of form and colour in the upper glaciers and snowfields, of which the ordinary tourist is utterly ignorant. In the panoramas from the loftiest peaks, the neighbouring mountain forms may sometimes be dwarfed into comparative insignificance. But such views have an unrivalled capacity for receiving various expressions from every change from morning to noon, or noon to evening light, and from every shift of cloud or vapour, and these, owing to the multiplication of mountain huts, it is in many cases no longer difficult to spend hours in watching with a certainty of regaining shelter before nightfall. Moreover, the early-rising forced on those who attempt snow expeditions introduces a traveller to many beautiful effects in nature he might otherwise never suspect.

It is not, however, necessary to decide here whether the advantages and delights of mountaineering outweigh its dangers.

[*Switz.*]   c

We have to deal with the obvious fact that the desire to undertake difficult and adventurous expeditions in the high Alps is yearly becoming more common amongst our countrymen. By many hardy exploits they have proved their aptness for this new description of sport. But several fatal accidents, and a still larger number of hairbreadth escapes, have shown the necessity of insisting on increased caution to inexperienced travellers who are liable to be led into danger by the spirit of imitation. Mountaineers who well understand their own pursuit, who have ascertained by continued practice the limits of their own strength and endurance, who know what the dangers of the high Alps are, and how they may best be avoided, do not require, and would not accept advice. Those who, with little or no knowledge and experience, wish to engage in a pursuit wherein they may at any moment risk, not only their own lives, but also those of their companions, may benefit by the teaching of their veteran predecessors, provided they will remember that no reading can dispense with the necessity for practical training, and some familiarity with the peculiar phenomena of the ice-region of the high Alps. The following paragraphs are condensed from the 18th chapter of ' Peaks, Passes, and Glaciers,' with such additions as recent experience has suggested.

The dangers of alpine expeditions may be divided into two classes—the real and the imaginary. Where a ridge or slope of rock or ice is such that it could be traversed without difficulty if it lay but a few feet above the level of a garden, the substitution on either side of a precipice some hundreds of feet in depth, or of a glacier crevasse, makes no real difference in the work to be done, though it may have a formidable effect on the imagination. Those who cannot remove this source of danger by accustoming themselves to look unmoved down precipices, and to fix their attention exclusively on the ledge or jutting crag to which they must cling with foot or hand, should avoid expeditions where a moment's nervousness may be a cause of danger.

The real dangers of the high Alps may be reduced to the following :—1, the *yielding of snow bridges* that cover crevasses, or of *snow cornices* overhanging precipices; 2, the risk of *slipping upon slopes* of ice, rock, or even turf; 3, the *fall of ice or rocks* from above; 4, the *slipping beneath the feet of a traveller of the upper layer of a steep snow-field*, which may bury him, or carry him over a precipice; 5, the *sudden approach* of bad weather.

It is a fixed rule of mountaineering, which can only be broken with risk to life, that on every steep ice or snow slope or snow-covered glacier, all the members of a party, including the guides, should be attached together with a stout rope. The best rope for the purpose, selected by a committee of the Alpine Club after careful examination, can be procured of Messrs. Buckingham, Broad Street, W.C. The use of the rope in crossing glaciers was known to the commercial travellers of the 16th century. Simler writes, in 1574: "Qui per Alpes iter faciunt peritos locorum qui ipsis præeant conducere solent: hosce fune cingunt, cui etiam aliquot ex his qui sequuntur se astringunt; qui vero præit longâ perticâ (pole) viam explorat, et diligenter in nivibus hiatus hos scrutatur, quod si forte imprudens in aliquem deciderit, a sociis qui eodem fune cincti sunt sustinetur etextrahitur."

The first to apply the rope to " mountaineering," in the strict sense of the word, were the guides of Chamonix, and it was their skill in its use which gave them their early pre-eminence as glacier guides. In remote parts of the Alps the local guide is still often ignorant of the proper use of the rope, and it is left to the traveller to insist on its adoption.

From covered crevasses almost absolute security is obtained by means of this precaution. In the *higher* region of the glaciers, chasms of considerable width are often completely bridged over by a covering of snow, so that no indication of their existence is seen on the surface. The bridges often yield under the weight of a man's footsteps; in such a case an unroped man, unless he is arrested by his outspread arms and ice-axe, must fall into the chasm, in which case, if alone, his chance of life is faint indeed. But if several travellers are tied together with a stout rope, as it is in the highest degree improbable that a majority of them should fall at the same moment into the same crevasse, no appreciable danger from this cause need be incurred. Even two travellers tied together may with proper attention diminish this risk, but real security is obtained only when they are three or more in number. It is because he cannot be protected from this danger that a man who goes alone over the névé of a glacier incurs a risk which must be called unjustifiable. *The rope, to be of any service, must be kept nearly tight*, and its proper management requires teaching, but is soon learned. Its proper use is to check and prevent a fall, rather than to pull a man out of a crevasse. When a party consists of four persons or more, the interval should be 15 ft. between every two; when of three, 18 or 20 ft.; when two alone, 30 or 40 ft.

One of the most terrible accidents of recent years, that on the Lyskamm in 1877, was caused by the giving way of a snow cornice, and narrow escapes from similar accidents have been frequent.

This danger can only be avoided by care, constantly observing the character of the crest being traversed, and keeping, where necessary, at a distance from the edge. The leader may often be unable to see what he is standing upon, but the last man, from 40 to 100 feet lower down, can generally watch from moment to moment his advance, and give timely warning when he draws too near the danger. It is in descending that this risk is most to be guarded against.

For surmounting steep ice-slopes by cutting steps the axe is the proper instrument. Considerable practice is required to use it for this purpose with effect, and comparatively few amateurs acquire much proficiency.

The ice-axe, however, has many other uses and advantages. It is frequently of service in clearing out or deepening steps which the leader has made, and in ascending or descending steep ice or snow it is employed as an anchor. The novice should choose an axe with a broad blade, but should avoid burdening himself with too heavy a weapon. After a few weeks in the Alps, he will be competent to select his own from among the approved models. Tools so made are to be procured complete in London of Messrs. Hill, 4, Haymarket. Ice-axes can also be obtained in Switzerland, at Chamonix, and elsewhere. At Evolena a light and convenient axe is made.

There are many ice-slopes where *the fall* of one of the party must inevitably drag down all his companions. There are very few where competent companions cannot prevent a fall. The rope, it is sometimes assumed, only increases the general danger on steep slopes. This is a mistake, arising from an imperfect knowledge of how to use it. Properly managed, it arrests *a slip* before it has time to become *a fall*. The instantaneous check gives time to recover to the traveller who has missed his footing. This, of course, is only the case when the rope is handled by experienced climbers who know how to keep it almost taut, while allowing one another sufficient liberty of movement. Where slopes of this nature have to be traversed, it is for those concerned to consider the extent of the peril, and their own capacity. In doing this they should give full weight to the increased risk caused by inexperience in any one of them. There is, perhaps, no act of prudence more irksome to the mountaineer than to decline to take with him, on an expedition of serious or unknown difficulty, an athletic youth who is new to the mountains. Whenever such a question arises, the lesson of the Matterhorn should be recalled to memory.

The danger arising from ice and fragments of rock falling across the track may, to a great extent, be avoided by a judicious choice of route. Experienced mountaineers learn to recognise the positions where ice detached from a higher level descends over a precipice or a steep slope. They either avoid such spots altogether or are careful to pass them early in the morning, before the sun has loosened the impending masses, or late in the day, after his rays have been withdrawn.

Several accidents, however, have occurred within the last few years from the fall of séracs and stones, in places generally held free from danger, which should induce great care in selection of a route by the guides. This danger, being often difficult to recognise, is sometimes unduly despised, both by guides and travellers. On slopes or crags, exposed to rockfalls, the rope somewhat increases the risk, as it may be struck, or impede a traveller from suddenly leaping, and it may, therefore, be dispensed with, unless the danger of doing so seems greater than that likely to be incurred by its use.

The ordinary risks of alpine adventure are seriously increased during bad weather, and new dangers may then assail the traveller. Masses of rock are detached from their previously firm resting-places, and come thundering down across the track. Falling snow obscures the view and effaces the footprints, so that it soon becomes equally difficult to advance and to retreat. The new snow forms a coating on the steep slopes of ice and rock, and renders them, for a time, highly dangerous. Worst of all, when snow is accompanied by violent gusts of wind, the *tourmente,* or snow-whirlwind, bewilders the traveller, half-blinded by the fine dust-like snow, and benumbs his limbs with its biting breath. A reasonable man will avoid bad weather in the high Alps whenever it can be foreseen, or resort to an immediate retreat when unexpectedly attacked by it. Attention to the bearings of the compass and to land-marks when the appearance of the weather becomes doubtful will generally enable a party to retrace their steps. The tendency of second-rate guides to put off facing the storm by refusing to descend at once should be resisted. An error of judgment of this kind led, in 1870, on Mont Blanc, to the most fatal of all alpine accidents. Bad weather may last for days, and those who cannot face it with unimpaired powers will scarcely find the effects of many hours' exposure counteracted by the energy of despair. Few summer travellers have an idea of the possible terrors of the Alps in bad weather.

On glacier expeditions a single traveller *must* take two guides, or a guide and porter. On easy snow and ice expeditions, it is enough if the first and last man on the rope and every alternate climber is a guide or a practised mountaineer. *Two tiros must never be roped next one another,* Neglect of this rule led, in 1878, to the fatal accident on Monte Cevedale, one of the safest and easiest snow-peaks in the Alps for a properly constituted party. On really difficult peaks inexperienced men have no business at all; to qualify themselves to ascend these, they are bound to learn steadiness and the rules of the craft by attempting easy snow-climbs under the care of experienced mountaineers. Those who cannot find experienced friends to take care of them, or afford a proper complement of guides, learn to climb at the risk of their own lives and of their guide's or porter's. No economical motive can be an excuse for reckless proceedings, which are condemned by all true mountaineers.

In addition to the requisites of an ordinary traveller, and to the indispensable rope and ice-axe, the mountaineer must provide himself with the following articles :—

A pair of neutral-tinted spectacles, framed in wire, for snow work.

A linen mask, for protection from sunburn, which in some cases causes very painful blistering of the face. A veil is far less serviceable and interferes with the eyesight. Cold-cream for the same purpose. To be really efficacious, this should be applied from time to time during the day. The small zinc bottles sold at Lloyd's, 3, Egg-street, Leicester Square, are very convenient.

Woollen or skin gloves with the hair turned inwards, to keep the hands warm. The best are made with a bag for all the fingers.

A knitted bonnet to protect the ears from frost-bite, also useful for sleeping in chalets or huts.

Gaiters (these are not indispensable). The best are the cloth gaiters used by the Swiss guides. They should strap, not button.

A light plaid is serviceable. Another excellent form of wrap is a knitted woollen waistcoat or jersey.

The mountaineer is subject to two special physical discomforts, mountain-sickness and frost-bite.

Mountain-sickness is a general feeling of collapse, coupled, sometimes, with violent headache and vomiting. Like sea-sickness, which it much resembles, it is very capricious in its attacks, and is felt unequally by different constitutions, and even by the same constitution at different times. The traveller who, on first ascending above 10,000 feet, feels its very unpleasant symptoms, should not be too easily discouraged. Habit will probably do much to cure him, and ten days later he may find himself breathing with delight the air of 15,000 feet. Those who *on European mountains* suffer permanently are a small minority. There is little doubt that above 12,000 feet the capacity of the human frame for strong exertion diminishes, but it has been abundantly proved that, in the majority of cases, the diminution is too small to be noticed, except by careful comparison. Mountain-sickness is a reality; but the name is often used as a dignified cloak for indigestion and want of training.

Frost-bite is a very serious danger to the mountaineer. Dr. C. Allbutt gives the following directions for its treatment. First rub the part affected gently with snow, then rub more briskly with cold water. This should be done out of doors away from wind, or in a cold room. The same principles should be followed when the sufferer is insensible from cold. Gentle rubbing with soft woollens in a cold room should be tried first, and when swallowing power returns, a little weak warm wine and water administered. The patient should next be put in a cold bed in a cool room. Hot bottles and a warm room are fatal kindness.

§ 7. ALPINE CLUBS.

The influence of these organisations on alpine travel has been, and is, too important to allow of their being passed over without some notice.

It 1857, two or three Englishmen, feeling it would be an advantage to those who met during the summer in Switzerland to meet also at home, determined to arrange social meetings in London, at which alpine knowledge might be exchanged and extended, and friendships formed in the mountains cemented. This was the origin of The Alpine Club, which was formally founded in 1858. Association led to the publication of a joint volume, under the title of ' Peaks, Passes, and Glaciers,' by its members; and its immense success secured the prosperity and popularity of the new society.

It now numbers nearly 500 members, meets once a month from December to June, and issues a quarterly journal devoted to " mountain adventure and scientific research." Its members have also published many books and maps illustrating the alpine region (see *post*). The qualification required for membership is such a number of mountain expeditions or such contributions to alpine literature, science, or art, as the Committee consider sufficient. The club-rooms are No. 8, St. Martin's Place, W.C. The Club has steadily endeavoured to diminish the dangers inseparable from its favourite pursuit by providing climbers with the best implements, and pointing out the most essential precautions. On two occasions it has brought a powerful influence to bear on the French Government, with the object of modifying the abuses which had made the rules of the Chamonix guides a danger to tourists.

The most important and unexpected result of the formation of the Alpine Club has been the spirit of imitation it has roused on the Continent. Switzerland, Austria, and Italy founded Alpine Clubs in 1863; France in 1874. The Austrian Club united some years ago with the German; but an independent Club has been set up at Vienna. The Vosges, the Carpathians, and the Pyrenees have each their own society. These bodies have been presided over by statesmen or men of science or letters (S. Sella, Herr von Sonklar, M. Joanne), number their members by thousands, and are organised in local lodges or sections, which meet frequently. They publish journals and annual volumes, and once a year hold a festival, generally in some Alpine or sub-Alpine town. They are distinguished from the English Club by the fact that no qualification beyond respectability is required for membership.

If our own Alpine Club can boast of having conquered the High Alps, the foreign clubs may be said to have organised the territory thus won from nature. Favoured by their position near the mountains, these societies have devoted their energies to the instruction of peasants to act as guides, and to the provision of huts where the climber may sleep before making his ascent. They have thus placed many great peaks within the reach of men, or even women, of moderate powers. They have brought the remotest valleys into communication with the world, and given an impulse to local improvements of every description. By their publications and the maps they have produced, they have added largely to our knowledge of the Alps, their history and natural phenomena, and they have succeeded, not only in Teutonic lands, but also in Italy, and to some extent in France, in creating a genuine taste for healthy adventure among the youth of the nation. In almost every considerable sub-alpine town of N. Italy, the traveller will find rooms belonging to the local branch of the Italian Club, containing maps and books relating to the district. Access to these is liberally allowed to foreigners.

§ 8. ROUTES TO SWITZERLAND, AND SKELETON TOURS.

English travellers generally enter Switzerland either by Geneva, Pontarlier, or Bâle. Geneva is reached viâ Paris and Mâcon, London to Paris viâ Boulogne, 8 hours; Paris to Mâcon, $5\frac{1}{2}$ hours; Mâcon to Geneva, 4 hours. Pontarlier is the frontier station where the lines for Neuchâtel and Lausanne separate. Neuchâtel is reached in about 11 hours, Lausanne in 13 hours from Paris. Through carriages run from the pier at Calais to Switzerland, viâ Paris, as well as viâ Rheims.

Bâle is reached by direct train from Calais viâ Amiens and Rheims in 16 hrs. [Travellers intending to break the journey at Rheims are warned that they will have to change carriages at a small country station 3 miles outside the town; Laon is therefore preferable as a sleeping-place.]

Bâle may also be reached from Paris viâ Delle in $10\frac{1}{4}$ hours. Those who do not object to a long passage may prefer the Ostend route. A train of through-carriages runs from Ostend viâ Brussels, Luxembourg, Metz, and Strassburg to Bâle in 19 hours.

A cheaper but slower route is by Rotterdam and the Rhine.

From Bâle the traveller may go by express trains—

To Lucerne in $2\frac{1}{4}$ hrs.
To Lugano in $7\frac{3}{4}$ hrs.
To Milan viâ the St. Gothard in $10\frac{1}{4}$ hrs.
To Berne in $3\frac{1}{4}$ hrs.
To Thun in $4\frac{1}{4}$ hrs.
To Zürich in $2\frac{1}{2}$ hrs.
To Geneva by Bienne, Neuchâtel, and Lausanne in 8 hrs.
To Schaffhausen in 2 hrs.
To Constance in $3\frac{1}{4}$ hrs.

Friedrichshafen may be reached—

London to Cologne, $15\frac{1}{4}$ hours; Cologne by Frankfort, Stuttgart, and Ulm to Friedrichshafen, 16 hours.
From Friedrichshafen the traveller may go to Zürich by Romanshorn, or to Ragatz or Coire by Rorschach, steamer and rail.

Travellers going first to Chamonix will go by Paris, Geneva, or Pontarlier and Lausanne; those to Berne and the Oberland by Neuchâtel or Bâle.

The direct route to Zürich and the Engadine is by Bâle and Chur. The St. Gothard line offers an alternative route which will be preferred by those who wish to avoid the 11 hrs. drive over the bleak Julier Pass. The rail is left at Como, whence there is a steamer to Colico and rail to Chiavenna. Chiavenna to St. Moritz is a drive of 6¼ hrs.

At Paris the stations of the Northern of France and the Eastern (the Bâle line) are close together. All the others are half-an-hour's drive or more apart.

Skeleton Tours.—For the guidance of travellers, skeleton tours are here given, adapted to the convenience and taste of persons of different degrees of bodily strength, and using different modes of conveyance. They are framed so as to show what may be done within a given time; but no sounder advice can be offered to those who desire real and thorough enjoyment in travelling than carefully to abstain from doing all that is possible in the time at their disposal. The grand scenes of nature cannot be fully apprehended at a glance, and the impression which will be retained of such as have been seen repeatedly, and under varying conditions of weather and light, will be far more prized than the crowd of imperfect images that can alone be carried away in the course of a hurried advance from one place to another.

The traveller visiting the Alps for the first time with a month at his disposal, will do well to be content with seeing the Oberland and Chamonix; with six weeks he may include Zermatt. A visit to the Engadine will link itself naturally with the Italian Lakes, whence the traveller may turn to the southern valleys of Monte Rosa. Though further details, as to Savoy and Piedmont, will be found in the Introduction to the second portion of this Handbook, no attempt has been made to confine the skeleton routes given below, within the *political frontiers* of Switzerland.

Routes for carriage travellers have been placed first, followed by several suitable for the general tourist, who can ride and walk when needful. A specimen tour for young men, who, having engaged a good guide, wish to qualify themselves as mountaineers, has been added.

Each traveller must, however, decide for himself where to halt, and the following outlines may be used on that understanding for any portion of the alpine chain which it is desired to explore.

CARRIAGE TOUR: about six weeks of easy travelling. A few easy excursions, which may be accomplished in a *chaise-à-porteurs*, are given in italics.

Lucerne.
Vitznau, by steamer.
Ascend Rigi, and return. (Rly.)
Flüelen, by steamer.
Drive to Andermatt, and return.
Lucerne, by steamer or road.
Visit Engelberg.
Meiringen, by Brunig Pass.
Visit the Reichenbach and Giessbach.
Steamer to Interlaken.
Lauterbrunnen, and thence by *Wengern Alp* to Grindelwald; returning to Interlaken.
Thun.

Berne, }
Fribourg, } Rly.
Lausanne, }
Visit Vevey and Chillon, by steamer.
Geneva.
Sallanches.
Chamonix.
Montanvers.
Fléyère.
Tête Noire to Martigny.
Aigle. (Making an excursion to Sepey, and Hôtel des Diablerets, in the Val des Ormonts.)
Brieg (Rly.).

Bel Alp.
Domo d'Ossola, by Simplon Pass.
Baveno.
Borromean Islands.
Luino, by steamboat.
Lugano.
Monte Generoso.
Steamer to Porlezza; thence to Menaggio, and to Varenna or (by boat) Bellaggio.

Como and back.
Chiavenna.
Splügen or Thusis by Splügen Pass.
Coire or Ragatz, visiting the Baths of Pfäffers.
Wesen.
Rappersweil, and steamer to Zürich.
Schaffhausen.

From Chiavenna the route may be varied as follows:

St. Moritz, by Maloja Pass.
Pontresina.
Drive to Bernina Pass.
Albula Pass to Tiefenkasten.
Schyn Pass to Thusis.

Visit Via Mala and to Chur and Ragatz.
Visit Pfäffers Bad.
Rail to Glarus and Stachelberg.
Rail to Zürich.

ROUTE BY BRIDLE-PATHS AND CARRIAGE-ROADS, including much of the fine scenery of the central Alps. Three months. It is assumed that wherever there is a good carriage-road it should be used. A few excursions partly on foot are given in italics. By dividing this route at Martigny it supplies two tours of ordinary length.

Bâle to Lucerne, direct; or by Schaffhausen and Zürich.
Ascend the Rigi from Arth [rly].
Descend to Vitznau [rly] or to Weggis.
Return to Lucerne.—Ascend Pilatus and sleep.—Descend to Alpnach.
By Stanz to Engelberg.
Joch Pass to Meiringen.
Baths of Reichenbach.
Pass of the Great Scheideck.
Faulhorn.
Grindelwald.
Excursion to the Lower Glacier of Grindelwald.
Wengern Alp to Lauterbrunnen.
Mürren and Fall of Schmadribach.
Interlaken.
Excursion to the Giessbach.
Thun.
Saanen, by the Simmenthal.
Vevey, Montreux-Territet, or H. Rigi Vaudois, by the Dent de Jaman Pass. [Or from Thun to Kandersteg, over the Gemmi to Leukerbad, and down the Rhone valley to Lake of Geneva.]
Castle of Chillon.
Lausanne.
Geneva.
Excursion to the Salève.
Chamonix.
Montanvers. Chapeau.

Brévent.
Martigny, by Tête Noire Pass.
Orsières.
Aosta, by St. Bernard.
Ascent of the Becca di Nona. Descent to Cogne.
Ascent of the Pousset.
Val Savaranche, by Col de Lauzon.
Courmayeur.
Ascent of the Cramont.
Châtillon.
Gressoney St. Jean.
Inn on the Col d'Ollen.
Alagna.
Varallo.
Excursion up Val Mastalone.
Orta, by the Col di Colma.
Over Monte Motterone to Baveno.
Ponte Grande in the Val Anzasca.
Macugnaga.
Excursion to Macugnaga Glacier.
*Mattmark or Saas, by the Monte Moro Pass.**
Sion.

* Those who fear to undertake the Pass of the Moro may vary the route by going from Varallo by Val Mastalone to Val Anzasca, returning to Baveno, thence by steamer to Locarno or Magadino, by Bellinzona to Airolo and over the St. Gothard and Furca Passes to the Upper Valais. From Viesch to the Eggischhorn, thence to Zermatt, returning by Visp to Brieg, and thence by the Simplon to Domo d'Ossola.

Evolena and Arolla.
St. Luc, in Val d'Anniviers, by Col de Torrent.
Zmeiden, in Turtman Thal, ascending *Bella Tola* on the way.
St. Niklaus in the Vispthal, ascending *Schwarzhorn.*
Zermatt.
Riffelberg and Gorner Grat.
Ascent to Schwarzsee and *Hörnli.*
Visp, in the valley of the Rhone.
Bel Alp.
Eggischhorn Hotel, by *crossing the Aletsch Glacier* and Rieder Alp.
Ascend the Eggischhorn.
Visit Märjelensee and *Aletsch Glacier.*
Brieg.
Domo d'Ossola, by Simplon Pass.
Canobbio, by Val Vigezzo.
Luino.
Lugano.

Excursion to Monte Generoso.
By Porlezza and Menaggio to Bellaggio, on the Lake of Como.
Varenna.
Lecco, by the Lake.
Como, by Erba.
Colico, by steamer.
Chiavenna.
Andeer, by Splügen Pass.
Coire, by Via Mala.
Ragatz and Pfäffers.
Wesen, by Wallenstadt.
Baths of Stachelberg.
Excursion to Ober Sand Alp.
Altdorf, by Klausen Pass.
Brunnen.
Glarus, by Muotta Thal.
St. Gall.
Rorschach.
Friedrichshafen.

From Chiavenna the Engadine may be visited (see previous route), or from Bellaggio the following route may be taken.

Como, by steamer.
Lecco, by Erba, rail to Bergamo and Lago d'Iséo.
Steamer to Lovere.

Drive by Val Camonica to Edolo.
Aprica Pass to Le Prese.
Bernina Pass to Pontresina, &c.

TOUR FOR MODERATE PEDESTRIANS, keeping to the higher parts of the Swiss and Savoy Alps. It is assumed that some days of rest should be allowed to intervene, and that the passes or ascents marked in italics should not be attempted without guides.

Engelberg.
Ascend the Titlis, and sleep at the Inn on the Engstlen Alp.
To Im Hof, and Grimsel Hospice.
Sidelhorn and Oberaar Glacier.
Strahleck Pass to Grindelwald.
Faulhorn.
Inn on the Wengern Alp.
By Lauterbrunnen to Mürren.
To Kandersteg, *by the Tschingel Glacier and Gasteren Thal.*
Leukerbad, by Gemmi Pass.
Ascend Torrenthorn ; descend to H. Nesthorn in the Lötschenthal.
By *Lötschlücke* from H. Nesthorn, to the Eggischhorn.
Eggischhorn, *Aletsch Glacier.*
Bel Alp.
Sparrenhorn.
Saas.
Excursion to Fée Alp; sleep at Mattmark.

Macugnaga by Monte Moro.
Excursion to Macugnaga Glacier.
Sleep at Ponte Grande.
Varallo, by the Baranca Pass and Val Mastalone.
Alagna.
Excursion to Pile Alp and Val di Bours ; sleep at Col d'Ollen.
Gressoney.
Ascend the Grauhaupt.
Breuil, *by the Cimes Blanches,* or in two days by Brussone and Châtillon.
To Riffelberg Hotel, *by the St. Théodule Pass.*
Excursions about Zermatt.
Sleep at St. Niklaus.
By Augstbord Pass (Schwarzhorn), to Zmeiden in the Turtman Thal. Visit the Turtman Glacier.
By Zmeiden Pass, or Pas du Bœuf, with ascent of Bella Tola, to St. Luc.
Zinal. Visit the *glacier,* or Arpitetta Alp.

Evolena or Arolla, by Col de Torrent.
Col de Collon to Prérayen (or by *Otemma Glacier* to Inn at Mauvoisin, and next day by Col de Fenêtre to Aosta).
Aosta.
Becca di Nona.
Courmayeur.

Ascend the Cramont.
To Chamonix, by the *Col du Géant, Grands Mulets.*
Cross *Buet* to Sixt.
Col de Sageroux to Champéry.
Pas de Morgin to Thonon.

Tour of three weeks in Eastern Switzerland for riders or moderate walkers.

Ragatz.
Davos, by Prätigau.
Bergün, by Sertig Thal.
Pontresina, by Albula.
[Piz Languard, Surlej Fuorcla, Fex Thal, &c.]
Old Bernina Pass to Poschiavo.
Canciano Pass to Chiesa.
Muretto Pass to Maloja. Visit Albigna glacier, and cross to Val Bondasca

and Promontogno.
Madriser Pass.
Avers Thal to Splügen.
Lugnetz Thal to Ilanz.
Ascend Piz Mundaun.
Drive to Trons, Lavazjoch to Disentis.
Sandgrat to Stachelberg.
Elm, Segnes Pass, to Flims and Reichenau.

Tour for good walkers, with a glacier guide.

Geneva.
Sixt.
Over Buet to Chamonix.
Grands Mulets.
Jardin.
Col du Tour, Col du Sonadon, Glacier Pass to Arolla, Col de Bertol to Zermatt (high-level route).
Ascend Monte Rosa.
Alphubel Pass to Saas.
Zwischbergen Pass to Simplon.
Ascend Monte Leone.
Bel Alp.
Ascend Aletschhorn.
Eggischhorn.
Ascend Finsteraarhorn.
Mönch Joch to Grindelwald.
Lauteraarjoch to Grimsel.

Or Bel Alp.
Beichgrat to Lötschenthal.
Petersgrat to Lauterbrunnen.
Wengern Alp.
Grindelwald.
Mönchjoch to Eggischhorn.
Oberaarjoch to Grimsel.
Grimsel, by Galenstock, to Furka.
Maderaner Thal.
Clariden Pass to Tödi hut.
Ascend Tödi, descend to Dissentis.
Camadra Pass to Olivone.
Cross Piz Valrhein to Splügen.
By Averserthal to Promontogno.
Bondasca Pass to Baths of Masino.
Sissone Pass to Maloya.
Pontresina.   Tour of the Bernina.
Lower Engadine, Piz Linard.
Silvretta Pass to the Prätigau and Ragatz.

§ 9. SELECTED LIST OF BOOKS AND MAPS.

The following works are selected from the long catalogue of works on the Alps as likely to interest and instruct Swiss travellers :—

BEATTIE, W.—'Switzerland,' illustrated by W. H. Bartlett. 1836.
———— 'The Waldenses,' illustrated by W. H. Bartlett and W. Brockedon. 1838.
BERLEPSCH.—'The Alps; or, Sketches of Life and Nature in the Mountains.' Translated by Leslie Stephen, 1861.
BONNEY, Rev. T. G.—'The Alpine Regions of Switzerland and the Neighbouring Countries,' 1868.
———— 'Outline Sketches in the High Alps of Dauphiné,' London, 1865.
BONNEY, Rev. T. G.— 'Lake and Mountain Scenery of the Swiss Alps, illustrated by G. Closs and O. Fröhlicher, with text by T. G. Bonney. 1874.

BROCKEDON, W.—'Illustrations of the Passes of the Alps,' 2 vols., 1828.
—————— 'Journals of Excursions in the Alps,' 1843.
BUTLER, S.—'Shrines and Sanctuaries,' 1877.
COLEMAN, E. T.—'Scenes from the Snowfields: being Illustrations from the Upper Iceworld of Mont Blanc,' 1859.
DENT, C.—'Above the Snowline Mountaineering Sketches between 1870 and 1880,' 1885. Longmans.
FORBES, JAMES D.—'Travels through the Alps of Savoy and other parts of the Pennine Chain, with Observations on the Phenomena of Glaciers,' 1843.
—————— 'Norway and its Glaciers, with an Appendix on the Alps of Dauphiné,' &c., 1853.
—————— 'The Tour of Mont Blanc and Monte Rosa' (abridged from the 'Alps of Savoy'), 1855.
—————— 'Occasional Papers on the Theory of Glaciers,' 1859.
FORBES, Sir J.—'A Physician's Holiday,' 1849.
FRESHFIELD, DOUGLAS W.—'Italian Alps; Sketches from the Mountains of Ticino, Lombardy, the Trentino, and Venetia,' 1875. Longmans.
FRESHFIELD, MRS. H.—'A Summer Tour in the Grisons and Italian Valleys of the Bernina,' 1862. Longmans.
GEORGE, H. B.—'The Oberland and its Glaciers Explored and Illustrated with Ice-axe and Camera,' 1866. Longmans.
HINCHLIFF, THOMAS W.—'Summer Months among the Alps, with the Ascent of Monte Rosa,' 1857. Longmans.
KING, Rev. S. W.—'The Italian Valleys of the Pennine Alps,' 1858. Includes also many of the valleys of the Graian Alps. Murray.
LATROBE, C. S.—'The Alpenstock; Sketches of Swiss Scenery and Manners,' 1825–26.
MORELL.—'Scientific Guide to Switzerland,' 1867. Smith and Elder.
RUSKIN's (PROFESSOR) 'Modern Painters' (vol. 4) contains the most eloquent descriptions of Alpine scenery yet written.
SMITH, ALBERT.—'Mont Blanc,' 1852.
STEPHEN, LESLIE.—'The Playground of Europe,' 1871. Longmans.
TSCHUDI, F. VON.—'Sketches of Nature in the Alps,' 1858.
TYNDALL, PROF. JOHN.—'The Glaciers of the Alps,' 1860. Murray.
—————— 'Mountaineering in 1861.' Longmans.
—————— 'Forms of Water,' 1876. Macmillan.
WALTON, E.—'Peaks and Valleys of the Alps, with text by T. G. Bonney. 1867.
—————— 'Peaks in Pen and Pencil.' 1872.
—————— 'The Bernese Oberland, with text by T. G. Bonney. 1874.
WILLS, ALFRED.—'Wanderings among the High Alps,' 1856. Bentley.
—————— 'The Eagle's Nest in the Valley of Sixt, and Excursions among the Great Glaciers,' 1860. Longmans.

The following works contain the history of the conquest of the Alps:—

'Peaks, Passes, and Glaciers,' 1st and 2nd series, 3 vols., by Members of the Alpine Club, 1859 and 1862. Longmans.
'Vacation Tourists,' vol. 1, for 1860, edited by F. Galton. Macmillan.
'The Alpine Journal,' vols. 1 to 8 (continued quarterly), 1863–78.
WHYMPER, E.—'Scrambles in the Alps' (beautifully illustrated), from 1860 to 1869. Macmillan.
'The Alpine Guide,' by John Ball. A mountaineer's handbook, admirably compiled and divided into 13 sections (2s. 6d. each). No longer kept up to date. The introduction (a separate pamphlet, price 1s.) contains a valuable paper by Mons. Desor on the Geology of the Alps. Longmans, 1876.

A mass of information is contained in Dolfuss Ausset's 'Matériaux pour l'Étude des Glaciers' (8 vols.), and in the annuals of foreign Alpine Clubs :—

'Jahrbuch des Schweizer Alpenklub.' Berne. Dalp.
'Bollettino del Club Alpino Italiano.' Turin. Candeletti.
'Annuaire du Club Alpin Français.' Paris. Hachette.
'Zeitschrift des Deutscher Alpenklub.' Munich. J. Lindauer.
'Annuaire de la Société des Touristes du Dauphiné.' Grenoble. F. Allier.

The following French and German books are recommended :—

DE SAUSSURE.—'Voyages dans les Alpes.' Partie Pittoresque; 1 vol.; Jullien, Geneva.

DURIER, C.—'Le Mont Blanc.' Genève. Sandoz et Fischbacher, 1877. An excellent history of Mont Blanc.

HEIM, PROF. A.—'Handbuch der Gletscherkunde.' Stuttgart. Engelhorn, 1885. An elaborate and impartial summary of glacier theories, and the observations on which they have been based.

JOANNE's Guides : 'La Suisse,' 'Les Alpes Françaises,' and 'La Provence, Alpes Maritimes.' Ponderous, but full of recent and accurate information.

PEYER, G.—'Geschichte des Reisens in der Schweiz. Eine cultur-historische Studie.' Basel. Detloff, 1885. Readable sketches of life at the Swiss Baths in the Middle Ages, and of early Alpine travel.

STUDER, G.—'Ueber Eis und Schnee. Die Höchste Gipfel der Schweiz und die Geschichte ihrer Besteigung.' Berne. Dalp, 1869–71. A complete summary of the history of mountaineering.

STUDER, PROF. B.—'Geschichte der Physischen Geographie der Schweiz bis 1815.' An admirable handbook and key to old Swiss literature. Berne. Stämpfli, 1863.

TÖPFFER, A.—'Premiers Voyages en Zigzag.' Paris.
————————— 'Nouveaux Voyages en Zigzag.' Paris.
Humorous sketches of the travels of a Genevese schoolmaster and his boys in the days when Zermatt and Pontresina were remote and unvisited.

TSCHUDI, IWAN VON.—'Schweizerführer.' A skeleton guide-book, full of accurate and minute information compressed into the smallest possible space.

TUCKETT, F. F.—'Hoch Alpen Studien.' Leipzig, Liebeskind, 1874. The collected papers of the well-known English mountaineer, not published in England in this form.

The following are useful local Handbooks :—

The sections of the 'Alpine Guide.' Longmans. 2s. 6d. each.
The 'Zermatt Pocket-book,' by J. M. Conway. Stanford. 2s. 6d.
'Pontresina and its Neighbourhood,' by Dr. M. Ludwig. Stanford. 2s. 6d.
'The Engadine,' by M. Caviezel. Stanford. 5s.
'Davos-Platz, by one who knows it well.' Stanford. 2s. 6d.
For local Handbooks dealing with the Italian and French Alps, see the Introduction to the second section of this volume.

The following foreign works on Swiss history can be recommended. The article 'Switzerland,' from the *Encyclopædia Britannica*, is about to be published separately.

ALBERT RILLIET.—'Les Origines de la Confédération Suisse.' Georg. Genève et Bâle, 1869. 2nd ed. 7 fr. 50 c. An accurate popular summary of the early history of Swiss confederation, and of the legends connected with it.

W. ÖCHSLI.—'Vaterländische Geschichte.' Zurich, 1885 (with 8 maps). 3 fr. 50 c.

K. DÄNDLIKER.—'Lehrbuch der Geschichte des Schweizer-Volkes.' Schulthess. Zürich, 1875. 2 fr. 50 c. Short and trustworthy handbook.

J. STRICKLER.—'Lehrbuch der Schweizer Geschichte.' Orell, Füssli, and Co. Zürich, 1874. 2nd ed., 6 fr. More detailed than the last—*the* Swiss history for travellers and students.

A. DAGUET.—'Histoire de la Confédération Suisse.' Georg. Genève et Bâle, 1879. 7th ed. In 2 vols., 6 frs. a vol. Handsome edition of a well-known book, brought up to present standard of historical research. Vivid and interesting, with copious references to original authorities and recent literature.

Alpine Maps.

The traveller who does not leave the high-road may be contented with a good general map. But the pedestrian and the climber will find themselves well repaid in independence and in instruction for the slight trouble of carrying about the sheets of the Government Topographical Atlas containing the districts they intend to visit, or at least such a map as that lately issued by the Alpine Club (see below). The Federal Survey of Switzerland, in twenty-five sheets, executed under the superintendence of General Dufour, and completed by Colonel Siegfried, is a magnificent work, and renders intelligent travellers independent of a *local* guide. The old Piedmontese and Lombard maps, executed by the Italian and Austrian Governments, have been superseded by a new and accurate survey, the results of which are published at present only in cheap and somewhat roughly executed lithography. The new French map is generally excellent, though the glacier explorer will detect some serious errors in the ice region; the 'Carte Militaire de la Frontière,' on the same scale, has the advantage of taking in the Italian side of the chain, but in this it only follows the old and very incorrect Piedmontese map. Mr. Adams Reilly's clear and accurate maps of Monte Rosa and Mont Blanc are unfortunately out of print. The Alpine Club map, in four sheets, was long the only trustworthy map of the Alps of Piedmont and Lombardy, and though on somewhat too small a scale, is useful for pedestrians in these regions.

The following details are extracted from the catalogue of Messrs. Stanford, of Charing Cross :—

Swiss Government Map, scale 1·57 mile to an inch; sheets, 35 by 26 inches, sold at 2s. 9d. and 1s. 6d. (Dufour-Karte.)

The above Map, geologically coloured, publishing in sheets at from 7s. 6d. to 56s. 6d. each.

Swiss Government Topographical Atlas on the scale of the original survey: Alps, 1·26 inch to a mile; lowlands, 2·53 inches to a mile; publishing in 549 sheets, 17 by 13 inches; 1s. 6d. per sheet. (Siegfried-Karte.)

French Government Map, scale 1·26 mile to an inch; sheets, 38 by 26 inches, sold at 2s. 6d. and 4s. 6d. each.

Carte Militaire de la Frontière des Alpes, scale 1·26 mile to an inch; coloured, and with contour lines; sheets, 18 by 13 inches, sold at 2s. each.

Italian Government Map, $\frac{1}{50000}$, in sheets, sold at 1s. each.

The following general maps are recommended :—

The Alpine Club Map of Switzerland, produced under the superintendence of the Alpine Club, including the Italian and French Alps within its limits. An admirable work, 4 miles to the inch; in 4 sheets, 42s., coloured.

Small Government Map, 3·94 miles to the inch; in 4 sheets, 3s. 6d. a sheet. An excellent map for those who do not intend to go beyond the Swiss frontiers, but not comparable outside them to the Alpine Club Map.

Mayr's Alpine Map, 7·10 miles to an inch; mounted in two divisions. In
case, 18s. 6d.

Leuzinger's Map of Switzerland, 6·31 miles to an inch; in case, 12s.

Ziegler's Hypsometrical Map of Switzerland, 6 miles to an inch; with letter-
press and Index, in case, 17s.

———— General Map of Switzerland; with explanations in French and
German, and Alphabetical Index; 6 miles to an inch; 39 by 28 inches;
in case, 12s. 6d.

Studer and Escher's Geological Map of Switzerland, 6 miles to an inch; in
case, 20s. A smaller map by the same, folded, 3s.

§ 10. ALPINE ART.

Prof. Ruskin (who, in 'Modern Painters,' [*] urged artists to attempt the
delineation of snow, and has himself drawn snow mountains with wonderful success) has lately declared that the brilliancy of snow scenery places
it outside the proper field of art—and many artists agree with him. Their
opinion is, however, based on an imperfect acquaintance with the many
and constantly shifting aspects of the snowfields and glaciers and their relations to clouds and mists, and has been practically contradicted by the
best work of the late Elijah Walton. While studies of snow and ice, such
as those of Mons. Loppé, will as a rule appeal to a limited class and be
admired only by those whose memories they excite, there is no reason why
mountain landscapes should not be successfully dealt with by art—why
pictures of the Alps should not be painted which should convey the impressions of beauty and sublimity we derive from nature herself. But
painters will not succeed in representing to others the characteristic aspects
of Alpine scenery, until they are content to live amongst the mountains
long enough to understand them themselves. A landscape made up of a
few hurried memoranda from the Alps, mixed up with impressions derived
from English shires and scenery, will be certain of failure. Unless an
artist is prepared to spend many seasons—springs and autumns, as well as
summers—in the Alps, he had better, therefore, leave them alone altogether.

There are many travellers, however, who, without aspiring to be artists,
desire to bring away with them topographical memoranda, and to these
the following Hints on Sketching in the High Alps, from the experience
of an artist, may be found useful. "Sketching in Alpine valleys can
be carried on as easily as in England or Wales, but there are special
difficulties attending painting in the High Alps.

"Travellers who, in crossing glacier passes or ascending the higher peaks,
find themselves among scenes of strange and wonderful beauty, must, however, often wish to make pictorial notes which will aid their memory as no
writing can. A large number of people can sketch the forms of mountains
with tolerable accuracy, but find these outlines prove uninteresting to their
friends, and, when hurriedly made, they often become almost unintelligible
to themselves. My practice in the Alps, when I could only snatch a few
minutes on an *arête* to note the shape of a distant mountain, or the lines
of a snow cornice, has been to sketch simply in pencil: in the evening,
however, or on the next wet day, to clear up and develop this rough
sketch with pale thin washes of colour, taking care that *every pencil-mark
should be visible*. By this method I can see at any time what was done
on the spot, and what was merely remembered.

"Adopting this plan, the amateur can bring out the forms of his peaks

[*] See vol. i. pp. 281-4; vol. iv. p. 246; and 'Notes on Turner's Drawings,' p. 117.

by tinting in the sky or cloud colour, and then with a few touches the rocky bones of the mountain will show out from the surrounding snows. Equally easy is it to define where the dark belts of forest end, and where the grass can no longer find sustenance among the rocks. The beginner will do well to use much bluish-grey in his distances, and to avoid all strong greens, except in the foreground, even although the distant hill may seem to his eyes verdure itself. If the sketcher has had little previous knowledge of water-colour, he should limit himself to a few quiet broken hues, giving himself more play in colour as he grows in power.

" The materials needed are a sketch-book or block, 8 or 9 inches by 6, and a colour-box, 5 inches by 2½, to hold a few half-cakes of moist colour. Some of the most useful colours are cobalt, light red, rose madder, indigo, crimson, lake, gamboge, burnt sienna, yellow ochre, Vandyke brown, and cadmium yellow. Of course, two or three brushes, a couple of pencils, and a piece of india-rubber will be also required. All, how-ever, can be easily pocketed, and are thus always available ; more bulky sketching apparatus will probably be placed on the porter's shoulders, and not be so readily obtainable when wanted.

" For the use of this system of tinted pencil outlines the highest authority can be quoted. Professor Ruskin wrote in 1878 : ' Between the years 1840 and 1845 Turner went every summer to Switzer-land, finding, it seemed, new strength and pleasure among the scenes which had first formed his power. Every day on these excursions fur-nished him with many more subjects for complete pictures than he could at all sufficiently express, and he could not bear to let any of these escape him. His way was, therefore, to make rapid pencil note of his subject on the spot ; and, it seems, at his inn in the evening to put so much colour on this outline as would recall the effect to his mind.' "—*A. W.*

Alpine scenery—and particularly the scenery of the snow-world—is peculiarly well-suited for photography, which has achieved some of its most complete successes in the High Alps. The amateur who desires to try his hand will find full directions in the chapter on photography, by Mr. W. F. Donkin (who has himself photographed the panoramas from many of the least accessible pinnacles) in the ' Hints for Travellers,' pub-lished under the authority of the Royal Geographical Society (Stanford, 1883). The apparatus needful for taking views capable of enlargement into pictures of any size can be carried in the form of a knapsack.

§ 11. THE ALPS—THEIR GROUPS, PEAKS, PASSES, GORGES, AND VALLEYS.

In order to travel with advantage in a country previously unknown, something more seems necessary than a mere detail of certain lines of road, and an enumeration of towns, villages, mountains and inns. The following sections have been prepared with a view to furnish such pre-liminary and general information as may enable the traveller to turn his time to the best account.

Switzerland owes its chief attraction, the sublimity and diversified beauty of its scenery, to the presence of the Alps—the loftiest mountains of Central Europe, the dorsal ridge or backbone, as it were, of the Continent. These run through the land, and occupy, with their main trunk and minor spurs and offsets, a great part of its surface. They attain the greatest height along the S. frontier-line of Switzerland, and on the north of the

Rhone valley. Opposite them, on the N., the minor chain of the *Jura*, forming the N.W. boundary of Switzerland, extends from Geneva to near Constance, in a direction roughly parallel to that of the greater range. Before the introduction into Switzerland of railroads, it was from the apex of this advanced guard, as it were, of the Alps, or from one of the intermediate outlying hills, that the traveller, on entering the country, obtained his first view of the great central chain. From the brow of the hill, at the further extremity of a landscape composed of undulating country—woods, hills, villages, lakes and winding rivers—sufficient of itself to rivet the attention, he discovered what, if he had not before enjoyed the glorious spectacle, he would probably take for a fleecy cloud floating high above the horizon. The eye, unaccustomed to objects of such magnitude, fails at first to convey to the mind the fact that these white masses are mountains 60 or 70 m. off.

There are many points on the Jura whence the semicircular array of alpine peaks, presented at once to the eye, extends for more than 120 m., and comprises between 200 and 300 distinct summits, covered with snow or bristling with bare rocks, having their interstices filled with glaciers.

The wise traveller approaching the Alps for the first time will not hesitate, in order to obtain this view, to give up a day or two to driving over the Jura.

Before proceeding to give some details as to their principal features and phenomena, it is desirable to say a few words of the Alps themselves, and their division into groups. This great chain, the watershed of central Europe, extends from the Gulf of Genoa on the S.W. to the sources of the Save on the E. Within 40 miles of the Mediterranean its peaks rise to a height of over 10,000 feet, and throughout the portion of the range with which we are here concerned, the summits of the main chain seldom sink below this level, and the gaps between them, or passes, none of them sink below 6000 feet.

Owing, however, chiefly to the facilities afforded by deep transverse valleys, the Alps have never formed a permanent barrier, as the Caucasus did up to the present age, to the passage of commerce or armies.

All arrangements of a *chain* into separate groups must be more or less arbitrary and unsatisfactory. The portion of the Alps included in this Handbook may, however, best be divided into the following groups :—

I. *The Maritime Alps*, extending from the Col' d'Altare on the Alessandria-Mondovi Road to the Col de l'Argentière, at the head of Val Maira.

II. *The Cottian Alps*, extending northwards from the Col de l'Argentière to the Mont Cenis Pass.

III. *The Dauphiné Alps*, lying W. of the last-named, and between the valleys of the Durance and the Romanche.

IV. *The Graian Alps*, extending from the Mont Cenis Pass northwards to the valley of the Dora Baltea and the pass of the Little St. Bernard, and bounded on the W. by the valleys of the Isère and the Arc.

V. *The Pennine Alps*; the main chain from the little St. Bernard to the Simplon, including Mont Blanc and the subsidiary groups N. and W. of it.

VI. *The Bernese Alps*; the great range which extends parallel to the main chain from the Lake of Geneva along the N. side of the valley of the Rhone to the sources of that river. It is bounded on the E. by the gorge in which the Reuss descends from the St. Gothard.

VII. *The Glarus, or North Swiss Alps,* form the natural continuation of the last-named group, and extend eastwards N. of the valley of the Vorder Rhein, from the valley of the Reuss to the trench of the Lake of Wallenstadt.

VIII. *The Sentis, or Appenzell Alps,* are a comparatively small and low group, lying between the present course of the Rhine below Sargans and the Lake of Wallenstadt.

IX. *The Lepontine Alps.* The main chain between the Simplon Pass and the Splügen is known by this name. It includes the Rheinwald group, which supplies the main source of the Rhine, and the ranges of Ticino.

X. *The Rhœtian Alps* extend from the Splügen to the trench of the Adige. On the N. they are limited by the Arlberg Pass and on the S. by the valley of the Adda, and the passes of the Aprica and the Tonale. Only a portion of them is dealt with in this volume.

XI. *The Bergamasque Alps* lie between the Lake of Como, the Val Tellina, the Aprica road, and Val Camonica. They are sometimes considered as a section of the Lombard Alps, but are of a wholly different geological formation from the neighbouring Adamello group.

Alpine Peaks.—The following is a table of some of the most remarkable summits in these groups. The numbers indicate the district to which each belongs :—

	Feet.		Feet.
Rocca dell' Argentera, I.	10,617	Finsteraarhorn, VI.	14,026
Cima di Gelas, I.	10,433	Aletschhorn, VI.	13,803
Aiguille de Chambeyron, II.	11,155	Jungfrau, VI.	13,671
Monte Viso, II.	12,605	Schreckhorn, VI.	13,394
Pic des Écrins, III.	13,462	Wetterhorn, VI.	12,166
Meije, III.	13,081	Galenstock, VI.	11,956
Ailefroide, III.	13,000	Titlis, VI.	10,627
Mont Pelvoux, III.	12,973	Tödi, VII.	11,887
Roche Melon, IV.	11,621	Oberalpstock, VII.	10,925
Pointe de Charbonel, IV.	12,373	Glärnisch, VII.	9,584
Grand Paradis, IV.	13,300	Sentis, VIII.	8,215
Grivola, IV.	13,028	Monte Leone, IX.	11,696
Grande Casse, IV.	12,668	Piz Valrhein, IX.	11,148
Ruitor, IV.	11,480	Blinnenhorn, IX.	10,932
Mont Blanc, V.	15,784	Basodine, IX.	10,748
Monte Rosa, V.	15,217	Piz Bernina, X.	13,294
Dom, V.	14,942	Piz Zupo, X.	13,120
Lyskamm, V.	14,889	Piz Roseg, X.	12,936
Weisshorn, V.	14,804	Monte della Disgrazia, X.	12,074
Matterhorn, V.	14,705	Cima di Piazza, X.	11,713
Dent Blanche, V.	14,318	Piz Kesch, X.	11,211
Grand Combin, V.	14,164	Piz Linard, X.	11,208
Grandes Jorasses, V.	13,799	Cima del Largo, X.	11,162
Aiguille Verte, V.	13,527	Monte Redorta, XI.	9,980
Fletschhorn, V.	13,176	Presolana, XI.	8,202
Buet, V.	10,207		

The following summits are easy of access, and command fine *distant* views of the snowy Alps :—

Summits.	near	Summits.	near
Chaumont	Neuchâtel.	Pilatus	Lucerne.
Generoso	Lake of Como.	Rigi	Lucerne.
Hoherkasten	Weissbad.	Salvatore	Lugano.
Moléson	Bulle.	Sentis	Weissbad.
Motterone	Baveno.	Weissenstein	Soleure.
Niesen	Thun.		

Of the distant views the Rigi is the most accessible and very fine.

The following peaks command noble panoramas. Those marked with a † are the more laborious. None are difficult in the proper sense of the word :—

Peaks.	near	Peaks.	near
Besimauda	Pesio.	Grand Tournalin	Breuil.
†Cima di Gelas	S. Martino Lantosca.	Grauhaupt	Gressoney.
		†Pizzo Bianco	Macugnaga.
Monte Frioland	Crissolo.	Schilthorn	Mürren.
†Roche Melon	Lanslebourg or Susa.	Faulhorn	Grindelwald.
		†Titlis	Engelberg.
†Grandes Rousses	Bourg d' Oisans.	Stockhorn	Meiringen.
		Torrenthorn	Leukerbad.
Aig. du Plat	La Bérarde	Sparrenhorn	Bel Alp.
Becca di Nona	Aosta.	Eggischhorn	Viesch.
Pousset	Cogne.	Sidelhorn	Grimsel.
Cramont	Courmayeur.	Sentis	Weissbad.
†Pointe Percée	Sallanches.	†Basodine	Tosa Falls Inn.
Brévent	Chamonix.	†Piz Centrale	St. Gothard.
†Buet	Sixt.	Piz Mundaun	Ilanz.
†Pointe de Vouasson	Evolena.	Schwarzhorn	Davos.
†Pigne d' Arolla	Arolla.	†Piz Corvatsch	Silvaplana.
Bella Tola	St. Luc.	Piz Ot	Samaden.
Schwarzhorn	Zmeiden.	Piz Languard	Pontresina.
†Cima di Jazzi	Zermatt.	Piz Chiampatsch	Tarasp Bad.
Gornergrat	,,	Monte Nero	Chiesa.
†Mettelhorn	,,	Piz Sassalbo	Poschiavo.

For a *near view* of alpine scenery, amidst the recesses of the mountains, the localities which afford a concentration of grand and sublime objects are the passes and valleys of the *Bernese Oberland*, those round *Monte Rosa*, especially the valleys of Zermatt, Saas, and Macugnaga, and those round the base of *Mont Blanc*. It is in these three districts that the combination of fine form and great elevation in the mountains—of vast extent of glacier and snow-field, with the accompaniments of the roar of the avalanche and the rush of the falling torrent—are most remarkable. In the Bernina group the ice scenery is singularly fine, and accessible even for the most moderate walkers. Dauphiné redeems the barrenness of its valleys by the superb forms of its rock peaks. The Graian and North Swiss Alps contain varied and attractive scenery, and travellers who have visited the more frequented districts should not omit Stachelberg and Cogne.

Wherever the Alps break down towards Italy, a succession of the most delightful landscapes meets the eye. The foot of Monte Viso, the Italian valleys of Monte Rosa, Val Maggia near Locarno, the valleys round the head of Lago d'Iséo, display this class of scenery in perfection. Those who have not visited Monte Generoso have still to see the most *beautiful* of all subalpine views. . .

Alpine Passes.—No part of the Alps is more interesting, either in a picturesque or in an historical point of view, than the passable gaps or notches in the ridge of the great chain, and in the minor mountain buttresses branching from it, whereby this colossal wall of mountains may be scaled, and a direct passage and communication maintained between northern and southern Europe, as well as between one valley and another. It has been through these depressions that the great tide of population has poured since the earliest times; from these outlets have issued the barbarian swarms which so often desolated, and at last annihilated, the Roman Empire. There are more than 50 of these passes over the Swiss portion of the alpine chain alone, or immediately communicating with the Swiss frontier.*

In seeking a passage over the Alps, the most obvious course was to find out the valleys which penetrate farthest into the great chain, to follow the rivers to their sources, and then to take the lowest traversable part in order to descend on the opposite side. . The variety and sudden transitions presented by such a route are highly interesting. In the course of one day's journey the traveller passes in succession from one stretch of valley to another by a steep ascent and defile, from the climate of summer to winter, through spring. The alteration in the productions keeps pace with that of the temperature. Leaving behind him stubble-fields, whence the corn has been removed and housed, he comes to fields yet yellow and waving in the ear ; a few miles farther and the crop is still green ; yet higher, and corn refuses to grow. Before quitting the region of corn he enters one of dark, apparently interminable forests of pine and larch, clothing the mountain-sides in a sober vestment. Above this the haymakers are collecting the short grass, the only produce which the ground will yield. Yet the stranger must not suppose that all is barrenness even at this elevation. It seems as though Nature were determined to make one last effort at the confines of the region of vegetation. From beneath the snow-bed, and on the very verge of the glacier, the profusion of flowers, their great variety, and surpassing beauty, are exceedingly surprising. Some of the greatest ornaments of our gardens, here born to blush unseen,—gentians, violets, anemones, and hare-bells, intermixed with bushes of the red rhododendron, the loveliest production of the Alps, scattered over the velvet turf, give it the appearance of a carpet of richest pattern. The insect world is not less abundant and varied,—thousands of winged creatures are seen hovering over the flowers, enjoying their short existence, for the summer at these elevations lasts but for 3 or 4 weeks : a premature winter soon cuts short this brief season of animal and vegetable activity. Above this region of spring, with its gush of waters, its young herbage and vivid greensward, its hum of insects just burst forth, and its natural flower-beds glittering with rain-drops, that of winter in Lapland or

---

* The late Mr. Brockedon carefully illustrated them, both with pencil and pen, in his beautiful work entitled 'The Passes of the Alps,' 2 vols. 4to. Their history has not yet been fully written in England. See the 'Jahrbuch für Schweizerische Geschichte.' Höhr, Zürich, 1878–9 (article by Oehlmann), and recent Jahrbücher of the Swiss Alpine Club (articles by Dübi).

Siberia succeeds. The traveller may form an idea of the height he has reached by observing the vegetation. Vines disappear at 2000 feet, generally sooner; oak-trees and wheat at 3000 feet; beeches and barley at 4000 to 5000 ft.; pines and firs at 6000 to 7000 ft. Above 9000 ft. flowering plants are very rare, but up to 11,000 feet they are found in sunny crevices. Above 11,000 feet a few blackened lichens alone preserve the semblance of vegetable life. It must of course be understood that in favourable situations these limits will be exceeded; in unfavourable situations they will not be reached. At the summit of a high pass and amongst the glaciers the rarefied air is icy cold, and exercise and quick motion are necessary to keep up the circulation of the blood. The agreeable murmur of falling water, which has hitherto accompanied the traveller incessantly, here ceases,—all is solitude and silence, interrupted only by the shrill whistle of the marmot, or the hoarse cawing of an ill-omened raven. The ptarmigan starts up from among the broken rocks on the verge of the snow-field at the traveller's approach, and the lämmergeier (the condor of the Alps), disturbed in his repast on the carcass of a sheep or cow, may sometimes be seen soaring upwards in a succession of corkscrew sweeps till he gains the ridge of the Alps, and then disappears.

Such are the remarkable gradations which the stranger encounters in the course of a few hours, on a single pass of the Alps; but the most striking change of all is that from the region of snow and ice on the top of the mountain, to the sunny clime and rich vegetation of Italy, which await the traveller at the S. foot of the chain.

The works of Nature, however, will not entirely occupy the attention and wonder of the wanderer in such a pass; at least a share will be demanded for admiration of the works of man. The great highways, passable for carriages, over the high Alps, are, indeed, most surprising monuments of human skill and enterprise in surmounting what would appear, at first sight, to be intended by Nature as insurmountable. These proud constructions of art thread the valleys, cross the channels of rivers on long causeways, skirt the edge of the precipice, with walls of rock towering over them, and torrents thundering below. Where the steep and hard surface of the cliff has not left an inch of space for a goat to climb along, they are conducted upon high terraces of solid masonry, or through a notch blasted by gunpowder in the wall of rock. In many instances a projecting buttress of the mountain has blocked up all passage for ages, saying "thus far and no farther:" the skill of the modern engineer has pierced through this a tunnel or gallery; and the difficulty is vanquished, without the least change in the level of the road.

Sometimes an impediment is eluded by throwing bridges over a dizzy gorge, and shifting the road from side to side, frequently two or three times within the space of half a mile. Often the road reaches a spot down which the winter avalanches take their habitual course, sweeping everything before them, and which, even in summer, appears reeking and dripping with the lingering fragments of snow. Will not so irresistible an antagonist arrest the course of this frail undertaking of man? Not even the avalanche;—in such a situation the road either buries itself in subterranean galleries, driven through the mountain, or is sheltered by massive arcades of masonry, sometimes half a mile or three-quarters of a mile long. Over these the avalanche glides harm-lessly, and is turned into the depths below.

Every opportunity is seized of gaining, by easy ascents, a higher level for the road; at length comes the main ascent, the central ridge, to be surmounted only by hard climbing. This is overcome by a succession of zigzag terraces, called *tourniquets* or *giravolte*, connected together by wide curves, to allow carriages to turn easily and rapidly. So skilful is their con-struction, with such easy bends and so gradual a slope, that in many alpine roads the drivers, *with horses accustomed to the road*, trot down at a rapid pace. Sometimes as many as 50 of these zigzags succeed one another without interruption; and the traveller, as he passes backwards and forwards, hovering over the valley, is as though suspended to a pendulum, and swinging to and fro. The road itself has a most singular appearance, twisted about like an uncoiled rope or a ribbon unwound.

The travelling-carriage descends sometimes rapidly and without inter-ruption for hours. A drag of tempered iron is quickly worn down, in that time, as thin as the blade of a knife, so great is the friction; and it is usual to substitute for the iron drag a wooden sabot, formed of the section of a fir-tree, with a groove cut in the centre to admit the wheel.

The winter's snow usually falls upon the alpine passes more than 5000 ft. high about the second week in October (sometimes earlier), and continues till the first or second week in June. Yet even after this, the passage across the neck or Col, as it is called, is not stopped, except for a few days, until the snow can be cleared away. On some of the minor passes, indeed, traversed by a mere rough footpath or bridle-path, the traffic is much increased after the fall of snow, which, by filling up depressions and smoothing the way, permits the transport of heavy merchandise on sledges, which move easily over the surface as soon as it is hardened.

Along the lines of the great carriage-roads strong houses are erected at intervals, called *Maisons de Refuge, Case di Ricóvero*, occupied by persons called Cantonniers, who are employed in mending the road and keeping it free from snow, and are also paid to assist travellers in danger during snow-storms.

As near as possible to the summit of the pass a *Hospice* is frequently erected, often occupied by a band of charitable monks, as in the case of the Great and Little St. Bernard, the Simplon, Mt. Cenis, &c. The direction of the road across the summit of the ridge is marked by a line of tall poles, which project above the snow, and, from being painted black, are easily recognised. Bells are rung in tempestuous weather, when the *tourmente* is raging and the mist and falling snow hide the landmarks, that the sound may aid when the sight fails.

The morning after a fall of snow labourers and peasants are assembled from all sides to shovel it off the road. Where it is not very deep, it is cleared away by a snow-plough drawn by 6 or 8 oxen. As the winter advances and fresh falls occur, the snow accumulates, and the road near the summit of a pass presents the singular aspect of a path or lane cut between walls of snow sometimes 10 or 20 ft. high. Carriages are taken off their wheels and fastened upon sledges; ropes are attached to the roof, which are held by 6 or 8 sturdy peasants running along on each side, to prevent the vehicle upsetting and rolling over the slippery ice down a precipice. More commonly, however, travellers are transferred to light narrow one-horse sledges, each carrying two passengers, by which communication is kept up, except during storms, when no living animal can withstand the fury of the elements. In this manner very high passes are crossed in the depth of winter with little risk. The spring is a season during which far greater danger is to be apprehended, from the avalanches which then fall.

The Swiss are essentially a road-making nation, and had good roads when those of continental Europe generally were still execrable. They bestow an amount of care and expense in avoiding hills and steep declivities which should make an Englishman ashamed of the state of things in the hilly parts of England.

The first carriage-road over the Alps was that of the Simplon, made passable for wheels by the Maréchal de Catinat, at the end of the 17th century, and converted into a military highway by Napoleon in 1807. In the Middle Ages travellers either rode or were carried in litters, and all commerce was carried on with mules or pack-horses. The Mont Cenis, the St. Gothard, the Julier and Bernina, and the Brenner, were then the principal routes. In the 17th century the Simplon was also used, and most amusing accounts of their passage have been left us by Lassels in his 'Voyage of Italy,' and Evelyn in his well-known 'Diary.' In earlier times, the Moro and St. Théodule were used for purposes of commerce.

The following are the principal carriage-passes over the alpine watershed now in use in the part of the Alps comprised in this volume :—the Col di Tenda, Col de l'Argentière, Mont Genévre, Mont Cenis, Little St. Bernard, Simplon, St. Gothard, Lukmanier, San Bernardino, Splügen, Maloja, Bernina. The Col du Lautaret, the Brunig, Furka, and Oberalp: the Fluela, Albula, and Julier, in Canton Graubünden, and the Aprica and Giogo di Castellone, in the Bergamasque Alps, are fine roads crossing lateral ridges. The recently constructed road over the Col du Galibier, between Briançon and St. Michel de Maurienne (8721 feet), surpasses in height all other roads in Europe except the Stelvio (9177 feet, Dufour ; but 9042 feet, new Austrian survey).

The most frequented, or finest, mule-passes are the Col della Finestra, in the Maritime Alps, the Col de la Traversette, under Monte Viso, the Col de Lauzon in the Graian Alps, the Col de la Seigne, and Col de Balme, near Mont Blanc, the Great St. Bernard, the Augstbord Pass from the Turtmann Thal to St. Niklaus, the Rawyl, Gemmi, Wengern Alp, Great Scheideck, and Grimsel, in the Bernese Alps, the Joch Pass, near Engelberg, the Klausen, near Altdorf, the Gries Pass, in the Lepontine Alps, the Muretto and Canciano, in the Bernina group.

The most famous glacier-passes are the Brèche de la Meije and Col du Selé, in Dauphiné, the Col du Géant, those forming the so-called "High-level Route" from Chamonix to Zermatt, the Lysjoch (14,040 feet), the Col d'Hérens, the St. Théodule, Alphubel, and Weissthor, near Zermatt; the Tschingel, the Mönch Joch, the Strahleck, and the Oberaarjoch, in the Bernese Oberland; the Sandgrat, near the Tödi; and the Sella Pass in the Bernina group.

Alpine Gorges and Valleys.—Especially deserving of notice are some of the avenues leading up to these passes ; in many instances mere cracks or fissures, cleaving the mountains to the depth of two or three thousand feet,

The *Schyn Pass* and *Via Mala* are two of the finest scenes of this kind among the Alps. As valleys shut in by towering precipitous mountains, the Lauterbrunnen valley, the Gasterenthal near Kandersteg, and Val Bavona in Canton Ticino, are without rivals. The gorges of the Via Mala, the Schyn, the Lukmanier in the Grisons; of Schöllinen; of Gondo; of the Via Mala Bergamasca, in Val di Scalve; of Val Verzasca and Val Canobbina, near Lago Maggiore; and of Val Mastalone, near Varallo, deserve mention. The gorges of Pfäffers, of Trient, and of the Gouffre de Bousserailles, in Val Tournanche, are singular narrow fissures.

Beautiful *Swiss Valleys* are the Vale of Hasli, near Meiringen, the Simmenthal, the Vale of Sarnen, the Kanderthal, the Prätigau, the valleys of Gruyères, and Ormonts—all distinguished for their quiet pastoral character, and the softness and luxuriance of their verdure—"The rock-embosomed lawns, and snow-fed streams," spoken of by Shelley. And here it may be remarked that the traveller in Switzerland must not suppose that beauty of scenery is confined to the High Alps: the undulating country between the Alps and Jura, which, though still greatly elevated above the sea, may be called the Lowlands, abounds in unobtrusive beauties —hills tufted with wood, from which picturesque rocks project at intervals, slopes bursting with rills, and meadows which, by the aid of copious irrigation, yield three crops of grass a-year, presenting at all seasons a carpet of the liveliest verdure, and of a texture like velvet;—such are the beauties of these lowland scenes. The frequent hedge-rows, the gardens before the cottages, and the neatness of the dwellings—the irregular, winding roads, free from the straight monotony and everlasting avenues of France and Germany—remind one frequently of England. There are, besides, among the Jura, many scenes of grandeur; such especially are presented by the Val Moûtiers, between Bâle and Bienne; the pass of Klus, at the foot of the Ober-Hauenstein; and the Lac de Joux.

The most beautiful valleys of the Savoy and Italian Alps are referred to in the Preface to the second portion of this work.

§ 12. GLACIERS.*

Glaciers (Germ. *Gletscher*: Ital. *Ghiacciajo*) are amongst the most remarkable objects in nature: to them alpine scenery owes much of its strangeness and sublimity. Glaciers may be described as streams of ice fed by the snow which falls above the summer snow level. Their size and length depend mainly on the extent of their snowy reservoirs, and on the amount of snow that falls on them. 'Glaciation is primarily dependent on distribution of moisture and temperature.' Where long troughs lie under the snowy peaks at a comparatively high elevation the glaciers attain greater dimensions than where deep valleys abut on the snowy chain, for every foot of descent increases the ablation of the ice.

The snow which falls upon the summits of the high Alps is at first a dry and loose powder. The action of the sun by day and of frost by night gradually converts this into a granular mass, as the minute particles are

* The best information respecting glaciers is to be found in Professor Forbes's 'Travels in the Alps,' already alluded to, in Agassiz' 'Études' and 'Recherches sur les Glaciers,' Tyndall's 'Glaciers of the Alps,' and more recent works, and Forbes's 'Occasional Papers on the Theory of Glaciers.' A complete résumé of glacier theories is contained in Dr. A. Heim's 'Gletscherkunde,' Zürich, 1885. Local names for glaciers—in Tyrol, Firn; in Carinthia, Käs; in the Grisons, Vadret; in part of Italy, Vedretto; in the Valais, Biegno; in Piedmont, Ruize or Roesa (whence Monte Rosa); in the Pyrenees, Serneille.

aggregated together in irregular roundish grains. In this state the entire mass appears white and opaque, but the separate grains are transparent. In the course of successive years, as one layer accumulates over another, pressure begins to act on the lower portions. The separate grains being brought into contact adhere together, until the whole becomes seemingly solid, but in reality granular, ice. The accumulation of snow, partly transformed into ice, in the upper regions, may be many hundreds of feet in thickness, and the pressure on the undermost part is therefore enormously great. The glacier ice yields to this pressure, and is gradually forced downwards on the slopes of the mountain into the hollows which afford the easiest channels for its descent. The upper part is called in German *Firn*, in French *Névé*, the term *Glacier* (Gletscher) being confined to the lower limbs of more solid ice. The Firn, or Névé, is a region of complete desolation ; no animal intrudes upon it save the chamois, and only the scantiest lichens appear on the rocks around it. The Firn occurs only at a height where the snow which falls in the winter does not entirely disappear in the course of the following year ; while that which falls on the lower glacier is almost always melted in the course of the summer, and never combines with the ice.*

The glaciers of the Swiss Alps are estimated at 471, and the surface covered by them at 712 square miles. The great Aletsch Glacier is 15 miles long, and covers 50 square miles. The Lower Grindelwald Glacier has descended to 3500 feet above the sea; the Chamoni Glaciers to 3660 feet. These are the lowest points reached by alpine ice in recent times. They vary from a few square acres to miles in extent, covering, in some instances, whole districts, filling up entirely the elevated hollows and basins between the peaks and ridges of the Alps, and sending forth arms and branches into the inhabited valleys, below the region of forests, and even below the level at which corn will grow.

It is such offsets of the glacier as these that are presented to the view of the traveller from the villages of Chamonix, Zermatt, and Grindelwald. These, however, are, as it were, but the skirts and fringes of that vast everlasting drapery of ice which clothes all the upper region of the Alps. These fields or tracts of uninterrupted glacier have been called "Seas of Ice" (Mers de Glace, Eismeeren), and there are five such among the central and southwestern Alps, which merit especial mention; that in the Dauphiné Alps, that round Mont Blanc, that extending from Mont Velan to Monte Rosa, that round Piz Bernina, in Canton Graubünden, and that of the Bernese Oberland, round the Finsteraarhorn, which covers 137 square miles. Extensive glaciers are found also in the Graian, St. Gothard, Lepontine, and Glarus Alps.

* A serious error is conveyed by the common expression, "the line of perpetual snow," or, "where snow never melts." There is no spot on the Alps where snow does not melt under the influence of a summer sun at mid-day. It melts even on the top of Mont Blanc; but there, and on the summits of the other high Alps, the duration of the sun's heat is so short, that very little is melted during the year, and, for the same reason, there is very little moisture in the air, and, consequently, very little snow can fall : and the greater part of this is carried to a lower level by the storms which often rage round the mountain tops. What is called "*the snow line*" does not depend on elevation alone, but on all the circumstances which affect the quantity of snow that falls during a year, and the quantity that melts during the same period. It is the limit at which the quantity melted in the year exactly equals the quantity that has fallen. Independent of a certain amount of variation from one season to another, it varies with the latitude, with the exposure to certain winds, and even on the two sides of the same mountain, being generally higher on the S. side than the N. The snow will likewise rest longer, and extend lower down, upon a mountain of granite than upon one of limestone, in proportion as the two rocks are good or bad conductors of heat, and this is the case even in contiguous mountains, members of the same chain.

The greatest thickness of the glaciers has been commonly estimated at
between 600 and 800 ft. The greatest depth of the Mer de Glace, on
the N. flank of Mont Blanc, is estimated by Forbes at 350 ft. Saussure had calculated it at 600 ft. Agassiz assures us that there are holes
in the Aar glacier 780 ft. deep.

Notwithstanding their great extent and solidity, the glaciers are undergoing a perpetual process of destruction and renovation. The lower
portions descending into the valleys are gradually dissolved by the increased temperature which prevails at so low a level. The summer sun,
aided by warm wind, acts upon the surface, so that, in the middle of
the day, it abounds in pools, and is traversed by rills of water.

The cause of the movement of glaciers has been much discussed and
variously explained. De Saussure supposed that it proceeds from their
weight alone, and that they slide down the inclined surface of the valleys,
aided by the ice melting below, in contact with the earth. Others believed that the descent was caused by dilatation of the glacier, in consequence of the water that penetrates the mass of ice, alternately thawing
and freezing. The theory of their motion now generally accepted by
scientific men is that of Professor J. D. Forbes, modified in some respects
by the subsequent researches of Professor Tyndall.* Without adverting to
disputed points, which are discussed in their works, it may be said that
by the pressure of its own enormous weight the accumulated snow of the
higher regions is converted into glacier-ice and moved downwards. It is
plastic so far as it yields to pressure, moulding itself to the form of the
channel through which it moves, but it cannot be stretched : with tension
it breaks, and thus crevasses are formed. The centre of the ice-stream
moves quicker than the sides, which are retarded by the friction of the
rocks, &c., and, for the same reason, the top moves faster than the bottom.
The rate of progression varies very much in different glaciers, according
to the slope and the mass of ice. Opposite the Montanvert the quickest
moving part travels in summer about 30 inches a day, in winter 16 inches.

The surface of the mountain, which forms the bed of a glacier, however
hard, is subjected to an extraordinary process of grinding and polishing
from the ice constantly passing over it. The harder fragments of rock,
such as granite and quartz, interposed between the glacier and the
mountain, act like diamonds on glass, and scratch deep and long grooves.
The seat of ancient glaciers, which have now entirely disappeared, may
still be discovered by the furrows left behind them on the rocks. These
furrows and the rounded polished surfaces (roches moutonnées) are very
remarkable above Guttannen on the Grimsel road. The motion of a glacier
may be admirably observed at Rosenlaui, where the foot of the glacier,
being on a surface of rock, marks its advance or retrogression daily by
the heaps of rubbish it pushes forwards, whilst on the rocks above may
be seen the moraine of former years when the glacier was larger.

The nature of the upper surface of the ice depends partly upon that of
the ground on which it rests : where it is even, or nearly so, the ice is
smooth and level ; but whenever the supporting surface becomes slanting
or uneven, the glacier begins to split and gape in all directions. As
it descends a steep declivity or precipice, as in the lower glacier of
Grindelwald, the entire mass is cleft by deep and wide fissures, which

* See, for an account of various theories, 'Alpine Journal,' vol. iv. p. 411; vol. xii. pp. 219
and 300. See also Croll, 'Climate and Time,' p. 495.

generally intersect each other, leaving crags, obelisks, and towers of ice of the most fantastic shapes, varying in height from 20 to 80 ft. Being unequally melted by the wind and sun, they are continually changing their form and crumbling away. After the difficulties are passed, these aiguilles and obelisks of ice, being pressed together at the bottom of the descent, close up, and, as soon as the mountain-bed below them is level, the surface of the glacier again becomes nearly smooth and compact.

The *Crevasses*, or fissures, which traverse the upper portion of the glacier, before it becomes entirely fractured and disruptured, run in a transverse direction, never extending quite across the ice-field, but narrowing out at the extremities, so that, when they gape too wide to leap across, they may be turned by following them to their termination. These rents and fissures are the chief source of danger to those who cross the glaciers. In the upper regions the crevasses are concealed by a treacherous coating of snow; and many a bold chamois-hunter has found a grave in their depths. Ebel mentions an instance of a shepherd, in 1787, who, in driving his flock over the ice to a high pasturage, had the misfortune to tumble into one of these clefts. He fell in the vicinity of a torrent which flowed under the glacier, and, by following up its bed under the ice, succeeded in regaining the surface with a broken arm. The man's name was Christian Bohren: he was living in 1849, and acted as guide to the upper glacier of Grindelwald. More melancholy was the fate of M. Mouron, a clergyman of Vevey: he was engaged in making some scientific researches upon the glacier, and was in the act of · leaning over to examine a *moulin* (a well-shaped aperture in the ice, formed by the action of a stream of water, when the staff on which he rested gave way; he was precipitated to the bottom, and his lifeless body was not recovered for some days. It may be hoped that the attention often directed to this subject by fatal accidents may induce travellers to adopt the precautions already urged in § 6.

The crevasses exhibit in perfection the beautiful *azure blue* colour of the glacier; the cause of which has not been satisfactorily accounted for. It is the same tint of ultramarine which the Rhone exhibits at Geneva, after leaving all its impurities behind it in the lake; and travellers have observed the same beautiful tint in footmarks and holes made in fresh-fallen snow, not more than a foot deep, among the high Alps. —*See* Tyndall's 'Glaciers of the Alps.'

The traveller who has only *read* of glaciers is often disappointed at the first sight of them, by the appearance of their surface, which is rough, tossed about in hillocks and gullies, and, except when covered with fresh-fallen snow, or at very great heights, has none of the purity which might be expected from fields of ice. On the contrary, it usually exhibits a surface of dirty white, soiled with mud, and often covered with stones and gravel. Such beds of stone, dirt, and rubbish are common to most glaciers, and, when accumulated in continuous masses, are called *Moraines*, running along the glacier in parallel lines at the sides (called *lateral* Moraines, German *Gandecken*); or in the middle (*medial* Moraines, in German *Guffer*), and *terminal* or end Moraines. They are formed in the following manner:—The edges of the glacier receive the fragments of rock detached from the mountains by the destructive agency of moisture and frost; but as the glacier itself is constantly descending, this fallen rubbish goes along with it, increased from behind by the débris of each succeeding winter, so that it forms a nearly uninterrupted line from the top of the ice-field to the bottom, thus forming a lateral moraine. Wherever the glacier from one valley meets that of another, the moraines from the two unite and form one, running down the centre of the united glacier instead of along its margin, as before, thus forming a medial moraine. Such a confluence of moraines is well seen on the glacier of the Aar (Route 27); and upon the great glacier of Gorner descending from Monte Rosa six or eight may be seen running side by side, each traceable to its origin by the nature of the rocks composing it (Route 127).

" The moraines remain upon the surface of the glacier, and, unless after a very long or very uneven course, they are not dissipated or in-gulfed. On the contrary, the largest stones attain a conspicuous pre-eminence; the heaviest moraine, far from indenting the surface of the ice, or sinking amongst its substance, rides upon an icy ridge as an excrescence, which gives to it the character of a colossal back-bone of the glacier, or sometimes appears like a noble causeway, fit, indeed, for giants, stretching away for leagues over monotonous ice, with a breadth of some hundreds of feet, and raised from 50 to 80 ft. above its general level. Almost every stone, however, rests upon ice; the mound is not a mound of débris, as it might at first sight appear."—*Forbes.*

The *terminal moraines* are heaped up often to a height of 80 or 100 ft., and sometimes much higher: the moraines in the Allée Blanche and on the glacier of Blaitière at Chamonix must be 500 or 600 ft. high. Not unfrequently there are 3 or 4 such ridges, one behind the other, like so many lines of intrenchment. The broken stones, sand, and mud, mixed with shattered fragments of ice, of which they are composed, have an unsightly appearance, being perfectly barren of vegetation; but each heap is, as it were, a geological cabinet, containing specimens of all the neighbouring mountains. The glacier, indeed, has a natural tendency to purge itself from impurities, and whatever happens to fall upon it is gradually discharged in this manner. It likewise exerts great mechanical force, and, like a vast millstone, grinds down not only the rock which composes its channel, but all the fragments interposed between it and the rock; forming, in the end, a sort of stone-meal. The extent of the moraine depends on the character of the strata of the mountains around the glacier: where they are of granite, or other hard rock, not easily decomposed by the weather, the moraine is of small extent; and it is largest where the boundary rocks are of brittle limestone and fissile slate. The researches of Swiss naturalists (Agassiz and Charpentier) have discovered extensive moraines, not only in the lower part of the Valais, but even on the shores of the Lake Leman, at a height of not more than 200 or 300 ft. above it; indicating that, during some anterior condition of our planet, the valley of the Rhone was occupied by glaciers, in situations at present 40 or 50 m. distant from the nearest existing ice-field, and 3000 or 4000 ft. below it. The existence of boulder-stones, so common on the Jura and elsewhere, is now generally attributed to glaciers, the boulders having been carried as moraine to their present position.[*]

* See an interesting paper on the Ancient Glaciers of Switzerland and North Wales, by Professor Ramsay, in ' Peaks, Passes, and Glaciers;' also published separately.

A singular circumstance occurs when a single large mass of rock has fallen upon the glacier; the shade and protection from the sun's rays afforded by the stone prevent the ice on which it rests from melting, and, while the surface around is gradually lowered, it remains supported on a pedestal or table, like a mushroom on a stalk, often attaining a height of several feet; at length the stone falls off the pillar and the process recommences. The glaciers of the Aar furnish fine examples of these *tables des glaciers*, as they are called. The surface of the glacier has been ascertained to lose 3 ft. by melting in as many weeks of fine warm weather. An exactly opposite phenomenon occurs when a small stone, not more than an inch thick, a leaf, or an insect, rests upon the ice. As it absorbs the sun's rays with greater rapidity than ice, not merely its surface but its entire substance is warmed through, and instead of protecting it melts the ice below it, and gradually sinks, forming a hole to a considerable depth, and generally a pool of water, of which the traveller is often glad to avail himself: these little pools are generally frozen over at night, and form natural compasses, as a little rim of ice generally remains throughout the day on the N. side.

The occurrence of Red Snow, which at one time was treated with incredulity, is common among the High Alps, and is produced by "infusoria of the genus *discercœa*, having a silicious carapace and two trumpet-shaped appendages which form their organs of motion."—*T. G. Bonney*. In the state of germination it imparts a pale carmine tint to the snow: this increases, as the plant comes to maturity, to a deep crimson blush, which gradually fades, and, as the plant decays, becomes a black dust or mould. By collecting some of the coloured snow in a bottle, and pouring it on a sheet of paper, the form of the plant may be discovered with a microscope, as soon as the water has evaporated.

The most careless observer can hardly fail to be struck by the evident races of the oscillations of the alpine glaciers. The period of their greatest extent is marked by the gigantic moraines of the North Italian plain, particularly remarkable round the mouth of Val d'Aosta and at the foot of Lago di Garda. Within the historical period we find no record of any such extension of the ice, nor, since the Great St. Bernard was a frequented route, and many other high passes constantly used in Roman times, does there seem much ground for the generally held belief in a diminution of the average total amount of ice in the Alps during the past 2000 years. The glaciers would appear, however, to have certain secular periods of advance and retreat; but their uniformity is broken by numerous exceptions. Thus, for instance, from 1850 to 1860, the Zermatt glaciers continued to advance, while those of Chamonix and the Oberland were in rapid retreat. The causes, alike of the secular oscillations and of their exceptions, have not yet been satisfactorily ascertained. The former are bound up with the general meteorological conditions of our planet, and a recent writer has endeavoured to trace a connection between their periods and those of sun-spots; the latter are probably connected with the relative severity of the winter, the heat of the summer, and the local snow-falls, which in many years vary greatly in different portions of the chain. In support of these suggestions, it should be noted that during the period of the first advance of the glaciers of which we have any record, the Lake of Constance was three times frozen over. During the latter half of the 16th century there was a continuous progress of the ice, which made a great impression on the Swiss mind, and gave rise to an exaggerated belief as to the small extent of the glaciers at an earlier date, and as to lost passes. It has been shown that if many passes fell into disuse, it was quite as much from the decline of enterprise as from the growth of the ice. Simler's 'Descriptio Vallesiæ,' first published in 1574, contains a description of snow-travelling, which shows that alpenstocks (*baculi Alpini*) crampons, snow-spectacles (*vitrea conspicilia*), and the rope, were well known and frequently used. Throughout the 17th century the ice seems to have remained comparatively stationary. From 1703 to 1723 it advanced. In 1750 the glaciers were again at their smallest. Towards the close of the century they were advancing, and in 1816–20 attained their maximum. In 1850–60 they were in great beauty, and had pushed far downwards. Between 1860–80 they lost ground with great rapidity, throughout the Alps. In the basin of the Rhone alone the revision of the Swiss survey in 1880 showed that one-twentieth of the whole surface covered by ice 27 years previously had been laid bare. The Chamonix Glaciers and many others in the western and central have in the last five years (1880–5) remained stationary or begun to advance, and it appears probable that the glacier system of the Alps is again entering on a period of increase.*

Professors Agassiz, Forbes, and Tyndall have made interesting experiments and observations upon the movement and rate of progress of the glaciers; but Hugi was the first observer who attempted to measure their advance. In 1827 the latter noted the position of numerous loose blocks lying on the surface of the lower glacier of the Aar, relatively to the fixed rocks at its sides. He also measured the glacier and erected signal-posts on it. In 1836 he found everything altered; many of the loose blocks had moved off and entirely disappeared, along with the ice that supported them. A hut, which he had hastily erected, to shelter himself and his companions, had advanced 2184 ft. A mass of granite, containing 26,000 cubic ft., originally buried under the snow of the névé, which had become converted into glacier, had not only been raised to the surface, but was elevated above it, in the air, upon two pedestals, or pillars, of ice; so that a large party might have found shelter under it. A signal-post, attached to a mass of granite, had not only made as great an advance as the hut, but the distance between it and the hut had been increased 760 ft. by the expansion of the glacier. In 1839 M. Agassiz found that Hugi's cabin had advanced 4400 ft. from the position it originally occupied, when first built in 1827; and in 1840 it was 200 ft. lower. Hugi's observations on the Aar glacier give as its rate of motion 240 ft. per annum. The more precise observations of Professors Forbes and Tyndall have ascertained the daily motion of the ice on the Mer de Glace, and proved that it proceeds regularly, not by fits and starts, but accelerated in speed by thaws and retarded by frosts, and that the motion is different in different parts of the glacier. The advance of the ice-field of the Mer de Glace is calculated at between 600 and 700 ft. yearly, or nearly 2 ft. a day. The most recent and elaborate measurements of glacier oscillations have been carried out on the Rhone Glacier by the Swiss Federal Staff.

* See for further statistics an article in 'Petermann's G. Mittheilungen' (vol. xxiv. No. x.), for October 1878, by Professor H. Fritz, and Prof. Forel's valuable papers on the 'Variations Périodiques des Glaciers des Alpes,' Bern. Staemfli.

The "veined structure" of glacier ice was long since observed. The walls of a crevasse are often found to be built up of alternate parallel layers of white and blue ice. The white ice is the least compact and easily crumbles. Professor Tyndall has shown, by conclusive experiments and observations, that these veins are the result of pressure. They are only seen where the glacier has been subjected to severe lateral pressure.

It is highly interesting to consider how important a service the glaciers perform in the economy of nature. These dead and chilly fields of ice, which prolong the reign of winter throughout the year, are, in reality, the source of life and the springs of vegetation. They are the locked-up reservoirs, the sealed fountains, from which the vast rivers traversing the great continents of our globe are sustained. The summer heat, which dries up other sources of water, first opens out their bountiful supplies. When the rivers of the plain begin to shrink and dwindle within their parched beds, the torrents of the Alps, fed by melting snow and glaciers, rush down from the mountains and supply the deficiency; and, at that season (July and August), the rivers and lakes of Switzerland are fullest.

During the whole summer, the traveller who crosses the glaciers hears the torrents rustling and running below him at the bottom of the azure clefts. These plenteous rills gushing forth from their sub-glacial beds, are generally all collected in one stream, at the foot of the glacier, which, in consequence, is eaten away into a vast dome-shaped arch, sometimes 100 ft. high, gradually increasing until the constant thaw weakens its support, and it gives way and falls in with a crash. Such caverns of ice are seen in great perfection, in some years, at the source of the Arveiron, in the valley of Chamonix, and in the glaciers of Grindelwald. The streams issuing from glaciers are distinguished by their turbid dirty-white or milky colour. The waters collected by the melting of the ice from all parts of the surface of a glacier often accumulate into torrents, which, at length, precipitate themselves with a thundering noise into a hole or fissure, often of very great depth, called a *Moulin*. This is formed whenever a stream encounters a crack in the glacier. The fall of the water scoops a vertical shaft which moves onward with the ice until the surface cracks again in the same place, when the operation is repeated. The most accessible glaciers are those of Grindelwald, Chamonix, Zermatt, and Pontresina. The great Aletsch Glacier has, since the building of mountain inns in its vicinity, been much visited.

The following striking passage from Professor Forbes's 'Alps,' p. 386, will form a good conclusion to this account of glaciers :—" Poets and philosophers have delighted to compare the course of human life to that of a river; perhaps a still apter simile might be found in the history of a glacier. Heaven-descended in its origin, it yet takes its mould and conformation from the hidden womb of the mountains which brought it forth. At first soft and ductile, it acquires a character and firmness of its own, as an inevitable destiny urges it on its onward career. Jostled and constrained by the crosses and inequalities of its prescribed path, hedged in by impassable barriers which fix limits to its movements, it yields groaning to its fate, and still travels forward seamed with the scars of many a conflict with opposing obstacles. All this while, although wasting, it is renewed by an unseen power,—it evaporates, but is not consumed. On its surface it bears the spoils which, during the progress of existence, it has made its own; often weighty burdens devoid of beauty or value, at times precious masses, sparkling with gems or with ore. Having at length attained its greatest width and extension, commanding admiration by its beauty and power, waste predominates over supply, the vital springs begin to fail; it stoops into an attitude of decrepitude—it drops the burdens, one by one, which it had borne so proudly aloft—its dissolution is inevitable. But as it is resolved into its elements, it takes all at once a new, and livelier, and disembarrassed form : from the wreck of its members it arises 'another, yet the same '—a noble, full-bodied, arrowy stream, which leaps rejoicing over the obstacles which before had stayed its progress, and hastens through fertile valleys towards a freer existence, and a final union in the ocean with the boundless and the infinite."

§ 13. ALPINE RIVERS, LAKES, AND WATERFALLS.

Rivers.—The Central Alps give birth to some of the greatest streams of Europe. The Rhone and the Rhine both have their origin in the St. Gothard group. The Inn flows from the glaciers of the Bernina. The Po rises under Monte Viso, and is the only great alpine river which has not its original source in a glacier.

Lakes.—Lakes are very numerous in Switzerland, and add to alpine scenery a charm which is not found in the, in some respects, more sublime landscapes of the Caucasus or Himalaya. The most remarkable are, the Lake of Lucerne, which exhibits both beauty and stern grandeur; Wallenstadt, Thun, and Brienz, the Lake of Geneva, or Lac Leman, distinguished for its great extent and diversified character, at one end bold and mountainous, at the other soft and smiling : it occupies an intermediate rank between the Swiss and Italian Lakes. The latter, that is to say, Maggiore, Lugano, Como, Orta, Iseo, and Garda, may be included in an alpine tour. Their character is soft and smiling; blessed with a southern climate, their thickets are groves of orange, olive, myrtle, and pomegranate; and their habitations villas and palaces. There are also, scattered about the Alpine chain, many high tarns, such as the Dauben See on the Gemmi, and the lakes of the St. Gothard. The most important lakes of this class are those of the Upper Engadine.

By some geologists the formation of even the largest lake-basins in the alpine regions has been ascribed to the erosive action of ice during the time of the greatest extension of the ancient glaciers. Owing to the nature of the rock or to local circumstances causing the ice to excavate, basins are supposed to have been produced in certain parts of valleys and not in others. This theory was advocated by Prof. Ramsay (Quart. Jour. Geol. Soc. xviii. 185) and has since then gained numerous supporters. Several geologists, however, no less familiar with mountains, as Mr. Ball, Mr. W. Mathews, and Prof. Bonney, consider that the theory is not applicable to the greater alpine lakes. The last named has pointed out difficulties in its application in the above Journal (xxix. 382 ; xxx. 474).

Waterfalls.—The attempt to fix an order of precedence for alpine waterfalls is not likely to meet with general approval, because much of the interest connected with them depends on the seasons and the weather, as well as on the taste of the spectator. Waterfalls, which in spring or after rains are magnificent spectacles, are reduced at the close of a dry summer to insignificant driblets. In Switzerland, waterfalls of some pretension are as numerous as blackberries. The traveller, after a time, is *pestered* by them, and will hardly turn his head to look at a fall which, if it were in England, would make the fortune of a watering-place. There is a certain similarity in all falls of water; and when the curiosity has been satisfied by the sight of three or four, they cease to be appreciated except as features in a landscape. It may therefore be useful to specify a few which are worth seeing for their own sake.

The Fall of the Rhine, at Schaffhausen, deserves the first rank, from the volume of water; but it is rather a cataract than a cascade—it wants height.

Fall of the Tosa, in the Val Formazza: remarkable for its volume of water, great height, and fan-like form.

Fall of the Aar, at Handeck, combines a graceful shoot with great elevation; an abounding torrent, and a grand situation.

The Staubbach, or Dust Fall: a thread or scarf of water, so thin that it is dispersed into spray before it reaches the ground; beautiful, however, from its height and graceful wavings.

Schmadribach, wild and impetuous, at the head of the valley of Lauterbrunnen.

Giessbach, a series of cascades in a pine-wood, on the lake of Brienz.

Fall of the Sallenche, a simple out-pour near Martigny.

Reichenbach Falls, with both beauty and dash, near Meiringen.

Fall of the Madesimo, remarkable for height, on the Splügen.

Stäubibach, a grand fall on the Klausen pass.

Falls of the Reuss at the Devil's Bridge.

Fall of the Sandbach above the lower Sand Alp, Canton Glarus. This fall would rank high for grandeur were it easier to see it from a favourable point of view.

Fall at Turtmann.

Fall of the Ordlegna torrent near Vico Soprano.

Fall of the Inn, below the Lake of St. Moritz.

Falls of the Serio, at the head of Val Seriana.

Most of these waterfalls are in the track of travellers. Others, worthy to rank with any but the first three, are to be seen in remote districts.

§ 14. LANDSLIPS, AVALANCHES, SNOW-STORMS, FLOODS.

Landslips.—These catastrophes are sometimes included under the heading of avalanches. They arise when, owing to the decay of the rock or the excessive saturation of the soil after heavy rains, great masses of the mountain-side break away and fall, carrying down ruin on all below them. The site of a downfall of this nature is seen in the Illgraben, above Sierre in the Rhone valley. The most famous historical instances of such a calamity are the destruction of Pleurs in 1618, the fall of the Rossberg, celebrated by Byron, in 1806, and the fall of one of the peaks of the Diablerets in 1714. In 1877 a large portion of a mountain, near the Little St. Bernard in the Tarentaise, gave way. The ruin was not sudden, but went on for weeks. The clouds of dust which rose from the débris were seen by travellers on Mont Blanc. In 1881 a large part of the village of Elm in Canton Glarus was destroyed by a fall of rock.

[*Switz.*]

Avalanches (Germ. *Lawinen*) are those accumulations of snow which precipitate themselves from the mountains, either by their own weight or by the loosening effects of the sun's heat, into the valleys below, sweeping everything before them, and causing, at times, great destruction of life and property. The fearful crash which accompanies their descent is often heard at a distance of several leagues.

The natives of the Alps distinguish between several different kinds of avalanches. The *Staublawinen* (dust avalanches) are formed of loose fresh-fallen snow, heaped up by the wind early in the winter, before it has begun to melt or combine together. Such a mass, when it reaches the edge of a cliff or declivity, tumbles from point to point, increasing in quantity as well as in impetus every instant, and spreading itself over a wide extent of surface. It descends with prodigious rapidity, and has been known to rush down a distance of 10 miles from the point whence it was first detached; not only descending one side of a valley, but also ascending the opposite hill by the velocity acquired in its fall, overwhelming and laying prostrate a whole forest of firs in its descent, and breaking down another forest on the opposite side, so as to lay the heads of the trees up the hill in its ascent. *Slide-avalanches* (*Schleichlawinen* or *Schlipfe*) slip down from inclined surfaces often without disturbance of the surface, and it is only when they begin to roll over and bound that they become *Schlag-* or *Grundlawinen*.

Another kind of avalanche, the *Grundlawine*, occurs in spring, during the months of April and May, when the sun becomes powerful, and the snow thaws rapidly under its influence. They fall constantly from different parts of the mountains, at different hours in the day, accordingly as each part is reached by the sun: from the E. side between 10 and 12, from the S. side between 12 and 2, and later in the day from the W. and N. This species is more dangerous in its effects, from the snow being clammy and adhesive, and partly converted into ice by the pressure of the fall. Any object buried by it can only be dug out by the most arduous labour. Men or cattle overwhelmed by the *Staublawine* can extricate themselves by their own exertions; or, at any rate, from the snow being less compact, may breathe for some hours through the interstices. In the case of the *Grundlawine*, the sufferers are usually either crushed or suffocated, and are, at any rate, so entangled that they can only be rescued by the aid of others. Such avalanches falling upon a mountain-stream, in a narrow gorge, are often hollowed out from beneath by the action of the water, until it has forced a passage under them; and they sometimes remain for the whole summer, serving as a bridge, over which men and cattle may pass.

The avalanches have usually a fixed time for descending, and an habitual channel down which they slide, which may be known by its being worn perfectly smooth, sometimes even appearing polished, and by the heap of débris at its base. The peasants, in some situations, await with impatience the fall of the regular avalanches, as a symptom of the spring having fairly set in, and of the danger being over. In some places the lower end of a glacier falls at long intervals of years and displays an avalanche on the hugest scale. Those near Randa, near Giétroz in the Val de Bagnes, and on the side of the Altels, are examples.

Danger arises from avalanches either by their falling unexpectedly, while persons are traversing spots known to be exposed to them, or else (and this is the more fearful source of catastrophes) when an unusual accumulation of snow is raised by the wind, or when the severity of the season causes the avalanche to desert its usual bed, and the whole mass descends upon cultivated spots, houses, or even villages. There are certain valleys among the Alps in which scarcely any spot is totally exempt from the possible occurrence of such a calamity, though some are naturally more exposed than others. The Val Bedretto in Canton Tessin, the Maienthal in Canton Uri, and many others, are thus dreadfully exposed. To guard as much as possible against accidents, very large and massive dykes of masonry, like the projecting bastions of a fortification, are, in such situations, built against the hill-side, behind churches, houses, and other buildings, with an angle pointing upwards, in order to break and turn aside the snow. In some valleys great care is bestowed on the preservation of the forests clothing their sides, as the best protection of the district below them from such calamities. These may truly be regarded as sacred groves; and no one is allowed to cut down timber within them, under pain of a legal penalty. Yet they not unfrequently show the inefficiency even of such protection against so fearful an engine of destruction. Whole forests are at times cut down and laid prostrate by the avalanche. The tallest stems, fit to make masts for a first-rate man-of-war, are snapped asunder like a bit of wax, and the barkless and branchless stumps and relics of the forest remain for years like a stubble-field to tell of what has happened.

A mournful catalogue of catastrophes, which have occurred in Switzerland, since the records of history, from avalanches, might be made out if necessary; but it will suffice to mention one or two instances.

In 1720 an avalanche killed, in Obergestelen (Valais), 84 men and 400 head of cattle, and destroyed 120 houses. The same year 40 individuals perished at Brieg, and 23 on the Great St. Bernard, from a similar cause.

In 1749 the village of Ruèras, in the Tavétsch Thal, was carried away by an avalanche; 100 men were overwhelmed by it, 60 of whom were dug out alive; and several of the houses, though removed to some distance from the original site, were so little shaken that persons sleeping within them were not awakened.

In 1808, after a snow-storm of three days' continuance, an enormous avalanche detached itself from the top of the precipices above Trons, in the valley of the Vorder Rhein; it crossed the valley and destroyed a wood and some chalets on the opposite alp; recoiling, with the force it had acquired, to the side from which it had come, it did fresh mischief there, and finally reached Trons, and buried many of its houses to the roof in snow.

In 1827 the greater part of the village of Biel, in the Upper Valais, was crushed beneath a tremendous avalanche, which ran down a ravine, nearly two leagues long, before it reached the village.

One of the most remarkable phenomena attending the avalanche is the blast of air which accompanies it, and which, like what is called the wind of a cannon-ball, extends its destructive influence to a considerable distance on each side of the actual line taken by the falling mass. It has all the effect of a blast of gunpowder: sometimes forest trees, growing near the sides of the channel down which the snow passes, are uprooted and laid prostrate, without having been touched by it. In this way the village of Randa, in the Visp-Thal, lost many of its houses by the blast of a mass of glacier, which fell in 1720. The E. spire of the convent of Disentis was thrown down by the gust of an avalanche which fell more than a quarter of a mile off.

Travellers visiting the Alps between the months of June and October are little exposed to danger from avalanches, except immediately after a snow-storm; and, when compelled to start at such times, they should pay implicit obedience to the advice of the guides. It is a common saying, that there is risk of avalanches as long as the burden of snow continues on the boughs of the fir-trees, and while the naturally sharp angles of the distant mountains continue to look rounded.

It is different with those who travel from necessity in the spring, and before the annual avalanches have fallen. Muleteers, carriers, and such persons, use great caution in traversing exposed parts of the road, and with these they are well acquainted. They proceed in parties, in single file, at a little distance from one another, in order that if the snow should sweep one off, the others may be ready to render assistance.

The avalanches, seen and heard by summer tourists on the sides of Mont Blanc and the Jungfrau, are of a different kind from those described above, being caused only by the rupture of a portion of the glaciers, which give way under the influence of a mid-day sun, and of certain winds, during the summer and autumn, when other avalanches, generally speaking, have ceased to fall. They differ, also, in this respect, that, for the most part, they do no harm, since they fall on uncultivable and uninhabited spots. It is more by the roar which accompanies them, which, awakening the echoes of the Alps, sounds very like thunder, than by the appearance which they present, which is simply that of a waterfall, that they realise what is usually expected of avalanches. Still they are worth seeing, and will much enhance the interest of a visit to the Wengern Alp, the Cramont (on the S. side of Mont Blanc), or the borders of the Mer de Glace; especially if the spectator will bear in mind the distance at which he is placed from the objects which he sees and hears, and will consider that, at each roar, hundreds of tons of solid ice are broken off from the parent glacier, and in tumbling many hundred feet are shattered to atoms and ground to powder.

The *Snow-storms*, *Tourmentes*, or *Guxen*, which occur on the Alps, are much dreaded by the chamois-hunter, the shepherd, and those most accustomed to traverse the High Alps: how much more formidable must they be to the inexperienced traveller! They consist of furious and tempestuous winds, somewhat of the nature of a whirlwind, which occur on the exposed promontories, the summit-ridges, and elevated gorges of the Alps, either accompanied by snow, or filling the air with that recently fallen, while the flakes are still dry, tossing them about like powder or dust. In an instant the atmosphere is filled with snow; earth, sky, mountain, abyss, and landmark of every kind, are obliterated from view, as though a curtain were let down on all sides of the wanderer. All traces of path, or of the footsteps of preceding travellers, are at once effaced; and the poles planted to mark the direction of the road are frequently overturned. In some places the gusts sweep the rock bare of snow, heaping it up in others, perhaps across the path, to a height of 20 ft. or more, barring all passage, and driving the wayfarer to despair. At every step he fears to plunge into an abyss, or sink overhead in the snow. Large parties of men and animals have been overwhelmed by the snow-wreaths on the St. Gothard, where they sometimes attain a height of 40 or 50 ft. These tempests are accompanied almost every year by loss of life; and, though of less frequent occurrence in summer than in winter and spring, are one reason why it is dangerous for inexperienced travellers to attempt to cross remote and elevated passes without a guide.

The guides and persons residing on the mountain-passes, from the appearance of the sky, and other weather-signs known to them, can generally foresee the occurrence of tourmentes, and can tell when the fall of avalanches is to be apprehended.

Floods.—In most of the Swiss valleys traces are to be seen of terrible floods, which have from time to time poured down from the mountains, and devastated tracts of land more or less large. These floods usually occur at the melting of the snow in spring, but may happen at any time of year when, either from excessive rain, or from the too rapid melting of the snow, or from the bursting of a dam formed by fallen ice a mountain torrent swells beyond its usual proportions, and carries down stones, earth, huge rocks, and trees, sweeping everything before it till it reaches the valley, when it spreads out, often covering acres of fertile land with rubbish, and ruining the land for ever. There is hardly a year in which some part of Switzerland does not suffer from this cause. A flood in the autumn of 1852 converted the valley of the Rhone below Martigny into a lake, and covered hundreds of acres of land with rubbish, which in 1856 remained untouched and uncultivated. The flood on the same day carried away all the bridges but one in the valley of Chamonix; whilst, above Sallanches, the river left its bed, and cut out a channel 30 or 40 ft. wide, and 6 or 8 ft. deep, through the fertile land and down to the bare rock. Great floods are described in Rte. 56 and Rte. 136. The upper part of the valley of the Rhone is now a desert in consequence of floods, and traces of great floods may be seen in the valley of the Rhine and in the vale of Sarnen, and, in fact, in nearly every valley. Those who have once seen the recent effects of a flood will soon detect them continually, though the grass and bushes in a few years conceal the traces from those who do not know where to look for them.

§ 15. ALPINE FAUNA AND FLORA.

Wild animal life is not abundant in the Alps: it is rather conspicuous by its absence; and nothing can be imagined more lonely and lifeless than those mountain solitudes from which man and his herds are absent. Near the mountain-top a herd of chamois are occasionally seen, fixed like statues, or galloping across the ice; lower down the marmot's whistle is heard, the croak of the raven, and in the woods the merry "curr" of the nutcracker; perhaps the chough wheels overhead, the squirrel, or black salamander, crosses the path; but, as a rule, few living things are met with. The list of Swiss animals, however, includes several quadrupeds, and some interesting birds, as may be seen in a visit to Stauffer's museum at Lucerne.

Among quadrupeds are the following: The *Brown Bear*, now confined to
Tyrol and parts of the Engadine and Trentino, where the creeping-fir
(Pinus pumilio) shelters it most effectually. The *Lynx*, a most destructive
animal, but very rare. The *Wild Cat*. The *Wolf*, found principally in
the Jura and the Maritime Alps. The *Steinbock, Bouquetin* or wild goat
(Capra Ibex), preserved on the Italian mountains by the late King of
Italy (extinct in Switzerland) (see Rte. 146), the *Chamois*, the *Fox,
Badger, Otter*, brown and blue *Hare, Squirrel*, &c. The *Marmot*
(Arctomys marmota) enlivens the wastes of rock and coarse grass immediately under the snowfields, and is abundant though persecuted. His
shrill whistle announces the approach of a traveller, who, if he be quick,
may see the little animal scuttling away to his hole. When undisturbed,
"they take up their position on some flat piece of rock, exposed to the
sun, where they bask and play, scratching and combing themselves."
About the middle of October the marmot retires to his winter quarters,
a chamber well lined with moss and hay, and, rolling himself into a ball,
goes to sleep for six months. Another and much smaller rodent, the
Arvicola nivalis, lives at a still greater height than the marmot, in oases
of rock and herbage amidst the mountain-ice.

Of Alpine birds the *Lämmergeier*, or Lamb Vulture, is the monarch of
the Alps, with wings sometimes 9 ft. span; the *Raven* (Corvus corax) will
sweep on a lonely height in circles round the traveller's head; the *Chough*
with a red bill, and the *Alpine Chough* with a yellow bill, frequent the
peaks. The *Nutcracker* feeds on the pine-cones and fills the woods with its
cheerful though harsh note, sounding like "crack" and at times like "curr."
There is the *Ptarmigan* near the snows, the *Jay* and *Blackcock*, in the
forests; and, among smaller birds, the white-breasted *Swift, Alpine Accentor,
Redstart, Snow Finch, Pastor*, and *Wall Creeper* (Tichodroma muraria).
The last is a beautiful little bird, with wings of crimson and black.

Of reptiles there is the *Alpine Frog*, with orange belly, said to be very
good eating; and the slimy black lizard called *Salamander*.

The Alpine *flora*, of such various soils and climates, is necessarily most
abundant and diversified, but is past its prime in the travelling season of
August. It is seen to perfection in early June, before the cattle have
entered upon the Alps, but when the carpet is spread for them, and
flowers by myriads seem to elbow the lingering snow-wreaths from the
ground. In July many mountain sides are belted with dense masses of
the greater Gentian, or ablaze with the *Alprose* (Rhododendron hirsutum
and Ferrugineum), which may be called the national flower of Switzerland, as the Blue-bell is of Scotland. The *Edelweiss* (Gnaphalium
Leontopodium) is another special favourite, like the Alprose a theme of
the poet, and associated with many a pathetic legend. It is the emblem
of purity, and is given by the Tyrolese youth to his affianced bride. In
August the well-watered rich green meadows are covered with the lilac
Lily (Crocus autumnalis), and the Alps to the snow-line spangled by the
deep-blue star of the smaller Gentian.

For further details on the subject of this section, see Tschudi's 'Thierleben
des Alpenwelt,' Bonney's 'Alpine Regions,' Morell's 'Scientific Guide to
Switzerland,' J. C. Weber's 'Die Alpen-Pflanzen Deutschlands und der
Schweiz,' and Christ's 'Das Pflanzenleben der Schweiz.'

§ 16. POPULATION, ARMY, EDUCATION, RIFLE-MATCHES, WRESTLING, COSTUMES, TOWNS.

Population.—Switzerland covers 15,900 square miles, and on the 1st December, 1880, its population was 2,831,787. Of these 1,567,000 were Protestants, 1,085,084 Rom. Catholics and Christians of other denominations, and 7036 not Christians, mostly Jews, the proportion of whom has doubled in the last ten years.

0·695, or 367,065 families, speak German; 0·234, or 123,438 families, speak French; 0·054, or 28,697 families, speak Italian; lastly, 0·017, or 8905 families, belong to the Romansch language spoken in a part of the Grisons.

On the subject of the *moral condition of the Swiss*, and of their character as a nation, there is much variety of opinion. The Swiss with whom the traveller comes into contact, especially the German portion of them, are often either polyglot waiters, grasping landlords, or slow-witted and churlish peasants. This disposes the superficial traveller to dislike and to take very little interest in the people amongst whom he is travelling; he has also perhaps heard something of their time-serving, their love of money, and their readiness to fight for any paymaster in former times, while he knows little of the most interesting portions of Swiss history, and is absolutely ignorant of the nature of the Swiss constitution. Looked at as a nation, the Swiss are deserving of our study and admiration, as the heirs of a freedom which has, like our own, been handed down from father to son through many centuries. The late Mr. Grote, the historian of Greece, in the preface to his admirable Letters on Switzerland wrote, "The inhabitants of the twenty-two cantons are interesting on every ground to the general intelligent public of Europe. But to one whose studies lie in the contemplation and interpretation of historical phenomena they are especially instructive; partly from the many specialities and differences of race, language, religion, civilization, wealth, habits, &c., which distinguish one part of the population from another; comprising between the Rhine and the Alps a miniature of all Europe; and exhibiting the fifteenth century in immediate juxta-position with the nineteenth; partly from the free and unrepressed action of the people, which brings out such distinctive attributes in full relief and contrast. To myself in particular they present an additional ground of interest from a certain political analogy (nowhere else to be found in Europe) with those who prominently occupy my thoughts, and on the history of whom I am engaged—the ancient Greeks." A living historian, Mr. E. A. Freeman, in the opening chapter of his small work on 'The Growth of the English Constitution,' has called attention to the fact that in the meetings of the Landsgemeinde of Uri, Appenzell, and Glarus, the tourist may see before his eyes a survival of the oldest form of Teutonic government, such as it was practised by our own forefathers in the days of Tacitus.

Army.—There is *no regular army* in Switzerland, nor, with the exception of a Federal staff, is there any one who makes the army his exclusive profession. Every able-bodied Swiss is, however, a soldier, and liable to military service between the ages of 20 and 45. On attaining the age of

20 he is trained for 28 or 35 days, and entered in the *Élite*, but he may not be called upon to serve, as only 3 per cent. of the population are required from each canton. These are drilled every subsequent year for about a week, and have occasionally to attend one of the large biennial camps of instruction. In April, 1869, the army was divided into three descriptions of service, according to age, viz. the *Élite* or *Bundesauszug* (20 to 32), 85,138; the *Reserve* (33 to 40), 50,559; and the *Landwehr* (41 to 45), 64,323. Besides these there is a 4th class, the *Landsturm*, or army of defence, which comprises all men fit for service above 45. There is a crack corps of riflemen called *Scharfschützen*. The following is the last estimate (1872) of the strength of the Swiss army, exclusive of the *Landsturm*: *Élite*, 84,045; *Reserve*, 51,102; *Landwehr*, 65,562. Total, 200,709.

Education.—Switzerland has 4 Universities,—Bâle, Zürich, Berne, and Geneva; 3 Academies,—Geneva, Lausanne, and Neuchâtel; 7 lycées; 32 "écoles normales," and a large number of establishments for secondary education. There are 7000 primary schools. The new Federal Constitution renders primary instruction gratuitous and obligatory. Many of the cantons, in addition, require attendance at supplementary courses, up to the age of 16, 17, or 18. The number of pupils is 400,000, or 1 in every 6 inhabitants. The amount of instruction given differs, however, enormously in the various cantons, as will be seen by the following table of the rates annually levied for educational purposes per head.

	fr.	c.		fr.	c.
Bâle (city)	7	30	Graubünden	1	5
Geneva	4	40	Ticino	0	95
Zürich	3	25	St. Gall	0	85
Schaffhausen	2	90	Zug	0	75
Soleure / Neuchâtel / Vaud	2	40	Obwald (Unterwalden)	0	50
			Appenzell (Inner Rhoden)	0	45
Berne	2	20	Glarus / Valais	0	40
Bâle (district)	2	5	Appenzell (Ausser Rhoden)	0	35
Lucerne	1	80	Uri	0	30
Aargau	1	75	Schwyz / Niederwald (Unterwalden)	0	25
Fribourg	1	30			
Thurgau	1	25			

The Swiss mountaineers are skilful marksmen at short ranges with the rifle, and, like their neighbours the Tyrolese, meet constantly to practise and engage in trials of skill. There are clubs or societies in almost every valley and parish, and constant matches between them; besides which, every year, a *grand Federal Rifle Match* is held near one or other of the large towns, at which all the best shots from the whole of Switzerland meet to contend for a prize. The late Lord Vernon gained the *first* prize at the Federal Match held at Bâle, 1849.

Annual *contests in wrestling* also (called *Schwingfeste*) are held in different parts of Switzerland. The cantons which distinguish themselves for skill in this and other athletic exercises are Berne, Appenzell, and Unterwalden.

Costumes distinguishing the people of each canton, and in some districts of each valley, were nearly universal before 1830. They are now disappearing, but may still be seen in the Bernese Oberland, the Valais, &c., and the women in many cantons have peculiar head-dresses. The men are usually attired in brown undyed homespun cloth.

§ 17. CHALETS AND PASTURAGES, RANZ DES VACHES, SWISS HUSBANDRY.

From the mountainous nature of Switzerland and its high elevation, the greater part of the surface, more than 1800 ft. above the sea, which is not bare rock, is pasture-land. The wealth of the people, like that of the patriarchs of old, in a great measure lies in cattle and their produce, on which account the pastoral life of the Swiss deserves some attention. The bright verdure of the meadows which adorns the valleys of Switzerland is one of the distinguishing features of the country; and the music of the cow-bells, borne along by the breeze, is one of the sweetest sounds that greet the traveller's ear.

The Alps, or mountain-pasturages (for that is the meaning of the word Alp in Switzerland and Tyrol) are usually the property of the commune; in fact common land, on which the inhabitants of the neighbouring town or village have the right of pasturing a certain number of cattle, the regulations as to which are often very curious. In the Italian Alps the lower pastures are known as *monti* or *primesti*, the higher are the *alpi*. In the German Alps the latter word, in the French Alps the former ("montagne") is used generally for mountain-pasturages.

" In the spring, as soon as the snow has disappeared, and the young grass sprouts up, the cattle are sent from the villages up to the first and lower pastures. Should a certain portion of these be exhausted, they change their quarters to another part of the mountain. Here they stay till about the 10th or 12th of June, when the cattle are driven to the middle range of pastures. That portion of the herds intended for a summer campaign on the highest Alps remain here till the beginning of July, and on the 4th of that month generally ascend to them; return to the middle range of pastures about 7 or 8 weeks afterwards, spend there about 14 days or 3 weeks, to eat the aftergrass; and finally return into the valleys about the 10th or 11th of October, where they remain in the vicinity of the villages till driven by the snow and tempests of winter into the stables.

" That portion of the cattle, on the other hand, which is not destined to pass the summer on the higher Alps, and are necessary for the supply of the village with milk and butter, descend from the middle pastures on the 4th of July into the valley, and consume the grass upon the pasturage belonging to the commune, till the winter drives them under shelter. The very highest Alpine pasturages are never occupied more than 3 or 4 weeks at the furthest."—*Latrobe.* The tourist in the higher Alps continually meets the flocks and herds migrating from one pasture to another, or to the valley below.

Sometimes the owners of the cattle repair in person to the Alps, and pass the summer among them along with their families, superintending the herdsmen, and assisting in the manufacture of cheese; and in some parts there are whole villages inhabited only temporarily; but in general only a sufficient number of men to attend to the herds and to make the cheeses remain with the cattle, in which case the cows or goats belonging to each owner are tried twice a-year, *i. e.* the amount of cheese produced in a day or two by each is ascertained ; then at the end of the season the cheese made is divided among the owners in the proportions indicated by the trial. The best cheeses are made upon pastures 3000 ft. above the sea-level, in the vales of Simmen and Saanen (Gruyères) and in the Emmenthal. The best cows there yield, in summer, between 20 lbs. and 40 lbs. of milk daily, and each cow produces, by the end of the season of 4 months, on an average, 2 cwt. of cheese.

The life of the cowherd (Fr. *Vacher*, Germ. *Senner*) is by no means such an existence of pleasure as romances in general, and that of Rousseau in particular, have represented it. His labours are dirty, arduous, and constant; he has to collect 80 or 90 cows twice a-day to be milked, to look after stragglers, to make the cheese, and keep all the utensils employed in the process in the most perfect state of cleanliness. The cowherd has generally, as assistants, a friend (*Freund*), who acts as a carrier to the low country, and a lad (*Kuhbub*). In some parts the herdsmen live for many months almost entirely on milk and cheese, not eating 10 lbs. of bread or potatoes in the time. The cattle are frequently enticed home at milking-time by the offer of salt, which they relish highly, and which is considered very wholesome for them. The allowance for a cow is 4 or 5 lbs. in a quarter of a year. The *Stoss* is an extent of pasture sufficient for the maintenance of 1 cow, or 1 colt, or 4 calves, or ¼ of a horse.

The *Chalet* (Germ. *Sennhütte*) in which the herdsman resides is literally a log-hut, formed of trunks of pines, notched at the extremities so as to fit into one another at the angles of the building, where they cross : it has a low flat roof, weighted with stones to keep fast the shingle-roof and prevent its being blown away by the wind. A building of this kind is rarely air-tight or water-tight. The interior is usually blackened with smoke and very dirty, boasting of scarcely any furniture, except, perhaps, a table and rude bench, and the apparatus of the dairy, including a huge caldron for heating the milk. A truss of hay, in the loft above, serves the inmates for a bed. The ground around the hut on the outside is usually cut up by the feet of the cattle, and the heaps of mud and dung render it difficult to approach the door.

There is another kind of *chalet*, a mere shed or barn, in which the hay is housed until the winter, when it is conveyed over the snow in sledges down to the villages below. A pastoral Swiss valley is usually speckled over with huts of this kind, giving it the appearance, to a stranger, of being much more populous than it is in reality : in the Simmenthal alone there are said to be 10,000 chalets. This large number is necessary, because everything—goats, sheep, cattle, horses, and food—must be put under cover for some months during the snow.

The herdsmen shift their habitations from the lower to the upper pasturages, as their cattle ascend and descend the Alps, at different seasons, and they sometimes have 2 or 3 places of temporary abode. The experienced traveller is careful to inquire beforehand what chalets are occupied ; otherwise when in search of repose or refreshment, after a long day's journey, he is liable to the disappointment, on approaching what he conceives to be a human habitation, of finding that it is a mere hay-barn, or else a deserted chalet; and he may learn, with much mortification, that he has still some tedious miles to trudge before he can reach the first permanently occupied dwelling. What an agreeable contrast to reach a well-appointed chalet of the better sort, where delicious milk cooled in the mountain stream, fresh butter, bread, and cheese, are spread out on a clean napkin before the hungry and tired stranger!

Ranz des Vaches.—It is not uncommon to find the Ranz des Vaches spoken of, by persons unacquainted with Switzerland and the Alps, as a single air, whereas it is a class of melodies prevailing among and peculiar to the Alpine valleys. Almost every valley has an air of its own. Those of Appenzell and the Gruyère country are the most celebrated. Their effect in producing home-sickness in the heart of the Swiss mountaineer, when heard in a distant land, and the prohibition of this music in the Swiss regiments formerly in the service of France, on account of the number of desertions occasioned by it, are stories often repeated, and probably founded on fact.

These national melodies are particularly wild in their character, yet full of melody; the choruses consist of a few remarkably shrill notes, uttered with a peculiar falsetto intonation in the throat, called *yodelling.* They originate in the practice of the shepherds on the Alps, of communicating with one another at the distance of a mile or more, by pitching the voice high. The Ranz des Vaches (Germ. *Kuhreihen*), literally *cow-call,* derives its name from the summons of the herdsman to his cattle at milking-time. From the wide alpine pasture the cows come marching home, in obedience to the voice, or the notes of the *Alphorn,* a simple tube of wood, wound round with bark, five or six feet long, admitting of but slight modulation, yet very melodious when caught up and prolonged by the mountain echoes. In some of the remoter districts, from which the ancient simplicity of manners is not altogether banished, the Alp-horn supplies, on the higher pastures, where no church is near, the place of the vesper-bell. The cow-herd, posted on the highest crest, as soon as the sun has set, pours forth the first four or five notes of the Psalm, "Praise God the Lord;" the same notes are repeated from distant Alps, and all within hearing, uncovering their heads and bending their knees, repeat their evening orison, after which the cattle are penned in their stalls, and the men betake themselves to rest.

A word may be said on *Swiss Husbandry* to draw the attention of such persons as take an interest in the subject, to one or two practices peculiar to the country. The system of irrigation is carried to a very great extent and perfection; streams from the mountain-torrents are sometimes led for miles, even from one valley into another, and turned over the meadows by means of trenches and sluices. The drainings of dunghills, cow-houses, and pigsties are not allowed to run to waste, but are carefully collected in a vat by the farmer, and at the fit moment carried out in carts to the fields, and ladled over them, very much to their benefit, and to the equal disgust of the olfactory nerves of all who pass; the air, far and near, being filled with this truly Swiss fragrance. The industry of the people and their struggles for subsistence, in some of the high valleys, are truly wonderful. The grain-crops are wretched, but the grass is sweet and good. (See § 11.) In the best and lowest pasturages they get three crops a-year. The cattle feed on the high mountains during the summer, and are supported in chalets by the hay of the valley during the long winter. An Englishman accustomed to buy everything, can hardly realise the domestic economy of a Swiss peasant. He has his patches of wheat, of potatoes, of barley, of hemp, of flax, and, if possible, of vines; his own cows, his own goats, his own sheep. On the produce of his own land and flocks he feeds; his clothes are of homespun, from the wool of his sheep; his linen and the dresses of the women of his family are made from his own flax or hemp, frequently woven by the women of his own family. The timber he requires for his house or for firing is supplied from the land of the commune or parish, either for nothing or for a very small sum. What little money he requires is derived from the sale of cheese. The interior economy of a Swiss village is very interesting: it is only by ingenious contrivances for saving labour and by amazing industry that it is possible for the inhabitants to maintain themselves in such a climate.

§ 18. GOÎTRE AND CRETINISM.*

" Quis tumidum guttur miratur in Alpibus?"—*Juvenal.*

Goître is a swelling in the front of the neck (of the thyroid gland, or the parts adjoining), which increases with the growth of the individual, until, in some cases, it attains an enormous size, and becomes "a hideous wallet of flesh," to use the words of Shakspeare, hanging pendulous down to the breast. It is not, however, attended with pain, and generally seems to be more unsightly to the spectator than inconvenient or hateful to the bearer; but there are instances in which its increase is so enormous that the individual, unable to support his burden, crawls along the ground under it. On the N. of the Alps women appear to be the principal sufferers from this complaint, and in the Valais scarcely a woman is free from it, and it is said that those who have no swelling are laughed at and called goose-necked. At Domo d'Ossola it seems more prevalent among the men. Val d'Aosta is its principal seat.

Various theories have been resorted to, to account for goître: some have attributed it to the use of water derived from melting snow; others, to the habit of carrying heavy weights on the head; others, again, to filthy habits; while a fourth theory derives it from the nature of the soil, the confined air of deep valleys, or the use of spring-water impregnated with calcareous matter.

As the goître occurs in Derbyshire, the Lake District, Yorkshire (especially at Settle, in the limestone district of Craven), Notts, Somerset, Surrey, Hants, &c., where no permanent snow exists, and no rivers spring from glaciers—also in Sumatra, and in parts of South America, where snow is unknown—it is evident that the first cause assigned is not the true one; as for the second and third, they would equally tend to produce goître in the London porters, and in the inhabitants of the purlieus of St. Giles's. Goître is found only in certain valleys; nor, when it does occur, does it exist throughout the valley. It appears in one spot; higher up it is unknown, and in another situation, a mile or two distant, perhaps it is

* Cretin = Chretien, a name resulting from the mediæval belief that the Deity particularly protects these.

again prevalent. A curious example of this is afforded by the valley leading up to the Great St. Bernard. Goître is unknown above Liddes; abounds at Verchères, 800 ft. lower down; and is almost universal at Orsières: had the disease depended upon the glacier-water, it would, of course, be more prevalent near the glaciers, and in the upper part of the valley.

On the annexation of Savoy to France, the question of goître was seriously taken up by the Government, on account of the number of the exemptions from military service claimed in consequence of this malady. The conclusion arrived at was that the deformity was produced by drinking tainted or naturally impure water. Consequently steps were taken, by analysing wells, to point out which should be avoided, by cleansing villages and by dosing the schoolchildren with lozenges containing iodine. " It is said that out of 5000 goîtrous children who were so treated, in the course of eight years, 2000 were cured, and the condition of 2000 others was improved; and that the number of cures would have been greater had not the parents opposed the care of the Government in order to preserve the privilege of exemption from military service." *

Cretinism, which frequently occurs in the same localities as goître, is a more serious malady, inasmuch as it affects the mind. The cretin is an idiot of the worst sort, deformed in body as well as mind. His countenance is misshapen as well as vacant; his head is disproportionately large; his limbs are stunted or crippled; he cannot articulate his words with distinctness; and there is scarcely any work which he is capable of executing. He spends his days basking in the sun, and from its warmth appears to derive great gratification. When a stranger appears, he becomes a clamorous and importunate beggar, assailing him with a ceaseless chattering; and the traveller is commonly glad to be rid of his hideous presence at the expense of a few centimes. Cretins, however, are now somewhat diminished in number, and some of the worst are confined, so that the traveller is not pestered by them as he used to be.

The causes of cretinism are still obscure; but there is little doubt that intermarriage must be counted as a principal agent in the continuation of this terrible curse.

§ 19. LAKE-DWELLINGS.

Pfahlbauten—Constructions lacustrines.—A short account of these curious relics of the ancient inhabitants of Switzerland forms a natural preface to an historical note on the country.

The Lake of Zürich was, in the winter of 1854, very low. Near Obermeilen the inhabitants took advantage of this circumstance to enclose a part of the lake. In so doing, they found in the mud heads of piles, staghorns, stone implements, and other pieces of handiwork. This induced further researches, and the result has been most remarkable. Undoubted traces have been discovered of a large population living on the shallow borders of the lakes, both in Switzerland and in North Italy. The habitations in some places stood on piles, as in the Eastern Archipelago; in other places, on artificial islands, like the Irish crannoges. From such habitations many things would naturally fall or be thrown into the water, and have thus been more or less preserved in the mud. In fact, an incre-

* ' Bollettino del Club Alpino Italiano,' No. 13, 1869, quoted in Mr. E. Whymper's ' Scrambles,' Chap. XVI., p. 303. See also the remarks on Cretinism in the same chapter.

dible quantity and variety of objects have been found and described— stone-axes and stone-knives in great numbers, bone pins and needles, string, cloth, bread, corn, rude pottery, bones of wild and of domestic animals, personal ornaments, fishing implements; in fact, enough to give a tolerable notion of the life and habits of the ancient inhabitants.

The number of these lake villages is very great; between twenty and thirty have been discovered in the Lake of Geneva, and upwards of forty in Neuchâtel.

They are probably to be found in every lake and peat-moss in Switzerland; and it is remarkable that on the great lakes they are usually opposite to the existing villages on the shore.

The most worthy of notice, perhaps, are at *Moosseedorf*, near Berne; *Robenhausen*, or the lake of Pfäffikon, where the settlement seems to have been burnt twice, and each time rebuilt: *Wangen*, on the Untersee, where there must have been a manufactory of stone tools; *Nidau*, near Bienne; *Wanwyl*, near Sursee; *Zug*; *Concise*, on the lake of Neuchâtel, &c.

The age of these dwellings has been the subject of much controversy. In some are discovered objects in iron and bronze, and pieces of Roman workmanship. In most places, however, stone takes the place of iron and bronze, probably indicating a higher antiquity. The latest may well have been in existence when Cæsar crossed the Alps, and the oldest may be two thousand years older. No theory to explain why the habitations were so built has as yet obtained general admission.

Collections of the objects found are to be seen at the public museums at Neuchâtel and at Berne. M. Désor, a professor at Neuchâtel, and Col. Schwabe, at Bienne, have also good collections.

The principal works on the subject are, Lyell's 'Antiquity of Man;' Lubbock, 'Prehistoric Times;' Troyon, 'Habitations lacustres;' Désor, 'Constructions lacustrines;' and Keller, 'Lake Dwellings.' The last has been translated into English, and is a most complete record of the discoveries up to the time when it was published.

There is not much to be seen at most of the places where the objects have been found; but, in 1875, the Lake of Bienne was lowered several feet. In doing this the piles of the old villages were brought to view, but would probably not long support the exposure to the air. Photographs were taken, and may be seen at the Museum in Berne.

§ 20. HISTORICAL SKETCH.*

The dwellers in the lake villages described in the last section were probably of Celtic race. It is uncertain whether they had disappeared before the Roman Conquest. The two principal tribes whom the Romans found in possession of the country were the Rhæti and the Helvetii, the former of obscure origin. The latter, a Celtic race, after inflicting some serious reverses on the Roman arms, were subdued by Julius Cæsar, B.C. 58. Augustus carried on the work of conquest, and in B.C. 5 was able to erect on the trophy at Turbia an inscription, preserved for us by Pliny,

* For a list of authorities, see *ante*, p. xlv. In the following section Swiss towns are spoken of by their historical names in place of the corrupt French forms, which have unhappily become naturalised in England, and have consequently been retained in other parts of this work.

recording the complete subjugation of all the alpine tribes from sea to sea. They were absorbed into the Roman Empire, their country was traversed in every direction by Roman roads, and prosperous towns— Aventicum (Avenches), Augusta Rauracorum (Kaiser-Augst), Vindonissa (Königsfelden, near Brugg in Aargau), arose at the foot of the mountains. Roman rule and order was maintained for 300 years. As the Empire grew weak, Helvetia was overrun by hordes of Burgundians and Alemanni (A.D. 450). Their limits may be roughly traced in the present division of languages between the German and French (or, as the present inhabitants prefer to call them, Romance) Cantons.

Under the domination of the Frank kings of the Merovingian dynasty, order was restored to the country, and Christianity was preached, chiefly by Celtic monks from Ireland, St. Gallus, St. Columbanus, and others. Great monasteries arose at Disentis, Pfäffers, St. Gallen, and Einsiedeln, which became centres of progress and learning, where the monks at once preserved the precious remains of antiquity, and taught improved methods of agriculture. The Roman roads were again used: " xenodocheia," or hospices, afforded shelter to the traveller, who had nothing as yet to fear from the Saracenic brigands, who made their appearance in the tenth century; so that at this period the Alps were a far less formidable barrier than in the Middle Ages.

Modern Switzerland formed part of the empire of Charles the Great. Even the mountain fastnesses of Uri were civilised and prosperous, so that Lewis the German granted them to one of his daughters, an abbess at Zürich. At the break up of the Carlovingian Empire, what is now East Switzerland fell to the eastern, West Switzerland to the western Frankish kingdom. In 888 Count Rudolf founded the kingdom of Transjurane Burgundy, including all Switzerland W. of the Reuss; and this territory, which, with Provence added to it in 933, constituted the kingdom of Arles, became in 1032, partly by bequest partly by conquest, part of the Empire. But in this outlying region the real power was in the hands of a number of petty nobles and wealthy abbots, of whom the counts of Zähringen were chief. When the last of this race died (A.D. 1218), the dignity of imperial bailiff was given now to one now to another of the local counts. Meantime the towns were rapidly growing in power : Zürich, Basel, and Bern were free imperial cities. Bern gave the municipal franchise to every householder, and offered an asylum to all who fled from the tyranny of the neighbouring nobles.

In 1273 Rudolf of Habsburg was raised to the Imperial throne. Himself a noble of the region which is now Aargau, he found his advantage in securing the aid of the hardy mountaineers and the wealthy towns by granting them special privileges.

On August 1, 1291, Uri and Schwyz (which had earlier in the century acquired the privilege of *Reichsfreiheit*, or immediate dependence on the Empire), and Nidwald, fearing the encroachments of the House of Austria on Rudolf's death, formed a perpetual alliance to maintain their several local rights and privileges. Profiting by the quarrel between Adolf of Nassau, the " Rex Romanorum," and Albert of Austria, they induced the former to ratify their charters. Adolf was slain in battle, and Albert did not ratify his charters, but while maintaining the rights of his family, did not enforce them by violent means. In 1308, the year of the alleged conspiracy of the Grütli, Albert appears from the contemporary authorities to have been on particularly good terms with the Confederates, and soon after Uri formally declared itself " a good friend of the Duke of Austria." In 1309 King Henry VII. of Lützelburg confirmed the charters of Uri and Schwyz, and gave Unterwalden a charter confirming all privileges previously conferred by his predecessors. As Unterwalden had before enjoyed no such privileges, the effect was to place it in the same position as Uri and Schwyz—*i.e.* grant it the *Reichsfreiheit.* Henry also appointed a single imperial bailiff for the three districts, thus cementing their union. On Henry's death a struggle for the imperial power took place between Lewis of Bavaria and Frederick of Austria. The latter prince, unable to retain his feudal rights in the three Cantons peaceably, had recourse to arms. The Confederates, on the other hand, fought not against the imperial authority, which they never dreamt of renouncing, but against a local lord who held that he had been unjustly deprived of his rights by the Emperor. The result was the famous battle of Morgarten, 15th November, 1315, in which the chivalry of Austria suffered utter defeat at the hands of the Swiss footmen. In the following year Lewis, as Emperor, formally declared the Dukes of Austria stripped of all their rights over the Drei Länder.

Such is the true story of the first assertion of Swiss independence.

The picturesque legends which have made of the first years of the 14th century the heroic period of Swiss history, the story of Tell and Gessler, of the meeting at the Grütli, have been reluctantly abandoned by all serious historical students. They were unknown to the contemporary chroniclers, and first appear in a work of the 15th century, the ' White Book of Sarnen.'

In 1339 the citizens of Bern, under Rudolf of Erlach, completely defeated at Laupen a combination of nobles, and secured the independence of their town. Between 1332 and 1353 the three humble mountain cantons were reinforced by the accession of Luzern, Zürich, Glarus, Zug, and Bern. In 1386 and 1388 the disastrous routs of Sempach and Näfels put an end to the Duke Leopold of Austria's hopes of making himself master of the eight confederates.

Intestine quarrels now broke out in the Confederacy. Between 1440 and 1450 a fierce war, arising out of the disputed inheritance of the Counts of Toggenburg, was waged between Zürich and the other confederates. The French came to the aid of Zürich, and in the bloody combat of St. Jakob, near Basel, the Dauphin, afterwards Louis XI., was taught to respect Swiss valour. He was not slow to profit by the lesson, and thenceforth used his best endeavours to entangle his dangerous rival, Charles of Burgundy, with such stubborn foes. That ambitious prince, anxious to reconstitute the old kingdom of Burgundy, readily turned his arms against the ' Schwyzers,' as the confederates now began to be popularly styled. He was disgracefully defeated in the three battles of Grandson and Morat (1476), and Nancy (1477). In 1481 at Stanz, after a violent altercation between the city and mountain cantons, which threatened to break up the Confederacy, and was appeased by the influence of Niklaus von der Flüe, Solothurn and Fribourg were added to the state, and a fresh league was made between the united cantons. But common danger again proved a more effectual guarantee of concord than any number of good resolves recorded in solemn parchments. In 1499 the allies had to defend their liberties against the Emperor Maximilian I. They were completely victorious. The Emperor freed the league from the jurisdiction of the Imperial Chamber, and from this time dates the practical independence of the Confederation, though it was not legally recognised till 1648. Basel, Schaffhausen and Appenzell were now admitted into the Confederation, which received no further increase until 1798. At this time (1499), perhaps the crowning point in Swiss history, Wallis, St. Gallen, Neuchâtel, Mühlhausen, and the 3 leagues of the Graubünden, were in alliance with the Confederates. Switzerland, respected abroad, was at leisure to follow at home the pursuits of peace. Swiss baths had become places of resort and expense for health- and pleasure-seekers. The schools, which had existed since Charles the Great's time at Zürich, and the university, founded at Basel, A.D. 1460, became the rivals of the old monasteries as seats of learning and research. In these, medical science was pursued, and the connection of medicine with herbs led to the first mountain exploration, while the spirit of physical inquiry fostered conduced to a general questioning of Nature. The story of the first ascent of Pilatus (see p. 56) illustrates admirably the change which about this time came over the national intelligence.

Unfortunately the martial spirit, which had been roused by the necessities of self-defence, found vent in mercenary service abroad. The battle of Marignano (1515) was the most famous of the many combats in the wars of Italy in which the Swiss were engaged, and they acquired by cession from the Duke of Milan (1512) as the reward of their bravery, or rather, perhaps, of their treachery, the Italian districts which they still hold. But the country was demoralised. "The common people in town and country were drawn away from honest labour, to idleness, lewdness, and warlike undertakings, and reckless and abandoned habits prevailed everywhere."

The 16th century was a time of internal troubles. On one side of the country, Zwingli at Zürich, on the other, Calvin at Geneva, led the revolt against Rome, which took political shape in the "Christian League" of Bern and Zürich. The Roman Church found an earnest and formidable champion in Cardinal Borromeo, Archbishop of Milan, the great Catholic reformer and leader of the Counter-Reformation, who in 1586 was successful in uniting the seven Catholic cantons in the Golden or Borromean League.

During this and the succeeding century the religious discords consequent on the Reformation, threatened to undermine the foundations of the state. Bern, Zürich, Basel, and Schaffhausen adopted the reformed religion; Appenzell and Glarus were divided; Luzern, Schwyz, Uri, Unterwalden, Zug, Fribourg and Solothurn adhered to the old faith. Geneva, shaking off, with the aid of Fribourg and Bern, the supremacy of the Counts of Savoy, though not yet a member of the Confederation, threw her influence on the side of the Reformers. Bern and Fribourg conquered the Pays de Vaud (1536). At the close of the period of the Reformation, Switzerland was divided into two religious leagues, holding separate Diets, the Catholics at Luzern, the Protestants at Aarau. The Protestant cantons allied themselves with France, the Catholic with Spain and Rome.

It was not until the class of the Thirty Years' War, in 1648, that the absolute independence of Switzerland was formally recognised by the Emperor in the Peace of Westphalia.

The troubles of the times were added to in 1653 by a revolt of the peasants, whom the Free Cantons retained in a state of serfdom, which was put down with great slaughter.

After numerous disputes and wars, the religious contest culminated in the war of Toggenburg, in which 150,000 men are said to have been brought into the field. The decisive Protestant victory of Villmergen was followed by the Peace of Aarau (A.D. 1712), which established absolute equality between the cantons. From this time up to the French Revolution, Switzerland, though the field of constant disputes and squabbles between parties, was free from internal wars.

During this time and the preceding period of civil war the democratical character of many of the cantons had been impaired. Bern, Solothurn, Luzern, Fribourg and Basel, were controlled by close oligarchies. In some cantons the rulers were local great families, in others the trading guilds. In the rural cantons alone, the ancient and simple institutions continued to flourish.

The French Revolution found Switzerland rife with the elements of disorder. In many of the large towns, and in several of the cantons the popular liberties had been abridged to the advantage of small oligarchies. The neighbouring, but still independent, city of Geneva first caught flame from the fires lighted at Paris in 1789. The democratic party which had been put down by violence, triumphed, and executions and proscriptions marked its revenge. Within the Confederation troubles soon broke out, fomented by French emissaries. From intrigues the French Republic proceeded to violence. Mühlhausen and Basel were annexed to France, and in 1798 a French army marched on Bern, which opened its gates. The conquerors declared the old Confederation dissolved, and decreed in its place an Helvetic Republic after the French model. It was received sullenly by the lowland states and cities. But the mountain cantons, Schwyz, Uri, Unterwalden, Zug, Glarus and Appenzell, were not disposed to exchange their immemorial rights for any work of French constitution-mongers. They attacked the French with a fury worthy of the days of Sempach. Defeated, they submitted only to rise again, exasperated at fresh interferences with their ancient customs. Unterwalden resisted to the uttermost, men, women and children joining in the desperate final combat. The French general and army rendered themselves infamous in history by their cruelties. All who bore arms were put to the sword, the town of Stanz was given to the flames, and the whole district was abandoned to pillage and massacre.

For the next few years, while the armies of Austria, Russia, and France fought and perished among their mountains, the Swiss, stunned by the crash of arms, looked on with indifference. After the Peace of Amiens, the French garrisons were withdrawn; anarchy followed, for the new constitution, which substituted a centralized state for the old loose Confederation of 18 cantons, or administrative districts, satisfied no party. In 1803, Napoleon, now First Consul, intervened. A commission of Swiss delegates assembled at Paris under his supervision, and framed a new constitution, known as " The Act of Mediation," which revived the old cantonal constitutions. At this time six new cantons, Graubünden, St. Gallen, Aargau, Thurgau, Ticino, and Vaud, were added to the Confederacy;

and henceforth the name 'Die Schweiz,' already in popular use, supplanted in formal documents the original title of "Upper League of High Germany."

No work of Napoleon could hope for any respect from the Congress of Vienna. The wave of reaction which passed over Europe rose into Switzerland. The towns seized the opportunity to reclaim unequal privileges; the patricians and the oligarchies resumed their former sway. In 1815 the "Federal Pact" was signed at Zürich, adding Geneva, Valais, and Neuchâtel to the number of the Cantons, now raised to twenty-two. By the Treaty of Paris, at the end of the year, the neutrality and independence of Switzerland within its present limits, were guaranteed by all the great European Powers.

A period of great material prosperity now opened for Switzerland, which has continued to the present day. In the previous century, Rousseau had preached the beauties of mountain scenery, De Saussure and Bourrit had rendered the Montagne Maudite of past ages "the famous Mont Blanc," and, in consequence of their writings, Gibbon had found his retreat invaded by an army of "visitors to the glaciers." But the Napoleonic wars stopped travellers. When peace again opened the Continent to our countrymen, they invaded it in increased numbers and with greater energy. Byron's powerful verse aided to establish the popularity of the Lake of Geneva and the Alps. The new roads Napoleon had made across the mountains were largely used, and their construction incited the Swiss to imitate them elsewhere. The whole country was thrown open, and each travelling-carriage, as it rolled through, left behind it a deposit of foreign gold. The Swiss found it no longer necessary to take service under foreign princes, in order to obtain opportunities for gain or even pillage.

The country was prosperous, but it was not contented. The reaction of 1815 was an impotent attempt to dam the stream of progress, and it was only a question of a few years when the barrier should give way. In 1830 the popular feeling became too strong to be resisted : the oligarchies had to yield, and the cantonal constitutions were roughly but peaceably revised.

In May, 1833, an attempt to revise the "Federal Pact" was defeated by the Catholic and aristocratic cantons. In 1841, the democratic party triumphed in Geneva; in 1843, the aristocrats obtained the upper hand in Valais. In the same year, Luzern, having admitted the Jesuits to control public education, was attacked by bodies of franc-tireurs belonging to the opposite party. She repulsed them with loss, and, to protect herself from further violence, formed, in defiance of the Federal Pact, an alliance with six other Catholic cantons, known in history as the *Sonderbund*, or Separate League. After some hesitation, the Federal Diet, in 1847, determined to dissolve by force of arms the illegal combination of the Catholic cantons. The Federal army, under the command of General Dufour (well-known to every Swiss traveller as the head of the survey which has produced the most beautiful and accurate of Ordnance maps), numbered 100,000. The Catholics could only bring half that number into the field, and the struggle was happily short.

The time had now come for a revision of the Federal Pact. A new constitution, which, with certain modifications, is still in force, was framed. It converted the Confederation from a *Staatenbund*, i.e., a mere treaty alliance of neighbours, to a *Bundestaat*—a single state, each of whose members retains a certain amount of independence. The supreme legislative power is vested in a Federal Assembly, which meets yearly, consisting of two bodies—the Nationalrath, or National Council, and the Ständerath, or Council of States. To the former every 20,000 or fraction over 10,000 citizens elect a member; to the latter each canton sends two members, and the half cantons (see p. 5) one apiece. Elections for the Nationalrath are triennial. Those to the Ständerath are held variously every year, every second, or every third year, and the deputies are elected in some cantons by the Grand Council, in others by universal suffrage. No Federal law can be made without the concurrence of both bodies. They retain in their own hands the power of peace and war, of making treaties, and of regulating the coinage, but are not allowed to keep up a standing army.

The Executive power is given to a council of seven members, known as the Bundesrath, and elected for three years by the Federal Assembly. Its president is the head of the state, but is merely a chairman, and has no special authority. The Supreme Court of Justice is elected by the Federal Assembly, and consists of nine judges, with nine deputy-judges, holding office for three years. It determines all disputes between the Cantons, or between the Cantons or individuals and the State. It sits at Lausanne.

The Federal authority is strengthened by a provision that no canton may maintain a force of more than 300 men, or make separate alliances with another canton or with a foreign state. Every Swiss of the age of 20 is liable to conscription, has a vote for the Federal Assembly, and is eligible as a member of it. The order of Jesuits are forbidden to have any establishments in the Republic. No new bishopric can be founded without the consent of the State. All forms of religious worship are free. Freedom of the press and the right of petition are guaranteed.

After an attempt in 1872, defeated by the jealousy in the 'Suisse Romande' of a centralising policy, a revision of the Constitution was, in 1874, passed by a majority of the Cantons and of the people, in accordance with the provision by which no revision could take effect without a direct appeal to the nation. Its effect was, on the one hand, to tighten the Federal Bond at the expense of the separate Cantons by introducing greater uniformity in the military and the educational system; on the other, to increase the power of the people at the expense of the Federal Assembly, by providing that, on the demand of 30,000 citizens, any law passed by the Assembly must be submitted for ratification to the popular vote. In pursuance of this provision two laws were met, in 1876, by a popular veto. By a further provision 50,000 citizens can demand to have an alteration of the Constitution submitted to the popular vote.

The penalty of death had been abolished for some years in Switzerland, but in 1879, owing to the increase of violent crime, it was decided by a small majority of the popular vote to leave to each Canton the power to re-enact it.

In 1876 the annual income amounted to 1,691,080l., and the expenditure to 1,737,720l., of which 614,441l. were spent on the army. The interest paid on the National Debt in the same year was 47,680l.

Switzerland, after a period of unexampled commercial prosperity, has recently been suffering from the effects of over-speculation. Many large hotels have been closed, or sold at an immense loss, by their first owners; railroads have paid decreasing dividends, or none at all; and the Corporations of large towns have found difficulty in meeting their liabilities.

LIST OF CANTONS.

Date of entrance into the Confederation.	Cantons.	Extent in square miles.	Population in 1880.	Language by Households.			
				German.	French.	Italian.	Romansch.
A.D. 1291	Uri . . .	420	23,744	3,367	..	1	..
1291	Schwyz .	338	51,109	9,895	2	21	..
1309	Unterwalden .	262	27,321	6,284	..	13	1
1332	Luzern . .	586	134,708	24,820	28	15	..
1351	Zürich . .	684	316,074	59,295	85	16	9
1352	Glarus . .	279	34,242	8,173	1	3	8
1352	Zug . . .	85	22,829	4,054	2	9	..
1353	Bern . .	2,543	530,411	83,688	16,633	49	1
1481	Fribourg .	563	114,994	6,056	16,682	24	..
1481	Solothurn .	254	80,362	15,239	65	2	..
1501	Basel . .	184	123,478	19,275	257	6	1
1501	Schaffhausen .	115	38,241	8,187	18	..	..
1513	Appenzell .	152	64,827	14,605	3	2	..
1803	St. Gallen .	758	209,719	41,215	40	31	1
1803	Graubünden .	2,665	93,864	9,347	29	3,024	8,740
1803	Aargau . .	501	198,357	39,405	36	5	..
1803	Thurgau .	268	99,231	20,006	8	13	..
1803	Ticino . .	1,033	130,394	108	16	26,320	5
1803	Vaud . .	1,180	235,349	1,535	48,957	160	..
1815	Valais . .	1,988	100,190	6,378	13,459	164	..
1815	Neuchâtel .	250	102,744	2,628	17,045	80	5
1815	Geneva . .	91	99,712	978	20,209	121	7
	Total . . .	15,179	2,831,787	384,538	133,575	30,079	8,778

§ 21. GLOSSARY.

The following are some common words and names.

Abendglühen—Evening sunset glow.

Ach—Brook.

Aiguille—Needle-like rock, generally of granite. In Ital. *Uja:* in the Graian Alps, *Ouille.*

Alp (or *Alm*)—Mountain pasturage.

Alpenglühen—Glow of the Alps by sunrise or sunset.

Alpi—In the Italian Alps, the upper pastures as distinguished from the lower known as *Monti.*

Arête—Ridge, Cumberland Edge.

Arolla—Name of the Pinus cembra in Piedmont and Valais. In the German Switzerland, *Arven.*

Balm—German for a small cave used by shepherds. *Beaume* in French.

Bergschrund—A crevasse, like a fosse, at the foot of a snow-peak. It is the crack formed where the névé in downward movement touches the stationary snow and ice plastered on the face of the mountain and is often 20 to 50 ft wide and of very great depth.

Caire—A rocky peak, S.W. Alps.

Casera—A large chalet in the Lombard Alps.

Calotte—Cap.

Camoscio— } Italian names for the
Camozza— } chamois.

Canale—A valley in the Italian Alps.

Chalet—A summer residence of herdsmen and cattle, improperly applied to any wooden house by travellers. The word ought not to be written with a circumflex on the a.

Clapier—Slope of loose broken stones, the Cumberland scree.

Cluse—Defile.

Colma — Top, height: Italian = *Kulm*, German.

Combe—Valley.

Couloir—A steep gulley, on the side of a peak or ridge.

Crevasse—A rent or fissure intersecting a glacier, and produced by the motion of the ice. In German, *Schrund*.

Eck—Corner.

Enge—Narrow place.

Etret—A narrow defile.

Firn—The higher region of a glacier, where the snow is passing into ice. In Fr. *Névé*.

Ferner—Glacier-clad chain.

Flüh—Cliff.

Furca—⎫
Furka—⎬ Fork—common name for passes which resemble a forked opening or furrow.

Gau—District.

Gems—German for chamois.

Geröll—Bed of loose stones. Screes.

Gestad—⎫
Staad—⎬ Landing-place or harbour.
Stad—⎭

Glacière—Cave containing ice. In old Swiss books the névés are called Glacières, as distinguished from the " Glaciers " which descend into the valleys.

Graben—Path of falling stones. In the Grisons a stony chasm or ravine: *tobel* is a ravine on a larger scale.

Grat—Ridge.

Hübel—⎫
Hügel—⎬ Hill, hillock, e.g. Alphubel.

Isola—Village between two streams.

Joch—Yoke. Hence mountain pass.

Jodeln—To shout in a falsetto, like Swiss cowherds.

Lauine or *Lawine*—Avalanche.

Lause—Piedmontese and Dauphiné *patois* —slate.

Lei (or *Lex*)—An enclosed pasture, found in Aléfroide, La Lex Blanche, and Pigne de l'Allée.

Lücke—Gap in a ridge = *Limmi* in Gadmenthal = *Fenêtre* or *Brèche* in French.

Mail—*Mal*. A peak, Maritime Alps.

Malga—Herdsman's hut in the Lombard Alps.

Mandron—A chalet in the E. Alps, classical Mandra.

Margaria—Shepherd's hut and fold in Maritime Alps, whence the manure is carried in autumn to the valley.

Margum—A small chalet in the Engadine.

Mayen—Chalet.

Montets—Common name for an ascent in a defile. Les Montets.

Moulin—Well-like aperture in a glacier, caused by the action of water.

Nachglühen—Afterglow of the Alps.

Nant, a stream.

Névé—See *Firn*.

Ouille—Aiguille: used in the Graian Alps.

Palü (Romansch.)—A swamp.

Parei—Savoyard patois for a wall of rock.

Peigne—⎫
Pigne—⎬ Comb or crest.

Piz—A peak.

Pousset—Projecting point.

Roesa—*Ruize*. Piedmontese for glacier, hence Monte Rosa (called Monts Roeses in MS. of XVIII. century) and Ruitor and Roisebanque.

Rua—Hamlet in Piedmontese Alps.

Scharte—A notch in a rocky ridge.

Scheideck — Ridge, separating valleys; literally dividing edge, from *scheiden* to divide, and *Eck*, corner.

Schrund—Gulf, crevasse.

Senner— *Vacher*—Cowherd.

Serac—Tower of a glacier ice-fall, icecastle ; name derived from a thin cheese which splits into rectangular pieces.

Staffel—Step.

Steinbock—German for the ibex. *Bouquetin* (Fr.). *Stambecco* (Ital.).

Stoss—Pasture of small extent.

Stunde—One hour's walk, or a league.

Tines—Les Tines. Common name for a defile.

Tobel—See *Graben*.

Tritt—Step.

Uja—For Aiguille in the Italian Alps.

Vastera—A pasture. Maritime Alps.

Wand—Wall of rock.

Wyl—Village.

Za Zan or *Cia*—A pasture belonging to the Commune ; frequent in the Pennine Alps ; according to Professor Ascoli the same word as the Latin *campus*.

§ 22. ABBREVIATIONS, &c., EMPLOYED IN THE HANDBOOK.

The points of the compass (not magnetic) are marked by the letters N. S. E. W.

(*rt.*) right, (*l.*) left,—applied to the banks of a river. The right bank is that which lies on the right hand of a person whose back is turned towards the source, or to the quarter from which the current descends.

Distances are, as far as possible, reduced to English miles; when miles are mentioned, they may be understood to be English, and feet to be English feet.

Where there is a railway, the distances at the head of the chapters are measured from the first station or terminus. On other roads the distances are measured from each place to the next place mentioned.

The names of Inns precede the description of every place. The best Inns are placed first.

† Denotes a pier and landing-place for steamers.

In order to avoid repetition, the book commences with a chapter of preliminary information; and to facilitate reference to it, each division or paragraph is separately numbered.

Each Route is numbered with Arabic figures, corresponding with the figures attached to the Route on the Map, which thus serves as an Index; at the same time that it presents a *tolerably* exact view of the great and minor roads of Switzerland.

Eng. Ch. S., English Church Service on Sundays.

MAPS AND PLANS.

ERRATA.

Page 47. **Flüelen.** The *Urnerhof* is closed.

„ „ Right-hand column, 5th line from foot of page, *for*
" 20 minutes " *read* " 40 minutes."

HANDBOOK FOR SWITZERLAND.

CORRECTIONS AND ADDITIONS, 1887.

ERRATA.

Page xiii., second paragraph:

Mr. **Edward Stanford**, Charing Cross, is one of the chief *Passport Agents* in London.

Page 155, first column,—Neuchâtel :

The **Pictures** have been removed from the Musée to a *Gallery* built expressly for them on the shores of the lake.

elds
s
e
,
e-
dee
e

s-
st
l.
ly

at
h
y
h)
he
d
he
e-
w
t.
g

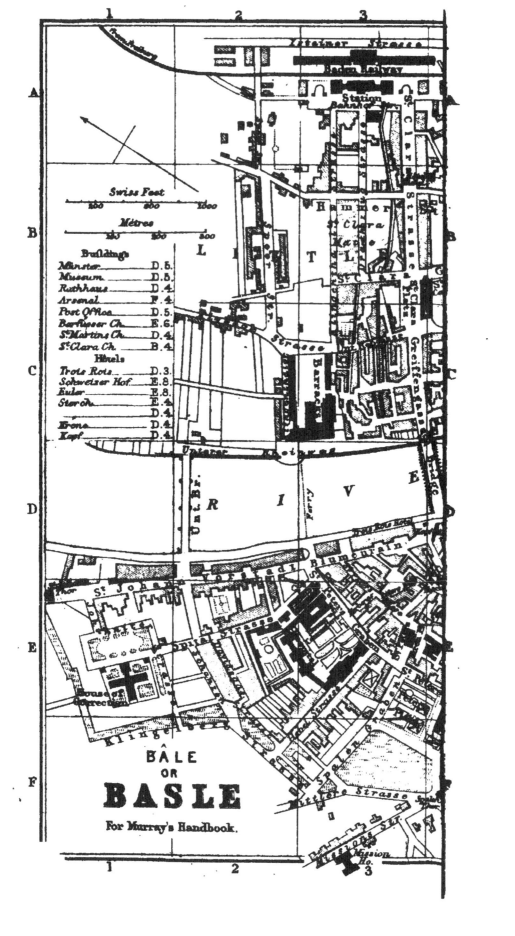

BÂLE
OR
BASLE
For Murray's Handbook.

SECTION I.

SWITZERLAND.

ROUTE 1.

BÂLE * TO BERNE, BY THE MÜNSTERTHAL
AND BIENNE—RAILWAY.

BASLE or BÂLE (Germ., Basel; Ital., Basilea).—*Hotels :* Trois Rois, on the bank of the Rhine, fine view, preferable for those who halt for more than a night ; Storch, Centralhof, Schiff. Near the Centr. Rly. Stat. ; Euler, Schweizerhof, both good houses; H. National, H. Hofer. In Little Bâle, on rt. bank of the river, are the H. Krafft, good and moderate; H. Schreider, opposite the Baden rly. stat. There is an excellent *Buffet* at the Centr. Rly. Stat. Requisites for washing can also be procured—a convenience to the traveller who arrives from Paris by the night train. He should remember that his watch will be wrong here. (See p. 5.)

Eng. Ch. S.

Physician : Dr. Jung.

Bookseller : Georg (near the Post Office), has a very complete collection and catalogue of old Alpine literature, and works relating to Swiss history.

Fiacres to the hotels, 1 fr. 50 c., to Klein Basel 2 fr.

Bâle is divided by the Rhine into Great Bâle on the l. bank and Little Bâle on the rt., connected by a wooden bridge, 680 ft. long, partly on

---

* Where the French forms of the names of Teutonic towns have been naturalised in England, they have been reluctantly retained by the present Editor.

[*Switz.*]

stone piers. Great Bâle is situated on high, sloping banks, overlooking the Rhine, which rushes past in a full broad flood of a clear light green; and the view from it is bounded by the hills of the Black Forest on the one side, of the Jura on the other. Its appearance is still that of an old German town. Great Bâle and Little Bâle, with a few miles of territory, form the half-canton called Basel-Stadt. Pop. (68,000.). The city is the residence of many rich merchants, bankers, and families of ancient descent. It is one of the principal gates of Switzerland, and has become of still greater importance since the Central Alpine line over the St. Gothard has been completed. There are few towns better worth a day's halt.

Starting from the bridge and ascending a narrow street, the first turning l. from the bridge, we pass l. the very unpretending University, rt. the Museum (see below), and shortly reach

The *Münster* (open 2 to 4, at other times 50 centimes), on the high bank of the Rhine, distinguished by its 2 spires (about 220 ft. high) and by the deep red colour of the sandstone, is very picturesque and interesting. It was begun by the Empr. Henry II. in 1010, and consecrated 1019; but the oldest parts now existing are probably of the 12th cent. It was mostly rebuilt in the beginning of the 14th century, after an earthquake in 1356.

B

The architecture is a mixture of the Romanesque and Pointed. The W. front, with its towers, its equestrian statues of St. George and St. Martin, and other almost grotesque carvings, is striking. The porch of St. Gallus in the N. transept, with figures of Christ in judgment, the Evangelists and John the Baptist, and a bas-relief of the wise and foolish virgins, is probably of the 12th cent. The interior was restored 1857, apparently with care and fidelity. The large organ was built 1858. It is occasionally played from 6 to 7 P.M., adm. 1 fr. The pulpit (1324–1486) is of one piece of stone, and an elaborate piece of work. The choir, with its four remarkable columns, is raised to make room for the crypt. In the choir were held the public meetings of the Council of Bâle. It contains the tomb of the Empress Anne (1281), wife of Rudolf of Habsburg, and round the nave, on the N. side, are many others of noble and royal persons ; also one or two quaint stone carvings let into the wall, particularly one of St. Vincent. Against a pillar opposite the *Font* (1465) is the *monument of Erasmus.* In the crypt are other tombs, mostly of the aristocratic families of Bâle, and also the coffins of six of the family of Baden Durlach. A staircase leads out of the choir into the Chapter-house, or *Conciliums Saal,* in which meetings of the committees of the Council of Bâle, were held between 1431 and 1449. It is a low room, with 4 Gothic windows, and distinguished not only in an historical point of view, but as being quite unaltered since the day of the Council, except the restored ceiling. It is now a museum, and contains ancient musical instruments, some pieces of furniture said to have belonged to Erasmus, and the six remaining fresco fragments of the original Dance of Death, painted on the walls of the Dominican Church in 1409, in remembrance of the plague. The Dance of Death has been attributed without cause to Holbein, since it existed at the time of the Council of Bâle, at least 50 years before his birth. Underneath the Conciliums Saal is the *Chapel of St. Nicholas,* in which many military curiosities are preserved, also most of the pictures and objects which were removed from the church at the recent restoration. Also the *Lällenkönig,* a head which, until 1839, was in a window of the town at the end of the bridge, and was made to put out its tongue and roll its eyes in derision of the inhabitants of Klein Basel. The inhabitants of Klein Basel are said to have put up on their side, in revenge, a figure making an indecent gesture of contempt.

On the S. side of the Church are extensive and picturesque *Cloisters* — a succession of quadrangles and open halls — which, with the space they enclose, served for centuries as a burial-place for the rich burghers, and are filled with their monuments ; among which are those of the three Reformers, Œcolampadius (Hausschein), Grynæus, and Meyer, and that of the great Hebraist Buxtorf. The cloisters were constructed in the 14th centy., and extend to the verge of the hill overlooking the river. They may have been the favourite resort of Erasmus.

Bernouilli is buried in *St. Peter's Church.* Œcolampadius first preached the Reformation in *St. Martin's Church.*

Behind the Münster is a *Terrace,* called *Die Pfalz,* 75 ft. above the river, commanding a beautiful view over the Rhine, the town, and the Black Forest hills, among them the Blauen. Close to it is the Club called *Lesegesellschaft,* with a library of 30,000 books. Returning towards the bridge, we come to the

Museum (Picture gallery *open* Sun. 10–12, Wed. 2–4 ; collection of engravings Thurs. 2–5 ; at other times 1 franc adm. Nat. Hist. collections open every day with fee. Library, week days 10–12). The most interesting of its contents are a collection of *Paintings and Drawings by the younger Holbein*—formed chiefly by his friend Boniface Amerbach, whose portrait is one of Holbein's masterpieces. *Obs.* the Passion of Christ, in 8 compartments, full of life, but harsh in colour; also 8 sepia drawings of the same subject;—a dead Christ, formerly in the Münster; a Last Supper, Holbein's Wife and Children, with countenances full of grief (1526); portraits of Erasmus, of Froben the printer, excellent—of a Mlle. von Offenburg, inscribed "Lais Corinthiaca," very good; the same lady as Venus with Cupid; two representations of a School, painted 1517, as a sign for a schoolmaster's door in the town of Bâle. Holbein's table—a table painted in his youth with scenes from the life of a Swiss burgher family. Here also are portraits of Luther and his wife, by *L. Cranach;* and of Zwingli; also the following works—102, the Baptist preaching, *Breughel;* 117, Street Musicians, *Honthorst;* 195, Man's Portrait, *Sir A. More;* 216, Madonna, Child and Saints, *L. Mazzolini;* 282, Adoration of the Shepherds, *Mabuse;* and good pictures by *Calame* and *Vautier.*

Among *Holbein's Drawings* are—his own portrait—*a work of the very highest excellence;* heads of the family Meyer —a beautiful pen-and-ink drawing, sketched for the celebrated picture now in the Dresden Gallery; original sketch for the picture of the family of Sir Thomas More—the names of the different personages are written on their dresses; 5 sketches for the frescoes which formerly decorated the Rathhaus in Bâle, with one or two fragments of the frescoes themselves; sketches in ink for glass windows, for the sheaths of daggers, for the organ in the Münster; the Costumes of Bâle; &c. &c. Holbein* was born at Augsburg in 1494 or 95, and removed 1520 to Bâle: his circumstances were by no means prosperous; he was even reduced to work as a housepainter. Erasmus, writing from Bâle a letter of introduction for the painter to one of his friends, complains that "hic frigent artes," and the want of

encouragement drove Holbein to seek his fortune in England, 1526, where he met with high patronage, and died of the Plague 1543. His native city showed its esteem for his talents by granting him a salary of 50 gulden per an., and by making him a citizen and member of the Painters' Guild.

Among other things deserving notice are the bronzes, pottery, coins, &c., from Augst, site of the Roman *Augusta Rauracorum,* 7 miles from Bâle; a silken embroidered banner, given by Pope Julius II. (1515) to the Bâlois; some old church-plate—part of the Dom-Schatz—a silver cup of open work is the oldest piece (13th cent.); St. Anne with the Virgin and Child; and a relic-box with reliefs, 13th century; a suit of chain-mail, once gilt, with plate-mail beneath it, worn by Charles the Bold at the battle of Nancy.

A copy of the 'Praise of Folly,' with illustrations by *Holbein,* and also autographs of Luther, Melancthon, Erasmus, and Zwingli, are exhibited in cases.

The *Library* contains 95,000 volumes —among them, the Acts of the Council of Bâle, 3 vols., with chains attached to the binding, many important MSS., of which there is a catalogue, and a few of the books of Erasmus.

The *University* of Bâle, in a poor building, nearly opposite the Museum, founded 1460, was the first great seminary established in Switzerland: it enjoyed a high reputation under Erasmus, and numbered among its professors in more recent times the names of *Euler* and *Bernouilli,* the mathematicians, who were natives of Bâle. *Schönbein,* the discoverer of gun-cotton and of ozone, was a professor.

Returning to the main street at the bridge, the Eisengasse, and ascending it, we pass on the rt. the *Fischmarkt,* a small square with Gothic fountain, and turning l. into the Freiestrasse reach the Market-place and

Rathhaus, a late Gothic building date 1508. The exterior is painted

* See Kugler's 'Handbook of Painting,' vol. ii., German School.

The frieze displays the emblazoned shields of the original cantons. The armorial bearing of canton Bâle is said to represent the case of a cross-bow. On the old staircase open rt. some ancient and almost unaltered rooms now employed as offices, and l. the Great Council-Room (*Stadt-Rathssaal*) ornamented on the walls and roof with humorous reliefs carved in wood by *Mat. Giger* (1609), and by painted windows bearing the coats of the 13 old Swiss cantons, with supporters. At the foot of the stairs is a statue of Munatius Plancus, the founder, according to tradition, of Bâle and of the Roman colony of Augst.

In the same street, rt., is the *Post Office*, a very ancient building, formerly the custom-house, with a new front. Passing through it, and observing the back, we see opposite, up a courtyard, the *Schmiede-Zunft*, or Smiths' Hall; and in the same street is another old hall, the *Gärtner-Zunft*; and in the town many others of the guilds or Zünfte, dating usually from the 16th cent., and almost unaltered. The interiors are worth a visit, and the attendants are glad to show them for a small payment.

Not far off towards the W. of the town is the *Arsenal* (Zeughaus).

A little way from the Arsenal are some very ancient corn stores, and beyond them the fountain called *Spahlenbrunnen*, with the figure of a bagpiper, copied from a design of Holbein or Albert Dürer, and of elegant workmanship. Beyond this is the *Spahlenthor*, i.e. St. *Paulusthor* (1400), which retains its advanced work or *Barbican*, similar to those which formerly existed at York, and, with its double portcullis and two flanking towers, is particularly picturesque. The town was surrounded with regular fortifications of early date, preserving the mediæval gates. The fortifications have since 1850 been mostly levelled and converted into streets. The Alban Thor, at the E. of the town, is left standing, and a garden has been laid out

around it. There is a stork's nest on the roof.

The *Barfüsserkirche*, in the Spitalgasse, is a noble building, well worth examination. *St. Elisabeth* is a modern Gothic church of some interest. *St. Leonard's Churchyard* and cloister are very quiet and pretty. *Bernouilli* is buried in St. Peter's Ch. Œcolampadius first preached the Reformation in *St. Martin's Ch.*

Erasmus resided in the house *Zur Luft*, No. 18, Baümleingasse, and Frobenius printed in it one of the first Bibles. The building called Kirschgarten was erected by the father of the distinguished African traveller, *Burckhardt*, who was born here.

A handsome *Hospital* has been built on the site of the palace of the Margraves of Baden.

Down to 1798 the clocks of Bâle went an hour in advance of those in other Swiss towns. This singular custom, according to one tradition, arose from a conspiracy to open the gates to an enemy at midnight having been defeated by the clock striking 1 instead of 12. According to another account, the clocks were put on at the time of the Council, in consequence of the unpunctual habits of the Fathers of the Church.

Since the Reformation, Bâle has been regarded as the stronghold of Methodism in Switzerland. It possesses many well-endowed religious benevolent societies and institutions. The Protestant Missionary and Bible Society has its head-quarters here. Attached to it is the School for Missionaries at *St. Chrischona*, 4 m. from Bâle. The spirit of trade has always gone, however, hand-in-hand with that of religion—and Bâle has been called a city of usurers; 5 per cent. was styled a "Christian usance" (einen Christlichen Zins), and a proclamation of the magistrates (1682–84) denounced those who lent money at a discount of 4 or 3½ per cent., as "selfish, avaricious, and dangerous persons."

Like many other Swiss towns, Bâle is much indebted to the liberality of its citizens, who continually bestow gifts and legacies for the public benefit. The Münster has been restored, and the Museum built and endowed by private means alone.

There is very good trout and grayling *fishing* in the Birs, and also in the Wiese, about 3 m. from Bâle, on the rt. bank of the Rhine.

Affenthaler, *Klingelberger*, and *Markgräfler* are 3 good Baden wines, grown on the W. slopes of the Black Forest. Bâle *Leckerli* is a ginger cake.

Railways.—A. CENTRAL STATION. —Direct line to Paris, by Delle and Troyes. To Calais, express in 15 hrs. (French time is 26 min. behind, German time 4 minutes faster than, that of Bâle.) To Strassburg; to Lyons, in 1 day, by Belfort, Besançon, and Dijon; to Olten, Zürich, Lucerne, Berne, Neuchâtel and Lausanne. B.—BADEN terminus in Little Bâle or Klein-Basel, N. of the Bridge; to Freiburg, Baden, Heidelberg, Frankfurt; to Schaffhausen, the Rhine Fall, and Constance (Rte. 7). The two stations are connected by a loop line with a bridge over the Rhine.

History.—The first building known to history on the site of Bâle was a Roman fort erected A.D. 358. After the destruction of the neighbouring town of Augusta Rauracorum in the 5th century, a bishop fixed his seat beside the old fortress. A town grew up under the walls of his palace, and, despite numerous calamities from sword, earthquakes, and pestilence, rapidly increased in importance. Its bishops were ranked by Charles the Great among his great nobles. Its history throughout the middle ages consists chiefly of struggles between the bishops and the townspeople, in which the latter were ever gaining ground. In 1356 an earthquake destroyed all but a hundred houses. Those left standing were attacked by fire, and so utter was the ruin of the city that it was proposed to rebuild it on a new site. From 1431-43 the Council of Bâle sat; and one of the prelates who attended it, afterwards Pope Pius II., has left us a description of the new city and its citizens. In 1460 the University was founded by a bull of the same Pope, on the model of that of Bologna. In 1501 the town joined the Swiss Confederation. The bishops shortly afterwards retired to Pruntrut, and the town enjoyed for many years great prosperity and was the seat of much commercial and intellectual activity. Holbein, Erasmus, and the reformer Œkolampadius were among its citizens.

During the 17th century the governing oligarchy ruled with a tight hand, and a prolonged struggle ensued between the lower classes and their oppressors. By the beginning of the 18th century the population had decreased by one-half. After the close of the Napoleonic wars Basel-Stadt arrogated to itself a permanent majority of three to two members in the Great Council. Basel-Landschaft waited its opportunity, and in 1831 revolted. The Federal troops occupied the district, and the Diet decreed the separation of the two disputants. The citizens declined to see their ancient power thus curtailed and marched against their neighbours. They were severely defeated, leaving 400 dead on the field. The Federal army now intervened in overwhelming force, and the separation of Basel-Stadt and Basel-Landschaft into two independent half-cantons was carried into effect in 1833. The peculiarity of the half-cantons is that each sends an independent member to the Ständerath in place of the whole canton returning two.

Owing to its position at the junction of the various lines converging on Switzerland, Bâle has, since 1850, grown rapidly in wealth and population. Its manufactories turn out yearly 2,000,000*l*. worth of ribbons. Its growth has, as usual, been effected at the sacrifice of much of its picturesqueness; the old walls are gone, and the charm of the solitary bridge has been interfered with by two modern rivals. The interior of the old city still, however retains its former character, and the view from the Cathedral terrace cannot easily be destroyed.

Environs. — On the Val Moutiers road, 10 min. from the Aeschen Thor (the S. Gate), a monumental group by the sculptor Schlöth was erected 1872 to the memory of the Swiss who fell in the *Battle of St. Jacob*, 1444. (Rte. 3.)

On the same road, near Dornach, 4 m. are *Arlesheim*, residence of the Bishops of Bâle between 1678 and 1792 ; and the *English gardens* of the *Château of Birseck*.

About 3 m. from the town, just within the German frontier, is *Hüningen*, once a strong fortress, afterwards under the French a great establishment for pisciculture. 21,600,000 impregnated eggs were distributed by its agency in 3 years. It is near the stat. of St. Louis, on the l. bank of the Rhine.

The salt-works of *Schweizerhalle* are 3 m. S.E. of the town on the l. bank of the Rhine. They were established by the Baron von Glenck of Gotha, who began a series of borings in 1821 to reach the salt-bed which extends below the cantons of Aargau, Schaffhausen, Berne, and even Valais. He was successful in 1835, and had a concession of the beds for 70 years on paying a tax of one-tenth of the raw produce, and supplying the canton at the rate of 2 fr. 70 c. the cwt. The total produce is 207,000 cwt.

Augst (Rte. 5), site of a Roman town, is a little further up the Rhine, 1½ m. from Pratelen, the first stat. on the Swiss rly.

BÂLE TO BERNE.

				Eng. m.
Delémont Junct.	.	.	.	25
Sonceboz Junct.	.	.	.	43
Bienne Junct.	.	.	.	53
Berne	.	.	.	76

This finely engineered line will be taken by those who wish to see something of the beauties of the Val Moutiers. With stoppages at the different junctions, the journey takes nearly 5 hours.

The *valley of the Birs*, commonly called the *Val Moutiers* (*Münsterthal*,

in Germ.), through which this excellent road passes, is one of the most romantic in the Jura. It consists of a series of narrow and rocky defiles, alternating with open basins, covered with black forests above, and verdant meadows below, enlivened by villages, mills, and forges. A road was originally carried through the Val Moutiers by the Romans, to keep up the communication between Aventicum (Rte. 46), the Helvetian capital, and Augst (Rte. 5), their great fortified outpost on the Rhine.

On leaving Bâle the road and rail pass the scene of the memorable fight of *St. Jacob* (Rte. 3).

4 m. farther, near *Reinach*, on the opposite bank of the *Birs*, is another battle-field—that of *Dornach* —where the Swiss gained a victory over a much larger Austrian force in 1499, during the Suabian war. The bone-house, near the Capuchin convent, is filled with skulls gathered from the field. In the ch. of Dornach *Maupertuis* the mathematician (d. at Bâle 1759) is buried. A monument, set up to his memory by his friend Bernouilli, was destroyed by the curé of the village, who was in the habit of repairing his kitchen floor with slabs from the churchyard. It has been replaced by a fresh monument at the expense of canton Soleure.

Beyond *Aesch* the ruin of the *Castle of Angenstein* is seen l., and *l'Evêché*, that part of the canton Berne which anciently belonged to the Prince Bishop of Bâle is entered; the valley contracts, and increases in picturesque beauty. *Zwingen* and its castle are passed, and l. a road by the Passwand to Ballstall and Olten.

Lauffen,—a curious, old, and dirty walled village. *Inn*, Sonne.

Soyhière (Germ. *Saugern*), *Inn* (Croix Blanche). Here is the division of languages: part of the inhabitants speak German, part French.

A contracted pass, the rocks of which on the rt. are surmounted by a convent, leads into the open basin of

Delémont Junct. Stat. (Delsberg) (*Inns*: Faucon, good ; Ours. [From this a line branches off to *Porrentruy* (G. Pruntrut), (*Inn*: Ours), a Jura town of 5500 Inhab., chiefly Catholics, and thence to Monbéliard in France. The line passes by the foot of Mont Terrible.] Fine view of the Jura and gorge of Moutiers. The bishop-princes of Bâle had a palace here. In the neighbourhood of *Bellerive* many Celtic remains have been found, particularly at Creux Belin and Roche de Courroux, opposite Vorbourg.

Courrendelin (Germ. *Rennendorf*. *Inn*: Cerf). Here we enter a defile higher, grander, and more wild than any that have preceded it. This is, properly speaking, the commencement of the Val Moutiers. Precipices overhang the line, and forests of fir cover the mountains above. In the midst of the gorge are the iron furnaces and forges of Les Rondes, supplied with ore in the shape of small granulated red stones, varying from the size of a pea to that of a cherry. The rent by which the Jura has been cleft from top to bottom, so as to allow a passage for the Birs, exhibits marks of some great convulsion, by which the strata of limestone (Jura-kalk) have been thrown into a nearly vertical position. The gorge terminates in another open basin, in the midst of which lies Moutiers. [Direct road to the Weissenstein and Soleure branches off beyond the gorge, about 1 mile before reaching]

Moutiers Grandval Stat., or *Münster* (*Inn*: Cerf, fair), a village of 1250 Inhab., named from a very ancient *Münster* of St. Germanus on the height, founded in the 7th century, and now fast falling to ruin. [There is a good car-road from Moutiers to the *summit of the Weissenstein* (Rte. 2), a distance of 10 m. (3 hrs.), up-hill nearly the whole way, but fit for the cars of the country, one of which, drawn by 2 horses, may be hired to go and return for 20 fr. It passes Grandval (Grossau) and Gänsbrunnen. Diligence daily to Olten in 6¼ hrs., passing Gänsbrunnen.]

At the upper end of the basin of Moutiers the old road went through another defile, equally grand, at the bottom of which the Birs foams and rushes, overhung by perpendicular cliffs and funereal firs.]

Court. — The valley to the E. of Court, called Chaluat (Tschaywo), is inhabited by the descendants of the Anabaptists, expelled from Berne in 1708–11. They speak French, and are distinguished by their industry and simple manners.

Malleray (*Inn*: Lion d'Or, capital trout).

Tavannes Stat., or Dachsfelden = badger's field, 2523 ft. (*Inn*: Couronne, pretty good).

[From Delémont to Tavannes there is a road along the *valley of the Sorne,* through *Bassecourt.* It passes the ironworks of *Untervelier* (2 hrs. 40 min.), built in a narrow gorge ; then ascends through the gorge of *Pichoux,* in 2 hrs. to *Bellelay* on a bleak tableland (3500 ft.). This was formerly a convent of Premonstratensian canons, built in 1136 ; it is now converted into an excellent brewery and a glass manufactory. Cheeses, called *têtes de moines,* are exported. Hence 1 hr. down to Tavannes.]

[The carriage-road quits the valley, mounting up a steep ascent, in the middle of which it passes under the singular archway in the solid rock, called

Pierre Pertuis (Pertusa = bored through). Probably a natural opening, enlarged by one of the Roman Duumvirs. The partly defaced inscription on the N. side is read as follows by Gruter :—

```
NVMINI AVGV
   STORVM
VIA . FACTA . PER
C . . VR . . . . VM . PATERNVM
II . VIR . COL . HELVET
```

"In honour of the Cæsars this passage was made by * * * Paternus, Duumvir of the Colony of the Helvetii." The archway is about 40 ft. high and 10 or 12 thick, and marked the boundary which separated the Rauraci, whose territory extended to Bâle, from the Sequani. It was fortified by the Austrians in 1813. Here is the watershed, 2834 ft., dividing the streams of the Birs from those of the Suze.]

The railway passes by a tunnel, nearly a mile long, to

Sonceboz Junct. Stat. — Change of carriages for Bienne (*Inn:* Couronne, good, R. Restaurant)—in the Protestant and charming Val St. Imier (Germ. Erguel), up which a rly. runs to Chaux de Fonds (Rte. 50). The engines on it are of a peculiar construction, in order to surmount the heavy gradients. Many of the inhabitants, as in other villages of this neighbourhood, are employed in watch-making. [The *old* road to Bienne descends the valley along the l. bank of the *Suze*, which forms several small cascades. The projecting rock of Rondchâtel was occupied in feudal times by a fort, and held by the powerful Bishops of Bâle, to whom it gave the command of this pass. *The View* from the *old road* on the last slope of the Jura, over Bienne and its lake, with St. Peter's Isle, and the district watered by the Aar, Emme, and Zihl, backed in clear weather by the snowy range of the Alps, from Mont Blanc to the Titlis, is exceedingly beautiful. On the bare limestone slope of the Jura, close to the road, are many granite boulders. (See § 12.)]
The line now follows the river to

Rencherette Stat. Thence by two other tunnels into another valley, then by a lofty bridge over the foaming stream of the *Scheuss*. Soon after this is a fine view over the lake, and the line descends through rocks and by cuttings and tunnels, crossing the canal of the Scheuss to

Bienne Junction Stat. (G. *Biel*). Good Buffet (*Inns:* *Couronne; Schweizerhof; Croix-Blanche). An industrious town, and Junction station of the Central and Berner-Staats Rlys. (Pop. 11,623), and prettily situated at the mouth of the valley of the Suze, at the foot of the Jura, here mantled with vines, and about half a mile from the foot of the lake of Bienne (Rte. 48). It is approached by several shady avenues. Bienne, having been ruled by bishops of Bâle (1272–1285), became a free Imperial city in 1285. The citizens formed a perpetual alliance with Berne in 1352, for the defence of their liberties, in revenge for which the town was burnt by its liege lord. The Reformation further weakened the connection between the town and its ecclesiastical ruler, and at the beginning of the 17th century his authority became nominal.

The low country near Bienne, known as Seeland or Das grosse Moos, in the triangle between the three lakes of Neuchâtel, Bienne, and Morat, was formerly subject to frequent inundations, and little better than a great swamp. Since 1868 it has been reclaimed by a series of great engineering works, at a cost of 560,000*l.*, of which 200,000*l.* are contributed by the State, under the direction of the engineer La Nicca. From Aarberg to the Lake of Bienne, and from the Lake to Buren, two canals, each more than 5 m. long, have been cut. Through these the Aar now flows. All three lakes have been connected by canals, and their surfaces lowered 7 ft.

[The *Chasseral* (or Gestler), one of the highest mountains of the Jura, may be ascended from Bienne. It is 5279 ft. above the sea. The view embraces Mont Blanc on the rt., the Bernese Alps and Pilatus and Rigi. There is a carriage-road as far as the village of Nods, about 3 hrs.; thence a footpath, about 1 hr., to the top. You may descend to Neuveville on the lake and rly. viâ Nods.]

From Bienne, railway to Neuchâtel, Yverdon (Rte. 49), Lausanne and Geneva; to Soleure and Olten.

The Rly. from Bienne to Berne (4 trains daily, 1 hr. 10 or 20 min.) crosses at Brügg Stat. the new Aar, which flows out of the Lake of B. at *Nidau* (*Inn:* Bär), the port of Bienne, with an old castle. It next crosses the old bed of the Aar by a lattice-bridge 800 ft. long, near Busswyl Stat. (fine view on l.), and ascends its rt. bank to

Lyss Junct. Stat. Here the direct line from Soleure to Morat, Lausanne and Yverdon is crossed (see Rte. 46). Then follow the Stations of Suberg, Schüpfen, and Münchenbuchsee.

Zollikofen Junct. Stat. Here the Central rly. from Olten (Rte. 4) falls in. A little N. of this lies

Hofwyl, long well known as the agricultural and educational institution of the late M. de Fellenberg. The surrounding district was little better than a bog when M. de Fellenberg settled here in 1799; but he gradually brought it into cultivation; and an English agriculturist, who had been sent abroad to investigate the state of farming on the Continent, reported that here alone he had seen really good ploughing.

The rly. leaves on rt. the picturesque peninsula of *Enge,* nearly surrounded by the Aar. At Tiefenau a lofty *Road-bridge* of 3 arches, a noble structure, has been thrown over the river. Nearly opposite the N. extremity of the Enge lies *Reichenbach,* which belonged to Rudolph of Erlach, the hero of the battle of Laupen (1339), murdered here, in his old age, by his son-in-law, Jost von Rudenz, with the very sword which he had wielded at that glorious victory. The assassin was pursued, as he fled from the scene of his crime, by the two bloodhounds of the aged warrior, which broke loose at their master's cries. They tracked the murderer's footsteps of their own accord, and after some hours returned with gore-stained lips, and nothing more was heard or known of Jost von

Rudenz. Rudolph was buried at the neighbouring church of *Bremgarten,* where a stone in the N. wall of the chancel marks the spot.

The great bridge over the Aar carries the rly. on the top, and the carriage-road on a lower story, into

BERNE Terminus. (Rte. 24.)

ROUTE 2.

BÂLE TO OLTEN, SOLEURE AND BIENNE, BY OENSINGEN :—RAILWAY.—THE WEISSENSTEIN.

	Eng. m.
Olten.	
Soleure	29
Bienne	42

As far as Olten the railway is described in Rte. 3. A new line of rly. was opened in 1876, avoiding Herzogenbuchsee. It follows the valley of the Dünnern to

Oensingen Stat. The rly. crosses a ridge into the valley of the Aar,
Wargen Stat. to

SOLEURE Junction (Germ. *Solothurn*). A short branch line leads to the Berne line at *Burgdorf* (*Inns:* Couronne, good and moderate; Cerf; Bargezi, opposite the stat., moderate). Soleure, the capital of the canton, is prettily situated on the Aar, at the foot of the Jura range, 1397 ft. above the sea, and has 7700 Inhab. In the middle of the 17th century it was surrounded by fortifications of great extent, which took 60 years to complete, and consumed vast sums of money. They are now removed for the most part. It is on the whole a dull town, with little trade and few manufactures, except of lenses and mathematical instruments. At the end of the principal street, approached by a flight of steps, flanked by fountains representing Moses striking the rock, and Gideon wringing the dew from the fleece, stands the

Minster of St. Ursus (the saint was a soldier of the Theban legion), in the Florentine style, finished 1773, by Pisconi, of Ancona; it is distinguished by its size, and on the whole is handsome. In the Sacristy are some fine Missals.

The *Jesuits' Church* (Jesuiten Kirche) has a genuine Holbein, Christ on the Cross, 1522.

The *Clock Tower* (Zeitglockenthurm), in the market-place bears a German inscription, which attributes its foundation to a period 500 years before Christ; it may owe its origin to the Burgundian kings. It is square, and constructed of the most solid masonry, rough outside, originally without window or other opening, for 80 feet. If we are to believe the two Latin verses on the front of this building, Soleure is the most ancient city in N.W. Europe except Treves:

In Celtis nihil est Solodoro antiquius, unis
  Exceptis Treviris, quorum ego dicta soror.

By the side of the clock are some quaint figures. One raises a sceptre at the striking of the hour, and at every quarter Death turns his glass.

The *Arsenal* (Zeughaus), a gable-fronted house (b. 1580), not far from the Minster, contains the most extensive and curious collection of ancient armour in Switzerland. Here are shown numerous standards, taken by the Swiss in their victories over the Burgundians and Austrians, at Sempach, Morat, Nancy (bearing the portrait of Charles the Bold—with St. George and the Dragon), and Grandson. Some of these, in order to preserve them, have been fastened to pieces of coarse canvas; the yellow flag with the Imperial eagle was brought from Dornach. Among 800 suits of armour are many French and Burgundian. There are a few suits of chain-mail, and a great many of the commoner sort worn by serving-men or Landsknechts. More than 100 heads are said to have fallen under an *executioner's sword* here preserved. Several specimens of wall pieces, or long swivels, for the defence of a fortress, are curious. Some of the armour is for sale. On entering a room on the second floor the visitor may be astonished by an automaton soldier, who turns his head and presents arms as the door opens.

The *Museum*, in the Orphan Asylum (Waisenhaus), close to the bridge over the Aar, contains the finest collection of Jura fossils in existence—15,000 specimens, chiefly from quarries near Soleure. There are nearly thirty specimens of fossil turtle, rarely found elsewhere, together with teeth and palates of fish, and numerous fragments of saurians, derived from a formation which is believed to correspond with the Portland stone of England. The jaws of mammalia are said to come from the same locality (?). A suite of specimens of the rocks of the Alps was collected in numerous journeys by Professor Hugi, a native of Soleure, to whom belongs the merit of forming and arranging this cabinet.

The *Art Union* (Kunst - verein) possesses a Madonna, by the younger Holbein.

The Roman Catholic Bishop of Bâle lives here. The clergy are numerous and powerful, both in the town and canton. There are several convents.

Soleure was long the head-quarters for enlisting Swiss recruits in the foreign service of France, Spain, the Pope, and Naples, in which countries a body-guard of Swiss was always maintained. The town of Soleure was an ancient Imperial city, but had been long allied to Berne, and in 1481 became, with its surrounding country, a Swiss canton. Until 1798 the government of Soleure was the closest and the worst in Switzerland. It was partially restored in 1814, but completely altered and rendered democratic in 1831, and has been since repeatedly modified.

Thaddeus Kosciusko, the Polish patriot, spent the last years of his life here; his house, where he died, 1817, is near the Post-office, No. 10, Bieler-strasse. His entrails were interred in the churchyard of Zuchwyl, 1 m. E. of Soleure, under a monument inscribed "Viscera Thaddei Kosciusko." His body was sent to Cracow, and buried in the Cathedral.

About 2 miles N.E. of Soleure lies the *Hermitage of St. Verena*, at the end of a pretty valley, which cuts through a hill between the town and Jura range. It is about 1 m. from the Bâle gate to the entrance of this valley, which is hemmed in by rocks, embowered in trees, and traversed by a sparkling rivulet. A path which runs up it, was originally formed by a French émigré, who, at the outbreak of the Revolution, sought an asylum here. It winds through the wood, passing here and there a boulder stone which bears an inscription—one to *Gressly*, the geologist; another to *Gluz-Blozheim*, the historian. The valley abounds in caves and grottoes, partly artificial, and at its further extremity, within a natural shelf of over-arching cliff, stands the little *Chapel of St. Verena*, and opposite to it, built against the rock, and approached by a flight of steps, one to St. Martin. The scene is very pretty. The valley opens by a kind of portal to a rolling expanse of meadow, beyond which rises the craggy front of the Jura. A good path runs from the chapel to the Weissenstein, ascending by a limestone cleft up which the telegraph wire is carried. St. Verena was a pious maiden who accompanied the Theban legion, and, according to the legend, suffered severe temptation in this solitude, from the devil, who, on one occasion, was on the point of carrying her off, when she saved herself by clinging fast to the rock, where the hole made by her finger-nails still remains. On the way to the hermitage, near the village of St. Nicolas, are the *Wengenstein*, one of the boulder stones so numerous on the flanks of the Jura, occupying a pretty point of view, and the *Château of Waldeck*, of which the old-fashioned gardens, laid out in terraces, are worth notice.

[*The Weissenstein.*—The most interesting excursion in the neighbourhood of Soleure is that to the hotel on the Weissenstein (8 m., 3 hrs.) (Whiterock, so named from its cliffs of limestone). There is a good carriage-road (omnibus in the afternoon from the rly. stat., 2-horse carriages 20 francs) passing through the villages Langendorf and Oberdorf, behind which it is carried up through a wood in a series of zigzags. To the rt. of this road is a direct path by which pedestrians may reach the top easily in 2½ hrs. (guide or porter 5 fr.; 3 more if he is detained for the night); the path starts from the Hermitage of St. Verena.

The hotel was built at the expense of the town, and occupies a beautiful and commanding position on the brow of the mountain, 4209 ft. above the sea, and in the midst of green slopes, which, stretching far away, afford the most delightful walking and riding. The house has 80 bedrooms, but it is so favourite a pension (6 fr. per day) as to be occasionally filled by its Swiss and German visitors. It is rented by the landlord of the Couronne at Soleure. The dairy is supplied by 60 cows, fed on the mountain, so that milk and cream may be had in perfection.

In the summer invalids resort hither for the benefit of the fine air, or the "cure de petit lait" (goats'-whey), which is recommended in certain complaints. But the greater number of visitors come for the view, remaining on the summit one night to enjoy the sunset and sunrise.

The *Röthifluh*, 4587 ft., ½ hour's walk E., or the *Hasenmatte* (Hare's-pasture; 4754 ft.), 2 hours' walk W. of the inn, command magnificent *distant* prospects of the Alps. The great chain of snowy peaks is seen extending for 200 miles, from the Säntis to Mont Blanc. Immediately in front rise the giants of the Bernese chain—the Schreckhorn, Finsteraarhorn, Mönch, Eiger, and Jungfrau.   In the foreground, amidst a varied expanse of wooded hill and verdant dale, are the lakes of Morat, Neuchâtel, and Bienne, while the silvery Aar, on which stands the town of Soleure, winds at the foot of the mountain. *See Keller's* panorama on the terrace of the hotel.

The path to Bienne, over the *Hasenmatte*, is a charming walk of 6 hours. The carriage-road to the Weissenstein from Soleure passes the hotel, and after mounting through a wood descends the opposite side, to Moutiers (Rte. 1).]

Quitting Soleure, the railroad runs by the Aar, and along the S. base of the Jura. The inn on the Weissenstein is for some time a conspicuous object.

On rt. lie the Baths of *Grange* (*Grenchen*), a large building.

Bözingen (Bonjean), on the river Suze, has ironworks of repute.

Bienne Junct. (Rte. 1).

ROUTE 3.

BÂLE TO LUCERNE, BY OLTEN—RAILWAY.

	Eng. m.
Liestal	8
Läufelfingen	18
Olten	25
Sursee	43
Lucerne	59

4 or 5 trains a day, in from 3½ to 4½ hrs.

The Central Swiss Railway starts from the S. side of Bâle, a mile from the bridge, and traverses the Jura, through very beautiful scenery, to Olten; whence its branches diverge to Berne and Bienne, Lucerne and Zürich. Take a seat on the right-hand side of the carriage.

The rly., on quitting Bâle, crosses the valley of the Birs on a lattice-bridge of 3 arches, a little N. of the battlefield of *St. Jacob*, where, on the 26th of Aug. 1444, 1500 Swiss had the boldness to attack, and the courage to withstand, a French army twentyfold more numerous, commanded by the Dauphin, afterwards Louis XI. According to the story only 10 of the Swiss escaped unwounded, and all but about 50 were left dead on the field, along with thrice their own number of foes.   This almost incredible exploit spread abroad through Europe the fame of Swiss valour ; and Louis, the Dauphin, wisely seeing that it was better to gain them as friends than to oppose them as enemies, courted their alliance.   The Swiss themselves refer to the battle of St. Jacob as the Thermopylæ of their history.   The vineyards near the field produce a red wine, called Schweizer Blut (Swiss blood).   A little beyond this place the men of Bâle were in 1833 drawn into an ambuscade by the men of Liestal and defeated with considerable slaughter.   The rly. runs for some miles along the flat land of the Rhine valley, then leaving it, turns to the rt. up the valley of the little river Ergolz.

Pratteln Junct. Stat.   Here the rly. to Zürich turns off to the l. (Rte. 5).

Liestal Stat. (*Inns :* Falk; Schlüssel).   Liestal was always opposed to its connexion with the town of Bâle, and was finally separated from it in 1833.   It is an uninteresting place of 3871 Inhab., and since the separation has become the seat of government of Bâle Campagne (or Baselland), which includes 53 parishes, with about 36,000 Inhab.   In the Council-room (Rathsstube) are curious paintings and sentences on the walls, and Charles the Bold's cup taken at Nancy.

The rly. now enters a mountain valley, and follows the curves of the stream. The scenery is very pretty; in the bottom are bright green meadows, dotted with white houses; on the sides of the hills fir and beech forests, and here and there above them limestone cliffs.

Sissach Stat. (*Inn :* Löwe). Rt., or 7 m. S., at the foot of the *Bölchenfluh*, 2923 ft., in a neighbourhood abounding in beautiful walks, are the *Baths of Eptingen.* The Rly. now ascends by a gradient of 1 in 50, and several side valleys are crossed on bridges, the line constantly rising until it looks down upon the village of

Sommerau Stat. (*Inn:* Halbmond), beyond which is a tunnel 900 ft. long; l. rise the ruins of the Castle of *Homburg*, the scenery becoming wilder and more picturesque, and the mountains higher.

Läufelfingen Stat. (*Inn:* Sonne). Close to this the tunnel under the *Unter-Hauenstein* is entered. It is 1½ m. long, and was completed in 3 years : at one accident, in 1857, 52 men were buried alive. The tunnel is 1860 feet above the sea. [The old carriage-road ascends to the head of the pass, 2280 ft., by a series of zig-zags, descending in a similar manner on the other side, and commands a * *View* of the great chain of the Alps, which is lost to the traveller by the rly. Those who would not miss it will quit the train at Läufelfingen, walk or drive over the mountain (*Inn* at the summit), and rejoin the rail at Olten.]

On emerging from the tunnel we enter the pretty valley of *Trimbach;* and commence a rapid descent, with distant view of the Appenzell mountains. Soon afterwards we open a wider valley, and, looking over Olten, obtain in clear weather the first glimpse of the snowy *Bernese Alps.* The rly. makes a curve of more than half a circle, and, crossing the river Aar, reaches

Olten Junct. Stat. (Good Buffet). Lines diverge hence in half-a-dozen directions, and the traveller must take care that he finds his way to the right train. (*Inns:* H. Wyss; Schweizerhof, close to stat.) A town very prettily situated in a valley of the Jura, and said to be the Roman *Utlinum.* Pop. 4000. Here are the ironworks of the Central Rly. Omnibuses to *Frohburg,* a watering-place with whey baths.

Railways.—To Zürich, by Aarau and Baden, 2 hrs. ; to Bienne by Soleure, 2½ to 3 hrs.; to Berne, 2 to 3 hrs.; to Lucerne, 2 hrs.

Aarburg Stat. (*Inn:* Krone), a neat town of 1930 Inhab., almost entirely rebuilt since a conflagration in 1840. Its *Citadel,* although it has bomb-proof casemates hewn out of the rock, serves only as a military store-house and prison, but it forms a picturesque object in the landscape. Outside the town is an extensive cotton factory, and a suspension wire bridge over the Aar.

Here the rail branches to Berne (Rte. 4), though the carriages are changed at Olten.

The Lucerne line leaves the Aar and enters a pretty vale, distinguished by its verdant pastures, and its substantial-looking houses, the walls of which are often covered with thin plates of wood overlapping each other like fishes' scales. Rt. and l. a varied outline of wooded heights, and the rocky front of the Jura.

Zofingen Stat. (*Inns:* Rössli; Ochs), a cheerful-looking town with 4465 Inhab. and manufactures of silk and cotton. Its *Library* contains autograph letters of Swiss reformers, a cabinet of coins and drawings by members of the Swiss Society of Artists. Near the Schützenhaus (shooting-house) are some magnificent lime-trees, in the branches of which a ball-room has been constructed. Zofingen is supposed to be the Roman *Tobinium.* Remains of the period have been turned up here, particularly the foundations of a villa, of which a mosaic pavement is still in good preservation. A fragment of the castle of *Reiden,* and a solitary tree perched on a rock beside it, become conspicuous before reaching

Reiden Stat. The Parsonage was originally a house of the Knights of Malta.

Dagmersellen Stat. (*Inn:* Löwe,

good). The village was the birth-place of the sculptor *Kaiser*.

Nebikon Stat.

Wauwyl Stat. Rt. the little *Mauen-see*, in which remains of *lake-dwellings* have been found. The ruined castle of Pasteln is seen in the distance.

Sursee Stat. (Inns: Sonne ; Schwan); an old walled town, whose gate-towers still bear the double-headed eagle of Austria. The *Rathhaus* is much dila-pidated, but a good specimen of the German-Burgundian style. The gene-ral outline resembles the old Tolbooth of Edinburgh.—Sursee is 1 m. from the N. end of the *Lake of Sempach*, which has no pretensions to great beauty, but is pleasing, and interesting histori-cally, as near the scene of the *Battle of Sempach* (9 July, 1386)—the second of those great and surprising victories by which Swiss independence was es-tablished. It was fought on the E. shore, behind the little town of Sem-pach. In 1805 a portion of the water of the lake was let off, in order to gain land ; thus the lake is diminished in extent, and its form somewhat altered from what it was at the time of the battle. The rly. runs along its W. shore. View of Pilatus and Rigi.

Nottwyl Stat. At *Büttisholz*, a vil-lage about 3 m. W. of this Stat., and on the rt. of the road, may be seen a mound, called the *English barrow*, said to contain the bones of a number of Free Companions, who fell here in a fight, 1375. They were chiefly English, nicknamed *Gugglers*, from their high-crowned caps of iron, and formed part of a numerous and splendidly equipped host, which had invaded Switzerland under Ingelram de Coucy, to claim the marriage-por-tion of his mother, Catherine, daughter of Duke Leopold of Austria. A band of 3000, whilst pillaging in this neigh-bourhood, were attacked and defeated by the sturdy peasants of Entlebuch, who rode back triumphant to their chalet homes on English steeds, and clad in the bright armour of their foes.

Sempach Stat. About 2 m. from the rly. stat. is the town of

Sempach (Inns : Kreuz ; Adler); and 2 m. farther a small chapel, erected to commemorate the victory of Sempach (A.D. 1386), on the spot where Leopold of Austria (son of the Duke of the same name who had been defeated 71 years before at Morgarten) lost his life. The names of those who fell, both Austrians and Swiss, were inscribed on the walls, which also bear a rude fresco representation of the noble devotion of *Arnold of Winkelried*—

> He of battle-martyrs chief !
> Who, to recall his daunted peers,
> For victory shaped an open space, "
> By gath'ring, with a wide embrace,
> Into his single heart, a sheaf
> Of fatal Austrian spears.—*Wordsworth.*

According to Tschudi's 'Chronicon Helveticum' (Tschudi died 1572), he was a knight of Unterwalden, who, observing all the efforts of the Swiss to break the ranks of their enemies foiled by their long lances, ex-claimed, "I will open a path to freedom : protect, dear comrades, my wife and children." He then rushed forward, and gathering in his arms as many lances as he could grasp, buried them in his bosom. The confederates were enabled to take advantage of the gap thus formed before the Austrian lancers had time to extricate their entangled weapons from his body. In order to oppose the Swiss, who fought on foot, many of the Austrian nobles had dis-mounted to form a serried phalanx ; but the armour which rendered them almost invulnerable on horseback, and which, while they remained united and in close column, had formed so impenetrable a barrier to the attack of the Swiss, now that their ranks were broken, disabled them from coping with their light-armed and active foes. 600 nobles were slain, and more than 2000 common soldiers ; while the entire force of the Swiss, who achieved this victory, is said not to have exceeded 1400 men. The conquerors founded masses for the souls of those who fell, foes as well as friends, and they are celebrated even now on the anniversary of the fight, which is a popular festival.

The earliest references to this *Heldenthat* are found in an interpolated notice in a Zürich chronicle (1438 or later), and a popular song of the latter half of the same century.

The approach to Lucerne is charming, between fir-trees and mossy knolls. On the l. is the Rigi; on rt. the serrated ridge of the gloomy Pilatus.

Emmenbrücke Stat. Here the Emme is crossed, and we reach the banks of the green and limpid Reuss, rushing out of the lake of Lucerne and spanned by a light bridge of the Zürich rly. The old battlemented wall of the town, flanked at intervals by a number of tall watchtowers, is seen descending to the margin of the river, and the railway passes through a tunnel to

LUCERNE Terminus, on W. or left side of the river, opposite the Promenade and Quay (Rte. 15). Many of the steamers call here.

ROUTE 4.

OLTEN TO BERNE, BY THE CENTRAL SWISS RAILWAY.

	Eng. m.
Olten.	
Herzogenbuchsee	43
Burgdorf	53
Berne	68

Trains in 3½ to 4½ hrs.

As far as *Aarburg Junct. Stat.* the line is the same as in Rte. 3. It then diverges and follows the course of the Aar through fertile but uninteresting country to

Herzogenbuchsee Junct. Stat. (*Inn*: Sonne), a town of some 2346 Inhab. Rail to Soleure.

Near *Riedwyl Stat.* a wooded valley is entered.

Burgdorf Junct. Stat. Buffet. (French, *Berthoud*) (*Inns*: H. de la Gare; H. Guggisberg; Bär). Here a line from Soleure falls in. A thriving town

(6580 Inhab.) of large arcaded houses. and opulent public institutions, and pleasantly situated at the mouth of the fertile Emmenthal (Rte. 22). In the old castle Pestalozzi first established his school. View of the Bernese Alps from the ch., and a much more extensive one from the Lueg, a hill 2 hrs.' walk.

Hindelbank Stat.

In the church of *Hindelbank* are monuments to the noble family of *Von Erlach*, whose château stands on the hill to the l., and also the *Monument of Madame Langhaus* by a Swedish sculptor named Nahl. Its merit has been much exaggerated. The epitaph was written by Haller.

Zollikofen Junct. Stat. Here the rly. to Bienne (Rte. 2) falls in. A short distance beyond is *Ruete*, rt., an agricultural institution.

At *Wylerfeld* (a fine view l. of the Bernese Alps) the rlys. from Thun (Rte. 25) and Lucerne (Rte. 22) fall in.

The Aar is crossed by a lofty bridge, having a passage for the rail above, and the carriage-road below. The bridge is a fine work and well deserves a visit, though it is far surpassed by the bridge at Fribourg. It is 540 ft. long, in 3 spans, and rests on 2 stone pillars. Immediately after passing the bridge is

BERNE STAT. (Rte. 24).

ROUTE 5.

BÂLE TO ZÜRICH, BY THE BÖTZBERG RAILWAY.

	Eng. m.
Pratteln	5
Rheinfelden	10
Brugg	35
Turgi	37
Baden	40
Zürich	55

This rly. follows the Lucerne rly. (Rte. 3) as far as Pratteln and then turns off to the left. It crosses the river Ergolz into canton Aargau at

Kaiser Augst, near the site of the Roman city *Augusta Rauracorum.* There are indications of an amphitheatre, and many columns, tombs, and fragments have been found, mostly of the Lower Empire. The city *Walls* were three miles in circumference when it was destroyed by Attila.

Rheinfelden Stat. (Inns: Zum Schützen, in the town, good: H. Dietschy and Couronne, in a pretty garden above the town on the Rhine, and a bath-house supplied with brine from the saltworks, good; moderate—Pension 5 fr. a day.)

This is an old Swiss town, 2400 Inhab., now included in Canton Aargau, on the l. bank of the Rhine, here crossed by a covered wooden *Bridge,* resting in the centre on a rock rising out of the water. On this once stood *The Stein,* a strong castle now replaced by a garden (good view over river). Down to 1744 Rheinfelden was a frontier fortress, and was besieged in turn by Bavarians, Swedes, Austrians, and French. Part of the old wall remains, and 6 of the *Towers,* on one of which a wheel is provided by the town for the storks to build on.

Duke Bernard of Saxe Weimar gained a battle here in the Thirty Years' War (1638) in which the Duc de Rohan, the French leader of the Protestants, perished.

Between Rheinfelden and the Rapids of Laufenburg, the most productive *Salmon Fishery* on the Rhine is carried on.

The success of Baron v. Glenck at Schweizerhalle (Rte. 1) induced other companies to bore for salt. At Rheinfelden brine was reached in 1845 at a depth of 351 ft., and below it a bed of rock salt, 80 feet thick, in the Muschel Kalk. The brine pumped up is almost saturated, containing 26 per cent. of salt.

The rly. follows the valley of the Rhine to *Stein* station.

Beyond *Effingen* station the line tunnels under the *Bötzberg,* and then descends into the valley of the Aar, which it crosses before reaching

Brugg Junct. Stat. Rly. to Olten (Rte. 6). *Brugg (Inns:* Rössli; Rothes Haus) belonged to the House of Habsburg, and is a picturesque old place, its entrances guarded by high conical-roofed towers. The *Schwarze Thurm* (Black tower) is a Roman building of the age of the Lower Empire. Brugg is the birthplace of *Zimmermann* (On Solitude), physician to Frederick the Great.

The country around is interesting. In the plain, a little below the town, three of the principal rivers which drain the N. slopes of the Alps, the Limmat, Reuss, and Aar, form a junction, and, united under the name of Aar, flow towards the Rhine, into which they fall about 10 miles below Brugg, at a place called Coblenz. Close upon this meeting of waters, and on the triangular tongue of land between the Aar and Reuss, stood

Vindonissa, the most important settlement of the Romans in Helvetia, as well as their strongest fortress on this frontier. In the 3rd, 4th, and 5th cents. it was ravaged by Vandals, Alemanni, and Huns, and in the 6th cent. destroyed by Childebert, king of the Franks, and scarcely any portion of it now appears above ground; but traces of an amphitheatre, of an aqueduct, which conveyed water from the Brauneggberg, 3 m. off, foundations of walls, broken pottery, inscriptions, and coins, have been turned up from time to time, and its name is preserved in that of the village of *Windisch.*

" Within the ancient walls of Vindonissa, the castle of Habsburg, the abbey of Königsfeld, and the town of Bruck have successively arisen. The philosophic traveller may compare the monuments of Roman conquests, of feudal or Austrian tyranny, of monkish superstition, and of industrious freedom. If he be truly a philosopher, he will applaud the merit and happiness of his own time."—*Gibbon.*

1½ m. E. of Brugg stands the *Abbey of Königsfelden* (King's field), founded, 1310, by the Empress Elizabeth, and Agnes, Queen of Hungary, on the spot where, two years before, their husband and father, the Emperor Albert, was assassinated. The convent, a group of gloomy buildings, was suppressed in 1528; part of it is now used as a farm-house, part as a hospital and mad-house; the rest is falling to decay. The dilapidated *Church* contains some very fine painted glass, and numerous pavement tombs, with coats of arms, of a long train of nobles who fell in the battle of Sempach. The large vaults were the burial-place of many members of the Austrian family, including Agnes, and Leopold who fell at Sempach, but their remains were removed into the Austrian dominions in 1770. According to tradition, the high altar stands on the spot where Albert fell. He had crossed the ferry of the Reuss in a small boat, leaving his suite on the opposite bank. He was attended only by the four conspirators. The chief of them, John of Suabia, his nephew—who had been instigated to slay him by the wrong he endured in being kept out of his paternal inheritance by his uncle—first struck him in the throat with his lance. Balm ran him through with his sword, and Walter von Eschenbach cleft his skull with a felling stroke. Wart, the fourth, took no share in the murder. Although the deed was so openly done, in broad day, almost under the walls of the Imperial Castle of Habsburg, and in sight of a large retinue of armed attendants, the murderers were able to escape in different directions; and the retainers took to flight, leaving their dying master to breathe his last in the arms of a poor peasant who happened to pass.

A dire vengeance was wreaked by the children of the murdered monarch; not, however, upon the murderers—for, with the exception of Wart, the only one who did not raise his hand against him, they all escaped—but upon their families, relations, and friends; and 1000 victims are believed to have expiated, with their lives, a crime of which they were totally innocent. Queen Agnes ended her days in the convent of Königsfelden, which she had founded and endowed with the confiscated property of those whom she had slaughtered. The building in which she passed 50 years

of her life was destroyed; that which is shown as her cell is not so in reality. About 2 m. from Brugg, on a wooded height called Wülpelsberg, stand the remains of the

Castle of Habsburg, or Habichtsburg (Hawk's Castle), the cradle of the House of Austria, built by Count Radbod of Altenburg, 1020, an ancestor of the family. A mere fragment of the original building now exists. The tall, square keep of rough stones has walls 8 ft. thick; and beneath it a dungeon, to be entered only by a trap-door in the floor above. The view from it is picturesque and interesting; the eye ranges along the course of the three rivers, over the site of the Roman Vindonissa and Königsfelden, the sepulchre of imperial Albert: on the S. rises the ruined *castle of Braunegg*, which belonged to the sons of the tyrant Gessler; and below it is Birr, where *Pestalozzi*, the teacher, died, and was buried. It takes in at a single glance the whole Swiss patrimony of the Habsburgs—an estate far more limited than that of many a British peer—from which Rudolf was called to wield the sceptre of Charlemagne. The House of Austria was deprived of its Swiss territories by papal ban, 150 years after Rudolf's elevation: but it is believed that the ruin has again become the property of the Austrian Emperor by purchase.

3 m. S.E. of Brugg, on the river Reuss, are the *Baths of Birmensdorf*. The waters are saline and purgative.

On quitting Brugg, the rly. leaves the Aar. It traverses *Oberdorf* (near which are scanty remains of a Roman amphitheatre), and crosses the river Reuss to

Turgi Junction Stat., where the branch from Waldshut (Rte. 6) falls in. (A large cotton manufacture here.) Since this line was opened, travellers from Mannheim or Heidelberg may reach Zürich by the express train in 9 hrs., without changing carriages.

Hence the rly. keeps the l. bank of the Limmat to

Baden Stat. (*Inns:* Engel, good; Waage (Balances); Bahnhof: the best hotels are at the Baths, more than ¼ m. distant). This ancient walled town, of 3700 Inhab., is squeezed within a narrow defile on the l. bank of the Limmat, here crossed by a wooden bridge. The ruins of the Castle of *Stein* overlook it from a rocky eminence, now tunnelled by the rly., and worth ascending for the singular view. The castle was anciently a residence and stronghold of the Austrian princes. Here were planned the expeditions against the Swiss, which were frustrated at Morgarten and Sempach. At length when the Pope, in 1415, excommunicated the Archduke Frederick, the Swiss took it and burnt it. In the *Rathhaus* of Baden the preliminaries preceding the treaty of peace which terminated the war of the Spanish Succession, were arranged by Prince Eugene on the part of Austria, and by Marshal Villars for France, in 1712.

Baden in Aargau, like its namesakes in Baden and Austria, was frequented by the Romans, who called it *Thermæ Helveticæ*. It was sacked and destroyed by Cæcina. Tacitus mentions it as "in modum municipii extructus locus, amœno salubrium aquarum usu frequens."—*Hist.* i. 67. In the middle ages the waters were very celebrated and much frequented. Poggio Bracciolini, who visited them on his way to the Council of Constance, says, "Persæpe existimo et Venerem ex Cypro et quicquid est ubique deliciarum ad hæc balnea commigrâsse."

The *Baths* (*Inns:* Neue Kuranstalt, 1875, beautifully situated and well spoken of; Verenahof; Freihof; Limmathof; Schiff; Schweizerhof), on the borders of the Limmat, ¼ mile below or N. of the town, are resorted to between June and September by numerous visitors, chiefly French and Swiss. The waters are warm and sulphureous, having a temperature of 118° Fahr. There are 19 springs and a copious outflow.

The Swiss Baden, though not equal in beauty to those in other parts of Europe, has considerable attractions. The rocky heights on each side of the river—the one surmounted by the ruined castle, the other partly covered by vineyards—form a portal through which the Limmat runs. Before this gorge was formed, Baden and the country above it must have been a vast lake.

There are agreeable walks for invalids by the side of the Limmat, and many pleasant excursions—the most interesting being that described above, to Schinznach (8 miles), by Windisch, Königsfelden, and Habsburg. The *Baldegg*, 1876 ft., commands a panoramic view.

Roman relics are constantly discovered in this district. Gambling must have been a prevailing vice among the visitors to the baths, and the Roman Legions stationed here, if it is true that a neighbouring field has obtained the name of *Dice Meadow* (Würfel Wiese), from the quantity of dice dug up in it.

The railroad passes by a tunnel 800 feet long, under the Stein or Castle hill, and runs along the l. bank of the Limmat. The Cistercian convent of *Wettingen*, a vast building with many courts, gardens, &c., surrounded by a wall, is situated in an angle formed by the river on its rt. bank. It was suppressed by the council of the canton (Aarau), 1841, and is now a seminary. Its *church*, founded 1227, contains tombs of some early counts of Habsburg and Kyburg, the stone coffin in which the body of the Emperor Albert was interred for 14 months after his murder, painted glass, carved stalls, &c. The railway makes a great bend here.

Schlieren Stat.

Altstetten Stat.

Dietikon Stat. The stately building l. on the height surrounded by vineyards is a Kelterhaus (wine-press) of the convent of Wettingen. Near this village the French, under Massena, crossed the river, Sept. 24, 1799—a masterly movement, which led to the defeat of the Russians and the capture of Zürich.

The landscape becomes very animated in the neighbourhood of Zürich. The distant Alps are seen on the rt. and the long ridge of the Albis, terminating towards Zürich in the Uetli-berg, crowned with its *Inn.* The Sihl river is crossed.

ZÜRICH STAT. In Rte. 9. Station on the former Schützenplatz.

ROUTE 6.

OLTEN, BY AARAU AND BRUGG, TO WALDSHUT—RAILWAY.

This is in part the old line of rail-way from Bâle to Zürich.

Olten Stat. (Rte. 3).

Aarau Stat. (*Inns :* Storch ; Ochs), the chief town of Canton Aargau or Argovie, which was first included in the Confederation in 1803, having pre-viously formed a subject province of canton Berne, contains 5940 Inhab., and is situated on the rt. bank of the Aar. Simond called it, in 1817, "an odious little place;" but it has much improved and increased since then. It lies at the base of the Jura, here partly covered with vineyards. There are many cotton-mills.

The *Rathhaus*, in which the can-tonal councils are held, has been re-built. In the *Parish Church* Pro-testant and Catholic services are per-formed alternately.

Heinrich Zschokke, popular historian and novel-writer, and the *Meyers*, the first explorers of the glaciers of the Bernese Oberland, resided here. When the armies of the French Revolution took possession of Switzerland in 1789, and destroyed its ancient form of government, Aarau was made for a short time capital of the Helvetian Republic.

Rapperswyl Junct. [From here a branch line runs to *Lenzburg, Bremgar-ten*, and *Muri*, a celebrated Dominican convent. The vast building has since 1841 been converted into a cantonal school.]

Schinznach Stat., 10 min. walk from *Schinznach-les-Bains*, also called *Habs-burger Bad*, a much frequented water-ing-place. The establishment, under the direction of M. Moser, consists of an hotel and pension with 350 beds and 160 baths. 200 persons frequently

join the table-d'hôte, 1 P.M., 3 fr. The waters are most efficacious, and deserve to be better known to the English. Dr. Amsler is an excellent physician. Drs. Zurkowski, medical resident, and Hemmann, are also in daily attendance. Season from June to September; prices reduced from September to May. The sulphur springs, among the strongest known in Europe, issue from highly tilted stratified rocks, at about 20 ft. below the surface of the drift of the valley of the Aar, and are collected in a shaft at the temp. of about 90° Fahr., and distributed by machinery. Sul-phur, salts of soda, and magnesia are united in these waters, which are effi-cacious in the treatment of diseases of the skin, mucous membrane, respi-ratory organs, wounds, and rheuma-tism. The neighbourhood is pretty, and winding paths, under the shade of trees, lead up the hill to the *castle of Habsburg*, the ancient seat of the im-perial family of Austria. At a short distance is the wooded eminence and château of *Wildegg* (Col. d'Effinger), at the foot of which is a saline and bitter spring containing iodine and bromide of sodium. Among the *excursions* may be mentioned the ascent of the *Gyslifluh*, 2539 ft., commanding a fine view of the Alps, and over which there is a pleasant walk to Aarau.

Brugg Junction (Rte. 5).

Beyond Brugg the rail descends the valley of the Aar and crosses the Rhine to Waldshut (Rte. 7).

ROUTE 7.

BÂLE TO SCHAFFHAUSEN [THE RHINE FALLS], BY WALDSHUT. — BADEN RAILWAY.

	Eng. m.
Bâle.	
Rheinfelden	10
Säckingen	20
Laufenburg	26
Waldshut	35
Schaffhausen	65

Terminus at the Baden Stat., in

Klein Basel, 3 to 3½ hrs. to Schaff-hausen.

This railway runs on the rt. or Baden side of the Rhine, and was extended 1863 to Schaffhausen and Constance.

Grenzach Stat. Excellent wine grown here.

The rail approaches the Rhine, which presents a beautiful appear-ance, white here and there with rapids. At Rheinfelden (Rte. 5) it rushes, breaking and foaming, through a pas-sage called *Höllenhaken.*

Säckingen Stat. has a fine *Abbey Ch.* with 2 towers, modernized and ador-ned with stucco within.

Klein-Laufenburg Stat., charming view over the Rhine, the rapids, and covered wooden bridge leading to Laufenburg. It was a favourite sub-ject of *J. W. Turner.*

Laufenburg (Inn : Post), a town on the l. bank of the Rhine. The river flows in a deep-sunk channel, rugged with rocks which fret its bright blue-green waters ; it is here interrupted by more rapids and falls, in German called *Laufen,* whence the name of the place. Small boats can only pass them by unloading their cargoes above, and being let down gradually by stout ropes, held by men stationed on the bank. There is a productive salmon-fishery here.

Albbruck Stat., at the mouth of the *Alb Thal*—a striking gorge, leading towards St. Blaise Abbey, well worth exploring. *See* HNDBK. FOR N. GER-MANY.

Waldshut Junct. Stat. (Inns : H. Blum ; H. Kuehnen ; H. Schätzer, all near the station and good. Rebstock in the town, reasonable), a walled town of 2340 Inhab., on the skirts of the Black Forest. [A branch of the Swiss Central Rly. crosses the Rhine to a small village called Coblenz (Conflu-entia), where the Rhine is joined by the Aar. It ascends the rt. bank of the Aar to Turgi Junct. Stat. (Rte. 6). Another line (Nordostbahn) runs

through Eglisau to Winterthur (Rte. 9).]

The Baden railway leaves the Rhine and proceeds along a tole-rably level but dull and uninter-esting country, enlivened only by occasional distant views of the moun-tains.

Thiengen Stat. In a cave near the station have been found some un-polished flint implements, a reindeer-horn with a figure on it : in a lower layer were mammoth-bones.

FALLS OF THE RHINE.

At *Erzingen Stat.* the Baden terri-tory is quitted, and Canton Schaff-hausen entered.

Neuhausen Stat. The most conveni-ent for visiting the *Falls of the Rhine,* and for those intending to pass the night in the neighbourhood.

Inns : Schweizerhof (10 minutes' walk), and directly facing the Fall, with garden descending the steep, wooded bank of the river ; Belle-vue, another large and good house, in a somewhat similar position, adjoining the stat. The obliging landlord of the Schweizerhof has ac-quired the exclusive right of fishing, and both his house and the Bellevue are favourite *pensions. Boats* to cross the Rhine and to ascend the central rock which divides the Falls. [On the opposite bank of the Rhine are H. du Château Laufen, within the walls of the castle, and, at Dachsen Stat., H. Witzig, a small chalet-like house, without view of the river, but good and reasonable.]

The stat. on the rt. bank of the Rhine is *Neuhausen,* near the Falls ; on the l. bank *Dachsen,* nearly a mile beyond the Falls. The distance is a short 3 miles from Schaffhausen, and there are carriages and omnibuses, or the trip may be made by boat. The usual course from the Schweizer-hof is as follows:—Descend to the old Schloss or Castle of *Wörth,* now a Restaurant and Ferry-house, where a tariff of the boatmen's fares hangs on the wall (3 frs. for 1 person to the central rock and back—less for more than one).   Here the Fall can be viewed through a camera obscura.

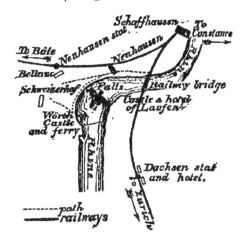

By boat to the central rock, which is ascended by rude stairs.   Then land on the opposite shore, in the grounds of *Schloss Laufen* (1 fr. admission for 1 person—less for more than one).   From the castle descend to the rly. bridge, which has a side walk for people on foot.   Return by path, L from the end of the bridge to the hotel. Those afraid of the water can walk round by the rly. bridge.   Persons coming from Zürich, who wish to go on to Constance the same day, can alight at *Dachsen* stat. (the guard will arrange about luggage), walk or ride (an omnibus) to Schloss Laufen, and thence to Schaffhausen.

It will take at least 2 hours to see the falls properly.

The garden of *Schloss Laufen* is situated on a rocky promontory, and in it are platforms and kiosks, from which views are obtained.   Rough stone and wooden steps lead to a rude balcony, called *Zum Känzeli* and to a projecting stage—*Zur Fischetz*, of iron bars, thrown out from the vertical cliff, and actually overhanging the roaring shoot.   Though perfectly secure, it trembles under the impulse of the water.   Here, covered with the spray, the traveller may enjoy the full grandeur of this *hell of waters*; and it is only by this close proximity, amidst the tremendous roar and the uninterrupted rush of the river, passing with

the swiftness of an arrow above his head and beneath his feet, that a true notion can be formed of the scale of this cataract.   The best time for seeing the Fall is on a sunny morning, when the iris floats within the spray, and in the month of July, when the river is usually most full.   The Rhine above is about 300 feet broad; the height of the fall varies from 60 feet on one side to 45 on the other; but, including the rapids, the entire descent is not less than 100 feet.   The river below the Fall is 1180 ft. above the sea.   An isolated pillar, standing in the middle of the stream, divides the fall.   This pinnacle appears eaten away by the constant friction of the water; but the rock is hard, and the waste of it within the memory of man has not been perceptible.

The river, after its leap, forms a large semicircular bay, as it were to rest itself, the shore of which is perpetually chafed by the heaving billows.

Arrangements are made for illuminating the Falls by night.

The discharge of water is about 80,000 cubic feet per second, and the broken nature of the river-bed is such that, during the low water in the early spring of 1848, 1858, and 1880, men were able to cross it by leaping from rock to rock.

At Neuhausen on the rt. bank are works, the machinery of which is worked by the water.

It is a fact worth noticing that no classic or ancient author mentions the Rheinfall.

About 3 m. below the falls is the island of *Rheinau*, a very pretty spot, with fine abbey ch. and Benedictine monastery (now a lunatic asylum). In the ch. are curious silver ornaments and busts of the 17th century.

SCHAFFHAUSEN STAT. at the Oberthor, near the Promenade.   (*Inns*: in the town—Krone, excellent; H. Muller; Post; Riesen; all good; Rheinischer Hof, near the station.   For hotels at the Falls see last page.)

Schaffhausen (Pop. 11,800, chiefly Prot.) stands on the right bank of the Rhine, just above the spot where the rapids commence. It was originally a landing-place and storehouse, at which the portage of goods began and ended, and owes its origin and name to the boat or *skiff houses*, here erected. It is distinguished above almost every other town in Switzerland by the antique architecture of its houses, whose fronts and projecting oriel windows are decorated with carvings and stucco-work. Many of them were originally entirely covered externally with fresco paintings, but of these there are now few examples : the house called Zum Ritter, nearly opposite the Krone inn, is one of the most remarkable. The *halls* of the ancient *Guilds*, or *Zünfte*, are worthy of attention on account of their quaint inscriptions and allusive ornaments. The wall and turreted gateways of the town have been preserved, and furnish picturesque subjects for the pencil. There are a few manufactures of iron, silk, and cotton. The water power is used to set in motion *turbines* for working factory machinery.

The Münster, Prot.—originally the church of the Abbey of All Saints—was founded 1052–1100. It is in the Romanesque style, remarkable for the solidity of its construction, and as exhibiting an unaltered specimen of that style. The arches of the nave are supported by single circular columns, and those in the centre of the transept by square piers of the most massive kind. It has been badly restored. The cloister attached to the church contains a number of monuments of the magistrates and patrician families, but everything is covered with plaster and whitewash.

The *Museum* contains a fine collection of objects of natural history and illuminated missals, &c. In the " Cantonsarchiv " is preserved the famous Schaffhausen onyx, a cameo attributed to the time of Nero. Permission to inspect it may be obtained at the Rathhaus.

On the height above the town rises the *Castle* called

Munoth (Munitio?), built 1564-90. It is provided with bomb-proof casemates 18 feet thick, and is a curious specimen of the transition style of fortification. There is a wide spiral passage by which it was possible to ride up the interior of the tower, and there are subterranean passages. The whole is shown for a small fee.

Frederick, Duke of Tyrol (Emptypurse), conveyed away Pope John XXIII. from the justice of the Council of Constance, 1415, and kept him safe in the castle of Schaffhausen, for which he was placed under the ban of the Empire.

The public walks (*Fäsenstaub*) outside the town on the W. side command fine views of the Rhine, near which is the new R. C. Church.

There are baths close to the Rhine and a swimming-bath in the river.

The *Town Library* contains the collection of books of the Swiss historian *Johann von Müller*, who was born here, and to whom there is a monumental bust on the Vesenstaub; also a *Museum* of antiquities, painted glass, church-plate, carvings, &c., from old convents.

Railways to Winterthur and Zürich, to Bâle, and to Constance.

Steamer to Constance : in about 4 hrs.—return journey in 1 hr. less.

Diligences to Donaueschingen and Freiburg (on the road to Strassburg and Frankfort).

Omnibus to the Falls (1 fr.).

ROUTE 8.

SCHAFFHAUSEN to CONSTANCE—RAIL.—
LAKE OF CONSTANCE.

There are two routes. A. along N. bank of Rhine: rly. 5 trains daily, 1½ to 2 hrs. B. by *steamer*: express boat in 3½ hrs.

A. The *Railway*, on the *N. side of the Rhine*, takes a N. direction by Herblingen Stat. to Thaingen, where it enters Baden and proceeds to the Lower Lake near Radolfszell.

Singen Junction (for Winterthur and

Darmstadt) — (*Inn:* Krone). Near this place you pass under *Hohentwiel*, a castle of the Dukes of Würtemberg, dismantled by the French in 1800. The lofty rock upon which it stands gives it the appearance of an Indian hill-fort. N. of it are the castles *Hohenkrähen, Hohenhöwen.*

Radolfszell Stat. (*Inn:* Krone or Post, good), a desolate town, with a fine church, in the true German-Gothic style.

The scenery is agreeable, often striking. The woods abound in splendid butterflies. Collections may be bought at Singen and Radolfszell.

Reichenau Stat., opposite the island of *Reichenau*, which is about 3 m. long, and connected with the mainland by a bridge. It contains the ruins of the castle of Schäpfeln, and at Münster the church of a Benedictine abbey.

Passing along the isthmus between the Lower Lake of Constance and the bay of Ueberlingen, the rly. reaches the Rhine opposite Constance.

The Rhine here, suddenly contracted from a lake to a river, is crossed by a handsome *Iron Bridge*, which also gives passage to the high road.

Passing the Insel Hotel, formerly a Dominican monastery, the line enters

Constance Stat. (See next page.)

B. By steamer about 4 hrs. On the l. bank of the Rhine are the ancient Nunneries of *Paradies* and *Catherinenthal;* the former belonged to the order of St. Clara, the latter to that of St. Dominic; they are now respectively a hospital and almshouse. The Austrian army under the Archduke Charles crossed the Rhine at Paradies 1799.

Diessenhofen (*Inn:* Adler). Here in 1800 the French crossed the Rhine on their way to Hohenlinden.

Wagenhausen (*Inn:* Ochs, clean).

Stein am Rhein (*Inns:* Schwann; Krone) a town belonging to Canton Schaffhausen, and united by a wooden bridge with a suburb on the l. bank. The old Guildhall, with pointed windows, and the houses Zum Ochsen, Zum Weissen Adler, are curious. The *Abbey of St. George* is a very ancient foundation. The owners of the castle of *Hohenklingen*, on a rocky height, were originally the feudal seigneurs of the town. In 1633 Marshal Horn crossed the river at Stein to lay siege to Constance. Stein is on the railway from Winterthur to Darmstadt by *Etzweilen.*

3 miles E. of Stein, at a height of between 500 and 600 feet above the Rhine, are the *Quarries of Oeningen,* remarkable for the vast abundance of fossil remains of terrestrial and fresh-water animals found in them, including mammalia, birds, reptiles, fishes, shells, insects, and plants, some of them identical with species now living. The most curious discovery is that of the perfect skeleton of a fossil fox, made by Sir Roderick Murchison: a very large tortoise had previously been brought to light. The beds in which the quarries are worked consist of marls, limestones, shales, and building-stone. They are freshwater deposits belonging to the Upper Miocene period. 900 species of insects and 470 plants have already been made out.

At *Wangen* the remains of a large lake-village have been discovered.

Above Stein the Rhine expands into a lake called *Untersee* (lower lake) connected again by the Rhine with the Obersee or Lake of Constance. The road passes *Mammern*, a favourite watering-place, below the ruined castle of Neuburg; and then *Feldbach*, a Cistercian nunnery, before reaching

Stekborn (*Inns:* Löwe; Sonne.)

Near the village of *Berlingen* a pretty *château*, which belonged to the Duchess of Dino, appears; and a little further that of *Arenenberg*, for some time the modest campagne-built residence of the Duchess of St. Leu (Hortense, ex-Queen of Holland), who died there, and of her son Prince Louis (late the Emperor Napoleon III.), before he made his attempt at Strassburg. It was sold in 1843 to a Neuchâtel gentleman, but in 1855 repurchased by the Emperor. The view from the garden over the Untersee is charming.

Ermatingen, known for its pickled salmon-trout. Here a boat can be procured to visit the *Isle of Reichenau*, anciently famed for its Benedictine Monastery, suppressed in 1799, founded by one of the successors of Charlemagne, of which the *Church* (partly Romanesque) and Treasury remain. In the Treasury are the shrine of St. Fortunata, an ivory ciborium, a cope, a crosier, and a missal of the 10th century.

(*Inn*: Krone, at the adjoining village of Münster.)

Iznang, a village on the W. shore of the Untersee, is the birthplace of *Mesmer*, the originator of mesmerism.

The castellated monastery of *Gottlieben*, on the l. of the road, built by the Bishops of Constance 1250, on the Rhine, at the point where it enters the Untersee, is remarkable for having been the prison of John Huss and Jerome of Prague, who were confined within its dungeons by order of the Emperor Sigismund and Pope John XXIII. The latter was himself transferred a few months later to the same prison, by the Council of Constance. This ancient building, restored by Louis Napoleon, now belongs to Count Beroldingen.

Petershausen, on the rt. bank of the Rhine, was a free abbey of the Empire. The iron bridge which carries the rly. and a carr.-road from Petershausen across the Rhine to Constance, is flanked by statues of the Grand-Duke Leopold, Duke Berthold the 1st of Zähringen, Bp. Conrad, founder of Constance, and Bp. Gebhard, founder of the monastery of Petershausen.

CONSTANCE, or CONSTANZ. (*Inns:* Insel Hotel ; H. and Pension Constanzerhof, both new and good ; H. Halm, opposite the station ; Hecht ; Krone, near the harbour ; Badischer Hof, in the upper town.) (E. C. S.)

Constance, a city of 13,270 Inhab., is remarkable for its antiquity, its streets and many of its buildings having remained unaltered since the 15th century. It has been a bishopric since the 7th century, and in the middle ages was raised to the rank of an Imperial city. From 1559 to 1805 it was subject to the House of Austria. Although situated on the l. or Swiss bank of the Rhine, it now belongs to Baden. It occupies a projecting angle of ground where the river flows out of the *Bodensee*, or *Lake of Constance* ; its agreeable position and interesting historical associations make amends for the want of life perceptible within its venerable walls. It has of late, however, revived considerably ; the Government have formed a harbour ; and several manufactories of cotton and muslin have sprung up. The ancient Episcopal State, numbering 87 bishops, was terminated in 1802, and in 1805 Constance was ceded by Austria to Baden.

The *Cathedral* or *Münster* (R. C., badly restored) is a handsome Gothic structure, founded 1052, rebuilt in the 16th cent.; the tower at the W. end, with spire of open work, in 1850-57; the oak doors of the main portal are carved with reliefs of the Passion of our Lord, by Simon Baider, 1740. The choir-stalls, by Nich. Lerch of Strassburg, are of the 15th century. The nave is supported by sixteen pillars, each of a single block, and dates from the 13th century. The spot where Huss stood, as sentence of death by burning was pronounced on him, is pointed out near the W. end of the nave. *Robt. Hallam*, Bp. of Salisbury, who presided over the English deputation to the council, is buried in front of the high altar, under a *brass.* St. Conrad's Chapel, restored, is at the N.E. end of the cathedral. Beneath the ch. is a very ancient *crypt.* Two sides of the *Cloisters*, whose arches are filled in with beautiful tracery, are yet standing. To the E. of the cathedral is a detached chapel, perhaps a baptistery, in the centre of which is a Gothic Holy Sepulchre.

In the *Sacristy* are some missals, plate and relics, also a beautiful Gothic fireplace and piscina; in the *Vestry* room, a range of cupboards of carved oak, none of a later date than the 15th century; in the *Chapter-house* the Vincent mediæval antiquities, rich in glass-paintings. There is a beautiful view from the tower.

The *Dominican monastery*, now the Insel Hotel, is the place where Huss was confined previous to his execution. The church is in the early style of German Gothic. The cloisters are perfect. The rly. passes the little island upon which this building stands.

In the *Hall of the Kaufhaus* (built 1388, as a warehouse), close to the lake, the *Council of Constance* held some of its sittings 1414–18, in a large room supported by wooden pillars. The room is painted in fresco, to illustrate the history of Constance. That famous assembly, composed, not of bishops alone, like the ancient councils, but of deputies, civil and ecclesiastical, from the whole of Christendom, including princes, cardinals (30), patriarchs (4), archbishops (20), bishops (150), professors of universities and doctors of theology (200), besides a host of ambassadors, inferior prelates, abbots, priors, &c., was convened for the purpose of remedying the abuses of the Church. It deposed the infamous John XXIII. and Benedict XIII., and elected Martin V. It was by the act of this council that John Huss and Jerome of Prague were seized and executed, in spite of the safe-conduct granted to the former by the Emperor Sigismund, the president of the assembly.

The *house* in which *Huss* lodged, bearing a rude likeness of him, is in the Paulsstrasse, near the Schnetzthor. He was imprisoned soon after his arrival in the monastery of Gottlieben, whence he was removed to a more irksome dungeon, affording scarcely room to move.

On the field, outside the town, in the suburb of Brühl, in which he suffered martyrdom, with a fortitude which moved even his judges and executioners to admiration, a monument is erected to his memory, as well as to that of his friend and fellow-sufferer, Jerome of Prague,

The *Chancery Court* (Kanzlei-Gebäude), in the principal street, is interesting for its architecture (1590), and its frescoes by Ferd. Wagner. The *Guildhall, Zum Rosen Garten,* has a collection of local antiquities. Here are preserved the chairs occupied by the Emperor and Pope at the Council; fragments of the dungeon in which Huss was confined; also the car on which he was drawn to execution; the figure of Abraham, which supported the pulpit, from the Münster, and which the people mistook for Huss, and defaced accordingly, and some other relics of the council, still remain in the hall, besides a collection of Roman and German antiquities, dug up in the neighbourhood, remains of lake-dwellings and local fossils.

The *Lyceum* contains fossils from Oehningen. There is a capital Swimming Bath at the *Ecole de Natation* in the lake.

The *Angler* can find no better quarters in Switzerland for lake fishing.

Excursions to Reichenau (*see above*), *Mainau,* and *Schloss Heiligenberg,* in Baden. The *island* of *Mainau,* about 4 m. N. of Constance, is a well-cultivated little estate, with no want of trees. The house was once a commandery of the Knights of the Teutonic Order. It was purchased, 1853, by the Grand Duke of Baden. From the garden terrace there is a view over the lake of the mountains of the Vorarlberg and Appenzell, among which the Sentis is pre-eminent. Mainau is approached by an iron bridge ¼ m. long, connecting it with the shore; there is an inn on the island.

From the Belvedere on *Hohenrain,* 1 hour's walk on the road to Mühlheim, is a fine view of the Alps.

Railway to Schaffhausen and Bâle (Baden line).

Railway (Rte. 66) or *steamer* to Romanshorn and Rorschach, thence by rail to St. Gall or Coire and Zürich. Also railway by Stein and Etzweilen to Winterthur, Zürich, &c.

Lake of Constance, or *Boden See*.

Steamboats 4 times a day to Friedrichshafen, Rorschach and Bregenz; 5 times to Lindau. For time and place of starting see time-tables, which will be found at all the inns. It is 2½ hours from Constance to Lindau, and 1½ to Rorschach or Friedrichshafen. Friedrichshafen to Romanshorn 1 hr.; to Rorschach 1½ hr. Romanshorn to Lindau, 1½ hr.

The lake of Constance, called by the Germans *Boden See*, and anciently by the Romans *Lacus Brigantinus* (from Brigantia, the modern Bregenz), separates Switzerland from Germany, and is bordered by the territories of 5 different states—Baden, Würtemberg, Bavaria, Austria, and Switzerland. It is 1306 ft. above the sea, 42 m. long, from Bregenz to Ludwigshafen; about 8 m. wide between Friedrichshafen and Romanshorn, the broadest part; and 1027 ft. is its greatest known depth; it abounds in fish, of which 25 species have been enumerated.

The main tributary of the lake is the Rhine, which flows out under the walls of Constance. Its accumulated deposits have formed an extensive delta at the upper end, and are annually encroaching.

The banks, either flat or gently undulating, present little beauty of scenery compared with other Swiss lakes; but they are remarkably fertile. The S. shore is studded with a picturesque line of ruined castles of the middle ages, and behind them are the cliffs of the Sentis. Towards the E. end of the lake the eye is riveted by the grandeur and beauty of the distant snowy chain of the Vorarlberg.

The water, on an average, is lowest in the month of February, and highest in June and July, when the snows are melting: it sometimes rises a foot in 24 hours at that season. The lake, like that of Geneva, is subject to sudden rises and falls, the origin of which is still obscure.

———

On quitting Constance by steam-boat, rt. is the suppressed Augustine convent of *Kreuzlingen*, now turned into an agricultural school, with 70 or 80 pupils. The edifice dates from the end of the Thirty Years' War, in the course of which the preceding building was destroyed.

The *Church* possesses a remarkable example of wood-carving by a Tyrolese, representing the Passion, with many hundred small figures; also a vest embroidered with pearls, the gift of Pope John XXIII. in 1414.

The canton of Thurgau, or Thurgovie, which occupies the S. shore from Constance to Arbon, is distinguished for its surpassing fertility. Instead of rocks and mountains, and alpine pastures, the characteristics of other parts of Switzerland, this canton presents richly-cultivated arable land, waving with corn and hemp; the place of forests is supplied by orchards; it is, indeed, the garden and granary of Helvetia. The country is at the same time thickly peopled, abounding in villages and cheerful cottages.

The nunnery of *Münsterlingen*, about 4 m. further, was suppressed in 1838, and converted into an hospital. The *old* convent near the water was the scene of the reconciliation between the Emperor Sigismund and Duke Frederick of Austria, 1418.

Romanshorn (Rte. 10) — (*Inns*: H. Bodan and Römerhorn, good)—Terminus of the Rly. from Winterthur and Zürich. It is the chief port of communication by steamer with

Friedrichshafen, on the N. shore of the lake (*Inns*: Deutsches Haus, near the Rly. stat. with garden, first-rate; Krone; König von Würtemberg; Seehof). Here is the *Villa* of the King of Würtemberg, formerly the convent of Hofen, in which he usually passes a part of the summer. During the absence of the royal family the *Gardens* are open to the public. Friedrichshafen is the terminus of the Stuttgart Rly., which joins the Baden Rly. at Bruchsal. The rly. runs down to the side of the steamer, and luggage-trains are carried bodily across the lake to Romanshorn. The *Riedle* is a pretty wood with roads and walks.

Arbon (*Inns:* Bär, near the station, good; Engel; Kreuz), a picturesque walled town close upon the lake. The Romans under Augustus built here, upon the high road from Augst and Vindonissa to Bregenz, a fort, which they called *Arbor Felix*. It was abandoned by them to the Alemanni in the 5th century. The *Castle*, on an eminence overlooking the lake, was built 1510, but its tower is said to rest on Roman foundations. The *Church*, lately restored, contains some good glass. The *belfry*, detached, was boarded, not walled, on the side nearest the castle, in order that no force hostile to the lords of the castle should be enabled to shelter in it, or annoy the castle from thence. St. Gallus, an Irish monk, the founder of the great monastery of St. Gall, is said to have died at Arbon (A.D. 640), and the place was a favourite residence of Conradin of Hohenstaufen.

Lindau (*Inns :* Bayerischer Hof, good; H. Reutemann; Deutscher Haus), 5000 Inhab., is the terminus of the Bavarian Rly., 5 hrs. from Augsburg. It is an interesting old town, on an island, surrounded by ramparts. (See HANDBOOK FOR SOUTH GERMANY.)

Railway open from Lindau to Bludenz by

Bregenz Stat. 3600 Inhab. (*Inns:* Oesterreichischer Hof, on the lake; H. Montfort; Weisses Kreuz; Krone; Schweizerhof); the Roman *Brigantium*, chief place in the Vorarlberg. Pedestrians intending to travel from Switzerland into the Tyrol may find it a good plan to pass their heavy luggage at the Austrian custom-house here, and forward it by rail to Innsbruck or Botzen. (See Rte. 67, and HANDBOOK FOR SOUTH GERMANY.)

Rorschach (Rte. 65). *Terminus* of the *Railways* to St. Gall (Rte. 65) and to Ragatz and Coire up the val-ley of the Rhine (Rte. 66). A short distance from Rorschach is the mouth of the Rhine, E. of which is the Vorarlberg in Austrian territory.

ROUTE 9.

SCHAFFHAUSEN TO ZÜRICH—RHEINFALL RAILWAY.

Schaffhausen.						Eng. m.
Dachsen	.	.	.	.	.	3
Andelfingen	.	.	.	.	.	7
Winterthur	.	.	.	.	.	18
Effretikon	.	.	.	.	.	24
Wallisellen	.	.	.	.	.	30
Zürich	.	.	.	.	.	35

6 Trains daily, in 2 to 2 hrs. 20 m.

After leaving Schaffhausen, the rly. crosses the Rhine by a long *stone bridge* in the midst of the foaming rapids just above the fall. It then passes under the Castle of Laufen, by tunnel, on emerging from which a rapid view of the Falls may be caught on the rt.

Dachsen Stat. (Hotel Witzig) about 10 min. walk from the Falls and Schloss Laufen hotel. (See Rte. 7.) The rly. keeps for a short distance above the wooded bank of the Rhine, forming a road wonderfully picturesque; but the river soon winds away, and the rail proceeds through a fertile country towards the valley of the Thur, making a great bend to pass that river near

Andelfingen Stat. Beyond this it ascends a considerable incline, to cross the ridge between the valleys of the Thur and the Töss, and affords a fine view on the rt. before descending into the broad vale of the Töss.

Winterthur Junct. Stat. (Buffet) (*Inns:* Löwe, best; Krone; Adler;

Sonne), a manufacturing town of 13,600 Inhab. (chiefly Protestants), consisting of long parallel streets, crossed by smaller ones at right angles. The new house of Assembly for the Canton is a large and handsome building. The Post Office and School-house are also handsome. The School-house contains the *Public Library*, and *Museum*, with a collection of Swiss animals, and coins, &c., from the adjacent village of *Oberwinterthur*, site of the Roman *Vitodurum*.

The weaving of cambric, the printing of cotton, and the manufacture of machinery, are thriving branches of industry here.

This is the junct. stat. of the *Rorschach* and *St. Gall* line with that of *Romanshorn* (Rte. 10), and of the line through Stein and Singen to *Stuttgart*. There are also lines to *Waldshut* by *Eglisau* and to *Rapperschwyl* by the *Töss Valley*.

It is a pleasant walk to the *Castle of Kyburg*, nearly 4 m. S. of Winterthur, on a height to the l. of the rly. Strangers are admitted. It is memorable in history as an ancient possession of the House of Austria, inherited 1264, by Rudolf of Habsburg, on the failure of the line of powerful Counts of Kyburg, who flourished between the 9th and 13th cents. Here Rudolf and other emperors often resided, and here they kept the regalia of the empire. The Castle passed from them 1375, yet the Emp. of Austria still retains the title of Count of Kyburg. From 1452 to 1798 it was occupied by a Zürich bailiff (Landvogt), and is now private property. It is furnished in antique style; contains a picture gallery, chamber of torture, and old chapel with original frescoes on its walls. Fine view from the towers.

After leaving Winterthur the rly. follows the rather picturesque valley of the Töss, passing rt. the ancient Dominican *Convent of Töss* (now a factory), the retreat of the Empress Agnes after the murder of her father, Albert of Austria. Here her daughter-in-law, Elizabeth of Hungary, took the veil, and died in the odour of sanctity: her monument, with the arms of Hungary, is visible in the existing church. The cloisters, built with the church in 1469, are ornamented with fresco paintings of Bible subjects; left is seen the castle of Kyburg.

The rly. crosses the Töss, and passes into the valley of the *Glatt*, which flows from the *Greifen-see*; on the l. there is a view of Glärnisch and other mountains.

Effretikon Junct. Branch rly. to Pfäffikon, and thence to *Wetzikon*, on the rly. to Rapperschwyl (Rte. 13).

Wallisellen Junct. Rly. to Rapperschwyl, &c. (Rte. 13).

Oerlikon Junct. Branch rly. along the valley of the *Glatt* to *Bülach*, and thence in progress to Schaffhausen.

Shortly after leaving Oerlikon a tunnel under the hill of Weid is traversed; on emerging from it the Limmat is crossed, and, after making some very sharp curves, the rly. reaches

Zürich Station—one of the handsomest and largest in Switzerland—at the extremity of the Bahnhof Strasse, which reaches to the lake.

Inns: first-class—H. Baur au Lac: H. Bellevue, command fine views over the lake; H. Victoria; H. National, both near the station; H. Bauer Stadt; H. Central, on the river.

Second-class: H. Habis; H. St. Gotthard; Stork and H. Schwert (Epée), both on the Limmat; H. Schweitzerhof.

Post-Office.—Bahnhof St.

Strangers' Office of Information (Bureau des Étrangers): on the ground-floor of the Exchange. Open daily, gratis, 9–12 A.M. and 2–5 P.M. Established by the Municipality and Public Bodies for the benefit of visitors.

English Service on Sundays in St. Ann's Church, near the Botanical Garden. R. C. Church in Ausser-Sihl.

Railways — To Bâle by Aarau and Olten; to Romanshorn and Constance; to Schaffhausen; to St. Gall and Rorschach; to Coire and the Engadine; to Ragatz, St. Gall, Bregenz, and Innsbruck; to Berne; to Zug and Lucerne.

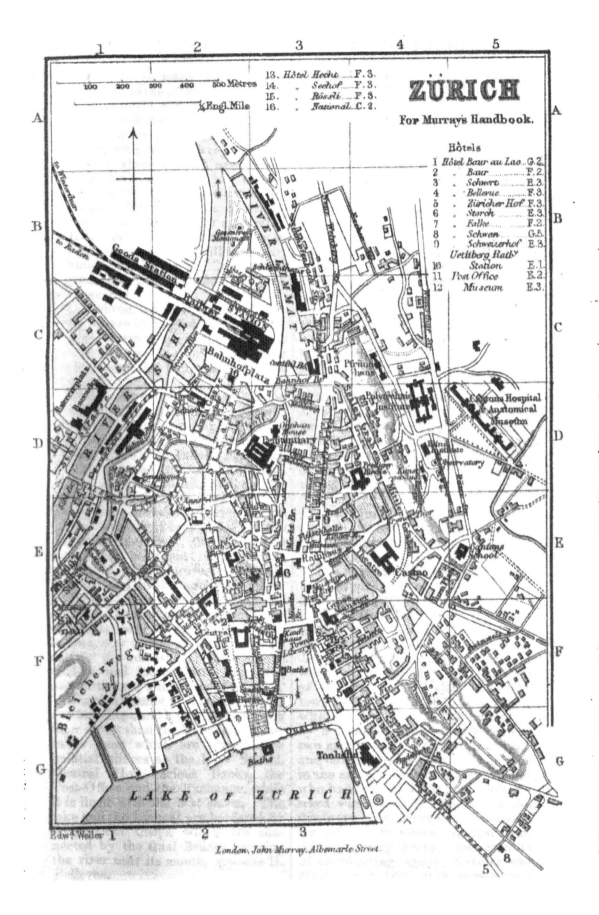

ZÜRICH

For Murray's Handbook.

13. Hôtel Hecht ... F.3.
14. " Seehof ... F.3.
15. " Rössli ... F.3.
16. " National ..C.2.

Hôtels

1. Hôtel Baur au Lac .. G.2.
2. " Baur ... F.2.
3. " Schwert ... E.3.
4. " Bellevue ... F.3.
5. " Züricher Hof. F.3.
6. " Storch ... E.3.
7. " Falke ... F.2.
8. " Schwan ... G.5.
9. " Schweizerhof .. E.3.
10. Uetliberg Rail? Station ... E.1.
11. Post Office ... E.2.
12. Museum ... E.3.

LAKE OF ZÜRICH

Edw? Weller

London, John Murray, Albemarle Street

Steamboats go many times a day from Zürich to the other end of the lake (Rapperschwyl), and to all places on the borders of the lake.

The *Museum* Club, close to the Unter Brücke, contains a capital reading-room, where English newspapers and Reviews are taken in; besides more than 300 of the best Continental journals. Travellers can be introduced for a few days by a member or Innkeeper. Open 9 A.M. to 9.30 P.M.

Booksellers: Albert Müller, Cäsar, Schmidt, and Meyer and Zeller, have a good collection of guide-books and photographs.

Lilienkron, chemist, in the Wein Platz, makes up English prescriptions.

Baths (swimming) in the lake near the H. Baur au Lac for men, and for women near the Bauschanze, in the Limmat.

Zürich, the seat of a university, the most important manufacturing town of Switzerland, and capital of a canton distinguished for prosperous industry, has 87,000 Inhab., nearly all Protestants, and lies at the N. end of the lake of Zürich, and on the banks of the Limmat, just where it issues from the lake in a rapid crystalline stream; it is bounded on the W. by another river, the Sihl. The flourishing condition of Zürich is visible in the improvements going forward and in the number of new buildings. The banks of the Lake and the Limmat, and the neighbouring hills, are thickly dotted with houses, now united with the town itself by the removal (in 1833) of the useless and inconvenient ramparts, and forming a wide circle of suburbs.

Zürich abounds in handsome modern buildings, and no Swiss town has a finer street than the Bahnhofsstrasse, in or near which are placed such palatial edifices as the Boys' School, Central Hof, various Banks, the Post-Office and the Exchange, while it is lined with the best shops. The lake and the Limmat are bordered by magnificent *Quays*, which are connected by the Quai Brücke crossing the river near its mouth, opposite H. Bellevue.

Zürich is divided by the Limmat into the *Kleine Stadt* (l. bank) and *Grosse Stadt.* (rt.)

One old ch. deserves a visit, the *Gross-Münster*, on the rt. bank of the Limmat, surmounted by 2 W. steeples, one of which is called Charlemagne's Tower, and bears a crowned figure supposed to represent that monarch. It is a massive Romanesque edifice of the 11th and 12th cents., and worthy of respect as the scene of Zwingli's bold preachings of Reformation in the Church, and amendment of morals. The exterior has been extensively repaired. The interior has some curious bas-reliefs of the 12th cent., but is severely plain and covered with whitewash. The door will be opened on knocking. It has no W. entrance, and ends square to the E. Its nave is supported on square pillars and round arches: beneath is a very perfect crypt. *See* the very fine N. doorway with detached shafts and the adjoining *cloisters* raised upon small low triple arches, with slender columns and capitals of various patterns. They have been restored.

The *Frau-Münster* (13th centy.), close to the Minster Bridge, has been completely modernised.

The house in which *Zwingli* passed the last six years of his life is No. 1 in the Gross-Münster Platz.

The *Peterskirche* (with the large clock), on the l. bank of the Limmat, had for its minister, for 23 years, *Lavater*, the author of the renowned work on Physiognomy, who was born at Zürich. On the capture of the town by the French army, he was shot, within a few steps of his own door, by a French soldier, to whom, but two minutes before, he had given wine and offered money, and while he was in the act of assisting another soldier who had been wounded. A high reward was offered by Massena for the discovery of the murderer: but Lavater refused to inform against him. After lingering through three months of excruciating agony, Lavater expired, Jan. 2, 1801, at the parsonage:

his grave is marked by a simple stone in the *churchyard*.

The *Augustiner-Kirche*, a well-restored ch., contains 2 modern frescoes by Deschwanden.

The *Town Library*, close to the *Münsterbrücke*, in a building formerly a church (Wasserkirche), contains, in addition to 120,000 printed volumes and 4000 MSS., 100 vols. of autograph letters of early Reformers; 3 Latin letters of *Lady Jane Grey* to Bullinger, in a beautifully clear and regular hand — Zwingli's Greek Bible, with marginal notes (chiefly Hebrew) by himself; a Roman inscription, giving the ancient name of Zürich, *Turicum*; a bust of Lavater, by *Dannecker*, a portrait of Zwingli and his daughter, by *Hans Asper*; a model in relief of a large part of Switzerland, superior to that at Lucerne; some fossil bones from Oehningen, including one described by Scheuchzer as a human skull, though in reality a portion of a salamander—fossils of the Glarus slate, chiefly fishes, from the Plattenberg, and a most interesting collection of antiquities from the *Swiss Lake Dwellings*, first discovered at Obermeilen on the L. of Zurich, and described by Prof. Keller.

The *Arsenal*, a modern building near the Sihl river, contains some ancient armour and early breech-loading and rifled guns, the sword and armour of Zwingli. There are several tattered standards, taken by the Swiss from their enemies, including one of Charles the Bold of Burgundy. But this collection is inferior to those in several other Swiss cantons.

One of the handsomest modern buildings is the *Polytechnic Schools and University*, situated on the hill, near the Great Hospital, designed by Semper, built 1860–64. It is a national school for pupils above the age of 17, supported by a yearly grant of 250,000 fr. from the Confederation. Each pupil pays but 115 fr. for a year's instruction, which is so practical, good, and cheap, that foreign pupils contribute about two-thirds of the total number.

The *University*, established 1832-3, when many professors, expelled from other countries for their political opinions, repaired hither as teachers. The terrace in front commands a fine view. The *Library* contains many original MSS. of the early reformers; and the *Museum* collections of geology, zoology, and botany, including the Herbarium of Conrad Gesner. A little higher on the hill is the *Observatory*. The *Chemical Laboratory* near this is one of the best appointed in Europe.

The chief attraction of Zürich lies in the *Walks* and *Promenades* in and about the town, and the splendid views they command S. of the Alpine Chain. Pre-eminent among these are the Broad Quays which line the lake and Limmat and the Upper Bridge across that river, the Public and *Botanic Gardens* which are well maintained, and the terraces on the heights on either side, as the Hohe Promenade above H. Bellevue. Of course the higher you ascend the wider the views over lake and mountains.

The most prominent and interesting of the peaks beginning at the E., are the Sentis in Appenzell, barely visible; Glärnisch and Tödi, in Glarus, Achselberg and Mytha in Schwyz, and Uri Rothstock and Albis.

On the *Platz* Promenade the triangular piece of ground at the junction of the Limmat and Sihl, N. of the Rly. Stat., planted with shady avenues, is a simple monument to the memory of *Solomon Gessner*, author of 'The Death of Abel.'

History.—A Roman station, Castrum Turicense, probably gave rise both to the town and its name. In 1218 Frederick II. declared Zürich a free Imperial city. Rudolf of Habsburg, as its general, destroyed several of the neighbouring castles, and afterwards, as Emperor, accorded the town important privileges. The Zürichers, under their aristocratic leaders, fought against the Confederates at Morgarten. A democratic revolution in the city in 1336 under Rudolf Brun led to a change of policy, and in 1351 Zürich entered into perpetual alliance with the Forest Cantons. At this time its prosperity rose to a great height, owing to its position on the road to Italy and the activity of its inhabitants. Its medical schools were celebrated, and it was, with Bâle, the chief seat of intellectual activity in Switzerland and one of the centres of the Reformation, which commenced, under the guidance and preaching of Ulrich Zwingli, in 1519, and naturally occasioned much bitterness in a town where domestic quarrels have always been very violent. Zürich had already, at an earlier period, afforded safe and hospitable shelter to Arnold of Brescia, when driven out of Italy for inveighing against the temporal power of the Pope. It was the asylum of many eminent English Protestants banished by the persecutions of the reign of Queen Mary: they met with a friendly reception during their exile. The first *entire English version* of the Bible, by Miles Coverdale, was printed here in 1535. Zürich was the scene of an important battle in Sept. 1799, when 37,000 French under Massena drove out the Russians under Korsakof, and compelled them to fall back upon the Rhine with a loss of 13,000 men. "Eternal glory to Massena!" exclaims M. Thiers: "he saved us at a moment more perilous than that of Valmy or of Fleurus."

The principal *Manufactures* are those of silk, the hand-weaving of which occupies many thousands in the town and along the shores of the lake, though giving place to the power-loom. There are numerous cotton-factories. There is a large paper-mill, 1 m. S. of the city on the river Sihl. The cotton and silk goods made in the neighbourhood, and in other parts of the canton, are the object of an extensive commerce with Germany and Italy, and compete in price with English goods. Escher Wyss & Co.'s. *manufactory of machinery* employs 700 persons. Most of the iron steamers plying on the Swiss lakes are made by

him, and boats, engines and all, are carried in pieces over the St. Gothard to the Italian lakes.

Zürich is the native place of *Hammerlin* the reformer; of *Gessner* the poet, and Conrad *Gessner* the naturalist; of *Lavater;* and of *Pestalozzi* the teacher.

Environs. *a.* The 'Restaurant' *Zur Weid*, on the *Käferberg* through which the Winterthur rly. passes by tunnel, 1 hr.'s walk on the Baden road, has a fine view of the Alps, town, and vale of the Limmat. Other good points are the Karolinenburg, the Forster, the Jacobsburg and the Schlössli, all on the *Zürichberg*, ½ an hr.'s walk to the N.E.

b. The *Uetliberg*, 5 m. W., and 2864 ft. high, one of the Albis range, commands a fine view of the Oberland and Appenzell mountains. A railway (½ hr., return-ticket 3 fr.) starts from a station on the Sellnau, near the Botanical Garden. There are no cog-wheels, but the engine and carriages are very light, and the adhesion to the rails is found sufficient, though the last incline is 1 in 14. The railway is about 6 m. long, 3 of them level, and in the last 3 m. it rises 1000 ft., through woods, and commands pretty views.

The *Hotel* Uetliberg is close to the summit, a restaurant (Uto-Kulm) on the top. On the S. slope is the H. Uto-Staffel. In the summer the place is a crowded holiday resort from Zürich. The station is about 200 ft. below the hotel, and 300 ft. below the summit.

From the Uetliberg to the *Albis Inn* (Rte. 14) is a pleasant walk of 3 hrs.

ROUTE 10.

ROMANSHORN TO ZÜRICH, BY WINTER-
THUR—RAILWAY.

		Eng. m.
Romanshorn.		
Weinfelden Stat.	. .	14
Mühlheim Stat.	. .	19
Frauenfeld Stat.	. .	25
Winterthur Stat.	. .	35
Wallisellen Stat.	. .	46
Oerlikon Stat.	. . .	48
Zürich Stat.	. . . .	51

5 Trains daily, in 4 hrs.

Romanshorn (Buffet) (*Inns:* Hôtels
Bodan and Römerhorn, united, good,
with garden), a town of 3640 Inhab.,
and the principal corn-market for
the supply of the Alpine districts
of N. Switzerland. It is a station on
the rly. which runs from Constance
along the S. shore of the lake, and is
the terminus of the N.E. Rly. from
Winterthur, and station for the
steamers from Friedrichshafen, Lindau, and Bregenz (Rte. 8). From
the ancient château of the abbot of
St. Gall, on the heights, there is a
fine view over the lake (Rte. 8).

Weinfelden, celebrated for its wines.
The council of the canton Thurgau
sits here.

Mühlheim.—Between this place and
Constance is *Hohenrain*, a hill commanding an extensive view.

Frauenfeld (*Inns:* Schweizerhof;
Falke), the chief town of canton Thurgovie (Germ. Thurgau), has 5800
Inhab., and is situated on the river
Murg, which sets in motion the wheels
of several cotton, dyeing, and printing
mills. The *Castle*, on a rock fronting
the Murg, was built in the 11th century, by one of the vassals of the
Counts of Kyburg.

On a hill to the S. stands the Capuchin monastery founded in 1595,
now occupied by only 7 or 8 brethren.

Winterthur Junct. Stat. (see Rte. 9).

ZÜRICH (Rte. 9).

ROUTE 11.

CONSTANCE TO WINTERTHUR, BY ETZ-
WEILEN—RAILWAY.

Trains in 2½ hrs.; distance 90 m.
The line runs through a fruitful district, passing many picturesque towns
and castles.

The train follows the Rhine, passing through *Gottlieben* Stat., with its
monastery, and *Ermatingen* Stat., near
which is Arenenberg (see Rte. 8).

Berlingen (stat.).

Stekborn (stat.).

Mammern (stat.). Here is a large
pension, with baths.

Eschenz (stat.).

Burg (stat.), a suburb of the picturesque town of Stein (see Rte. 8).

The rail leaves the Rhine and turns
S. to

Etzweilen Junction. Here the line
from Singen falls in.

Stammheim is the only place of any
importance between this and Winterthur.

Near *Dorlikon* the line passes over
a lofty bridge.

Winterthur Station (see Rte. 9).

Zürich (Rte. 9).

ROUTE 12.

ZÜRICH TO BERNE—RAILWAY.

		Eng. m.
Zürich.		
Baden	. . . . . .	15
Aarau	. . . . . .	31
Herzogenbuchsee	. . .	56
Berne	. . . . . .	80

Trains in 4 to 5½ hrs.: distance about
80 m. The line is circuitous: as far
as Olten it is the same as to Bâle.
At Olten it joins the Bâle and Berne
line (see Rtes. 4, 5, and 6).

There is an alternative rte., viâ
Lucerne and the Emmenthal.

ROUTE 13.

A. ZÜRICH TO RAPPERSWEIL, BY STEAMER.

B. ZÜRICH TO ZIEGELBRUCKE, BY VALE OF GLATT. RAILWAY.

C. ZÜRICH TO SARGANS, BY RAIL. LAKE OF WALLENSTADT.

	Eng. m.
Rapperswell (by water) . .	19
" (by rail) . .	26
Wesen (by rail) . .	18
or	
Wesen (by direct rail) . . .	36
Wallenstadt (by rail) . . .	12
Ragatz (by rail)	13

This is the direct route to Coire, the Splügen, Davos, and the Engadine.

There are numerous steamers on the lake, and the traveller can take advantage of them as far as Rapperschwyl (see local time-tables). It is a pleasant voyage of 2¼ hrs. to Rapperschwyl.

The railway along the S. shore of the Lake of Zürich will be taken by those to whom time is an object, in place of the circuitous rly. route to Rapperschwyl.

The *Lake of Zürich* has no pretensions to grandeur of scenery; that must be sought for on the steep and romantic shores of the lakes of Lucerne and Wallenstadt; but it has a charm peculiarly its own—that of life and rich cultivation. Its borders teem with population, and are embellished and enlivened at every step by the work of man. The hills around it are less than 3000 feet above the sea, and descend in gentle slopes to the water's edge; wooded on their tops, clad with vineyards, orchards, and gardens on their sides, and carpeted below with verdant pastures, or luxuriantly waving crops of grain. But the principal feature in this landscape is the number of human habitations. The hills from one extremity to the other are dotted with white houses, villas of citizens, cottages, and farms, while along the margin of the lake, and on the high road, they gather into frequent clusters around a church, forming villages and towns almost without number.

Every little stream descending from the hills is compelled to do duty by turning some mill; at the mouths of the valleys enormous factories are erected, and thus the shore of the lake, on either side, has almost the appearance of one uninterrupted village.

The effect of this lively foreground is heightened by the snowy peaks of the Sentis, Tödi, and Glärnisch, which are seen at different points peering above the nearer hills. The charms of the Lake of Zürich inspired the Idylls of Gessner : they are celebrated in an ode of Klopstock, and in the prose of Zimmermann. The lake is 1341 feet above the sea, about 26 miles in length from Zürich to Schmerikon, and not more than 3 broad at the widest part, between Stäfa and Wädenschwyl. The greatest depth is 640 ft. The principal river falling into it is the Linth, which flows out at Zürich, under the name of Limmat.

Scarcely any of the villages or towns on the lake are remarkable except as the seats of flourishing industry. A few only of the principal places are enumerated below. The banks are distinguished as rt. and l., in reference to the course of the Limmat.

l. The high ridge rising on the W. of Zürich, and bordering the lake for more than 12 miles, is the *Albis*.

rt. *Kilssnacht (Inn:* Sonne, excellent)—not to be confounded with its namesake on the Lake of Lucerne.

l. *Rüschlikon :* behind it are the baths of *Nidelbad*, 340 ft. above the lake.

rt. *Erlenbach*, in the midst of vineyards. 2 m. beyond it is a huge boulder-stone called *Pfugstein*, visible from the boat.

l. *Thalwyl (Inns:* Adler ; Krone). An elegant church has been built on a terrace, whence there is a lovely view of the lake, with the mountains of Appenzell and Glarus in the background. Lavater is said to have written a portion of his work on Physiognomy at the parsonage of Oberrieden, about 3½ m. farther on.

[*Switz.*]

D

1. *Horgen Stat.* (*Inns:* Meyerhof, good; pleasant garden; Löwe, clean), a prosperous little town of 5200 Inhab. [Here passengers bound for Lucerne or the Rigi, by way of Zug, may land. The road goes by a beautiful ascent and descent to *Sihlbrücke;* thence to Zug. The distance is about 12 m. (Rte. 14B.)]

rt. *Meilen* (*Inns:* Löwe ; Sonne) and *Obermeilen,* scattered villages of 3000 Inhab., chiefly silk-weavers, with a Gothic church, built 1490-9. In the lake opposite Obermeilen the first discovery of the ancient lacustrine dwelling-places, which have attracted so much attention, was made. See *Introd.,* § 19.

l. *Wädensweil* (Rail to Einsiedeln, see Rte. 72); (*Inn:* Engel, good), a pretty village of 6200 Inhab., containing silk factories. The ruined *Castle,* ½ hr.'s walk, was the residence of powerful barons of the same name.

l. *Richterschwyl* (*Inns:* Drei Könige ; Engel). Here is one of the largest cotton factories on the lake. The village is built on the boundary line of cantons Zürich and Schwyz, and at the point where the lake is broadest. Hence an excursion may be made to the whey-cure establishment of *Hutten* (1¼ m.), and to the top of the *Gottschallenberg* (3743 ft.). Zimmermann resided here as physician, and in his work on 'Solitude' justly praises the extreme beauty of Richterschwyl.

rt. *Stäfa* (*Inns:* Sonne ; Löwe), an industrious village, the largest on this side of the lake, with 3800 Inhab., by whom much silk and cotton are woven. Goethe resided here, 1797. The boundary of canton Zürich here crosses the lake. It has been calculated that the number of inhabitants on the shores, hence to the town of Zürich, a distance of 16 miles, is not less than 12,000.

On approaching Rappersweil and its long bridge, the little isle of *Ufnau* becomes a pretty feature of the landscape. It belongs to the abbey of Einsiedeln, and has some celebrity as the retreat and burial-place of Ulrich von Hutten, a Franconian knight, the friend of Luther and Franz of Seckingen, distinguished equally for his talents and chivalrous bravery, but withal a bit of a roué. His satirical writings contributed not a little to the spread of the Reformation, but raised up against him such a host of enemies that he was forced to fly from the court of Charles V., and take refuge from their persecution, first, with Franz of Seckingen, and, after his death, in this little island. Zwingli had procured for him an asylum here, in the house of the curé, where he died a fortnight after his arrival (1523), at the age of 36. He was buried by a faithful friend, but all record of the spot in which he lies has long since disappeared.

The *Bridge of Rappersweil* is one of the longest in the world : it extends from the town to a tongue of land on the opposite side, completely across the lake, a distance of 4800 ft., or more than ¾ of a mile. It is only 12 ft. broad, is formed of loose planks laid (not nailed) upon piers, and is unprovided with railing at the sides, so that only one carriage can safely pass at a time. It was originally constructed by Leopold of Austria, 1358 : the existing bridge dates from 1819. It has been superseded by a bridge which carries road and railway.

Rappersweil Stat. (*Inns:* H. du Lac Freehof ; Schwan, both good; Post). This is a very picturesque place (2640 Inhab.), still partly surrounded by walls, and surmounted by an old *Castle* (Die Grafenburg). The *Church* contains some antique sacred vessels, and the Castle a Polish historical museum. From the Castle terrace called *Lindenhof,* there is a delightful view.

N.E. of Rappersweil is the *Bachtel* (3671 ft.), with a small *Inn* at the top, which is visited chiefly by those who drink the waters at *Gyrenbad,* a bathing-place N.W. of it, between Wetzikon and Bubikon. A tower 95 ft. high has been built for the view. The Bachtel is most conveniently reached from Rappersweil by way of the Rüti Stat. from which it is about 1½ hr. Mines of lignite are worked at Dürnten and Köpfnach at the foot of the mountain.

B. *Zürich (or Schaffhausen) to Zie-gelbrücke*—by the Vale of the Glatt. *Railway.* About 2 hours.

Wallisellen Junct. Stat. (Rte. 9), where the line to Winterthur diverges l.; by *Dübendorf* and *Nänikon*, following the *Glatt Thal*, a valley teeming with manufacturing industry: industry which has expanded its hamlets into villages, mixed with white cotton factories and the handsome mansions of their owners. At the E. end the Glarus mountains rise into view with grand effect. Rt. is passed the *Greifen See*, and castle of the same name, in which a garrison held out bravely for Zürich against the Swiss Confederates under Reding in 1444.

Uster Stat. (*Inn:* Kreuz) with an ancient castle; and *Wetzikon Stat.* [Branch line to Effretikon (Rte. 9) and Winterthur], remarkable for the lacustrine deposits found in the neighbourhood, especially at *Robenhausen* by the small *Pfäffikon See.* Rude structures have been discovered 6 ft. below a layer of peat, and with them bones of 3 species of urochs; also chamois, bisons, beavers, boars, &c., with remains of apples, pears, and cherries. *View* of Alps of Glarus, near

Bubikon Stat. l. rises the *Bachtel.*

Rüti Junction. Another line from Winterthur by the valley of the Toss here falls in. The Rly. does not approach the Lake of Zürich until near *Rappersweil Stat.* (see preceding page).

Schmerikon Stat. (*Inns:* Rössli; Seehof; Adler), at the E. extremity of the Lake of Zürich. The castle of *Grynau*, rt., stands on the *Linth*, a little above its entrance into the lake.

Schänis Stat. (*Inn:* Hirsch), an ancient town. Fine old glass and armour in the church.

Uznach Stat. (*Inns:* Ochs; Linth-hof, both fair), on an eminence, the summit of which is occupied by a tower of the ancient castle and by that of the church. There are mines of brown

coal at *Oberkirch*, to the E. in a hill 1500 ft. high. Near Uznach is a large cotton-mill, driving 24,480 spindles.

The railway now leaves the lake and runs through the marshes of the Linth. This river, coming down from the valley of Glarus, formerly ran directly into the Lake of Zürich, and by its floods devastated the whole of the lower district. In 1807 the scheme of Conrad Escher of Zürich was adopted. The Linth was turned into the Lake of Wallenstadt, where its fury is now spent, and the stones and gravel brought down are deposited. At the same time a wide canal was dug between the lakes, by which the surplus water was carried off into the Lake of Zürich. The works cost 60,000*l.*, and have proved perfectly successful. The well-earned name of *Von der Linth* was bestowed on Herr Escher and his descendants.

Ziegelbrücke Junction. Fine view towards Glarus. Here we join the direct line from Zürich.

C. *Zürich to Ziegelbrücke and Sargans Railway*, by S. shore of the lake. About 2 hours. The line skirts the lake to Lachen, with beautiful views.

Horgen Stat. Here a portion of the line and the station fell into the lake soon after it was first opened. Near the *Au* station is a hotel on a peninsula overlooking the lake.

Wädensweil Junct. Branch line hence to Einsiedeln in 1 hour (Rte. 72).

Richterswyl Stat., opposite Rappersweil.

Lachen Stat. (*Inns:* Bär; Ochse). [Hence there is a path to Glarus by the *Wäggithal* and over the *Karrenegg Pass.* There is an inn at Hinter Wäggithal. From Vorder Wäggithal the Schwändi Scheideck leads to Näfels.] Here the line leaves the lake and traverses a marshy plain. Crossing the Linth Canal, it joins the Rappersweil line at Ziegelbrücke. Hence it is 1¼ hr. to Sargans, 2¼ hrs. to Coire (Rte. 81). Rly. to Glarus and Linthal branches rt. (Rte. 74), before reaching

Wesen Junct. Stat. (Buffet) (*Inn:* Zum Speer, good, charmingly situated on the height to the l.). The stat. is at a little distance from the village and lake.

Wesen (*Inns:* Schwert H. and Pension, comfortable, on the lake H. & P. Rossli ; H. & P. Mariahalden, both good), a village at the W. extremity of the lake of Wallenstadt, and in the midst of scenery of great magnificence. Above it are some remains of a fort, and a cavern called the *Ghosts' Chamber* (*Geisterstube*). Pleasant walks on the banks of the Lake.

[The ascent of the *Speer*, 6417 ft., is made in 3½ hrs. : it commands a noble view, particularly of the Glärnisch and Tödi. There is a good *Inn*, with 40 beds, half an hour below the top. From the summit the traveller may reach Nesslau in the Toggenburg (Rte. 71) in 2½ hrs. The Speer is the farthest E. of several similar points on a ridge.

A pass without any difficulty from Wesen to *Wildhaus* between the *Leistkamm* and the *Gulmen* may be accomplished, including the ascent of the Gulmen, in 7 or 8 hours' walking.]

The railway next crosses the Linth canal and the new course of the Linth, and reaches the shore of the *Lake of Wallenstadt* or *Wallensee*, 1386 ft. above the sea, about 10 miles long and 1¼ broad, and at its greatest depth 600 ft. Its scenery is grand, but somewhat wanting in variety. Its N. shore consists of colossal cliffs of lime and sandstone, regularly stratified, and so nearly precipitous that there is room for no road, and only for a very few cottages at their base, while their steep surface, almost destitute of verdure, gives to this lake a savage and arid character. The S. side consists of more gradually sloping hills covered with vegetation and overtopped by the tall bare peaks of more distant mountains. Here there are several villages, and a path, very rough and irregular as far as *Mühlehorn*, runs along it. Before the railway was made there were steamers on the lake. In Jan. 1851 the steamer was submerged by a squall, and every soul on board—14 in all—perished. It was fished up from a great depth.

The precipices along the N. bank vary between 2000 and 3000 feet in height, and the stranger is surprised to learn that above them are situated populous villages and extensive pastures crowded with cattle. Such a one is the village of *Amden* (H. and P. Leistkamm, good and moderate), containing 1280 Inhab., nearly 1500 feet above the lake. It is approached by a new road, replacing a narrow and steep path, sloping upwards from Wesen along the face of the mountain. Several waterfalls precipitate themselves over this wall of rock, or descend, by gashes or rents in its sides ; but they dwindle into insignificance by the end of summer. A beautiful excursion may be made from Wesen or Wallenstadt to these villages.

Quinten is the only village on the N. shore of the lake. At the mouths of the streams and gullies, on the opposite side there are several, such as *Terzen* and *Quarten*, whose names clearly refer to the ancient military occupation of this district by the Romans. Prima and Secunda (*Primsch* and *Siguns*) are farms E. of the lake, near Flums Stat.

Until the railway was made there was no road on either side of the lake. The railway runs along the S. shore, crossing the ravines by bridges, and penetrating the headlands by tunnels, 9 in number. Fine views of the lake are obtained at intervals.

Mühlehorn Stat. (*Inn:* Tellsplatte). Here is a large cotton-mill. Hence a delightful walk of about 3 hrs. over the shoulder of the mountain to Mollis in the valley of Glarus.

Murg Stat. (*Inns:* Kreuz ; Rössli), at the mouth of the Murgthal, a glen leading up to the

Mürtschenstock (8012 ft.). The summit of this mountain, apparently inaccessible, is traversed through and through by a cavern, which, though of large size, looks from the lake like the eye of a bodkin. The hole is best seen when abreast of the village of Mühlehorn; by those not aware of the fact, it might be mistaken for a patch of snow. This peak is said to be a favourite resort of chamois.

The N.E. extremity of the lake is bounded by the 7 picturesque peaks of the *Sieben Churfirsten.* At their feet lies

Wallenstadt Stat. — village a mile from the station—(*Inns:* Zum Churfirsten at the Stat., good; Hirsch; Seehoff); a scattered township of 2830 Inhab.; nearly ½ m. from the lake, of which it commands no view. The flats of the valley around and above it are marshy, and the neighbourhood was formerly very unhealthy, so long as the irregularities of the Linth obstructed the passage of the waters of the lake. A large trade in timber has sprung up on the shore N. of the lake.

[A steep and rugged path by the side of the Churfirsten, commanding magnificent views, leads over the *Hinterruck* in 6 hrs. to Wildhaus (Rte. 71). There is a beautiful walk by the villages N. of the lake, Sael, Quinten Amden, to Wesen.]

There is considerable beauty in the valley of the Seez, and there are rich iron-mines, interesting to visit, in the *Gonzen* above Sargans; their yearly yield is 50,000 cwt. As the ore is hematite, everything belonging to the miners is reddened, even their cats. A good climber will enjoy a scramble to the top of the *Gonzen,* a panoramic point of view. A ladder of 50 steps, chained against the face of a cliff, has to be surmounted.

Mels Stat. (*Inn:* Melserhof). On rt. the Seez comes down the Weisstannen Thal, a valley leading by the pass of the Rieseten to Matt and by the Ramina or Foo Pass to Elm in the Sernf Thal (see below).

Sargans Junct. Stat. (Buffet, Hotel Thomal, near the station), some way from

Sargans (*Inns:* H. Thoma; Löwe), a picturesque old town at the foot of the *Gonzen,* on an eminence crowned by a *castle,* formerly seat of the Counts of Werdenberg-Sargans. It stands upon the watershed dividing the streams which feed the

Rhine from those which fall into the lake of Wallenstadt; and this natural embankment is so slight (about 200 paces across and less than 20 feet high) that, as the deposits brought down by the Rhine are constantly raising its bed, it is not impossible, though scarcely probable, that the river may change its course, relinquish its present route by the lake of Constance, and take a shorter cut by the lakes of Wallenstadt and Zürich. It was calculated by Escher von der Linth, from actual measurements, that the waters of the Rhine need rise but 19½ feet to pass into the lake of Wallenstadt; and it is, indeed, recorded that the river, swollen by long rains in 1618, was prevented taking this direction only by the construction of dams along its banks. Geologists argue, from the identity of the deposits of gravel in the valley of the Upper Rhine with those in the vale of Seez, that the river actually did pass out this way at one time. The rly. from Winterthur, St. Gall, and Rorschach falls in here (Rte. 66).

[From Sargans and Mels there are 2 passes by the *Weisstannen Thal* to the Sernf Thal, on the way to Glarus or Stachelberg, and another to the Calfeuser Thal, a pleasant roundabout rte. to the Baths of Pfäffers and Ragatz. The Weisstannen Thal, which is entered through a gorge, is bounded l. by the savage summits of the *Grau-Hörner,* of which the highest point, the *Piz Sol,* is about 9340 ft. It is a drive of 3 hrs. to *Weisstannen* (*Inn:* Alpenhof, fair), at the junction of the Seez with the stream flowing from the Piz Sol. Here the two passes to the Sernf Thal divide.

a. Rieseten Grat (6 hrs.). The pass lies between the *Faulenstock* (N.) and *Härten* (S.) The descent is down the Rieseten Alp and the Krauchthal to *Matt* in the Sernf Thal.

b. Ramina, or *Foo Pass,* 6772 ft. (10 hrs.). The path turns l. up the Unterseezalp and Foo Alp to a pass between the *Foostöckli* (N.) and *Scheibe* (S.). The descent lies down the Ramina Alp to *Elm,* in the Sernf Thal.

c. The 3rd pass leads to *Vättis,* opposite the mouth of the Calfeuser Thal, above the Baths of Pfäffers, in 11 hrs. from

Weisstannen. 2 rtes. pass over the mountain, the easiest being up the valley running S. from this village.

The pass commands a fine view of the Sardona glacier. Descent into the Calfeuser Thal.

St. Martin.

Vättis.]

The remainder of this route up the valley of the Rhine, by

Ragatz Stat. to

Coire (or Chur) *Terminus* is described in Rte. 81.

ROUTE 14.

A. ZÜRICH TO ZUG AND LUCERNE—RAILWAY.

B. ZÜRICH TO ZUG, BY HORGEN (LAKE OF ZUG).

	Eng. m.	hrs.	min.
Zug	18 =	1	30
Lucerne	19 =		50

Most travellers now take the railroad, thus missing the fine views of the old Albis road—which is, however, noticed below as an excursion. It is 17½ m. by it to Zug.

At *Altstetten,* about 3 m. from Zürich, the Zug Rly. leaves the Olten line and makes a sharp turn to the S. round the base of Uetliberg, the hotel on which is conspicuous. It then ascends a valley by the side of a green hill.

Birmensdorf Stat. Pretty view of the town below.

Affoltern Stat. (*Inn:* Krone).

[From this may be made the ascent of the *Albis.*

Albis. Inn: Hirsch, with moderate accommodation and a magnificent prospect. The best point of view, however, is the *Signal* (Hochwacht, 2887 ft., called also Schnabel), a height off the road, about a mile above the inn: it takes in nearly the whole of the Zürichersee. Between the foot of the mountain and the lake the vale of the Sihl

intervenes. Its wooded slopes were the favourite retreat of the pastoral poet Gessner. In 1799 they were occupied by two hostile armies—that of the French under Massena, who encamped on the slope of the Albis, and that of the Russians, who were on the rt. bank of the Sihl. They watched each other for more than 3 months; until Massena, by a masterly movement, crossed the Limmat, cut off part of the Russian force, and compelled the rest to retreat.

On the W. are seen the little lake of Türl, the Baths at Wengi, near Aeugst, and at a distance of 10 miles the beautiful convent of Muri in Aargau (now an agricultural school). S. of the lake is the church of Kappel, where Zwingli died; farther off the lake of Zug, and behind it the Rigi and Pilatus, disclosing between them a little bit of the lake of Lucerne. The grandest feature, however, is the snowy chain of the Alps. The view has been engraved by Keller.]

Metmenstetten Stat.

[About 3 m. from this is *Hausen,* and near it *Albisbrunn,* about 2000 ft. above the sea, a large and handsome water-cure establishment, under the management of Dr. Brunner. Travellers are also received. It is a pleasant residence among green pastures and fir-trees, with a beautiful view of the Bernese Alps.

Beyond *Hausen* is *Kappel,* where Zwingli, the Reformer, attending the Zürich Protestants to battle, was killed by a man of Unterwalden, Oct. 11, 1531. The church of Kappel, formerly attached to a convent, is of the 13th cent.]

Soon after leaving Metmenstetten the Rigi and the Oberland mountains come into view, and the tall slender spire of Cham church is seen. Near *Cham* (*Inn:* Rabe) the rly. turns to the l., and runs into

Zug Stat., close to the town.

†*Zug* (*Inns:* Hirsch, good; Löwe, well situated on the lake; Bellevue; Ochs, in a very old house; Schiff; H. de la Gare), the capital of canton

Zug, in size the smallest state of the Confederation, has 4924 Inhab., and is prettily situated at the N.E. corner of the lake. It has an antiquated look, partially surrounded by its old walls, and a deserted air, which the rly., now connecting it with Zürich and Lucerne, may perhaps remove. Its inhabitants, are chiefly occupied with agricultural pursuits. The rich crops, vineyards, orchards, and gardens, on the borders of the lake, proclaim a soil not ungrateful to the cultivator.

There are some old arms in the *Arsenal*, and a standard taken at Arbedo in a battle between the Swiss and Milanese, 1422.

The *Ch. of St. Michael*, outside the town, like many of the churches in the Roman Catholic cantons, has a *bonehouse* attached to it, containing many hundred skulls. It is the custom for relations to cause the skulls of the dead to be taken up, cleaned, labelled with their names and date of birth and death, and then placed in the bonehouse. The skulls are no longer visible. The *Cemetery* is filled with quaint gilt crosses, and the graves are planted with flowers. The large building near is a nunnery and school.

St. Oswald, with the tall spire, is of German Gothic, and has some good stone figures on the buttresses. Near it is a Capuchin monastery.

There are, near the lake, some dirty narrow streets of very old houses.

On the *Zugerberg* (3222 ft.) are two large and comfortable *hotel-pensions*, *Felsenegg* and *Schönfels*, 1½ hr. from Zug by a good carriage-road. Omnibus twice a day from the stat. They command a beautiful view of the Lake of Zug; pension 4 to 5 fr.

Schönbrunn, Baths and Pension, 1½ m. W. of Zug, 2329 ft. Comfortable, in a natural park.

From Zug, the trains run back on the Zürich line nearly as far as

Cham Stat. (*Inn:* Rabe). The slender spire of the ch. is very remarkable. At this village is a large establish-

ment for condensing milk, which is largely exported to England.

The Rigi is now seen on the l., and Pilatus in front. The country improves, and the line enters the valley of the Reuss just before *Gislikon* Stat. The valley here is very pretty. Just beyond *Ebikon* Stat. is the little lake of *Rothsee*. The rly. then crosses the Reuss by a light-looking bridge, and joins the line from Olten (Rte. 3) just before entering the tunnels leading to *Lucerne* (see next Rte.)

B. *Zurich to Zug by Horgen (Lake of Zug).*

Horgen (Inns: Meyerhof, pleasantly situated; Löwe). To this place see Rte. 13. Carriages for Zug (12 or 14 fr.: 3 hrs.' drive) are generally to be found on the quay. A brown coal or lignite is found here; not fit, however, for steam-boilers. The road immediately begins to ascend by a series of zigzags, affording fine views over the lake; and from the pension *Bocken* (an old château), about ¼ m. l. of the road, a still finer view is obtained. The ascent occupies full 1½ hr., after which the descent is at once commenced, the road running for the most part along the rt. bank of the *Sihl*, crossing it at the village of

Sihlbrücke, by a covered bridge, which connects the cantons Zürich and Zug. [A good road leads l. (2½ hrs. on foot) to Egeri and its lake. The new watering-place of *Schönbrunn* (Pension 33 to 52 fr. per week) is half-way. The waters are cold, about 44° Fahr. *Egeri (Inn:* good but homely quarters) is a thriving town, from its cotton manufacture and embroidery. The *Lake of Egeri*, 2383 ft., is pleasing in scenery, and its shore memorable as the battlefield of *Morgarten* (Rte. 72). Zug may be reached from Egeri in 1½ hr. by following the river which flows from the lake, as far as the paper-mill; by then crossing it and keeping above Allenwinden.]

From the ridge beyond Sihlbrücke, the Rigi and Pilatus are first seen.

Buar (*Inn:* Lindenhof), a village with a cotton-mill which has 60,000 spindles, and 642 windows. [A path through the forest leads direct to Schönbrunn.]

A straight level road leads to *Zug* (see above).

The Lake of Zug, whose surface is 1369 feet above the sea, is 8 m. long, 2½ m. broad, and of a maximum depth of 1280 ft. Its banks are low, or gently-sloping hills, except on the S., where the Rigi, rising abruptly from the water's edge, presents its precipices towards it, forming a feature of considerable grandeur, in conjunction with the Pilatus. The *Rufi*, or *Rossberg*, 5190 ft., in the S.E. corner, is also lofty and steep; the lake, at its base, is not less than 1200 ft. deep.

Steamers, which touch first at Immensee and then at Art, run 3 or 4 times a day (Rte. 18).

† *Immensee. Inn:* H. du Rigi, comfortable and moderate. Omnibus to Küssnacht, by Tell's Chapel, through the *hohle Gasse* (Hollow Way).

† *Art* (*Inns:* Schwarzer Adler, good; Hôtel du Rigi; Sonne), a village of 2447 Inhab., occupies a charming position on the lake of Zug, between the base of the Rigi and the Rossberg. There is a Capuchin monastery here. In the *Treasury* of the *Church* are preserved a richly-worked crucifix and chalice of silver, which belonged to Charles the Bold, and were left by him on the field of Grandson, besides some gaudy priests' robes.

One of the railways up the Rigi starts from Art, and there is also a mule-path to the top.

An excellent road to *Art* winds round the base of the Rossberg, famous for the catastrophe caused by the fall of a portion of it (see Rte. 18). Near the chapel of *St. Adrian* a small monument has been erected on the spot where the arrow is supposed to have fallen which Heinrich von Hunenberg shot out of the Austrian lines into the Swiss camp, before the battle of Morgarten, bearing the warning words, "Beware of Morgarten." It was in consequence of this that the confederates occupied the position indicated, and it contributed mainly to their victory on that memorable field. *Morgarten* (Rte. 72) lies within this canton, about 14 m. S.E. of Zug, on the lake of Egeri.

ROUTE 15.

LUCERNE TO WEGGIS, VITZNAU, BRUNNEN, AND FLÜELEN. LAKE OF LUCERNE.

Lucerne *Terminus.*

Lucerne (Luzern). *Hotels:* Schweizerhof; Luzernerhof; Stadthof; Grand H. National—4 very large first-class houses; Englischerhof; Beau Rivage—all excellent. Schwan; H. St. Gothard, at the Rly. Stat., and H. du Lac, near the Stat., both good; Schweizerhaus, outside the town; H. de l'Europe, on lake, out of town—Bus from stat., fine view, and comfortable; H. du Rigi; moderate charges. In the old part of the town, Balances, Rössli, Engel, Krone.

Pensions—Neu-Schweizerhaus, Morel, Seeburg (Müller)—on the Küssnacht road; Suter, Victoria and Wallis, the highest—on the Gütsch; Château Stutz (2 m.), a lovely spot; Belvedere; Sonnenberg, 1 hr, 1000 ft. above the lake. All good. In 1868 Q. Victoria occupied P. Wallis.

Eng. Ch. S. in the Germ. Protestant Ch. Scotch Free Ch., service in the Maria Hilf Church.

Lucerne, chief town of the canton, lies at the lower end of the lake of Lucerne, and is divided into two parts by the river Reuss. Its population is 17,921, nearly all Rom. Cath. The town and convent were granted by Pepin in 768 to the abbots of Murbach in Elsass. In 1291 an abbot sold his rights to the Emperor Rudolf of Austria. In 1332 Lucerne joined the Forest Cantons as the fourth member of the Confederation (see *Introd.*)

It is not a place of any considerable trade or manufacture, but their absence is more than compensated by the beautiful scenery in which it is situated, on the shore of the finest and

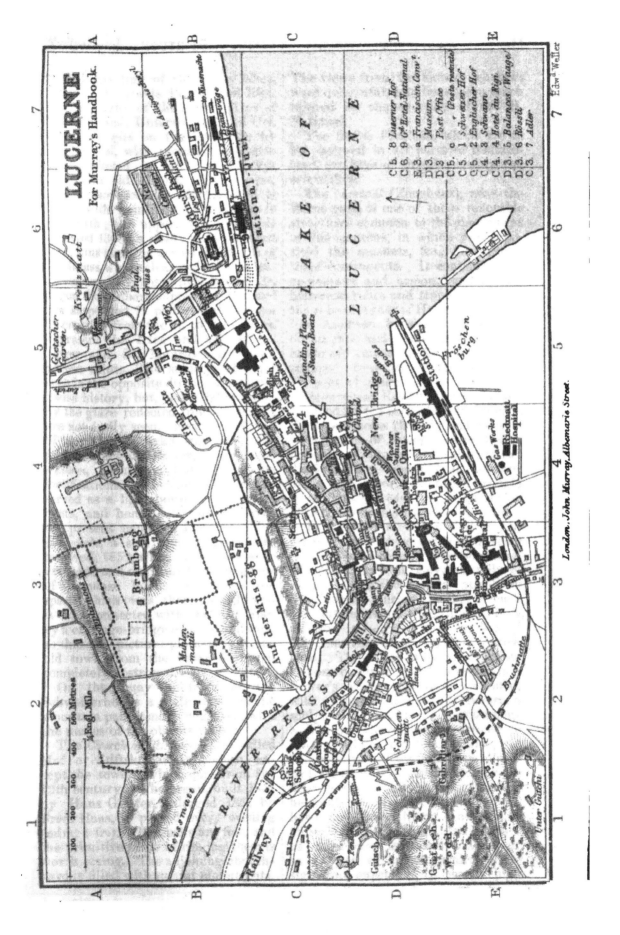

LUCERNE.

For Murray's Handbook.

LAKE OF LUCERNE

C.5. 8 Luzerner Hof
C.6. 9 Gd Hotel National.
E.3. a Franciscan Convt.
D.3. b Museum
D.5. Post Office
C.5. c (Posta restante)
C.5. 1 Schwaner Hof
C.5. 2 Englischer Hof
C.4. 3 Schwann
C.4. 4 Hotel du Rigi.
D.3. 5 Balances / Waage
D.3. 6 Rössli
C.3. 7 Adler

London, John Murray, Albemarle Street.

Edwd Weller

most interesting of the Swiss lakes, between the giants Pilatus and Rigi, and in sight of the snowy Alps of the Oberland, Unterwalden, and Uri. It is still girt on the land side by a long *wall*, with picturesque *watch-towers*, erected in 1385; and it has 2 curious old *bridges*. The lowest, the *Spreuerbrücke*, or *Mühlenbrücke*, is hung with paintings of the Dance of Death; the upper, or *Capellbrücke* (erected 1303), a shady walk on a hot day, runs slanting across the mouth of the Reuss, whose clear and pellucid sea-green waters glide swiftly beneath it. From the timbers supporting the roof are suspended 77 pictures; those seen in crossing from the rt. to the l. bank represent the lives and acts of St. Leger and St. Maurice, Lucerne's patron saints. The subjects of those seen in the opposite direction are from Swiss history, but, being lighted only by the glare reflected from the water, are not easily seen. Near the W. end of the Capellbrücke stands a very picturesque watch-tower, called *Wasserthurm*, forming a link of the old fortifications. It is said to have once served as a light-house (*Lucerna*) to boats, and hence some have derived the present name of Lucerne. The *Hofbrücke*, a still longer bridge, was removed, 1852, when the shores were extended and embanked. A long row of immense hotels stands on the space which was then gained, and is now connected with the Rly. Stat. by a carriage-bridge of stone and iron, so that the picturesque aspect of the old town from the water has been completely destroyed.

On the quay in front of the Schweizerhof is a plate on which the mountain panorama is engraved, with the names of the objects visible.

The *Church of St. Leger*, also called Hof or Stiftskirche, is modern, except the towers, which date from the 12th century. The organ, built 1651 by Hans Geister, enlarged 1862 by Fred. Haas, is played every evening (adm. 1 fr.). The bells are fine, and the primitive mode of ringing them is worth seeing. The adjoining church-yard is filled with quaint monuments.

The views from the cloister windows were delightful, but have been much injured by the erection of the H. National.

The *Gothic Fountains*, which are to be observed in all parts of Switzerland, are here of singular beauty and originality.

The *Arsenal* (Zeughaus), near the Berne gate, is one of those venerable structures common to the chief towns of the cantons, in which are deposited the muskets, &c., for arming their contingents. It contains some cross-bows and armour, and several historical relics and trophies, such as the robe of Agnes of Hungary, the yellow Austrian banner, and pennons of knights and nobles, taken at the battle of Sempach; the coat of mail stripped from the body of Duke Leopold of Austria, who fell there; the iron cravat, lined with sharp spikes, destined for the neck of Gundoldingen, the Schultheiss (bailiff) and general of the men of Lucerne, who died in the hour of victory. Here also are two Turkish flags captured at Lepanto, and a long Moorish standard brought from Tunis, 1640, by a knight of Malta, who was a native of Lucerne.

The most interesting *sight* of Lucerne is the **Monument to the memory of the Swiss Guards* (*Löwendenkmal*), who defended the Royal Family of France from the popular attack on the Tuileries during the first French Revolution, August 10, 1792. It is situated in a garden, $\frac{1}{4}$ m. behind the Luzerner Hof, on the Zürich road. The design is by Thorwaldsen (whose original model is shown in a carver's shop opposite), executed, with a slight variation, by Ahorn, a sculptor of Constance. It represents a lion of colossal size, wounded to death, with a spear in his side, yet endeavouring in his last gasp to protect from injury a shield bearing the fleur-de-lys of the Bourbons, which he holds in his paws. The figure, hewn out of the living sandstone, is 28 ft. long and 18 high, and whether as a tribute to fallen valour, or as a work of art of admirable design and execution, it merits high praise. Beneath it are carved the names of the officers who fell in defending the Tuileries, Aug. 10 and on Sept. 2 and 3, 1792. The rock is mantled with fern and creepers, forming a natural framework to the monument ; and a streamlet of clear water, trickling down, is received into a basin-shaped pool, in which the sculpture is reflected. One of the few survivors of the Swiss Guard long acted as guardian of the monument. The cloth for the altar of the little chapel adjoining was embroidered expressly for it by the late Duchess d'Angoulême. Close to the garden is

Stauffer's collection of Swiss birds and quadrupeds, well set up and grouped, full of life and spirit, and probably, after that of Berne, the most complete collection of the kind in Switzerland : charge, 1 fr. each person. There are several specimens of the *Steinbock*, now extinct in the Swiss Alps. Among the birds are the *Lämmergeier*, or great vulture ; the *Alpenrabe*, or raven of the Alps, and the *Mauerläufer*, or rock-creeper.

Gletscher Garten. Near the Lion Monument, and well worth a visit (1 fr.). Here were found (1872–5) by the accidental baring of the hillside, within an area of 60 yards, 16 *pot-holes*, such as are formed in the rock beds of rapid rivers and underneath glaciers by streams twirling round stones in their vortex. One of these rock basins is 18 ft. deep and 27 feet in diameter, and the actual round stone which by their revolutions drilled the holes in the rock, still remains, affording proof of the existence of glaciers on this spot in a former age of the globe. " The native rock is sandstone, the circular stones limestone."—*F. W.*

Similar cavities in the rock, called Giant's Pots (Strudellöcher), formed by the action of stones washed by water, occur in the Jura and in Scandinavia. A small collection of lacustrine remains, found at Baldegg in 1873, are also exhibited. A model in relief of a part of Switzerland, by Gen. Pfyffer, is also shown here.

Meyer's Diorama is on the way to the Lion.

Physicians : Dr. Otto Stecker, 315 Kapell Platz, highly spoken of ; Dr. Steierlin—both have studied in England ; Dr. Steiger, Dr. Nager : all these speak English.

Pharmacie Anglaise, Place de la Chapelle ; Stierlin, Zürcher-strasse.

A handsome *Casino* and *Café* near the Hôtel National.

Turkish Bath in the Zürcher-strasse.

Post and *Telegraph-office*, behind the Englischer Hof.

There are many pretty *walks* and *points of view* near Lucerne ; one of the most interesting of the latter is the

Drei Linden (Three Lime-trees) on a natural terrace, ¼ hr. above the ch. Go through the ch.-yard. Another is the villa *Allenwinden*, perched on the hill outside the Weggis gate, from which it may be reached in 15 minutes, by a path winding up outside the town wall. The *Gütsch*, close to the town (tramway 2 min.), and *Gibraltar*, both on the S. side of the Reuss, also command a fine prospect. A point 50 minutes' walk E. from the town, called "The Little Rigi," is also recommended.

At *Kriens*, 3 m. S.W., are ironworks, and a silk factory. The castle of *Schauensee* crowns a hill behind it.

There are three lines of *Steamers* on the lake.—1. To *Flüelen*, calling at the villages on the way, including *Vitznau*, the starting-place of the Rigi Rly. ; 2. To *Küssnacht*, corresponding with a diligence to Immensee ; 3. To *Stanzstadt* for Engelberg, and *Alpnachgestad* for the Brünig. They start from the pier in front of the principal hotels. (See local timetables.)

Railways to *Bâle*, *Berne*, by *Langnau*, *Zug*, *Zürich*, and *Schaffhausen*, and to *Italy* viâ the *St. Gothard*.

The Rigi may be visited on the way to Flüelen, see Rte. 16.

Ascent of Pilatus, see Rte. 17.

Routes from *Lucerne to the Oberland*: —*a.* direct, by the Brünig Pass: *b.* circuitous, by Engelberg and Joch Pass (2-horse carr. Stanzstad to Engelberg 11 fr.: 2-horse carr. 20 fr.): *c.* leave

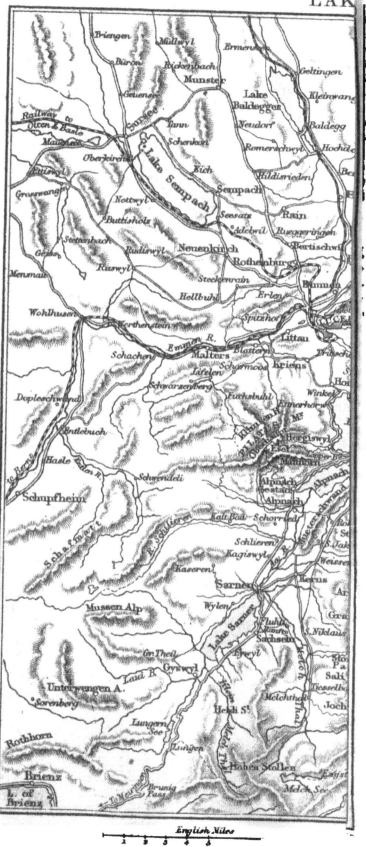

English Miles

1 2 3 4 5

Lucerne by 6 A.M. boat, breakfast
at Altdorf, and by Surenen Pass to
Engelberg: *d.* breakfast at Sarnen
and by Storegg Pass or Jöchli Pass
to Engelberg; or by the Melchthal
to Engstlen: *e.* by Wasen and the
Susten Pass.

No one should leave Lucerne without exploring its *Lake*, called in
German *Vierwaldstätter See*, Lake of
the 4 Forest-Cantons. It is one of
the noblest in Europe, and the mountain scenery at the farther end of it,
called the bay of Uri, is unrivalled
in any other alpine lake. Much additional pleasure will be derived if
the traveller who understands German
will take Schiller's 'Wilhelm Tell' as
a pocket companion.

Steamers 7 times a day between
Lucerne and Flüelen (26 Eng. m.)
in 2 hrs. 40 min., express boats in 2
hrs. 15 min; 7 times a day to Stanzstad and Alpnach; 4 times to Küssnacht. *Fare*—1st class, 4 fr. 50, to
Flüelen. Return-ticket for 3 days,
6 fr. [Beware of the porters at the
landing-place; there is a printed
tariff for their services.]

Boats may be hired at all the ports
on the lake, and are convenient when
the steamer's time is not suitable. The
charges are fixed by tariff, which may
be seen at the inns, but the men expect a trinkgeld.

The *winds* on the lake are capricious
and variable, blowing at the same
time from opposite quarters in different parts of it, so that the boatmen
say that there is a new wind behind
every promontory. The most violent
is the S., or *Föhn*, which occasionally
rushes so furiously down the bay of
Uri as to prevent the progress of a
row-boat, and to render it difficult for
even a steamer to make headway.
During fine weather, in summer, the
N. wind blows on the bay of Uri from
10 A.M. to 3 or 4 P.M., when it dies
away, and is succeeded by the S. The
boatmen, in coming from Lucerne, en-
deavour to reach Flüelen before the
wind turns.

The *Lake of Lucerne*, or *of the Four
Forest Cantons* (Vierwaldstätter-See),

so called from the cantons Uri, Unterwalden, Schwyz, and Luzern, which
exclusively form its shores, is distinguished above every lake in Switzerland, and perhaps in Europe, by the
beauty and grandeur of its scenery.
It is also interesting historically. Its
shores are a classic region—the sanc-
tuary of liberty. On them occurred
those memorable events which gave
freedom to Switzerland, and here the
first Confederacy was formed.

The lake lies at a height of 1437 ft.
above the sea: it is of very irregular
shape, assuming, on the W., the form
of a cross. Its bays are navigated by
separate lines of steamers, and are
each named after some town or village:
thus the W. branch is properly the
lake of Lucerne; then come the
bays of Alpnach on the S., Küssnacht
on the N., Buochs, stretching E. and
W.; and lastly, the bay of Uri, running N. and S., entirely enclosed by
mountains.

Quitting Lucerne, the steamboat
soon arrives abreast of a promontory
on the l., called *Meggenhorn*, and
the handsome château of M. Hofer.
Here is a small island, the only one
in the lake. Thus far the shores of
the lake are undulating hills, dotted
with villas—a smiling scene to which
the dark ridge of Pilatus adds a feature
of grandeur. After doubling the cape
of the Meggenhorn, the bay of Küssnacht opens l., that of Alpnach rt.,
and the traveller finds himself in the
centre of the *Kreuztrichter*, the cross
or transept (so to call it) of the lake.
From this point Pilatus appears to
advantage, and, beyond, the three
peaks of the Wetterhörner appear
over the Brunig.

Looking up the bay of Küssnacht,
the castle of Neu Habsburg is seen
l. perched on a cliff; the mass of the
Rigi occupies the other side of the
bay. Its sides are girt with forest,
below which runs a fringe of
field and orchard; above, it is
clothed to its very summit with pastures, feeding a hundred flocks;—an
agreeable contrast to its neighbour
Pilatus. After passing the promontory of *Tanzenberg*, on which is *Her-*

tenstein, with charming pensions, and with its charming Mountain Hotel, the village of

* † *Weggis* (*Inns:* H. and P. Bellevue; H. du Lac; H. Post; 20 minutes above, Kuranstadt Regelbeck ; Lion d'Or), ½ hr. from Lucerne, appears in sight. Before the construction of the rly. it was the point from which the Rigi was generally ascended. On the opposite (S.) side of the lake are the precipices of the *Bürgenstock* (see p. 61) with its excellent hotel. They belong to Unterwalden, but the ledge of meadow at their base to Lucerne.

† *Vitznau* (*Inns:* H. Pfyffer; H. Rigibahn ; H. Rigi ; Restaurant at the station). Terminus of the Rigi Rly. (Rte. 16). Vitznau is connected with Weggis by carriage-road.

Two rocky headlands projecting from the Rigi on one side, and the Bürgenstock on the other — significantly called the Noses (Nasen) — appear from some points to close the lake ; but the strait between them is about 1 m. wide. When through these narrows, the noses seem to overlap each other, and the traveller enters, as it were, a new lake shut out by mountains from that which he has traversed. This oval basin is called the *Gulf of Buochs*, from the little village at the end of the W. bay, behind which rise the *Buochserhorn* and *Stanzerhorn*.

† *Buochs* (*Inn:* Kreuz), a small village burnt by the French in 1798. Carriages to Engelberg and to Stanz can be got here.

† *Bekenried* or *Beggenried* (*Inns:* Nidwalder Hof ; Sonne, good and clean ; Mond ; H. Unterwald), a pretty and popular watering-place, where the council of the 4 Forest cantons formerly held their meetings. Carriages may be hired here, and there is an omnibus daily through Buochs for *Stanz* (6 m.). It is a charming walk from Bekenried to the Seelisberg Hotel, 2½ hrs., by the bathing-place of *Schönegg*, 2 m., Em-

metten (a waterfall), and the Seelisbergersee. The road is fit for small 1 horse-carriages, 13 fr.

On the opposite shore, at the foot of the Rigi, nestles

† *Gersau* (*Inns:* H. Müller, large and good ; Hof. Gersau ; Sonne), which, with the strip of cultivated land behind it, formed, for four centuries, an independent state, undoubtedly the smallest in civilized Europe.

Its entire territory consisted of a slope leaning against the side of the mountain, produced probably by the earth washed down by two torrents. The whole extent of land cannot measure more than 3 m. by 2, which would make a very small *parish* in England ; scarcely an acre of it is level, but it is covered with orchards, and supports a population of about 2000.

It is recorded that the people of Gersau bought their freedom from a state of villenage in 1390, with a sum of 690 lbs. of pfennings, scraped together after 10 years of hard toil, to satisfy the Lords of Moos, citizens of Lucerne, whose serfs they had previously been. They maintained their independence apart from any canton, and were governed by a landammann and council, chosen from among themselves, until the French occupied Switzerland in 1798, since which they have been united with canton Schwyz. Though Gersau possessed a criminal jurisdiction of its own, together with a gallows long left standing, no instance of a capital execution occurred during the whole of its existence as a separate state.

There is something very pleasing in the aspect of Gersau on the margin of its quiet cove, shrouded in orchards and shut out from the rest of the world by precipices. Its broad - brimmed cottages are scattered among the fields and chestnut woods ; some perched on sloping lawns, so steep that they seem likely to slip into the lake. The village, facing the S. and well-sheltered, is so warm, that it has been called the Nice of Switzerland. The hotel is open all the winter,

* This mark (†) denotes a landing-place of the Steamers,

From Gersau to Flüelen a carriage-road has been made at an enormous expense. It is called the *Axenstrasse*, and is a wonderful piece of engineering. The views from it are very fine.

A path leads up the Rigi in 3 hrs. to the *Rigi Scheideck Hotel* (Rte. 16). To the rt. is the commanding point of the *Hochfluh* a climb of 3½ hrs. The chapel of *Kindlimord*, on the Brunnen road, commemorates the murder of a child by its father.

Gersau is reached in about 1¼ hr. from Lucerne. As soon as it is left behind, the bare peaks of the Mythen (Mitre) start into view,—the town of Schwyz is seen at their feet, 3 m. inland, and on the shore Brunnen.

The boat next calls at

† *Treib*, an old wooden boat-house, on the opposite shore, the pretty landing-place for

Hotel Sonnenberg (Curhaus and Pension, an immense establishment, *Eng. Ch. S.*), above the village of *Seelisberg*; carriage-road to the hotel (1-horse carr. 6 fr.), and a tolerable char-road from Bekenried. The house can also be reached by a foot-path of ¾ of an hour from Grütli. The hotel is about 1200 feet above the lake, beautifully situated on the brow of a precipice, under the *Niederbauen* or *Seelisberger Kulm* (6323 ft., 3 hrs.' ascent, practicable for ladies), and looks directly down on the blue waters of the Bay of Uri, across them to the Frohnalpstock, and up the lake to Flüelen and the conical Bristenstock. It is surrounded by woods.

[A charming walk, with view of the Uri Rothstock, leads to *Bauen*, on the lake, 1 hr.; whence a boat can be taken to Flüelen; or a path to Altdorf by Seedorf; or to *Isenthal*, 2¼ hrs. from Bauen, in the valley of Isenthal.

From Isenthal the *Schönegg Pass* (6652 ft., between the *Brisen*, N., and *Kaiserstock*, S.), leads in 3 hrs. to the Engelberg valley at Wolfenschiessen, 1¼ hr. from Stanz.

The *Uri Rothstock*, 9620 ft., may be ascended, or crossed to Engelberg from Sonnenberg, by sleeping at *Isenthal* (*Inn*: Adler, rough, kept by the guide Imfanger). The mountain is of limestone. 2 valleys run towards it from Isenthal, Grossthal, W., Kleinthal E.—so you can ascend by one and return by the other. The Grossthal gives the easiest access. The ice is reached in 4 hrs. from Isenthal; the summit, accessible only on the S. side, in 6 hrs. About 4 hrs. are required for the descent to Engelberg; 2 hrs. across the *Blümlisalpfirn*, a névé lying between the Uri and Engelberg Rothstock (9251 ft.); then down the Rothstock gl. to the head of the *Horbisthal*, leading to Engelberg.]

From Treib the boat crosses to Brunnen, opening the promontory of Treib, where the *Mythenstein* rises from the water, and the *Bay of Uri*, in all its grandeur, bursts into view.

†*Brunnen* (*Inns*: Waldstätterhof, very good; Goldener Adler; Rössli; Hirsch; P. Aufdermaur, recommended. There are many pensions here. P. Mythenstein is well situated. On the Brändli is H. Axenfels, and higher up H. Axenstein on the *Axenberg* (¼ hr. from Brunnen) with room for 300 guests, in a large park, commanding a fine view and highly recommended; *Eng. Ch. S.*). Brunnen is the port of canton Schwyz. Its position in reference to the scenery of the lake is most fortunate, commanding a view along two of the finest reaches. It was once an important mart for Italy, and its warehouse of early times still stands by the water-side. It is called *Sust*, and bears a rude painting of the three Confederates, commemorating the alliance which was formed on this spot between the Forest Cantons in 1315, after the battle of Morgarten. Aloys Reding here raised the standard of revolt against the French in 1798.

The *Stoss*, a spur of the Frohnalpstock, with a large *Hotel Pension*, 4200 ft. above the sea, 2¼ hrs. S.E., and the *Frohnalpstock*, 5787 ft., 1½ hr. S. of the Stoss, command magnificent views over the Alps of Glarus and Uri. On the higher grass slopes of the mountain are some dangerous holes. A steep path leads from the summit to Sisikon and the valley of Riemenstalden.

The *Gross Mythen* (6244 ft.) can be ascended in about 4 hours from Brunnen, 2¾ to the point called *Holz-egg* (a small *Inn*), whence it is 1¼ to the top (another *Inn*, kept by the proprietor of the Bellevue at Ricken-bach). The best path is by Ricken-bach, where horses and guides can be procured. No guide is needed. The bare sides of the Mythen were formerly covered with wood, which was destroyed by fire in the dry summer of 1800.

By the Axenstrasse it is 7 m. to *Tell's Chapel* (1-horse carriage 5 fr.). About 1 m. on the road the sweet-scented *cyclamen* (*Europæum*) grows abundantly in the month of July.

Diligences for Schwyz, Einsiedeln, and Goldau Station. Carriage to Flüelen, 2 hrs., 1-horse 6 fr., 2 horses 12 frs.

Opposite Brunnen, the lake changes at once its direction and character. Along the bay of Uri, or of Flüelen as it is sometimes called, it stretches nearly N. and S., and its borders are the buttresses of lofty mountains. On the E. runs an almost unbroken preci-pice of the grandest dimensions with twisted strata descending sheer to the water, here in places more than 1100 ft. deep. Until 1865 the E. side of the Bay of Uri was impassable. It was first invaded by the telegraphic wire, which ran from rock to rock, but it is now traversed by a magnificent road—the *Axenstrasse* (so named from the *Axen-berg*, 6830 ft.), which connects Brun-nen with Flüelen, a distance of about 8 m. It was commenced by the Swiss Government after the union of Savoy with France, when it was considered advisable to improve the communica-tion between the Cantons. Below the road, in a series of tunnels and em-bankments which somewhat impair the beauty of the once pathless shores, runs the railroad. To reach Flüelen from Brunnen or Schwyz it was formerly usual to make a long cir-cuit; but there was a difficult path

by Morschach, Sisikon, and Tellen-rüth to Altdorf, which was actually traversed by the French General Le-courbe, with his army, in pursuit of Suwarrow, in the night, by torchlight, 1799. The want of boats to carry his troops across the lake compelled him to attempt this daring exploit.

The steamer on leaving Brunnen passes rt. the headland of Treib, and then the *Mythenstein*, which bears this inscription to the bard of Tell's country:

"Dem Sänger Tells,
FRIEDRICH SCHILLER,
die Urkantone, 1860."

About a mile beyond, the preci-pices recede a little, leaving a ledge, formed by earth fallen from above, and sloping to the water. A few walnut and chestnut trees have here taken root, and the small space is occupied by a meadow conspicuous among the surrounding woods from the brightness of its verdure. This is *Grütli* or *Rütli*, the spot pointed out as the rendezvous of the 3 legendary founders of Swiss freedom,— *Werner Stauffacher*, of Steinen, in Schwyz; *Erni* (Arnold *ab der Halden*) of Melch-thal, in Unterwalden; and *Walter Fürst*, of Attinghausen, in Uri, who are reported to have met in the dead of night, on this secluded spot, on the 7th November, 1307, to form a plan for liberating their country. It is possible that consultations may have been held here, but the whole tale of the oath and the details are not sup-ported by evidence, and are due to the fancy of Tschudi and Johannes von Müller; the older authorities do not agree as to the members of the con-spiracy. The expulsion of the Aus-trian bailiffs in 1308 is now con-sidered to be a transfer to that year of similar events which had occurred 50 years before.

According to popular belief, the oath of the Grütli was followed by a miracle, and 3 springs gushed from the spot upon which the confede-rates had stood. In token of this every stranger is led to a little hut built over the sources, and is invited to drink from them to the memory of the founders of Swiss freedom. The Grütli was purchased in 1859 for the nation by a voluntary subscription, in order to save it from being turned into a tea-garden.

A small scar may be observed on the face of the opposite precipice of the Frohnalpstock, formed by the fall of a piece of rock. The fragment which has left such a trifling blemish was about 1200 ft. wide; when it fell it raised a wave which overwhelmed 5 houses of the village of Sisikon, distant 1 mile, and 9 of its inhabitants were drowned. The swell was felt at Lucerne, more than 20 miles off.

The steamer passes the hamlet of Sisikon, at the entrance of the valley of Riemenstalden, through which is a charming walk over a low col to Muotta, 5½ hrs.

On a shelf at the foot of the Axenberg, called the *Tellen-Platte*, on the margin of the water, and at times lapped by it, stands

TELL'S CHAPEL, a row of ¾ hr. from Grütli (*Inn:* H. Tellsplatte, 300 ft. above the lake, beautifully situated; small, but comfortable). Here, according to the story, Tell sprang on shore from the boat in which Gessler was carrying him a prisoner to Küssnacht (Rte. 18), when a sudden storm on the lake had compelled him to remove Tell's fetters, in order to avail himself of his skill as steersman. The building as it stood up to 1879 was obviously of much later date, but it is said that a chapel was built here by canton Uri in 1888 (first mentioned by Tschudi, who died in 1572), and in the firm belief of the country-people to the memory of the brave archer. The walls having given way, the chapel was rebuilt in 1879. The original form has been strictly preserved, and the walls decorated with frescoes from the story of Tell by the Swiss artist, Stuckelberg. Once a year, on the first Friday after the Ascension, mass is said and a sermon preached in the chapel, which is attended by the inhabitants on the shores of the lake, who repairing hither in boats, form an aquatic procession. The Tell legend is first found in the MS. preserved at Sarnen, and known from the colour of its binding as the 'Weisses Buch,' written between 1467 and 1476, and in a poem the 'Tellenlied,' written about 1474. See W. Vischer's 'Die Sage der Befreiung der Waldstätte,' 1867, Leipzig. The story was much improved by Tschudi of Glarus in the 16th cent. Doubts were already thrown upon it in the 18th cent.; but the legend was warmly taken up by Schiller the poet, and by Müller the historian, writing in 1808. Since that time a more critical spirit has arisen, and the old chronicles have been more closely studied. The result is that Tell has been banished from authentic history. Exactly similar legends, or sagas, of the 10th cent. are found in Norway and Denmark, and our Clym of the Clough shoots at an apple on his son's head—

" But Cloudeslè cleft the apple in two,
His son he did not nee."

10 min. beyond Tell's Chapel, on the Axenstrasse, is a long tunnel through the cliffs of the Axenberg, nearly 400 ft. above the lake, and with beautiful views through the side openings. Here the cretaceous strata of the precipices are marvellously contorted, and similar contortions appear on the other side of the lake. The depth of the lake, opposite Tell's chapel, is 800 ft. After rounding the cape on which it stands, Flüelen and the conical Bristenstock appear. On the W. shore are the Isenthal and snowy peaks of the *Uri Rothstock.* The steamer stops at the landing-place of the large H. Urnerhof, a few hundred yards before reaching

Flüelen (Inns: Urnerhof, large house on the lake, away from the village, best ; Krone ; Flüelerhof ; Kreuz ; Adler), the port of canton Uri ; it is 20 minutes from Tell's chapel. Here begins the carriage-road over the St. Gothard. (Rte. 34.)

Omnibuses to Altdorf, 1½ m.

Those who wish to ascend the *Uri Rothstock* may take a boat to Isleten, whence it is 5 m. to *Isenthal* (see p. 45).

ROUTE 16.

ASCENT OF THE RIGI TO RIGI KULM, KALTBAD, AND STAFFEL, BY RAILWAY FROM VITZNAU OR ART. PATHS FROM ART, GOLDAU, IMMENSEE, KÜSSNACHT, GERSAU.

The Rigi is a broad-backed steep-sided mountain-mass, about 9 to 10 m. in length by 3 to 4 m. in breadth, cut off from the neighbouring ranges by the lakes of Lucerne, Zug, and Lowerz, and the vale of Schwyz.

Its highest point (the Kulm) attains 5931 ft. above the sea. Other summits are the Rothstock, 5460 ft., the Staffel, 5229 ft., and the Scheideck, 5406. "The mountain is in great part composed of nagelflue, a conglomerate belonging to the miocene period, which has undergone violent disturbance since its original deposition. Near the Rigi Scheideck the strata are actually reversed—the cretaceous and eocene rocks overlying the miocene conglomerate. The flora is not particularly rich."—*J. Ball.*

The classical derivations of the name from "Mons Rigidus" or "Regina Montium," are probably afterthoughts. The latter, however, can be traced back to the 15th centy., when Albert von Bonstetten, in one of the earliest works on Swiss geography, spoke of the Rigi as the centre, not only of the Swiss Confederation, but of Europe. The upper part of the mountain is a vast pasturage supporting 100 chalets, in summer, with 3000 cows. In very early times a certain sanctity was attributed to this upper region, and holy hermits are said to have retired there, whose songs of praise to the Deity often reached the herdsmen's ears. In 1689, a chapel, dedicated to Our Lady of the Snow, was built (Maria zum Schnee). It soon became a place of pilgrimage; and homely inns suited to the pilgrims' needs grew up round the shrine. After a time, it was found that the efficacy of the pilgrimage in restoring health was much increased by a residence in the pure mountain air and on a mountain diet. The pilgrims gave place to patients, and a "cure de petit lait" was established.

The Napoleonic wars checked the growing taste for mountain travel. Immediately on the restoration of peace, tourists of all nations, English in particular, flocked to the Alps. One of the first signs of the times was the erection of a small inn on the Rigi-Kulm, which was replaced in 1848 by a larger building. Somewhat later, Albert Smith made "the Rigi" a household word in England, and in the last twenty years the number of visitors to the mountain has increased enormously, and facilities for making the ascent, unknown elsewhere, have been provided. The 9 mule and footpaths which converge from every direction on the Kulm, have been supplemented by two railways, while a third line follows the crest from the Kaltbad to the R. Scheideck. In the summer of 1872, nearly 87,000 tickets were distributed by the Vitznau line alone.

Large hotels and pensions, containing, in all, lodging for 3000 guests, have been built on the upper part of the mountain. A considerable number of persons reside in the lower hotels for health, but the majority of visitors to the Kulm are attracted by the celebrated panorama seen from the top.

Comparisons or estimates of mountain views, which depend largely for their beauty on weather and light, can rarely be made with profit. It may be possible, however, to point out the reasons which have given the Rigi its peculiar celebrity. Many mountains share its position on the verge of the lowlands and the Alpine region, and from not a few summits of equal elevation, the snowy range presents itself in a more imposing aspect. But it would be difficult to select a mountain so completely isolated and commanding so varied a prospect over the lakes which lie at the feet of the great range, from which so large a proportion of the horizon is fringed with glacier-clad summits. These do not equal in apparent height the rampart which impends over Piedmont; no single mass rivals in graceful majesty Monte Rosa from Monte Generoso; nor can the atmosphere of Central Switzerland compare with that which transfigures Italian hills. But if less romantic, the Swiss view possesses charms of its own in the brilliant verdure of the foreground, the immediate contrast between the rich plain and the shining lakes on the one hand and the stern mountains of Uri on the other, and the admirable combinations into which the panorama divides and arranges itself.

By most visitors the view will be best enjoyed on some other part of the mountain than the actual "Kulm," where the natural features of a mountain top are dwarfed and distorted by two huge and ugly edifices. Nor, however conducive it may be to other forms of enthusiasm, does a crowd generally prove agreeable to the lover of mountains. The summit of the Rigi is often occupied by several hundred, and seldom by fewer than fifty visitors.

So long, however, as a thousand Alps lie open to the ordinary traveller, it is, perhaps, ungenerous to grudge the sacrifice of a single mountain to the infirm, the hurried, and the indolent. Nor can even the elbowing and noisy crowd, the bands of itinerant musicians, the sound and flying of champagne corks, the din and bustle of railways, the smell of petroleum gas, and the many other distracting or stupefying elements of the scene, altogether take away the natural charms of this beautiful mountain. If the actual Kulm has been hopelessly vulgarized there remain quiet nooks

[*Switz.*]

among the pine-forests, grassy knolls overlooking the still depths of the lakes, where the traveller may remind himself of the days when the Rigi was the home of herdsmen, and the haunt of but a few eccentric tourists.

Owing to the uncertainty of the atmosphere at high elevations, travellers should prepare themselves for disappointment, since the trouble of an ascent is often repaid with clouds and impenetrable mist, instead of a fine sunrise and extensive prospect.

The Rigi Railways.

The rlys. are now used by the majority of travellers, and they are therefore described here first. There are three lines on the mountain (see map, p. 43):—

i. From Vitznau to the Kulm, 1½ hr., 7 fr.

ii. From Art to the Kulm, 1½ hr., 8 fr.

iii. From the Kaltbad to the Scheideck, 7 fr.

Luggage over 10 lbs. is charged at the rate of 1 fr. per 100 lbs. Descent takes the same time, about half fare is charged. Trains are despatched on the arrival of every steamer, and frequently during the day. Travellers from Lucerne mostly take the Vitznau route, but for picturesque effect it is best to ascend from Art, descending to Vitznau. Circular tickets are issued at Zürich for the ascent of the mountain. In fine weather there are "sunrise" and "sunset" trains from the Klösterli to the Kulm.

The gradient over about one-third of the line is 1 in 4, *i.e.* for every 4 ft. of length the line rises 1 ft. This is exceedingly steep, much steeper, in fact, than would be practicable for horse-carriages on ordinary roads, and in this consists the extraordinary character of the railway. To ascend or descend such a gradient by ordinary

E

railway appliances would be impracticable; stationary engines and ropes would be difficult of application and highly dangerous, and it has therefore been necessary to adopt a system of propulsion which, though it was tried in the infancy of railways, has never been used in their practical development, namely, the rack and pinion. Two rails are laid down on the ordinary plan, and on a 4 ft. 8 in. gauge; between them is placed a continuous iron rack in the openings of which engage the teeth of a pinion or toothed wheel, worked by the locomotive, and the revolution of this wheel causes the ascent of the train.

The engine is made as light as possible, there being no necessity, as on ordinary railways, to procure adhesion by weight on the wheels. Those employed on the Vitznau line have little resemblance to an ordinary locomotive, the boiler being built so as to have a vertical position when on the steep gradient, so that it slopes considerably when standing at the stations. This mode of construction has been abandoned, as unnecessary, on the Art line. Each engine propels only one light carriage, holding about 50 passengers; when a greater number have to be conveyed, other engines are despatched at intervals, always pushing, not drawing, the carriage. The speed, both ascending and descending, is purposely kept very slow, not much exceeding 3 m. an hr.

The great point aimed at was to ensure safety, which, with such an extraordinarily steep gradient, was a difficult problem. It has, however, been carefully studied, and the ingenious arrangements made with this object are worth a short description. Collisions at such a slow speed are not to be feared: the dangers are of two other kinds. In order to provide against the engine or carriage getting off the rails, there are on both clips which embrace two projections on the middle or rack-rail; so that if the flanges of the wheels should run off their rails the vehicle cannot get away.

In order to obviate the more serious risk of the train becoming unmanageable and running down, it has been necessary to devise a scheme, which is most ingenious and perfectly effective. The carriage is provided on one of its axles with a cogged-wheel similar to the driving-wheel on the engine, and double-clip breaks, worked by powerful screws, are applied to drums fastened on this shaft; so that by screwing these tight a hold is obtained on the rack-rail, and the carriage is held up with great security. The locomotive is provided with a similar break on its free axle, while the driving-axle has a still more powerful break adapted to the shaft of the engine, so giving a double security in case of the accidental fracture of any part of the machinery. With these breaks the train, while running down at the slow speed adopted (not exceeding 4 m. an hr.), can be brought to a stand almost instantaneously, and firmly held in its place on the steepest part of the incline. Another very ingenious contrivance is also adopted in running down hill; the steam being entirely shut off, the pistons, worked by the motion of the train, are made to compress the air in the cylinders, and to drive it through an aperture capable of regulation; this acts as a break, and serves to regulate and control the speed. The rack is strongly formed in wrought iron, and the pinions working into it are of cast steel, these materials giving the best security against fracture.

As an additional precaution, the carriage, in ascending, is not coupled and dragged behind the engine as on ordinary railways, but is loose, and is pushed on in front. By this arrangement if anything should happen to the engine and it should run down, it need not take the carriage with it, as the latter can be stopped by its own break, and will remain where it is till help can be procured. In running down the carriage follows the engine by its own weight, and the same security is obtained.

Vitznau Railway (for steamers to Vitznau, see Rte. 15). The views over the lowlands are very fine, and seats on the l. hand should be looked for. This line was constructed as far as the Staffel in 1871, and to the Kulm in 1873. The first portion of the line is the steepest. Mounting behind the village, the train traverses the steep slope seen from the lake. After passing a tunnel, it crosses on a light iron *Viaduct* a ravine opening upon a precipice many hundred feet deep, commanding noble views of the lake and distant ranges.

Freiberg, a watering and passing station. The line is double hence to the Kulm.

Romiti-Felsenthor Stat.

RIGI KALTBAD STAT., 4698 ft. (3261 ft. above the Lake of Lucerne, and 2½ hrs. from Weggis, by mule-path).

The handsome, well-furnished *Hotel* affords accommodation for 140 guests; house well warmed; table-d'hôte and good cook; a healthy situation, with view down upon the lake and over the mountains, and sheltered from the N. and W. (breakfast at 8, dinner at 12, tea at 4, supper at 8). Reading-room. Baths and whey. Post to and from Lucerne daily. Rly. and Telegraph stat. Season from June to the middle of September. The society is chiefly German.

H. Bellevue, close to the stat., is a perfectly comfortable house and pension, with more moderate charges.

Walks to the Känzeli or Pulpit, fronting Pilatus (10 min.), and on to the Rothstock, the W. point of the mountain, 5460 ft. above the sea, grand sunset view, 1½ hr.; to the Kulm, 1 hr.; to Klösterli, ¾ hr.; to the Dossen over Vitznau, 1½ hr.; to Rigi Scheideck, 2 hrs.; to the Stalactite Caves on the road to Vitznau, 1 hr.; to Weggis, 1½ hr.; to Art, 2 hrs.

In the olden time it was the custom for patients at the Kaltbad to lie down in the bath with their clothes on, and afterwards to walk about in the sun until they dried on the back; but this method is no longer regarded as essential to effect a cure.

The spring is called the *Sisters' Fountain*, from a tradition that 3 fair sisters sought refuge here from the pursuit of a wicked and tyrannical Austrian bailiff, and spent the remainder of their days amidst the clefts of the rocks in the exercise of piety.

[Here the line to the Rigi Scheideck branches off.

Rigifirst Stat., with a large hotel. The line next runs along the N. slopes of the Schild, crossing again to its S. flank before reaching

Unterstellen Stat. A small pension on a shelf overhanging the Lake of Lucerne.

Rigi-Scheideck Stat. The hotel, 5405 ft., is a large establishment with fine public rooms, and a chapel for all creeds.]

Staffelhöhe Stat. The *Staffelhaus* (5229 ft.) is a very good and moderate *Inn*, with table-d'hôte twice a day for 300 to 400 persons, and sleeping accommodation to match. It is ½ an hour's walk below the Kulm, so that those who rest here must get up half an hour earlier next morning if they wish to catch the sunrise from the top.

Staffel Stat. Junction of Art and Vitznau rlys.

Kulm Stat. (see below).

Art Railway.

From *Art* (see Rte. 14), the train runs at a good pace to Oberart and Goldau, where the cog-wheel system begins. Traversing the remains of the Rossberg "bergfall" (Rte. 18), it ascends to

Kräbel watering station. The Kräbelwand is now overcome by an incline of 1 foot in 5, commanding fine views over Lowerz. The train then runs along the side of a ravine through rocks and woods to

Klösterli Stat., which takes its name from a small *hospice*, Klösterli, inhabited all the year by 3 or 4 Capuchin brothers, who do the duty of the adjoining church of Sta. Maria zum Schnee, being deputed by the fraternity at Art on this service. The church is surrounded by a group of inns and pensions, the best of which (the *Schwert* and *Sonne*) are sometimes resorted to by invalids, to drink goat's-whey. The situation is sheltered and without distant view.

The line continues to station Rigi-Staffel (see above), and then ascends steeply to the

Summit of the Rigi.

The *Kulm*, or culminating-point of the Rigi, is of some extent, destitute of trees, but covered with turf. A few feet from the top, at a height which exceeds that of the most elevated mountain in Britain, 5931 ft. above the sea-level, and 4478 ft. above the Lake of Lucerne, stand two vast inns, *H. Rigi Kulm* and *H. Regina*, offering every comfort, at prices not in excess of the hotels on the lake below. It is fair to remember that the constant pressure of a crowd of hungry and impatient guests must try to the very utmost the patience and activity of the entire household. Travellers not on foot should bring cloaks with them, as the cold is often intense; and the thermometer marking 76° in Lucerne at midday, has been 37° on the Rigi at sunset, and 31° at sunrise. The houses are warmed with stoves even in summer. In 1855 the landlord paid to the canton for a piece of ground on which the new building stands (96 ft. by 55 ft.), no less than 54,000 fr., or more than 2000*l*.

During the height of summer the Kulm inns are crammed to overflowing every evening; and sometimes it is not easy to procure beds, food, or even attention. In the evening the guests are collected at a table-d'hôte supper; after which most persons are glad to repair to rest. The inmate is roused about an hour before sunrise by the harsh sounds of a long wooden horn, which is played until every particle of sleep is dispelled.

Long before dawn an assemblage of many hundred persons is often collected on the Rigi Kulm, awaiting the sunrise. A faint light in the E., which gradually dims the flickering of the stars, is the first token of the morning; it soon becomes a streak of gold, and is reflected in a pale flush upon the snows of the Bernese Alps. Summit after summit suddenly catches a rich roseate hue; the dark space below is next illuminated; forests, lakes, hills, rivers, towns and villages, are gradually revealed, but look cold and indistinct until the red orb surmounts the horizon, and darts his beams across the landscape. The shadows are then rolled back, as it were, and in a few moments the whole scene is glowing in sunshine. The view is best seen during the quarter of an hour preceding and following the first appearance of the sun; after that, mists often begin to curl up and shroud parts of it from the eye.

The most striking portion of this wonderful panorama, which is said to extend over a circumference of 300 miles, is undoubtedly the lakes of Lucerne and Zug; the branching arms of the former extend in so many different directions as to bewilder one at first, and both lave the base of the mountain so closely that the spectator might fancy himself suspended in the air above them, as in a balloon, and think, by one step from the brow of the precipice, to plunge into them. The peculiar greenish-blue tint which sheets of water assume when seen from a height has also something exceedingly beautiful. Eight other lakes may be seen from the Rigi, but they are so small and distant as to "look like pools; some almost like water spilt upon the earth."

On the N. side the eye looks down into the lake of Zug, and the streets of Art; at the end of the lake upon the town of Zug, and behind it the spire of Kappel, where Zwingli, the Reformer, fell in battle. This is backed by the chain of the Albis, and through gaps in its ridge may be discerned a few of the houses of Zürich, and two little bits of its lake. Over the l. shoulder of the Rossberg a peep is obtained into the lake of Egeri, on whose shores the Swiss gained the victory of Morgarten. The N. horizon is bounded by the range of the Black Forest hills.

The prospect *on the W.* is more open and map-like. Close under the Rigi lie Tell's chapel, on the spot where he is said to have shot Gessler, and the village and bay of Küssnacht. Farther off, nearly the whole canton of Lucerne expands to view;—the Reuss winding through the midst of it. Lucerne, with its coronet of towers, is distinctly seen at the W. end of the lake; and beyond it the lake of Sempach, the scene of another triumph of Swiss valour. On the l. the gloomy Pilatus cuts the sky with its serrated ridge. The remainder of the W. horizon is occupied by the Jura.

On the S. the Rigi forms the foreground, and touching the opposite mountains of Unterwalden, only allows here and there a small portion of the lake of Lucerne to be seen. On this side the objects visible in succession, from rt. to l., are the lakes of Alpnach and Sarnen, buried in woods, by the side of which runs the road to the Brünig; the Stanzerhorn and Buochserhorn at the entrance of the Engelberg valley, and behind them the white chain of the high Alps of Berne, including the Wetterhorn, Jungfrau, Eiger, and Finsteraarhorn. Nearer are the Titlis (the highest peak in Unterwalden), Uri Rothstock, and the Bristenstock above Amsteg on the road of St. Gothard.

On the E. the Alpine chain continues to stretch along the horizon, and includes the pre-eminent peaks of the Tödi, on the border of the Grisons, of the Glärnisch, in Glarus, and of the Sentis, in Appenzell. In the middle distance, above the lake of Lowerz, lies the town of Schwyz, the cradle of Swiss freedom, backed by the two sharp peaks called, from their shape, the Mitre (Mythen). Above them peers the crest of the Glärnisch; and to the rt. is the opening of the Muotta Thal, famous for the bloody conflicts between Suwarrow and Massena, where armies manœuvred and fought on spots which before the shepherd and chamois hunter alone used to tread. Farther to the l. rises the Rossberg,—the nearest mountain neighbour of the Rigi. The whole scene of desolation caused by its fall (see Rte. 17); the chasm on the top, whence the ruin came; the course of the terrific avalanche of stones, diverging and spreading in its descent; the lake of Lowerz, partly filled up by it, and the pools formed in the valley by the stoppage of the watercourses, are at once displayed in a bird's-eye view.

The very distant bare peak seen above the top of the Rossberg is the Sentis in Canton Appenzell.

The Spectre of the Rigi is an atmospheric phenomenon not unfrequently observed on the tops of high mountains. It occurs when the cloudy vapours happen to rise perpendicularly from the valley beneath the mountain, on the side opposite to the sun, without enveloping the summit of the Rigi itself. Under these circumstances the shadows of the Rigi Kulm and of any person standing on the top are cast upon the wall of mist in greatly magnified proportions. The shadow is encircled by a halo, assuming the prismatic colours of the rainbow, and this sometimes doubled when the mist is thick.

Mule-paths up the Rigi.

These once-frequented paths are now little used. They are all broadly-marked horse-tracks, and can hardly be missed.

The tariff for horses had been a subject of local conflict before the establishment of railways. Ten francs up is a fair price for a horse ; a boy to show the way can be found for a couple of francs, but is scarcely needed by a traveller in the least accustomed to mountains.

Many travellers will prefer to walk down the mountain, and a few may wish to explore paths which the railways have restored to their primitive quiet. The principal routes to the top formerly in use are therefore given here.

a. Ascent from Goldau, or Art.

	hrs. min.		hrs. min.
Goldau, or Art		Staffel	0 45
Untere Dächli	1 0		
Maria zum		Kulm	0 40
Schnee	0 50		

Goldau (Rte. 18) may be reached from *Art* by rail (see above). It is generally preferred as a starting-point, and all things considered it is the better of the two, because the ascent from Art, before it joins the Goldau track, is steeper. There is an advantage in ascending the Rigi from this side, because the path runs along a deep gully in the mountain, the sides of which protect the traveller from the afternoon sun (a thing of importance), and shut out all view of the great Alpine chain until the Staffel is reached, so that surprise aids the effect of the glorious vision when it bursts upon the sight.

From Goldau the path strikes at once up the Rigi; at first across fields strewn with blocks from the Rossberg, which, by the force acquired in their descent of that mountain, were actually carried up the opposite slope.

A small public-house, called *Untere Dächli*, is a good point for surveying the fall of the Rossberg in the vale of Goldau. The long train of earth and rocks can be traced stretching across to the lake of Lowerz, a part of which it filled (see Rte. 18). The steep footpath from Art falls into our road. Here begin "the Stations," a series of 13 rude pictures fastened upon poles, each representing an event in our Lord's Passion, and leading to the pilgrimage ch. Mary-of-the-Snow. At the chapel of Malchus, which contains the Bearing of the Cross, the route from Lowerz falls in, and soon afterwards there is a steep short-cut rt. leading to the Kulm, but avoiding Maria zum Schnee and the Staffel. Pedestrians sometimes go that way, but the track is ill-marked and the ground so rough that it is

generally found to take more time than the regular path.

The ascent from *Art* is by a steep path which falls into that from Goldau in about an hour.

b. Ascent from Immensee.

This track is rather less steep, and about a mile longer, than that from Art or Goldau; but as it lies in great part along a projecting ridge or spur of the mountain, it is much exposed to the afternoon sun, and therefore hot. Those who have not dined at the inn at Immensee may find good bread, milk, butter, &c., at a neat chalet below the steeper part of the ascent. About half-way up, this joins the path from Küssnacht.

c. Ascent from Küssnacht.

Küssnacht is reached by steamer from Luoerne, and the ascent requires 3 hrs. to mount, 2½ to descend. It is by a horse-path, as long as that from Goldau, and in some places more steep. A toll is paid on this road for the animals. By a détour of ½ an hour, Tell's Chapel (see Rte. 18) may be visited in going or returning. Leaving Küssnacht and passing on the l. the ruins of Gessler's Castle (Rte. 18), the path is carried in zigzags up the steepest part of the mountain, then through forest, and across the pastures called Seeboden. The lake of Lucerne is in sight almost the whole way. The horse-path emerges on the brow of the hill in front of the Staffel inn, but a steep footway strikes off l. some distance below, and leads direct to the very top.

d. Ascent from Weggis.

Weggis.	hrs. min.		hrs. min.
Heiligkreuz	1 0	Staffel	0 40
Kaltbad	1 0	Kulm	0 40

It is best to *descend* from the Rigi top *to Weggis*, and there take the steamer.

Weggis is the spot where those who

approach the Rigi by water from Lucerne, and do not ascend by rly., land. The steamer to and from Lucerne and Flüelen touches here 6 times daily (¾ hr. from Lucerne). A carriageroad, winding round the foot of the mountain, connects Weggis with Küssnacht, and with Vitznau.

The horse-path up the Rigi from Weggis is steeper than the three preceding: 3½ hrs. up; 2½ down. It commences opposite the landing-place, and keeping to the rt. winds nearly on a level through orchards towards a wood, where the ascent properly begins; the path rising to the little chapel of *Heiligkreuz* (Holy Cross), a resting-place and point of view. The path then mounts by a kind of stair-way, and reaching a romantic hollow, is carried under a natural arch (called *Hochstein* or *Felsenthor*), formed by 2 detached blocks of nagelflue (pudding-stone), holding suspended a third. These fragments illustrate the tendency which this rock has to split, and to this cause may be attributed a torrent of mud, which, in the year 1795, descended upon Weggis. It advanced slowly, taking a fortnight to reach the lake, so that the inhabitants had time to remove out of its way. It is supposed to have been produced by springs, or rain-water, percolating the cracks of the nagelflue, and converting a layer of clay beneath it into mud. Had there been any great fracture in the nagelflue, it is probable that a large portion of the mountain would have given way and slipped down into the lake, since the strata of the Rigi slope at a very steep angle, and a catastrophe similar to that of the Rossberg might have ensued. As it was, the softened clay was squeezed out, and formed this deluge of mud, traces of which are still visible.

A little beyond the arch the track enters the region of pasture, turns l. or N., and at the point where a branch diverges to Klösterli, comes to the *Cold Bath* (kaltes Bad), where a source of very pure cold water, 41° Fahr., issuing out of the rock behind the inn, supplies the bathing establishment of *Rigi Kaltbad* (see above).

The path, after leaving the Kaltbad, ascends a rough pasture to the W. angle of the mountain, leaving on the left some projecting spurs, which furnish admirable points of view, in some respects superior to that from the summit. Then turning N.E. across a wooded steep, it reaches the *Staffel* (see above).

Whatever route may be chosen for the ascent, there can be no doubt that the descent should be made to Weggis. The varied and exquisite views of the Lake of Lucerne and the opposite ranges of Uri and Unterwalden are often found to leave a more permanent impression than the panorama from the summit.

e. *Ascent from Gersau.*
5½ hrs.

The ascent lies up a combe, through meadows and orchards, and by a cascade—the *Röhrlibach*—to the little inn of *Unter Gschwend* (1¼ hr.). After passing the chapel of St. Joseph, and taking care to keep to the l., a winding track leads up grassy slopes, in 1¾ hr., to the Rigi Scheideck (see above). From this hotel to Rigi Kulm is 2¼ hrs.

ROUTE 17.

ASCENT OF PILATUS, A. BY HERGISWYL, B. BY ALPNACH-GESTAD.

Pilatus has altogether 7 summits, exceedingly rugged and precipitous, viz.: from W. to E. the *Widderfeld*, 6747 ft. *Tomlishorn*, 6997, *Gemsmättli*, 6435, *Klimsenhorn*, 6555, and *Oberhaupt;* S. of this the *Esel*, 6962 ft., and *Matthorn*, 6675.

The mountain is in itself more interesting than the Rigi. The summit of the former is the highest point of an extensive down, the tops of Pilatus are true mountain-peaks, girt by imposing precipices. The view from Pilatus is unlike, and in some respects superior to, that from its rival. The various lakes arrange themselves less picturesquely in the panorama. On the other hand, the Oberland peaks are nearer and better seen, and the Lake of Lucerne displays its cruciform shape and many bays to greater advantage.

According to a wild tradition of considerable antiquity, this mountain, which down to the 15th cent. was known as 'Fractus Mons' or 'Frakmund,' derives its name from Pilate, the Roman governor of Judæa. Pilate, according to the legend, disgraced by the Emperor, committed suicide in prison at Rome. His body was cast into the Tiber. Storms and floods visited the city until the corpse was recovered, and sent off to Vienna in Gaul, where it was thrown into the Rhone. Here, however, the elements again broke loose. The body was removed to the Lake of Geneva, with a similar result, and finally to the little mountain-lake on the Mons Fractus, since known as Pilatus. Even here the wicked spirit could not rest from evil-doing. Storm and rain enveloped the mountain, the lake burst its banks, alps were ruined, and herds swept away. At last a travelling scholar confronted the ghost, and by his magic forced him to accept a pact by which, on condition of one day's freedom, he was to remain at rest for the remainder of the year. The bargain was kept. The land was at peace, but yearly on Good Friday the shepherd who approached the haunted tarn saw, seated on a throne of rock above the water, a terrible figure clad in the red robes of magistracy. Whoever beheld this vision died in the course of the year. The mountain, in consequence, laboured under a very bad reputation. From its position as an outlier, or advanced guard of the chain of the Alps, it collects the clouds which float over the plain from the W. and N.; and it is remarked that almost all the storms which burst upon the lake of Lucerne gather and brew on its summit. This frequent assemblage of clouds was attributed to the disturbance of the unquiet spirit by rash intruders. So prevalent was this superstition, that in 1337 six priests suffered several months' imprisonment for ascending the mountain. In 1518 four of the most enlightened men of the time obtained leave from the Government of Lucerne to ascend Pilatus. Strange to say, they returned to confirm the legend. It was not until 1555 that Conrad Gesner, the first naturalist of his day, ventured not only to climb the mountain but to dismiss its legend as an "Aberglaube." Thirty years later, the popular belief was still strong enough to give solemnity to the proceedings of the Stadtpfarrer of Lucerne, who, before a crowd of witnesses, flung stones and rubbish into the lake without raising anything more than a ripple.

According to some, the name Pilatus is only a corruption of *Pileatus* (capped), arising from the cap of clouds which rarely quits its barren brow, and which is sometimes seen rising from it like steam from a caldron. The peasants profess to be able to foretell the weather from the shape of these clouds and have a saying,—

> " Hat Pilatus seinen Hut
> Dann wird das Wetter gut.
> Trägt er aber einen Degen,
> So giebt's wohl sicher Regen."

" If Pilatus wears his hat, the weather will be good; but if he wears a sword (the long cloud called *stratus*), it will surely rain."

Pilate's lake is a mere pool, sometimes dry, on the Bründlen Alp, far from the beaten tracks. The way to it is by *Kriens* (3 m.); then up through forest 1½ hr. to *Hergottswald*, beautifully situated with a small *Inn*, and in 2½ hrs. more to the Bründlen Alp. Above the tarn on the Widderfeld, is a stone called *St. Dominik*, and on the cliff below it the cavern *Dominiksloch*. The crest of Pilatus is 1½ hr. from the lake.

The mountain consists entirely of nummulite limestone and sandstone; the strata incline to the S., and abound in fossils, especially near the summit. It is rich in rare plants.

Ascent by Hergiswyl.

This route should be preferred for the ascent by those who are equal to the short walk from the Klimsenhorn to the Esel.

The road to the Brünig (Rte. 19) passes by *Hergiswyl* (*Inn:* Rössli; horses for the ascent), to which place a little steamer runs twice every morning from Lucerne. At other times it can be reached by row-boat, in 2 hrs., or carriage in 1½. Horses may be procured. A bridle-path, made at an expense of 1000*l.*, leads up the mountain meadows and pasture, and by a series of steep zigzags, in 3½ hrs. to the Joch or Col, 6287 ft., connecting the Klimsenhorn with the Oberhaupt. Here is the

Hôtel of the Klimsenhorn—very comfortable. The *flora* of Pilatus is particularly interesting, and a lover of flowers might well spend some time here. Extensive view from the Klimsenhorn, 5 min. walk, and from the *Tomlishorn*, about 1 hr. distant from the inn. A well-made path leads upward to the foot of the *Oberhaupt* (30 min. walk), where it stops, for the ridge itself cannot be climbed. It is, however, bored through by a natural and nearly vertical fissure about 40 ft. deep, called the *Kriesiloch*, in which a commodious ladder, or rude staircase is placed. On emerging from this the whole range, hitherto hidden, of the Bernese mountains suddenly bursts upon the traveller. There are few more striking scenes in Switzerland. A descent of 5 min. leads to the *Bellevue Hotel*, about 6750 ft.,—a good house, visited in 1868 by Queen Victoria, who ascended from Alpnach. It stands on the depression between the *Oberhaupt* and the *Esel*. The latter summit is 5 min. above the hotel. Though not the highest peak of the mountain, it commands, owing to its advanced position, the most picturesque panorama, and is the most frequently visited. The face of Pilatus overhanging the lake and the ridge between the Tomlishorn and Oberhaupt are very precipitous, and

tourists are warned against attempting short cuts without the aid of a guide. The mountain has been the scene of several fatal accidents.

Ascent from Alpnach-gestad.

4 hrs. From *Alpnach-gestad* (Rte. 19) a mule-path leads by the Emsigen Alp to the Esel. It commands fine views of the lake. On all the routes a half-way shed offers refreshment to the tourist.

[A *Railroad* on the cog-wheel system is in construction from *Alpnach-gestad* to the Esel (1886).]

ROUTE 18.

LUCERNE TO SCHWYZ—THE ROSSBERG.

Lucerne.		Eng. m.
Küssnacht	. . . . .	7¼
Art	. . . . .	5¼
Goldau } Rail	. .	2
Lowerz }	. .	2
Schwyz }	. . . . .	4¼
		—
		21

A railway is in construction to Küssnacht, and there is also a road. The pleasantest way is to go by steamer to Küssnacht, carriage or omnibus to Immensee, steamer to Art, and then take a carriage or the Railway.

Steamers from Lucerne 4 times a day, in 55 min., to Küssnacht.

A good *post*-road to Schwyz.

The road to Küssnacht runs nearly all the way in sight of the lake of Lucerne, and of the Alps of Uri and Unterwalden. On a headland at the angle of the green bay of Küssnacht, stands *Neu-Habsburg*, a modern castle, adjoining a ruined stronghold of the Imperial family, destroyed, 1352, by the Lucerners.

Küssnacht (*Inns:* H. du Lac (See-hof) ; Adler), 3¼ hrs. from the top of the Rigi. The road to Immensee (2 m.) lies through the *Hollow Way*, and on rt. a ruined wall used to be pointed out by the name of *Gessler's Castle*. The *Hollow Way* (hohle Gasse) was a narrow green lane, between high, wooded banks, which have been partially destroyed in making the new road. This is the place where, according to the tale, Tell, after escaping from Gessler's boat on the lake of Lucerne, lay in wait for his enemy, and shot him as he passed, with his unerring arrow. It is somewhat unlucky that researches into the archives of Küssnacht have clearly proved that the ruin called Gessler's Castle never belonged to him.

Tell's Chapel is seen by the roadside. By a singular anomaly a place of worship, originally dedicated to "The Fourteen Helpers in Need" (Our Saviour, the Virgin, and Apostles), now commemorates a traditional deed of blood, which its supposed connection with the origin of Swiss liberty appears to have sanctified in the eyes of the people, so that mass is periodically said in it, while it is kept in constant repair, and bears on its outer wall a fresco representing Gessler's death.

†*Immensee Stat.* on rly. to Lucerne (*Inn* : H. Rigi, comfortable). The road turns off before it reaches this village, and both it and rly. (see 34 A) skirt the lake of Zug to

* *Art* (see Rte. 14).

Goldau Stat. (*Inn* ; Rössli (Cheval Blanc), good, but dear). The church contains a painting from memory of the Rossberg and of Goldau before its destruction. If it may be relied on, it would seem that the part of the ridge which fell was somewhat higher than the rest, and carried a crest. On the church door is a curious lock, with 5 bolts, said to have belonged to the former church, and to be 700 years old. One of the Railroads up the Rigi, starting from Art, begins the ascent at Goldau. (See Rte. 16.)

FALL OF THE ROSSBERG.

> "Mountains have fallen,
> Leaving a gap in the clouds, and with the shock
> Rocking their Alpine brethren ; filling up
> The ripe green valleys with destruction's splinters ;
> Damming the rivers with a sudden dash,
> Which crush'd the waters into mist, and made
> Their fountains find another channel—thus,
> Thus, in its old age, did Mount Rosenberg."
> *Byron.*

On approaching Goldau the traveller may perceive traces of the dreadful catastrophe which buried the original and much larger village of that name, and inundated the valley for a considerable distance with a deluge of stones and rubbish. The mountain which caused this calamity still remains scarred from top to bottom : and nothing grows upon its barren surface ; but in the course of years the valley itself has in many places become green, and the fallen rocks bear trees, lichens, and vegetation, and the great similarity to mountain valleys in general shows how often in past ages such catastrophes must have happened, though no record of them has been preserved.

The *Rossberg*, or Rufiberg, is a mountain 5190 ft. high ; the upper part of it consists of a conglomerate formed of rounded masses of other rocks cemented together, and called by the Germans Nagelflue, or Nail-rock, from the knobs and protuberances which its surface presents. From the nature of the structure this kind of rock is very liable to become cracked, and if rain-water or springs penetrate the fissures they will not fail to dissolve or moisten the beds of clay which separate the nagelflue from the strata below it, and cause large portions to detach themselves from the mass. The strata of the Rossberg are tilted up from the side of the lake of Zug, and slope down towards Goldau. The slanting direction of the seams which part the strata is well seen on the road from Art. Within the period of human record destructive land-slips had repeatedly fallen from the Rossberg, and a great part of the piles of earth, rock, and stones, which deform the face of the valley, derive their origin from such catastrophes of ancient date; but the most destructive of all appears to have been the last. The summer of 1806 had been very wet, and on the 1st and 2nd of Sept. the rain had been incessant. Towards 2 o'clock in the afternoon the face of the mountain began to move, and a mass estimated to be a league long, 1000 ft. broad, and 100 ft. thick, slipped down into the valley below, overwhelming the villages of Goldau, Busingen, and Rothen, and a part of Lowerz; the rich pasturages in the valley and on the slope of the mountain, entirely overwhelmed by it and ruined, were estimated to be worth 150,000*l.*; 111 houses, and more than 200 stables and chalets, were buried under the débris of rocks, which of themselves form hills several hundred feet high. More than 450 human beings perished, and whole herds of cattle were swept away. Five minutes sufficed to complete the work of destruction. The inhabitants of the neighbouring towns and villages were first roused by loud and grating sounds like thunder: they looked towards the spot from which it came, and beheld the valley shrouded in a cloud of dust; when it had cleared away, they found the face of nature changed. The houses of Goldau were literally crushed beneath the weight of superincumbent masses. Lowerz was overwhelmed by a torrent of mud. Such a mass of earth and stones rushed at once into the lake of Lowerz, although 5 m. distant, that one end of it was filled up, and a prodigious wave passing completely over the island of Schwanau, 70 feet above the usual level of the water, overwhelmed the opposite shore, and, as it returned, swept away into the lake many houses with their inhabitants. The village of Seewen, situated at the farther end, was inundated, and some houses washed away; and the flood carried live fish into the village of Steinen. The chapel of Olten, built of wood, was found half a league from the place it had previously occupied, and many large blocks of stone completely changed their position.

Those who desire a near view of the landslip should ascend the *Gnypenstock,* whose summit may be reached in 3 hours from Art. It is the W. point of the Rossberg: E. of it is the *Wildspitz,* the highest point, 5190 ft.; further E. the *Kaiserstock.*

The church and one of the inns at Goldau stand on the site of the village which was overwhelmed; its inhabitants, thus destroyed in the midst of security, are said to have been remarkable for the purity of their manners and their personal beauty. The church contains two tablets of black marble inscribed with the names of some of the sufferers, and with particulars of the sad event. The railway and road traverse the talus or débris, which extends from the top of the Rossberg far up the Rigi on the rt. They pass through hillocks of rubbish, calculated to be 30 feet deep hereabouts, but near the centre of the valley probably 200 feet, and winds among enormous blocks of stone now moss-grown, and with herbage springing up between them. These mounds and masses of rock enclose numerous pools, arising from springs dammed up by the fallen earth.

Lowerz (Inns: Rossli; Adler), standing on the margin of the *Lake of Lowerz,* round the S. shore of which the road is carried on an embankment, lost its church and several of its houses in the same catastrophe. The lake (length 2½ m.; breadth ¼ m.) was diminished by one-quarter in consequence of the avalanche of mud and rubbish which entered it, and its waters were thrown up in a wave 70 feet high to the opposite bank, so as to cover the picturesque island, and sweep away a small chapel which stood upon it.

[Near the village of Lowerz a footpath strikes up the Rigi, shorter than going round by Goldau for travellers approaching from Schwyz or Brunnen. In about 3 m. it falls into the path from Goldau (Rte. 16).

The Kulm may be reached by it in 3 hours by those who dislike the Rly.]

Seewen (*Inns:* Rössli, fair ; Kreuz), a village at the E. end of the lake, resorted to for its chalybeate springs and baths. A direct road to Brunnen turns to the rt. ; it is 1½ m. shorter than that by Schwyz, but not good.

Schwyz Stat. (*Inns:* Rössli, clean and reasonable ; Kreuz ; Hirsch, good ; H. Hediger ; Pension Jütz, 10 min. walk, comfortable, and prettily situated ; H. Bellevue at Rickenbach, 1 m., at the foot of the Mythen) is a mere village, though the chief place in the canton — "the heart's core of Helvetia"—from which comes the name Switzerland, and contains 6543 Inhab. (nearly all Roman Catholics), including the adjoining scattered houses and villages, which all belong to one parish. It lies picturesquely, about 3 m. from *Brunnen* (Rte. 15), its port on the lake of Lucerne, at the foot of the double-peaked *Mythen*.

Adjoining the *Parish Church*, a modern building, finished 1774, is a small Gothic chapel, called *Kerker* (prison), erected, according to tradition, at a time when admission to the church was denied the people by a ban of excommunication from the Pope. It was built in great haste, half of it within three days, and the mass was secretly administered within it.

In the *Cemetery* of the parish church is the grave of *Aloys Reding*, the patriotic leader of the Swiss against the French Republicans, in 1798. "Cujus nomen summa laus," says his epitaph.

The *Rathhaus*, a building of no great antiquity or beauty, in which the Council of the canton holds its sittings, is decorated with portraits of 43 Landammänner, and a carved ceiling. It contains a relief-map of the Rossberg landslip.

In the *Arsenal* are banners taken by the Schwyzers at Morgarten, and others borne by them in the battles of Laupen, Sempach, Kappel, and Morat; also a consecrated standard presented by Pope Julius II. to the Schwyzers.

The *Archiv* (record-office) is a tower of rough masonry several stories high, probably once a castle: its walls are remarkably thick, and enclose some gloomy dungeons.

Schwyz possesses a Capuchin convent, and a Dominican nunnery, founded 1287. A Jesuit convent, built 1847, on the hill, has never been occupied.

Model of the valley of Muotta, illustrating the French and Russian campaign, at M. Schindler's.

There are fine roads to *Sattel*, near the Egeri-See, and to Flüelen by Brunnen and the Axenstrasse. Up the Muotta Thal runs a carriage-road as far as Muotta, on the route of the Pragel Pass (Rte. 73).

The Schwyzers first appear in history in the 12th cent. The natives of this district quarrelled with the tenants of the monks of Einsiedeln about a right of pasturage. The Emperor, to whom an appeal was made, took the part of the monastery, and the indignant Schwyzers formed with their neighbours a league in defence of their ancient rights, which was the origin of the Swiss Confederation.

The name Swiss (Schwyzer) was first given to the inhabitants of the three original Forest cantons after the battle of Morgarten, their earliest victory, in which the men of Schwyz had prominently distinguished themselves, but did not form part of the formal style of the confederation till 1803.

At *Ibach*, a village on the Muotta (through which the road to Brunnen passes), may be seen the place where the Cantons-Lands-Gemeinde—consisting of all the men of the canton — formerly met in the open air to choose their magistrates, from the Landammann down to the lowest officer. Here they used to deliberate and vote on the affairs of the state, decide on peace or war, form alliances, or despatch embassies——a singular example of universal suffrage and the legislation of the masses. (See Rtes. 34 and 72.) The business was opened by prayer, and by the whole assembly kneeling, and taking an oath faithfully to discharge their legislative duties. Since 1833, the General Assemblies of the canton have been held every second year at Rothenthurm, on the road to Einsiedeln. At present the meeting of the local assembly of the 'Kreis-Gemeinden' only is held here.

The *Gross Mythen*, 6244 ft., and *Klein Mythen*, 5955 ft., of pyramidal form and separated by a cleft, are so named from their fancied resemblance in shape to a *Mitre*. The highest point, on which is a small *Inn*, is reached by a good path in about 3 hrs. from Schwyz. In the view the Uri Rothstock, being the nearest of the great Alps, is the most conspicuous. The Klein Mythen flanks the summit of the *Hacken Pass*, a short cut to Einsiedeln in 4 hrs.

ROUTE 19.

THE PASS OF THE BRÜNIG.—LUCERNE TO MEIRINGEN OR BRIENZ.

	Eng. m.
Hergiswyl (by road)	5
Gstaad	5
Alpnach	1
Sarnen	3¼
Sachseln	2
Lungern	8¼
Top of Brünig Pass	3¼
Meiringen	6
[or Brienz	7]

A carriage-road was opened 1861, across the Brünig Pass to Meiringen, Brienz, or Interlaken, traversed by open public carriages twice daily in each direction.

There is a carriage-road from Lucerne to *Gstaad*, passing through *Winkel* and *Hergiswyl*, also traversed by diligences. Most persons prefer going by steamer as far as Gstaad, and there taking the diligence or hiring a carriage. Diligence fares, from 8·50 fr. Carriage from Gstaad to Brienz, one horse, 20 fr.; 2 horses, 32 fr. In the season there are plenty of carriages waiting to be hired.

Steamer to Alpnach-Gstaad in 1 hr., 7 times daily. Diligence on to Brienz in 6 hrs., to Meiringen in 5½ hrs. Passengers booked through on board the steamer, or at the post-office (next door to the Englischer-hof), Lucerne. Leaving Lucerne in the morning, Brienz is reached in about 7 hrs., in time for steamer to Interlaken, and thence by steamer and rly. to Berne.

The steamer touches at Hergiswyl station for Pilatus (see Rte. 17).

Stanzstad (*Inns:* Freihof; Winkelried; Rössli), a small village under the *Bürgenstock*, on the margin of the lake, with beautiful view of Pilatus. It is the usual starting-point for Engelberg, and distinguished by its picturesque watch-tower, 5 centuries old. In 1315, a little before the battle of Morgarten, a vessel laden with Austrian partisans was crushed and swamped by a millstone hurled from the top of this tower.

The beautifully situated and well-managed *Hôtel - Pension Bürgenstock*, 2772 ft. above the sea, 1335 ft. above the lake, is an up-hill drive of about 1½ hr. by a good carriage-road. Ascent of Stanzerhorn and Buochserhorn (see below). *Omnibuses* to Bekenried and Engelberg, both passing through Stanz (Rte. 31).

The boat next passes through a strait between the village of Stanzstad and the spur of Pilatus called *Lopper*, into the beautiful and retired gulf of the lake of the Four Cantons, known as the Lake of Alpnach. An embankment has been thrown across the opening, with a bridge (Achen-brücke) in the centre, which is raised to let the steamer pass.

On the opposite, or E. shore of the Alpnach lake, is seen the *castle of Rotzberg*, said to have been taken by the Swiss confederates on New-year's Day, 1308. The story is that one of the party, the accepted lover of a damsel within the castle, being, according to the practice of Swiss lovers even at the present time, admitted by a ladder of ropes to a midnight interview with his mistress, succeeded in introducing, in the same way, 20 of his companions, who found no difficulty in surprising the garrison. The loves of Jägeli and Anneli have, from that day forth, been celebrated in Swiss song.

The boat touches at *Rotzloch*, which has a *Pension*, with baths, belonging to Herr Blättler, and then proceeds to

Gstaad, or *Alpnach - am - Gstaad*, 11 m. by road from Lucerne, at the S. end of the bay, the port for the Brünig. The name *Gstaad* or *Staad* signifies a landing-place (*Inns* : Pilatus, good, kept by the owner of the inns on Pilatus, horses and porters at fixed tariff ; Stern ; Rössli). Path to Pilatus, see Rte. 17.

Alpnach (*Inns* : Schlüssel ; Sonne), a scattered village of 1600 Inhab. at the foot of Pilatus. The extensive forests which clothe the sides of the mountain belong, for the most part, to Alpnach, and would be a source of wealth to its inhabitants if they could be got at more easily. It was with a view of turning to account the fine timber, that the *Slide of Alpnach* was constructed. This was a trough of wood formed of nearly 30,000 trees, fastened together lengthwise, 5 or 6 ft. wide at the top, and 3 or 4 ft. deep, extending from a height of 2500 ft. to the water's edge. It was planned by an engineer from Würtemberg, named Rupp. The course of this inclined plane was in some places circuitous; it was supported partly on uprights; and thus was carried over 3 deep ravines, and in two instances passed underground. Its average declivity did not exceed 1 foot in 17, yet this sufficed to discharge a tree 100 ft. long and 4 ft. in diameter, in the short space of 6 minutes, from the upper end of the trough into the lake below, a distance exceeding 8 m. The trees were previously barked, and rudely dressed with the axe. The bottom of the trough was kept wet by a rill of water trickling down it, and thereby diminishing the friction. Professor Playfair, who wrote a most interesting account of the slide, says

that the trees shot downwards with the rapidity of lightning, and a noise like thunder. Though the utmost care was taken to remove every obstacle, it sometimes happened that a tree stuck by the way, or, being arrested suddenly in its progress, leaped or bolted from the trough with a force capable of cutting the trees growing at the side short off, and of dashing the log itself to atoms. To prevent such accidents, watchmen were stationed at regular distances along the sides during the operation of discharging the wood, and a line of signals, similar to those in use on modern railways, were established, showing when anything went wrong. The timber was collected on the lake and floated down the Reuss into the Rhine, where it was formed into rafts, and sold in Holland. Napoleon had contracted for the greater part of it, to supply his dockyards; but the peace of 1815, by diminishing this demand, rendered the speculation unprofitable, and the slide, having been abandoned, was taken down in 1819. Similar slides, nearly as long, are common throughout the great forests of Tyrol and Styria.

The *Ch. of Alpnach*, with a slender spire, was built with timber brought down by the slide.

The road ascends the valley along the left bank of the Aa to

Sarnen (*Inns* : Goldener Adler, Obwalderhof, both fair ; Schlüssel ; Sarnerhof). This village, of 4903 Inhab., is the capital of the division of the canton called Obwalden, and the seat of the Government. It is pleasingly situated at the end of the lake of Sarnen, at the foot of an eminence called *Landenberg*. No vestige of the castle said to have stood on it now remains: the terrace which marks its site, and commands a most beautiful view, has since 1647 served for the annual *Landesgemeinde*, or convocation of the men of the canton, who meet to elect their magistrates. Adjoining it is the public shooting-house. The upper half of the village was burnt some years ago. The lower half is ancient; and there is a bridge across the river nearly 300 years old.

The *Rathhaus* contains, in its council chamber, portraits of the landammänner from 1381 to 1824. There is one picture, better than the rest, of Nicolas von der Flüh, a patriot, and at the same time a peace-maker, having spent his life in allaying the dissensions between the cities and mountain cantons, which in 1481, after the war with Charles the Bold, threatened the destruction of the Confederation. After an active life, in which he acquired fame as a soldier in the field, and an adviser in council, at 50 years of age, he retired into the remote valley of Melchthal, where, at Flühli, he passed his time as a hermit in a humble cell, in exercises of piety. His reputation, however, for wisdom as well as virtue, was so high that the counsellors of the confederacy flocked to him in his solitude to seek advice, and his sudden appearance before the Diet at Stanz and his conciliating influence prevented the dissolution of the confederacy. After enjoying the respect of men during his lifetime, he was honoured after his death (1487) as a saint.

In the archives here preserved is the famous 'Weisses Buch,' which (reproduced in Etterlin's Chronicle in 1507) is the earliest document (written 1467 and 1476) wherein the legendary history of the origin of the Swiss Confederation is found.

The valley of Sarnen, rich in orchards, and bounded by gently sloping hills, is quiet and pleasing.

[The path by the Melchthal to Engstlen, and the Storegg and Jöchli passes to Engelberg are described in Rte. 20.]

The road skirting the E. shore of the Lake of Sarnen traverses the pretty village of

Sachseln (*Inns*: Kreuz, good ; Engel, comfortable). In this neighbourhood lived *Nicolas von der Flüe*, during the first 50 years of his life, cultivating his paternal acres. His farm was situated under a precipice, whence his sobriquet *von der Flüe* (of the Rock); his real name was Löwenbrugger. Within the *Church*, his remains are preserved. His bones lie, but do not repose, in a glass case above the high altar, the shutters of which are opened for travellers, and are also withdrawn at stated seasons to exhibit the relics to crowds of pilgrims. Within the ribs, where the heart was, there is now a jewelled cross, and from the breast hang several military orders gained by natives of Unterwalden in military service, but offered up to the use of the dead saint, who is known to the peasants by the name of *Bruder Klaus*. There is a wooden figure in the transept, clothed with the saint's veritable robes. The walls are lined, by devotees, with votive tablets to St. Nicolas, recording miracles supposed to have been performed by him.

[From Sachseln it is an agreeable variety to go through the Klein Melchthal to a col whence the *Hohenstollen* can be easily ascended, and down the other side to the Melchsee, and so to Engstlen ; 10 to 11 hrs.]

The village *Gyswyl*, about 4 m. from Sachseln, was half swept away in 1629 by the torrent Lauibach, which brought so much rubbish into the valley as to dam up the waters of the Aa. A lake, thus created, lasted for 130 years, when it was let off by an artificial canal into the lake of Sarnen.

[The summit of the *Brienzer Rothhorn* (7917 ft.), just over Brienz, and celebrated for its view, may be reached in 6 hours from Gyswyl; the path, at least for the first 3 hours, is good; the descent on the other side into the Emmenthal above Sörenberg is not so good (see Rte. 25E).]

The steep ascent of the *Kaiserstuhl* has to be surmounted before the road reaches a higher platform in the valley occupied by the *Lake of Lungern*. This was formerly a beautiful sheet of water, embowered in wood, but the dwellers on its shores, less influenced by the picturesque than by the prospect of acquiring 500 acres of good land, tapped it in 1839, lowering its surface about 120 feet, and reducing it by nearly one-half. The cost of this enterprise was about 2000*l.* and 19,000 days' labour performed by the peasants. The old limits of the lake can still be distinguished, and the mouth of the tunnel is visible from the road.

The bare *Wylerhorn* (6520 ft.) towers above the plain beyond the head of the lake.

Lungern (*Inns:* Lion d'Or; Brünig, good), about 10 m. from Sarnen, a timber-built village, the last in the valley, situated at the foot of the Brünig, and originally at the S. end of the lake, is now some distance from it. The carriage-road was made in 1865. It is doubtful whether the old mule-path is now practicable even for pedestrians.

The carriage-road leaving the old mule-path l. runs in well-constructed zigzag sweeps through the forest to the summit of the pass, 3648 ft., whence the ascent of the *Wylerhorn* on the rt. can be made in 2 hrs.

Shortly before reaching the culminating point of the road, there is a charming view down the valley of Sarnen backed by Pilatus, with the Lungern See in the foreground. A little beyond the brow, the still finer view of the valley of Hasli, with the *Kirchet* stretching across it, shut in by the broken peaks of the Engelhörner on one side, and by the Plattenberg on the other side, with a range of snowy summits between them.

The *Hotel Brünig*, a post-station, is well placed near the top of the Pass. Close to a small tavern, formerly a toll-house, the road to Meiringen turns off on the l. The town is seen below, seated on the rich flat which forms the bottom of the valley. On the opposite precipices streaks of white mark the waterfalls of the Reichenbach, Oltschibach, and others.

1 hr. takes the traveller down the

steep descent, cut in places out of the face of the mountain, to *Brienzwyler* bridge on the road from Brienz to Meiringen (Rte. 25E). On a cliff rt., a curious instance of contorted strata may be noticed. It is about 3 m. on a level to

Brienz. (Rte. 25E.)

———

ROUTE 20.

Pedestrians bound from Lucerne to Meiringen or Engelberg, may vary their route in an agreeable way by the *Melchthal*, which opens E. of Sarnen (Rte. 19). At its mouth, close to the chapel of *St. Niklaus*, stands an isolated tower. one of the most ancient buildings in the canton, dating from the earliest Christian times, erected probably as a belfry. Melchthal was the native place of *Arnold an der Halden*, one of the reputed conspirators of Grütli (Rte. 15). Nearly opposite the chapel is a hill called the *Ranft*, the site of the hermitage of *Nicolas von der Flüh* (see Rte. 19) The scenery of the Melchthal, which lies between the range of the *Hohenstollen* (8150 ft.) and the *Lauberstock* (8516 ft.) is pretty and pastoral, but the entrance of the valley is a wooded defile. Countless chalets cover the slopes. There is a carriage-road, as far as the village of *Melchthal* (*Inn :* Kaplanei, clean), 7 m. Two paths lead direct to *Engelberg* from the Lower Melchthal.

a. *Storegg Pass* (6703 ft.) turns off l. just beyond the bridge 1 m. from the Ranft and 4 m. from Kerns or Sarnen. It is steep at the top and badly marked. The Col lies between the *Salistock* (7528 ft.) and *Bockistock,* and is about 3½ hrs. from Sarnen. The descent leads in ½ hr. to the *Lautersee*, a small lake on the l.; and in 1 hr. more to the junction of the Jöchli road (see below), ¾ hr. from Engelberg.

(b) *Jöchli Pass* (7136 ft.): the turn is from the end of the char-road, 1 m. beyond *Melchthal.* Steep zigzags lead up grassy slopes in 2 hrs. to the Col, where there is often snow, and the Titlis range opens to view. The path passes through a narrow gap, deep in moss and with many flowers. Then a descent of 1¼ hr. to the junction of the Storegg route, and ¾ hr. on to *Engelberg* (Rte. 31).

The way to *Engstlen* (about 4½ hrs.) on the Joch Pass, lies up the very picturesque and well-wooded Melchthal (horsepath) to the chalets of *Melchalp* on the *Melchsee* (6432 ft.), where it turns l. This is a large pool lying in the midst of a rich alpine pasturage, studded with chalets. The path traverses meadows for an hour. The descent to Engstlen is steep, and the path may easily be missed, so that the traveller without a guide will do well to hire a boy from one of the chalets to set him on the right track.

From the chalets of Melchalp pedestrians have two fine routes to Meiringen. Instead of turning l. to the cross, they may keep along the stream, and follow it up the slope rt. It leads in 1 hr. to a Col opening into the Klein Melchthal, and commanding a view of the Titlis, Sustenhorn, Galenstock, Pilatus, and Wetterhorn. From this col another at the head of the same valley, and at about the same elevation, is visible. Pass to it along the flank of the *Hohenstollen,* without descending (2 hrs.). The view here is splendid. The E. flank of the Oberland mountains is thrown into view from top to bottom, and many snowpeaks are seen. The Hohenstollen can be ascended by easy slopes. Descent of 2 hrs. from the second col to Meiringen. A more direct way is over the *Laubergrat* (7352 ft.) between the Glockhaus and the Lauberstock. It is reached by an easy ascent of 1¼ hr. from the Melch See. The view of the Oberland peaks from the summit is magnificent.

———

ROUTE 22.

LUCERNE TO BERNE OR THUN, BY THE ENTLEBUCH—RAIL.

The distance is 60 m., and the trains take about 3½ hrs. The line was opened in August, 1875.

After emerging from the tunnel under the Gütsch, the Berne Rly. leaves the line to Olten, turns sharp to the l., and begins to ascend the valley of the *Kleine Emme,* which is here a rocky defile.

Soon after passing *Malters* Stat., the river is crossed. Near this the democratic Free Corps were in 1845 defeated by the men of Lucerne, a conflict which foreshadowed, but was reversed in its results by, the war of the Sonderbund.

[From this the *Bramegg Pass* leads through a rich and fertile valley, past the baths and hotel of *Farnbühl,* commanding a fine view, and falls again into the main line at Entlebuch.]

The rly. follows the l. bank of the stream through a narrow valley, passing tunnels, and making many sharp curves past

Wohlhausen Stat., on the Emme, to

Entlebuch Stat. A village of 3000 Inhab., situated in a wide green valley at the W. foot of the Bramegg (3645 ft.) (*Inns*: H. du Port, Drei Könige), prettily situated on a slope, with the torrents Entle and Emme roaring beneath it.

The vale of Entlebuch is about 30 m. long, and flanked by mountains covered with wood and pasture. The men of the valley are celebrated as the best wrestlers in Switzerland. They hold 4 or 5 great matches, called *Schwingfeste,* between the months of June and Oct.; the chief on the first Sunday in Sept., when they try their skill against the athletes of the neighbouring valleys. The Bernese highlanders are formidable rivals. The Entlebuchers have been long renowned for their courage and independence. In 1405 Lucerne bought this valley from Austria, along with the feudal rights of the nobles over it, substituting a Lucerne bailiff.

The *Napf*, 5194 ft., rising W. of Entlebuch, can be ascended in about 3 hrs. The *Menzberg*, with *Kurhaus* and Pension, abuts upon the slopes of the Napf above Wohlhausen.

Schüpfheim Stat. (*Inn:* Adler), a large village at the junction of the Weisse Emme and Wald-Emme, the latter flowing from the *Brienzer Rothhorn*. On the *Schafmatt*, l., at the pilgrimage-chapel of *Heiligkreuz*, a wrestling-match is held on the 29th Sept., and on the *Schüpferberg*, rt., another on the following Sunday.

A carriage-road leads from here to *Sorenberg* (10 m.), whence there is a path over the Brienzer Rothhorn to Brienz, in 6½ hrs.

The rly. again crosses the stream, and rises rapidly to

Escholzmatt Stat. (*Inns:* Löwe, good; Krone), a scattered village, in a high situation, 2800 ft. above the sea.

Near Trübschachen is a handsome hospital for 100 orphans and 300 paupers.

Langnau Stat. (*Inns:* Hirsch, quiet and good; zum Emmenthal, clean) is the principal place in the *Emmenthal* (Pop. about 7200), an extensive, fertile, and industrious valley, famed for its cheeses (made on the high pastures and exported all over Germany), and for its manufacture of linen. Its meadows are of the brightest green; the cottages neat and substantial, with pretty gardens before them. The Grosse Emme, which traverses it, and its tributaries, at times commit serious devastation.

The Ilfis is crossed, and afterwards the Emme, before reaching

Signau Stat. (*Inn:* Bär, tolerable), a pretty village, with a ruined castle above it. For the next few miles there is nothing remarkable until the

range of the Bernese Oberland comes into view on the l.

The road then runs through a wood of fine firs.

Gümligen Junct. Stat. on the rly. from Berne to Thun (Rte. 24).
BERNE *Terminus* (Rte. 24).

ROUTE 24.

BERNE TO THUN.

BERNE (table-d'hôte at the Buffet, 2 fr. 50 cents.).—*Hotels:* Bernerhof, close to the Federal Hall, first-class, excellent; table d'hôte 5 fr.; H. Bellevue, well managed and comfortable—these hotels command the view of the Alps; Falke; Mohr; both in the street, old established, quiet and comfortable; Schweizerhof, Zähringerhof —these houses are close to the Rly. Stat.; H. Victoria, on the Schänzli, outside the town, with fine view; H. des Boulangers, good; Storch; Schmieden, rough and homely. The *Abbayes*, or houses of the guilds, such as the Distelzwang,* or Abbaye aux Gentilshommes, the Abbaye des Tisserands, and the Abbaye du Singe, are no longer used as inns.

Pensions. — The Pension Jäggi at la Villette and the Pension Mattenhof are well recommended: also P. Bremgarten, outside the town.

Booksellers.—Dalp and Co., opposite the station, are agents for the sale of the Dufour maps, and the publications of the Swiss Alpine Club, and have a good stock of maps, views, photographs, &c. Beck's photographs of the snowy region are remarkable.

Post and Telegraph Office near the station, to the N. of it.
Eng. Church Service on Sunday in the Cathedral.
Railways to all parts of Switzerland.

* *Zwang*, a local word for guild: Distel, thistle, the emblem of the gentlemen who held their meetings or club under this sign.

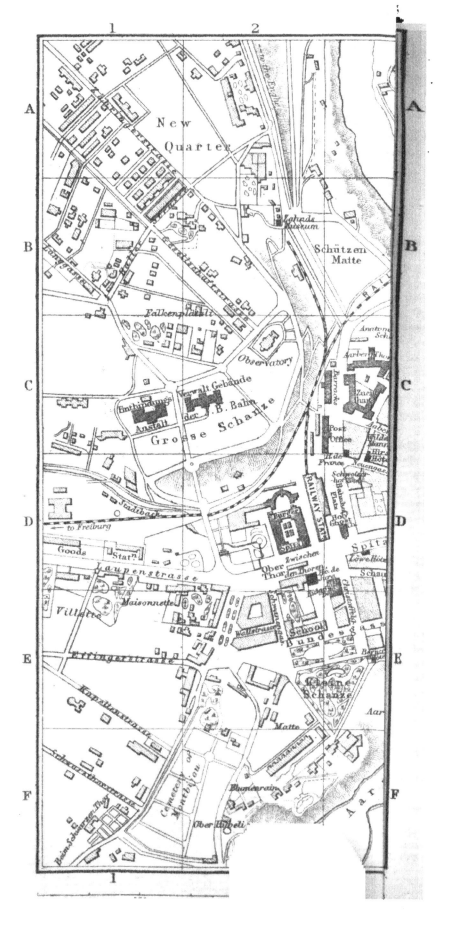

See route-map. Diligence to Gurnigel Baths.

The *sights of Berne* may be taken in a walk through the town in the following order :—Starting from the rly. stat., walk E., down the principal street (called in consecutive portions of its length Spitalgasse, Marktgasse, Kramgasse, and Gerechtigkeitsgasse), along its arcades and under its clock tower, to the Nydeck Bridge, and over it to the Bears (Bärengraben), 1¼ m. from the rly. stat. In returning diverge to the l., into the Junkern Gasse, to see the Münster Platz (Minster and view), and again to the Bundes Rathhaus (Federal Council Hall). The Münster is half-way between the rly. stat., and the Bundes Rathhaus is close to the stat. Finally, crossing the Aar by the rly. bridge, ascend to the *Schänzli,* the best point of view near Berne, and return by the new Botanic Garden and rly. bridge to the station.

Berne, capital of the most populous, and of the second in size, of the Swiss cantons (Pop. 530,000; all but 80,000 are Protestants), and, since 1849, permanent seat of the Swiss Government and Diet, and residence of most of the foreign ministers, contains 44,000 Inhab.

Berne is built on a lofty sandstone promontory, nearly encircled by the winding Aar, which flows in a deep gully, with steep and in places precipitous sides (Stalden). The inconvenient descent and ascent by which the town could alone be reached from the E. formerly, has been remedied by three lofty *Bridges.* The (Nydeckbrücke), partly of granite, derived from the erratic blocks of the Kirchet near Meiringen is 900 ft. long, and the central arch over the Aar 150 ft. wide and 93 ft. high. The Kirchenfeld Bridge (completed 1883) was built by an English company. Berne, on this elevated platform, 1700 ft. above the sea, is imposing at a distance, and there is something striking in the views of the interior, from the town being built of massive stone. It has this peculiarity, that almost all the houses rest upon arcades (Lauben), which form covered walks, and are lined with shops and stalls, like " the Rows " in Chester. The lowness of the arches, however, and the solidity of the buttresses supporting them, render these colonnades gloomy and close. The chief street of shops and business runs through the town, along the top of the ridge. Overhanging the Aar, and removed from the main streets, are the residences of the patricians, which look really like " gentlemen's houses."

Berne is well supplied with water. In 1868 a brook called the Gasel was diverted from its natural course, and made to flow into the town. The streets have their rills, and numerous *Fountains,* each supporting some quaint effigy. One of these, the *Kindlifresser-Brunnen* (Ogre's fountain), on the Corn-house-square, receives its name from a figure (probably Saturn) devouring a child, with others stuck in his girdle and pockets ready for consumption. Some support armed warriors, such as David : another is surmounted by a female figure; but the favourite device is *the Bear.* Thus, the *Bärenbrunnen* in the principal street has a bear in armour, with breast-plate, thigh-pieces, and helmet, a sword at his side, and a banner in his paw: the *Schützen Brunnen,* the figure of a Swiss cross-bowman of former days, attended by a young *bear* as squire; and the Morat gate (Ober-Thor) two granite *bears,* larger than life, standing as sentinels.

In the principal street, which extends from the Ober-Thor (Higher Gate) and Rly. Stat. to the Nydeck Bridge are 2 antique watch-towers and the *Käfichthurm* (cage tower), now used as a prison. The *Clock-tower* (Zeitglockenthurm) stands nearly in the centre of the town, though, when originally built, in 1191, by Berthold V. of Zähringen, it guarded the outer wall. Its droll clockwork puppets are objects of wonder to an admiring crowd of idlers : three minutes before the hour, a wooden cock crows and flaps his wings; in another minute a procession of bears passes round a seated figure of a bearded old man: the cock then crows again. The hour is struck on a bell by a fool with a hammer, while it is counted by the bearded figure, who turns an hour-glass, raises his sceptre, and opens his mouth; a bear inclining his head at the same time. The cock then crows once more in conclusion.

The great charm of Berne is the *view of the Oberland Alps*, which the town and every eminence in its neighbourhood command in clear weather. From the *Münster Platz*, a terrace, planted with shady rows of trees, overlooking the Aar, six snowy peaks of the great chain are visible, and from the Enge, outside the town, at least a dozen rise into view.

The Münster Platz, supported by a wall of masonry, is 108 ft. above the Aar; yet an inscription on the parapet records that a young student, mounted on a spirited horse, which had been frightened by some children, leaped the precipice, and reached the bottom with no other hurt than broken ribs. The horse was killed on the spot. The rider became minister of Kertzers, and lived to a good old age.

Here is a bronze *Statue* of *Berthold V. of Zähringen*, founder of Berne, by Tscharner of Munich; his esquire is a bear. Opposite the W. door of the Münster a spirited equestrian *Statue* of *Rudolph v. Erlach*, the conqueror at Laupen, with 4 bears at the corners.

The *Münster* (entrance at W. door, 50 c.), of Flamboyant Gothic, by begun 1421, and finished 1457, was Matthias v. Steinbach, son of the builder of Strasbourg Cathedral; and many of the ornaments, such as the open parapet running round the roof, and varying in pattern between each buttress, are not inferior in design or execution to those o Strasbourg. The chief ornament is the great *W. portal*, bearing sculptured reliefs of the Last Judgment, flanked by figures of the wise and foolish Virgins, &c. (date, 1475-85). The interior is in admirable preservation, and has never suffered restoration. The organ dates from 1727, but was much enlarged in 1851, by way of rivalry to that at Fribourg. It is played on daily during the season (8 P.M., adm. 1 fr.). In the windows, and on the roof, are the coats of the aristocratic burghers of Berne. 3 tall windows of very fine painted glass in the choir deserve notice; (date, end of 15th cent.), particularly the "wafers-window," with a symbolical representation of the Eucharist. The stalls in the choir (1512) are well carved with figures of the Apostles on one side, and prophets on the other. Along the walls are tablets, bearing the names of 18 officers and 683 soldiers, citizens of Berne, who fell fighting against the French, at Grauholz, near Zollikofen, 1798. There is also a monument erected by the town, in 1600, to Berthold of Zähringen. The tower 234 ft. high, can be ascended ($\frac{1}{2}$ fr.). The exterior of the cathedral has been lately restored and repaired.

The *University*, founded in 1834, is near the cathedral. There are about 320 students, belonging chiefly to the medical faculty.

Natural History Museum, Waisenhausgasse. Open, free, Tues., Sat., 2 to 5; Sun., 10.30 to 12.30: strangers may obtain admittance at all times by paying 50 c. On the ground floor is the collection of minerals.

The geology of Switzerland may be studied in the very complete series of fossils collected by *M. Studer* and others. There are a number of beautiful specimens of all the rarest minerals from St. Gothard, and several plans in relief of various parts of Switzerland.

On the first and second floors is the zoological department; there are stuffed specimens of the bear at all ages. The lynx of the Alps, and the steinbock or bouquetin, both from the Bernese chain, are interesting for their rarity. Here is deservedly

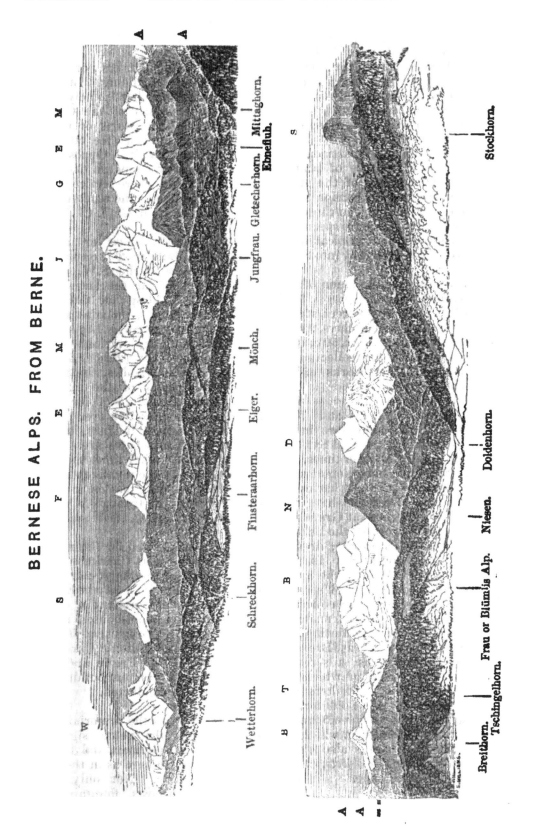

BERNESE ALPS. FROM BERNE.

Wetterhorn. | Schreckhorn. | Finsteraarhorn. | Eiger. | Mönch. | Jungfrau. Gletscherhorn. | Mittaghorn. Ebnefluh.

Breithorn. Tschingelhorn. | Frau or Blümlis Alp. | Niesen. | Doldenhorn. | Stockhorn.

preserved the skin of *Barry*, one of the dogs of St. Bernard, who is recorded to have saved the lives of 15 human beings. A chamois with three horns, one growing out of the nose ; a specimen of a cross breed between the steinbock and domestic goat, which lived 7 years; a wild boar, of gigantic size, are also worth notice.

In the *Ornithological* department are the lämmergeier (vulture of lambs), the feathered monarch of the Alps, inferior in size to the condor alone among birds. In addition to those native to the country, there are specimens of several foreign and tropical birds which have found their way into Switzerland.

In the corridor is the fauna of the Pile-dwellings Period.

Opposite, in the same street, stands the *Art Museum* (free Tuesdays, 9 to 6, Sun. 10½ to 12, other times, 50 c. each person), a considerable collection of landscapes and other works of the Swiss school.

The *Historical Museum* and *Town Library* of 70,000 volumes, are in the Kesslergasse (free, Tues. and Sat. 3 to 5; Sun. 10.30 to 12, at other times, 1 fr. a head). Here are some Roman antiquities ; the Prie Dieu of Charles the Bold, and part of his tent-hangings, captured by the Bernese at Grandson; the pointed shoes worn by the Bernese nobles in the 16th century ; dresses, &c., from the South Sea Islands, brought over by Weber, the artist, who accompanied Capt. Cook's expedition. Also a very large collection of tapestry, taken at Morat, made for Charles the Bold from paintings by Roger v. der Weyden, at Brussels. Some early rifled guns; a series of headsman's axes, each of which has cut off 100 heads ; 750 halters prepared by Charles the Bold for the Swiss; armour from Laupen, found in a hollow on the Bramberg, which was the battlefield. There is also a good collection of *lacustrine objects*, chiefly from the Lake of Bienne.

On the N. side of the town is the *Roman Catholic Church*, by the archi-

tects Deperthes of Rheims and Müller of Fribourg.

Near it is the *Rathhaus*, or Town-hall, a 16th-cent. building. In it are offices, and some handsomely-fitted rooms for meetings of the Council of the Canton, for courts of justice, &c. ; but the interior (fee 50 c.) is scarcely worth a visit. Opposite the Town Hall is the modern *Church* of the *Old Catholics*, where service is performed according to the tenets of that division of the Rom. Cath. Ch.

The *Bundes - Rathhaus* or *Federal Council Hall*, built 1852-7, on the cliff above the Aar, at the S.W. corner of the town, by far the largest and handsomest building in the town (Stadler, architect), includes all the departments of the Swiss Legislature, the Diet, and the various Public Offices. The Diet (*Bundesversammlung*) consists of 2 bodies, the *Ständerath* (44 Deputies of the 22 Cantons) and *Nationalrath* (1 for every 20,000 Inhab. or fraction over 10,000), who meet generally in July, in separate halls. The debates are open to the public. At other times the building is shown by the doorkeeper. The roof of the building may be ascended for the *view*. In front is a marble *fountain*, with allegorical statue of *Berne*.

Berne is celebrated for the number and excellence of its Charitable Institutions: they are, perhaps, more carefully attended to than any in Europe. There is a public granary in case of scarcity, two orphan-houses, an Infirmary, and an extensive *Hospital*, bearing the inscription " Christo in pauperibus." The Prison and Penitentiary is an enormous building and said to be well conducted.

The *bear* forms the armorial badge of the town, the name signifying "bear" in old German, and he is as great a favourite here as in the house of Bradwardine. Not only is his effigy on sign-posts, fountains, and buildings, but for several hundred years living specimens had been maintained when the French revolutionary army, on taking possession of Berne, 1798, led them away captive, and deposited them in the Jardin des Plantes, where one, the celebrated Martin, became the favourite of the French metropolis. But when the ancient order of things was restored at Berne, one of the first cares of the citizens was to replace and provide for their ancient pensioners. There is a foundation for the support of the bears. After having been reduced to one, their number has been again increased, and the animals removed from the Aarberg Gate to a commodious den at the Nydeck Bridge. In 1861 an Englishman was destroyed by the large male bear, having fallen in a fool-hardy attempt to pass along the wall separating the two dens.

The fortifications of Berne have been converted into *Promenades.* The banks of the Aar, as seen from them, especially from the *Grosse Schanze,* outside the Aarberg Gate, are most picturesque; and, the Alps, when visible, form a surprising background.

The mountains, however, as well as the city, are better seen from the *Enge,* a terrace walk 20 min. N. of the Rly. Stat., outside the town gate, (but not beyond the river), the favourite resort of the citizens. On the way to it, is the *Shooting-house.*

There is a pleasant footpath through the Enge-wald to the castle of *Reichenbach,* once the residence of Rudolph von Erlach.

The *Schänzli,* a promenade at the end of the hill nearest the railway bridge, is the best point of view for the Alps. It is reached in ¼ hr.'s walk from the stat., by the magnificent rly. bridge (for carriages also), and past the *Botanic Garden* on the rt. bank of the Aar. There is a good Hôtel-Pension here.

The *Gurten,* the ridge above the Aar to the S. of the town, is another good point for a view of the Alps. On the top is an *Inn.*

At *Tiefenau,* ¼ hr. N. of Berne, near the Aar bridge, is an ancient Gallic battle-field, whence swords, rings, spear-heads, &c., have been collected.

The *Casino,* a handsome building close to the Bundes-Rathhaus, contains a reading-room and ball-room. There is also a *Theatre* in the town.

History of Berne.—The town was founded in 1191 by Duke Berthold V. of Zähringen. "Bern" is the German form of Verona, and Dietrich von Bern = Theodoric the Great. Both cities were subject to the Zähringen dynasty. In 1218 Berne became a free city of the Empire. The battle of Laupen, in 1339, in which its forces, under Rudolf von Erlach, annihilated a combination of nobles, secured its independence. It joined the Swiss Confederation in 1353, having been for many years an ally. From being a city of refuge for the oppressed, it, like many other Swiss towns, passed under the rule of an exclusive and conservative oligarchy, who repressed liberty both at home and abroad. It held Aargau, Vaud, and other districts, as tributaries, and is reported to have governed them tyrannically. The government latterly fell into the hands of a small number of patrician families, who lost their power in 1798, partly recovered it in 1814, and lost it again in 1831. A Von Erlach led the Bernese to the battle of Laupen in 1339, and a Von Erlach led them against the French in 1798. Until 1848 the Swiss government was carried on at Berne, Zürich, and Lucerne alternately, the governing canton for the year being called the Vorort. Since that date Berne has been the sole capital of the Confederation.

The special trades of canton Berne are *watch-making,* and in the Bernese-Oberland, *wood-carving,* now an important industry. Between Thun and the Grimsel there are said to be 2000 carvers, earning on an average 2 fr. a day, some much more, and there are schools for teaching these people to draw and model. The wood of the linden is chiefly used.

Berne to Thun, by Rly.

1 hour 7 min. by rly., five trains a day. Travellers going to Interlaken or Meiringen should take through-tickets. The rly. crosses the Aar, passing rt. the Botanic Garden and Schänzli, and at Wyler separates from the line to Bâle. In fine weather the snowy Alps are in sight nearly the whole way. The scenery of the valley of the Aar is pleasing. The river itself runs at some distance on the rt., and is rarely visible.

Gumligen Junct. (see Rte. 22).

Münsingen Stat. [From this point the *Belpberg* (rt.), with fine view, can be ascended in 2 hrs., the path passing the Aar by ferry. From the top, called *Harzern Spitze*, descent can be made to a small *Inn* on the *Gerzensee*, 3 m., and thence to the Kiesen Stat.]

Kiesen Stat. for Gurnigelbad, a large bathing-establishment with good accommodation.

Beyond Münsingen

The *Stockhorn* and the *Niesen*, two limestone mountains, forming, as it were, the advanced guard of the high Alps, become conspicuous. The Aar is crossed near *Uttigen Stat.*

Thun Stat., on l. bank of the Aar. Passengers bound for Interlaken, and not wishing to stop at Thun, proceed 1 m. further (5 min.) to

Scherzligen Terminus, on the Aar, where travellers step on board the steamer.

Thun, Fr. *Thoune.*—(*Hotels :* outside the town—Grand Hotel de Thoune, a magnificent building on the banks of the Aar ; H. Bellevue, a large establishment, with beautiful grounds, well-managed, English chapel. Pension, 9 to 12 fr. Table-d'hôte, 5 fr. ; Pension Baumgarten, clean and pleasant ; —in the town, Freienhof, frequented by Swiss officers ; Kreuz ; Krone ; Falke.—Campagne and Pension Itten,

S. of the town, comfortable, and moderate charges ; beautiful views.

Physicians. — Dr. F. Ris, speaks English. Dr. Köller.

The charges for vehicles and saddle-horses throughout the Bernese Oberland have been fixed by a tariff (price 40 c.) which is hung up in the principal inns and in the lake steamers. The voituriers are also bound to produce the tariff when called for. As it is subject to changes, travellers are recommended to consult that for the current year.

Thun is one of the most picturesque towns in Switzerland (about 5130 Inhab., almost all Prot.). It is situated about a mile from the lake, partly upon an island between two branches of the river Aar, which here rushes out of it blue but clear as crystal. Many of the houses are built upon arcades, as at Berne, and pre-eminent above the other buildings rises a *church*, reached by a staircase from the bridge up the hill-side, and a picturesque feudal *castle* of the Counts of Kyburg (1429), now the Court-house and the prison and a promenade. There are remains of the mediæval walls of the enceinte, seen in various places, but particularly on each side of the *Berne Gate*, a square tower. The old *Beguinage*, close to the Town-house, has some Gothic windows. Thun enjoys considerable trade, and in the 14th cent. reckoned 70 noble families within its walls. It is a very curious old town, and from its position and beautiful environs one of the most agreeable residences in Switzerland. It is supplied with excellent water, which flows through 25,000 ft. of pipes from a reservoir on the Homberg.

Close to the Rly. Stat. is the *Military College* of the Swiss Confederation. Here also are the principal artillery and cavalry barracks. Reviews take place every summer.

The view from the *Churchyard terrace* "along the lake, with its girdle of Alps (the Blümlis being the most conspicuous), fine glaciers, and rocks

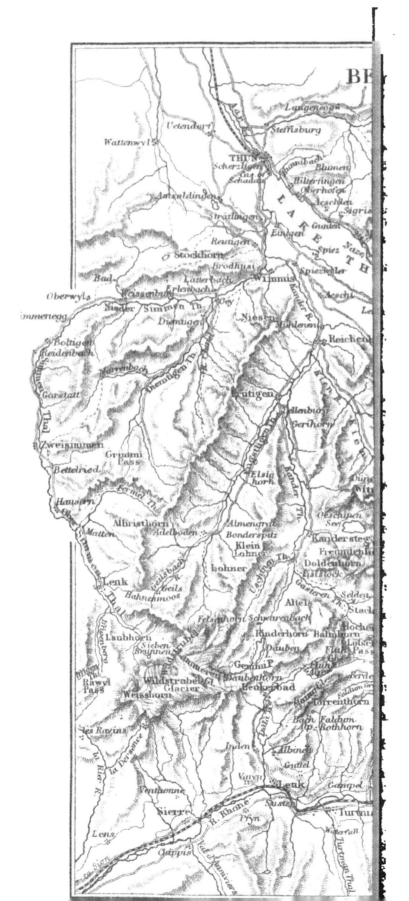

wooded to the top," is mentioned by Byron. On leaving the church, go through the court of the castle, and descend by a flight of wooden steps to the town.

A very extensive prospect is gained from the *Pavillon de St. Jacques* or *St. Jakobshübeli*, about ¼ mile above the Bellevue. The Doldenhorn, Blümlis Alp, Altels, Jungfrau, Mönch, and Eiger are seen. The *Kohlern Schlucht*, 6 min. walk from the hotels, is a picturesque ravine with cascades.

The *Church of Aeschi* (fine view), about 3 hrs.' drive, on the S. side of the lake, is a pleasant excursion (see Rte. 37). The situation is beautiful.

The *Château Schadau* is a Gothic building, erected (1850) by M. de Rougemont, of Paris, in a beautiful garden, a part of which is open to the public on Sunday evenings. The castle faces the lake, just where the Aar issues from it, and is close to the little Gothic Church of *Scherzligen*, to which there is a ferry from the rt. bank of the river.

Diligence to Saanen daily.

Excursions to the summits of the *Niesen* and *Stockhorn*, and *Thuner Rothhorn*, to the *Baths of Blumenstein* and the *Fallbach* waterfall, 6 m. W., to the frequented Hotel and *Baths of Gurnigel* further W., 3783 ft. above the sea. 2½ hrs. to *Wattenwyl* (*Inns:* Bär; Post), thence 2 hrs. to Gurnigel (see Rte. 42). To the baths of *Weissenberg*, in the Simmenthal, by Spiez. To the *Aeschi Allmend*, descending to Leissigen, on the S. shore of the lake.

The *Niesen* (7763 ft.) commands one of the finest panoramic views in the Bernese Alps. There are 3 bridle-paths up: N. from Wimmis, S. from Frutigen, E. from Heustrich-Bad on the Frutigen road. Omnibuses daily to *Heustrich-Bad*; steamboat to Spiez, about 4 m. from Wimmis. A carriage-road of 7 m. (1-horse carr. 7 fr.) leads from Thun across the entrance of the Simmenthal to *Wimmis* (*Inn:* Löwe, comfortable). (Diligence to Brothausi, 1½ m. short of Wimmis.) The ascent takes about 4½ hrs.; the descent 3. The charge for a horse from Wimmis to the sum-

mit and down again the same day is 15 fr. If kept all night 20 fr., but it will be of little use in the descent. Close to the top is a clean wooden hotel, with 24 beds.

The *near* view embraces the snowy mountains of the Oberland from the Altels and Rinderhorn on the W. to the Wetterhorn on the E.—the finest object being the Blümlis Alp at the head of the Kienthal. The more distant view comprises the summit of Mont Blanc and the Dent du Midi; in the valleys the eye rests on the lakes of Thun and Brienz, on the town of Thun, and the villages of Brienz and Interlaken. A panoramic view has been published by Deck of Berne.

The *Stockhorn* (7195 ft.) is ascended by a steep path in 3½ hrs. from Erlenbach, 8¼ m. on the Simmenthal road. The lake of Thun is admirably seen. There is a longer path from Amsoldingen, 3½ m. from Thun.

The *Thuner Roth-horn* (6700 ft.), on the N. side of the lake, commands a splendid view. It may be reached through Gunten and Sigriswyl. On the descent the *Justi Thal* and Schafloch may be visited.

ROUTE 25.

THE BERNESE OBERLAND.

The magnificent highland district described in this route is the very heart of Switzerland, and should be omitted by no one who wishes to form an idea of the noblest scenery of the Central Alps. At Zermatt or in Dauphiné the peaks are bolder and more fantastic; Mont Blanc is a more majestic mass than any other Alpine mountain: but nowhere are the grandeur of the snows and the pastoral beauty of the lower hills of Switzerland brought into such striking juxtaposition as in this region. It was here that Byron "repeopled his mind from nature," and gathered many of the ideas and images which he has interwoven in his tragedy of 'Manfred,' and that Tennyson found the scenery for the exquisite alpine Idyl in 'The Princess.'

A. *Lake of Thun—Thun to Interlaken*—Steamboats between Thun and *Därligen Rly. Term.*, 4 times a day, in 1 hr. 40 min. Fare 2 fr. and 1 fr. They start from the Freienhof, calling at H. Bellevue and *Scherzligen* Rly. Stat. On the passage they touch at *Oberhofen* and *Gunten* (N.), at *Spiez* and *Faulensee* (S.). A good road runs to Interlaken (about 15 Eng. m.), along the S. shore. There is a shorter and very fine carriage-road also on the N. side of the lake. Beyond *Merligen* (*Inn*: H. du Lion) (whence it is a pleasant walk across the Justithal, visiting the *Cave of St. Beatus* on the way, to the Beatenberg) the road is cut through romantic scenery at the foot of precipices to Neuhaus.

The lake is about 11 m. long, and 2 broad, with a maximum depth of 780 ft. It is 1837 ft. above the sea. The banks near Thun are covered with villas and vineyards, with woods above them; further on, its N. shore is precipitous. On the N. shore is the Rothhorn (see above). The S. shore is more striking. Here the *Stockhorn* and pyramidal *Niesen* stand sentinels at the entrance of the Kanderthal and Simmenthal. The river Kander, conducted into the lake by an artificial channel formed in 1714, has deposited within less than a century and a half, a delta of several hundred acres. The progress and extent of this recent formation, so interesting to geologists, have been ably investigated by Sir C. Lyell.

On entering the lake the spire of the *Chartreuse Château* may be seen N., at the mouth of the ravine of the Hünnibach, which forms within it

some small but pretty cascades. A little farther on stands the modern *Château Huneck* (Baron Parpart), a short distance from *Hilterfingen*, with a spire, and *Oberhofen* (several pensions), where Count Pourtales has a château, conspicuous by its square tower. Strangers are allowed to walk in the castle grounds. At *Gunten*, N., are some pensions. On the S. side of the lake, in the distance, is seen the whitewashed tower of *Strättlingen*, and on a projecting tongue of land, close by, a picturesque château, for the last 3 cents. the property of the family of von Erlach. It has also a rude Romanesque *church*, with the arms of von Erlach on the windows.

Close to the landing-place of *Spiez* is the *Spiezerhof*, a large hotel, with view of the Niesen. Near Spiez is the large Pension Schöneck, and on the hills above it *Krattegen* (Restaurant), with a beautiful view of the Lake.

Diligences in connection with the steamers to Zweisimmen and Lenk and to Frutigen. Guides and horses for the Niesen.

On leaving Thun the giants of the Bernese Oberland come into view. The Eiger, Mönch, Jungfrau, Ebnefluh, &c., rise in front, beyond Spiez, the Faulhorn and Schreckhorn appear on their left. The ch. of Aeschi is seen on a slope under the Niesen, S.

Faulensee, landing-place for Faulenseebad, a large *pension*. A curious small church, possibly of the time of St. Beatus.

[Behind *Merligen* is the entrance to the *Justi Thal*: between 2 and 2½ hrs.' walk up it, in the cliffs forming its W. boundary, is a cave called *Schafloch*, which in the height of summer always contains *ice*. Such ice wells are not uncommon in the Jura, and in other parts of the world. For as air when it is cold is denser than when it is warm, all depths that do not admit of ventilation become receptacles of the coldest air. It subsides into them, and, once there, cannot be displaced. This cave has 2 branches; that in which the ice occurs runs straight from the entrance for about 60 ft., when it suddenly narrows, and dips down 12 or 15 ft.; the whole length of the cavern is about 800 yards. Lights must be taken.]

Off the Nase promontory, which juts out from the *Beatenberg* N., the lake is 720 ft. deep.

N. Farther on, in the face of the mountain overhanging the lake, is the *Cave of St. Beatus*, above a small cascade, which may be seen leaping into the lake. St. Beatus, according to tradition was a native of Britain, who converted the inhabitants of this part of Helvetia to Christianity. Being minded to take up his residence on the shore of the lake, he fixed his eyes upon a grot well suited to a hermit, but at the time occupied by a dragon. The monster, however, was easily ejected simply by hearing a notice to quit addressed to him by St. Beatus. The anchorite was in the habit of crossing the lake on his cloak, which, when spread on the water, served instead of a boat. A rivulet issues from the cave, and is subject to sudden rises, which fill the cavern to the roof, and cause a loud report. The cave may be reached in 15 min. from the shore. The path to the cave leads through private property, but permission is accorded to strangers.

The steamer now stops at a village called *Därligen* (Pension Schätz), on the S. shore of the lake, and about 3 m. from Interlaken. The passengers and luggage are transferred to a railway (called the Bödeli Rly.), which carries them to Interlaken Stat., where at least 25 omnibuses from as many hotels will be found in waiting, with chars, porters, and guides besides. The rly. is continued to Bönigen, on the lake of Brienz (Rte. 25E), but its utility is not very obvious, as the station is 10 minutes' walk from the principal hotels, and the old plan of one transfer by omnibus was quicker and easier. There is a second station at Interlaken (*Zollhaus*), about a mile further, which is nearer to *H. du Lac* and *H. des Alpes*, but has not so good a supply of omnibuses, carriages, &c.

Interlaken.—*Hotels*: Victoria, hand-some; H. des Alpes, frequented by English; pension, 7 to 10 fr. a day; Jungfrau, also a very large house; du Casino; Interlaken; Beaurivage; Ritschard, a German house; Schweizerhof, the same; Belvedere: all on the Höheweg, and all with gardens and a view of the Jungfrau. Deutsches Haus; H. Oberland and H. Wyder, also large hotels; H. du Pont and H. Belvedere, comfortable; on the bank of the Aar; H. Unterseen, in the Place of Unterseen; H. Beausite, outside Unterseen; H. du Lac, at the E. end of Interlaken. About a mile off, on the Kleine Rugen, is H. Jungfraublick (large and good). These are all somewhat cheaper than the hotels on the Höheweg. All the hotels will take people *en pension*, price 6 to 10 fr. a day. H. Bellevue. There are also pleasantly situated pensions at Bönigen, on the Lake of Brienz.

Interlaken (1860 ft.) and the adjoining village Unterseen stand on a perfectly flat piece of land called Bödeli, no doubt formed by the rubbish brought down by the torrent from the valleys of Grindelwald and Lauterbrunnen, and occupying the space between the lakes of Thun and Brienz, whence the name of Unterseen and its Latinised form Interlaken. The piece of land is about 4 m. long from lake to lake, and about 2 m. from mountain to mountain. The *Harder* mountain, on the N. side, rises almost precipitously from the flat land. On the S. side opens a wide valley, through which the snowy Jungfrau is seen as in a frame, and it is to this superb view that Interlaken owes its celebrity. For the last 50 years the town has been growing, and now consists of a broad straight avenue of fine walnut-trees with fields on the S. side, and on the N., facing the Jungfrau, a row of large hotels. This is called the *Höheweg*, or Promenade. Near the middle is the *Kursaal*, an outdoor café, where there is music in the evening (for which every visitor is charged in the hotel bill 50 c.). Near the E. end of the Höheweg, beautifully placed amongst fine walnut-trees, are the church and old convent of Interlaken.

Interlaken was the site of an Augustinian convent (founded 1133), containing 40 nuns and 50 canons regular, which became the possessor of all the adjoining valleys. The nunnery grew notorious for irregularities, and in 1488 was dissolved by the Pope. In 1528 the monks surrendered all their possessions to the Canton of Berne, which governed them by means of a bailiff.

Interlaken may be described as the capital of the tourist's Switzerland. It possesses some features of a capital, which travellers will value variously, large hotels with every luxury, gay shops and a promenade crowded with elegantly-dressed company. Dust and heat must be added. The situation, though charming, is somewhat low and confined, and in the summer months the climate is decidedly relaxing. Those who seek bracing air must then go on to the Beatenberg, Grindelwald, or Mürren. Lovers of nature will see Interlaken at its best in May, June or October, when the crowd is absent and the woods are in full beauty. But in clear weather the view of the Jungfrau repays at all seasons a visit to this fashionable resort.

Adjoining Interlaken on the N., and across the river, is the ancient village of

Unterseen (12,000 Inhab.), composed (except the *Castle* on the market-place, and *Rathhaus*) of wooden houses, many of them brown from age. The *church-tower* has an old pack-saddle roof.

Seiler's factory of *Parquet floorings* is worth a visit.

Excursions. (a) The wooded slopes of the *Harder*, on the other side of the Aar. Keep to the paths, and beware of the slippery grass slopes, one of the real dangers of Switzerland. Several visitors have been killed here by falling over the cliffs below. (b) The *Rugen*, about 2 m., commands a very beautiful view. The path ascends from the Jungfraublick hotel, and winds to the top, branching in various directions through the wood.

(c) The old *Castle of Unspunnen*, rt. of the Lauterbrunnen road, beyond Matten, is within an easy walk. (d) The old ch. of Ringgenberg and the remains of the castle, about 2 m. from Interlaken on the road to Brienz, beautifully situated on a rocky knoll, overlooking the lake of Brienz and a little lake where the last lord of the castle is said to have been drowned. (e) The *Heimwehfluh*, ¼ hr.'s walk, commands a charming view of the two lakes and the Jungfrau. (f) The *Beatenberg*, 3450 ft.; H. Alpenrose; H. des Alpes, good pensions. A drive of 7 miles. (g) The *Scheinige Platte*, 6180 ft., which crowns the E. portal of the Lauterbrunnen valley, has one of the finest views of the Oberland range, and also commands the valleys of the two Lütschine. The path is easy. A carriage takes ½ hr. to Gsteig. The same horses are used for the ascent, which leaves the Lauterbrunnen road immediately behind the ch. of Gsteig, 3 hrs. from the *Inn* on the Scheinige Platte (H. Alpenrose, small, good), close to the *shining* slate-rock which gives a name to the spot. The Oberland Mountains are seen from the Wellhorn to the Blümlis Alp. The path to the inn is good, thence a rough path, not fit for horses, leads along the flank of the Gumihorn in ½ hr. to the *Taubenhorn*, whence the view is panoramic. The descent can be made to Zweilütschinen in about 2 hrs. The Iselten Alp, close to the inn, is a good specimen of a Swiss "sennerei." It feeds 400 cows and 200 oxen. There is a horse-path from the Scheinige Platte in 3 hrs. to the Faulhorn. (h) Another excursion, for climbers, is to the *Suleck*, 7910 ft., W. of the Lauterbrunnen valley. The top is difficult, but may be reached in 3½ hrs. by the village of Isenfluh, or by Saxeten, in the Saxeten Thal. (i) The churchyard of *Aeschi*, 1000 ft. above the S. shore of the lake of Thun, commands a splendid view. You leave the road to Thun at Leissigen, and take a good road l., for an ascent of 4 m.

The Giessbach is reached by steamboat. Lauterbrunnen, with the Staub-bach, and Grindelwald with its gla-ciers, are within a day's excursion.

By the *Saxeten Thal*, which falls into the valley of the Lütschine above Gsteig, Mühlenen and Reichen-bach in the Kander Thal, may be reached by the *Renggli Pass*, 6168 ft. The Saxeten Thal is known for its *Enzian Wasser*, a spirit distilled from the root of *Gentiana lutea*.

Christen's is an old established Library. *Urfer* has a good supply of maps.

The *English Church Service* is per-formed every Sunday twice in the choir of the old conventual church of Interlaken by an English clergyman. There is a Rom. Cath. chapel, and a Scotch Free church in the same build-ing.

Physicians—Drs. Strasser, Eber-sold, and Frohlich.

Diligences—to Grindelwald in 3 hrs.; to Lauterbrunnen in 2 hrs; Brienz to Lucerne in 6½ hrs.; Brienz to Meiringen in 1¾ hr.

There is a *printed Tariff* for carriages and horses. But the tariffs are fre-quently altered and are in the height of the season disregarded.

On many excursions (as to Mürren, Scheinige Platte, Wengern Alp, &c.) it is customary to drive as far as the road will permit, then to take out the horses and saddle them for the as-cent.

B. *Interlaken to Lauterbrunnen*, 7½ m.—*Mürren.*

						Miles.
Matten	.	.	.	.	.	1
Mühlenen	.	.	.	.	.	1
Zweilütschinen	.	.	.	.	.	2½
Lauterbrunnen	.	.	.	.	.	2½

[These rtes. may be reversed, and by commencing at Meiringen the

beautiful pass of the Great Scheideck is certainly seen to more advantage.]

About 2 hours' walk : a drive of 1½ h. Diligence from the post-office. [Pedestrians may avoid a part of the dusty road by ascending the *Heimwehfluh* on the rt.] Crossing a tract of meadow-land, on which wrestling-matches are periodically held, the road reaches *Matten*, where it divides, rt. being the shortest to Mühlenen, l. ½ m. longer by Gsteig. The former passes rt. the *Castle of Unspunnen* : it is in a dilapidated state, but a square tower, with flanking round turret, rises picturesquely above the surrounding brushwood. It is the reputed residence of Manfred, and its position in front of the Alps renders it not unlikely that Byron may have had it in his eye. The real owners of the castle were the barons of Unspunnen, lords of the Oberland, from the Grimsel to the Gemmi.

At *Gsteig* (*Inn:* Kreuz) the ascent of the *Scheinige Platte* (described above) commences.

Leaving, at the entrance of the Saxeten Thal, the village of *Mühlenen*, whose inhabitants are sadly afflicted with goître (§ 18), the road plunges into the gorge of the torrent *Lütschine*, overhung rt. by the Rothenfluh.

At the hamlet of *Zweilütschinen* (*Inn:* Bär), about 2 m. from Mühle-nen, the valley divides : the l. branch, from which flows the Black Lütschine, is the valley of Grindelwald (Rte. 25D) ; the rt., traversed by the White Lütschine, is the valley of Lauter-brunnen.

The latter is remarkable for its depth, contracted width, and precipices of limestone, which enclose it like walls. Its name is derived from the number of streamlets which cast them-selves from the cliffs, looking at a distance like so many pendulous white threads.

[From this point a pedestrian going

to Mürren can climb aloft and pursue his way along the mountain. The first turning rt. leads up to *Isenfluh* (whence the Suleck is ascended) and a path runs onward from it to Mürren in 3 hrs.]

The road to Lauterbrunnen passes under a precipice, called *Hünenfluh* (from Hüne, giant), whose face displays singular contortions in the limestone strata. If the clouds permit it, the summit of the Jungfrau is now seen; and soon afterwards, surmounting a steep slope, we reach

Lauterbrunnen. Inns: H. Staubbach, good and moderate: English spoken, and horses kept. Capricorne (Steinbock), H. Lauterbrunnen; both good.

Christian and Ulrich Lauener, of Lauterbrunnen, are celebrated guides. Johann Lauener (Christian's son), Ch. and J. von Almen, Joh. Gertsch, Ulr. Linder, Jac. Lauener, and F. Fuchs, are also recommended.

(Travellers should be on their guard against the personation of celebrated guides, sometimes attempted by inferior men of the same surname.)

This village contains about 2100 Inhab., dwelling in chalets, widely scattered along both banks of the torrent. It lies 2613 ft. above the sea, but so sunk between mountains that, in summer, the sun does not appear till 7 o'clock, and in winter not before 12. About 30 "wreaths of dangling water-smoke" hang from the edge of the ramparts which form the sides of the valley; and, when their tops are enveloped in clouds, appear to burst from the sky: but many disappear in summer. These minor falls are eclipsed by that of the

Staubbach, distant about 600 yds. from the inn. It is one of the loftiest in Europe, measuring between 800 and 900 feet; and from this cause, and the comparatively small body of water, it is shivered by the wind into spray long before it reaches the bottom

(whence its name — literally, *Duststream*). Those who expect in the Staubbach the roar and fury of a cataract, will be disappointed; but, in the opinion of many, these wants are atoned for by other beauties. The friction of the rock, and the resistance of the air, retard the descent of the water, giving it, when seen in front, the appearance of a lace veil suspended from the precipice, and imitating, in its centre, the folds of the drapery. When very full, it shoots out from the rock, and is bent by the wind into flickering undulations. Byron has described it admirably, both in prose and verse :—

"The torrent is in shape, curving over the rock, like the *tail* of a white horse streaming in the wind—such as it might be conceived would be that of the 'pale horse' on which Death is mounted in the Apocalypse. It is neither mist nor water, but a something between both : its immense height gives it a wave or curve—a spreading here or condension there — wonderful and indescribable."— *Byron's Journal.*

Wordsworth has called the Staubbach "a sky-born waterfall;" and when the clouds are low, it literally appears to leap from the sky. In winter, when nearly arrested by frost, a pyramid of ice is formed by the dripping of the water, increasing gradually upwards in the manner of a stalagmite, until the icicle reaches nearly half-way up the precipice.

Lauterbrunnen to Mürren.

2 to 3 hrs. Horse, 12 fr.; after 5 P.M., 15 fr.; returning by the Sefinen Thal, 15 fr. No guide required. The ascent is best made in the afternoon, when the sun is off. About 200 yards beyond the Capricorn inn, on the road to the Staubbach, the mule-path to Mürren turns off to the rt. It is a broad, well-marked mule-track, and at once begins to rise quickly, turning first to the right and then to the left. The ascent is steep, lying chiefly

through pine woods, and Jungfrau, Mönch, and Eiger come more and more into view. After a little less than an hour, the stream of the Staubach is crossed above the fall. A chalet for refreshment has been built at the spot. The path continues very steep, and after passing a saw-mill, in a little more than an hour from the Staubbach (2 hrs. from Lauterbrunnen), comes out on an open pasture. Less than 20 min. walk on level ground brings the tourist to H. des Alpes, and 3 min. more brings him to H. de Mürren. These hotels are both very good and comfortable, *Eng. Ch. S.* in a small ch. The hamlet (5348 ft., or 2735 ft. above Lauterbrunnen) is a cluster of old black wooden houses and haybarns. At *Gimmelwald*, 4300 ft., 25 min. below Mürren, is a good pension, *H. Schilthorn*, overlooking the wild gorge of the Sefinen Thal.

The tourist may vary his route by descending through the lower part of the *Sefinen Thal* to Stechelberg, 5 m. from Lauterbrunnen. The path is easily found.

Mürren is on a tolerably wide shelf at the top of the precipices which bound the Lauterbrunnen valley. Immediately facing it are the monotonous precipices of the *Schwarz Mönch*, a buttress of the Jungfrau, which is seen from here in its least beautiful aspect. This defect in the view is made up for by the noble circle of peaks (*Mittaghorn, Grosshorn, Breithorn*) encircling the head of the Lauterbrunnen valley. There are several pretty walks round Mürren. (*a*) Through the meadows to the S. to H. Schilthorn (25 min.). (*b*) The path to the *Schilthorn* (see below). (*c*) Among the woods on the path to Lauterbrunnen. (*d*) To the Fern Valley.

The *Schilthorn* (9748 ft.) is about 3½ hrs. due W. of Mürren. Horses can go for the first 2½ hrs. The last hour is a rough scramble up rocks, and though the track can be found without a guide, many people would prefer to have one. Ladies frequently make the ascent. The path turns out from the middle of the village, and passes a conspicuous chalet with a white basement. Just beyond the chalet, the path goes to the rt. through two gates, and then rises by steep zigzags past a new chalet up a steep buttress of the mountain. It then goes up a ravine, and across an alp, at the top of which is a fine view. Then through a dreary valley, usually patched with snow. At the end of this valley the two peaks of the Schilthorn appear in front. Here, 2 hrs. from Mürren, the horses are left. The path goes along a ledge to the rt., then crosses the stream from the glacier, and goes up by the monument to Mrs. Arbuthnot, who, making the ascent with her husband, was struck dead by lightning in 1865, then keeps to the L up a ridge of rocks to near the top of the Little Schilthorn, and then to the top of the Great Schilthorn. The view is very fine. The Blümlis Alp is a noble object, but the great peaks of the Oberland are not so imposing as from the Faulhorn.

The return may be varied by descending over rough shale to the path in the Sefinen Thal, about an hour longer than the other route.

Upper Valley of Lauterbrunnen.

Carriage-road to Stechelberg, 5 m.

	Miles.
Trümelbach	2
Stechelberg	3
	Hrs.
Trachsellauinen	¾
Schmadribach	1¼

Although comparatively little visited, the upper part of the valley possesses scenery of the highest order. The fall of the *Schmadribach*, 7 hrs. there and back (*Inn:* H. Schmadribach, at Trachsellauinen), has impressed many a traveller even from a distance, when climbing the Wengern Alp, and has well repaid a nearer acquaintance, but it was unfortunately injured in 1870, when an avalanche cut it into 2 cascades. It is a large body of water, which, issuing from the glacier, throws itself over a precipice of 200 ft. and makes two more leaps, before reaching the bottom of the valley. The road for some way from Lauterbrunnen runs nearly on a level, below magnificent cliffs from which dangle numerous cascades of the Staubbach character.

The curious little fall of the *Trümelbach*, leaping from a ravine under the Jungfrau, may be visited by the way. The road as far as *Stechelberg* (new *Inn*) is practicable for a small carriage; beyond that place it is so narrow that horses can alone go for another ¾ hr., as far as the hamlet of *Trachsellauinen* (2½ hrs. from Lauterbrunnen), opposite which will be seen the remains of an avalanche, called by the same name, which falls annually from the Jungfrau, and spreads its ruins over a surface of many hundred acres. An hour farther, in which there is a steep ascent, stands a single chalet, near the foot of the lower fall; from which there is ½ an hour's sharp ascent to the foot of the upper fall. Deciduous trees cease below Trachsellauinen; thence the way lies generally through pine forests, and the pasturage is abundant to a much greater height. Above towers the snowy chain, which, running S. and then W. from the Jungfrau, rises in the summits of the Gletscherhorn, Mittaghorn, Grosshorn, Breithorn, and *Tschingelhorn*, passing on in an unbroken line of ice to the Gemmi.

If the path hitherto taken to the upper fall be still further followed, it leads in ¾ hr.'s sharp ascent to the rt., to the high pasture of the *Steinberg*, close to the Tschingel glacier. The view of the Jungfrau from this point is most magnificent. It is quite possible to descend from the Steinberg to Mürren without going into the Lauterbrunnen valley. The track is not difficult to find. It enters the bridle-path to Mürren near the fine fall of the stream issuing from the Sefinen Thal.

[From Trachsellauinen the traveller may cross to Ried in the Lötschen Thal, by the easy glacier pass of the Petersgrat, or the more difficult Wetterlücke (see Rte. 35).]

Lauterbrunnen to the Gemmi involves the long détour by the lake of Thun, or the passage of the fatiguing double pass of the *Sefinen Furke and Dündengrat*, or of the easy glacier *Tschingel Pass*. The last is to be preferred (see Rtes. 35, 36).

The *Jungfrau* can be ascended by the *Roththal* (about 12 hrs. from Lauterbrunnen to the top) by means of a couloir which comes half-way down towards the Roththal glacier. The climb is difficult, and in one part exposed to avalanches. A guide was killed by one in 1872. Those who ascend this way, go down to the Aletsch Glacier.

The *Lawinen Thor* (Avalanche-gate), a very difficult passage between the Jungfrau and Gletscherhorn, first accomplished by Prof. Tyndall and Mr. Vaughan Hawkins in 1860. They spent 7 hrs. on the rocks, and 19 hrs. between Lauterbrunnen and the Eggischhorn. A hut has been built in the Roththal, 4 hrs. above Trachsellauinen, to facilitate these ascents; but they are not to be recommended even to mountaineers.

The ice-crest has been crossed at other spots further W., but the *tours de force* of a party of skilled climbers are not in this work reckoned as passes.

C. *Lauterbrunnen to Grindelwald,*—a. *By the carriage-road.*—b. *By the Wengern Alp.*

Both Lauterbrunnen and Grindelwald may be visited in one long day from Interlaken, returning in the evening. If the Wengern Alp route is chosen, a carriage may be hired at Interlaken, and the saddle-horses used to draw it, saddles being taken. Boys run the carriage back to the junction of the Grindelwald road.

a. By the high-road the time occupied in going from Lauterbrunnen to

Grindelwald is about 2 hrs.—the distance about 10 m. It is necessary to return down the valley as far as Zweilütschinen, then, crossing the White, to ascend, by the side of the Black Lütschine. The Eiger and Wetterhorn are noble features in the scenery, but the loftier Schreckhorn is only seen for a short time. On approaching Grindelwald the lower glacier appears in sight.

b. In fine weather there is no more interesting ride among the Alps than that over the *Wengern Alp* and *Little Scheideck.* The view of the Jungfrau, Mönch and Eiger is one of the most glorious near views of snowy mountains, and avalanches are seen and heard in the greatest perfection. No one should abandon the expedition without an effort. The pass takes from 5 to 7 hrs., so, if an early start be made, there is time for a long enjoyable halt on the Col. The path is constantly traversed by ladies on horseback, or in chaises-à-porteurs (§ 2). Those who are at all able to walk need take a horse to the summit only, for which one day is charged; for the whole journey, 1½ day.

The bridle-path turns off at the chapel nearly opposite the Staubbach, and after crossing the river ascends steep zigzags, which command the Silberhorn (Silverhorn) and summit of the Jungfrau, and the splendid perspective of the valley of Lauterbrunnen, closed by glaciers. After nearly an hour of toilsome ascent, it reaches a more gradual slope of meadow land and the hamlet of *Wengern,* with pensions belonging to Ulr. and Chr. Lauener. The valley of Lauterbrunnen, beneath whose precipices the traveller may have previously walked with some little awe, presents from this height the aspect of a mere trench; the Staubbach is reduced to a thread, and its upper fall, and previous winding, before it makes its leap, are exposed to view. An Alpine horn is here played as travellers pass, and the track winds to the rt. round the shoulder of the hill, and through a pretty belt of forest, and then,

becoming steep, crosses slopes of grass towards the Jungfrau, which rises to the view in a magnificent expanse of snow and glacier. It is quite a surprise, for so colossal are its proportions, that the effect of distance is lost, and it appears to be within gunshot of the spectator.

About ½ hr. short of the Col (where there is also an *Inn*) is the *H. de la Jungfrau,* a convenient midday halting-place with excellent table-d'hôte, 4 fr., directly facing the Jungfrau. The opposite precipices are channelled with a deep furrow, down which the avalanches descend. They are most numerous a little after noon, when the sun and wind exercise the greatest influence on the glacier in loosening masses of it, and causing them to break off.

The attention is first arrested by a roar, not unlike thunder, and in half a minute a gush of white powder, resembling a small cataract, is perceived issuing from one of the upper grooves or gullies; it then sinks into a fissure, and is lost only to reappear at a lower stage; soon after, another roar, and a fresh gush from another gully, till the ice, reaching the lowest step, is precipitated into the gulf at the foot of the mountain. By watching attentively, the separation of the fragment from the glacier may be seen, and before the sound reaches the ear. Sometimes the ice merely slides down the surface, at others it turns over in a cake; but in an instant it is shattered to pieces, and, in passing through the different gullies, apparently ground to powder. Independent of the sound, which is awful, there is generally nothing grand or striking in these falling masses: and, indeed, it is difficult, at first, to believe that the echoing thunder arises from what appears so slight a cause; but the spectator must bear in mind that the distance is 1 m. and that at each discharge tons of ice are hurled down the mountain, and that the seeming dust to which it is reduced includes blocks capable of sweeping away the largest trees, if such stood in their course. During the early part of summer many such discharges may be seen in an hour; in cold weather they are less numerous.   The avalanches descend into the valley of Trümmleten, the uninhabited ravine dividing the Jungfrau from the Wengern Alp, far deeper than travellers along the bridle-track have any idea of; and, on melting, send forth a stream which falls into the Lütschine, a little above Lauterbrunnen.

[*Near View of the Avalanches.*—Mr. F. Galton drew attention in 1863 to the view by the side of the gully immediately facing the Jungfrau hotel,

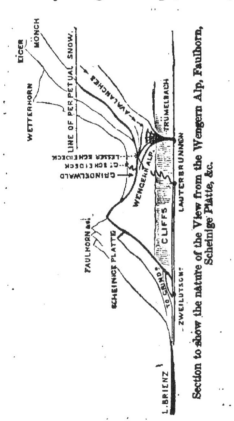

to which the avalanches from the Jungfrau converge, a point which may be reached in 1¼ hr. from either hotel quite easily and safely by descending into the Trümleten valley, crossing the stream by a bridge, traversing a narrow band of avalanche snow fallen from the Eiger, and then mounting to the gully.   The path is simple and easy, save up two low terraces of rock, where the absence of foot-hold (steps might be quarried) necessitates the assistance of a guide and rope. On arriving at the side of the gully the traveller, in perfect safety, may see the avalanches sweep by like a waterfall.   First a prodigious roar is heard, then a storm of ice-balls tears through the opening and dashes forth upon a long slope of ice and snow.   Down this they slide swiftly, with a hissing noise.   Gushes of water accompany each discharge.   The ice-cliffs that supply the avalanches tumble 2000 ft. before they reach the head of the gully, which itself is 1000 ft. high: consequently the fragments have time to be ground into shivers ; but, for the most part, they are rounded into balls from 1 to 2 ft. in diameter.   These, with the finer débris, form a slope extending nearly 2000 ft. in additional descent, from the foot of the passage to the almost inaccessible depths of the valley.]

A part of Byron's 'Manfred' was either written or mentally composed on the Wengern Alp.   He says in his Journal, "Heard the avalanches falling every five minutes nearly.   The clouds rose from the opposite valley, curling up perpendicular precipices, like the foam of the ocean of hell during a spring tide—it was white and sulphury, and immeasurably deep in appearance.   The side we ascended was not of so precipitous a nature; but, on arriving at the summit, we looked down upon the other side upon a boiling sea of cloud, dashing against the crags on which we stood—these crags on one side quite perpendicular.   In passing the masses of snow, I made a snowball, and pelted Hobhouse with it."—*Swiss Journal.*

A day ought to be spent on the Wengern Alp in thoroughly enjoying the grand scenery.   Those who sleep at one of the inns on the mountain are, in fine weather, well rewarded by the glorious sunset and sunrise views, far more sublime than those seen from the Rigi.

Beyond the Jungfrau Hotel the track is tolerably level, and in about

2 miles the col is attained (6788 ft.). *Inn:* H. Bellevue, most obliging people. A good stopping-place for a day or two. The view is one of the noblest in the Alps, including, besides the Jungfrau, Mönch, and Eiger, the Wetterhorn, and distant Alps E. and W. Travellers should on no account omit walking ¼ hr. towards the Mönch, to the verge of the intervening valley. They should walk past the flagstaff, following the ins and outs of the small spurs in their way, till they arrive suddenly on the edge of a cliff overlooking the deep Trümmleten Thal. The grandeur of the range greatly rises in the estimation of those who have seen it from this point of view. The Jungfrau, Mönch, and Eiger stand like watch-towers on the edge of terrific cliffs, which to an unpractised eye appear almost vertical, and bold must have been the man who first ventured to scale them : but they are not quite so steep as they look.

Beyond the valley of Grindelwald towers the Wetterhorn (Peak of Storms), 12,165 ft. The glaciers, which cling to these mountains, and fill the hollows between them, extend without interruption from the Gemmi to the Grimsel, and from Grindelwald nearly to the villages of Viesch and Mörel, in the Valais. The extent of this glacier-field has been calculated to be 115 square miles, or about one-sixth of all the glaciers among the Alps.

Between the Jungfrau and Mönch are the *Guggi Glacier* and pass of the *Jungfrau Joch*, first achieved, 1862, by Messrs. George, L. Stephen, Hardy, and Moore, with six guides. The first day they were obliged to return for a ladder; on the second they accomplished what must always be a passage of some peril. Their course lay up the buttress of the Mönch, and then by the Guggi glacier to a plateau of some size, scarcely seen from the inn (3 hrs. up). Above this they encountered very serious difficulty and danger. The only course was by the steep ice-fall, among huge and tottering séracs, which at any moment might have

fallen and overwhelmed the party. At length they reached the bergschrund, in places 30 ft. wide, crossed it with their ladder, and gained a view of the final ridge. This was a curtain of névé, pierced in the centre by a patch of rocks. To the rt. the wall was tried, but found too perilously steep, and the only course was to the l. of the rocks where the slope was a little less, but heaped with towers and cut by a maze of crevasses. At one point they had to climb a sheer cliff of ice by their ladder, but this was the last difficulty, a smoother slope leading to the summit—8¾ hrs. from the Wengern Alp.

The descent from the Jungfrau Joch to the Wengern Alp has been effected, but it is always a somewhat hazardous enterprise.

A hut has been built near the Guggi Glacier for the use of mountaineers—1½ hr. from H. Bellevue.

Between the Mönch and Eiger are the *Eiger Glacier* and the difficult *Eiger Joch*, first passed in 1859.

The *Jungfrau*, or Virgin (13,671 ft.)—which is separated from the Giant by the Monk—received her name in the last century from the unsullied purity of the snow, or because her crest was then deemed inaccessible to human foot. Like most of the high peaks, she has lost her claim to the title on the latter score, the summit having been reached for the first time as early as 1811, by the brothers Meyer, of Aarau; in 1828 by 6 peasants from Grindelwald; and, in August, 1841, by M. Agassiz, of Neuchâtel, and Professor Forbes, of Edinburgh.

Since that time many ascents have been made from the Aletsch side, and a few from the Roththal and the Wengern Alp. The latter route is long and laborious, and in the lower portion (as in crossing the Jungfrau Joch) the traveller is exposed to some danger from the fall of huge masses of "sérac" on the Guggi glacier.

The beautiful secondary peak of the *Silberhorn* (12,106), has also been

G 2

climbed, both by the Guggi glacier and the steep cliffs which face Lauterbrunnen.

The *Mönch* (13,465) rises on this side in a tall cliff of rock and ice, and can only be climbed from the North in rare conditions of the snow. Its summit is usually reached from the S. side (see Rte. 29).

The favourite expedition for climbers is the ascent of the *Eiger* (13,045 ft.). It is a long, but not very difficult rock-climb, but the last half-hour lies along a sharp ice-crest, and requires steadiness in all the party. An incapable traveller was here only saved by the strength of his guide a year or two ago. The great advantage of this ascent is, that the climber starts from good quarters, at the very foot of his peak, and has no tiresome preliminary wandering over rough ground. The time taken varies, according to the state of the mountain, from 9 to 14 hrs.

Ordinary travellers will content themselves with the ascent of one of the easy crests which rise N. of the H. Bellevue, the *Lauberhorn* (1½ hr.'s walk) or *Tschuggen*, whence they may descend to the path leading to the inn on the Männlichen (see below).

The descent to Grindelwald is at first steep. It passes within sight of a weather-worn forest. Byron describes " whole woods of withered pines—all withered; trunks stripped and barkless; branches lifeless; done by a single winter — their appearance reminded me of me and my family."

In descending into the valley, the Wetterhorn is seen in front; on the l. the Faulhorn, surmounted by its inn; on the rt. the upper glacier of Grindelwald, issuing from a gorge. About half-way from the pass is the H. des Alpes, a good chalet *Inn*.

Those who have already traversed the mule-path, may find charming footways to the N. of it through the woods, with a superb view of the Schreckhorn, a peak difficult to see to advantage elsewhere.

Grindelwald.—Hotels: Bär, excellent; Adler, good, with garden and Pension; Pension Schönegg; Eiger; Burgener; Zum Gletscher. Pension Finsteraarhorn, and several others. *Eng. Ch. S.* in summer.

The village of Grindelwald, consisting of picturesque wooden cottages, widely scattered over the valley, stands at a height of 3460 ft. above the sea, from which cause, and its vicinity to the glaciers, the climate is cold and unstable even in summer. Its inhabitants are chiefly employed in rearing cattle, of which 6000 head are fed on the neighbouring pastures; and many act as guides.

Guides. — Ulr. Almer, first-rate; Hans and Johann Baumann, P. Egger, Peter Baumann, all excellent; P. Schlegel, P. Kaufmann, U. Kaufmann, P. Inabnit, U. Wenger (employed at Adler Hotel); Christian Bohren, Ulrich Rubi : all fair men.

Grindelwald owes its celebrity to its position under the Wetterhorn, to the beauty of the views from the Great Scheideck and Wengern Alp, and to its *Glaciers*, which, as they descend below the level of the village, are easily accessible. Three great mountains form the S. side of the valley— the Eiger, or Giant; the Mettenberg (Middle Mountain), which is, in fact, the base or pedestal of the magnificent Schreckhorn; and the Wetterhorn (Peak of Tempests). From the sides of the Mettenberg stream down the two glaciers of Grindelwald. They are branches of that field or sea of ice mentioned above as occupying the table-land and high valleys of the Bernese Alps. Their chief beauty as a feature of the landscape arises from contrast, the white ice being fringed by dark forest and pasture.

In some years, a quarry of ice, to supply the markets of Paris and elsewhere, is established at Grindelwald, and is in full operation after the busy season of the year. Hundreds of workmen hew squared blocks, which are wheeled to the village, and thence sent to their destination.

Excursions.

The Lower Glacier (a tramway now leads from the glacier to the bridge over the Lütschine, where the path to the Wengern Alp branches off) forces its way out between the Eiger and Mettenberg, and descended some years ago to a point only 3200 ft. above the level of the sea. In 1850, it projected far into the valley, and the pressure in the narrow passage between the Eiger and Mettenberg drove the ice up into pinnacles of great size and beauty. Since that time this glacier, like nearly all the Swiss glaciers, has retreated nearly half a mile, and has sunk some 300 ft., leaving a large surface of bare rock. The retreat of the ice exposed ancient marble quarries, worked before some previous advance of the glacier. A grotto or passage is cut in the ice, in order to exhibit the beautiful blue colour. It is about 20 min. from the village. A path runs along the cliff on its E. margin, beneath the precipices of the Mettenberg, commanding a view of the minarets of the ice-fall, and affording means (a ladder) of paying a visit to the *Eismeer* (Ice-sea), or level part of the glacier, *one of the pleasantest excursions on the Alps;* with a local guide, occupying 5 or 6 hrs. It is the beginning of the Strahleck Pass (Rte. 27B), and a lady may be carried to the ladders in a chaise à porteurs. On the *Bärenegg,* 2 hrs. from Grindelwald, is a châlet, where beds and provisions can be obtained. The Eismeer, and the path to it, offer to those who cannot mount great heights a very grand near view of the snow-region of the Alps; the cultivated valley is hidden, and little visible but the peaks of the Eiger, Schreckhorn, and Viescherhörner, streaming with ice. To the W. is the steep and broken névé leading to the Mönch Joch, and below the slopes of the Viescherhörner, surrounded by glacier, the *Heisse Platte* (Hot Plate), a rock so called because

snow or ice never rests upon it. In 1821 M. Mouron, a clergyman of Vevey, was lost in one of the crevasses of the Eismeer. Fair walkers will be tempted to cross the ice to the Zasenberg, a slope at the foot of the Viescherhörner, which feeds a few sheep in summer.

On the path to the chalet a depression in the rocks, called *Martinsdruck,* is pointed out to the traveller, and opposite to it, in the crest of the Eiger, a hole—called *Martinsloch*—through which the sun shines twice a-year. Once on a time, according to the legend, the basin now occupied by the Eismeer was filled with a lake, but the space between the Mettenberg and the Eiger being much narrower than at present, the outlet from it was constantly blocked, and inundations produced, which ruined the fields of the peasants in the valley. At length S. Martin, a giant, came to their rescue; he seated himself on the Mettenberg, rested his staff on the Eiger, and then, with one lusty heave of his brawny back, not only burst open the present wide passage between the two mountains, but left the marks of his seat on the one, and drove his walking-stick right through the other.

On the Eiger side is the *Nellenbalm,* a cavern chapel to St. Petronilla. 1 hr.

The *Upper Grindelwald Glacier* may be visited in going over the Scheideck. That glacier has also retreated, and sunk so that it no longer projects into the valley, and is scarcely worth a visit in its lower portion. The upper icefall is one of the finest in the Alps (see Rte. 27).

The *Männlichen,* between the valleys of Grindelwald and Lauterbrunnen, over the junction of the two streams, is a fine point of view, preferred by some good judges to the Wengern Alp, with an *Inn* on the summit. Easy slope from Grindelwald; on the other side very steep slopes, down which a path leads to Wengern. Small mountain *Inn* on the top. As soon as the snow has left the top it is covered with flowers. Horse there and back 15 fr. This excursion can be combined with the Wengern Alp. Ascent from Grindelwald 3½ to 4 hrs., Männlichen to Wengern Alp 1½ hr.

The *Faulhorn* (*faul*, rotten, from the shaly nature of its summit slopes) is a mountain 8800 ft. above the sea, situated between the valley of Grindelwald and the lake of Brienz, and commanding, from its summit, a celebrated *near* view of the Bernese Alps. It may be reached from Grindelwald, from the Great Scheideck, the easiest ascent; from the Scheinige Platte; or from the Giessbach. It is 4½ hrs. from Grindelwald, and 3¼ hrs. from the Scheideck. There is an *Inn* half-way up from Grindelwald (H. Alpenrose).

Ladies may be carried from Grindelwald in chaises à porteurs, with 4 bearers to each chair, at 6 fr. each; or if the party sleep on the Faulhorn, 9 fr. *A guide* to the top is 8 fr.: a horse 17 fr. up and down; 25 fr. if the night is passed on the top; 35 fr. is charged from Interlaken by the Scheinige Platte. The *Inn* on the summit has 24 beds, and is fair but dear. In the height of the season you must secure beds beforehand, or be early on the top. The path from Grindelwald leads over the Bach Alp, by the side of a small lake, 1000 ft. below the summit. The Faulhorn view of the Bernese Alps far surpasses that from the Rigi. On the other hand, though the lakes of Thun and Brienz are both partly seen, they afford but a poor equivalent for the wide expanse of blue water which bathes the foot of the Rigi. Easy path in 3 hrs. from the Faulhorn to the Scheideck *Inn*.

Those who cannot reach the summit of the Faulhorn will be well repaid for mounting its slope for an hour or two on the road to the Scheideck as far as the small *Inn* which offers refreshment and beds.

The *Mettenberg*, 10,443 ft., between the Lower and Upper Grindelwald glaciers, is a remarkably fine point of view. This is the best expedition for good walkers who, without wishing to undertake a difficult ascent, desire to make a close acquaintance with the ice-world and the great peaks. It is an expedition of 10 to 11 hrs.

The *Wetterhorn*, so well known for its wall of rocks and beautiful pyramid of snow, has 3 peaks—the glittering point to the N. 12,149 ft., S. of it the *Mittelhorn*, 12,166 ft., and S. of that the *Rosenhorn*, 12,107 ft. The two latter rise from a field of névé, called the *Wettereismeer*, the snows of which feed the Gauli and Rosenlaui glaciers. The Rosenhorn was first ascended in 1844 by M. Desor and his friends; the Mittelhorn on July 9, 1845, by a Scotchman, Mr. Spier; and the Wetterhorn proper in 1844, by two of M. Desor's guides, and in 1845 by Professor Agassiz and a large party, and in 1854, from Grindelwald by a new route, by Mr. A. Wills, who has given an interesting account of it in his 'Wanderings among the High Alps.' The last is remarkable for its wonderful view down upon the Scheideck, and is the peak now generally ascended. The usual rte. is identical with that to the Lauteraar Joch (Rte. 27B) as far as the *Weisshorn* hut, above the old Gleckstein Cave, where the night can be passed. Thence a scramble leads to the ridge connecting the Wetterhorn with the Mittelhorn, and a very steep climb up the final slope, at an angle of 50° to 58° (in 5 hrs. from the hut), lands the traveller on a crest so sharp that, in some years, there is scarcely a place for a man to rest on. It is possible to descend to Rosenlaui, or by the Gauli Joch.

The *Schreckhorn*, 13,386 ft., lying far back in the mountain solitude, was long invested with a certain mystery. In 1842 M. Desor reached the S. peak of the Schreckhorn block, known as the Lauteraarhorn, from the Finsteraar glacier. The highest peak was left for Mr. Leslie Stephen who, in 1861, climbed it from the Lower Grindelwald glacier. It is a difficult rock-climb, only to be attempted by first-rate climbers with good guides. The tracks of falling stones should

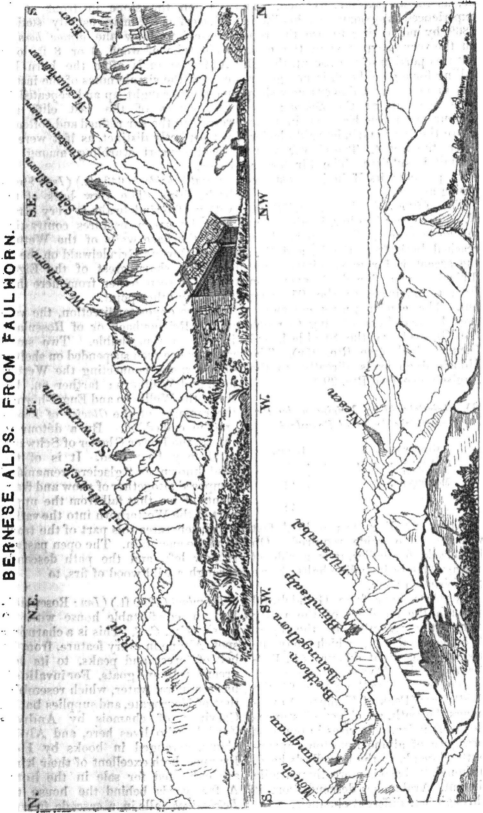

BERNESE ALPS. FROM FAULHORN.

be, as far as possible, avoided. An experienced cragsman lost his life in 1869, by neglecting to use the rope on the very sharp crest of the peak, but this portion of the ascent, though calling for a good head, is not generally dangerous. Climbers now sleep in a new hut at the *Schwarzenegg*, ½ hour from the Kastenstein Cave, above the lower Grindelwald glacier, before the ascent. The view from the summit is sublime. The Finsteraarhorn presents itself in its most imposing aspect.

The *Little Schreckhorn*, 11,473 ft., N. of his great brother, is almost as savage in aspect. The top has been reached both from the E. and W.; the ascent is for good climbers not difficult, and a fine day's excursion from Grindelwald or the Bärenegg hut. The glacier passes commonly used by travellers wishing to reach the Grimsel are the Strahleck and Lauteraarjoch (see Rte. 27B.) The Mönch Joch leads directly to the Eggischhorn (see Rte. 29.)

D. *Grindelwald to Meiringen, by the Great Scheideck and Rosenlaui.*

Grindelwald.	Hours.
Scheideck	3
Rosenlaui	2
Meiringen	2¼
	—
	7¼

About 20 Eng. m.; 6 hrs.' fast walking. No guide required. On horseback, for ladies, it is a ride of at least 9 hours, including halts; horse to Meiringen 25 fr.

The first hour from Grindelwald through the meadows of the valley brings the traveller to the *Upper Grindelwald Glacier*, which may be visited by a slight détour. (*H. Wetterhorn*, small.) The ascent afterwards is easy, and during the whole of it the *Wetterhorn* (Peak of Tempests) overhangs the path, an object of stupendous sublimity. It rises in one vast precipice of alpine limestone, apparently close above the traveller's head, although its base is more than a mile distant. Avalanches descend from it through four different channels,

Upon the slope in front of the Wetterhorn a man usually stations himself to blow the *alpine horn*, a rude tube of wood, 6 or 8 ft. long. A few seconds after the horn has ceased, the simple notes of the instrument are caught up and repeated by the echoes of the vast cliff, and return to the ear refined and softened, yet perfectly distinct, as if it were an aërial concert warbling among the crags.

Great Scheideck (6434 ft.) (*Inn:* Steinbock, fair). The view back of the valley of Grindelwald is very striking: its green pastures contrasting with the bare walls of the Wetterhorn. Beyond Grindelwald on the l., rises the sharp crest of the Eiger, which is seen better from here than from any other point.

In the opposite direction, the vale of the Reichenbach or of Rosenlaui, is not so remarkable. Two small glaciers are seen suspended on shelves of the range connecting the Wetterhorn and Wellhorn; farther on, between the Wellhorn and Engel-hörner, the remains of the *Glacier of Rosenlaui* lie embedded. By a détour to the rt., the Lower Glacier of Schwarzwald may be visited. It is of the kind known as " glaciers remaniés," composed altogether of snow and fragments of ice that fall from the upper part of the Wetterhorn into the valley which separates this part of the track from the mountain. The open pasture is now left, and the path descends through a wild wood of firs, to

Rosenlaui (4300 ft.) (*Inn:* Rosenlaui-Bad, a comfortable house with 80 beds). *Eng. C. S.* This is a charming spot, Alpine in every feature, from its belt of forest and peaks, to its soft green knolls and goats. For invalids it has a mineral water, which resembles that of Harrogate, and supplies baths. Carvings of chamois by Andreas Zurfluh, who lives here, and Alpine plants, arranged in books by Herr Brunner, both excellent of their kind, are exhibited for sale in the hotel. A few yards behind the house the *Reichenbach* falls in a cascade from a rocky cleft. On the opposite side of the valley a path winds up the steep forest in 1 hr. to the *Glacier of Rosenlaui,* smaller than those of Grindelwald, but formerly celebrated for the purity of its surface, and transparent azure of its crevasses. It has now so far retreated as to be scarcely worth a visit to the foot. A steep path on the l. of the glacier leads in about ½ an hour to the summit of a cliff which projected over it, and bent its course considerably. It forms a good point of view. The torrent which issues from this glacier rushes through a remarkable chasm in the mountain side. It is, in places, so narrow as to escape notice until a bridge is reached, when the water is seen raging 300 ft. below.

[From Rosenlaui the *Schwarzhorn,* a higher summit of the Faulhorn range, may be reached in 4½ hrs. (for 3 hrs. horsepath). The view is finer than from the Faulhorn, and the excursion is strongly recommended. A guide is essential.

The ascent of the *Wetterhorn* can be made from here by fair mountaineers as easily as from Grindelwald in about 6 or 7 hrs. A hut with sleeping-room for 30 persons has been built nearly halfway on the rocks of the Dossenhorn. The Grimsel is reached by the laborious glacier pass of the *Renferjoch.*]

The path to Meiringen runs by the side of this stream, first crossing a charming little green plain, carpeted with soft turf, like that of an English lawn, dotted with chalets and girt by forest heights. The view from this point deserves particular notice : it is a favourite subject for the pencil. The Wetterhorn, Wellhorn, and craggy peaks of the Engel-hörner, form a most picturesque mountain group.

Below this the valley contracts, and numerous waterfalls dangle from its sides : one, from its tenuity, is called the Rope-stream (Seilbach) ; and now a bird's-eye view opens into the vale of *Hasli,* or Meiringen, which, in comparison with the narrow glens of Grindelwald and Lauterbrunnen, deserves the name of a plain, though bounded by lofty mountains.

The latter part of the descent is steep and rugged, paved with slippery stones, and travellers are usually invited to dismount, and proceed on foot. The stream goes down nearly 2000 ft. in a succession of seven leaps, the celebrated *Falls of the Reichenbach.* The upper fall is a short distance l. of the road, near the hamlet of Zwirghi. A small fee is exacted for the liberty to cross the meadow and enter the hut called Belvedere. But the fall is best seen from a headland shooting out in front of the bare cliff over which the cataract dashes. A little lower is the less imposing *Kesselfall;* and lower still another, by which the stream gains the level of the valley. This is just behind the Reichenbach hotel, and is illuminated with coloured fires every night during the season. The effect is beautiful.

The *Reichenbach Hotel,* 2 hrs. from Rosenlaui, a comfortable house, with hot and cold baths, preferred by some to the inns at Meiringen; *H. des Alpes.* These hotels are distant about ⅓ m., by a road and bridge over the Aar, from

Meiringen (1968 ft.) (*Inns:* Sauvage, very good; Couronne; Bär). Meiringen is the chief place in the vale of Hasli (2800 Prot. Inhab.). It has suffered greatly from the disastrous fire of February, 1879, which destroyed a large portion of it. Its situation, in the midst of a truly Alpine valley is picturesque. The precipitous and wooded mountain sides, streaked with cascades, and here and there overtopped by some snow-peak, are beautiful features. A stone dyke 1000 ft. long protects the village from the Alpbach, which, subject to sudden rises, and cutting through loose shaly strata of lias marl, has more than once threatened to bury Meiringen.

The *English Church* was erected 1868.

Wood-carving is a thriving industry here, as well as at Brienz, and a visit to one of the workshops is interesting. The dealers will pack and forward articles to England.

The *Falls of the Alpbach*, on the E. side of the valley, is best seen about 9 on a sunny morning, when a *triple bow*, or iris, glimmers in the spray. The inner iris forms nearly a complete circle, and the outer are more or less circular as the water is abundant or not. The spot whence it is visible is within the rain from the cataract. Near the fall, and on a rock above the village, is the ruin of the *Castle of Resti*: it belonged to an ancient and noble family, to whom the praise is given of never having tyrannized over their dependants. There is a fine view from the ruin.

The men of *Hash* are celebrated for their athletic forms and strength, and generally distinguish themselves in the *Schwingfeste*, or wrestling matches which they hold every year with their neighbours of Unterwalden and Grindelwald. The first Monday of Aug. is the day, and it is kept as a fête, with national songs and dances. The women enjoy the reputation of being prettier, or rather less plain, than those of other Swiss valleys. Their holiday costume is not ungraceful, a bodice of black velvet reaching to the throat, starched white sleeves, a yellow petticoat, and a round black hat, worn on one side of the head, and allowing the hair to fall in long tresses down the back.

Glacier Guides.—Melchior Anderegg, Johann Jaun, Johann von Bergen, Kaspar Maurer, Andreas Jaun, A. Jaun. These men are at the head of their profession, and are generally engaged before hand. There are many other good men. Inquire at the inns.

At Meiringen converge the carr.-roads—*a*, from Interlaken and Brienz; *b*, from Lucerne by the Brünig (Rte. 19); *c*, from Guttannen on the way to the Grimsel (Rte. 26), the Falls of

Handeck are on the way thither; and the *Bridle-paths; d*, the Joch Pass from Engelberg (Rte. 33); *e*, the Susten from Wasen on the St. Gothard (Rte. 32); and *f*, the Great Scheideck from Rosenlaui and Grindelwald.

E. *Meiringen to Interlaken, by Brienz and the Giessbach.—Rothhorn.*

1½ hr. drive or 9 Eng. m. to Brienz; 1-horse carr. 7 fr.; 2-horse 14; *diligence* three times daily (2½ fr.). Thence to Interlaken by road, or N. shore, 1-horse carr. 8 fr.; 2-horse 15 fr., or steam-boat in 1½ hr., calling at the Giessbach.

The road down the valley passes the *Wandelbach* and *Oltschibach* and other cascades leaping down the wall of rock. After proceeding for about 4 m. along the l. bank of the Aar, it crosses the river by an iron bridge near *Brienzwyler* (5½ m.), where the branch of the Brünig road leading to Brienz (Rte. 19) descends into the valley. The Aar flows between stone dykes through marsh and flat meadow-land; but near its influx into the lake of Brienz, the form of the mountains on its l. bank is grand. In skirting the margin of the lake, the road crosses heaps of débris, covering acres of land once fertile. A torrent of mud, in 1797, destroyed a considerable part of 2 villages near Kienholz; and a landslip from the Brienzergrat, the mountain immediately behind Brienz, overwhelmed, in November, 1824, 40 acres of land, and swept 6 persons into the lake.

Brienz.—Inns: L'Ours, not recommended; Croix Blanche, at Tracht, ½ m. There is also an hotel at *Kienholz*, the Bellevue, about a mile towards Meiringen. Carriages may be hired, and on the arrival of the steamer from Interlaken with passengers for the Brünig (Rte. 19), the noise and bustle are marvellous. Brienz is a village of 2600 Inhab., at the E. end of the lake, on a narrow ledge at the foot of the mountains, remarkable for wood-carving, which employs 600 persons, for its beautiful position, and vicinity to the Giessbach Falls. The *Lotte*, a fish of the lake (Gadus mustela), is good eating.

[From Brienz the traveller may ascend the *Rothhorn*, 7713 ft., the highest point of the chain bounding the lake on the N., in about 4 hrs. by walking, in 5 on a horse (15 fr.), and in 6 in a chaise à porteurs. The path lies at first through forest-trees, chiefly beech, but including many oaks; to these succeed larch, and above them one-third of steep ascent over a barren tract. Views are obtained through vistas in the forest of the lake of Brienz. The Rothhorn is higher than the Rigi, and not so high as the Faulhorn. It takes 2 or 3 hrs. to descend. The view comprises the Bernese Alps, the lake of Brienz close under the mountain, and a peep of the lake of Thun, the vale of Hasli, nearly to the Grimsel, the Titlis and Sustenhorn, the lake of Sarnen, a considerable part of the lake of Lucerne, Pilatus, the Rigi, and a portion of the lake of Zug. The lake of Constance also appears, and a long strip of the lake of Neuchâtel. There is a path from the summit to Lungern (Rte. 19), and another to the Emmenthal.]

Lake of Brienz.—Giessbach Falls.

A *Steamer* 4 times daily, in 1 or 1½ hr., between Brienz and Bönigen, the port of Interlaken, touching 4 times at the Giessbach, once at Oberried, twice at Iseltwald, and twice at Bönigen. Fares, 2 fr. and 1 fr. A row-boat takes about 3 hrs. to Interlaken, including a visit to Giessbach. Boat 10 fr.; to the Giessbach only, waiting 1 hr. and back, 4 fr.

The Lake of Brienz is about 9 m. long, 2 wide, and 1781 ft. above the sea; near the mouth of the Giessbach, 500 ft. deep, but in the deepest part 2140 ft. Its surface is about 30 ft. higher than the lake of Thun. It is inferior in variety and beauty to most of the Swiss mountain lakes.

The carriage-road from Meiringen and the Brünig skirts the N. shore, between Brienz and Interlaken. There is a pretty footpath along the S. side by the Giessbach, and a carriage-road from Iseltwald to Interlaken.

It takes 25 minutes to row from Brienz to the outlet of *the Giessbach*, where travellers begin to ascend the very steep though excellent road, that leads in 20 min. to the *Falls*. They are a series, leaping step by step from the top of the mountain; and, though inferior in height to the Reichenbach, surpass it in beauty, as they break their way through a rich forest of fir. The Giessbach is one of the prettiest of waterfalls: there is nothing wild about it, and the immediate contact of green turfy knolls and woods has the effect of a park scene. You can easily pass behind the second fall by a gallery constructed beneath the shelving rock; and the effect of the landscape seen through this curtain of water is singular. The best of the falls are close to the hotel, though the highest, about 1000 feet above the lake, is worth a visit. To land and see all the falls will take a full hour and a half. The excellent

Giessbach Hotel, approached in 5 min. by an ingenious wire railroad (fare up and down 1 fr.) is finely situated 400 ft. above the lake, gay and cheerful, even to the waiters, who are maidens prettily dressed in the costumes of their native valleys. Pension, 7 fr. The mountain side forms its garden, and is a network of paths running through the woods to the best points of view. Hotel is lit by electric light and the Falls are illuminated every night from June to September. Although the idea may be distasteful, the effect is beautiful; 1 fr. per head is charged for it in the Hotel bills, but only for the first night. Good specimens of Swiss carving may be purchased of the Kehrlis, descendants of the school-master who first opened the Giessbach to the world. A smaller house, *Hôtel Beausite*, recommended, stands a few minutes walk higher.

[An excursion on foot may be made to the *Hinterberger See*, a small lake high up amongst the mountains.

There is a footpath to Meiringen, and a long but pleasant one to the

Faulhorn; 2 hrs. on the way is the
H. P. Axalp.]

At *Iseltwald*—a charmingly situated village and steamboat station—are several pensions.

Near the foot of the lake, on the N. shore, are seen the ch. and castle of Ringgenberg, and a little beyond is the ruined castle of Goldswyl, near the place where the Aar runs out of the lake.

Bönigen (two cheerful-looking pensions). This is the port of Interlaken, and passengers are transferred to the Bödeli railway. The rly. crosses the Zweilütschinen torrent, and then runs over the plain to

Zollhaus Stat., which is nearer to the ch. and to some of the hotels than the Interlaken station. The rly. then crosses the Aar by a skew lattice-bridge, runs under the precipices of the Harder, crosses the Aar again, runs right through a part of the village, and reaches

Interlaken Stat. (Rte. 25, A).

ROUTE 26.

A. MEIRINGEN TO THE RHONE GLACIER. GRIMSEL PASS.

B. RHONE GLACIER TO HOSPENTHAL OR ANDERMATT. FURKA PASS.

Meiringen or Reichenbach.

	Hours.
Imhof	1
Urweid	1
Guttannen	1¼
Handeck	1¼
Grimsel Hospice	2¼
Rhone Glacier	2¼

A. *Meiringen to the Rhone Glacier. Grimsel Pass.*

A good carriage-road is completed to Urweid. Over the pass there is a much-frequented bridle-path.

This is an important line of communication, and one of the grandest of the old mule-passes. The characteristic of the Grimsel is savage *rock* scenery.

Above Meiringen the vale of Hasli contracts, and is crossed by a limestone hill nearly 800 ft. high, called the *Kirchet*, which appears at one time

to have dammed up the waters of the Aar, as a lake in the basin of Imhof. At the present day they flow through a very remarkable chasm, cut through this barrier from top to bottom, and known as the *Finsteraar Schlucht*. It is easy of access by means of another water-worn channel—a cavern, which runs down by a steep but quite practicable descent to the river. A sign-post directs the traveller "Zur Finsternaar Schlucht." The beautiful scenery at the entrance of the cavern, and the grandeur of the perpendicular rocks, 300 ft. high, where the path emerges upon the margin of the Aar, are well worth the delay of half an hour. On the surface of the Kirchet lie erratic blocks of granite, vestiges, it is supposed, of that ancient time when a glacier filled the valley, and marked it with those grooves which are seen on its rocky sides (see § 12).

The road now descends by zigzags into the retired green valley of Upper Hasli. In front rises the *Mährenhorn* (9593 ft.), a beautiful feature of the pass: rt. appears the opening of the *Urbachthal*, from which there is an ill-traced path along the W. slope of the valley of the Aar to Guttannen. The road now crosses the river to

Imhof (*Inn:* H. Imhof, good; H. Alpenhof), a village at the junction of the paths of the Grimsel, Joch, and Susten. A carriage-road is carried up the last to Gadmen (Rte. 32).

[The following are some of the glacier expeditions from the *Urbachthal*, a valley rich in magnificent scenery, but little known, though opening on one of the best travelled paths. A chalet at its higher end has been fitted for mountaineers. 1. The *Gauli pass* to the Grimsel, about 15 hrs.; col just E. of the *Ewig Schneehorn:* steep descent to the Lauteraar gl. by rock and couloirs. 2. The *Bergli Joch*, between the Berglistock and *Rosenhorn* (one of the Wetterhörner) to Grindelwald. 3. The ascent of any of the peaks of the Wetterhörner, descending to Grindelwald or Rosenlaui. 4. The *Wetterlimmi*, E. of the Berglistock to Rosenlaui, descending from the Wettereismeer by the Rosenlaui gl. 5. The *Weitsattel*, over the *Engel-hörner*, between the Stellihorn and Dossenhorn, a direct but difficult pass to Rosenlaui. 6. *Hangendhorn*, on W. side, near the Wetterlimmi. Ascent by Hangend Gl. and rocks, about 5 hrs. from the chalet. View of the Wetterhörner. 7. *Ritzlihorn*, on E. side, over Guttannen; loose stones, but otherwise easy ascent of 5 hrs.; view of Finsteraarhorn. S. of Imhof is the *Triftlimmi* (Rte. 27) to the Rhone Gl. hotel; carriage-road as far as Mühlestalden.]

Beyond Imhof the road enters a defile below the Mährenhorn, where the fine scenery of the Grimsel begins. The road passes through tunnels. Beyond the gorge *Urweid* (Inn), where the carriage road now ends, is reached. The stream is here crossed, and a rocky shoulder rounded. Thence the traveller rises through meadows to

Guttannen (*Inn:* Bär, good, very civil people, a far better sleeping-place than Handeck). The village has been twice burnt and once inundated in this century. Rt. are the steep slopes of the *Ritzlihorn*, l. the *Furtwang Sattel*, leading to Gadmen, or by the Stein-limmi Joch to Stein, or by the Trift Joch to the Rhone gl. The *Mähren-horn*, N., and the *Steinhaushorn*, S. of the Furtwang, may be ascended from Guttannen. The *Gelmerlimmi*, a high glacier pass, gives access to the upper region of the Rhone Glacier.

The path now rises through the zone of forest, passing here and there the stream, which rolls in magnificent volume down the valley. On the steep and pretty ascent through the wood to Handeck the traveller turns aside to view the Fall, but it can be only imperfectly seen there.

Handeck (a rough *Inn*), 4528 ft. It is a beautiful spot, and close to the *Fall of the Aar*, one of the finest cataracts in Switzerland, from its height (more than 200 ft.), the quantity and rush of water, the gloom of the gorge into which it precipitates itself, and the wild character of the rocky solitude.

A little bridge has been thrown across the stream, not more than 5 or 6 ft. above the fall, and the view from this point is exceedingly impressive and stimulating. So plentiful is the rush of water that it reaches more than half-way down in one unbroken glassy sheet before it is tossed into foam; and what adds to its beauty is, that another stream (the Erlenbach or Handeck), pouring in from the W. takes precisely the same leap, mingling its tributary waters midway with the more powerful column of the Aar. Between 10 o'clock and 1 the iris hovers over the fall.

The forest of fir through which the route has wound for a considerable distance, now dwindles away into a few dwarf bushes, and the rough stones are mantled by the creeping fir (Pinus Mughus) bilberry and Alpine rose or rhododendron. About 2 m. above Handeck, a very remarkable place is reached—the *Böse Seite*, or *Helleplatte*, where the path crosses the bare bed of an ancient glacier, a polished and convex slope of granite (roche moutonnée), furrowed by the action of ice and stones, and extending for a space of nearly $\frac{1}{4}$ m. Professor Agassiz has here left his autograph chiselled on the rock. It used to be customary and prudent to dismount, and cross this bad bit of road on foot, since the surface, though cut into grooves to secure a footing for the horses, was very slippery; but a broad path, with stout posts and rail on the side of the abyss, is now carried over. On the opposite side of the valley is the fall of the *Gelmerbach*, the stream of the Gelmer glacier, flowing from a little lake called the *Gelmer See*.

There is but one human habitation between Handeck and the Hospice, the chalet of *Räterichsboden*, where the valley expands once more into a basin evidently once a lake-bed, with a marshy bottom, affording herbage for some goats and pigs. Beyond this the path rises above the Aar, the valley becomes a glen, walled by rocks; at its narrowest point the paved path crosses the torrent, the glen of the Aar glacier opens on the rt. to the Oberaarhorn, and turning a corner, the traveller suddenly finds that he has reached

The *Hospice of the Grimsel*, 5492 ft. (a good mountain *Inn*), originally a monastery, and after the Reformation supported by the neighbouring communes, in order to shelter those who travelled from necessity, and to afford gratuitous aid to the poor. The present hospice is modern, its predecessor having been feloniously burnt by the innkeeper in 1852. It is a grim building of rough masonry, designed to resist a weight of snow. It contain 50 beds, in cells, the lower tier over a stable for goats and cows; but the kitchen affords good fare, better far than might be expected in a spot more than 6000 ft. above the sea, and far removed from any other human dwelling. The establishment includes a man cook, washerwoman, and cobbler, and they have clothes to lend to drenched travellers. It is occupied by the innkeeper from March to November. One servant passes the winter in the house, and two dogs, to detect the approach of wanderers, for even in the depth of winter the hospice is resorted to by traders from the Hasli-thal and Valais, who exchange the cheese of the one for the wine and spirits of the other. Its situation is as wild as can be conceived, in a hollow, about 950 ft. below the summit of the pass, surrounded by walls and slopes of granite, on which the marks of ancient glaciers are seen 2000 ft. above the present bed of the valley. The rocks are broken, scarcely varied by patches of snow, which never melt even in summer, and by strips of grass and green moss, which shoot up between the stones, and are eagerly browsed by a flock of 150 goats. A considerable supply of peat is dug from a bog within a few yards of the door. In the bottom of this naked basin, close to the house, is a black tarn, or lake. Although entirely covered with snow in winter, it is rarely frozen, as it is supplied from a warm spring. Beyond it lies a small pasturage, capable of supporting for a month or two the cows belonging to the Hospice, and the servants' cross the lake twice a-day, in a boat, to milk them. It is a landscape worthy of Spitzbergen or Nova Zembla. This wilderness is the haunt of the marmot, whose shrill whistle frequently breaks the solitude; and the chamois, become rare of late, still frequents the neighbouring heights; both animals contribute at times to replenish the larder of the Hospice.

On the 22nd March, 1838, the Hospice was overwhelmed and crushed by an avalanche, which broke through the roof and floor, and filled all the rooms but that occupied by the servant, who succeeded with difficulty in working his own way through the snow, along with his dog, and reached Meiringen in safety.

In August, 1799, the Grimsel was the scene of a remarkable skirmish. The Austrians were encamped upon it with the view of preventing the French from penetrating into the Valley of the Rhône. They had possession of the whole declivity from the summit to the Hospice, with a force of rather less than 1500 men. The French under General Gudin, consisting of about 3600 men, were posted in the neighbourhood of Guttannen. The Austrian commander, Colonel Strauch, naturally relied upon the strength of his position, and the French General also considered it impregnable to an attack in front. He was therefore placed in a situation of great anxiety by receiving positive orders from Massena, to force the pass on the 14th of August. Fahner, the landlord of the Inn at Guttannen, then undertook to guide the French over the mountains and glaciers E. of the valley—the *Gelmer, Gersten*, and *Nägelis Grätli*—to the summit of the Grimsel in rear of the Austrian position.

The next morning, early, Gudin confided about 400 men to the guidance of Fahner; and himself advanced with the main body and attacked the Austrian position in front—with the characteristic impetuosity of French soldiers. The Austrian commander was convinced that the attack could not succeed in this direction, but drew down the greater part of his force to repel it and some sharp fighting ensued. Suddenly the Austrians were alarmed by firing on the heights to their rear; and its continuance, together with the impetuous advance of Gudin produced a panic which ended in a disorderly flight up the Grimsel, and over the pass in the direction of Obergestelen. The number of the killed is supposed not to have exceeded 150, of which the French composed a fifth part. The wounded Austrians were necessarily left to their fate, the nature of the ground rendering it impossible for such of their companions as escaped to remove them, and the French troops passed directly over into the valley of the Rhone.

The source of the Aar lies in two enormous glaciers, the *Ober* and *Unteraar-Gletscher*, to the W. of the Hospice. The peak seen from the Hospice is the *Agassizhorn* (12,960 ft.), which is also visible from Grindelwald. The Unteraar is the best worth visiting, and may be reached in 1½ hr. from the Hospice. It is about 9 m. long, and 1 to 2 broad and remarkable for the evenness of the surface and the rareness of crevasses. At about 5 m. from its lower end it divides into two branches. The rt., to the traveller ascending, is the *Lauteraar Glacier*; the l., the *Finsteraar Glacier*. The two are separated by a rocky promontory called *Abschwung*, which forms the base of a huge ridge, rising at the centre to the formidable *Schreckhorn*, and ending over Grindelwald with the Mettenberg. On the S. side of the Finsteraar Glacier, which leads to the Strahleck pass, is the still more imposing summit of the *Finsteraarhorn*, the highest of the Bernese Alps. Owing to its great dimensions, and the ease with which it may be traversed in most directions, the Unteraar Glacier has long attracted those who wished to study the phenomena of glaciers. In 1827 Hugi erected a rude hut on the ice

near the foot of the Abschwung. In 1840 the remains of this hut were found by Agassiz to have advanced about 4600 ft. In the following year Agassiz and a party of scientific friends established themselves on the medial moraine in an equally rude shelter, which they styled the Hôtel des Neuchâtelois, and here they continued during several successive seasons to carry on observations. A more secure and convenient dwelling was provided by M. Dollfuss-Ausset of Mulhouse. It has been in turn replaced by a substantial hut, on the l. bank of the glacier, 4 hrs. from the Grimsel.

A *Panorama* of the Grimsel and neighbouring peaks and glaciers may be obtained from the *Little Sidelhorn* (9075 ft.), the mountain just W. of the top of the pass; its summit may be reached in 3 hours from the Hospice. The ascent is easy and the view magnificent. The descent may be made to the Oberaar glacier, and thence by rough ground to the lower end of the Unteraar glacier, and the path to the Hospice.

The *Gross Sidelhorn*, further W., is rough and steep towards the top, but otherwise not difficult. It is 9449 ft. above the sea.

The *Juchlistock*, cresting the wall of rock on the N. side of the Aar valley opposite the Sidelhorn, and almost directly over the Hospice, is another fine point of view. The first stream on the rt. leads to a gap in the ridge, along which it is a short scramble to the top.

The *Galenstock*, 11,798 ft., is an easy glacier expedition from the Grimsel (5 or 6 hrs.) From the top of the Grimsel pass the Nägelis Grätli, on the l., is climbed and crossed to the Rhône glacier. The passage of the ice presents no difficulty, and the way then lies straight up the mountain. Crystals of topaz are often found. Descent may be made either to the Furca or Rhone Glacier hotel. A good guide is necessary. In the first ascent a fatal accident nearly happened through the giving way of a snow cornice.

[For the glacier-passes leading to

Grindelwald, the Egischhorn, and the Gadmenthal, see Rte. 27.]

The bridle-path between the summit of the Grimsel and the glacier of the Rhone called *Maienwand*, is steep, and better descended on foot. Guide not necessary in fine weather, except perhaps to show where the paths to the Rhone glacier and Obergestelen diverge.

The summit of the Grimsel pass (6446 ft. above the sea, 950 ft. above the Hospice) is 2 m. by a steep path, marked near the top by tall poles to guide the wayfarer in the snow. Here the path divides. The rt.-hand track, formerly in general use, leads directly to Obergestelen, that on the l. to the Rhone glacier, and a pedestrian should be careful not to miss the turning. Just beyond it is the dismal tarn called *Todten See*, or Lake of the Dead, from the corpses of French and Austrian soldiers, who were thrown into it by way of burial. It is surrounded by a bleak and barren waste of granite. The path now reaches the culminating point of the road, and begins at once the descent of the *Maienwand* (celebrated for its flowers). The first portion of the way is the worst of the whole, being very steep and often muddy, but it soon brings the traveller in sight of the Rhone glacier, snowy Galenstock, and zigzags of the Furca. The dislocation of the ice-fall, the spreading out of the glacier below, and the system of crevasses are well seen from this point. [By keeping to the l. on the descent, the pedestrian with a guide may avoid part of the Maienwand, and cross the glacier to the Furca road.] At the foot of the Maienwand the traveller finds himself on the highway, which connects the valleys of the Rhine and Rhone, and at a large and excellent inn the

Hôtel Belvedere, 5750 ft., a centre between the Furca, Grimsel, and Eggischhorn ; a dinner always about 1 P.M., when the diligences arrive. *English and R. Catholic Ch. S.* Behind the inn are two tepid sources which dispute with the glacier torrent the title of Source of the Rhone.

Rhone Glacier, one of the grandest in Switzerland, fit cradle for so mighty a stream. It formerly filled the head of the valley from side to side, and appeared piled up against the shoulder of the Galenstock, whose tall peak rises behind it. It is now much shrunk, and, from the measurements of Swiss engineers, it appears that in the 19 years before 1876 the glacier had retreated a quarter of a mile and sunk 300 feet. The annual decrease from 70 to 100 ft., has lately been indicated by lines of black paint on the rocky bed.

The belt of mountains is well seen by a walk on the glacier to the foot of the ice-fall.

The heights above the sea, in Eng. ft., of the Rhone at various points in its course are as follows :—At foot of glacier, 5750 ; at Brieg, 2302 ; at Sion, 1630 ; at Lake of Geneva, 1230 ; at Fort de l'Ecluse, 1066 ; at Seyssel, 802.

A path leads up the mountain side (l. from the hotel) to the higher reaches of the Rhone glacier, whence there is a glorious view of the Galenstock and ice-fields—a pleasant afternoon stroll.

[The *pass of the Rhone and Trift Glaciers* to Stein on the Susten, or to Imhof, may be broken by passing the night at the Swiss A. C. hut above the ice-fall of the Trift. The descent of the rocks by the side of this ice-fall—particularly near the bottom—is the principal difficulty (Rte. 27A.).

The *Galenstock* may be ascended from this hotel or the Furca; with greater ease from the latter.]

Diligence daily from Andermatt over the Furca to Brieg (Rtcs. 26B, 28). Rhone Glacier to Brieg, 12 **fr.** 50 cent.; to Andermatt, 8 fr. 50 cent. Two-horse carriage to Hospenthal, 50 fr.

B. *Rhone Glacier to Hospenthal or Andermatt. Furca Pass.*

The *Inn* of the Glacier of the Rhone is on the diligence-road from Brieg to Andermatt. The diligences take about 12 hrs. over the whole distance, and about 4½ hrs. from the Rhone Glacier to Andermatt, dining at the *H. du*

Glacier. 1-horse carriage from the Rhône Glacier to Andermatt 25 fr., 2-horse 50 fr.

The carriage-road over the Furca from Obergestelen to Andermatt was completed by the Swiss Government in 1867, at the small cost of 255,000*l.*, and is much admired as a magnificent specimen of road-making. It ascends by bold zigzags to a great height, and abuts at some of the angles upon the edge of the precipice overhanging the glacier, and thus commands a near view of an ice-fall, and its yawning crevasses, at the elbow of one of these zigzags is a small Inn. Except the Stelvio, no other carriage-road brings you into such intimacy with a glacier. From the higher terraces, views, entirely lost on the old path, open out, of the Alpine chain from Monte Leone to the Weisshorn, and of the dark Oberland giants, the Schreckhorn and Finsteraarhorn, which are beautifully seen from this road. The steepest part of the ascent is mastered by 7 sweeping zigzags, which bring the traveller to the summit of the pass, or *Fork* between two peaks, from which it receives its name of

Furca, 7992 ft. above the sea (*Inn :* H. de la Furca, Müller's, with 50 beds, a very good inn, where Q. Victoria staid 3 days in 1868).

[The mule-path up the Furca is dull and without view. The carriage-road is far finer. The path on the descent to Hospenthal is also dull and tedious.

A direct rte. from the Furca Inn to the Grimsel, across the higher part of the Rhone gl. and near Nägelis Grätil, is a delightful walk of 3½ hrs.]

The *Galenstock* (11,798 ft.), whose summit is seen glittering on moonlight nights from the windows of the inn, can be ascended without much difficulty in 4 hrs. with a good guide ; 2 hrs. snow and ice. The snow cornice must be carefully avoided. Guide 15 fr. The view is most magnificent, as the mountain stands like a watch-tower, looking down the long vale of the Rhone, and on this account supersedes its slightly higher neighbours,

the Rhonestock and Dammastock. Just under it is the Trift glacier ; between it and the Gletscherhorn the Tiefen glacier. Finsteraarhorn, Schreckhorn, Sustenhorn, and other great peaks, are well seen. It is possible to descend to the Grimsel.

Furcahorn (1 hr. above the *Inn*) at sunset or sunrise is the common excursion. For the higher of the two Furcahörner, 2½ hrs., up and down, a guide might be required.

E. of the pass the carriage-road keeps high up on the side of the mountain, and the views from it over the Siedeli glacier are fine. The *Inn* Zum Tiefengletscher is the only house between the Furca Hotel and Realp. Hence there is a pass, the *Winterlücke,* to the Geschenen Alp (see Rte. 34). The descent into the valley of Urseren is effected by the new road in a long series of serpentine windings, from which are views over the monotonous vale of Urseren.

Realp (*Inn :* H. des Alpes ; Zur Post). Glacier pass to Oberwald (see Rte. 28). Realp is 9 m. from the Furca, and about 4 m. of dull level road from

Hospenthal, on the St. Gothard (*Inns :* Meyerhof, a large and excellent hotel ; Goldener Löwe, civil landlord), or 2½ m. farther to Andermatt (Rte. 34).

From Hospenthal to the Furca, in a carriage, 3½ hrs. ; Furca to the Rhone glacier, 1 hr.

ROUTE 27.

THE GLACIER PASSES LEADING TO OR FROM THE GRIMSEL.

Besides the bridle-road leading over the Grimsel there are several passes in different directions, suited to those who are in good condition for walking, and accustomed to ice.

A. *Gadmenthal to Grimsel. Trift Limmi.*

About 12 or 18 hrs.

This fine pass by the Trift and Rhône glaciers to the Grimsel or Rhône glacier hotel runs from *Stein* (landlord's son a good guide), or from Mühlestalden. 1 long day, or 2 by sleeping at the Trift-hut. From Stein (Rte. 32) it is a double pass. Easy ascent of 2 hrs. by the Stein and Steinlimmi glaciers, with *Sustenhorn* and *Thierberge*, l., to the *Steinlimmi-joch*, 8800 ft. Steep descent down débris and the *Drosi* glacier (directly opposite the Furtwang) to the Trift gl., where the rte. joins that from

Mühlestalden. Opposite this village opens the narrow gorge of the *Triftbach*, flowing from the Trift glacier. The glacier is reached in 2½ hrs., and the path mounts the shoulder of the *Windegg*, on the W. side of the ice-fall, E. of which rise the precipices of the *Radolfshorn* and *Gyglistock*, to a châlet, 3 hrs., where a night's rest on clean hay may be obtained. It is the point from whence the *Steinhaushorn* (10,350 ft.), overlooking the valley of Hasli, may most easily be ascended, or a passage made to Guttannen, by the *Furtwang*, 8700 ft., and *Steinhaus Alp.* For nearly an hour above the lower ice-fall the glacier presents no difficulty; it then rises steeply in shattered masses, and it is necessary to climb the rocks on the E. side—a spur of the Thierberge called Thältistock—formidable in appearance, but not really difficult. At the top, (4 hrs. from Mühlestalden) is the *Trift-haus*, a hut built by the Swiss Alpine Club (bring the key and firewood) furnished with cooking utensils, bags for sleeping, &c. It stands in a commanding position above the ice-fall, with grand view of the weathered peaks and wastes of snow. From this point two hrs. of gradual ascent lead to the summit of the flattened ridge which separates the Trift from the Rhône glacier, about 10,000 Eng. ft. Here the wild *Gelmerhörner*, rt., and l. the *Schneestock, Dammastock, Rhonestock*, and *Galenstock*, open to the view, and on the descent of the glacier the beautiful chain of the Upper Valais. The ridge to the l., between the Galen-

stock and Sustenhorn, overlooks the remote valley of Geschenen. The passes across it are noticed in Rte. 34. On the upper part of the Rhône glacier the rte. keeps to the l., and then crosses diagonally. There are many concealed crevasses. The best course to the Grimsel is by the Todten See, and on the same side of the glacier is the most direct path to the Rhône glacier hotel, but another way is under the Galenstock, and so down by the steep bank to the Furca road. With good guides a traveller may strike to the l. from the upper plateau of the Rhône glacier, along the slopes of the Galenstock, and reach the Furca Inn.

B. Grindelwald to Grimsel. Strahleck and Lauteraar Joch.

Strahleck, 12 to 14 hrs. Guide to the Grimsel 40 fr. This well-known pass is one of the grandest in the Alps. The time required depends altogether on the state of the snow. It is best taken from the Grimsel side, the ascent is less considerable, and the views (particularly of the Finsteraarhorn) are on the whole finer. The hard day's work may be broken by sleeping in the new Club hut on the Schwarzenegg, 4 hrs. from Grindelwald ; or at the Pavillon by the Aar Glacier, if the traveller attacks the pass from the Grimsel side; but the usual practice is to start early and walk through in one day.

The path, on leaving Grindelwald, ascends the grass slopes on the E. side of the Lower Grindelwald glacier, and then passes along the rocks overhanging the lower icefall. After descending a ladder near the Bärenegg hut clamped against the face of a cliff (Rte. 25c), the *Eismeer*, 2 hrs., is reached and followed on either bank, past the *Zäsenberg* châlets to the central icefall, 1½ hr. Here the rocks on the E. side are the shortest course, but they are difficult to reach when the ice is low, and the easier slopes on the W. are often preferred. Thus the traveller mounts (1 hr.) to the high plateau of névé—the *Ober Eismeer*—

where the grander scenery of the pass opens to view. On the l. the dark rocky peak of the Schreckhorn—Peak of Terror—on the rt. the cirque of the Viescherhörner; and in front, under the Strahlgrat, one of the wildest of ice-falls. Continuing along the glacier (which is here without crevasses), and passing immediately below two steep lateral glaciers, a nearly precipitous wall of snow is reached, forming the end of the valley, 1 hr. At this point the traveller turns to the left, and, by ascending for 2 hrs. snow slopes, steep enough to require roping and care, gains the top of the pass.

The summit of the Strahleck (Sunbeam corner) is, indeed, the perfection of wild scenery. Vegetation there is none, save a few of the smallest gentianellas. The height is 10,994 feet, and the pass lies in the very centre of the most elevated group of the Oberland Alps, between the Schreckhorn and Finsteraarhorn. The latter peak has been reached from this side by a steep snow-slope leading to its W. ridge, but is usually climbed from the hut on the Aletsch Glacier (see Rte. 29). The upper part of the Finsteraar Glacier is divided longitudinally by crags called the *Mittelgrat* or *Strahlgrat*, which are connected with the Schreckhorn by a transverse ridge. The Strahleck lies across this ridge, which terminates at the Mittelgrat. To the W. of it, under the Finsteraarhorn and Agassizhorn, a common névé unites the glaciers of Finsteraar and Grindelwald, forming the pass of the *Finsteraar Joch,* which is shorter but more difficult than the Strahleck, and better taken from the Grindelwald side.

The descent from the summit towards the Finsteraar Glacier by the well-known wall of the Strahleck, 800 ft. high, and sloping at an angle of about 48°, forms the principal difficulty of this expedition. Ordinarily, when proper precautions are taken, there is no real risk. Just below the steepest part a wide crevasse or *bergschrund* must be passed, but this is generally pretty well bridged over with snow;

the slope soon becomes less formidable, and before long the travellers may safely run or slide down to the *névé.* From the foot of the passage, which may occupy about 1 hr., the Abschwung, where the hut which replaces the Pavillon Dollfuss is situated, may be reached in 1½ hr.: thence to the hospice of the Grimsel will take a good walker 3 hours, two of them on the ice.

In 1866, at Christmas, Messrs. A. Moore and Walker, with 3 guides, crossed the Finsteraar Joch from Grindelwald and returned by the Strahleck, in 22 hrs. More recently the summits of the Schreckhorn, Wetterhorn and Jungfrau have been attained in January by Mr. W. A. B. Coolidge.

The pass of the *Lauteraar Joch,* at the head of the Upper Grindelwald glacier, leading under the rocky ledges and precipices of the Wetterhörner, is very striking in its scenery, and forms a worthy rival to the Strahleck. It requires at least 16 hrs.' walking, which can be divided by sleeping at the "Weisshorn" hut above the old Gleckstein Cave. As the Upper Grindelwald Glacier descends almost from its source in an impassable icefall, and the sides of the Mettenberg are nearly perpendicular, the path has to be carried among the crags of the Wetterhorn. It begins in a mere *geissweg,* or goat-track, called the *Enge,* which in 2½ hrs. leads by a dizzy rte. to a little slope of green and some rocks named *Platten.* From this point the traveller has to climb to another plateau—the *Schönbuhl*—commanding a most magnificent view, and then up rocks and ladders to the "*Weisshorn*" *Hut* (4½ hrs.). Here mountaineers who make this passage, or ascend the Wetterhorn, can pass the night. Above this spot rises another tier of precipices, which has to be surmounted in order to reach the névé. Hence it is comparatively plain sailing to the col, which lies on a steep ridge, 10,354 ft. above the sea, between the Schreckhorn and the *Berglistock,* 11,998 ft., which can be ascended from the col in about 2 hrs. The descent from the col to the Lauteraar Glacier is short but excessively steep, but this is the last difficulty. When the névé is gained it is a walk of some 6 hrs. to the Grimsel.

C. Grimsel to the Eggischhorn. Oberaar-joch.

14 hrs., including rest at the col. Guide, 35 fr.

This pass is a hard day's work, but the grandeur of scenery will well repay any traveller who may traverse it in fine weather.

It is advisable to start very early from the Grimsel, as the path on the Eggischhorn side is puzzling after dark. The shortest way from the hospice is by the Sidelhorn and Trübten See, but as this cannot be traversed by starlight, the ordinary rte. is to the Unteraar glacier, and then up the rough ground, l., to the valley of the Oberaar and chalets at the foot of the glacier. This is almost as easily traversed as the lower glacier (27, B), but the ascent to the Col (which presents no difficulty worth mentioning) is rather more rapid. Rt. are passed the *Zinkenstock*, and *Thierberg*, streaming with glaciers, l. the *Gross Sidelhorn* and *Löffelhorn*. The summit of the pass, 10,624 ft., is reached in 6 hrs., and hence the *Oberaarhorn*, 11,923 ft., if time permits it, should be ascended. It is easy, by a snow slope, in 1½ hr., and commands a very fine view. The Viescher Glacier is much cut up by crevasses, particularly the main stream, which runs N.W. by the Finsteraarhorn to the Almerhorn and Great Viescherhorn. From the Oberaarjoch the traveller descends the sloping névé of the smaller branch towards the point of junction at the base of the *Rothhorn*, where a hut has been erected. From this point there are two ways to the Eggischhorn. On reaching the ice on the other side of the hut it is possible (1) to traverse the Walliser Viescher Firn as far as the foot of the Grünhornlücke, to cross this gap on to the Aletsch Glacier, and thence by the ordinary Concordia hut route to the Eggischhorn (round

about as it may seem, this is perhaps on the whole the best way). (2) To keep along the *right* bank of the Viescher Glacier to a place known as "In der Trift." Here it is necessary to descend down a slippery watercourse to the glacier again, and if the exact spot is not hit, very great difficulty will be found in so doing, as the ice has shrunk away enormously. The glacier once reached there is no further difficulty, and the way leads now by glacier and now by moraine to the foot of the path leading to the Hotel de la Jungfrau. There are 3 ways up to the hotel, but the usual rte. is by a badly traced path, and watercourse, round the E. shoulder of the mountain. After dark it would be better to go by the Märjelen See and the mule-path over the ridge.

Studerjoch. In 1863 a pass parallel to the Oberaarjoch, but considerably higher, was made a little N. of the Oberaarhorn. A glacier hanging on the E. of the Studerhorn enables a climber to scale the cliffs from the Finsteraar glacier, and a descent is made to the Viescher glacier by an ice-slope and couloir. Grimsel to the col 7 hrs. An easier pass W. of the Studerhorn was made in 1868. It has been called the *Unteraarjoch*.

D. Grimsel to Meiringen, over the Lauteraar and Gauli Glaciers.

"We set out from the hospice of the Grimsel a little after 5 A.M. For some distance the route is the same as that of the Strahleck, but, instead of turning to the L up the Finsteraar gl., it inclines to the rt. along the Lauteraar gl. nearly to its head, where the ridge of the Lauteraarsattel runs across from the Schreckhorn to the Schneehorn. Here we turned to our rt., and commenced the ascent of the steep ridge of rock which, running from the last-named mountain, forms the boundary between the Lauteraar and Gauli glaciers. After having reached about half its height, we turned again to our rt. for some distance, parallel to the Lauteraar glacier, till we came to where the passage of the ridge is to be made. The ascent is up rock and loose shingle to the summit, which is very narrow. On the northern side the descent is down an extremely steep slope of hard frozen snow, which occupied nearly 1 hr. before we reached the Gauli glacier, down which we slid, and before 2 o'clock were off the ice. The route then is down the Urbach Thal, and in parts very steep. At Hof we struck in upon the road to Meiringen, and reached that town a little after 6 o'clock, having been 13 hrs., including stoppages, in coming by this pass from the Grimsel; 5¼ hrs. were upon the ice."—*R. F.*

The ascent to the Gauli Pass from the Lauteraar glacier lies between the *Berglistock*, N., and *Ewig Schneehorn* (eternal-snow horn) S., the first of the Oberland peaks ascended, reached in ½ hr. from the pass, and commanding magnificent views. N. of the Berglistock rise the 3 peaks of the Wetterhörner, and E. of them an opening in the ridge, called *Wetterlimmi*, enables the traveller to pass to the *Wettereismeer*, and to descend by the Rosenlaui Glacier to Rosenlaui.

ROUTE 28.

RHONE GLACIER TO BRIEG. UPPER
RHONE VALLEY.

Rhone Glacier to	Miles.
Obergestelen	6
Münster	4
Viesch	13
Brieg	12
	35

The diligences from Andermatt to Brieg halt for dinner at the Rhone Glacier Hotel, and take from it to Brieg 5 hrs. down, 7 hrs. up: fare 12 fr. 50 c. Carriage, 1-horse 30 fr., 2-horse 60 fr.

Soon after leaving the hotel, the carriage descends by the steep zigzags of the new road, from which the traveller sees before him, for many a mile, the valley of the Rhone. The

Upper Valais is one long undulating meadow, dotted with villages—little clusters of black timber houses round a church. The mountain sides are forested. The natives of the Upper Valais are a distinct and apparently superior race to those of the Lower. The language is German. As the traveller journeys onward he has a glorious object in view as far as Viesch —the snow-peak of the Weisshorn. On looking back, he sees the Galenstock, one of the *Pillars of the Sun*, above the sources of the Rhone.

3½ m. *Oberwald* (*Inn:* H. de la Furca). The highest village of the Upper Valais, 4456 ft. Some fair guides. [The *Gerenthal* here opens l., leading to the principal summits of the St. Gothard group. Glacier passes lead to the Hospice of All' Acqua, on the Nüfenen pass, or to Realp. Pizzo Rotondo, the highest peak (10,489 ft.), may be climbed.]

2 m. *Obergestelen* (Fr., Haut Châtillon). This village was burnt to the ground, Sept. 2, 1868, but is now rebuilt of *stone;* before, it was of wood. It is the depot for the cheeses exported by canton Berne to Italy, and a place of some traffic, as it lies at the junction of the roads over the Grimsel, Furca, Nüfenen, and Gries (Rte. 62).

In 1720, 84 men were killed here by an avalanche, and lie buried in one grave in the churchyard.

1½ m. *Ulrichen* (*Inn:* Zum Gries, homely). Opposite opens the valley of Eginen, leading to the Gries and the Nüfenen (Rte. 63).

2½ m. *Münster*, a Post stat. with 40 Inhab., and a good *Inn*, La Croix d'Or, in full view of the peak of the Weisshorn. 10 fr. for horse and carriage to Viesch, 18 fr. to Brieg; 20 fr. to Visp. From Münster the ascent of the *Löffelhorn* (10,138 Eng. ft.) may be made in about 5 hrs.' descent by Trützi Pass to Grimsel. The view of the Finsteraarhorn is singularly fine, but the panorama in other respects not equal to that from the Eggischhorn.

Reckingen, with a handsome ch.

4½ m. *Niederwald* (*Inn*). Some 2 m. further the traveller reaches the second great step of the Rhone valley, and descends through a wild wood of pines covering an ancient moraine of the Viescher glacier to

4 m. *Viesch* or Fiesch (*Inns:* H. du Glacier, Poste; H. des Alpes: both good. 1-horse carriage to Rhone Glacier, 20 fr.: a return often to be had for 10 fr.: and 2 persons are commonly taken for diligence fare. To Brieg 10 fr.), at the entrance of a side valley, blocked by the Viescher glacier, above which rise the peaks called the Walliser Viescherhörner. The tradition that a path once led up this valley, now entirely filled by the glacier, to Grindelwald is without any solid foundation.

Aernen, on the other side of the Rhone, is the burial-place of Prof. Tyndall's favourite guide—the brave *Bennen*, killed by an avalanche on the Haut de Cry, Feb. 1864.

[From Viesch are several passes through the Binnenthal to the Val Formazza(Rte. 61), Eggischhorn(next Rte.), or to Isella (Rte. 61).]

From Viesch the high road proceeds to

1½ m. *Laax* (*Inn:* Croix Blanche), and beyond it passes a romantic defile, where the road descends, by a series of zigzags, the third great step of the Rhone valley to the bridge of *Grengiols* or *Grängenbrücke*.

5 m. *Mörel* (*Inns:* H. des Alpes; H. Eggischhorn). Here the direct path to the Rieder Alp turns off (3 hrs.).

4 m. *Naters*, a village of 600 Inhab., in a beautiful situation and a milder climate, where the chestnut begins to flourish. Above it rises the ruined castle of Auf der Flüh, or Supersax.

The stream of the Massa, issuing from the Aletsch Glacier, here joins the Rhone. The volume of its waters is greater than that of any other glacier-stream in the Alps.

A wooden bridge leads across the Rhone to the great Simplon road at

1 m. *Brieg* (*Inns:* Trois Couronnes or la Poste; H. d'Angleterre; good). (Rte. 59.)

From Brieg the Bel Alp may be ascended in 4 hrs. Horse and man 15 fr. (see next Rte.).

ROUTE 29.

THE EGGISCHHORN, RIEDER ALP, AND BEL ALP. THE MÖNCH JOCH AND GREAT PEAKS OF THE OBERLAND.

The Eggischhorn—There are 4 ways of reaching the Eggischhorn.—*a*, from Viesch, 2½ hrs.; *b*, from Lax, 2½ hrs.; *c*, from Mörel, by the Rieder Alp, 5½ hrs.; *d*, from the Bel Alp, 4½ hrs. The first 3 are horsepaths.

a. From *Viesch*. For nearly an hour the path mounts by zigzags through a pine-forest, whose shade affords protection from the sometimes oppressive heat of the sun. The track is intersected by slides, which serve for the small sledges, in which cheeses, hay, &c., are conveyed from the upper pastures. About 10 m. walk to the l. of a small hut where refreshments are sold, are some curious pinnacles formed by the protection of large stones which ward off the rain, which has washed away the surrounding soil. Above the forest the path mounts by gentle slopes. The views are not very striking, but a little to the l. of the path the grand ranges which encircle Saas and Zermatt are seen, the most conspicuous peak being the exquisitely-pointed pyramid of the Dom, the summit of the Saas Grat (Rte. 122). The path winds along the eastern slopes of the Eggischhorn, and in 2½ hrs. from Viesch the traveller reaches the excellent

Eggischhorn Hotel. Eng. Ch. S., 7195 ft. It does not command so striking a view, but is better situated for glacier expeditions than the rival houses on the Rieder Alp and Bel Alp.

Permanent guides at the Hotel, A. Minnig, L. Seiler; both good.

Many excursions can be made.

a. The first object of attraction is, of course, the summit of the *Eggisch-*

horn—1½ hr. A bridle-path nearly to the top (9649 ft.).

Other panoramas may be more beautiful, but in one respect the view from the Eggischhorn is unrivalled. It displays in its entirety the largest glacier in the Alps.

The vast snow-fields which cover the southern flank of the Bernese Alps send down two great glaciers towards the valley of the Rhone. The lesser of these, the Viescher glacier, has been already referred to (Rte. 27, c). The greater, the *Aletsch glacier*—originates in the basin which is enclosed by the peaks of the Aletschhorn, Jungfrau, Mönch, and Walliser Viescherhörner. Its length, from the Mönch Sattel to the source of the Massa at its base, is about 16 m., with an average breadth of 1¼ m.; and by its extent and the uniformity of its slope, it far better deserves the name of a *Mer de Glace*, or *Eismeer*, than any other glacier in the Alps.

From the Mönch Sattel, between the Mönch and the Jungfrau, the main stream preserves for some 8 m. a nearly straight course, a little E. of S., until it abuts against a steep pyramidal mountain, which lies exactly in its course. By this it is deflected to the rt., or S.W.; its slope becomes somewhat more rapid, and its bed narrower, till it finally disappears from sight in the deep ravine of the Massa. The mountain which thus turns aside the flow of the Aletsch glacier is the *Eggischhorn* (probably from the German *Eckig*, Corner Peak). It commands a full view of the entire course of the glacier, and of the grand range of peaks which surround it, in itself an unsurpassed combination of grand natural objects; but, besides these, the panorama which it presents in clear weather includes many of the highest summits of the Alps. Taken in the order in which they present themselves, we have Mont Blanc; the Grand Combin, the peaks of Arolla, the Weisshorn, Matterhorn, Mischabel, Monte Rosa, Fletschhorn, Monte Leone; the range extending from thence to the St. Gothard; the Galenstock, Oberaarhorn, and Fin-

steraarhorn, succeeded by the Eiger, Mönch, and Jüngfrau. The traveller who comes from the valleys of Canton Berne, will scarcely recognise the magnificent peaks which hang over the Wengern Alp in the three snow hummocks rising out of the vast snow plain which is the source of the Aletsch glacier. The noblest feature in the view is the Aletschhorn, the second in height of the Oberland range, which rises in a stately pyramid immediately opposite the spectator. There is probably no other spot so easy of access from which all these summits are visible. Among other objects of interest the *Viescher glacier*, which is rather an ice-cataract than an ice-river (Rte. 27, c), should not be overlooked. It presents a striking contrast with the tranquil and scarcely ruffled flow of the great Aletsch glacier.

Looking downwards some 2000 ft., another remarkable and almost unique object is seen, which, however, requires a nearer visit to be fully appreciated. Immediately N. of the Eggischhorn the ridge separating the Aletsch and Viescher glaciers is depressed into a plateau, 2 or 3 m. in length, and nearly ¼ m. wide. On one side the Aletsch glacier rises above the level of this vale in steep cliffs of ice, forming a barrier to the outflow of water. Hence that which accumulates in summer, from the drainage of the surrounding mountains, forms a small lake called the *Märjelen See*, upon whose cold surface the blocks that fall away from the cliffs float as miniature icebergs. The cliffs rise about 50 ft. above the water, and are grounded at a depth varying from 34 to 97 ft. In order to prevent the lake from unduly encroaching upon the adjacent pasture, a channel has been dug, by which the surplus water escapes in the opposite direction; but from time to time the onward movement of the Aletsch glacier opens some sub-glacial channel, when the lake rapidly falls, leaving a whole fleet of icebergs stranded on the shore.

b. The *Märjelen See* is 2 hrs.' walk by a bridle-path from the hotel. This excursion is often combined with the ascent of the Eggischhorn and a visit to the Aletsch glacier, which is easy of access, and in that part pretty free from dangerous crevasses, but it is only after walking some miles upon its surface that a true impression can be formed of the extent of this sea of ice.

c. The *Aletsch Glacier.*—Travellers desirous to form a correct idea of the phenomena of the ice-world, may make such excursions as their powers enable them on this vast field. Its extent will be fully appreciated by those who can reach the huts on the upper glacier used as sleeping-quarters by mountaineers, or descend from the Märjelen See to the Bel Alp. Either will take some 5 hrs.; to the huts and back is a long day. Good guides are, of course, necessary. In a walk to the *Faulberg hut,* 5 m. from the Märjelen See, the *Walliser Viescherhörner* are seen rt., the *Olmen-horn* and *Dreieckhorn* l., and there is a grand distant view to the Zermatt mountains. Beyond the hut an opening, called the *Grünhorn Lücke,* points the way to the Finsteraarhorn, and divides the Walliser Viescherhörner from those of Grindelwald. To the N. are the summits of the Jungfrau (l.) and Mönch (rt.) with the rocks of the *Kranzberg* S. of the former, and those of the *Trugberg* S. of the latter—(Trugberg, *Deceitful Mountain,* because mistaken by Agassiz and his guides for the Jungfrau). The Faulberg hut was a great improvement on the old cave. A new hut, called the Concordia Hütte, has lately been erected half an hour higher up the glacier. The walk should be extended to the basin of névé. When not overcrowded, a night spent in one of these refuges involves no serious discomfort, and the traveller is rewarded by witnessing the most sublime effects of the snow-world.

d. A longer expedition is to the *Eiger Joch,* or depression separating the Mönch from the Eiger (to be preferred to the Jungfrau Joch); but it is a fatiguing walk, especially if there be fresh snow. The contrast afforded by the view over the green Alps of the Oberland and the plain of Switzerland, after having been so long confined to the Polar scenery of the fields of névé, is very striking. The first ascent of this difficult pass from the Wengern Alp was accomplished in 1859, by Messrs. Leslie Stephen and W. and G. S. Mathews, with Ulrich Lauener, J. B. Croz and M. Charlet, guides.

Of the glacier routes by which the traveller from the Eggischhorn may penetrate the icy wilderness, there are only three sufficiently practicable and useful to call for notice here. The Oberaar Joch already described (Rte. 27, c), the Lötschenlücke (Rte. 38, B), and the Mönch Joch.

The *Mönch Joch* is the most traversed of the gaps connecting the Eggischhorn and the valleys of the Lütschine, and the easiest, although the descent is sometimes difficult. (Guide 20 fr. to the col; 60 to Grindelwald.) The upper region of the Aletsch glacier had been attained from Grindelwald by this route in 1828, in one of the early attacks on the Jungfrau. The Mönch Joch was opened as a pass, thirty years later, by an English party. The traveller ascends the Aletsch glacier nearly to the base of the Mönch, and then crosses the ridge connecting the Mönch with the Viescher Grat; hence he descends the séracs of the S. branch of the Lower Grindelwald glacier to Grindelwald. It is a pass of about 16 hrs. But the distance is much shortened by sleeping at the "Concordia," or at the Bergli hut. The latter is on the N. side of the pass, 6 or 7 hrs. from Grindelwald.

From the Eiger Joch a very narrow arête, broken by teeth projecting from the ice, rises towards the summit of the

Eiger, 13,045 ft. This fine mountain, which stands out like a promontory towards the Grindelwald glacier, is usually ascended from the Wengern

Alp by the rocks of the N.W. face. (See Rte. 25, c.)

The *Mönch*, 13,468 ft., is a difficult mountain, the Trugberg ridge, generally selected for the ascent, being steep and narrow, and liable to be *corniched*, and near the top of ice. The first ascent was made by Herr Porges of Vienna, by the ridge falling to the Mönch Joch. The second successful attempt was in 1863 by Mr. Macdonald, with Chr. Almer and Melchior Anderegg. They started from the Faulberg cave, where there is now a hut, ascended by the S.E. or Trugberg ridge, and returned the same day to the Eggischhorn. In 1875, Rev. F. T. Wethered descended from the Mönch to the Little Scheideck ; difficult, and only practicable in very rare conditions of the snow.

The *Jungfrau*—13,671 ft. (guide 70 fr. ; porter 40)—requires a good climber, and experienced guides, but rewards the traveller with one of the most astonishing of mountain views. It was first climbed in 1811 and 1812 by 2 Swiss gentlemen, J. R. and H. Meyer, and again, 1828, by some Grindelwald guides, who were followed by Agassiz, Désor, Forbes, and G. Studer. The ordinary route is up the rocks of the Kranzberg, and a snow slope (with bergschrund) to the *Roththalsattel*, a dizzy crest, 12,946 ft., looking down into the upper valley of Lauterbrunnen, and 5 hrs. from the Faulberg. From this point a crest which varies exceedingly in character and difficulty according to the season, leads N. to the top, which is a little ridge of snow. (See Rte. 25, c.) ;

The *Finsteraarhorn*, 14,026 ft. (guide 60 fr.). This is on the whole the ascent most to be recommended to travellers who wish to practise climbing, and is not more difficult than Monte Rosa. The view is singular and somewhat monotonous in its grandeur. Owing to the secluded position of the peak, no valleys are visible, and the eye, weary of snow and ice, can find nothing green to rest on nearer than the distant lowlands of N. Switzerland. The honour

of first scaling the highest peak of the Oberland belongs to three guides employed by R. Meyer in 1812. They made the ascent by the very difficult Rothhorn ridge, never passed again until 1876. In 1842, Herr Sulger of Bâle, with 4 guides, reached the top by the route now generally taken. In 1857, he was followed by the Rev. J. F. Hardy, Messrs. Kennedy, Ellis, St. John and W. Mathews, with 5 guides.

The top is generally reached in 6 or 7 hrs. from the Faulberg. The way lies at first across the Viescherhörner by the *Grünhorn Lücke* (3 hrs.), 10,843 ft., where the *Gross Grünhorn* rises l. 13,278 ft. The Viescher glacier is then crossed (1 hr.) and the rocky ribs of the mountain assaulted. They are steep, but give good holding, and are climbed for about 1 hr., to equally steep snow-slopes, which land the traveller on the arête to the N.W. of the summit. This resembles that of Monte Rosa, having teeth which project from an icy edge, and is a work of about 2 hrs.

The Finsteraarhorn can also be reached from Grindelwald viâ the Lower Glacier and the gap at the foot of the N.W. ridge, known as the Agassiz Joch. Mons. Cordier, in 1876, ascended the Finsteraarhorn from the Rothhorn Sattel by an extremely difficult route, probably the same as that taken in 1812 by Meyer's guides.

The *Aletschhorn*, 13,803 ft. (guide 40 fr.), the second in height of the Oberland peaks, was first climbed by Mr. Tuckett in June, 1859. Starting from a cave in the Olmenhorn, the mountain E. of the Mittler Aletsch glacier, he reached a saddle between the Dreieckhorn and Aletschhorn in 2¾ hrs. From that point the climb westward was rather dangerous from fresh snow, and occupied 3½ hrs., 200 steps having to be cut in the final slope. The Aletschhorn is easier, and more commonly ascended from the Bel Alp (see *post*).

The Gross Viescherhorn, or *Almer-horn* (so named after the great guide), 13,281 ft., at the head of the great Viescher glacier, is the highest of the Viescherhörner, and commands a marvellous view. Its top was gained in 1862 from the Trugberg in about 4 hrs.; and in 1863 from the Mönch Joch in about 3½ hrs. by the N.W. arête. It has a splendid view of the Aletschhorn and Schreckhorn.

The traveller who has visited the Eggischhorn, and does not propose to venture on a high glacier pass, will do best if, in place of redescending to Viesch, he takes the horse-path leading along the S. slopes of the Eggischhorn ridge to the *Rieder Alp* (2 hrs.) 6726 ft. Here, on a level pastoral platform, commanding a beautiful view of Monte Leone, he finds an excellent small *Inn* and pension. The situation is not convenient for high ascents; but there are many charming strolls in the neighbourhood. One of these is the *Riederhorn* (1 hr.), commanding a glorious view of the Pennine Alps.
[From the Rieder Alp, a direct path leads to Mörel in the Rhone valley (ascent 2½ hrs.).]
Beyond the Rieder Alp, the path to the Bel Alp mounts slightly, and then descends through a wood (glorious views) to the Aletsch Glacier. The passage of the glacier is very easy, so that horses can, in most years, be got across. It takes about 20 min. Thence a steep ascent by a good zigzag path leads in 2½ hrs. from the Rieder Alp to the *Inn on the Bel Alp* (7130 ft.), with 70 beds, fairly kept (*Eng. Ch. S.*). It commands a magnificent view of the great Aletsch glacier, which sweeps round the cliff on which the house stands; and in the opposite direction the windows open upon the Monte Leone, Fletschhorn, Mischabel, Weisshorn, Matterhorn, and other well-known summits. The sunrise on this range is glorious. In the valley below are seen the road of the Simplon, and towers of Brieg, and W., close at hand, a rolling green Alp, which gives a long stretch of nearly level ground for exercise. Near the inn stands the chalet built by Professor Tyndall. A small tarn, 5 minutes W. of the inn, offers excellent bathing.

The chief excursions from the Bel Alp are as follows :—

The *Sparrenhorn*, 9889 ft., 2 hrs. up: horses can go two-thirds of the way. Fine view across the Ober Aletsch Glacier, to the Aletschhorn, a new side of which is here seen.
The *Gorge of the Massa*, just under the hotel to the E., and reached by a bridge some way down the Alp. 4 or 5 hrs. to go and return. With the aid of an ice-axe, and a guide, you may walk to it down the centre of the glacier. It is one of the wildest chasms in the Alps—fit receptacle for the leagues of ice and snow which are slowly descending towards this point.
To the W. is a nearly level walk along the face of the hill to the village of *Nessel* (easy 2 hrs.), commanding noble views across the Rhone to the opposite ranges, particularly of the Weisshorn. From Nessel it is possible to descend by Murrel to Visp. Horses can go all the way.
The *Ober Aletsch Glacier*, as far as the *Jägi Glacier*, a névé stretching from the Gross Nesthorn to the Aletschhorn, an excursion of 6 to 8 hrs., suitable for ladies, who may here enjoy, without much fatigue, the scenery of the high Alps. A fine and easy pass, the Beichgrat (see Rte. 38, c) leads to the Lötschthal.
The most attractive objects to the mountaineer at the Bel Alp, are *the Aletschhorn* (13,773 ft.) and the *Gross Nesthorn* (12,538 ft.). Both peaks command glorious panoramas, and it is hard to assign to either the preference. Neither peak can be called, in the strictest sense of the word, difficult. But both require a proper number of good guides [*see Introduction*, § 5], fairly practised climbers, all the ordinary precautions and due consideration of the state of the weather and the snow. From 10 to 13 hrs.' actual walking may be allowed for these ascents. The tariff price for each guide is 40 fr.
The *Unterbachhorn* (11,800 ft.) is sometimes ascended, chiefly for the

sake of the climb, a difficult but not very long one.

A good mule-path connects the Bel Alp with Brieg (4 hrs. up, 3 hrs. down) horse and man 15 fr. The ascent is very hot in the middle of the day. A steep path from Naters climbs to a hamlet—*Blatten*—(restaurant), thence a second ascent in zigzags up a long, in part pine-clad hillside, leads to the hotel.

ROUTE 31.

STANZ TO ENGELBERG. ENGELBERG TO ALTDORF, BY THE SURENEN PASS, THE TITLIS.

From Stanzstad—		Miles.	Hrs.	Min.
Stanz	} car.-road {	2¼	—	20
Engelberg		13¼	4¼	
Surenen Eck	} bridle-path {		4	
Altdorf			4	

Steamers 4 times daily from Lucerne to *Stanzstad*—the port of Stanz—between which places an omnibus runs.

Travellers coming down the lake should stop at Bekenried, or Buochs (Rte. 15).

There is a good carriage-road to Engelberg (4½ hours' walk; 1-horse carr., 12 fr.; 2 ditto, 20 fr.); thence to Altdorf, across the pass, a rough horsepath.

Stanz (*Inns:* Krone; Engel), capital of the lower division (Nidwalden) of Canton Unterwalden, with 2032 Rom. Cath. Inhab. It is charmingly seated among orchards at the entrance of the Engelberg valley, under the *Stanzerhorn*, 6230 ft., which can be ascended in about 3½ hrs. The *Buochserhorn*, opposite, is 5938 ft., and at a height of about 3800 ft. has the comfortable pension of *Nieder-Rischenbach.*

The *Rathhaus* contains portraits of the *Landammänner*, the coat of mail of Arnold of Winkelried, and several old banners, Swiss and French. It was in the Rathhaus of Stanz that the venerable Swiss worthy *Nicolas von der Flüh* appeased the dissensions of the Confederates, in 1481, by his wise and soothing counsels. In the existing building there is a picture representing him taking leave of his family. In the market-place and by the ch.-yd. are statues of *Arnold of Winkelried*, a native of Stanz, with the "sheaf of spears" in his arms (see Rte. 3), and on the road to Sarnen is a chapel to his memory. His house is also shown here, now occupied by a family named Kaiser, that of Winkelried being extinct. It is a large ancient farm-house, of which one portion, including a low archway with groined entrance and dwarf pillars, may be as old as the time of Winkelried. The field on which it stands is called in old records "the meadow of Winkelried's children." The *church*, with Romanesque tower and columns of black marble, contains 2 painted figures of Nicolas von der Flüh and his grandson. On the outer wall of the bone-house is a tablet to the memory of the unfortunate people of Nidwalden (386 in number, including 102 women and 25 children) who were massacred, in defending their homes, by the French in September, 1798. This part of Switzerland refused the new constitution tyrannically imposed on it by the French republic. The ancient spirit of Swiss independence, fanned and excited by the exhortations of the priests (which in this instance must be termed fanatic, as all resistance was hopeless and useless), stirred up this ill-fated community to engage an army ten times greater than any force they could oppose to it, and consisting of veteran troops. Their desperate resistance served only to inflame the fury of their foes. After a vain attempt made by the French to starve the Unterwaldeners into submission, " on the 3rd of September, 1798, General Schauenburg, the French commander, directed a general attack to be made, by means of boats from Lucerne, as well as by the Oberland. Repulsed with great spirit by the inhabitants, only 2000 strong, the attack was renewed every day from the 3rd to the 9th of September. On this last day, towards two in the afternoon, reinforcements having penetrated by the land side, with field-pieces, the invaders forced their way into the very heart of the country. In their despair the people rushed on them with very inferior arms. Whole families perished together ; 102 young women and 25 children were found among the dead, side by side with their fathers and brothers, near the chapel of Winkelried. 63 persons who had taken shelter in the church of Stanz were slaughtered there, with the priest at the altar. Every house in the open country, in all 600, was burnt down ; Stanz itself escaped through the humanity of a *chef de brigade.* The inhabitants who survived this day, wandering in the mountains without the means of subsistence, would have died during the ensuing winter if they had not received timely assistance from the other cantons, from Germany and England, and from the French army itself, after its first fury was abated." —*Simond.*

The attack upon Stanzstad was conducted by General Foy, afterwards prominent as a leader of the revolutionary party in France. That unfortunate village was totally consumed.

Kerns (*Inn* : Krone, good and cheap), a small village 7 m. beyond Stanz, on the way to the Melchthal. The pedestrian may make a short cut to Sachseln avoiding Sarnen. A mile and a half beyond Kerns the roads from Bekenried and Lucerne meet at Sarnen.

The road from Stanz to Engelberg follows the course of the Aa, gradually ascending, and passing *Wolfenschiessen,* 4 m., with its ruined castle, and

Grafenort, 2½ m., where there is a small inn. ¼ m. beyond this the valley contracts, and a new road (1873) is carried up the l. bank of a ravine, opposite the woods through which the steep old road passed. At the summit of the ascent the traveller beholds before him the green vale and village of

Engelberg, 3343 ft. (*Inns* : H. Titlis, with beautiful view, good; H. Sonnen-

berg, a large and well-managed house, moderate and comfortable, attentive landlord, *Eng. Ch. S.* ; Engel, the old house; both well kept by Catani; H. Engelberg; Pension Müller. All very good and reasonable. *Guides,* K. Hess, Joseph Hess, good, and others). This retired village, situated 3343 ft. above the sea, in a bracing air, and amid beautiful scenery, has long been a favourite summer residence, the visitors being chiefly German Swiss. The valley is hemmed in on all sides by lofty mountains topped with snow, and based by precipices from which, in winter and in spring, numerous avalanches are precipitated. In the midst of it, upon a verdant slope, rises the Benedictine Abbey, conspicuous among the ordinary habitations of the village. It was founded in 1120, and received from Pope Calixtus II. the name of *Mons Angelorum,* from a legend that the site of the building was fixed by angels—

"Whose authentic lay,
Sung from that heavenly ground, in middle air,
Made known the spot where Piety should raise
A holy structure to th'Almighty's praise."
Wordsworth.

Having been three times destroyed by fire, the existing edifice is not older than 1729. "The architecture is plain and unimpressive, but the situation is worthy of the honours which the imagination of the mountaineers has conferred upon it." The monastery is independent of any bishop or sovereign but the Pope himself, or his legate : its revenues, once considerable, were seriously diminished by the French, but it still possesses valuable alpine pastures, and the cheeses produced on them are stored in an adjacent warehouse and cellars which are worth seeing. It contains, at present, only 19 brothers, and many of the rooms are empty and closed : in its large *church* are numerous paintings by Deschwanden and other artists of the modern Swiss school. The Library is of some value, rich in Swiss early printed books and illuminated MSS. ; the roof of the apartment in which it is placed has been cracked by an earthquake. By the rules of the order no woman is allowed to enter the building.

The *Titlis*, the chief of the mountains which overhang this romantic solitude, rises on the S. to a height of some 7000 ft. above the valley, and 10,620 ft. above the sea-level. Its round snowclad summit is frequently ascended (7 to 8 hrs.), but more easily from Engstlen (Rte. 33) or from the new *Inn* at the Trüb See than from Engelberg. The climb is fatiguing, but not difficult or dangerous. As far as the Trüb See on the Joch Pass the traveller can ride. The ascent is then up the rough mountain side, and higher by a steep buttress, and a slope of débris with a precipice on the l. This leads to the glacier above the ice-fall, from which point it is 2 hrs. over snow to the summit. The view is superb. The Sustenhorn, Galenstock, Thierberge, Finsteraarhorn, and Schreckhörner, are well seen. The Titlis was the first snow-peak in the Alps ascended, having been reached in 1739 by a monk from the convent.

Excursions—1. Up the main valley towards the Surenen Pass for a nearer view of the Titlis and Spanörter, 10,515 ft., but at least as far as the fall of the Tätschbach ¾ hr. 2. To the head of the *Horbis Thal*, the valley running N.E. from the village, a grand cirque of cliffs surmounted by glaciers, 1½ hr. 3. To the top of the same cirque, on the way to the Rothgrätli. 4. N. by W. to the chalets of *Schwand* (2 m.), and down through the pine wood to the high road about 2 m. below Engelberg. 5. By the Joch path to the Gerstni Alp, and then at rt. angles, or N.W., to the Jöchli track, and return by it. 6. The *Widderfeldstock* (7723 feet), in the direction of the Jöchli, commands a fine view.

[The *Passes of the Storegg* and *Jöchli* (Rte. 20) lead by the Melchthal to Sarnen in 6 hrs.

The *Joch Pass* (Rte. 33) to Meiringen in 10 hrs.

For climbers there are the following glacier-passes :—1. To Isenthal on the lake of Lucerne over the *Uri Rothstock*, 9620 ft. ; or to Isenthal, by the Rothgrätli Pass, crossing a shoulder of the Engelberger Rothstock, and descending by a small piece of glacier. 2. To Stein on the Susten, by the *Wenden glacier*, a passage just below the magnificent precipice of the Titlis. 3. To Stein or Wasen by the *Grassen glacier*, W. of the Spanört. 4. To the Erstfelder Thal and St. Gothard road by the *Spanörter Joch*, 9823 ft., between the Gross and Klein Spanört, or by the *Erstfelder Joch*, 8635 ft., between the Gross Spanort and Schlossberg. The former pass is the higher and more difficult, but also the finer. The Gross Spanört (10,515 ft.) has been ascended from it by a stiff rock climb.]

The *Surenen Pass.*

In about 3 m. the path reaches the dairy belonging to the abbey, called Herrenrüti, where cheese is made: 50 cows are attached to it ; and the pastures refreshed by more than 20 springs rising upon them. From the steep sides of the Hahnenberg on the N.E., a beautiful waterfall bursts forth, called *Tätschbach*. The valley now winds round the base of the Stotzigberg in a N.E. direction below the precipices of the Spanörter and Schlossberg. [At the angle the track for the Wenden and Grassen glaciers crosses a bridge, the former climbing to an old moraine below the Titlis, the latter up slopes of grass and then steep smooth rocks.] Some chalets are next passed, and rough ground ascended to the pretty fall of the *Stierenbach*, where the stream is crossed to a level pastoral vale grazed by a herd of horses. Here beyond a little chapel and chalets the valley again sweeps to the rt., and soon afterwards l., while the path, traversing patches of snow, gains the summit of the pass, or *Surenen Eck*. It is a narrow ridge 7562 ft. above the sea, not more than 5 ft. wide, between a grand craggy precipice of the Blackenstock l. and the Geissberg rt. During the greater part of the ascent the Titlis shines forth, and a long line of peaks and glaciers extends from it uninterruptedly to the Surenen. Another view now opens out on the opposite side into the valley of Schächen, bounded in the extreme distance by the snowy top of the Glärnisch. On the E. side of the Surenen, the surface of snow to be crossed is often greater, and the descent is steeper. After traversing a desolate tract, the chalets of Waldnacht are passed; and at the end of the green valley the path divides, l. a very steep but direct descent, now a horse-track, leads to Attinghausen and Altdorf. On the rt. both path and stream suddenly fall into the wonderful gorge called *Bockischlund*, and are conducted into the valley of the Reuss at Rübshausen, about 2 hrs. from Amsteg and 1 from Altdorf. Those who cross the Surenen in the opposite direction without a guide, should be careful to cross the stream at the chapel mentioned above, and at the Stierenbach to take the l. of two paths.

In 1799 a division of the French army, under Lecourbe, crossed this pass with cannon to attack the Austrians in the valley of the Reuss, but were soon driven back the same way by the impetuous descent of Suwarrow from the St. Gothard.

Altdorf (Rte. 34).

ROUTE 32.

PASS OF THE SUSTEN, FROM MEIRINGEN OR REICHENBACH TO WASEN.

29½ m., 11 hrs.' walking. It is better to start from Hof.

In 1811, when the Valais was added by Napoleon to the French empire, a char-road was constructed by the Swiss from Meiringen to Stein, and on the side of Uri from Wasen to Fernigen, to enable the inhabitants of Canton Berne to convey their produce into Italy through Swiss territory. When the Valais had been restored to Switzerland this road was no longer wanted. It was allowed to fall into decay, and can now only be regarded as a bridle-path. There is a carriage-road as far as Gadmen. Charge for a horse 30 fr. No guide is required in clear weather. The pass, though little frequented, displays fine mountain scenery on the W. side, and enables a stout pedestrian to proceed in one day from Meiringen to Wasen; but the distance is almost too much, and it is usual to stop for the night at Stein. The word Sust means toll or custom-house.

The route of the Grimsel is followed from Meiringen as far as Hof (Rte. 26, A), where, quitting the side of the Aar, a road turns l. up the course of the Gadmen Aar, ascending the valley called, at its lower extremity, Mühlenthal, and higher up Nessel-thal. Opposite *Mühlestalden*, where reside the guides Weissenfluh, the narrow Triftthal opens from the S., with glimpses of the Trift glacier, up which lies a pass to the Grimsel (Rte. 27, A). Beyond is *Nesselthal*, very prettily situated, about 1 hr. from

11 m. *Gadmen* (*Inn*: Bär, tolerable). This village of 550 Inhab., 4101 ft. above the sea, is composed of 3 groups of houses, Eck, Ambuhl, and Obermatt, ¾ mile higher up. L. runs the wall of the *Gadmenfluh*, culminating in the Titlis, which rises at the head of the Wenden Thal. From Obermatt an ascent by zigzags through the forest leads to the rocks of the Urathhörner, round which the path winds above a great ravine — where the mountain side opposite will excite the admiration of the traveller—to the little *Inn* (humble, but pretty good) at

4¾ m. *Stein*, close to the Stein glacier, surrounded by wild heights, and looking W. down the valley to the Wetterhörner. Behind the house a curious cascade falls apparently from the top of an isolated rock. The char-road was not carried further than Stein, and a portion of it has been destroyed by the advance of the glacier, which has again retreated. The appearance of the glacier is remarkable, as it assumes a fan shape at its termination. From Stein the ascent of the *Sustenhorn* (11,529 ft.) may be effected in from 4 to 5½ hrs. up, the only difficulty being the sharp crest of snow at the top. (Kaspar Luchs, the landlord's son, a good guide, asks 15 fr.) The view extends from the Combin to the Bernina, the chief features being the Galenstock and eastern peaks of the Oberland.

The *Thierberg*, 10,410 ft., below which the traveller passes to the Sustenhorn, can be climbed more easily in 10 hrs. up and down.

The *Heuberg*, N.E., 8507 ft., is only 2 hrs. from Stein, by the top of the pass. The Titlis is shut out, but in other quarters a grand view lies open.

[The following glacier rtes. lead
a. To Geschenen. There are two passes. For both you climb the Thierbergli rocks ; then (*a*) turn l. and pass between the Sustenhorn and Steinberg, descending to a low point on the *Kehle* glacier ; (*b*) turn rt. and pass between Steinberg and Thierberg, and traverse the whole length of the Kehle glacier. The rt. pass is much longer and steeper, but also much finer.

b. To the Grimsel, or Rhone glacier notel, by the Steinlimmi, Trift, and Rhône glaciers (Rte. 27, A).

c. To Engelberg, by the Wenden glacier, crossing the ridge close to the precipice of the Titlis—the grand feature of the pass. The easy way to the glacier is to descend nearly to Gadmen, the shorter to climb over the Urathhörner, but the rocks on the other side are steep. About 6 hrs. to the col, and 4 down to Engelberg. From Engelberg to the col, 4½ hrs.; thence to Gadmen 2 hrs.; thence to Stein 3½ hrs. On the W. side of the Titlis there is a pass to Engstlen.]

From Stein a steep ascent of 1 hr. brings the traveller to

2 m. The *Susten Pass*, 7424 feet. The view is fine; the serrated ridges, and the many-pointed peaks of the mountains bounding the Maienthal, through which the descent lies, especially arrest the attention. There is always some snow on the E. declivity of the pass. The first chalets are met with on the Hundsalp. The stream of the Maien-Reuss,

issuing out of the Susten glacier (rt.), under the Sustenhorn, is crossed several times, until at the Hauserbrücke, a considerable distance below Fernigen, the unfinished char-road again commences. Near Fernigen the deeply engulfed and foaming Gurezmittlerbach is crossed. Lower down, 3 hrs. from the top of the pass, is the village of

6¾ m. *Maien,* where there is a poor *Inn.* Most of the houses in this valley are protected from avalanches by a stone dyke, or well-propped palisade of wood raised on the hillside behind them. Beyond Maien the road grows steep and stony, and passes, at a rugged spot, the remains of an hexagonal redoubt (Schanze), which was fortified by the Austrians, 1799, and stormed by the French under Loison, who forced the enemy up the vale of the Reuss, and, after five assaults, took Wasen, an important point.

3¾ m. *Wasen,* on the St. Gothard Rly. (Rte. 34). Fast walking *from* Wasen, 5 hrs. to the Pass; ¾ Stein; 2 Gadmen; 2 Hof; 1 Meiringen = total, 10¾ hours.

ROUTE 33.

THE JOCH PASS, FROM MEIRINGEN TO ENGELBERG.

	hrs.
Meiringen	
Imhof	1¼
Engstlen Alp	5¼
Joch	1¼
Engelberg	2¼
	——
	10¼

Horse to Engstlen 15 fr., to Engelberg 30 fr.

This pass, though practicable for horses, and a good deal used, is high and steep. It is a fine pass, with considerable variety of scenery, commanding beautiful views of the Titlis. As far as Hof it is the same as Rte. 26. The road of the Susten is then followed for nearly an hour to the junction of the Gentelbach with the Gadmenbach at Wyler. From this point there is a rapid ascent, with fine view back of the glaciers and peaks at the head of the Urbach Thal, to the pastures at the lower extremity of the Gentel Thal, in which is a pure spring, very grateful after the hot climb. The path then runs on the rt. bank of the stream (do not cross at the bridge) on a very gradual rise for 1½ hour, through delicious scenery, to the chalets of Jüngholz, where a cluster of streams, called *Jüngibrunnen*, spring from the mountain side. A little further it crosses the torrent (but not to go up to the rt.), and in 1½ hr. by a rough path, partly through pine forest, and by a beautiful waterfall of the Gentelbach, leads to the Engstlen Alp, and the well-known and excellent

Engstlen Inn and Pension (about 6100 ft.). The position is a very fine one, the near view of the range of the Titlis is magnificent; and in the distance are seen the 3 peaks of the Wetterhörner, and the Schreckhorn. The chief excursion is the ascent of

The *Titlis* (see Rte. 31). Guide 10 fr. From this convenient starting-point it is often accomplished by English ladies. A practised mountaineer will easily reach the summit in 4½ hrs., but it is well to start early to secure a frozen surface on the glacier. The old rte. was to descend to the rt. after passing the Joch, and to go up the buttress, as from Engelberg, but latterly a shorter path has been followed, by the rocks and glacier from the head of the Pass. About 300 yds. N.E. of the inn is a remarkable intermittent *Spring*, called *Wunderbrunnen*, which flows from spring to autumn, always running from 8 A.M. to about 4 P.M., when it ceases. In the opposite direction, under the Gadmenfluh, is the prettiest feature of the Alp—the *Engstlen See*—a short walk over knolls red with the Alpine rose and here and there shaded by an old pine. A day may well be spent in a ramble from the inn. One may climb the *Gwartlistock*, the rock close to the E.; or to the *Mittagslücke*, the gap in the Gadmenfluh; or to the

rock called *Razenstein* (after the landlord), in a wider glacier gap further E.

A pass leads to Sarnen by the Melchthal (Rte. 20), and another to Gadmen, called

The *Sätteli* (Little Saddle) in 4 hrs., or in 6 to Stein, but a guide should be taken. The path skirts the rocks at the extremity of the Engstlen See, and thence, bearing to the rt., ascends slanting to the summit, W. of the Tellistock (2½ hrs.); the view is over the Thierberge, Sustenhorn, and peaks about the Trift glacier. On the Gadmen side the descent is very steep, and by a mere goat-track. It takes a direction to the l. and leads to a shepherd's hut (½ hr.), where it divides; l. to Obermatt and Stein (Rte. 32), rt. to Gadmen and Hof. The remainder of the descent is rather less formidable and very picturesque, passing through fir-woods and commanding beautiful views of the valley.

From the Engstlen inn it is about 1 hr. to the top of the

Joch Pass, 7244 ft., whence the glaciers of the Titlis range, and the snowy peaks of the Uri Rothstock beyond Engelberg are well seen. The rocks to the l. are the *Grauhorn* and beyond it the *Wild Geissberg*. The descent to the *Trüb See* [*Inn* built by Herr Kuchler, a good botanist, good]—fed from the *Ochsenberg*, rt.—is by rough and steep ground. At the chalets the paths separate; riders pass to the l. of the lake, and make a long circuit of 2½ hrs. to Engelberg. Pedestrians keep the lake on their l., walking through the water where it spreads in shallow channels, and make straight for the low part of the opposite ridge, thus saving an hour. From the brow the church and buildings of Engelberg are plainly seen. There is a very steep descent down the *Pfaffenwand* by zigzags to pastures. These are crossed to the forest, which is steep to

Engelberg (Rte. 31).

ROUTE 34.

THE PASS OF ST. GOTHARD, FROM FLÜ-
ELEN, ON THE LAKE OF LUCERNE, TO
BELLINZONA.

9¾ posts = 78¾ miles.

	Eng. m.
Flüelen to Amsteg	10¼
Amsteg to Andermatt . . .	14¼
Andermatt to St. Gothard Pass .	9½
St. Gothard Pass to Airolo . .	7¼
Airolo to Faido	9¼
Faido to Biasca	13
Biasca to Bellinzona (Rly.) . .	14
	——
	78¾

For the *St. Gothard Railway and
Tunnel*, see Rte. 34A. For the benefit
of those who desire to explore at
leisure and in detail the scenery of
the old road—this Route is retained.

The Railway may be used as far
as Amsteg, where the ascent properly
begins.

This was anciently one of the most
frequented passages over the Alps, as
it offered to Northern Switzerland
and W. Germany the most direct and
practicable line of communication with
Lombardy, and the important cities of
Milan and Genoa. Not less than
16,000 travellers and 9000 horses
crossed it annually on an average, at
the commencement of the present
century; but being only a bridle-path,
it was almost entirely abandoned after
the construction of the roads over the
Splügen and Bernardino. The cantons
of Uri and Tessin, through which
the St. Gothard runs, at length became sufficiently alive to their own
interests to perceive the necessity of
converting it into a carriage-road. In
1820 the work was begun, and in
1832 finally completed and opened.
The expenses were defrayed by a
joint-stock company, formed in Uri
and the neighbouring cantons. The
construction of the road was intrusted
to an engineer of Altdorf, named
Müller. The carriage-road from Lucerne to Flüelen passes round by
Schwyz, and has been completed by
a fine work of engineering, called the
the *Axenstrasse*, from Brunnen to
Flüelen.

[*Switz.*]

At present the road is excellent,
not inferior to any other of the great
Alpine highways. In grandeur of
scenery, except near the summit, it
may vie with any Swiss carriage-pass.
Its points of chief interest are the
Gorge of Schöllinen, Devil's Bridge,
and Val Leventina, near Faido.

The road is now superseded as a
trade route by the Railway and
Tunnel.

The Canton Uri and the valley of
the Reuss possess an historical celebrity, as the theatre of the memorable
campaign of 1799, when the armies
of France, Austria, and Russia, dispos-
sessing each other in turns, marched,
fought, and manœuvred, on heights
whence the snow never disappears.

†*Flüelen* — Italian, *Fiora* — (*Inns*:
Urnerhof, 5 minutes from station, outside town on the lake, excellent;
Alder; Kreuze; Tell; close to the
steamboat pier; a small village at
the S. extremity of the lake of the
Four Cantons. Flüelen was formerly
rendered unhealthy by the marshy
ground produced by the deposits
of the Reuss at its entrance into the
lake. The marshes have, however,
been drained at a considerable expense, and the air is now pure and
good.

1½ m. *Altdorf* 1466 ft. (*Inns*: Adler,
Schlüssel (Clef d'Or), both good;
Löwe, fair; Krone, cheap). The
capital of Uri: it is a dull town of
2900 Inhab., without trade or manufactures. It is principally known by
the tradition that it was on the open
square of Altdorf that William Tell
shot the apple from his son's head.
The spot where he is said to have
stood and taken aim was marked by
a stone fountain, erected 1786, but in
1861 this was replaced by a colossal
plaster statue of Tell, a gift of the
riflemen of Zürich. The tall *Tower*,
ornamented with rude frescoes of Tell
and Gessler, has been stated to occupy
the site of the lime-tree upon which
Gessler's cap was hung, for all men
to do obeisance to it as they passed,
and to which the child was bound, to

serve as a mark for his father's bolt. It existed a withered trunk, as late as 1567.

In the *Rathhaus* are preserved flags taken at Morgarten and Sempach.

A lane crossing the Reuss at its junction with the Schächenbach leads to *Attinghausen*, the birthplace of *Walter Fürst*, one of the three liberators of Switzerland: a house is pointed out as his.

From this village there is a pretty path all the way to Amsteg along the l. bank of the Reuss.

W. of Altdorf is the *Surenen Pass* to Engelberg (Rte. 31).

On quitting Altdorf the road crosses the mouth of the Schächen Thal, traversing, by a bridge, the stream in which, according to the legend, William Tell lost his life in endeavouring to rescue a child from the waterfall of Bürglen. He plunged in, and neither he nor the child was seen again. Tell was said to be a native of *Bürglen* (*Inn* and Pension, Wilhelm Tell), a little to the L. of our road. The small *Chapel*, backed by an ivy-clad tower, rudely painted with the events of his life, was built about 1388, but there is no evidence to prove it was to commemorate Tell. It is said to be the spot where his house stood, near the churchyard. The inhabitants of this valley are considered the finest men in Switzerland. A path runs up it, and across the Klausen Pass (Rte. 76) to the baths of Stachelberg, and another over the Kinzig Kulm (Rte. 75), into the Muotta Thal.

In a field at *Schaddorf*, a little beyond the bridge, the parliament (Landsgemeinde) of Uri is held on the first Sunday in May. Every male citizen above the age of 20, except a priest, has a vote. The authorities of the canton, on horseback, with the Landammann at their head, preceded by a detachment of militia, with military music, and the standard of the canton, and two men in ancient costume, bearing aloft the two bull's horns of Uri, march to the spot in procession. From a semicircular hustings, erected for the purpose, the business of the day is proclaimed to the assembled crowd, and the different speakers deliver their harangues, after which the question is put to the vote by show of hands. When all affairs of state are despatched, the Landammann and other public officers resign, and are either re-elected or others are chosen in their place.

Beyond Altdorf the road passes through pretty meadows shaded with walnut-trees as far as Amsteg. L. rises the rocky wall of the Windgelle, a continuation of the Clariden-Grat, and Scheerhorn. A flat surface on the precipice returns a very distinct echo.

At *Erstfeld*, on the rt., opens the steep Erstfeldthal leading up to the glaciers of the Spanörterjoch. It contains very fine scenery, and two interesting but somewhat difficult passes, the *Erstfeldioch* (8 hrs.), and the *Spanörterioch* (10 hrs.), leading from it to Engelberg.

At *Klus* the road approaches the margin of the Reuss, and beyond, at the hamlet of *Silinen*, it is partly cut through the rock, passing under the ruins of a tower, formerly supposed to be the castle of *Zwing Uri* (Restraint of Uri), built by Gessler, to overawe the peasants.

9 m. *Amsteg* (*Inns*: Stern; Kreuz (Croix Blanche); Hirsch—all good country inns; *Guides*). This village is delightfully situated under the Bristenstock and Windgelle, 1713 ft. above the sea and, although not a post station, is a convenient place for those to stop at who cross the lake by the afternoon steamer from Lucerne. It stands at the mouth of the *Maderaner* or *Kärstelen Thal*, which stretches E. as far as the Hüfi gl. at the base of the Scheerhorn and Düssistock, a valley abounding in waterfalls and pine forests (see Rte. 83). [A track leads to Dissentis over the Kreuzli Pass, and a glacier pass over the Clariden Grat to Stachelberg. There is a good *hotel* near the Hüfi Glacier, 3½ hrs. from Amsteg. The lower part of the valley may be visited in less than 2 hrs. by walking to the

first bridge over its torrent and back.

The *Bristenstock*, 10,089 ft., and about 8000 ft. above Amsteg, is a difficult mountain to climb without a guide, as it has many ridges or arêtes, and in coming down the wrong one may be taken. This happened in 1857 to Messrs. Hardy and Kennedy, and led to an exciting but not pleasant adventure, as they had to pass the night on a ledge 3 ft. by 6. The ascent takes fully 12 hrs. up and down. The course from the inn to the top is S.E. by S., over the pasture by a sheep track to the tarn called *Bristen See.* The views from the Bristenstock are finer than those from any of the neighbouring mountains.

The *Kleine Windgelle* (the nearest to the St. Gothard road, and in the Maderaner Thal called the Grosse Windgelle), 9848 ft., was first ascended on the S.W. side; direct from Amsteg; but Mr. Sowerby, in 1862, found an easier way by the Golzern See and the hollow between the Great and Little Windgelle. Thence he climbed by a gully in the eastern precipices, and reached the top in 6¼ hrs. from Amsteg. In the hollow he found the limestone wonderfully weathered, split into chasms 50 ft. deep. The rocks of the Gross Windgelle are the grand feature of the view.

The *Gross Windgelle* (Kalkstock of the Maderaner Thal), 10,463 ft., was first climbed, 1848, by the small glacier and rocks facing S.W. Difficulty was experienced in passing from the ice to the rocks, and higher up a wall about 1 ft. in width had to be traversed between precipices. The ascent took 5½ hours from the Bernertsmatt Alp (4½ hrs. from Amsteg), but it has since been done in less time.

The *guides* Ambrose Zgraggen, Joseph M. and Melchior Trösch and Albin Baumann are recommended. A very pleasant walk from Amsteg is to ascend the alp on the opposite side of the valley of the Reuss by a path from the bridge over that river. It leads through beautiful scenery and commands a grand view of the Bristenstock. The *Grossgant*, 8000 ft., or the

Ottersbalm, a still finer point of view W. of it, may be climbed.]

At the bridge the road of the St. Gothard first crosses the Reuss and begins to ascend in earnest, having on the l. the river, in a deep channel, dashing from rock to rock, and high above the *Bristenstock*, rising in tiers of precipices.

Beyond *Intschi,* a second bridge carries the road to the rt. bank; and, after traversing a wood, a third, called Pfaffensprung (Priest's Leap), from a fable of a monk having leaped across the chasm with a maiden in his arms, brings the traveller to the torrent Maienbach, descending from the Susten Pass (Rte. 32). Two or three zigzags lead up to

7½ m. *Wasen* (*Inns*: Ochs, good and moderate ; H. des Alpes, good), on an eminence, at the mouth of the Maien-thal, and 1355 ft. higher than Amsteg. Fine view from the churchyard close to the Ochs. At the entrance is a chapel containing skulls of Wasen people arranged in cases like books. Overhead, to the W. are the rocks of the *Voralpstock*, and E. the *Felli Thal*, rich in crystals, leading by the easy *Felli pass* to the Oberalp See. Winding from side to side, the road slowly toils upward to

3¼ m. *Geschenen*, 3600 ft. (*Inns*: H. Geschenen, good ; H. du Cheval ; H. des Alpes). Hence diligences for Andermatt the Furca and Oberalp, run to correspond with the trains.

[Here a wild valley opens W., through which the torrent of the *Geschenen Reuss* descends from the five glaciers of the *Winterberge* and the great *Damma Glacier*. A walk of 3 hrs. leads to the Geschenen alp, a solitary hamlet at the foot of a fine amphitheatre of rock and ice. Passes lead rt. and l. to the Stein Alp (9 hrs.) and Realp (7 hrs.). The direct pass across the central portion of the range to the Rhone glacier and the Grimsel is exceedingly difficult, and only to be attempted by firstrate mountaineers and guides.]

Opposite Geschenen, where the rock is gneiss, the great tunnel of the *St. Gothard Railway* was commenced in 1872. The valley now contracts into the Schöllinen gorge, and is bounded for nearly 3 m. by high cliffs. The *Teufelsstein*, a fragment, skirted by the road, was dropped, according to the legend, by the devil. The valley here ascends steeply, and has been called by the peasants *Krachenthal* from the wild dashing of the Reuss. The road is much exposed in spring to avalanches. Here and there niches are cut in the rock for shelter, and a part of the road is roofed by a stone *gallery*. The gorge now grows narrower—a mere cleft in the mountain —the clamour of the torrent becomes a roar; a corner is turned, and the traveller beholds, in the midst of the spray of a cataract,

*The *Devil's Bridge*. Here rocks of granite, remarkable for the smooth nakedness of their surface, hem in the bed of the river on both sides; and so closely that on the left bank there is not an inch of space for the sole of a foot, except what has been hewn out of the cliff. For ages this must have been a complete cul-de-sac, until, by human ingenuity, the torrent was bridged and the rock bored through. The old bridge, a thin segment of a circle, spanning the abyss, suspended at a height of 70 ft. above the Reuss, had originally an air at once of boldness and fragility, much of which it has lost by the contrast with the towering and solid structure that has now superseded it. A commodious and gradually sloping terrace leads to the broad new bridge. It is of granite, the arch 25 ft. span, and was finished 1830. The construction of this part of the road presented great difficulties; the mines necessary for blasting the granite could only be formed by workmen suspended by ropes, and dangling in the air like spiders . The ancient bridge was first built by Abbot Gerald, of Einsiedeln, in 1118, so that, in the naming of it, the devil has received more than his due: it has been allowed to remain beneath the new bridge, though no longer of any use.

Within the last few years a despicable refreshment shed and large posters announcing illuminations of the fall have been allowed to vulgarise this striking scene. The landlord of the Bellevue at Andermatt is said to be responsible for this outrage.

During the extraordinary campaign of 1799, the defile of the Schöllinen was twice obstinately contested within the space of little more than a month. On the 14th of August the united French column, under Lecourbe and Loison, having surprised the Austrians, drove them up the valley of the Reuss, as far as this bridge, which, having been converted into an entrenched position, was defended for some time. At last even the bridge was carried by the French, On the 24th of the following September the tide of war took an opposite turn. Suwarrow, pouring down from the summit of the St. Gothard, at the head of 5000 horse and 18,000 foot, compelled the French, in their turn, to retire before him. The truth, however, seems to be that these passes were never forced, but that the attacking party always turned the position, coming down upon the flanks and rear of the enemy (see Rte. 26). The bridge itself was not blown up, but some of the arches leading to it were destroyed. For correct accounts of the extraordinary actions among these mountains, only Jomini, the military historian, can be relied on.

Immediately above, after passing the Devil's Bridge, the road is carried through a tunnel called the

2½ m. *Urnerloch*, or *Hole of Uri*. It is 180 ft. long, 15 high, and 16 broad. Previous to its construction, in 1707, the only mode of passing the buttress of rock which here projects into the river, so as to deny all passage, was by a shelf of boards, suspended on the outside by chains. By means of this the traveller doubled, as it were, the shoulder of the mountain, enveloped in the spray of the torrent, within a few feet of which the frail structure was hung. The Gallery of Uri was originally constructed by a Swiss engineer named Moretini ; but was only passable for mules, until, in reconstructing the St. Gothard road, it was enlarged to admit carriages.

Out of this gallery the traveller emerges into the wide pastoral valley of Urseren, which, in contrast with the savage gorge, and from the suddenness of the transition, has obtained from most travellers the praise of beauty and fertility. Taken by itself, however, it has little but its verdure to recommend it: owing to its great height, about 4700 ft. Few trees grow in it, and the inhabitants supply themselves with corn from more fortunate lands. The lower part was probably a lake, until a passage was opened through the rocks of Schöllinen. It was originally colonised, it is supposed, by the Rhætians. The old entrance was the pass of the Oberalp. Its inhabitants spoke the language of the Grisons, and the valley was a dépendance of the abbey of Dissentis. Down to the 12th century it had no direct communication with the lower valley of the Reuss. About that time, however, a path seems to have been opened; and the men of Urseren, allying themselves with those of Uri, threw off the yoke of their feudal lords. A mile from the gallery of Uri lies

1 m. *Andermatt*, or *Urseren* (Ital. *Orsera*) (*Inns:* H. Bellevue, a large house, very high charges, uncivil landlord (*Eng. Ch. S.*); H. du St. Gothard, moderate, recommended; H. Oberalp, good; Drei Könige (Post). It is a village of 660 Inhab., and the chief place of the valley, 4733 ft. above the sea; 20 min. walk from the Devil's Bridge. Honey and cheese here are excellent; and the red trout of the Oberalp See enjoy the reputation, with hungry travellers, of being the finest in the world. The *Church of St. Columbanus* is said to have been built by the Lombards. The great tunnel of the St. Gothard Rly. passes under it. Above the village, on the slope of the mountain of St. Anne, are the scanty remains of a forest, the last relic of that which perhaps at one time clothed the sides of the valley. The inhabitants had learned to value

it for the protection it afforded from falling avalanches. They therefore guarded it with the utmost care; but, in 1799, foreign invaders, reckless of the consequences, felled a great part of it, and consumed it as firewood. Trenches have been cut to break the upper slopes, and many young trees planted.

At Andermatt, Hospenthal, and Airolo, are many dealers in the minerals with which these mountains abound. The variety is surprising, and the mineralogist derives some of his rarest specimens from the Alps of St. Gothard.

[From Andermatt diverges l. the road over the Oberalp to Coire (Rte. 82), and it is the starting-place of the diligences over the Furca to the Valais (Rte. 26, B).]

2½ m. above Andermatt is

Hospenthal, or *Hôpital* (*Inns:* Meyerhof, good; pension during the summer (*Eng. Ch. S.*); Goldener Löwe).

Hospenthal receives its name from an hospice which no longer exists. Above the village rises a venerable tower, said to be, like the church of Andermatt, a work of the Lombards.

The road now turning to the l. quits the valley of Urseren, and begins to ascend by zigzags towards the summit of the St. Gothard. It may be reached in about 2½ hours from Hospenthal by a pedestrian, who may make a short cut by the old mulepath, paved with granite slabs, but grass-grown. The scenery is wild and dreary.

Under the name of St. Gothard are comprised, not merely the depression, or col, over which the road passes, but a group of mountains, exceeding in elevation the snow-line, situated between the cantons of Uri, Valais, Ticino, and Grisons; and containing the sources of the Rhine, the Rhone, the Reuss, and the Ticino, all of which, with many tributaries, rise within a circle of 10 miles, described from the summit of the pass.

The river Reuss may be said to fall, rather than flow, into the lake of the Four Cantons. Between the Hospice and Urseren it descends more than

2000 ft., and between Urseren and Flüelen 3000; the road crosses it for the last time by the bridge of Rodont, which marks the boundary of the cantons Uri and Ticino. The source is in the small lake of Lucendro, 1 m. rt. of the road. The Pass of St. Gothard (6936 feet above the sea) is a saddle in the granite central chain, overlooked by the *Sasso di San Gottardo*, E. (8983 ft.), the *Blauberg* further E. (9848 ft.), and *La Fibbia*, W. (8996 ft.). The Fibbia can be easily ascended in 3 hrs. from the inn, there and back. The pass is a desolate scene: the mossy ground covered with stones, and the road winding among tarns, some of which flow N., but the greater number are feeders of the Ticino, which gives its name to the Canton Tessin, or Ticino. A few minutes' walk below the summit are the

7½ m. *Inn* (and *Post-house*): H. du Mont Prosa, good, and the *Hospice* (rented by the same landlord), a massive and roomy building, constructed by the Canton Ticino, which has also erected several houses of refuge. It is designed for the accommodation of travellers, being fitted roughly as an inn, containing 15 beds. Attached to it is a warehouse for goods. In 1872 it received 8160 poor travellers, and distributed 24,635 portions, food and clothes, at an outlay of 9974 fr.; the receipts were 9870 fr. A very humble hospice and a chapel have existed on the St. Gothard since the 13th century, owing their origin to the Abbot of Dissentis, who sent a monk to this wild height to minister to the spiritual as well as physical wants of distressed travellers. In the 16th century St. Carlo Borromeo suggested the construction of a hospice on a larger scale, which, after his death, was built by his brother.

[Excursions may be made to the *Lago di Lucendro* or the *Pizzo Centrale* (9853 ft.). This peak, reached in 3½ hrs. from the hospice, commands a fine panorama. The *Monte Prosa*, a lower summit, also commands a fine view. There are glacier routes to the Furca Inn, 10 hrs.]

The passage in winter and spring is by no means free from danger: the snow is sometimes heaped in drifts 40 feet on the summit, and the descent towards Airolo is much exposed to tourmentes and avalanches (§ 14). A winter seldom passes without the loss of some lives, and melancholy catastrophes have occurred. The spot called Buco dei Calanchetti is so named from a party of glaziers from the Val Calanca, who, persisting in pushing on from the hospice, in spite of warning, were buried here beneath the snow.

The descent towards Italy displays skilful engineering; and the difficulties of a slope, much steeper on this side than on the other, have been overcome by a series of 28 zigzag terraces not exceeded in number and tortuous direction on any other Alpine pass. They begin a little beyond the hospice, and continue nearly all the way to Airolo. The gully down which the road passes is called *Val Tremola* (Germ. Trümmeln Thal), Trembling Valley, from its supposed effect on the nerves of those who passed it. Since the new road has been made, its terrors, whatever they were previously, have been much softened. A very pretty mineral, named from this locality, where it was first found, Tremolite, is abundant, and specimens of it occur even in the walls and loose stones at the road-side. On this pass many rare minerals are found, and may be purchased better than in any other part of Switzerland. The view up and down the vale of the Ticino and over the mountains on the opposite side is extremely fine.

7½ m. *Airolo*, 3868 ft. (Germ. *Eriels*) (*Inns:* Posta; H. Airolo; good; H. and P. Lombard), on the l. bank of the Tessin, near the junction of its 2 branches. The inhabitants both in habit and language, are Italian. It possesses a relic of antiquity: the stump of a tower called *Il Castello*, and Casa dei Pagani, built, it is said, by Desiderius King of the Lombards, A.D. 774. The Lombard kings constructed a line of similar forts all the way to Como, many of which will be passed in descending the valley.

The summit of the St. Gothard may be reached from Airolo in a *light* carriage in 2½ or 3 hrs.; by means of the old road and short cuts a pedestrian may ascend, and even descend, in less time than a carriage.

[Several paths diverge from Airolo. 1. Up the Val Bedretto to the *Nüfenen Pass* (Rte. 63): or, 2, from All' Acqua by the *S. Giacomo Pass* to the Val Formazza (Rte. 62): 3. By the *Uomo Pass* to Sta. Maria, on the Lukmanier Pass leading to Dissentis (Rte. 84): 4. A summer path, ascending by the N.W. side of the Val Canaria, and over the *Unteralp Pass* to Andermatt. The head of the Val Canaria is occupied by a small lake ; the scenery is wild and rugged. The *Nera Pass* leads from it into V. Maigels. A guide should be taken for these passes. 5. The *Passo di Campo Lungo* (5 hrs.) to Fusio at the head of one of the branches of Val Maggia diverges at Daziogrande, where there is no inn, so that travellers must start from Airolo or Faido (see Rte. 64).]

At Airolo is the S. opening of the *Great Tunnel of St. Gothard Rly.*

Just below Airolo, at the mouth of the picturesque glen of *Stalvedro*, is a Lombard tower of King Desiderius. This part of the pass was defended, Sept. 1799, against Suwarrow's army for 12 hrs., by 600 French, who effected their retreat over the Nüfenen into the Valais. 1 m. further is the waterfall of *Calcaccia*. The valley hence to Biasca is called *Val Leventina—Livinen Thal* in German. A few miles lower down the river threads another defile, named after a toll-house within it

Dazio Grande,—a rent in the Monte Piottino (Platifer), nearly a mile long, and one of the most picturesque scenes on the whole route. The old road threaded the depths of the gorge, supported for a great part of the way on arches and terraces, and crossing the river thrice on bridges. During the storms of 1834 and 1839, the Ticino swept away nearly the whole of these costly constructions. The new line runs at a higher level, out of the reach of inundations, and

escaped the great flood of 1868. The descent is less rapid than the old road. On emerging from the last tunnel the fall of the *Piumegna* is seen rt. Chestnut-trees first appear soon after quitting the defile of Dazio, and vines are cultivated at

9¾ m. *Faido* (*Inns:* Principe di Galles, or Prince of Wales; Angelo—both good; H. Vella; Sole), a post station and the chief place in the valley, with 778 Inhab., 2366 ft. above the sea.

A revolt of the people of the Val Leventina, in 1755, against their tyrannical lords and masters the cowherds of Uri, to whom they had been subject since the 15th century, was here terminated by the execution of the ringleaders, whose heads were fastened to the trunks of the chestnut-trees, in the presence of 3000 men of the valley. The troops of the Confederation had previously surrounded and disarmed this ill-starred band of rebels, and afterwards compelled them, on bended knees, to sue for mercy.

[A footpath crosses the mountain from Faido to the Lukmanier Pass (Rte. 85).

The *Campo Lungo Pass* to Fusio (Rte. 64) can be taken from here as well as from Airolo. Mountaineers will prefer to cross over *Piz Campo Tencia* (10,100 ft.), a fine view-point, with glaciers on its N.E. slope (ascent 5½ hrs.; beautiful descent to Broglio in Val Lavizzara, 3½ hrs.). The Federal map supplies any deficiency in local knowledge in the guides, few of whom know the mountain. The peak is ascended by a direct route up the ridge of rocks which falls from the highest summit.]

Through a highly cultivated tract the road reaches another fine defile full of chestnut-trees. At *Chironico* the glen of the same name leads to the wild and steep *Passo di Barona* and Val Verzasca.

7½ m. *Giornico* (Germ. *Irnis*) (*Inns:* Posta, dear; Cervo, clean; Corona, dirty), a village of 700 Inhab. It has a high tower, and 2 very old and curious churches, — *Santa Maria di*

Castello, of which the substructure is said to exhibit traces of a fort, attributed to the Gauls (?); and San *Nicolò da Mira*. The architecture is Romanesque, and the E. end offers an unaltered specimen of the choir raised upon a vault that can hardly be called a crypt. Both these churches are interesting examples of a very early form of Christian buildings.

Half-way to

2¼ m. •*Bodio* (*Inns*: H. de Ville (Posta); Bissone), a heap of large rocks (Sassi Grossi) serves as a natural monument of the victory gained in 1478 over the Milanese by the Swiss, who had made a foray across the St. Gothard as far as Bellinzona, under pretext of an injury—the felling of some trees belonging to Canton Uri.

[High and rough passes lead through Val Cramosina and Val d'Efra to Val Verzasca.]

The Val Leventina terminates a little beyond Pollegio, at the junction of the Val Blegno. After crossing the river from that valley the traveller reaches

3¾ m. *Biasca*, 1110 ft. (*Inns*: Posta; de la Gare). The village contains an ancient Romanesque *church*, situated on the slope of the hill. A chain of chapels, or Via Crucis, leads from it to the Chapel of St. Petronilla, whence there is a pleasing view. The valley from this point to the Lago Maggiore is called the *Riviera*.

Diligence daily to Disentis by the Lukmanier Pass (Rte. 85).

Below the junction of the rivers Moësa and Ticino—when the road from the San Bernardino falls in (Rte. 91)—stands *Arbedo*, memorable in history for the gallant stand by 3000 Swiss against 24,000 Milanese, commanded by the celebrated generals Della Pergola and Carmagnola 1422. The fight lasted from morning until nightfall, when more than half the Swiss had been killed. Near the Church of St. Paul, called Chiesa Rossa, from its red colour, about 2000 were buried under 3 large mounds, still distinguishable. Defeat was at that period so unusual to the Swiss, even from a greatly superior force, that they retired across the Alps abashed and discouraged.

The distant aspect of Bellinzona, surmounted by battlemented walls, which once stretched quite across the valley, and overhung by no less than 3 feudal castles, is exceedingly imposing and picturesque. It looks as though it still commanded, as it once did, the passage of the valley. The luxuriance of vegetation, and the magnificent forms of the mountains complete the grandeur of the picture.

14 m. *Bellinzona* (770 ft.) (Germ. *Bellenz*).—*Inns*: Angelo, clean and good; H. de Ville; H. Bellinzona.

Bellinzona, situated on the l. bank of the Ticino, here restrained by a long stone dam (Riparo Tondo), and crossed by a bridge of 14 arches, contains 2500 Inhab., and is one of the 3 chief towns of the canton Tessin, and becomes the seat of government alternately with Lugano and Locarno, for 6 years together. Within, it is Italian in its narrow and dirty streets, and in the arcades which run under its houses. It stretches across the valley to the river, so that the only passage lies through its gates. It is still a place of commercial importance — situated as it is at the union of 4 roads — from the St. Gothard, the Bernardino, and the lakes of Lugano and Maggiore. It is of still greater military consequence, as the key of the passage from Lombardy into Germany, and has been strengthened by modern fortifications. It became the fruitful cause of intrigue, contest, and bloodshed, between the crafty Italians and the encroaching Swiss.

The *three picturesque Castles* which still seem to domineer over the town, though partly in ruins, were built 1445 by Italian engineers for Philip M. Visconti. They subsequently became the residence of the 3 Swiss bailiffs deputed to govern the district, and were occupied by a garrison, and armed with cannon. The largest, called *Castello Grande*, or *San Michele*, on an isolated hill to the W. of the town, belonged to Uri, and now serves as an arsenal and prison, and there is a fine view from it (admission 1 fr.). Of the two castles on the E. the lower one, *Castello di Mezzo*, belonged to Schwyz, and the highest of all, *Castello Corbario*, to Unterwalden.

A few hours of Bellinzona will suffice; Locarno (Rte. 112) is a preferable halting-place. The traveller has the choice of two railroads to Milan: by the Lago Maggiore (Rte. 34B), or by the Lago di Lugano (Rte. 34A).

ROUTE 34A.

LUCERNE TO BELLINZONA, LUGANO, COMO, AND MILAN.   ST. GOTHARD RAILWAY.

175 m.   5 Trains daily in 9 h. 35 m. express, 12 h. 37 m. ordinary.

N.B.—In this route only such information as is likely to be needed by railway travellers is given. For a full account of the scenery and towns traversed, see Rte. 34.

This important Railway, begun 1872 and finished 1881, was designed to open a direct communication between W. Germany and Piedmont and Lombardy. The St. Gothard was from early times one of the most frequented passes of the Alps; and the piercing of the Tunnel through the main chain now renders it passable for goods and passengers throughout the year.

The carriages are entered at the ends, and the first-class have open side galleries excellent for seeing out of. Seats on the right-hand side (going S.) are to be preferred, and a carriage as far as possible from the engine, to avoid steam-clouds and coal dirt.

Most pleasure travellers will prefer the *Steamer* as far as Flüelen, 27 miles. Boats run 5 or 6 times a day in 2¼, express, to 2¾ hrs.

From Lucerne the line makes a slight detour by

11 m. *Rothkreuz* Junct. Stat. until a direct line by Küssnacht is opened to

5 m. *Immensee* Stat., on the W. shore of the lake of Zug (*Inn:* H. Rigi), at the N. base of the Rigi mountain. *Steamer* to Zug and Arth.

5 m. *Arth-Goldau* Stat. Arth (*Inn:* Adler), a village and port on the lake, l., is the terminus of one of the remarkable railways up the Rigi, which is crossed by our line near Goldau village. The rly. is carried for some distance through the midst of the tremendous débris of rock and rubbish brought down by the vast *Landslip* or *Fall* of the *Rossberg*, which buried this village in 1806, falling from a height of 3000 ft. The rly. skirts the N. shore of

The Lake of Lowerz, 3 m. long which was partly driven out of its bed by the landslip

Steinen Stat.

5 m. **Schwyz** Stat. (*Inns:* Rössli, and Hediger's H.) is at Seewen, about a mile from Schwyz. It is a town of 6250 Inhab., picturesquely situated at the foot of the singular mitre-shaped mountain—*the Mythen* (6244 ft.)—which has been conspicuous in the views all the way from Arth.

The rly. is carried along the l. bank of the Muotta, as far as its influx, into **The Lake of Lucerne** at

2½ m. *Brunnen* Stat. (*Inns:* Waldstädter Hof; Adler; Rössli), the port of the Canton Schwyz—situated on one of the loveliest spots on the lake, two of whose romantic bays it commands. The view is well seen from the height behind the town called the Gütsch.

Beyond Brunnen the rly. is carried along the base of the precipices and sheep pastures which form the E. shore of the grand Bay of Uri, all the way to Flüelen, traversing no fewer than ten tunnels between these two places, in a distance of 8 m. The longest of these, 2120 yds., is near.

4 m. *Sisikon* Stat. On the opposite shore, under the wooded heights of Seelisberg, is the green meadow of Rütli, the legendary scene of the oath of the 3 patriots, which led to the emancipation of the Forest Cantons, Nov. 7, 1307, close to 3 springs, which, it is said, sprung forth on this occasion. The meadow is the property of the Swiss Government.

A little further on the rly. passes *Tells Platte*, marked by a Chapel painted with frescoes, where, according to the legend, Tell sprung ashore and escaped from the boat which was carrying him to prison.

4 m. *Flüelen* Stat., a village at the S. end of the lake, on the shore (*Inn:* Urnerhof). l. above this, the Grup torrent enters the lake, usually a quiet stream, but after it had been bridged for the rly. it rose and swept away bridge and roadway clean into the lake. A gallery of masonry, paved above with big stones, now protects the line, and carries the stream overhead, allowing the torrent to spread innocuously. The rly. now enters the valley of the Reuss, running over the flat marsh on its rt. bank.

2 m. *Altdorf* Stat. (*Inn:* Post), a town of 2800 Inhab.—the capital of Canton of Uri, on the l., famed in the story of Tell as the place where he shot the apple off his son's head.

4 m. *Erstfeld* Stat., still on the flat. Here the line begins to ascend the slopes on the rt. bank of the Reuss to

3 m. *Amsteg* Stat. 1759 ft. high above the village (*Inns:* H. des Alpes; Post. The torrent from the Maderaner Thal, and shortly afterwards the Reuss, are crossed by lofty bridges.

Near *Intschi*, 2168 ft., the rly. is carried over a grand viaduct, and near this occurs the first of the very remarkable corkscrew or *Helix Tunnels*, bored in the rock in a circle or loop, with a radius of only 15 chains and a gradient of 1 in 43; thus the railway attains a sudden change of level and direction. By means of three of these loop tunnels on the N. and four on the level of the great centre tunnel.

The first loop is called the Gurtnellen, or *Pfaffensprung Tunnel*, from a legend that a monk once leaped over the gorge from the rock which this tunnel pierces. It is 1606 yds. long. The ordinary tunnels in this part of the line, cut in the rock or in the form of arched galleries of masonry, follow one another so closely that it would be unprofitable to enumerate them. The steepest gradient on the way up to Göschenen is from 23 to 26 per thousand.

11 m. **Wasen Stat.**, 2780 ft., a large village (*Inns:* H. des Alpes; H. Ochs), where those who have time to spare should alight, in order to inspect the wonderful works of the railway in the midst of wild alpine scenery, which is well seen from the *Churchyard*.

Beneath the village the rly. crosses by a fine lattice Bridge 250 ft. span over the Reuss to its rt. bank. It leaves Wasen behind until it reaches the 2nd *Helix Tunnel* of *Wattingen*, 1199 yds. long, bored in granite, after traversing which it recrosses the river to its l. bank and returns towards Wasen, but at a height above the sea of 3000 ft., and, still rising, and crossing the Mayen Reuss, flowing from the Susten, on the finest Bridge on the whole line, reaches the 3rd Helix of *Leggistein*, 1204 yds. long. Again it resumes its original direction up the valley, looking down upon Wasen far below. Thus the spectator from Wasen beholds the railway upon 3 different terraces intersected by bridges, tunnels, and other works, and is puzzled to see trains running backwards and forwards.

A long tunnel leads to

5 m. *Göschenen* Stat., 3500 ft. (H. Göschenen). Buffet. (Here the day express stops ½ hr.), an untidy village at the N. entrance of the great tunnel, where the workshops and waterworks for boring it were established.

One of the grandest scenes on the St. Gothard Pass is the Devil's Bridge over the Reuss, and the Urner Loch approached by the gorge of Schöllenen, one of the wildest in the Alps. They may be reached by following the old road for 3 m. from the station. Higher up, the Pass loses its interest, and the scenery is stern and dreary, until the summit is passed.

The St. Gothard Tunnel.

This stupendous opening, bored through the main chain of the Alps for a distance of 9½ m., 15 kilom. (i.e. 2½ kilom. longer than the Mont Cenis), runs N. and S. at an elevation of 3786 ft. above the sea-level, and about 4600 ft. below the topmost ridge of the mountain. It runs nearly directly under the Devil's Bridge. It was begun in Nov. 1872; the headings or borings from the 2 sides of the mountain met with wonderful exactness in Feb. 1880, *i.e.* in 7¼ years from its commencement, and it was opened for traffic 1882. The enterprising contractor was M. Jules Favre of Geneva, who died suddenly in the tunnel almost at the moment of its completion. The boring was effected by 26 drills moved by compressed air, piercing holes 4 ft. deep, which were filled with charges of dynamite. Each explosion brought down 2½ cubic metres of stone. The rock traversed was chiefly hard granite or gneiss, also schist and other rocks. Near the centre a stratum of wet shifting rock-rubbish, semi-fluid, was met with, which exercised great pressure, always descending, and was vanquished only by masonry supports, buttresses, and arches of enormous strength. The tunnel is lined throughout with masonry.

The tunnel ends near

10½ m. *Airolo* Stat., 3756 ft. (*Inns :* Post; H. Airolo), the first village on the Italian side of the Pass, on the river Ticino, whose course the rly. henceforth follows down the Val Leventina. Below Fiesso tunnels begin again, and between this and Faido are the 4th and 5th spiral tunnels of *Freggio*, 1712 yds., and *Prato*, and the rly. passes the rocky ravine of Dazio Grande.

12 m. *Faido* Stat., 2365 ft. (*Inns :* P. of Wales; Angelo).

Below Lavorgo the final and steepest descent is effected by several tunnels, including the two spiral ones of *Piano-Tondo* and *Trave;* the rly. whirling past superb scenery of rocks and forests and Italian Campanili, then crosses the river to

Giornico Stat., 1235 ft. (*Inns :* Cervo; Corona). This village contains an old Lombard, *Tower* of massive masonry, and a very early *Romanesque Church*, San Nicolo alla Mira.

By a lattice-girder bridge of two spans, each of 150 ft., the rly. recrosses the Ticino, and continues on its L. bank the rest of the way.

17 m. *Biasca* Stat., 1112 ft. Buffet (*Inn :* Grand Hotel), is situated opposite a fine waterfall at the mouth of the Val Blegno, leading to the pass of the Lukmanier (Route 85).

The rly., now in the level valley, is terraced along the base of the mountains through a country of exuberant fertility and dense vegetation, past the villages of Osogna and Claro.

Near the site of the battlefield of Arbedo the Val Mesocco opens out, and the road from the Bernardino Pass joins the St. Gothard route (Route 91).

121 m. **Bellinzona** Junc., Buffet, 761 ft. (*Inns :* H. de Ville; H. Bellinzona, good; Angelo; Schweizerhof); a picturesque town, 3670 Inhab., still surrounded by old walls and crowned by 3 *Castles*, was long regarded as the key to the entrance of Italy from Switzerland. It stands on the l. bank of the Ticino, and is one of the three capitals of Canton Tessin. It has a bridge of 10 arches over that river. There is a good view from Castello Grande. It was built, as well as the two other fortresses, 1445, by Italian engineers for Philippo Maria Visconti. They afterwards became the residences of the bailiffs of the canton.

Railways : to Locarno—to Magadino along E. shore of the lake, viâ Pino, Luino, and Sesto Calende, to Novara and Turin or Genoa (Route 34B, and *Handbk. N. Italy*, Route 14c. The drive from Bellinzona to Como is described in Route 114).

Soon after quitting Bellinzona, the rly. leaves the valley of the Ticino, and turning l. from the line to Sesto Calende and Locarno on the Lago Maggiore, commences the ascent along the side of the valley towards Monte Cenere. After traversing the slopes of the mountains for about four miles, crossing ravines on lattice bridges, and penetrating rocks in tunnels, the mouth of the Monte Cenere Tunnel, 3 m. in length and 1440 ft. above the sea, is reached; on emerging from it the train enters the valley of the Agno, a stream flowing into the N.W. bay of L. Lugano.

7¼ m. *Rivera Bironico* Stat. Henceforth the rly. follows closely the line of the old carriage road, among fertile hills, to

17 m. **Lugano** Stat. (see Rte. 115), on a hill ¼ hour's walk above the town. (Omnibuses do not meet all trains). It is about 19 m. from Como and 12

from Varese. The Lago di Como at Menaggio may be reached by steamer and tramway in 2½ hrs, and the Lago Maggiore at Luino in the same time (Rte. 115).

The rly. to (19 m.) Como follows nearly the direction of the old road, which runs by the water-side, under *Monte Salvatore.*

4 m. At *Melide* Stat. a promontory projects into the lake, from the point of which a stone causeway 2400 ft. long affords a passage for road and railway across the lake.

2 m. *Maroggia* Stat. [Here a road strikes up the hills l. to (2 hrs.) *Lanzo d'Intelvi*, where is a comfortable mountain hotel (H. Belvedere, open May 15 to Oct. 15), situated at a height of 1700 ft. above Lago Lugano, and commanding magnificent views of the lake and surrounding mountains, and M. Rosa in the distance. The road from Maroggia as far as *Arogno* 6 m. is fair (post carriage twice daily). The rest of the journey must be made in a small mountain carriage. A second road leads to *Rovio* (H. Rovio fair), whence there is a beautiful path to the H. du Monte Generoso (see below). See Rte. 114.]

After passing along the shore of the lake, the traveller quits it at
Capolago Stat.

5 m. *Mendrisio* Stat. (*Inn :* H. Mendrisio), has manufactories of paper, silk, and hats, and 2300 inhab. It is supposed to be the cradle of the once-powerful Milanese family Delle Torre, or Torriani. The wine of the country is stored in mountain caves, which form capital cellars. To the sulphureous baths of *Stabbio* is a drive of 20 min.

[Mendrisio, is the most convenient point for ascending *Monte Generoso*, 5561 ft., the Rigi of the Italian lakes, but with a far finer mountain view. A good bridle-path, practicable also for small chars, leads in 2½ hrs. to the excellent and well - furnished *Hotel* (H. du Monte Generoso), for 100 guests, built and managed by Dr. Pasta, 4000 feet above the sea. The views from the hotel, as well as that from the summit (an easy walk of ¾ hr.), are most magnificent. Monte Generoso, while commanding the lake scenery and the Alpine chain, from Monte Viso to the Adamello group, also overlooks the great plain of Lombardy and its cities, Milan with its Duomo, the courses of the Po and Ticino. Lago Lugano lies at its feet. A path from the hotel leads in 5 hrs. to *Argegno* on the lake of Como (Rte. 116). Pension at the Generoso hotel. *Eng. Ch. Service.* Mules and chars may be obtained for the ascent at the hotel at Mendrisio: mule with guide 4 fr. It is advisable to go on mule-back, if practicable, for the jolting of the chars on part of the road is intolerable.]

The Italian frontier and customhouse is reached at

5 m. *Chiasso* Stat. Buffet. The custom house officers here are troublesome and discourteous.

3 m. COMO Stat. (Rte. 116) outside the town and thence to

30 m. MILAN. (H. Cavour, H. Milan, H. de la Ville). See *Handbk. N. Italy*, Rte. 20.

ROUTE 34B.

BELLINZONA TO SESTO CALENDE—RAIL.

Leaving the Lugano line to ascend the hillsides on the l., and the Locarno line to cross the Ticino to the r., the train proceeds along the swampy level to *Magadino* (*Stat.*), 10 m., a wretched village. See Rte 112.

The shores of the lake are followed to *Ranzo-Gera*, 14 m. (stat.).

The frontier of Italy is now crossed. The first Italian station is *Pino*, 18 m. ; but the stoppage for customs' examination is made at

Luino, 26 m. (good buffet). Tramway and road to Lago di Lugano. Rte. 112.

Porto Val Travaglia Stat. (30 m.) A long tunnel under the Sasso di Ferro leads to

Laveno Junct. Hence there is a direct line to Milan.

The line to the foot of the lake runs through undulating country, often out of view of the lake, to *Sesto Calende Junct.* (50 m.).

Hence there are lines to Milan and Novara. The latter crosses the

Ticino on a magnificent bridge. The express to Rome takes the latter route. (See *Hdbk. to N. Italy*).

For further particulars as to the places on the lake, see Rte. 112. The steamboat will be preferred by all who are not pressed for time.

ROUTE 35.

LAUTERBRUNNEN OR MÜRREN TO THE LÖTSCHENTHAL, BY THE PETERS-GRAT, OR TO KANDERSTEG BY THE TSCHINGEL GLACIER.

The Schmadribach *Inn* at *Trachsellauinen* is the best starting-point, 2½ hrs. above Lauterbrunnen, 2 hours from Mürren. (Rte. 25, B.)

A good walker may easily perform the distance hence to Kandersteg in 8½ hrs. without halts, and to the H. Nesthorn in the Lötschenthal in about 9. It is about 1 hr. from the Schmadribach Inn to the Steinberg Alp and foot of the glacier. Its easy surface is traversed for about 20 min. to the ice-fall, where it becomes necessary to turn rt. to scale the neighbouring cliff. This is the steep face of rock called the *Tschingel Tritt*, ordinarily considered to be the main difficulty of the route. Below it lies an awkward slope and precipice. The rock, however, gives good hold, and few persons experience any real difficulty.

Above the Tschingel Tritt the ascent continues on rather steep slopes, for about 1½ hr., when the passage of the upper glacier commences. This is free of danger, if the rope is used. The silvery surface slants gently upward between the *Breithorn* on the S. and *Tschingelgrat*, and *Gspaltenhorn* on the N., until it stretches at the col, 9252 ft., between the E. cliffs of the *Blümlis Alp*, and a rock called the *Mutthorn*, or *Mittelhorn*, behind which rises the *Tschingelhorn*. The ascent from the moraine will have taken from 1½ to 2 hrs., but here, if time permits, it is well worth while to make a détour (scarcely ¾ of an hr.) to the *Gamchilücke*, an opening overlooking the Kien Thal (Rte. 36), and framing,

as it were a bird's-eye view of the plain of Switzerland and distant Jura. Directly below it the *Gamchi Glacier* slants steeply down and offers a possible, but difficult, path to the valley.

At the col the routes to the Lötschenthal and Kandersteg diverge. In the direction which the track has hitherto followed, the snow sinks towards the S.W. between the Blümlis Alp and the comparatively low and curiously level ridge of névé, which extends from the Tschingelhorn in the direction of the Balmhorn and Altels. Over this ridge, which forms the boundary between Berne and Valais, and is called the *Peters-Grat*, 10,550 ft., lies the route to the Lötschenthal.

A short descent, followed by a new ascent over moderate slopes of névé in a direction nearly due S., leads in about an hour to the summit. One wide crevasse is passed near the top, but the glacier shows no others. The ridge commands a magnificent view. In addition to the grand ranges which have been seen throughout the ascent, the traveller now finds himself exactly opposite the chain whose extremities are the *Aletschhorn* and *Bietschhorn*, which separates the *Lötschenthal* from the valley of the Rhone.

The broad snow-covered Peters-Grat throws out several arms of glacier which descend into as many lateral glens of the Lötschenthal. The usual course is to follow the E. side of the *Telli* glacier which descends nearly S. from the point at which the ridge is attained. The slope, at first gentle, soon becomes steep, and the ice, sometimes easy enough, is occasionally much crevassed and difficult. The grand views of the peaks are for a time concealed, and their place supplied by the wild rock scenery of the *Tellithal*. When the Lötschenthal has been gained, it is but a short walk to the little *Inn* at Ried—H. Nesthorn (Rte. 38).

[The more direct, but generally more difficult, pass of the *Wetterlücke* may also be taken from Trachsellauinen to the Lötschthal. The Breithorn glacier on the N. side is in some years so crevassed as to be extremely difficult. At other times it may, with a good guide, be easy to ascend. The descent on the S. side is easy. The *Breithorn* (12,382 ft.) is accessible from the pass.]

Descent to Kandersteg.—From the col, which forms the limit between the Tschingel and Kander glaciers, the névé at first inclines with a gentle slope towards the Gasteren Thal. This gradually becomes steeper, and after an hour's descent crevasses make it necessary to quit the glacier for the rocks on its S. or l. bank. Here there is a spring, at which it is usual to halt for refreshment. A steep and rough descent of about 2500 ft., with view of the magnificent ice-fall, and then a short passage over the lower end of the glacier, lead in 1½ hr. from this point to the châlets of the *Gasteren Thal*, opposite the glacier Lötschen Pass. The scenery of this wild and savage valley, enclosed by the cliffs of the *Doldenhorn, Balmhorn* and *Altels*, is of the highest order, and well deserves an excursion from Kandersteg by those who do not cross the pass. A track, used by the herdsmen, leads in 2 hrs. from these châlets, sometimes called Gasterendorf, or *Im Selden*, where milk, cheese, and, in case of need, hay to sleep upon, may be obtained, to *Kandersteg* (Rte. 37). Time, the reverse way, 11 hrs.

ROUTE 36.

LAUTERBRUNNEN OR MÜRREN TO KANDERSTEG, BY THE PASSES OF THE SEFINEN FURKE, AND DÜNDENGRAT.

Lauterbrunnen to	Hrs.
Mürren	2¼
Sefinen Furke	3¼
Kien Thal	1
Dündengrat	3¼
Oeschinen See	2
Kandersteg	1
	13½

This route leads through a succession of magnificent scenery. The *two* passes, however, if taken in one day, make it very laborious, and the de-

scent into the valley of Oeschinen is awkward after dark, although the path has been improved. The traveller, however good a walker he may be, will do well to allow himself 14 hrs. of daylight.

On leaving Lauterbrunnen there is a choice of routes: one by the valley, following the road to Stechelberg, and then to the right up the *Sefinen Thal*; the other and far better plan, to sleep at *Mürren* (Rte. 25, B), starting in good time on the following morning. From Mürren the traveller can either descend to the Sefinen Thal (for the purpose of enjoying its savage scenery) and pursue the upward path, which finally mounts rt. to the pastures, with a grand view on the l. of the precipices of the *Gspaltenhorn*, 11,260 ft.; or follow the direct track, round the shoulder of the Schilthorn, to the same point on the *Boganggen Alp*. Here, at a height of 6663 ft., is a group of chalets, and from these the track, passing a tarn, slants up steep débris to the

Sefinen Furke, 8566 ft., an opening in a very narrow chain of crags, connecting the *Gross Hundshorn*, 9607 ft. (and Schilthorn, 9728 ft.), with the *Büttlassen*, 10,463 ft., a buttress of the Gspaltenhorn—and along which chamois occasionally pass, as over a bridge, from the Blümlis Alp. The view is very fine, including the Faulhorn, and below it the Wengern Alp and its hotel, which is easily discernible; but the great features are the Jungfrau in the E., and the Blümlis Alp, or Frau, in the W. Far down lies the Kien Thal, and l., at its head, the *Gamchi Glacier*, by which a passage has been made to the *Gamschilücke*, and Tschingel glacier. The traveller will look with some interest down the apparently impassable rocks at his feet, and across to the ridge which he will soon have to climb, perhaps in the heat of the day. A mountaineer can now shorten the way by turning l. along the Büttlassen, descending to the Gamchi glacier, and then steering direct for the Dündengrat; but the ordinary course is to go a little way rt., and then down débris of shale so steep that caution will be necessary to avoid a slip. Below it is sometimes followed by a slope of snow, which lands the traveller on the greensward of the *Dürrenberg Alp* 1 hr. from the top (2 hrs. up). From this point the route taken by the guides leads to a bridge at the hamlet of Tschingel, on the *Bund Alp*, so low down the valley as to increase considerably the toil of the next ascent; and if the tourist is fatigued, or the sun much past the meridian, he will do well either to make up his mind to sleep at some chalets near the head of the Kien Thal, or else to take the opportunity which here presents itself of descending to the carriage-road at Reichenbach. But there is a short cut which will save an hour. The head of the Kien Thal is divided by a ridge, below which the torrent runs in a ravine, and, if the guide knows the way, this can be crossed near the foot of the glacier. The ascent to the

Dündengrat, 8619 ft., between the *Schwarzhorn* and *Blümlis Alp*, 12,041 ft., is steep, but over good ground, and a view is soon obtained of the pyramidal Niesen, and the lake of Thun beyond it. Near the top it becomes rather rough, and the stones are succeeded by a bed of snow, which adds a good deal to the fatigue of the last half-hour. From this to the top of the ridge is but one step, and the rest is down-hill. Here a hut has been built by the Swiss Alpine Club to facilitate the ascent of the *Blümlis Alp* (12,041 ft.). A magnificent view opens. The glittering Blümlis Alp, which is here quite close, with a triple glacier streaming down its side, and farther off the *Doldenhorn*, 11,965 ft., and the beautiful lake of *Oeschinen* encompassed by it, form a scene of wild and singular beauty. The descent from the high pastures to the level of the lake is practicable only by one route, where steps have been cut along the faces of the rocks. The path runs under a cliff, on the W. shore of the lake, and thence in 1 hr. through a pine wood to the Victoria Hotel at

Kandersteg (see Rte. 37), 1¼ m. from the H. de l'Ours and H. Gemmi at the foot of the Gemmi.

ROUTE 37.

THE GEMMI, THUN TO LEUKERBAD AND THE VALAIS.

Thun to			Stunden.	Eng. m.
Frutigen . .	}	Carriage-road	4½	14½
Kandersteg . .	}		2⅔	8
Schwarenbach	}	Bridle-path .	2¼	8
Leukerbad . .	}		2½	8
Leuk . . .	}	Carriage-road	2⅔	8
Susten. . .	}			
			15	46½

A carriage may be hired at Thun. A pleasanter and commoner route is to take the steamboat to Spiez, a very pretty place, close to which is a good *hotel*, the Spiezerhof. Hence 10 miles to Frutigen. Horse and guide for the Niesen 17 fr. But prices vary.

[This pass may also be taken from Interlaken. The high road to Thun is left a little beyond Leissingen, and a char-road mounts the hill to *Aeschi* (see further), and descends from thence to Mühlenen, about 4 leagues from Interlaken. Pedestrians may make a short cut.]

The Gemmi (pronounced Ghemmi) is one of the most remarkable mule-passes in the Alps.

The first part of the route lies along the beautiful shores of the lake of Thun. Near the tall tower of *Stretlingen* it crosses the Kander by a lofty bridge. That river originally avoided the lake altogether, and, flowing for some distance parallel to it, joined the Aar below Thun. Owing to the quantity of mud and gravel which it brought with it, and the slight inclination of its channel in this part of its course, it converted the surrounding district into an unhealthy marsh. This in 1714 was corrected at the expense of the canton, by turning the river into the lake through a canal, 3000 ft. long, and 272 ft. broad, and which, seen from the bridge in crossing, has much the appearance of a natural ravine. By this change the land on the banks of the Aar has been drained and made profitable, while the deposit brought down by the river into the lake has so accumulated as to form a delta, extending already nearly a mile from the shore.

The road passes the mouth of the Simmenthal (Rte. 42), guarded on one side by the *Stockhorn*, 7195 ft., and on the other by the *Niesen*, 7763 ft. (Rte. 25, A), two noble mountains, between which the valley opens out a scene of exceeding beauty, with the *Castle of Wimmis* standing as it were in its jaws.

5 m. *Wyler* [a road turns l. to *Aeschi*. The ascent of ½ hr. will be well repaid by the *view* from the *churchyard*. At your feet the Lake of Thun, with a peep into the singular Justi Thal on its N. side; beyond Thun the range of the Jura; l., close at hand, the rival mountains Niesen and Stockhorn; rt. the Lake of Brienz, Rothhorn and Pass of the Brünig, topped by the Titlis. S. the snowy giants of the Oberland. There is a carriage-road from Aeschi direct to Mühlenen.]

On the margin of the lake rises another picturesque castle, that of Spiez. Skirting the base of the Niesen, we enter the valley of Frutigen, remarkable for its verdure and fertility, and which may be said to exhibit Swiss pastoral scenery in perfection.

At Emdthal a road branches off to (10 min.) *Heustrichbad*, a large and good Pension. A mile further is

5 m. *Mühlenen* (H. and Pension Niesen). At *Reichenbach* (H. de l'Ours) the *Kienthal* opens to the S.E., and a view of the Blümlis Alp. Ascending by the side of the Kander, we reach

4½ m. *Frutigen* (*Inns*: Helvetia; Adler (Post); Bellevue, a pretty house outside the town, belonging to the landlord of L'Ours at Kandersteg— all good and reasonable, with view of the Altels). Frutigen (over 4000 Inhab.), is for the most part not older than 1826-7, at which time it was nearly destroyed in two consecutive conflagrations. There are many match manufactories here. Beyond it the valley divides—the *Engstligen Thal* leading W. to Adelboden (Rte. 40); the *Kander Thal* to the Gemmi.

[The ascent of the *Niesen* may be made from Frutigen by a bridle-path in 4 hrs., and there are 3 other commanding points much easier of access —the *Elsighorn*, between the valleys of the Kander and Engstligen; the *Ubliberg*, 1½ hr. to the E.; and the *Gerihorn*, to the W., over the Bellevue.]

The road, on leaving Frutigen, crosses the Engstligenbach by a bridge, from which there is a short cut into the Engstligen Thal (3 hours to Adelboden), and passes under the castle of *Tellenburg*, formerly residence of the amtmann, or bailiff of the district. It then crosses the Kander, and proceeds up its rt. bank into the beautiful *Kander Thal*, where the snowy Altels closes a long vista of romantic scenery.

At one of the prettiest spots, 3 m., will be found the

Hôtel Altels, at a hamlet called *Mittelholz;* and a little beyond it, deeply buried in a wood, the *Blausee* (a Pension), a tarn of exquisite transparency and blue colour, and well worth a visit. It is only 10 min. rt. of the road, which ascends steeply below crags, on one of which is the ruin of the *Felsenburg* tower. At a height of about 3800 ft. the traveller enters the vale of

Kandersteg. (*Inns:* H. de l'Ours; H. Gemmi; both good, and at the foot of the Gemmi, where the carriage-road ends. H. Victoria, in the centre of the vale, opposite the entrance of the Oeschinenthal.) Good guides with a tariff; F. Ogi, G. Reichen, recommended. *E. C. S.* From Kandersteg to Leukerbad is about 5 hrs.; the path is obvious, and there is no occasion for a guide. Kandersteg is the last village in the valley: its scattered habitations contain about 700 individuals. It is beautifully situated 3839 ft. above the sea, at the N. base of the Gemmi. Wood cut in the mountain forests is here set afloat in the Kander, and thus conveyed into the lake of Thun, where the logs are collected and separated by the various proprietors. The fern *Cistopteris montana* grows at Kandersteg and on the Gemmi.

[*Excursions.* — Those who are not obliged to hurry through should stop a day and make one, at least, of two excursions—either to the *Oeschinen See*, or to the *Gasteren Thal.* The entrance to the *Gasteren Thal* is directly behind the Ours hotel, through a gorge, where, just within the mouth, the Kander thunders in a long fall beneath a frail bridge and overhanging cliff. The path leads in 20 min. to the valley, where wall-like precipices rise to the *Fisistock* and *Doldenhorn* on the N., to the *Altels* and *Balmhorn* on the S., and enclose a level vale; a scene of striking and savage grandeur, which is hardly surpassed in the Alps. 4 or 5 hrs. will suffice to go to the highest chalets of *Im Selden* and back.

The *Oeschinen See* (horse 8 fr.) is about 1 hour E. of the Victoria Hotel. Here the traveller will find, hemmed in by precipices and glaciers, a large mountain tarn, which mirrors on its smooth surface the snowy peaks of the Blümlis Alp—one of the most beautiful scenes of the kind in Switzerland.

The *Blümlis Alp*, or Frau, consists of a group of 5 peaks, running N.E. and S. W., precipitous towards the Tschingel glacier, and of which the 3rd and 4th are the highest—*Weisse Frau*, 12,011 ft., *Blümlisalphorn*, 12,041 ft. In front, or to the N., are three minor peaks, *Wilde Frau*, *Blümlisalpstock* and *Oeschinen Rothhorn*. The first ascent was made by Dr. Roth and M. de Fellenberg, who reached the top of the Weisse Frau; the first ascent of the highest point by Messrs. Leslie Stephen and Stone, and Dr. Liveing. In two hrs. 55 min. they climbed the glacier from the Dündengrat, where a Club hut now facilitates the expedition, and passed behind, or to the S., of the Blümlisalpstock to a depression between the Rothhorn and Blümlisalphorn. From that point a long, narrow arête led to the top in 1 hr. 40 min. It was also ascended in 1874 without difficulty from the Tschingel glacier. The Doldenhorn, 11,965 ft., rises to the rt. of the Blümlis Alp, and is easier of ascent.

W. of the Ours hotel rises the unfrequented pastoral *Uschinen Thal*,

bounded W. by the *Lohner.* At its head is a passage under the rocks of the *Felsenhorn* to the Schwarenbac Inn, and in the opposite direction round the *Tschingellochtighorn* to Adelboden in 6 hours.

Two other passes lead to Adelboden (Rte. 40); 1, the *Bonder Grat*, N. of the *Lohner* (the gap and *Steinmann* are seen on the ascent of the Gemmi), and 2, *Almen Grat* (5 hrs.), up the rocks opposite the Victoria Hotel. These used to be scaled partly by a ladder, which still remains, but is no longer wanted, as steps have been cut. The track leads to an upland valley, which, however, can be reached by an easier path from the Ours over the shoulder of the mountain. From the summit (2 hrs. 50 min.) the view comprises the Blümlis Alp, Jungfrau, and Oeschinen Thal and lake.

The *Doldenhorn*, 11,965 ft., is a steep and difficult mountain. It was ascended in 1862 by Dr. Roth and M. de Fellenberg, on the N.W., which seems the only practicable side. From the glacier on the N. they gained the ridge connecting the mountain with the Klein Doldenhorn on the W., and so the summit. The *Freundenhorn*, between the Doldenhorn and Blümlisalp, was first ascended July, 1871.]

The Gemmi.

Immediately above the H. de l'Ours, the ascent of the Gemmi commences in earnest. The path lies for the first 1½ hr. through steep forest to the shoulder of the mountain, where it passes the boundary of cantons Berne and Valais, and commands a view up the grand Gasteren Thal. Running nearly on a level through the precipitous wood it soon emerges upon a tract of pasture, from which the Altels rises on the l., separated from the Rinderhorn by the Zagen glacier. The steep that follows was rendered desolate by the fall of an avalanche from the Rinderhorn in 1782, and the path winds upward for some distance, among fragments of rock to the solitary

Schwarenbach Inn (2¼ hrs.' walking),

kept by Andreas Anderegg, brother of the celebrated guide, Melchior, a mountain inn, with fair sleeping accommodation. In this gloomy spot the German poet Werner laid the scene of a still more gloomy tragedy, ' Der vier und zwanzigste Februar.' The extravagant and improbable plot has no foundation in fact.

[Mountaineers may make several excursions hence. The ascent of the *Altels*, 11,923 ft., about 6 hrs. up, and 3 down. The way is along the snow on the edge of the precipice overhanging the Zagen glacier, but the slope is steep and formidable, except to practised climbers. Behind the Altels rises

The *Balmhorn*, 12,100 ft., a mountain higher, but not quite so difficult. The route lies rt. of the Altels, to the ridge connecting the Balmhorn with the Rinderhorn. Thence along the arête to the top (5 to 6 hrs.). A descent, not difficult but long and fatiguing (1868), to Leukerbad has been accomplished by the wall of rocks. There is one place at which it is possible to pass from these rocks to the Fluh glacier.

It is possible to pass directly from the Balmhorn to the Altels, but the route is somewhat difficult.

The *Rinderhorn*, 11,372 ft., is the nearest to the Schwarenbach Inn. Guide to any of the three, 20 fr.

The *Wildstrubel*, 10,715 ft., can also be ascended from this place; or a pass made over it to An der Lenk, (4½ hrs. to the col. There is a little-known pass from Schwarenbach leading, in 5½ hrs., to Adelboden (Rte. 39). There are no difficulties, but it would be hopeless to find the way over the two cols without a guide.]

About 2 m. beyond Schwarenbach the Gemmi road reaches and runs along the margin of the *Dauben See*, supplied by the snows of the Wildstrubel, which often swell it so as to cover the path: for 8 months of the year it is frozen. Nothing can exceed the dreary aspect of the seared and naked limestone rocks on either side: they seem too barren for the lichen, yet their *flora* is interesting.

The top of the pass, 7553 ft. above the sea, is 1½ hr. from Schwarenbach. From the *H. Wildstrubel*, a small inn, a superb view is obtained of the chain of Alps beyond the Rhône, separating the Valais from Piedmont.

The highest summits, reckoning from the W., are:—the Pigne d'Arolla, the Mont Collon, easily recognised by the deep cleft in its side; the Dent Blanche. Then come three or four minor peaks at the head of the Val d'Anniviers. Above them are seen the Dent d'Hérens and Matterhorn, both peaks of bare rock. The series is terminated by the Weisshorn and the Mischabel, which is in itself a complete group of snowy peaks, and the most beautiful feature of the view. Between it and the Weisshorn there is just a peep of the Nordend and Höchste Spitze of Monte Rosa. Directly W. of the pass rises the Lämmeren glacier leading to the Wildstrubel, and in front the cliffs of the *Daubenhorn*, 9449 ft.

On beginning the descent the traveller finds himself on the brink of a precipice of about 1800 ft. It is principally upon the faces of a buttress of a vast wall that one of the most extraordinary of all the alpine roads, constructed in 1736-41, by a party of Tyrolese labourers, has been carried. Its zigzags have been ingeniously contrived, for in many places the rocks overhang the path, and an upper terrace projects farther out than the one immediately below it. When it was first made and consisted merely of a shallow groove in the rock, it must have been far more striking than at present. The improvements that have been carried on year after year have ended in making it a roomy and perfectly good mule-path, but it is, nevertheless, most imprudent to ride down it. It is about 2 m. in length.

The wonders of this descent are greatly increased to those who approach it from the side of Leukerbad.

" The upper end of the valley, as you look towards the Gemmi, has all the appearance of a cul-de-sac shut in by a mountain wall. Up to the very last moment, and until you reach the foot of the precipice, it is impossible to discover whither the road goes, or how it can be carried up a vertical surface. It is a mere shelf — in some parts a groove cut in the face of the cliff, just wide enough for a mule to pass ; and at the turns of the zigzags you constantly overhang a depth of nearly 500 ft." In a niche of the rock a large white cross has been placed to the memory of a French lady, who, falling from a mule, was killed here in 1861. Lower down remains of a hut are pointed out, in which, it is said, a hermit once lived. He had to climb to it up a pole.

The following rather amusing clause, relative to the transport of invalids, is copied from the regulations issued by the director of the baths:—" Pour une personne au-dessus de 10 ans il faudra 4 porteurs ; si elle est d'un poids au-dessus du commun, 6 porteurs : si cependant elle est d'un poids extraordinaire, et que le commissaire le juge nécessaire, il pourra ajouter 2 porteurs, et jamais plus." The *ascent* from the Baths to the summit takes 2 hrs. The first 20 min. are on flat ground.

Leukerbad—Fr. *Louèche-les-Bains*— not to be confounded with Leuk. *Inns:* H. des Alpes, best; E. C. S. Maison Blanche, well spoken of ; Bellevue; H. de France; Union; H. Brunner, cheap.

A *bath* costs 2 fr. There are 5 bath establishments attached to the hotels.

Leukerbad is a village of about 500 Inhab., situated 4642 feet above the level of the sea, *i.e.* higher than any mountain in Great Britain and at the end of a valley terminated towards the Gemmi by tremendous precipices, which will remind the traveller of a *cirque* in the Pyrenees. The hot springs (117° to 124° F.) attract a number of visitors, chiefly Swiss and French, during the season, viz. in July and August, though the inns are open from May to October. The baths and adjacent buildings have been three times swept away by avalanches since their establishment in the 16th cent.; and, to guard against a recurrence

of the calamity, a very strong dyke has been built behind the village. Such danger, however, is past before the bathing season begins. One of the first patrons of Leukerbad was the Cardinal and Bishop of Sion, Matthew Schinner.

The springs, to the number of 10 or 12, rise in and around the village, and nine-tenths of them run off into the Dala torrent without being used. *The chief spring of St. Lawrence* bursts forth in the middle of the village—a rivulet in volume, with a temperature of 124° Fahr. It is used after being slightly cooled. The other springs vary somewhat in temperature. They all contain only a small portion of saline matter, and seem to owe their beneficial effects less to their mineral qualities than to their heat and the mode of using them. The patient begins with a bath of an hour's duration, but goes on increasing it daily, until at length he remains in the water 8 hours a day—from 5 to 10 A.M., and 2 to 5 P.M. The usual *cure time* (kur) is about 3 weeks. The necessity of preventing the ennui of such an amphibious existence, if passed in solitude, has led to the practice of bathing in common. The principal bath-houses are divided into compartments, each about 20 ft. square, capable of holding 15 or 20 persons, and with two entrances, communicating with dressing-rooms, one for the ladies, the other for the gentlemen. Along the partitions runs a slight gallery, into which visitors are sometimes admitted. The stranger on entering will perceive a group of some 12 or 15 heads emerging from the water, on which float wooden tables holding coffee-cups, newspapers, snuff-boxes, books, and other aids, to enable the bathers to while away their allotted hours. The patients, a motley company, of all ages, both sexes, and various ranks, delicate young ladies, burly friars, invalid officers, and ancient dames, are ranged around the sides on benches, below the water, all clad in woollen mantles, with a tippet over their shoulders. It is not a little amusing to see people sipping their breakfasts, or reading up to their chins in water —in one corner a party at chess, in another an apparently interesting *tête-à-tête*; while a solitary sitter may be seen reviving in the hot water a nosegay of withered flowers. The temperature of the bath is preserved by a supply of fresh water constantly flowing into it, from which the patients drink at times. Against the walls are hung a set of regulations and sumptuary laws for the preservation of order and decorum signed by the burgomaster, who enforces his authority by the threat of a fine of 2 fr. for the highest offence against his code.

"Art. 7. Personne ne peut entrer dans ces bains sans être revêtue d'une chemise longue et ample, d'une étoffe grossière, sous peine de 2 fr. d'amende.

"Art. 9. La même peine sera encourue par ceux qui n'y entreraient pas, ou n'en sortiraient pas, d'une manière décente."

The hours of subaqueous penance are, by the doctor's decree, succeeded by one hour in bed.

Dr. Reichenbach, from Geneva, resides here in summer.

Excursions :—

a. The principal curiosity of the neighbourhood is the *Ladders* (Leitern). The broad terrace-walk S. of the bath-house is continued by a path through woods, which, in 1½ m., leads to the foot of a precipice, called Wandfluh, where 8 rough ladders are placed nearly perpendicularly against the face of the cliff. This is the peasants' road to *Albinen*, a village on the mountain, and before the Torrenthorn path was made was the only means by which the inhabitants, without a long circuit, could communicate with the baths. The ladders, which are pinned to the crevices of the rock by hooked sticks, are often awry, and rather unsteady. They are traversed at all seasons, day and night, by the natives—by children, as well as men and women, and their use has given rise to a Bloomerish modification of the dress of the female peasants. In climbing the mountains the petticoat is tucked up, and the wearers do not differ in appearance from boys. There is an easy path from Albinen to Inden, and another to Leuk and Susten.

b. A fine day may be well devoted to the *ascent of the Torrenthorn* (or *Mainghorn*), a mountain rising E. of Leukerbad. Horses can reach the summit (9679 ft. above the sea) in 3½ hours. It commands a wonderfully fine panorama—an unbroken series of peaks from Mont Blanc to the Simplon; with the Bietschhorn E. above the *Lötschenthal*, and at the head of that valley the principal Oberland peaks; with the Balmhorn, Altels, and Blümlis Alp on the W. and N. The ridge ends in a precipice, dropping to wild crags and the head of the small *Maing Glacier*. The first 1200 ft. is steep. Descent in 2½ hours.

From the Torrenthorn it is a beautiful walk to the Lötschenthal by the *Faldum Pass* between the Rothhorn and Laucherspitze. Down-hill all the way, 4½ hrs.; or 7½ from Leukerbad.

The *cascade of the Dala* (¼ hr.'s walk), is worth a visit, and the rocky pass, called *Felsen Gallerie*, on the way to Sierre, is a very striking scene. (See below.)

Above Leukerbad the valley terminates in the Fluh or Dala glacier, by which pedestrians may reach Kandersteg in 9 hrs. by the beautiful *Fluh Pass*. 3 hrs. to the glacier, which is traversed between two small ice-falls: ¾ hr. to the ridge by snow-slopes. Descent, steep at first, is made further to the rt. and leads to the track of the Lötsch pass. (See Rte. 38.)

There is a pass to Kippel, by the *Regizi Furke*, to the rt. of the Fluh pass. The col is reached in 4¼ hrs. from Leukerbad. The descent bears to the rt. until the streams are met, 1 hr. Then through trees and meadows to Kippel in 2½ hrs. from the col.

———

From the baths of Leuk to the valley of the Rhone is a fine carriage-road, following the course of the *Dala*, and well engineered, affording a beautiful drive. It descends by numerous zigzags, past the Baths of *Inden* (an *Inn:* and short cut for pedestrians l.), to the solid and lofty Dala bridge, 170 ft. above the torrent, whence is a mule-path to Sierre (see below). Hence it winds down the mountain, with beautiful views of the Rhone valley, in about 8½ m. (2½ hrs.' walk), to

Leuk—Louèche—(*Inn:* Couronne), a town of 1123 Inhab., with ruins of two castles, destroyed by the Valaisans in 1414 — picturesque, with a charming view, but not a place to stop at. The road zigzags down, crossing the Rhone, and falling into the great Simplon road about ¼ m. below the solitary inn at

Susten Stat. (*Inn:* H. de la Souste, good), Rte. 56, on the Valais railway.

A mule-path is carried direct from *Le Grand Pont* (the **Dala Bridge**) through Salgesch to Sierre, 12 m., and is a short cut for those who wish to *descend* the valley of the Rhône.

A little beyond the bridge the traveller finds himself beneath the shadow of a tremendous precipice, forming the corner of the Louèche valley. The path is carried along a narrow ledge, and beneath it is a gaping abyss; above, the rocks lean so far forward that stones falling from their tops would descend upon the road, and it is therefore partly protected by a roof. This spot is called the *Galerie,* and was the scene of a bloody combat in 1799, when the Valaisans defended it for several weeks against the French, effectually checking all attempts to pass, by rolling down stones and logs from above. A rough and steep descent leads from this, in about 1½ hour, to

Sierre, upon the Simplon road (Rte. 56).

Pedestrians going from Leukerbad to the *Val d'Anniviers* need not go through Sierre, but may reach the bridge across the Rhone by a footpath on l., 20 min. after passing the village of Salgesch, where lunch should be secured.

ROUTE 38.

THE LÖTSCHENTHAL AND ITS PASSES.—
A. TURTMAN TO KANDERSTEG, BY THE LÖTSCH PASS.
B. TURTMAN TO THE EGGISCHHORN, BY THE LÖTSCHLÜCKE.
C. TURTMAN TO THE BEL ALP, BY THE BEICHGRAT.

The Lötschenthal has been too much neglected by Alpine travellers. It abounds in fine scenery, leads to several interesting passes (Rtes. 35, 37), and has now, at *Ried,* a fair mountain inn, H. Nesthorn. There is a car-road for some distance. Mines of argentiferous galena were formerly worked on the Rothenberg above Goppenstein.

2 miles above Turtman a bridge over the Rhone leads l. in ½ m. to the village of *Gampel* (*Inn,* Lötschenthal, homely), at the mouth of the narrow and steep valley of the Lötschenthal, rising, not in terraces, but with a rapid and continuous ascent, mastered by a carriage-road as far as the old mines. Above Gampel the path enters a gorge. In about an hour there is a fall, not visible from the road, of no great height, but a large volume of water. Beyond the chapel of *Goppenstein* (4 m.), which has been often swept away by avalanches, the path crosses the Lonza to its rt. bank in a lovely scene of meadow, wood, and rock, after which the character of the valley is open and cheerful. At

2 m. *Ferden,* it turns sharply to the east, and the view along both branches of the valley is superb. The upper portion is wider and longer than that which has been passed, extending to the Lötschen glacier, a branch of the great sea of ice of the Bernese Alps, overhung by the Lauterbrunnen Breithorn on one side, and the Schienhorn, an offset of the Aletschhorn, on the other; while on the S. the Bietschhorn and Lötschthaler Breithorn rise steeply in icy peaks. The curé's house at

¼ m. *Kippel,* was for some years the sleeping-place of travellers. The curé was an active mountaineer, but is now an old man. Few of the people can speak anything but their own German patois. ¾ hr. above Kippel is

Ried (*Hotel Nesthorn*, a mountain inn, dear, 1884), at the foot of the Bietschhorn. Joh. and Jos. Siegen of Ried, Lehner of Kippel, and P. Siegen and J. J. Henzen of Blatten are recommended as guides. There is a fair tariff for the neighbouring expeditions, the chief of which is the ascent of the *Bietschhorn* (12,966 ft.), the pyramid conspicuous from Saas, and the Riffel. Owing to the extremely rotten character of the rock, the climb is one of the longest and most difficult in the Alps, and only suited for very steady climbers. A hut has been built 3 hours above Ried to facilitate the ascent.

[From Ried the passes of the *Petersgrat* and *Wetterlücke* (see Rte. 35) lead to Lauterbrunnen. Mountaineers proceeding to Visp and Zermatt may take the *Baltschiederjoch*, a fine pass (8 hrs.). From Ried a steep ascent over boulders leads to the gap immediately E. of the Bietschhorn. The descent lies over the Baltschieder glacier and through the long narrow glen of the same name. On the opposite W. flank of the Bietschhorn the *Bietschjoch*, a fine and easy glacier route, leads in 8 hrs. to the Rhône valley at Raron. There are two fine glacier passes to the Schwarenbach, the *Mildersteinjoch*, and *Andereggjoch* (8 to 10 hrs.). The first lies W. of the Rinderhorn, the second between the Rinderhorn and Altels.]

a. To Kandersteg by the *Lötschen Pass.* This pass between the Valais and the Canton Berne was formerly in much use, and remains of the mule-path, which was then carried across the entire way, are still to be seen. Since the construction of the Gemmi road a century and a half ago, this has fallen into decay, and the extension of the glaciers, which seems to have been universal at one time in this part of the Alpine chain, destroyed part of the old route. The pass is not difficult in good weather, but it is better suited for a mountaineer than

an ordinary tourist. It may be accomplished in 8 to 9 hrs.' walking from Ferden.

From Ferden the ascent to the Lötschen pass lies for about 2½ hrs. over pastures, bare stony slopes and beds of snow. The col (8796 ft.) is overhung by the grand precipices of the Balmhorn, which forms the eastern end of the Altels group. ["By giving 2 or 3 hrs. more to the excursion, a high peak to the E., called the *Hockenhorn*, may be ascended. Our guide did not suggest it till we had nearly reached the col, from which it is 1½ hr., chiefly over ice. Some very steep slopes are to be crossed, from which the eye plunges down right into the Gasterenthal, 5000 to 6000 ft. beneath. A singular and most striking scene occurs in passing round an insulated steeple of rock, rising out of the ice, with a pool of clear blue water at its foot. Between it and the peak lies a narrow isthmus of ice, sloping steeply down on either side; after passing this, the icy shoulder of the mountain is to be wound round, with empty space on two sides; and then the last ascent, up a sharp pile of stones, takes 15 min. The view is superb. To the S. and S.W. the Mischabel, the Matterhorn, and Mont Blanc, towering far above nearer mountains, are the leading objects. To the E. the Tschingelhorn and other points of the chain on which we stood, extending to the Jungfrau. To the W. a sea of lower mountains towards the Simmenthal, and an extensive view over the Bernese lowlands. Retracing our course for a good way, we then descended over bare rocks and beds of snow to the lower part of the Balmgletscher, and reached in a short 2 hrs. from the Hockenhorn the point where the direct route across the Lötschberg quits the glacier, after lying across it probably for 1½ to 2 m. Thence there is about 1¼ hr. of very steep descent into the Gasterenthal. The river is to be crossed by a bridge, which must not be missed: thence to Kandersteg, about 2 hrs."—*E. W.*]

Even without making the excursion to the ¦Hochenhorn, the view from the col is extremely fine, decidedly superior to that from the Gemmi, or any of the passes over the chain to the E. of it. In descending into the Gasterenthal there are some long slopes of snow, giving opportunity for a *glissade;* when the glacier is reached, which now covers over the old track, which is seen in places, it is advisable to keep to its W. side, nearest to the Altels, which towers over the valley. After nearly an hour's descent over the glacier the track emerges into the Gasterenthal near the chalets of Im Selden (Rte. 35). In 2 hrs. the traveller reaches Kandersteg (Rte. 37).

b. To the Eggischhorn by the *Lötschenlücke.*

Lötschsattel, or *Lötschenlücke,* 10,512 ft. (guide, 30 fr.). This is a long day's journey on snow and ice, but a most magnificent expedition, leading through the very heart of the Bernese Alps, and by a corridor, of which the sides are the Jungfrau and Mönch, Aletschhörner and Viescherhörner. In a favourable state of snow it is by no means difficult, and may be accomplished in 10 to 12 hrs. The middle part of the Lötschen glacier is crevassed from side to side, and the Aletsch glacier, at the angle under the Dreieckhorn, is a maze of hidden crevasses, but the rte. is free from danger with common care and knowledge.

Above the Hôtel Nesthorn the dark wooden village of *Platten* is passed, then wild pine-covered hillocks of old moraine. It is 1½ hr. to the foot of the glacier, near which a chalet has been fitted up with some comforts for travellers. To the rt. are the *Beich Grat,* and higher the precipices of the *Schienhorn* and *Distelhorn;* to the l. a magnificent icy amphitheatre, formed by the Ahnen glacier. The slopes of névé now become steeper, but are easily traversed to the *sattel* or *lücke,* a depression in the *Ahnen Grat,* about 5 hrs. from the inn.

The scenery here is extremely grand. On the N. is the range of the *Gletscherhorn* and *Mittaghorn,* neighbours of the *Jungfrau;* to the S. the

still higher group of the *Aletschhorn* and *Schienhorn,* enveloped in a shining coat of ice. An easy descent leads over gently sloping snow-fields to the main stream of the Aletsch glacier. If not pressed for time, the traveller will do well to push on to a point near the centre from whence diverge 4 great and nearly equal glacier highways, each about 2 m. in width, separating the surrounding peaks. S.W. is that which he has just descended; N.W. the branch from the *Jungfrau Joch,* between the Jungfrau and Mönch; N.E. the glacier coming down from the *Grünhorn-lücke,* over which lies the way to the Finsteraarhorn; finally, to the S.E. descends the great stream which carries down the accumulated ice of the tributaries. These vast *Allées Blanches* are symmetrically placed so as to form a cross, or, as one traveller has called it, "The Place de la Concorde of Nature." The guides, if they know the glacier well, will not fail to point out the *Concordia-Hütte,* and lower down a mere speck in the rocks on the l. hand in descending the main glacier, which marks the position of the old *Faulberg Hut.* In the latter adventurous travellers bent on ascending the great peaks usually pass the night. On reaching the curious *Märjelen See* the path on its N. bank is followed, and then the ridge of the Eggischhorn is crossed to the Jungfrau Hotel (see Rte. 29). To pass, 5½ hrs.; descent to Eggischhorn, 6½ hrs.

c. To the Bel Alp by the *Beichgrat.*

The *Beichgrat,* leading from Ried to the Bel Alp in 8 to 9 hrs., is an easy and useful glacier pass, traversing very fine scenery. The ascent on the Lötschthal side is steep; the descent lies over the Ober Aletsch Glacier, which spreads between the Aletschhorn and Gross Nesthorn. Both these noble peaks are splendidly seen, and the ice scenery of the Ober Aletsch is bold and varied. On leaving the ice a terrace path is found leading to the Bel Alp Hotel (Rte. 29). Good guides are required.

ROUTE 39.

PASS OF THE RAWYL.—THUN, OR IN-
TERLAKEN, TO SION OR SIERRE.—
THE GRIMMI.

The pass of the Rawyl begins at
Lenk, or An der Lenk, at the N.
foot of the pass, a good halting-place,
about 36 m. from Thun; diligence
twice a day from Thun, once from
Spiez, to Zweisimmen, and thence,
once a day, to Lenk, a 3 hrs.' walk.
Thence to Sion, over the mountain, is
10 hrs., or to Sierre 11 hrs. It is a
rough horsetrack, best on the Valaisan
side. The scenery on both sides of
the pass resembles that on the S. side
of the Gemmi, is but less savage.

The village of Lenk may be reached
from the lake of Thun by the Simmenthal, or by the Diemtigen Thal
and the pass of the Grimmi, a byeway accessible only to pedestrians;
or, thirdly, by Frutigen, the Engstligen Thal, and Hahnenmoos Pass,
a bridle-path. The scenery by the
Diemtigen Thal is inferior; and there
is little saving of time. From Interlaken the way by the Engstligen
Thal is decidedly shorter for pedestrians.

a. The road up the *Simmenthal* is
described (Rte. 42) as far as Zweisimmen. Thence the carriage-road is
continued, bearing to the l. up the
Ober Simmenthal, about 10 m., to An
der Lenk.

b. The route by the *Diemtigen Thal*
leaves the Simmenthal at Latterbach
10 m. from Thun. A path there
strikes off up the Diemtigen Thal,
crosses the Chirelbach, and follows
its l. bank through Diemtigen and
Narrenbach, then recrosses it to

Thiermatten, where there is an *Inn,*
about 4 hrs. from Latterbach, or 4½
from Wimmis, from whence a path
mounts the valley by the rt. bank.
About a mile farther it again passes
the stream, and, leaving it on the l.,
gradually ascends to the pass of the
Grimmi (6234 ft.)., 3 hrs. from Thiermatten. Descending through the *Fer-
mel Thal* (a fertile valley, only 6 m.
long), it reaches

Matten, in the Upper Simmenthal,
on the carriage-road leading from
Zweisimmen to An der Lenk, 4 m.
from

Lenk (*Inns:* Kuranstalt Lenk;
Hirsch, Bär), 3527 ft. The village is
in a charming situation at the foot of
the snow-crowned precipices of the
Wildstrubel. Five minutes beyond
is the sulphur-bath establishment and
hotel, *Kuranstalt Lenk.* The baths are
much frequented by the Swiss: closed
early in September.

Excursions. — The Simmen rises
about 6 m. above Lenk, at the foot of
the glacier of Räzli and precipices of
the Wildstrubel, from a source called
the

Sieben Brunnen, Seven Fountains
(2 hrs. up). It is a charming excursion.
By char-road to the foot of the mountain, at a saw-mill, where the Simmen
rushes down in one of the longest
and most furious cataracts in Switzerland (there is a foot-path up the
E. bank). Thence a mule-track
ascends the forest, passing several
falls in a deep dark chasm. The scene
from the green upland is both grand
and beautiful. Here, close to the
Sieben Brunnen, which spring out
from the mountain like a band of
brothers, stands a chalet where those
who ascend the Wildstrubel, or cross
it to Leukerbad, can pass the night.
The way up is through the firwood
behind the chalet. From the Sieben
Brunnen the traveller may visit the
Oberlaubhorn, 1½ hr., *Cascade d'Ifigen,*
40 min., and return to Lenk by the
Rawyl road, 1 hr. 10 min.

Other excursions from Lenk are to
the *Milkerplatte,* 2 hrs. up, and to the
Albristhorn, the highest point between
the Simmenthal and Engstligenthal.
This mountain rises N. of the Hahnenmoos pass, and is an ascent of
about 4 hrs.

The *Wildstrubel,* 10,715 ft., may be
ascended on a glacier rte. to the Gemmi, or to Sierre. The mountain has
2 peaks, of which the eastern is about
60 ft. higher than the western. The
latter is first gained by mounting the
track up the cliffs and the Amerten
Glacier; then E. by a snow-ridge to

the highest point. The descent to the Gemmi is down the long Lämmeren Glacier; to Sierre by the ice-field on the S. called La Plaine Morte. About 11 hrs. to Leukerbad or Sierre.

From Lenk are passes, the *Hahnemoos* to Adelboden (Rte. 40), and the *Trüttlisberg* to Lauenen and thence to Aigle (Rte. 40).

The path to Sion, by the *Rawyl*, is fit for a char for about 3 m. Instead of proceeding towards the source of the Simmen, it ascends the l. bank of its tributary, the Iffigenbach; and the gorge of that torrent is in places very grand. The solitary traveller should beware of losing time by crossing a tempting bridge about half-way to Iffigen, a little below a waterfall.

Iffigen (*Inn*), at the N. base of the Rawyl, near which the Iffigenbach makes a fine fall, a good 2 hrs.' walk from Lenk and 2½ hrs. from the summit.

From here the ascent of the *Wildhorn*, the highest point in the Bernese Alps W. of the Gemmi, may be made. The view is superb, and the climb presents no serious difficulty to a good walker.

A series of zigzags mounts the steep slope above Iffigen. They have been excellently constructed and are constantly kept in repair. The small cascades that used to fall on the path have been diverted, and the way throughout is so broad that the most timid person need not fear. From the brow of the precipice, looking N., a view expands over the valley of An der Lenk, and the green mountains of the Simmenthal.

The summit of the Rawyl pass, marked by a cross, and 7943 ft. above the sea, is probably 2 m. broad, covered with loose shattered fragments of slate and almost utterly bare of vegetation. When clouds lie on the height, the path over the stones is not easily traced, and it is tedious from the number of gullies, and the alternately crumbling and slippery nature of the clay-slate, which gradually changes into clay. A small lake is passed before reaching the brow of the S. declivity, which consists of precipices similar to those on the

side of Berne. Glorious view hence of the mountains beyond the valley of the Rhone, especially of the Weisshorn. A good zigzag path leads down to the chalets of Ravins in 1½ hr. Close to these chalets two large bodies of water burst from the cliffs. That on the rt. has a singular appearance, springing from a black cleft in 5 or 6 distinct columns, and then forming a fine wild tumble of foaming water. Though apparently clear when issuing from the rock, it has no sooner touched the ground than it becomes a river of mud. A large portion of it is a short way below separated, and conducted very ingeniously along the face of the mountain, at one part against a perpendicular cliff, till, after a course of several miles, it fertilises the meadows near Ayent.

Two paths branch off at the chalets of *Ravins;* the one leading in 5½ hrs. to Sierre; the other, on the rt. bank of the stream, through Ayent to Sion in 4½ hrs. The walk to Sierre is fatiguing, owing to the frequent ascents and descents. For about half an hour the rt.-hand path runs nearly on a level: it next rises to turn a rocky barrier, and then descends on *Ayent.* Foot-passengers can avoid this ascent by following the bank of the watercourse before mentioned, which saves nearly an hour. The most dangerous part takes 10 min. or ¼ hr. to traverse. The only way of passing is along trees supported by cross-bars on the face of precipitous rocks. The scene is very grand. The rock hangs over on the rt., and on the l. recedes beneath to a depth of 1000 ft. This track should not be attempted by persons in the least liable to giddiness.

The mule-path descends through a forest of fir, and unites with the footpath before reaching

Ayent, about 3 hrs.' walk from the summit.

Sion (Rte. 56), in 1½ hr.

The Rawyl is called Ravoué in the patois of the Valais.

ROUTE 40.

FRUTIGEN TO ADELBODEN, LENK
LAUENEN, AND GSTEIG—THE HAH-
NEMOOS—TRÜTTLISBERG—THE CHRI-
NEN.

This is a little-frequented but interesting route from Thun or Interlaken to Aigle in the Valais.

Starting from Frutigen (Rte. 37) a
road leads up the *Enstligen Thal* to
Adelboden, a small village (*Inn:* Adler,
tolerable). It is a prettily situated
place, with fine views of the Wildstrübel. In the ch.-yd. is a fine old
sycamore. There are passes to Kandersteg (Rte. 37), and there is a
curious but little-frequented pass
under the Wildstrübel to Schwarenbach on the Gemmi. It is about 6 hrs.'
walk over two cols, and past one of
the Wildstrübel glaciers. It would
be hopeless to find the way without a
guide round the head of the desolate
Kanderthal.

A little above Adelboden there is
a mule-path to the rt., leading up a
valley to the *Hahnemoos* pass. The
first part of the pass is on the rt.
bank of the torrent, which is then
crossed, and the path keeps the l.
side. The col (6404 ft.) is marshy.
There is not much view from it. The
first part of the descent is marshy,
and in 4 hrs. from Adelboden is
Lenk (Rte. 39).

The *Trüttlisberg* Pass is a mule-
path of 4 hrs. Beyond the church
of Lenk, the path, after traversing
meadows with the glaciers of the
Wildstrübel in view, ascends on
the N. side of the Wallbach Thal to
the chalets of Ober Staffel, which
are reached in 2½ hrs. 1 hour more,
a gentle rise over grass, along a shelf
or plateau cut off from the valley by
a precipice, brings the traveller to the
Trüttlisberg (6235 ft.), between the
Dauben, N., and the Rothhorn, S.,
with view of the rocky chain stretching from the Wildstrübel to the
Diablerets. A steep descent, in which
the eye dwells on the glorious Wildhorn, and a great waterfall, descend-

ing from the Gelten glacier, leads in
1¼ hr. to

Lauenen (*Inn:* Hirsch, poor). A fine
church. In *ascending* the Trüttlisberg,
a col N. of the Dauben is very likely to
mislead. It passes into a valley which
rejoins that of Lauenen at Gstaad.
Beware of descending into the hollow
to the l., and from the col keep to
the high ground l. The view from
Lauenen is magnificent. Round the
head of the valley circle the precipices of the *Wildhorn*, 10,722 ft., which
can be climbed from here, snowy
glaciers and cascades, and the Alps on
either side are green and beautiful.

The *Gelten Pass* affords a glacier
route over the shoulders of the Wildhorn to Canton Valais.

[From Lauenen there is a very
pretty carriage-road to Saanen in
1 hr.]

From Lauenen the *Chrinnen* pass
leads in 2½ hrs. to Gsteig. The mule-
path goes a little way down the valley,
then crosses the stream, and turns to
the l., leading over meadows by an
easy ascent to the col (5463 ft.) between the two *Windspillen*. Thence
an easy descent leads to
Gsteig (Rte. 41).

ROUTE 41.

PASS OF THE SANETSCH.—SAANEN TO
SION.

About 12 hrs. 31½ m.

This is a long, steep, and tedious
horse-pass. The village of Saanen
(or Gessenay), and the road between
it and Thun, are described in Rte. 42.
Carriage-road from Saanen to Gsteig,
about 9 m.

At *Gstaad* the road turns S. by the
valley of the *Saane*, the upper end of
which is called Gsteig Thal, to
Gsteig (Châtelet in French) (*Inn:*
Hirsch), the highest village in it

(3950 ft.), situated close under the lofty and precipitous Mittaghorn, and near the foot of the Sanetsch, the most westerly of the passes over the Bernese chain.

It is advisable to sleep at Gsteig, from which Sion is 8 hrs. The pass rises in a very precipitous manner, and often resembles that of the Gemmi. $\frac{3}{4}$ hr. above Gsteig the Saane makes a beautiful *fall*, clearing the face of the rock by at least 100 ft. In the evening it is crowned by an iris. The path follows the torrent to its source below the *Sanetschhorn* (9679 ft.), W., and *Arbelhorn* (9980 ft.), E. Lovely view looking back. After a climb of

2 hrs. the traveller enters a grassy plain, surrounded by abrupt mountains, and by a gentle ascent of 1 hr. gains

The *summit*, 7369 ft. above the sea, a wild, rocky, solitary plain 3 or 4 m. long, called *Kreuzboden*, barely relieved by a few patches of vegetation. To the W. the *Sanfleuron* glacier descends from the *Oldenhorn* nearly to the Kreuzboden. The pass is not a grand one, but the mountains of the great chain of the Alps are finely seen, from Mt. Velan and the Grand Combin to the Dent d'Hérens and Dent Blanche. The whole of the Val d'Hérens is seen directly in front. The descent is steep but grassy all the way down to the pine-forest, through which the road to Sion is long, but not unpleasing.

2 m. from the summit the *Morge* stream is crossed, and after 4 m. of bad winding road, passing a chalet, is again crossed by the Pont Neuf, a substantial stone bridge 200 ft. above the stream. "There is a very pleasing and grand view from this point. The slate-rocks rise on the E. about 2500 ft. Portions have been detached and stand upright from the valley, each the height of a small mountain. The hill on the W. is covered with fir-trees. A white horizontal line on the face of the slate mountain (rt.) is the wall of a watercourse constructed at the sole expense of a farmer's wife to supply her native village with water for irrigation, of which she had felt the want in her lifetime, and for which she left the whole of her fortune at her death." The descent continues for about 5 m. through the ravine of the Morge. Near its mouth is a ruined castle, and view over the valley of the Rhone and the Zermatt peaks. The only village,

Chandolin (humble *Inn*, good wine), is the first place from Gsteig where refreshments can be procured. Here and at Saviese are many narrow lanes, through which the way is intricate to find. A bed of anthracite is worked here. View, as you descend, of the 3 castles of

Sion (Rte. 56). (*Time from Sion*) walking to Chandolin $1\frac{1}{2}$ hr.; to summit of pass, 4 hrs.; to Gsteig, $3\frac{1}{2}$ hrs.

ROUTE 42.

THUN TO VEVEY, BY THE SIMMENTHAL; SAANEN, CHÂTEAU D'OEX, AND GRUYÈRES:—PASS OF THE DENT DE JAMAN.

$26\frac{1}{2}$ leagues = 79 Eng. m.

Thun	Leagues.		Eng. m.
Weissenburg . .	$4\frac{1}{4}$	=	14
Zweisimmen . .	$3\frac{3}{4}$	=	11
Saanen (Gessenay)	$2\frac{7}{8}$	=	9
Château d'Oex . .	$2\frac{3}{8}$	=	7
Montbovon . . .	3	=	7
Bulle	$3\frac{3}{8}$	=	10
Vevey	$6\frac{1}{4}$	=	19
	$26\frac{1}{2}$		

An excellent carriage-road. 10 hrs.' drive to Château d'Oex: Couronne at Zweisimmen, a good stopping-place. The valley abounds in rich cultivation, fields, orchards, gardens, and meadows reaching to the tops of the hills, with houses and villages lying along the banks of the river, varied with fir forests, rocky gorges and open basins, entirely of a pastoral character.

Diligence daily from Thun to Saanen, and next morning on to Château d'Oex; thence to the railroad at Bulle, and to Aigle by Sepey. Those who can walk or ride may proceed to Vevey from Château d'Oex, or Montbovon, by the Dent de Jaman pass.

6 m. The entrance to the Simmenthal lies, through a defile called *Port*, between the Stockhorn rt. and the Niesen l., and is approached from Thun by the road along the margin of the lake (see Rte. 37), and the banks of the Kander, as far as its junction with the Simmen, a little below the picturesque castle of Wimmis, which our road leaves 1 m. on the l.

Brothäusi at the foot of the Niesen (*Inn:* Hirsch).

About 3¼ m. farther is *Erlenbach* (*Inn:* Krone). From this parsonage Latrobe started on those Alpine expeditions which he has described in so admirable and interesting a manner in his *Alpenstock*. The *Stockhorn* (7195 ft., 3½ hrs.' ascent, with a complete view of the Lake of Thun) rises almost immediately behind the village of Erlenbach.

4½ m. *Weissenburg* has a good country *Inn.* [The *Sulphur Baths of Weissenburg*, 2930 ft. above the sea, are between 2 and 3 m. N. There is an ascent immediately on leaving the village, but after that the road winds through a beautiful defile till the Old Bath-house, singularly situated in a profound chasm, bursts upon the view, in a little nook between the boiling torrent Buntschi and the rocks. This building is now almost exclusively occupied by peasants, as a large *new Hotel* and bath-house of a superior class has been opened near the mouth of the gorge. This is well kept by an attentive landlord, and the charges are reasonable. The scenery around is highly picturesque. The waters contain sulphur, magnesia, soda, and iron, and are efficacious in removing internal obstructions. The source is ½ m. higher up the gorge, and the water (above 82° Fahr.) conveyed to the baths in wooden pipes carried along the face of the precipice.

Some way up the ravine the peasants have formed a pathway to the upper pastures, by cutting notches or rude steps in the face of the rock, and partly by attaching ladders to it. By this means they scale a dizzy precipice between 200 and 300 ft. high. The pedestrian bound for the upper Simmenthal need not retrace his steps to Weissenburg, as there is a short cut direct from the baths to Oberwyl, on the high road.]

The *Simmenegg* or *Enge* is a defile through which the road passes to 4½ m. *Boltigen* (*Inn:* Bär; trout-fishing here), a village situated under the *Mittagfluh*, 2726 ft. above the sea, a little to the S. of the old castle of Simmenegg. The ruined castle of Laubeck overlooks the road, which is now carried round the eminence, avoiding a steep ascent. The gorge of *Laubeck* is a grand scene. Near Reidenbach there. are coal-mines. [There is a carriage-road between Boltigen and Bulle, by *Jaun* and the *valley of Charmey*.] The river is crossed 3 times before reaching 6½ m. *Zweisimmen*, a village of 2200 Inhab. (*Inns:* H. Simmenthal, good; Krone, Bär), at the junction of the great and lesser Simmen. Here the diligence usually stops to dine. The village is prettily situated, and many persons stay here *en pension*. The *Castle of Blankenburg* crowns the height about a mile above it.

[A carriage-road l. runs up the Ober-Simmenthal, past (3 m.) St. Stephan (*Inn:* Alte Schweizer), to (2¼ m.) Matten and (3¼ m.) An der Lenk (see Rte. 39).]

The road to Bulle and Vevey now quits the Simmenthal by a very steep ascent, through beautiful scenery, in which rugged peaks of limestone are interspersed with grand forests of pine, and, turning to the S.W., crosses an elevated tract of pasture-land called the Saanenmooser, commanding fine views, till it descends upon 9 m. *Saanen* (Fr. *Gessenay*) (*Inns:* zum grossen Landhaus; Bär, Havswirth), the chief place in the pastoral valley of the upper Saane (Sarine), whose 3786 Inhab. are almost exclusively cattle-owners, or occupied in their dairies, and in manufacturing excellent cheese, exported to all parts of the world as Gruyères. A kind peculiar to the valley, too delicate to bear exportation, is called Fötschari-käse. [The ascent of the Sanetsch Pass (Rte. 41) is made from here, or, taking the carriage-road to Gsteig (9 m.), you may cross the Col de Pillon to the Hôtel des Diablerets and Sepey, in Val des Ormonts (Rte. 43). There is also a pleasant footpath leading to Gruyères over the *Grubenberg*; to Abläntschen 4 hrs.; then to *Jaun* 1½ hr. (Bellegarde in French), *Inn*, clean. And lastly down the valley of the Jaun.]

The road beyond this is hilly. A little below Saanen we pass out of Berne into Canton Vaud. German, the language of the upper extremity of the valley, is soon exchanged for a French patois, which is called haut Romand. The first Vaudois village, 2½ m., is *Rougemont* (Germ. Rothenberg—*Inn*: Kreuz). Its château was formerly a convent.

4½ m. *Château d'Oex* (Oesch) (*Inns*: H. Berthod, very good; H. Rosat, also very good, are large hotels and pensions, situated in their own grounds, 4½ to 6 fr. a-day. Ours, *Eng. Church Service*. There are other pensions). The village (2800 Inhab.) stands in a beautifully green open valley (3498 ft.), with pine-woods and rocks on each side, and the pensions are much and deservedly frequented.

The village was burnt in 1800, and is now chiefly of stone houses. The houses outside it are, however, of wood; many of them ancient, and very handsome and picturesque. On the mound where the Château stood is now a church, the walls of which seem to include part of the old castle.

[This is the centre of a rich pastoral district, too little known to English travellers. It has, of course, no pretension to the sublimity of the snowy Alps; but it is rich in quiet charms, and accessible at times of year when the higher valleys are closed. It is the home of the 'Ranz des Vaches,' and of the idyllic châlet life celebrated in Swiss romance—far less severe than that met with by the traveller at the foot of the glaciers.

There are many pretty walks in the woods, and many drives, a list of which is given in the hotels. From *Mount Cray* on the N., easy ascent of 2¼ hrs. over grass, there is a fine view extending to the chain of Mont Blanc. The next summit to the E. of the Cray, is called the *Prah*. It is 300 ft. higher, and commands a rather more extensive view. The commencement of the path can be pointed out at any of the pensions. Near the summit the ordinary Alpine flowers grow in great beauty and luxuriance. Eastwards of the Prah the range gradually rises in height, till after several points, with strange names—Bimi, Sofothi—it culminates in the *Vanil Noir* and *Dent de Brenleire*. These can be best reached by walking from Château d'Oex, up the Vallée de Vert Champ, to the opening of the Val de Morteys. Here there are several chalets where the night could be passed, or at all events a guide procured. The *Val de Morteys* is a very curious basin, of the kind frequent in this range, high up between the Vanil Noir and Dent de Brenleire, and famous for its rare flowers. Up to the opening of the Val de Morteys, the traveller bound from Château d'Oex to Jaun or Charmey follows the same path. Instead of diverging at this point, he follows it to the col, with the Dent de Brenleire on his l., the fine crags called Pertaboveys on his rt., and descends into the valley of the Jogne by a picturesque path. The path is well marked all the way. From Château d'Oex to the col is about 4 hrs. Thence to the Jogne, 1½ hr. Thence by the new road to *Charmey* (*Inn*: H. du Sapin, very fair) 1 hr.

On the opposite side of the Sarine valley the chief points are the *Rubli* and the *Gummfluh*. The former can be best ascended by walking up the Gerine valley to the chalets, just under the Gummfluh. Here a guide can be found, and it is necessary for any but really good climbers to take one, as there is a *mauvais pas* in climbing the rock. The view from the Rubli over the Oberland is very fine, as is also that from the Gummfluh. The easiest way of climbing the *Gummfluh* (8060 ft.) is to drive or walk to Etivaz, from whence a straightforward climb of about 4 hrs. will land you on the summit. Or it is possible for fair climbers, particularly if assisted by a guide, to climb directly to the summit from the last chalets in the Gerine valley. The longest way, but the most interesting of all, is to start from these chalets, ascend to the col between the Rocher du Midi, and the westernmost rocks of the Gummfluh "massif," then turn to the l., and after a short climb, cross the ridge, and descend a little on the other side till a point is reached, from which it is possible to walk fairly straight along the side of scree and broken rock till the col is reached which leads from Etivaz to Rougemont. This point is also made for by those climbing in the ordinary way from Etivaz, and from here an hour more is enough to reach the top. The view of the Oberland, particularly of the nearer points, such as the Wildhorn and Diablerets, is magnificent.]

Diligence to Sepey and Aigle. The traveller will notice, among other things, the great size of the cattle in this valley.

The Vevey rte. next crosses the stream from the Val d'Etivaz at *Moulins* (¾ m.). [Hence a carriage-road strikes off to Sepey, H. des Diablerets, and Aigle, Rte. 43. The pedestrian may strike off from the bridge at Etivaz (*Inn:* H. du Pont), and then up the Val d'Etivaz, and over a col at its head, or by another on the W. side of the mountain called the *Tête du Moine* (7713 ft.)] In 1¼ m. a road on the rt. leads across the river to *Rossinière* (H. et Pension du Grand Chalet de Rossi-

nière, highly praised; 4 fr. 50 c. a day). The beautiful gorge of *La Perte de la Tine*, between very grand rocks and pines, leads to

4 m. *Montbovon*, or Bubenberg (*Inn:* H. de Jaman, clean, civil people; opposite is the path to the col de Jaman)—which Byron calls "a pretty scraggy village, with a wild river and a wooden bridge:" it is situated in Canton Fribourg. A few horses are kept here for hire. It is better to order them from Vevey the day before.

[A horse-path over the romantic *Pass of Dent de Jaman* (Jommen Pass; there is a short cut at the angle of the road from La Tine), 4872 ft. above the sea, descending upon the Lake of Geneva, will bring the traveller to Glion, or Montreux Territet, in 4½ hrs. (2½ up, 1½ down). In ½ hr. it passes a deep glen by a bridge; in another 25 min. a chapel; 15 min. a small *Inn*; from which it is 1 hr. to the col, where there are stone chalets (wine and milk), and often a herd of enormous cows chewing the cud, each with a musical bell. On the descent, in 5 min. the path divides, to pass down different sides of a gorge, rt. to the hotel at *Les Avants*, a comfortable pension in a high pastoral basin, whence there is a car-road to Vevey in 3 hrs; l. to Glion and Montreux. The latter is for some distance exceedingly steep: lower down it becomes a char-road. Guide needless. Byron, who crossed this path, describes the whole route as "beautiful as a dream." "The view from the highest points (we had both sides of the Jura before us in one point of view, with alps in plenty) comprises, on one side, the greatest part of Lake Leman; on the other, the valleys and mountains of the canton of Freiburg, and an immense plain, with the lakes of Neuchâtel and Morat, and all which the borders of the Lake of Geneva inherit. The music of the cows' bells (for their wealth, like the patriarch's, is cattle) in the pastures, which reach to a height far above any mountains in Britain, and the shepherds shouting to us from crag to crag, and playing on their reeds, where the steeps appeared almost inaccessible, with the surrounding scenery, realized all that I have ever heard or imagined of a pastoral existence—much more so than Greece or Asia Minor, for there we have a little too much of the sabre and musket order, and if there is a crook in one hand, you are sure to see a gun in the other; but this was pure and unmixed—solitary, savage, and patriarchal. As we went they played the 'Ranz des Vaches' and other airs by way of farewell. I have lately repeopled my mind with nature."—*Byron's Journal.*

The view from the col is very beautiful—the blue expanse of the lake—green slopes decked with woods and rocks—the bold mountains at the mouth of the Rhône. To see the Oberland range you must climb the *Dent* itself, 6165 ft., a stiff 1 hr.'s work from the col. It is only accessible on the N. side. Below it is the pretty Lac de Jaman.

"Besides the Col de Jaman there are two less-known passes by which a walker can cross from the Sarine valley to the Lake of Geneva—the *Col des Chaudes*, and the *Col de Jortése.*

For both passes the Hongrin—the stream that issues from the Lac de Lioson above Lecherette, and runs down its retired upland valley to the Sarine at Montbovon, must be reached. From Les Moulins ascend the well-marked col, on the rt. of which is the Planachaux, taking the path on the l. of the road, just after crossing the bridge. 1½ hr.'s easy walking to this col by a well-marked but very stony path. Descend almost immediately and follow the path to the L, keeping continually downwards till in another hour the Hongrin is reached. Descend its course to a white house. Cross the bridge close to it for the *Col de Jortése* leading to Roche or Yvorne. A large wooden chalet known as *La Jointe* is soon passed. Here wine can be had, and possibly a guide, if one has not been already secured at Château d'Oex. His services will be useful in saving time, as the immense spongy pastures over which for 4 or 5 hrs. the way now lies are puzzling to a stranger, and there is nothing that can be called a path till close to the summit of the pass. The view of the Tours d'Ai and Mayen, whose precipices close in the left side of the valley, is imposing. About ½ hr. below the col is a chalet, which affords milk and bread. At Aux Agittes, a little on its further side, there is a private chalet residence. Here the traveller can either diverge to the l. and walk by Corbeyrier to Yvorne, or descend directly upon Roche, whence a train will take him to the lake side, or up the valley of the Rhone. A pedestrian intending to make out the way for himself without the help of a guide should allow at least 9 hrs. from Château d'Oex to Roche. In taking the path in the reverse direction, from Roche to Château d'Oex, be careful to turn to the l. after about ½ hr. through the wood, and not to be tempted into what begins as a path but ends as a timber shoot, a little further on. The view from the col is a fine one, and the whole country traversed is one little known."

"The *Col des Chaudes.* From the white house mentioned above, follow the Hongrin as directed for ¾ hr., to a lower bridge at a saw-mill. After mounting the first rise by a winding path, the well-marked col is directly in view: 1½ hr. should suffice to reach it from the Hongrin. The descent to Villeneuve will occupy about 2 hrs. The whole walk along the Hongrin is one of great beauty, and there are several pools suitable for a bathe. From Château d'Oex to Villeneuve is an easy walk of about 6 hrs. Chamois are fairly abundant on the Dent d'Avenaire, and Englishmen have been known to take up their quarters at the saw-mill for the purpose of shooting them. There are also plenty of trout in the Hongrin, but they will not easily be tempted by English flies. A few hints from a native would be useful to an intending fisherman."—*W. T. A.*]

The carriage-road from Montbovon to Vevey makes a long détour in its descent of the valley; circling round the *Moléson* (6578 ft.), it passes under the hills crowned by the castle and town of

7 m. *Gruyères*—German, Greyerz—(*Inn*: Fleur de Lys, fair). In the vicinity are the *Bains de Montbarry*, a cheap and good pension, pleasantly situated. This little place, of 375 Inhab., is picturesque from its position on the face of a hill, the top of which is crowned by the *Castle*, very commanding and well preserved. Its owners, the Counts of Gruyères, were sovereigns of the surrounding district down to 1554, when the family became bankrupt, and the creditors seized and sold the lordship to Berne, so that the last descendant died in a strange land. The castle has been sold to M. Rory, who has repaired it with taste. The gloomy antiquity of the interior corresponds with the character of the watch-towers, battlements, and loop-holes as seen from without. The walls are 14 ft. thick, the halls vaulted and dimly lighted; in one is a fireplace at which oxen were roasted whole. The *torture* chamber at the top of the stairs contained the rack, which had been used within the present century. The *Ch. of St. Théodule* (1254) has a monument, with marble effigies, of a Count of Gruyères, in singular costume. The inhabitants of the town are a lazy set, many of them pensioners of a rich *Hospital*. The peasants have good voices, and *yodel* to perfection.

The language spoken in this district, a dialect of the Romance (called, in German, Gruverin-Welsch) is thought to prove descent of the people from the Burgundians. It is a subject worthy of attention. The district is famous for its *cheeses*, and supplies a great part of the 40,000 centners (cwt.) which Canton Fribourg manufactures yearly, and which is chiefly exported under the name of Gruyères.

The watch-tower of *La Tour de Trême* was an outpost of the Counts of Gruyères. In the neighbourhood is the monastery of *La Part Dieu*, founded 1307 by Guillemette de Grandson, Dowager-Countess of Gruyères.

3 m. *Bulle*—Boll—(*Inns*: H. des Alpes, near the station, good; Cheval Blanc; Maison de Ville), one of the most industrious towns in the canton, terminus of a branch from the Berne and Lausanne rly. (Rte. 45). It contains 2500 Inhab., and is the chief depot for the cheese made in the valleys of the Sarine and of Charmey, and on the elevated plateau of which it is the centre. It is 2523 ft. above the sea; and if the ages inscribed on the tombstones form any test, it must be one of the healthiest places in the world. There is an old château, but the town is modern, having been burnt in 1805. It is 20¼ m. from Vevey. To Fribourg (17 miles) there are two roads, one on either side of the Sarine, by Favargny and La Roche. The latter is said to be the more picturesque. The former passes by the fine Abbey of Hauterive, founded in 1137, now an agricultural school.

[From Bulle or Gruyères the traveller may ascend the *Moléson* (6578 ft.), in about 4 hrs. It is a widespreading mountain, covered with cattle, and the summit difficult to find without a guide. E. are beautiful routes to Thun, through valleys little visited. An excursion in that direction can be made to the *Baths of Domène*, by carriage-road and horsepath, the former as far as Val Sainte. The road crosses the Sarine from *La Tour de Trême*, and at *Crésus* leaves rt. the *Valley of Charmey*, leading by Jaun to Boltigen in the Simmenthal. It then ascends to *Val Sainte*, formerly a Carthusian monastery, founded 1295 by Girard, lord of Charmey, now occupied by French monks. It is situated under the mountain called *La Berra*, on which wrestling-matches are held on the third Sunday in July. Hence over the pass of the *Chessalette* (4650 ft.) to the *Baths of Domène*, with cold sulphureous spring and lovely landscape, on the *Schwarze See* (3500 ft.), or *Lac d'Omeinaz*, a little lake surrounded by mountains. From Domène the *Ganterisch Pass* leads further W., in 6½ hrs., to the *Baths of Blumenstein*, another charming watering-place, 2005 ft. above the sea, from which there is a carriage-road to Thun. The *Hotel and Baths of Gurnigel*, 3783 ft. (Hauser Frères), can also be reached from the Ganterisch Pass. The Vallée de Bellegarde or Jaunthal, where the finest cheese is produced, may be visited from Bulle. From Bulle to Boltigen, in the Simmenthal, is a picturesque drive of 8½ hrs. At the village of Jaun there is a fair *Inn*.]

Near Vaulruz (a station on the Bulle line) are the *Baths of Colombette*, a name celebrated in the most popular of the Ranz des Vaches.

The coach road now turns S., skirting the base of the Moléson to

12½ m. *Châtel St. Denis*—Kastels—(*Inn*: Maison de Ville ; Pension Perrier, good), a picturesque village with an elevated castle on the l. bank of the Veveyse. ½ m. beyond it the road enters Canton Vaud, and is then carried by an easy descent in zigzags down the steep hill towards the beautiful lake Leman, passing the Hôtel Bellevue about 2 m. short of

8 m. *Vevey* (Rte. 55). The view from this road is nearly as fine as from the Jaman, so that the enormous bends will not be regretted, though they lengthen the journey.

———

ROUTE 43.

CHÂTEAU D'OEX TO AIGLE, BY THE VALLÉE DES ORMONTS.

	Miles.
Sepey	20
Aigle	7¼

Château d'Oex, in Rte. 42.

There is a comfortable diligence every day to Aigle in 7½ hrs., losing at least an hour by stoppages. Carriage 25 to 48 fr. The road is a magnificent specimen of engineering, and runs through very fine scenery. The first mile and a half of road runs down the valley to the village

of *Moulins.* The road here turns off to the left, leaving the Bulle road, and, after rising by two long zigzags, plunges into the defile of *Pissot* in the *Etivaz* valley. For full three miles the road is carried along a narrow ledge which has been blasted out of the rocks, and is perhaps 500 ft. above the stream, which can scarcely be seen in the rocky and wooded gorge below. There are few finer passes or bolder works in the Alps. After leaving the gorge, the road crosses the stream at *Eticaz* (*Inn* and Pension Hirsch), then doubles back and rises by a series of zigzags to

La Lecherette (Pension Oette), about 5300 ft. The road then runs through a tolerably level open valley, descending towards

Comballaz, 4416 ft. above the sea, with a sulphureous mineral spring (*Inn* : H. and P. de la Couronne, fair). The country resembles a magnificent park spread over mountains, emerald green to their tops. Excursions to the *Lac Lioson* (6135 ft.) and the *Pic de Chaussy* (7799 ft.), overhanging the lake, with view of the lake of Geneva, Dent du Midi, and Diablerets. Comballaz is seldom free from snow before the end of June. An easy pass leads over the hills to Montbovon (Rte. 42) in 4½ hrs.

A descent into the Vallée des Ormonts leads to

Sepey (*Inns*: H. des Alpes, H. Cerf, H. du Mont d'Or, H. des Trois Suisses, pensions of a homely kind, moderate in their charges, frequented by Swiss, from June to the end of August). It is a primitive village, very prettily placed, with beautiful view of the Dent du Midi.

At the hamlet of *Leysin*, (5056 ft.), 3 m. from Sepey there is a Pension.

[Ascents can be made of the *Tour d'Ay*, 7818 ft., *Tour de Mayen*, 7622, and *Pointe de Chamossaire*, 6953. Over the Chamossaire you may walk to Bex or Aigle by crossing the Grande Eau by a bridge 1 m. below Sepey, ascending the opposite slopes to La Forclaz, then to a cascade and *Lac de Serray*, 2¼ hrs., by fine forests. The chalets of Bretaye, immediately above the lake, afford cream and milk, and are about ½ hr. from the top of the mountain. 1½ hr. descent (Rte. 44) leads to Chésières (H. de Chésière, good) and *Villard*, 4000 ft. (H. du Grand Moveran ; H. de Chamossaire), whence there is a road to Ollon and Aigle (see Rte. 56).] .

The pasturages in this valley are celebrated, and the cheese, cream, and butter of Les Ormonts (Ormont-dessus above Sepey, and dessous below it) equal any in the canton.

The descent from Sepey to Aigle is very fine. The road is a magnificent piece of engineering, often running along a shelf in the rock, and the views from it are glorious.

At the bottom of the valley rushes the Grande Eau in a series of rapids and cascades. In the distance, beyond Aigle, the snowy tops of the Dent du Midi glisten in contrast to the dark forests of the Ormonts ; and the Pointe de Chamossaire, to the E., rears its grey peak above the pasturages and chalets. In the month of July the *laburnum* is found here in flower, and the rare fern *Asplenium montanum*.

Aigle (*Inns:* Gd. H. des Bains, a mile from the town, large and well-kept establishment; Beau Site ; Mon Séjour; Victoria, very good ; H. des Bains, hydropathic ; H. des Diablerets; H. Bellevue), a station on the Simplon Rly. (Rte. 56).

ROUTE 44.

SEPEY TO GSTEIG, BY LES DIABLERETS.

	Miles.
Les Plans	7
Gsteig	7¼

Between Sepey and Comballaz a branch road turns off from the Aigle road, and goes up the valley of *Ormont-dessus* to the Plan des Iles. At Vers l'Église there are several Pensions. Hôtel des Diablerets, E.C.S., good pension. Higher is *Les Plans* or *the Diablerets*, 3823 ft. above the sea, in full view of one of the grandest scenes in the Alps, the *Creux de Champ*,

the head of the valley of Ormont-dessus. It is surrounded by precipices and glaciers of the *Diablerets*, shaped like a horseshoe ; not unlike the Cirque of Gavarnie, in the Pyrenees, over which dash 5 or 6 waterfalls, the sources of the Grande Eau. The scenery is beautiful—green alps dotted with chalets, the Tour d'Ay and Tour Mayen to the W., forests on the heights, and far above them, tier upon tier, and streaming with ice, the rocks of the Oldenhorn and Diablerets.

The chief excursions are to the

a. Creux de Champ, about 2 hrs. there and back, passing through a forest (horse, 6 fr.). On the l., at the entrance of the basin, a path leads up the Prapioz alp to the glacier of *Sex-rouge*.

b. Cascade du Dard, falling from the Oldenhorn, rt. of the path to the Col de Pillon.

c. Tête du Moine, 7713 ft., N. of the hotel. On the other side it is craggy, and its shape very whimsical, whence the name. 3½ hrs. up; guide, 6 fr.

d. Lac d'Arnen (horse, 10 fr. ; guide, 5), a pretty mountain tarn, beneath a wood. It is reached by a col (2 hrs.), the second opening E. of the Tête du Moine (but not seen from the hotel), commanding a grand view of the Oldenhorn and mountains eastward. A path runs slanting to this col from the hotel.

e. Chamossaire, 6953 ft., the highest point of the range S. of Sepey. The way lies towards that village, and then up the alp to the *Lac de Serray*, 3 hrs. Thence to the top in about ¼ hr. without difficulty. A very beautiful view, including Mt. Blanc and the head of the Lake of Geneva. The descent to Villard down a wooded dale is most charming, and the mountain is best taken by crossing from the Diablerets to that place. Guide, 6 fr.

f. Oldenhorn, 10,250 ft.; about 7 hrs. up. Guide, 10 fr. A descent can be made on the other side, by the Sanfleuron glacier, sleeping at the Olden chalet, to the Sanetsch Pass.

g. Diablerets, 10,666 ft. One of the

easiest snow mountains, with a noble view. First ascended by the Rocher de Culand, on the W. side. In 1869 an ascent was made by the rocks above the Creux de Champ, the lower precipice being turned by the path leading to the Sexrouge glacier. The tariff for a guide is 12 fr., and 20 for crossing the mountain to Sion. The descent on the other side is down the great *Sanfleuron glacier.*

The *Col de la Croix* (5705 ft.) is a beautiful pass to Bex. 1½ hr. to the col, 2 down to Gryon, whence there is a carriage-road of about 3 hrs. to Bex. The path to the col ascends rt. at the entrance of the wood near the Creux de Champ, keeping N. of the stream. Carriage road in construction.]

From Plan des Isles the road mounts through charming rock and forest scenery to the *Col de Pillon* (5124 ft.) under the Oldenhorn, and then descends, passing a pretty waterfall, to Gsteig (Rte. 41).

ROUTE 45.

BERNE TO LAUSANNE, BY FRIBOURG (RAIL).

Stations.	Miles.
Flamatt	8
Fribourg	19¼
Romont	35¼
Oron	44¼
Chexbres (Vevey)	52¼
Lausanne	60

The country traversed is fertile and broken, and very pretty; distant views of the Alps are often obtained, and the descent to the lake of Geneva is very fine. The left-hand side of the train has the best view, but, as the train backs out of the station before starting, it is the right-hand out of the station. The line makes a great curve, and in a short time the Bernese Alps and the Simmenthal mountains appear on the l. About 3 m. from Berne is

Bümplitz Stat. The Sense, which divides Canton Berne from Fribourg, and comes from the Baths of Domène and Lac d'Omeinaz (Rte. 42), is crossed to

Flamatt Stat.
[Diligence twice a-day to 4 m. *Laupen*, by Neueneck (*Inn:* Hirsch), on the Sense. It is famous for the battle in which the Swiss confederates, under Rudolph of Erlach, defeated the mailed chivalry of Burgundy and Suabia, 1339. A tower, erected 1853, with a short inscription to commemorate the victory, stands near the spot where the main battle raged.]

There is a tunnel beyond Flamatt, after which the railway runs for some miles through a pretty little valley. It then passes through another tunnel and comes to

Guin Stat. Two miles beyond this the ravine of the Sarine is crossed by the great Grandfey Viaduct.

The towers and old walls of Fribourg are now seen on the l., and the train goes round the town to

Fribourg Stat., which is on the S.W. of the town, nearly a mile from the cathedral and bridge.

Fribourg can be seen in 3 hrs., and is well worth the excursion from Berne; or, stopping between 2 trains, walk or hire a carriage to the Grandfey bridge, and come back to the cathedral, after which the carriage is of no use.

Fribourg (*Hotels:* H. de Fribourg, about 5 min. walk from the stat., H. National, with a good view; both excellent) 11,546 Inhab., chiefly Rom. Cath., the capital of Canton Fribourg, situated on a promontory formed by the windings of the Sarine (Saane). Many of the houses stand on the very edge of the precipice overhanging the river, and their quaint architecture, the long line of embattled walls stretching up hill and down dale, varied by the chain of feudal watch-towers, and gateways of the ancient fortifications which still exist in a perfect state, together with the singular and romantic features of the gorge, make the distant view at once imposing and highly picturesque. The narrow dirty streets of the interior do not altogether correspond with these outward promises.

Fribourg was founded in 1175, by Duke Berthold of Zähringen, father of him who founded Berne, and was long a free town. It became subject to the House of Austria, and frequently fought against Berne. It was afterwards subject for a short time, about 1452, to the Dukes of Savoy. In 1481, it was admitted into the Swiss confederation, having done good service on its side in the battles of Morat and Grandson. It is now a stronghold of the Catholic party.

Down to 1847 Canton Fribourg presented a remarkable instance of a state with a constitution purely democratic, in which the chief influence was exercised by the hierarchy. The town of Fribourg was a stronghold of the Roman Catholic priesthood: it is the see of a bishop, who still styles himself Bishop of Lausanne, although, since the Reformation, the Canton Vaud is cut off from his diocese. It contained no less than 9 convents (5 for monks and 4 for nuns), 12 churches, and 10 chapels. The *Jesuits,* while interdicted from most other states of Europe, were here openly tolerated, having been recalled, in 1818, by a decree of the Grand Council of the canton. They were expelled in 1847.

The Suspension-Bridge over the Sarine, completed in 1834—engineer M. Chaley, of Lyons—should be crossed. The span of the catenary of the wire ropes is 870 ft., that of the chains of the Menai Bridge 570 ft. It was originally supported by 4 cables of iron wire ; two more have been added. It is well seen from the old road, and from the gorge of Gotteron.

The appearance of Fribourg from the Berne road and the wire-bridge is singularly striking and picturesque, its antique battlements and numerous towers crowning the summit of a precipitous rock above the gorge of the Sarine. The most conspicuous building is a large structure, with 5 stories and many windows, once a Jesuits' Pensionnat. Below are the Gothic tower and church of St. Nicolas.

Another Wire Bridge, 689 feet long and 317 high, has been suspended across the romantic gorge of Gotteron, on the opposite side of the river Sarine. It was finished in 1840. The wire cables are attached immediately to the solid rock on each side, and the point of suspension is higher on one side than on the other, which gives it the appearance of half a bridge. The object of this mode of construction is economy, the expense of building piers of solid masonry from the bottom of the valley being saved. Those not pressed for time should descend from the bridge to the stream over which it is thrown, and follow up its course for a mile or two. The soft sandstone rocks through which it has worn its way are picturesque both in form and colour, and the limpid purity of the water is varied and enhanced by constant rapids.

The *Cathedral Church of St. Nicolas* is a handsome Gothic building, chiefly in the Flamboyant style (date 1285–1500). The exterior was carefully restored in 1856. " The original charter by which Berthold of Zähringen in 1178 confirms the Monastery of Payerne in possession of the allodium in which the new church of St. Nicolas was built is preserved in the archives of Turin." St. Nicolas was made a Collegiate Church in 1512 by Julius II. The portal under the tower (date 1452, but the separate figures are of different dates) is surmounted by a bas-relief, representing the Last Judgment. In the centre stands St. Nicolas, his statuette was entirely gilt, and is among the more modern ; and above him is seated the Saviour; on the l. hand an angel is weighing mankind in a huge pair of scales, not singly but by lots, and an imp is maliciously endeavouring to pull down one scale, and make the other kick the beam.

The handsome interior has a nave of five bays, divided from the aisles by clustered columns supporting pointed arches. There is a triforium and a clerestory, but no transept. In the choir are quaint reliefs of saints on the backs of the stalls.

Certain magistrates of Fribourg, it is said, being imprisoned for a time, about 1449, at Fribourg in the Breisgau, learned to admire exceedingly the tower of the minster in that town, and longed to replace the meaner structure in their own Fribourg with something of equal grandeur; but it was not till 1470 that the work was entrusted to Georges du Jordil. The tower was brought to a termination in 1492, without the spire at first intended. It rises above the portal, at first quadrangular and then octagonal.

The windows of the nave were at one time filled with stained glass, portions of which found their way (it is not known how or when) to the Musée de Cluny at Paris. The stained glass of the apse was partly derived from the church of Hauterive.

The *Organ*, built by the late Aloys Moser, a native of the town (b. 1770, d. 1839), is one of the finest instruments in Europe. It was first played in 1834. A white marble bust of the artist surmounts a small "Gothic" monument below the organ. The organist plays on it for the gratification of travellers at 1.30 P.M., and 8 P.M., except on certain feast days and on Saturdays. Tickets are obtained at the hotels. The performance terminates with the imitation of a storm, from 'Der Freischütz,' introducing the howling of the wind, the roaring of the thunder, and a few flashes of lightning. The instrument

was enlarged in 1852 by Vogt, at a later date by Kyburg of Soleure, and 1872, by Merklin and Schütz, of Paris, and has 64 stops and 7800 pipes.

The Pensionnat, or Jesuits' School, the most conspicuous building in the town, was destined for the reception of about 400 pupils, many of them children of the Roman Catholic noblesse of France and Germany who were sent hither for their education. The School and Convent have been turned into a Cantonal school since 1848.

The ancient *Rathhaus* is a building of no consequence, dating from 1502–14. It stands on the site of the Duke of Zähringen's castle, which, according to the legend, had been carried off by the devil from Fribourg in Breisgau and dropped in his flight.

Before it is the ancient trunk of a *Lime-tree*, planted, according to tradition, on the day of the battle of Morat, in 1476. The story relates that a young Fribourgois, who had fought in the battle, anxious to bring home the good news, ran the whole way, and arrived on this spot, bleeding, out of breath, and so exhausted by fatigue, that he fell down, and had barely time to cry "Victory!" when he expired. The branch of lime which he carried in his hand was immediately planted, and grew into the tree, of which this decayed trunk, 20 ft. in circumference, is the remains. Till 1851 it gave the name of Lindengericht, or Court of the Lime Tree, to a popular tribunal for the settlement of disputes between the townsfolk and the country folk. Its branches are supported by stone pillars.

The *Cantonal Museum* contains a fine Roman Mosaic found at Cormerod, near Avenches, a collection of lacustrine objects and other antiquities.

A long flight of steps leads from

this down to the lower town and river side: it is called the *Rue Court Chemin*, and the roofs of some of its houses serve as pavement for the street above it, called *Rue Grande Fontaine*.

The Canton Fribourg is singularly divided between the German and French languages; and the line of separation, extending from the S.E. corner to the N.W., passes through the town of Fribourg, so that in the upper town French is spoken, and in the lower German. This distinction, however, is wearing out.

The walls and gates are perfect specimens of ancient fortification, and contribute, along with the general air of antiquity, to carry back the spectator to a remote state of society. One tower, near the Préfecture (thrown across the street, and now converted into a prison), has acquired the name of *La Mauvaise Tour*, because it contained the rack. Though the torture had been disused in the canton for many years, it was not legally abolished until 1830.

The *Grandfey Railway Bridge* is a wonderful structure. There is a very pleasant walk or drive to it, starting from outside the Morat gate, and lying all the way through an avenue of large trees, commanding fine views of the Sarine and of the mountains. It is about $1\frac{1}{2}$ m. from the Morat gate. At the bridge is a café.

The bridge was made in 1862, at Creuzot in France. It is a lattice-girder bridge, 13 ft. deep, 1092 ft. long, in 7 spans of 156 ft. each. The six piers are partly of stone, partly of iron lattice. The two middle piers reach 251 ft. above the stream, *i.e.* 50 ft. higher than the Monument, and 27 ft. higher than the towers of Notre Dame. There is a footpath under the rly.

About 3 m. lower down the valley of the Sarine is the *Grotto of Ste. Magdalene*, a hermitage and chapel cut out of the sandstone rock, by a native of Gruyères named Dupré, between 1670 and 1680. It is scarcely worth a visit.

21 m. S.E. are the *Baths of Domène*, in a charming situation, with moderate charges. There are boats on the lake (Lac Noir), the source of the Warme Sense, and excursions to the mountain *La Berra* (4 hrs. from Fribourg)—to *Jaun* $2\frac{1}{2}$ hrs.—and *Val Sainte* $2\frac{3}{4}$ hrs.

Diligences twice daily to Morat, about 10 m. (Rte. 46).

On quitting Fribourg Stat., the train overlooks (l.) the deep valley of the Sarine: beyond it is Mont Moléson. l. The Nunnery of La Fille Dieu, near

Romont Junction Stat. Branch to *Bulle* (4 trains daily, in 55 min.), chief town of the Gruyères district. *Romont* (*Inns:* Cerf, good ; Couronne) is picturesquely seated on one of the Jorat hills above the Glane. It possesses 2 of the mysterious *Round towers*, similar in construction to those in Ireland, with the entrance high above the ground, and 4 openings just below the roof facing the cardinal points. One tower, of graceful form, and in a very perfect state, stands detached on a mound outside the walls ; the other, which has been much altered, now forms part of the mediæval *Château* said to have been founded by the Kings of Burgundy in the 10th centy. Soon after leaving Romont, a glimpse of Mont Blanc may be gained, and, beyond

Vauderens Stat., of the Jura range.

Rue (*Inns:* H. de Ville ; Fleur de Lys), $1\frac{1}{2}$ m. W., is a picturesque town, with castle, in the vale of the Broye.

Oron le Château Stat. The *château* crowns a rock above it. *Oron la Ville* is below.

Beyond this is the summit-level (2080 ft.), near which the rugged peaks of the Dent d'Oche come into sight.

Palézieux Junct. Stat. Here the line from Soleure (Rte. 46) falls in.

Chexbres Stat. [This is the station for Vevey, and for the Hôtel Signal, an excellent house on the hill between Lausanne and Vevey, 10 min. from the station. *Omnibuses,* to and from every train; to Vevey, *fare* 1 fr., luggage extra; a drive of rather more than 1 hr. The return (ascent) takes longer. Fine views.]

On emerging from the rly. tunnel beyond Chexbres, a *magnificent view* on the L—Lake of Geneva, Valley of Rhone, Dent de Jaman, and other mountains.

The rly. then runs through several other tunnels and cuttings through tilted sandstone strata of the lower miocene.

Grandvaux Stat.

La Conversion Stat., above *Lutry* (*Inns:* H. de Ville; Couronne) on the lake.

A viaduct of 9 arches next carries the line over a valley through which runs the viaduct of the Sierre and Lausanne Rly. The 2 lines unite before entering

Lausanne Junct. Stat. (in Rte. 55).

ROUTE 46.

SOLEURE TO LAUSANNE, BY RAIL.—MORAT. AVENCHES.

	Eng. m.
Soleure.	
Lyss.	15
Morat	30
Palézieux	53
Lausanne	66

This rly., opened 1876, after leaving Soleure (Rte. 4), follows the valley of the Aar to *Busswyl,* a station on the line from Berne to Bienne. It keeps to this line as far as *Lyss Stat.,* and then branches off to the rt.

Aarberg Stat. (*Inn:* Krone), a town of 864 Inhab., on a rocky promontory, nearly surrounded by the Aar, which at times converted it into an island,

At this point the course of the river has been diverted (see Rte. 1). The road enters and quits the town by two covered bridges. View from the cemetery.

Morat — Germ. Murten — (*Inns:* Couronne; Aigle; Lion), a thriving town of 2360 Inhab., prettily situated on the E. shore of the lake of Morat. Its picturesque and arcaded streets are overlooked by an old *Castle;* and it is still surrounded by feudal walls and watchtowers—the same which, for 10 days, withstood the artillery of Charles the Bold. In the *Gymnasium* is a collection of arms, guns, and other relics of the fight.

The battle of June 22, 1476, which has rendered this otherwise insignificant town famous all over the world, was fought under its walls. The Swiss were drawn up along the heights a little to the S.W., and nothing could resist their impetuous charge. The loss of the Burgundians was immense : 15,000 dead bodies are said to have been left on the field, and many perished in the lake. The bodies of the slain were collected by the Swiss in an Ossuary, which, after standing 300 years, was destroyed in 1798 by the soldiers of the Burgundian Legion in the Revolutionary French army, anxious to efface this record of their ancestors' disgrace and defeat.

The scattered remains have now been collected and buried, and an *Obelisk* was set up over them (in 1822), by the canton, at the roadside, about ¾ m. S. of Morat, on the site of the bone-house. The inscription belonging to it, and one or two cannon, made of iron hoops, used in the battle, are still preserved in the *Town-house* of Morat.

The best view of the battle-field and lake is from the hill of *Münchenwyler,* near an enormous lime-tree, 36 ft. in circumference, and 90 ft. high, still in full vigour and luxuriant foliage : it is probably at least 600 years old, since, according to tradition, the Swiss held a council of war before the battle under its shade.

The *lake of Morat*, 1430 ft., is 6 m. long, 2½ broad: it is separated by a narrow flat tract of land from the lake of Neuchâtel, but empties itself into it through the river Broye.

[A *Steamer* runs twice daily from Morat to Neuchâtel, in 2 hrs., crossing the lake of Morat towards Mont Valles, 2270 ft. Near *Sugier*, where the steamer enters the channel of the *Broye*, between the lakes, is

Anet, or *Ins* (*Inn*: Bär), a village on an eminence, from which the Alps are well seen in clear weather, with the lakes of Morat and Neuchâtel near at hand. The lake of Bienne lies about 2 m. N. You overlook from this place the *Aarberger Moos*, a tract of morass, 9 m. long by 6 m. wide, drained in 1875. *Bretiége* (Brüttelen) is a watering-place at the foot of hills 2½ m. N.E. of Anet. A road runs from this to *Erlach* (Cerlier, *Inn*: L'Ours), a town of 1000 Inhab., on a spur of the *Jolimont*, remarkable for the number of snakes to be found upon it, and projecting into the lake, like a wall or causeway, towards *Rousseau's* (or *St. Peter's*) *Island*. The castle of Erlach was the cradle of the noble family of that name: among its members was Rudolf, the hero of Laupen in 1339.

The steamer here enters the lake of Neuchâtel, and crosses over to Neuchâtel. Rte. 48.]

Avenches Stat.—Germ. Wiflisburg— (*Inns*: Couronne; Maison de Ville), an ancient walled town of 1750 Inhab., situated in the S.W. angle of the area once occupied by *Aventicum*, the Roman capital of Helvetia. It appears to have existed before the time of Cæsar. It attained the height of its prosperity, and a population of 60,000, in the reign of Vespasian and Titus; and was destroyed, first by the Alemanni, and afterwards by Attila. The walls may be traced for nearly 4 m., in some places 14 ft. thick and 15 high; they extended to the lake, where they formed a small mole and harbour. The mo-

dern town fills but one-tenth of the space they enclosed—the rest is meadow-land or corn-field. About a mile before reaching Avenches the road from Morat is carried through a breach in these ancient fortifications. On the l. is seen a tower, which, though ruined, is the most perfect of the Roman edifices here. They owe their total destruction to their massy masonry having been for ages regarded as a quarry out of which the neighbouring houses and villages have been built. Close to the modern town, on the l. of the road, a solitary Corinthian column, 37 ft. high, is still standing, and has, for a long time, served the storks as a pedestal to build their nests on, whence it is called the Cigognier.

" By a lone wall a lonelier column rears
   A grey and grief-worn aspect of old days :
 'Tis the last remnant of the wreck of years,
   And looks as with the wild bewilder'd gaze
 Of one to stone converted by amaze,
   Yet still with consciousness ; and there it
       stands,
   Making a marvel that it not decays,
 When the coeval pride of human hands,
 Levell'd Aventicum, hath strew'd her subject
       lands."

Other traces of fallen splendour, such as the line of city walls, broken cornices, inscriptions, distinct remains of an *amphitheatre*, and fragments of an aqueduct, exist, and are interesting evidence of the extent of the largest Roman colony in Helvetia.

Tacitus has recorded the history of Julius Alpinus, the chief man of the city, who was condemned to death for aiding and abetting an insurrection against the Roman Emp. Vitellius, in ignorance of the murder of his rival Galba (A.D. 69).

1500 years after this event an Inscription was reported to have been found here, bearing these words:— "Julia Alpinula: Hic Jaceo. Infelicis patris infelix proles. Deæ Aventiæ Sacerdos. Exorare patris necem non potui: Male mori in fatis illi erat. Vixi annos xxiii. (I, Julia Alpinula, lie here—unfortunate child of an unfortunate parent, priestess of the Goddess Aventia. I failed in averting, by my prayers, the death of my father:

the Fates had decreed that he should die ignominiously. I lived to the age of 23.)"

The critical acuteness of the late Lord Stanhope destroyed the romance of this story by proving incontestably that the above pathetic epitaph, the cause of such poetic sympathy, is a *forgery* of the 17th century, and that no such person as Julia Alpinula ever existed.

The *feudal Castle* was built by a Count Wivilo, in the 7th century, whence Wiflisburg, the German name of Avenches. The country here is interesting by the richness of the cultivation, the beauty of the fruit-trees, and the comfort apparently enjoyed by the population.

Payerne Junct. Stat.—German *Peterlingen*—(*Inns:* Ours, very good; de la Croix Blanche; du Cerf). There are 2 churches in this walled town—the one, now turned into a *Halle au Blé*, is in the Romanesque style, and very ancient. Bertha Queen of Burgundy (A.D. 950), the founder of it and of the adjoining convent (suppressed since the Reformation, and now a school), was buried in it. The curiosity of the place is Queen Bertha's Saddle, a cumbrous machine kept in the *parish* church, from which it appears that, in her days, it was the fashion for ladies to ride *en cavalier*; but Bertha spun as she rode, having a distaff planted on the pommel. In the same church is Bertha's tomb, an antique sarcophagus discovered in 1818, now covered with a slab of black marble.

[There are rlys. to *Estavayer* on the lake of Neuchâtel, and thence to Yverdon, Rte. 49. To Fribourg, Rte. 45.]

The rly. continues to ascend the valley of the Broye, passing Henniez, to

Lucens Stat. (Lobsingen), with a castle, formerly a hunting-seat of the Bishop of Lausanne.

Moudon Stat.—Germ. *Milden*—(*Inn:* H. Victoria, not good). This town (1500 Inhab.) was the Roman *Minidunum*, whence its modern name. It has a Gothic church, recalling the Cathedral of Lausanne, and a tall

Tower of defence, attributed to Queen Bertha.

Palézieux Junct. Stat. Here the rly. joins that from Fribourg to Lausanne.

Lausanne. Rte. 55.

ROUTE 48.

BIENNE TO NEUCHÂTEL.

20 m. For the Rlys. converging at Bienne from Berne and Olten, see Rtes. 1 and 2.

About 1 m. S. of Bienne is

Nidau, a village on the lake, with a picturesque castle, flanked by round towers and surmounted by a tall square keep. The lords of Nidau, an extinct branch of the former lords of Neuchâtel, were foes of Berne; their stronghold now shows on its front the Bernese bear, painted of colossal dimensions, and is converted into the cantonal salt-warehouse. From the slope of the hill near Belmund a good view is obtained of the lake and of St. Peter's Isle. Rt., near a fir-wood, rises an obelisk, by way of monument to the Swiss who fell here fighting against the French 1798.

The recently deepened Zihl (Thièle), which drains the lake of Bienne, passes near Nidau. A lake-village has been discovered here.

Since the opening of the railway steamers have ceased to navigate the lake of Bienne. The trains run along its bank and command a fine view of it: but the Jura chain is hid.

6 m. *Twann Stat.* (*Inn:* L'Ours). Row boats may be hired here for a visit to St. Peter's Isle.

The *Lake of Bienne* (German *Bieler See*) is about 10 m. long, and nearly 3 broad. It is 17 ft. lower than the lake of Neuchâtel, whose waters it receives at its S. extremity by the Thièle, discharging them again at the N.E. corner, through a continuation of the same river. It possessed much quiet beauty of scenery, lately impaired by the artificial lowering of its waters, which has, however,

brought to light some interesting remains of lake-villages.

The Lake of Bienne owes its celebrity chiefly to Rousseau's residence
on it, and to his somewhat extravagant praises. The *Ile de St. Pierre*,
on which he took refuge for 2 months,
in 1765, after his proscription at
Paris, and his stoning at Motiers
(Rte. 51), is situated about 6 m. from
Bienne. Boats may be hired at
almost all the villages on the lake to
row to it. The island, a pretty object,
is a ridge of sandstone, rising 12 ft.
above the lake, and prolonged southwards, under water, to the hill
called Jolimont. It is crowned by a
grove of old oaks, the shade of which
in summer is refreshing.

Rousseau's room is preserved nearly
as he left it, except that its walls, doors,
shutters, and windows are scribbled
over with names of all nations. To
escape the importunities of curious
visitors he used to climb up by a stove,
through a trap-door (still shown)
into the garret, and frequently, when
informed by his host that a party had
come expressly to see him, refused to
appear—"Je ne suis pas içi dans une
ménagerie."

The most extensive peat-moss in
Switzerland lies on the S.E. shore of
the lake of Bienne. The Gothic abbey
of St. Jean is now a manufactory,
where the peat is transmuted into
benzine oil, petroleum, and pigments.
An ancient lacustrine village has been
dug out of the morass, 1000 ft. from
the present shore, near Möringen.

4 m. *Neuveville Stat.*—Germ. *Neuen-
stadt*—(*Inns:* Couronne, or Pension
Grether, out of the town on the S.
side, surrounded by as much shade as
the vineyards will afford), a thriving
little town of 1200 Inhab. (here French
is spoken), on the edge of the lake,
and foot of the *Chasseral*, whose summit
(5279 ft.) may be reached in 4 hrs.;
by carriage-road to the village of
Nods 3 hrs., path thence to summit
1 hr.

On the opposite side of the lake,

near its S. extremity, stands *Erlach*
(Cerlier), on the slope of the *Jolimont*.

Landeron Stat. is at a picturesque
old Swiss town near the mouth of
the naturally shallow river *Thièle*, or
Zihl, through which the waters of
the lake of Neuchâtel find their way
into the lake of Bienne.

Emerging from a tunnel the train
reaches
St. Blaise Stat. The line continues
to rise until it overlooks the whole lake.

NEUCHÂTEL Junct. Stat., high above
the lake—Germ. Neuenburg—(*Hotels:*
Hôtel Bellevue, a large building close
to the lake; Grand H. du Lac—
both excellent houses; Faucon; H.
de Commerce. The beautifully situated H. de Chaumont is 2 hrs. up the
mountain.)

English Church Service.
Neuchâtel, the chief town of the
canton (15,612 Inhab., Protestant and
Rom. Cath.), is built upon the steep
slope of the Jura, and along a narrow
shelf of alluvial deposits brought
down by the river *Seyon*, gained
by embankments from the water,
and by turning the river into a
tunnel cut for 500 ft. through the
rock. Several streets have been
built on the land thus acquired.
Except as the threshold of Switzerland, it has little to interest the
passing traveller: it has but little
trade, and not much activity, except
on market-days. To one newly arrived in the country, the first and
glorious view of the Alps from the
heights above the town, is a constant
delight; and, even should the sky be
clouded, Neuchâtel, with its picturesque old castle, its numerous white
country-houses, its vine-clad hills,
and blue expanse of lake, will be pronounced beautiful.

The French princes of the house of
Châlons (Longueville) were, at least
nominally, the sovereigns of this
little state: though the subjects
maintained jealously their privileges
and liberties, allowing their princes

but very limited authority. When the house of Châlons became extinct in 1707, the King of Prussia was chosen, as the nearest descendant by the female line of the former lords of Neuchâtel, to be stadtholder. The sovereignty of the house of Brandenburg was interrupted by Napoleon, who made Marshal Berthier Prince of Neuchâtel, but was resumed in 1815, and continued until 1857. Though long an ally of the Swiss cantons, Neuchâtel was not formally incorporated as a member of the Confederation until 1814. There was a great struggle in 1848 between the aristocratic and the democratic parties, the latter assisted occasionally by French sympathisers, when the constitution was settled upon the regular French republican model. In 1856, under the mediation of the great powers, the King of Prussia renounced his rights and title.

The *Old Castle* on the height, now converted into government offices, was originally the residence of the French princes.

The *Church*, adjoining the castle, is a Gothic building of the 12th century: but the E. end, in the round style, is older. Within the chancel is a Gothic monument, including 15 life-sized effigies, erected 1372 by one of the Counts of Neuchâtel; there is also a monument to *Farel*, the reformer, who was buried on the terrace in front. There is a pleasing view from the terrace S. of the ch. On the W. terrace is a statue of Farel, and a cromlech, discovered in 1876 near the Palafitte d'Auvernier.

In the Palais Rougemont, or *Musée*, N.E. of the town, is the *Picture Gallery* (admission ½ fr., free on Sunday), containing some very good productions of modern artists, chiefly natives of French Switzerland, as :— *Calame's* Monte Rosa, Rosenlaui, &c.; *Ch. Girardet*, Lady Claypole, and Cromwell; *Tschaggeny*, a Flemish bridal procession ; *Leopold Robert* (a native of Chaux-de-Fonds), Ch. of St. Paul at Rome after the Fire, Roman Oxen, also portraits of Frederick the Great and other Prussian

sovereigns. In an adjacent house is Challande's collection of stuffed *Alpine animals.*

The *College*, a handsome building near the lake, erected by the town, as a public school, contains a very interesting *Museum of Natural History*. The specimens of rocks and fossils illustrating the structure of the Jura are very complete and instructive. This collection owes much to the zeal and talents of Professor Agassiz, a native of Orbe in Vaud, whose discoveries in the history of fossil fishes have thrown so much light on that branch of study. He held the Professorship of Nat. Hist. at Neuchâtel 1838–1847.

The town has also built a *Ladies' School*, where a good cheap education is given to girls. The *Public Library* contains 70,000 vols., and among the MSS. 2000 letters written by J. J. Rousseau, 1760-1770.

A fine view from the *Observatory*, ½ hr. N.E. of Neuchâtel. *Swimming-bath* in the lake, E. of the Bellevue H.

The charitable institutions of this town, for which it is indebted to its own citizens, are on a very splendid scale. In 1786 one *David Purry* left his whole fortune of 4,000,000 of livres (166,000*l.*) to endow an hospital and poorhouse, and for other purposes connected with the improvement of his native town. He had quitted it a poor lad, without money or friends, had gradually, by industry and talent for business, increased his means, becoming, in turn, jeweller, owner of mines, banker, and, finally, millionnaire, at Lisbon, where he died. His *statue* has been set up in front of the Banque Cantonale by his fellow citizens.

The *Hôpital Pourtalès* is a similar monument of the benevolence and public spirit of a townsman. It is open to people of all religions and countries alike.

Several of the richest bankers, merchants, &c., in France, are Neuchâtelois by origin.

The *Lake of Neuchâtel* is 1427 ft.

above the sea (17 feet higher than the lake of Bienne), about 24 m. in length, 4 to 6 in breadth, and has a maximum depth of 488 ft. Its fluctuations are shown by a *Limnimètre*, on the walk by the Bellevue hotel. The greatest height recorded was on Jan. 8, 1802, when the lake rose 6¼ Swiss ft. above the ordinary level. The lakes of Neuchâtel, Bienne, and Morat, were bordered by 45,000 acres of marshland, unproductive, except of malaria, and almost unpeopled. The creative cause was the imperfect drainage of the country by the river Zihl (or Thièle), which, having a fall of only 12 ft. to the Aar, was frequently choked by freshets and the gravel brought down by that river. In Jan. 1802, it rose 3 inches above the lake of Neuchâtel; in 1837 3¼, when Nidau was so flooded that a large pike was caught at the Town Hall. In 1841, for 7 days, the stream ran towards its source at the rate of 4623 cubic ft. per second. In consequence of the great drainage works undertaken to remedy these evils (Rte. 1) the lake has been lowered several feet.

There are steamers to *Estavayer*, with its interesting old castle of Chilnaux, and to Morat (Rte. 46), by which pleasant excursions can be made. The snowy peaks of the Bernese Oberland are, in clear weather, well seen from the lake.

Those who would enjoy one of the finest distant views of the Alps, with the lakes of Neuchâtel, Morat, and Bienne in the foreground, and the long range of the Jura on the N., should ascend

The Chaumont (*Inns:* H. du Chaumont; H. du Château; comfortable and moderate; *Eng. Ch. Service*), the hill immediately above Neuchâtel. Diligences twice a-day both ways. It is about 2 hours' walk, by a good carriage-road to the hotel on the top, a point of a ridge, 3845 feet above the sea, running N. of the lakes for many miles, and attaining its greatest height in the *Chasseral*, N.E., 5279 ft. The view comprehends in clear weather the whole array of Alps, from the Titlis to Mont Blanc, and is said to be superior to that from the Weissenstein.

On the slope of the hill, about 2 m. above the town, and 820 ft. above the lake, lies the *Pierre à Bot* (toadstone), the largest boulder known on the Jura; it is situated in a wood near a farm-house, and measures 62 feet in length by 48 in breadth, and is calculated to contain 14,000 cubic feet. It is of granite, similar to that of the Great St. Bernard, from which part of the Alps it probably came, as there is no similar rock nearer at hand; yet it exhibits no symptoms of attrition, all its angles are perfectly sharp. The entire S. slope of the Jura, a limestone formation, is strewed with these granite blocks, which, from the nature of the stone, must have all been derived from the high Alps. Their presence was long a mystery, but is now pretty generally attributed to the operation of glaciers covering a large portion of Switzerland and carrying these blocks on their surface, or else to that of icebergs floating on a great lake or inland sea.

Those who dislike so long a walk may enjoy extensive and beautiful views of the Bernese Alps and Mont Blanc from the Noiraigue Stat. of the Pontarlier Rly. (Rte. 51), or from Les Hauts-Geneveys stat. of the Chaux-de-Fonds Rly. (Rte. 50).

The *Gorge of the Seyon*, immediately behind Neuchâtel, is a singular scene, and those who find little to amuse them in the town will not repent a walk to explore it, though its recesses are only to be reached by scrambling and climbing. It is a deep narrow fissure, which cleaves the Jura, and allows the river Seyon to escape from the Val de Ruz. The section it presents of the strata of the Jura limestone will prove particularly instructive to the geologist. In one spot they may be observed curved and fractured, probably by the upheaving force, which rent the mountain. Though at times a torrent sweeping everything before it, the Seyon is reduced in summer to a driblet of water, which exhales unwholesome effluvia. A tunnel, *de la Trouée du Seyon*, has therefore been made to carry its waters clear of the town into the lake. This public work was executed out of the Pury fund.

Chanélaz, 1½ m. from Auvernier Stat., is a Hydropathic establishment, very prettily situated at the foot of the Jura. Pension 6 to 8 fr. In its ponds fish-culture, particularly trout, is carried on by Dr. Vouga, Prof. of Nat. Hist. at Neuchâtel.

Longer excursions may be made to the *Chasseral* (Rte. 48) and the *Creux du Vent* (Rte. 51A).

The principal produce of the canton is *wine*; the best sorts resemble *ordinaire* Burgundy. The red wines of Cortaillod and Derrière Moulins, and the white grown between Auvernier and St. Blaise, are most in repute; they are agreeable as sparkling wines.

The chief *manufacture* is that of watches and clocks, of which nearly a million are exported annually : the central seats of it may be said to be the valley of Chaux de Fonds and Locle (Rte. 50) ; but much is done in the town of Neuchâtel, in Sonvillier, Sonceboz, and the large villages of the Val St. Imier; Sonvillier making 60,000 watches yearly, and St. Imier a still larger number. Most of the watches sold at Geneva are made in the canton of Neuchâtel; the dealers at Geneva contracting for all the good ones, and leaving the bad.

Railways to Locle and Chaux de Fonds;—to Paris, by Pontarlier and Dijon (Rte. 51A) (this is the most direct and the shortest route from Paris to Western Switzerland);—to Yverdon, Lausanne, and Geneva;—to Bienne, Bâle, and Lucerne;—to Berne and Thun. By these lines Neuchâtel is brought into easy and rapid communication with all the principal places in Switzerland. The station is about 200 ft. above the town.

Steamers twice a day to Morat in 1¾ hr., passing through a canal which connects the two lakes; also to Estavayer, a small town opposite Neuchâtel.

ROUTE 49.

NEUCHÂTEL TO YVERDON AND LAUSANNE.—RAILWAY.

Neuchâtel to Yverdon, 23 m. Rly. 1¼ h.

Yverdon to Lausanne, 26½ m. Rly. 1¼ hr.

The *Swiss Western Railway*. At first the line runs side by side with that to Pontarlier ; about a mile from Neuchâtel it crosses the glen of Serrières by a lofty viaduct. At the bottom of the gorge runs the road, over a handsome stone bridge built by Marshal Berthier. Near it is a little hamlet, composed of watermills, turned by a remarkable stream, rising in the head of the dell and falling into the lake, after a course of not more than half a mile. Though it remains, as it were, but a few minutes above ground, it rises in sufficient force and volume to turn a wheel within 200 yards of its source, and subsequently sets in motion several others, both above and below the bridge. It is fed from reservoirs within the mountain, and is probably to be identified with some of those singular streams which bury themselves in various places in caverns of the Jura.

The rly. descends towards

Auvernier Junct. Stat., where that to Pontarlier turns rt. Our line also quits the lake to rejoin it beyond Bevaix.

[About 1 m. farther is *Columbier*, once the seat of the Scotch Marshal Keith, the friend and general. of Frederick the Great ; he was governor of Neuchâtel. *Cortaillod*, by the water-side, produces one of the best red wines in the canton. The village Boudri, on the Reuse, was the birthplace (1764) of the demagogue *Marat*.]

Bevaix Stat.

Gorgier St. Aubin Stat. From this the ascent of the *Creux du Vent* (Rte. 51A) may be made in 2 hrs. Rt. of the next station is the well-preserved castle of *Vaumarcus*, beyond which the Canton de Vaud is entered.

Rly. crosses part of the lake on an embankment.

Concise Stat. (*Inn*: Écu de France). More than 800 stone axes, chisels, and other tools were dredged up from the lake near this in 1861.

Near *Corcelles* at the roadside rt. stand 3 upright blocks of granite, 8 to 10 ft. high, by some supposed to have been raised by the Swiss as a memorial of the victory of Grandson, but more probably of Druidic origin.

Grandson Stat. (*Inn*: Lion d'Or), a town of 1740 Inhabitants. The rly. passes through the enclosure of the venerable *Castle*, formerly seat of the barons of Grandson, now a cigar-factory. It is historically remarkable for having, before the first of three great battles, in which Charles of Burgundy suffered defeat at the hands of the Swiss, resisted for 10 days the assaults and artillery of the Burgundian army. When at length the garrison, reduced by famine and invited by the offer of free pardon, by a spy or deserter who had entered the castle by stealth, surrendered it, Charles caused them to be stripped and hung by hundreds on the surrounding trees, and as many more to be drowned in the lake. But two days afterwards, on the 3rd of March, 1476, he experienced the vengeance of the Swiss, in the memorable defeat of his army, 50,000 strong, by the confederates, who amounted to not much more than ⅓ of that number. He himself was compelled to fly for his life across the mountains, with only 5 followers. The spoil of his camp, which fell into the hands of the victors, included 120 pieces of cannon, 600 standards, all his jewels and regalia, costly hangings, and military chest; on that day gold and diamonds were dealt out by handfuls. The scene of the battle, marked by 3 rude pillars of granite, lay between Concise and Corcelles; but the final rout of the Burgundians was at the little river between the battlefield and Grandson.

The *Church* of Grandson, of the 10th or 11th centy., is very remarkable. The prior's stall of wood is worth notice. Farel preached the reformed doctrines from its pulpit. There is a path over the hills from Grandson to Motiers Travers.

The rly. skirts the lake and crosses the Thièle.

Yverdun Junct.— Ger. *Ifferten*— (*Inns*: H. de Londres ; Paon), a town of 6000 Inhab., at the S.W. extremity of the lake of Neuchâtel, at the spot where the Thièle falls into it. It is built upon the site of the Roman *Eburodunum*, whose name, with a little change, it still inherits.

The *Castle*, built in the 12th century by Conrad of Zähringen, is in the middle of the town, and is modernised and uninteresting. It became the school-house and residence of *Pestalozzi*, from 1805 to 1825. Although the founder of a system of education, and of many schools both in Europe and America, he was a very bad practical schoolmaster himself; and this establishment, the head-quarters as it were of his system, turned out a failure.

There are some pretty promenades by the side of the lake, and the town is picturesque.

A very delightful excursion may be made to the *Lac de Joux* (Rte. 52).

Diligence over the Jura to *Ste. Croix*, noted for the manufacture of musical boxes (50,000 in a year).

[Branch line to Payerne and Fribourg, 30 miles. The line follows the shore of the lake as far as *Estavayer* (12 miles), an ancient town, with a castle (steamer to Neuchâtel). The line now runs across a fruitful portion of the Swiss lowlands to Payerne Junction (Rte. 46) and Fribourg (Rte. 45).]

From Yverdon the rly. proceeds through a fertile and thriving country, along the valley of the Thièle, with fine views of the Jura range, and often a view of snow-peaks S. and E. Before coming to *Chavornay Stat.* the castle of *Champmont* will be observed on the rt. Soon after this the line passes by two short tunnels through the low range of hills which separates the valley of the Thièle, or Orbe, from that of the *Venoge.*

Cossonay Junct. H. du Grand Moulin, close to the stat. Here the line from Pontarlier (Rte. 51A) falls in. The ch. is prettily situated on a height. The rly. passes through a fine country to

Bussigny Junct. Stat., whence one branch goes to Morges and Geneva (Rte. 53), the other through some green and pleasant valleys, without any extensive view, to

LAUSANNE JUNCT. STAT. (Rte. 55).

ROUTE 50.

NEUCHÂTEL TO CHAUX DE FONDS AND LE LOCLE.

24 m. *Railway* by La Chaux de Fonds to Le Locle in about 2 hrs.

Neuchâtel is described in Rte. 4.

[The high-road to Chaux de Fonds runs directly through the profound chasm of the Seyon (Rte. 48).

Vallengin (*Inn:* Couronne) is the principal place in the fertile Val de Ruz. Its *Castle* (now a prison) is in part as old as the 12th century : its base is washed by the Seyon. The *Church*, a perfectly regular Gothic structure, was built by a Count of Vallengin, on his return from the crusades, in consequence of a vow made to the Virgin in a storm at sea that he would build a church upon the water; accordingly the stream of the valley is conducted under the building.

A steep and long ascent up the Tête de Rang leads to Hauts Geneveys.]

On quitting Neuchâtel Stat. the railway commands fine views l. of the Alps. It crosses the Seyon and near the two viaducts over the valley of Serrières penetrates a tunnel 1850 ft. long. Fine Alpine view on emerging.

Corcelles Stat., 2 short tunnels.

Chambrelieu Stat. See from it the line to Pontarlier (Rte. 51), nearly 1000 ft. below. The direction of the line is now reversed from S.W. to N., passing over the 2 small tunnels just mentioned.

Hauts Geneveys Stat. (Hôtel Renaud), 2944 ft. above the sea, the summit-level of the line.

Rt. grand view of Mont Blanc. The tunnel of Hauts Geneveys is 3259 mètres in length. It passes under the *Col des Loges*, which the high-road surmounts; close to it is

Convers Junct. Stat. [The rly. here joins a line from Bienne to Chaux de Fonds, by Sonceboz, Rte. 1.] Another tunnel between Convers and

La Chaux de Fonds Stat. (*Inns :* Fleur de Lys, good; Lion d'Or; H. National) a town of no less than 22,400 Inhab., but in a bleak and desolate valley, bare of wood and nearly destitute of water. From its great elevation, 3274 ft. above the sea, it is capable of producing only a scanty crop of oats. La Chaux de Fonds covers an area not less than that of the city of Oxford, each cottage being an isolated cube, surrounded by a croft or garden half an acre or an acre in extent; it was, however, burnt in 1794. Its inhabitants are reputed to be very rich. It is the chief seat of the manufacture of clocks and watches. This is not carried on in large factories, but in the separate dwellings of the workmen. Each man usually makes only one particular piece of machinery, leaving even the finishing of it to others. The number of persons here and at Locle, and in the neighbouring district, engaged in different branches of watchmaking is about 12,000; the wages vary from 2½ fr. to 10 fr. a day. 800,000 gold and silver watches, valued at 35 millions of francs, are now made yearly in Canton Neuchâtel. In 1774 the total number was 300. There are two *subterranean mills* here, turned by the stream of the valley previous to its sinking underground; the rocks have been blasted to afford space for the mills; but those at Locle are even more curious. *Diligences* to Porentruy;—to Sonceboz, by the Val St. Imier.

The *Doubs* (N. of Chaux de Fonds and Locle), which separates Switzerland from France, traverses one of those singular fissures common in the Jura limestone, and descends in a fall (*le Saut du Doubs*) 80 ft. high. Above the fall the river, dammed up by rocks, spreads out into a sort of lake called *Lac des Brenets* (H. du Saut du Doubs); below, for the space of nearly 6 m., it runs between rocks 800 or 1000 ft. high, presenting to the pedestrian both here and lower down, as far as Goumois and St. Ursanne, many scenes of beauty and interest, rendered accessible by paths made by the French Alpine Club.

The Rly. makes another bend to reach

Le Locle Stat. (*Inns:* H. du Jura; Trois Rois), another scattered village, 5 m. from Chaux de Fonds, occupied by an industrious population of 10,464 souls; the men chiefly watchmakers, the women lacemakers; rebuilt since a fire which consumed it in 1833.

The little stream of the *Bied*, which traverses the valley, loses itself, at a short distance from Locle, in a rocky chasm. This outlet, however, proved insufficient to drain the valley; and the district around the town was inundated at the season of the melting of the snows—and not much better than a morass at any time. To remedy this evil, a tunnel, 950 ft. long, was pierced through the screen of solid limestone which encompasses the valley, in 1802-6, and this now effectually carries off into the Doubs the previously stagnant waters. At *Le Cul des Roches*, a short distance from this artificial drain, and about a mile W. of Locle, the river disappears in a natural opening, sinking into the heart of the mountain, through a vertical abyss, more than 100 ft. deep. This water-power is rendered available by wheels constructed within the cavernous cleft, and the powerful machinery, impelled by the falling stream, moves a corn and saw mill.

"You go down flights of broken and slippery stairs, cut in the rock, to these mills, placed one under another, in very frightful situations undoubtedly, but rendered more so to the imagination of the beholder from the circumstances of darkness and ignorance of the means by which the works are secured, by the noise, the unfathomable depth below, &c."—*Simond*.

An excursion to *Saut du Doubs*, a waterfall 80 ft. high, 4½ m. N.W. of Locle, can be made in two ways. 1. A pretty char-road leads N.W. from La Chaux de Fonds to Les Planchettes; thence S.W. to Moron in ½ hr., and to the Saut ¾ hr., along the bank of the river, returning by Les Brenets and Le Locle. 2. A good carriage-road goes from La Chaux de Fonds to Le Locle, thence to the mill of Le Cul des Roches, *La Roche Fendue*, and the pretty village of the Brenets.

A special festival, called the *Fête du Saut du Doubs*, is celebrated on the first Sunday of the month of July, and draws thither sometimes 100 boats with music and feasting.

La Roche Fendue is an aperture bored in the rock, dividing Switzerland from France, commenced 1779, and only finished 1868, by which the road to Besançon is shortened by 6 m.: it opens a singular view over the Val de Doubs.

There is another road from Locle to Neuchâtel, by Chaux du Milieu, Les Ponts, then E. by the heights of La Tourne, and Corcelles.

ROUTE 51A.

PONTARLIER (IN FRANCE) TO NEUCHÂTEL, BY RAIL.

About 32 Eng. m. *Railway* (Franco-Suisse) opening direct communication between Paris and W. Switzerland. It passes through scenery of great interest, and is a pleasant way of reaching Switzerland. Seats on the rt. side of the carriage are best. Those who are going to Lausanne or

Geneva can take the direct line (Rte. 51 B).

Pontarlier (*Inns:* Poste; National; Croix Blanche), the last town in France, with the *douane*.

The Rail first ascends by the side of the river Doubs, which flows from the Lac de St. Point, about 4 m. S.W. It then turns E. through the pass of *La Cluse*, a mountain gateway fortified and capable of being closed. The defile is commanded (rt.) by a very elevated detached *Fort*, erected 1877, after the blowing up by dynamite of the old *Fort de Joux*, situated on the summit of a precipice, at the foot of which the old roads from Pontarlier and Salins, and those from Neuchâtel and Geneva, by Jougne, unite. The old fort was the prison of the unfortunate Toussaint l'Ouverture, when treacherously carried off from St. Domingo by command of Napoleon. He ended his days here, some say by violent means; but the sudden transition from the climate of the tropics to a dank dungeon on the heights of the Jura sufficiently explains the cause of his death, without the need of violence. Here also was confined, previously, another remarkable prisoner, *Mirabeau*, who was sent hither by virtue of a lettre de cachet obtained by his father, " l'Ami des Hommes," as he called himself, and the tyrant of his own family, as he proved himself. Mirabeau, having by his insinuating manners obtained leave from the governor to visit the town of Pontarlier on parole, made love to Madame de Monnier, the young wife of an old magistrate there, and eloped with her to Holland. She was the Sophie to whom he addressed some of his writings.

Here on Jan. 28–30, 1871, the army of Gen. Bourbaki, in the midst of snow and famine, made its last stand against the Germans. Then followed the Convention of Les Verrières, and the surrender of the whole body, some 84,000, to the Swiss.

Between the villages of *Verrières* [*Switz.*]

de Joux and *Verrières de Suisse*, the French frontier is crossed.

The country now becomes exceedingly romantic—the hills clothed with forests, the valleys carpeted with the richest grass, and sprinkled with neat cottages in the picturesque style of architecture peculiar to the Jura. Cheese, nearly as good as Gruyères, and sold under that name, is made on the upland pastures.

The descent from the summit of the ridge, 3060 ft., into the *Val de Travers* is through another narrow gorge, called *La Chaine*, because the passage was at one time stopped by a massy chain drawn across the road, and fastened to staples in the rock. This primitive fortification is said to have been a relic of the Burgundian wars, intended to arrest the artillery of Charles the Bold. The Val de Travers is celebrated for its *absinthe*. The wormwood and hyssop yearly collected amount to 100,000 lbs., of the value of 50,000 fr., and their distillation produces 370,000 litres of *absinthe*, which make 63,000 packages.

At the village of *St. Sulpice* the river Reuse, which waters the Val de Travers, rises out of the rock. This abundant source is said to be the outlet of the Lac des Tallières, situated about 5 miles N., among the hills. Several tunnels and viaducts are passed before reaching

Fleurier (*Inn:* Couronne, good) (2600 Inhab.), built on both sides of the Reuse, thrives by the manufacture of watches.

Boveresse Stat.

Couvet Stat. Omnibus to Motiers. *Diligence* daily to Le Locle by Les Ponts. Distilleries of Kirschwasser. At Presta, on the l. bank of the river, is a mine of asphalte worked by an English company. Stratum 12 ft. thick. Now used in London for paving.

Travers Stat. Far down, on the opposite side of the valley lies

Motiers Travers (*Inns:* Hôtel de Ville, good; Maison de Commune), a clean, thriving village inhabited by

M

watch and lace makers, in the meadows of the Reuse. It was the residence of *Rousseau* after his banishment from Geneva. In the house a desk is shown, at which he wrote his celebrated ' Lettres de la Montagne ;' and up-stairs, in a wooden gallery, two peeping-holes, through which he could observe people out of doors without being seen himself. He quitted the place under the pretence of persecution, and because the boys threw stones at his windows. Val de Travers, hemmed in by limestone precipices, is highly picturesque.

Noiraigue Stat. Near which is a remarkable cliff of tilted limestone. [From this the ascent of the *Creux du Vent* (S.), 4806 ft., may be made in 1 hr. ; descent to the lake of Neuchâtel by St. Aubin or Boudri. "Its summit is hollowed out into a vast and profound cavity, 1000 ft. deep, surrounded by an amphitheatre of limestone rock from the top to the bottom." It is more than 2 m. in circumference. " At times, when a change of weather is impending, the crater of the mountain is seen to become suddenly filled with a cloud of white vapour, working and rising and falling with an easy but perceptible motion, until the whole hollow presents the appearance of an immense caldron of boiling vapour, which seldom rises above the edge. If any escape, it is by the opening towards the defile ; and I have seen it repeatedly issue in a thin white line, and float gradually down the centre of the valley till imperceptibly diminished and dissipated."—*Latrobe.*

The echo produced by firing a gun within the Creux du Vent is like a scattered fire of musketry, or a succession of discharges from a battery; and the hollow may be called the very cradle of the winds, which appear to be perpetually blowing from it.]

The view now opens of the Lake of Neuchâtel, rt. ; far below is seen the viaduct of the Yverdon Railway, while high up overhead is the Stat.

of Chambrelieu of the Chaux de Fonds Rly.

Auvernier Junct. Stat., above the towns of Auvernier and Colombier. Here we meet the Neuchâtel and Yverdon line (Rte. 49); fine views of the Lake and Alps. Gradual ascent to the lofty *viaduct* over the gorge of Serrières. Above the gorge the Castle Beauregard is seen.

NEUCHÂTEL JUNCT. STAT. and Terminus (Rte. 48).

ROUTE 51B.

PONTARLIER TO LAUSANNE.—RAILWAY.

This line, opened in 1875, affords a very pleasant mode of reaching Switzerland.

From Pontarlier (2850 ft.), the line passes through the defile of Joux, along the line to Neuchâtel (Rte. 51A), turning off before *Frambourg Stat.* It then ascends through a mountain valley, well-wooded, and containing many water-mills. Here is the summit-level, 3406 ft., but there is no tunnel until after *Jougne Stat.* On emerging there is a fine view to the l. into a green and populous valley. Soon after this, the Swiss frontier is passed, and there is a remarkable descent to

Vallorbes Stat. (H. de Genève, close to the stat. ; Maison de Ville, recommended), a small town of watchmakers. Here is the Swiss custom-house.

The train backs out of the stat. and crosses a remarkable iron bridge over a deep ravine. This and the remaining part of the road are very fine.

Romainmotier Stat., in a level spot. The village is in a hollow. The ch. is one of the oldest and most interesting in Switzerland. It was built A.D. 753, and, despite some additions, retains it primitive character.

Beyond this the ranges of the snowy Alps may be seen in clear weather.

Orbe Stat. (Maison de Ville. Guillaume Tell), a very picturesque and ancient town of 1884 Inhab., built on a hill nearly insulated by the Orbe, which is crossed by 3 bridges. The lower bridge, on the road to the Vallée de Joux, is of great antiquity; the upper and modern one, of a single arch, 124 ft. span, is in use at present. Orbe was the Roman station *Urbigenum*, and a place of importance in the middle ages, under the Burgundian Kings, who had a *Royal Castle* here. The fair but cruel Brunhilda, Queen of the Franks, took refuge here, with her granddaughter, but was carried a prisoner to Worms, and there barbarously put to death. The three sons of Lothaire I. met here, in 855, to divide his kingdom. In 1475 the Swiss took Orbe by assault; but the *Castle* made a lengthened resistance. The garrison, yielding step by step, disputed the possession of each chamber, stair, and passage. The last remnant were pursued into a tower, to which the Swiss set fire, and the few who fell into their hands alive were thrown over the battlements. The site of the castle now forms the public promenade, whence in clear weather there is a view over the valleys of the Orbe and Nozon to the Bernese Alps. Two towers of the castle are still standing.

[About 2 m. above Orbe, near Montcherand, is a cascade of the Orbe; and 1 m. N.W. *Valleyres*, the summer residence of the Count and Countess Agénor de Gasparin. From Valeyres and Baulme a winding path, called *La Covatane*, leads through a rocky cleft to the valley of Ste. Croix, a nest of industrious watchmakers living at a height of 3000 ft. in a severe climate. A carriage-road winds along the N. side of the gorge, and crosses a ridge to the Val de Travers.]

From Orbe the rly. makes many sharp curves, and then passes through a very pretty valley to

Cossonay Junct. Stat. (H. du Grand Moulin, close to stat.). Hence to *Lausanne*, in Rte. 49.

ROUTE 52.

VALLORBES TO THE LAC DE JOUX.

This is an exceedingly pretty excursion, well worth taking by those who wish to see the best Jura scenery, and may be easily made from

Vallorbes Stat., Rte. 51B.

From Vallorbes to Le Pont ($4\frac{1}{2}$ m.) there is a good road on the N. slope of the Dent de Vaulion.

A path to the rt., about $1\frac{1}{4}$ m. from Vallorbes, leads in a mile to the *Source of the Orbe*, which comes out of a limestone rock at once a copious spring, and is no doubt the stream from the Lac de Joux. Near it is a cavern, *Grotte des Fées.*

3 m. from Vallorbes is the col (3350 ft.), whence the Dent de Vaulion (see below) may be ascended. From the col the road descends to

Le Pont (Inn: H. de la Truite, tolerable), a village, named from a bridge across the channel which connects the *Lac de Joux* with the small *Lac Brenet*. It is very prettily situated at the N. end of the Lac de Joux, and looks like an English village, with its neat roads, good houses, and green fields. There are guides, but only one or two horses, and no side-saddles. Care should be taken in walking amongst these mountains to avoid clefts in the limestone, but more particularly old wells dug for the flocks, and imperfectly covered. An unfortunate English gentleman, named Herbert, was drowned in one near the chalets of the Mont Tendre in 1837, and is buried at Mont Richer.

The *Vallée de Joux* contains another small lake, *Le Ter*, but is entirely shut in by high hills; so that these sheets of water have no visible outlet. There are, however, cavities in the beds of the lakes, called *entonnoirs*, through which the waters escape. These fissures are sometimes incapable of carrying them off, and thus inundations are caused in the valley. A tunnel, of no very great extent, migth drain the lake entirely.

M 2

The *Lac de Joux* is 3310 ft. above the sea, and at the feet of two of the highest summits of the Jura,—the *Mont Tendre*, on the S., 5512 ft., the *Dent de Vaulion*, on the E., 4877 ft. Its quiet aspect, surrounded by limestone cliffs, and woods of beech and fir, would, if it were more in the highway, make it a popular resort. There are several pleasant excursions.

a. To ascend the *Dent de Vaulion*, the summit of which is not visible from Le Pont, go along the high road towards Vallorbe for about a mile, until it opens into a little valley. Cross the meadow or marsh, and begin to ascend through the woods N.E. After a short walk through the wood the path follows a depression of greensward, between fir-trees and beeches. Beyond this there is no regular path, but you should continue to ascend, and the top will be reached in an hour's good walking from Le Pont. A guide is not absolutely necessary, but without one you will probably lose time. The N.W. side is a sheer limestone precipice of some 1500 ft., looking down into the green valley of the Orbe. N. is seen the range of the Jura, E. the Bernese Alps, S. the chain of the Pennine Alps to Mont Blanc ; the rest is concealed by the Mont Tendre. S.W. the lake and valley of Joux. There is a path to Vaulion on the S., and thence to Romainmotier Stat.

b. About 10 min. from the village of *l'Abbaye*, on the lake, 2 m. from Le Pont, by climbing up a steep and picturesque ravine, out of which a fine stream issues, a cavern, called *Chaudière d'Enfer*, will be found, into which, by crawling and using a rope, you can penetrate about 200 yds. to a little lake or pool. There are other unexplored recesses in the cavern. Guide at the inn, 2 fr.

c. Another ascent is to the *Mont Tendre*, 5512 ft. The path to it goes up on the l. bank of the ravine, behind l'Abbaye ; and the ascent occupies 3 hrs. from Le Pont. The view extends to Mont Blanc on the one side, and to Soleure on the other. There is a path down the opposite side, leading, in 2 hrs., to the village of Montricher.

d. Instead of returning to Vallorbes, there is a very pretty drive through country like an English park, by Vaulion—a village of shoe-makers—to Romainmotier Stat.

e. Or the excursion may be prolonged by either shore of the Lac de Joux to *Le Brassus*, a thriving town of watchmakers, and thence to *Les Rousses*, on the old post-road to Geneva, descending from which place there is a very fine view of the Alps.

f. Another route is to cross from Le Brassus by the *Asile de Marcheiruz* to the village of St. Georges, 3 hrs.' walk ; whence the *glacière*, or *Ice-cave of St. Georges*, is 1¼ hr.'s walk W. From St. Georges it is 3 leagues by a good road to Rolle, on the Lake of Geneva (Rte. 55).

ROUTE 53.

LYONS, OR MÂCON, TO GENEVA.— RAILWAY.

From Mâcon to Geneva, 114 m.; 2 trains daily, in 7 hrs., and the express in 4 hrs. 35 min. From Lyons, 100 m., 3 trains daily, in about 6 hrs., and the express in 4. The two lines join at the

Ambérieux Junct. Stat., 28 m. from Lyons, 42 m. from Mâcon. There are two express trains each way daily.

From Ambérieux the rly. ascends the rocky valley of the little river Serrant, making considerable curves, to

Tenay Stat., beautifully situated at the junction of three valleys. Soon after this the road passes between lofty cliffs and by a series of little lakes,

Rossilon Stat. Here the summit-level is reached, and the road, after passing a tunnel, begins to descend towards the Rhone. There is a fine view of distant Alps. The traveller passes under the *Grand Colombier,* 4733 ft., to

Culoz Junct. Stat., with good *buffet* (*Inns :* Croix Blanche ; Union). Here the line to Aix les Bains, Mt. Cenis, and Turin (Rte. 153) branches off. The rly. to Geneva henceforward keeps close to the Rhone, leaving it only at one point in order to cut off an angle.

Seyssel Stat., on the Rhone.

Pyrimont Stat. 1 m. hence is the *Malpertuis* ("pertuis" means a gorge), an abyss even more imposing than the Perte du Rhône. The river quietly flows at a depth of 600 ft. between walls of rock, sometimes not more than 14 ft. apart.

Bellegarde Stat., with the French *Douane.* (*Inns :* Poste ; Perte du Rhône.) This frontier town has doubled its pop. within the last 3 years, since the development of the important works of the Bellegarde Company. 10 min. walk from stat. is the *Perte du Rhone.* (See Geneva, excursion *f.*) In the gorge the Rhone is joined by the *Valserine,* which the rly. crosses on a viaduct ; far below are the old road and bridge. The rail next passes through the *Crédo Tunnel,* 2½ m. long, under the *Crédo,* 5328 ft., a mountain terminating the main chain of the Jura on the S. Beyond are the extensive fortifications of the *Fort de l'Ecluse,* overhanging the road. (See Geneva, excursion *f.*)

Collonges Stat. Here the bridge of the line to Evian is seen on the rt. (Rte. 57). This station is in a pass between rt. the *Vouache,* and l. the *Crédo,* which was fortified by Julius Cæsar.

The Swiss territory is entered a little beyond *Challex,* 7 m. from

Geneva Terminus, at the upper end of Rue du Mt. Blanc, a street leading to the lake and bridge.

GENEVA. (*Fr.* Genève ; *Germ.* Genf ; *Ital.* Ginevra ; from the Celtic, *Gen,* outlet, *ev,* river.) *Hotels* on the N. side of the Rhone : H. National, furthest from the town ; H. Beau Rivage—both first rate ; H. des Ber-

gues ; H. de la Paix ; H. d'Angleterre, H. and P. Richemont, all first class, on the quay ; H. de Russie ; on the S. side : H. Métropole, good ; well managed ; H. de la Poste ; Ecu de Genève ; H. de Lac. Second-class houses are : Schweizerhof and H. de la Monnaie, near the station ; Victoria, comfortable ; de Genève ; both in Rue du Mt. Blanc ; Balance, Rue du Rhone. Among the numerous *pensions,* Picard's, 2 Place Métropole ; Flœgel's, near the Salle de la Reformation ; P. d'Etrangers, No. 9 Quai du Mt. Blanc. Jacquemot, Rue du Lévrier, Reynold's, 22 Boulevard St. Gervais, P. Hägel ; are recommended. *Restaurants,* La Bourse, Rue de Stand ; Oder, Rue du Rhone.

Cafés : du Nord (also restaurant), on the Grand Quai du Lac, one of the best in Switzerland ; La Poste.

The *Post Office* is a handsome edifice near the Pont de la Coulouvrenière on the Place or Quai de la Poste. *Telegraph Office* on the first floor.

The principal Genevese Club is called the *Cercle de la Terrasse.* There are others called cercles.

British Consul resides here. The American (U.S.A.) Consul, has his office at 2 Rue des Paquis.

Railways : to Paris by Mâcon, expr. in 12 hrs. ; to Lyons ; to Lausanne ; to Berne ; to Brieg, on the Simplon Route ; to Neuchâtel ; to Aix-les-Bains, Chambéry, and Mont Cenis ; to Annecy.

Steamboats several times a day along the N. shore of the lake to Ouchy (Lausanne) and Villeneuve in 4 to 4½ hrs. Also along the S. shore in connexion with the Simplon Rly. at Bouveret in 5½ hrs. ; with 2 additional boats to Evian-les-Bains and Ouchy. Some steamers start from the N. shore, some from the S., and the traveller should ascertain which he is going by. Omnibuses, affording a good view of the country, daily at 10 and 11 A.M. and at 1.30 P.M. from the Grand Quai and Place du Rhone, for *Chamonix,* making the journey in 8 or 9 hrs. For *Sixt* at 10 A.M. and 1.30 P.M.; for *Thonon* 7 and 11 A.M.

Voituriers charge for a carriage with one horse 15 fr., with two horses 30 fr. for the day. 2-horse carriages to Chamonix at the same price per head as the post. *Fiacres*, holding 4, 2½ fr. the hour, 1½ fr. the course. When the driver has S. G. on his cap, 50 cents. the ¼ hr., within the town.

There are good shops in the Rue de la Corraterie. Bordier, in the Rues Basses, for English cutlery and household goods. Mrs. Lang, 8, Rue du Mt. Blanc, for " articles anglais " and needlework. "Old England," 9, Fusterie, Tailors, Drapers, and General Outfitters; English goods only. Les Sœurs Schneider, 16 Corraterie, for ladies' shoes; gloves. Mercier Au gant gris, 18 Corraterie. Wistaz, 6, Rue Cornevin, for cigars, tobacco, and snuff. Bastard, Rue des Allemands, is a good chemist.

G. Baker, Place des Bergues, keeps an English pharmacy.

Booksellers : Georg, 10, Corraterie, has a store of old works on the Alps; sells Swiss Government maps: Monroe, Grand Quai. Sandoz, Rue du Rhone; Mueller, 2, Molard, books in all languages, guides, handbooks, maps, &c.

English resident Physician : Dr. Williams, M.R.C.P., London, 1, Place du Lac.

Dr. Lombard is an experienced physician, studied at Edinburgh. Dr. Spiess, an accomplished physician, speaks English. 4, Cours des Bastions, Dr. Binet, Corraterie, 4, Haltenhoff, 20, Corraterie, is a first-rate oculist; and Colladon, Quai des Bergues, an aurist, studied in London.

A very reprehensible system has been established at some of the hotels, of appointing a Genevese medical practitioner on the staff of the hotel. Whenever "the English doctor" is asked for, some excuse is made for not sending for him, and the hotel doctor is recommended to be called in. British and American travellers should insist on having the doctor they select sent for, and not submit to this attempt at imposition.

Geneva is a handsome city, and is finely situated, but it contains very few remarkable buildings.

A *walk through Geneva* from the Rly. Stat. and back. To the Quai du Mont Blanc and the Bridge of Mt. Blanc, a good point of view to see the lake and Mont Blanc. Across the bridge to the National Monument, commemorating Geneva's reception into the Swiss confederation in 1814, and to the Jardin Anglais ; Palais de Justice, Place du Bourg de Four; Athénée; Botanical Garden; University Buildings, &c.; Public Library; Collections of Antiquities and Natural History ; Musée Rath; Promenade de la Treille ; Cathedral ; House of Calvin, 11, Rue des Chanoines, House of J. J. Rousseau, 40, Grande Rue; H. de Ville; Musée Historique Genevois, opposite ; Fountain of the Escalade (see History; at end of Rue des Allemands; over the Bridge des Bergues, visiting Rousseau's Island, to Rue du Mont Blanc, leading to the station. Duke of Brunswick's monument, Place des Alpes. Barracks and arsenal, Plainpalais ; École de Medicine, Plainpalais ; École de Chimie, Boulevard des Philosophes ; École des Arts Industrielles, Boulevard St. Gervais ; Ecole d'Horologie, Terraux du Temple.

Geneva, though the capital of the smallest of the Swiss cantons, except Zug, is the most populous town in the Confederation, since the city alone contains 50,000 Inhab., the majority Protestants. It is well situated, at the W. extremity of the lake of Geneva, where " the blue waters of the arrowy Rhone" issue out of it. The river divides the town into two parts; the old part on the rt. bank being called Quartier St. Gervais. The intensely blue colour of the waters of the Rhone, alluded to by Byron, is very remarkable, and resembles no-

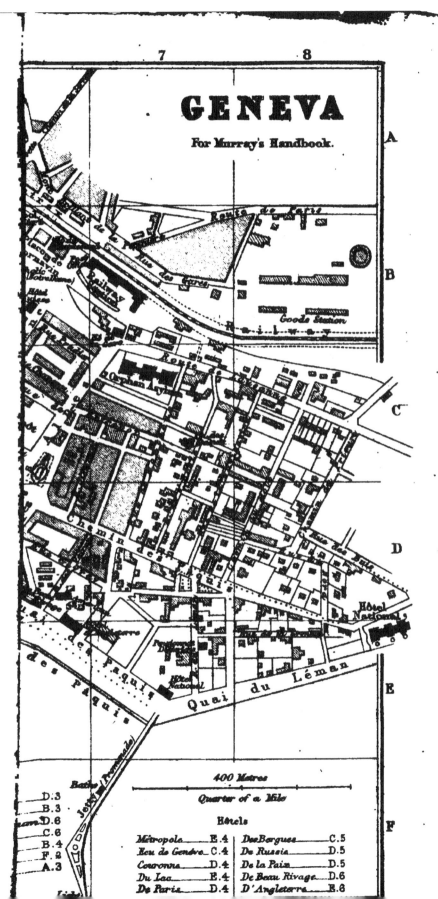

GENEVA

For Murray's Handbook.

400 Metres

Quarter of a Mile

Hôtels

Métropole	E.4	Des Bergues	C.5
Ecu de Genève	C.4	De Russie	D.5
Couronne	D.4	De la Paix	D.5
Du Lac	E.4	De Beau Rivage	D.6
De Paris	D.4	D'Angleterre	E.6

D.3
B.3
D.6
C.6
B.4
F.2
A.3

]
]
g
]
]
f
6
a
n

a

h
A
N
d
in
m

lir
du

ph
Spi
spe
Dr.
20,
and
aur

A
bee
hot
mec
the
doc
mac

thing so much as the discharge of indigo from a dyer's vat. The cause of it has not been satisfactorily explained. The extreme purity lasts but for a short space, since a mile below the town it is altered by the admixture of the waters of the turbid Arve.

Geneva, when seen from the lake, presents a very imposing appearance, in consequence of improvements, made since 1830, and continued since 1848 with great activity, for which it is indebted, in no slight degree, to the circulation of the gold of English travellers. Several new quarters have started up, displaying handsome fronts of tall houses, lined with broad quays towards the lake. The Quai du Mont Blanc is a continuation of Quai des Bergues, and forms a row of magnificent buildings. On the S. shore the unsightly houses which lined it have been refaced and beautified, while a broad belt of land has been gained and converted into a Garden and a line of Quais. Piers have been thrown out to form a harbour, and three handsome *Bridges* have been constructed. The longest of these, completed 1863, leads from the Quai du Mont Blanc to the Grand Quai and English Garden on the S. side. Another is united with a small island, formerly a part of the fortifications, on which is a very inferior statue of Rousseau, by *Pradier*. Pont de la Coulouvrenière, between the Boulevards Plainpalais and St. Gervais. Since 1848 the fortifications have been razed, those near the Porte de Rive partly thrown into the lake, so as to form the Quai des Eaux Vives, occupied by streets and houses.

Geneva was formerly divided into the upper and lower town; and this distinction, arising from the uneven nature of the ground, was perpetuated in the rank and condition of the inhabitants of the two divisions. The upper town consisted almost entirely of the large and handsome mansions of the burgher aristocracy, heretofore the senators and magistrates of the republic, between whom and the inhabitants of the lower town, consisting of shopkeepers, a strong social line was drawn. The Quartier de St. Gervais is the abode of the workmen, the seat of democracy after the French pattern—the Belleville of Geneva :— its streets are narrow, its houses lofty, and it has something of the air of the old town of Edinburgh.

The feuds arising between the high and low town would fill a long and amusing historical chapter: they often led to bloodshed; but the democrats below generally brought their exalted neighbours to reason by the simple expedient of cutting off the water-pipes, taking especial care to guard the Hydraulic Machine which furnished the supply to the upper town, and which is situated in their quarter. The disputes are now between the upper town and St. Gervais, the lower town siding sometimes with one, sometimes with the other.

On the island, in the middle of the Rhone, not far from the Hydraulic Machine, traces may, it is said, be discovered in the Tour de l'Ile of a Roman structure, supposed to be the foundations of one of the *towers* erected by Julius Cæsar, to prevent the Helvetians crossing the river. The earliest mention of Geneva occurs in his 'Commentaries,' where it is described as " the last fortress of the Allobroges, and nearest to the Helvetian frontier."

The *Cathedral*, or *Ch. of St. Pierre*, is of an extreme simplicity of architecture. Its fine Corinthian portico added on the outside is a blemish where it is placed, but the interior of the building possesses interest as a very early and uncorrupted specimen of the Gothic of the 11th century. The columns of the nave are clustered, and have grotesque capitals. In the apse at the E. end are three tiers of painted windows. The tower is of the 15th century. The church contains the monuments of Agrippa d'Aubigné, the friend of Henri IV., and grandfather of Mme. de Maintenon, and of the Duc Henri de Rohan, a leader of the French Protestants in the reign of Louis XIII., slain near Rheinfelden, 1638. A statue of plaster now replaces one of marble, ruthlessly destroyed at the French Revolution. The canopy of the pulpit is the same under which Calvin preached. During summer the organ, one of the finest in Switzerland, is played Mon., Wed., Sat., at 7.30 P.M. Ticket 1 fr.

A *Rom. Catholic Church* in the Gothic style has been built near the rly. stat.; and a synagogue (*Temple Juif*) in the Saracenic style near the Porte Neuve.

The *English Church*, near the Bergues Hotel.

The *American Episcopal Church*, stands behind the Hotels d'Angleterre and Beau Rivage.

Scotch Church Service in the Cathedral.

A *Greek Chapel* has been built in the Muscovite style, on the Tranchées.

The *Palais Électoral*, outside the Porte Neuve, is a fine building for elections, exhibitions, meetings, and festivals.

The *Musée Rath*, so named after its founder, General Rath, a native of Geneva, who acquired a large fortune in the Russian service, and who left the reversion of his fortune to found the Museum, is a building in the Greek style, close to the Porte Neuve, open Sun. and Thurs. from 11 to 3, other days, from 1 to 3; it contains a collection of pictures and other works of art, the greater part by native artists. The best are:—8. *Bassano*, Adoration of Shepherds. 11, 12. *Berghem*, Prodigal Son, and Abraham receiving Sarah. 21. *Caravaggio*, Four Singers. 48. *Helst*, Excellent portrait. 104. *Rubens*, Nymphs. 113. *Snyders*, Dog Saving a Heron. 134. *Wouvermans*, English Fleet burnt by De Witt. 18, 180, 183. *Calame*, Alps. *Diday*, *Hornung*, and *Töpfer* deserve to be mentioned. There is also a beautiful landscape (a lake) by *Thuiller*. A statue of the Greek captive girl by *J. Chaponnière*. A bronze statue of David by the same sculptor is an ornament to the promenade des Bastions opposite the Musée Rath.

The *New University*, in the Bastions and facing the Botanical Garden. In the rt. wing of this handsome building, is

The *Natural History Museum*, open to the public Sat. 1 to 3, Sun. 11 to 3. In it are the collections of botany and conchology, bequeathed by Delessert of Paris; the geology of Saussure, the fossil plants of MM. Brongniart and De Candolle, and those of M. Necker. Here also may be seen the native productions of Switzerland, specimens of the chamois, the bouquetin, and the fishes of the rivers and lakes; among them the *ferra*, the lotte, and a trout which weighed 43 lbs. from the lake of Geneva. Among the minerals is a cluster of smoked quartz, unequalled for size, from the Galenstock; there are also models of Lake Dwellings, and specimens of their contents.

In the basement is

The *Archæological Museum* (Cabinet d'Antiquités) (open Thursdays 1 to 4). It contains antiquities, some of them found in the neighbourhood, such as a silver buckler, with fine bas-reliefs, discovered in the bed of the Arve, inscribed "Largitas Valentiniani Augusti;" some instruments of sacrifice found near the rocks of Neptune in the lake; relics of the lacustrine habitations, amongst them a boat; seats have been in it, and the knobs against which the rowers rested their heels still exist. It has to be kept in a tank of water, to preserve it from crumbling to pieces.

In the left wing is the *Public Library*, open daily, except Sunday, 10 to 4; founded by Bonnivard (the Prisoner of Chillon), contains 73,000 volumes. *Curiosities:*—394 MS. letters of Calvin, almost illegible, but with fair transcripts (there is one addressed to Lady Jane Grey while a prisoner in the Tower); 44 vols. of his MS. sermons, 1549–60; 12 vols. of letters addressed to him, and many important documents relating to the Council of Bâle; several volumes of letters of Theodore Beza; the manuscript of the 'Noble Leçon,' a work of the ancient Waldenses; part of the account-book of the household of Philip le Bel, for 1308, written with a style upon waxed tablets, but now almost effaced ; a translation of Quintus Curtius, with beautiful illustrations, taken along with the baggage of Charles the Bold at Grandson ; Discourses of St. Augustine, a MS. on papyrus of the 7th century; Greek MS. of 4 Gospels (of 9th or 10th centy.), on vellum, with miniatures ; Marine Charts of Andrea Benincasa of Ancona, 1476 ; Letters of St. Vincent de Paul, J. J. Rousseau, &c.; French Bible, printed at Geneva, 1588 ; a Portrait of *Calvin*, said to be original, but of the signpost school.

Near the Museum is the *Pierre aux Dames* (see below), a curiously carved stone which stood near Troinex, 4 m. S. of Geneva.

The *Musée Fol*, in the Grande Rue, the gift of a Genevese gentleman, still living, has a large and valuable collection of antiquities, consisting of Etruscan pottery, gold ornaments, and other remains, besides objects of art, of the middle ages. Over the Musée Fol is

The *Société de Lecture*, with a Circulating Library of near 100,000 vols., and a large reading-room. Strangers are easily admitted to the latter.

The *Hall of the Reformation*, erected as a monument to Calvin, by private subscriptions amounting to 10,000*l.*, is set apart for educational and other meetings, lectures to working men, concerts, &c.

Museum of Fine Arts, the gift to the Society of Arts of Madame Eynard, called *Athenæum*, is a beautiful building near the Botanic Garden. It is the seat of the Soc. of Arts and of the Geographical Soc., and Soc. of "Physique et Histoire Naturel."

The *Palais de Justice*, where are all the Law Courts, formerly a convent, is in the Place du Bourg de Four. In it is a collection of Roman and early Christian inscriptions.

The *Monument* to the late Duke Charles of Brunswick, in the Jardin des Alpes, facing the lake, is a magnificent work ; it is surrounded by a garden with marble terraces and gigantic heraldic lions and sphinxes in red marble. The monument is a copy of one of the tombs of the Scaligers at Verona—the statues of the latter being replaced by those of the late Duke and of his immediate ancestors. The Duke died in 1873, leaving by will his fortune of 20,000,000 francs, 800,000*l.*, to the city of Geneva, on condition of this monument to him being erected in a conspicuous position, and giving the Scaliger monument as the model to be strictly followed.

The *Botanic Garden* behind the theatre, and near the Porte Neuve, deserves mention, as having been laid out under the direction of the eminent botanist De Candolle; but the funds are so limited that the collection of plants is of no great importance. The ground it occupies has also painful historical associations. This spot, in 1794, was the scene of horrible fusilades and butcheries.

The *Jardin Alpin d'Acclimatation*, 2, Chemin Daucet, Plainpalais, deserves a visit and the patronage of any travellers who desire to carry home healthy specimens of the Alpine flora. It has been founded by the ' Society for the Protection of Alpine Plants' to supply plants of the rarer species in vigorous health at low rates, and thus to counteract the impoverishment of the mountain flora, which has resulted during the last few years from reckless gathering by tourists, and wholesale uprooting for sale by professional plant-hunters, who have been known wilfully to destroy numbers of plants in order to increase the rarity and market value of their specimens.

Besides its connection with *Calvin* and *Rousseau*—the one by adoption, the other by birth—Geneva can boast of being the native place of many illustrious men, whose reputation may be styled European. The list includes *Isaac Casaubon, Estienne,* and *Scaliger; Lefort,* the friend and councillor of Peter the Great; *Necker,* the weak and ill-starred minister of Louis XVI., and father of Madame de Staël; the naturalists, *De Saussure* (who ascended Mont Blanc), *Bourrit, De Luc; Huber,* the biographer of the bee and ant; *De la Rive,* the chemist, and *De la Rive,* the physicist; *De Candolle,* the botanist; *Delolme* and *Mallet du Pan,* political writers; *Gallatin,* U.S.A.; *Rossi,* the Pope's minister, assassinated at Rome in 1849; *Dumont,* the friend and adviser of Mirabeau and Jeremy Bentham; *Necker,* the geologist; *Merle d'Aubigné* and *Sismondi,* the historians; *General Dufour,* the head of the Federal Staff during the execution of its magnificent survey; *Töpffer,* the writer. Among the living are *Alphonse de Candolle* and *Edmond Boissier,* botanists; *Plantamour,* astronomer; and *Raoul Pictet,* the Physicist.

Geneva may be regarded as the intellectual metropolis of Switzerland; and strangers who choose it as their residence, if provided with good introductions, will find, among the upper classes, a very agreeable society, including many individuals distinguished for their literary and scientific acquirements.

The staple manufacture of Geneva, from which it derives its chief commercial prosperity, is that of *watches, musical boxes,* and *jewellery.* The first watch was brought to Geneva in 1587, and at the end of the last century 4000 persons were employed within the town, and 2000 without the walls, on this manufacture. At present they are diminished to less than 3000, though, from improvements in the mechanical processes and increased skill of the workmen, the number of watches made is much greater than before, 100,000 being now manufactured annually. Upwards of 50 watchmakers' and 70 jewellers' workshops are kept in constant employment; and it has been calculated that in good years, 75,000 ounces of gold, 5000 marks of silver, and precious stones to the value of a million of francs, are used in them. A committee of master workmen with a syndic at their head, called *commission de surveillance,* is appointed by the government to inspect every workshop and the articles made in it, to guard against fraud in the substitution of metals not of legal alloy, and thus to prevent any deterioration in a branch of industry productive of so great an advantage to Geneva. There is a school for teaching watch-making. A good watch costs from 300 to 500 francs.

At the French custom-house, musical snuff-boxes, of Genevese manufacture, and watches pay a duty of only 5 fr. each.

A splendid *Theatre,* a diminished copy of the New Opera House at Paris, was erected 1879, alongside the Musée Rath, principally with some of the funds left by the Duke of Brunswick. Voltaire greatly shocked the prejudices of the citizens by acting plays, as it were under their very nose, at Les Délices and Fernex. Rousseau writes to him, "Je ne vous aime pas; vous avez corrompu ma république en lui donnant des spectacles." A *Conservatoire* de Musique, the gift of Bartaloni, the Paris banker, has also been erected near the same spot.

A *model of Mont Blanc,* the work of an artist named Séné, who employed 10 years upon it, is placed in a building erected for the purpose, in the Jardin Anglais. It is not equal to those of other parts of the Alps which embody the results of recent Ordnance Surveys.

On the Grand Quai du Lac, close to the place where the steamers land, a *Limnimètre* (lake measure) marks the rise and fall of the water, which amounts to 50 inches or more, and makes a very great difference in the appearance of the town.

In the *Cemetery* of *Plain-Palais,* a

little way beyond the Porte Neuve, rest the remains of *Sir Humphry Davy*, who died here in 1829, "I wish to be buried where I die, *natura curat suas reliquias*" (in his will), and near to him of *De Candolle*, the botanist, of *Dumont*, and *Pictet*, and of two English tourists who perished on the Col du Bonhomme in 1830. The site of Calvin's grave is marked by a plain slab, with the letters " J. C." carved on it, and is on the S.W. side of the cemetery, close to the pathway.

In the bed of the lake lie many granitic boulders, transported from the high Alps. Two of these, in the port of Geneva and a little to the S.E. of the Jardin Anglais, are so large as to project above the water. They are called *Pierres de Niton*, from a tradition that sacrifices were offered upon them to the god *Neptune* by the Romans. Indeed, instruments of sacrifice have been found near them.

History. Geneva is of Roman origin. In the middle ages up to 1530 it was governed by its bishop, with whom the citizens had many struggles. In 1401, the Counts of Savoy became powerful enough always to obtain the bishopric for one of their own family. One portion of the citizens, leagued together under the name of " Confederates," " Eidgenossen " (from which " Huguenot " is probably derived), after many struggles with the Counts or Dukes, in 1518 concluded an alliance with Fribourg and soon afterwards with Berne, and in 1530 compelled the Duke of Savoy to sign a treaty by which they regained their independence. After a sort of reign of terror Geneva was annexed to France in 1798. In 1815 it became a member of the Swiss Confederation, and the aristocratic government was re-established, but after many changes a democratic government supplanted it in 1846, every citizen having a vote. In 1846 the town had a balance in hand of 300,000 fr.; it is now largely in debt, and its accounts usually show an annual deficit. On the other hand, it should be said that many public improvements have been carried out under the new government.

Geneva may be said to possess a historical interest for intelligent travellers, far greater than that to be derived from the individual objects of curiosity contained within its walls. The influence which she has exercised, not only over Europe but over the world, by means of her children, or those whom she has adopted as her citizens, is quite out of proportion to the limited extent of a territory which one may traverse from end to end in a morning's ride. Voltaire ridiculed its diminutiveness by saying, " Quand je secoue ma perruque, je poudre toute la république ;" and the Emperor Paul called the disputes of its citizens a tempest in a tumbler of water : yet from Geneva emanated those religious doctrines from which Scotland, Holland, and a large part of France, Germany, and Switzerland, derive their form of faith, and which were transported by the Pilgrim Fathers to the opposite shores of the Atlantic. Here also were sown those political opinions which bore fruit in the English revolution under Charles I., in the American and the French revolutions.

It was in the year 1536 that *John Calvin*, the reformer, passed through the town a fugitive, on his way from Italy to Bâle. Two years had not elapsed since the Genevese had abolished Roman Catholicism, expelled their bishop, and adopted the Reformation. Farel, who was the means of introducing it, was then preaching at Geneva, and, aware of Calvin's talents and powerful eloquence, entreated him to remain. Calvin obeyed the call, and, in a short space, the itinerant preacher and foreigner was raised to be the dictator of the republic, ruling its turbulent democracy with a sway not more mild than that of the dukes of Savoy and bishops of Geneva, under which the citizens had groaned for ages, and from which the Reformation had at length released them. From the pulpit of St. Peter's Church, which became at once the tribune and judgment-seat of the reformer, he denounced the prevailing immorality of the town with such eloquence and force that profligacy was obliged to hide its head. His hearers, running into an opposite extreme, adopted a rigorous and puritanical austerity of manners, and every transgression of Calvin's code of morals was visited with punishment of the utmost severity. This artificial austerity has long since disappeared. The change of manners since the time of Calvin is, indeed, most remarkable. The theatre is open on Sundays; balls are given in the various "Brasseries" every Sunday evening; concerts are held in the electoral and other public places, all the cafés are open; in fact the bitter observance of the Sabbath has given place to general cheerful enjoyment of the day of rest from ordinary work.

The sumptuary laws enacted by Calvin were severe, but were rigidly enforced by the Consistory. They contained such enactments as the following: a dinner for ten persons was limited to five dishes; plush breeches were laid under interdict; violations of the sabbath were followed by a public admonition from the pulpit; adultery was punished with death; and the gamester was exposed in the pillory, with a pack of cards tied round his neck.

Geneva, thus become the metropolis of Calvinism, and "the Rome of Protestantism," was resorted to by many foreigners, who sought refuge here from religious persecutions in their own country. Among a number of English and Scotch exiled by the cruelties of the reign of Queen Mary, was John Knox. He was made a citizen of Geneva in 1558, and did not finally quit it till 1560. Calvin died in 1564, at the age of 55, after 23 years of uninterrupted power: he was buried in the *cemetery of the Plain-Palais*, but he forbade the Genevese to mark with a monument the spot where his remains were laid, but

the spot nevertheless is pointed out, and is marked by a plain slab.

The Duke of Savoy, for many years after his authority within the town had been destroyed, was engaged in repeated open contests with the citizens; nor did he omit to maintain, within the walls, spies and secret partisans, in the hopes of regaining possession by surprise. The street called *Corraterie*, at the period in question, A.D. 1602, the town ditch, was the scene of the most memorable of these attempts, known in Swiss history as *the Escalade*. The Savoyards had already despatched a messenger announcing to their commander the capture of the town; but the citizens, though completely taken by surprise, were by no means seized with the panic which such an occurrence was likely to produce. Every man, armed as he might be, issued out into the streets; the small body of Savoyards who had gained the ramparts were quickly overpowered; the first gun fired from the walls, by a chance shot, swept away three of the ladders; and the enemy on the outside, on approaching the Porte Neuve, found that, instead of being blown up, it was strongly guarded, with the portcullis down. The storming party, thus unexpectedly attacked, and at the same time cut off from their friends, were quickly killed or made prisoners. Those who fell alive into the hands of the Genevese were hung next day as house-breakers: 67 heads were planted along the ramparts, but many more than these fell in the ditch and outside the town. The venerable Theodore Beza, at that time 80 years old, gave out from the pulpit next day the 124th Psalm, which has been sung ever since on the anniversary of the Escalade.

Geneva remained independent, but its history during the 18th century is a long record of internal struggles between the aristocratic party, who kept all power in their own hands, and the people, who struggled to retain old privileges and obtain new ones. In 1782 France, Berne, and Piedmont united to impose the yoke on the popular party after a successful revolution.

In 1792–5 there were fresh troubles, ending in the acceptance of a Democratic constitution, which after only three years was upset by the French occupation. In 1814 Geneva was added to the Swiss Confederation. In 1847 the Democratic constitution now in force was carried by a large popular vote.

Jean Jacques Rousseau, son of a watchmaker of Geneva, first saw the light in a house, No. 40, Grande Rue. The accident of his being shut out of the town one evening, on his return from a walk, induced him to fly from his native town, as he feared to face his master next morning. His book, the *Émile*, was burnt, in conformity with an order of the Council of Geneva, by the common hangman, in front of the Hôtel de Ville, in 1762. The instigators of this act were Voltaire and the Council of the Sorbonne, who, by a singular coincidence, in this instance acted in unison. The Council at the same time issued a warrant for the arrest of the author.

Environs of Geneva.

a. *Junct. of Arve and Rhone.* b. *Salève.* c. *Voirons.* d. *Diodati.* e. *Fernex.* f. *Perte du Rhone. Bellegarde, &c.* g. *Divonne.* h. *The Dôle.* i. *Reculet.*

Omnibuses run to St. Julien, Mornex, Fernex, every hour, to Vandoeuvres and Sacconnex 5 times a day, and in summer to the Voirons 2 days a week. There is an American tramway also, which runs from Carouge through Geneva up to Chêne and back every ¼ hr. with a branch tramway from the Pl. du Molard over the Rue du Mont Blanc to the rly. stat.

The rides, walks, and views in the vicinity are delightful, and almost endless; but the great charm of every prospect is the *Mont Blanc* and Alps of Savoy, when they deign to show

themselves, which they do not, in perfect distinctness, more than 60 times a year on an average. There cannot be a more majestic sight than that of Mont Blanc and its surrounding Aiguilles, when tinged with the pink hue which the rising or departing sun sheds upon them. One of the finest views of Mont Blanc is from the garden of Baron Adolf Rothschild's villa at *Prégny* (see next page).

a. The *junction of the Arve with the Rhone* is well worth visiting, and is best seen either from the tongue of land between the two rivers, which is reached on foot along the l. bank of the Rhone by the gasworks, or from the grounds of a country-house called Châtelaine, on the rt. bank of the Rhone, about 1½ m. beyond the Porte de Cornavin. On the way to it, Les Délices, a country-house of Voltaire, is passed. A fine view of the junction is also obtained from the Bois de Batie, on a cliff overhanging the rivers. This may be reached by a walk on the left bank of the Rhone, by crossing a footbridge over the Arve and ascending a narrow footway to the Bois, which has been laid out as a public garden.

The Arve is in summer a wide and turbid torrent fed by the snows and glaciers of Mont Blanc. The pellucid blue waters of the Rhone, driven on one side by the furious entrance of its new ally, for a long time refuse to mix with it, and the line of separation between the blue and white water is distinctly marked for some distance.

b. On the S. side of Geneva rises the *Mont Salève* (4537 ft.), a long line of limestone precipices, seeming to impend over the town, though it is, in reality, 5 m. off, and within the French territory. The S. side is a gentle slope, covered with verdant pasture and sprinkled with houses, and the whole of this vast inclined plane, facing the Alps, is strewn with fragments of rock, identical with that of which Mont Blanc is composed.

The summit of the Salève, 3300 ft. above the lake, is frequently scaled by the inhabitants of Geneva, who make picnic parties to enjoy the view. The shortest road to it is by Carouge and Veirier (taking the junction of the Arve on the way: there is a shorter road back, 3 m.), whence a very steep path, practicable only on foot, partly formed by steps cut in the rock, and called *Pas de l'Échelle*, leads up through a remarkable gap in the mountain to the village of Monnetier 2½ m. Those who cannot walk may reach Monnetier by a carriage-road, which makes a détour of 8 m. from Geneva, through the beautiful village of

Mornex (*Inns:* Écu de Genève; H. de Savoie; H. Bellevue, P. Bovet, and many others) on the S. slope of the *Petit Salève*. The pleasantest way is to drive to Monnetier, thence to ascend the Petit or the Grand Salève on foot, and to descend the Pas de l'Échelle on foot to Veirier, whither the carriage may be sent round to wait for the party.

Monnetier is a comfortable stopping-place (*Inns* and *Pensions*—Péréard, Reconnaissance, and de l'Ermitage, commanding beautiful views, kept by civil people, and prices reasonable). From thence to the top is about an hour. Near the summit are the Chalets des Treize Arbres, so called from the presence of a few trees. The view extends S.E. up the valley of the Arve to Mont Blanc; N.E. over the lake; N.W. to Geneva, the Rhone, and the Jura; W. the eye follows the valley of the Rhone as far as the gap in the Jura, through which the river forces its way into France. The stony path has been superseded by a good carriage-road, made at the expense of a Genevese, M. Naville, whose residence, Grange Gaby, crowns the top of the Salève. Danger formerly arose from attempting to descend through a promising cleft, where a very steep slope ends in a precipice. For any one accustomed to mountains there is no danger; but in 1853 one English gentleman was killed, and his companion broke his thigh, in wandering about, after losing their way. *La Grande Gorge* is frequented by botanists, who find in it several rare plants. The ascent was formerly difficult, but a sort of path has now been made, and is kept in repair by the Alpine Club of Geneva. Archæologists have been busy on the Salève, searching for troglodytes, and no less than 38 caverns have been discovered. The most interesting are the *Grotte des Trois Fées d'Archamp*, and that of *Aiguebelle*, on the N. face of the Petit Salève.

c. Les Voirons (H. et P. l'Ermitage, not recommended), E. of Geneva, is another beautiful point of view. There is a carriage-road to the top from Bons on the N. side, and from Boëge on the S. side, and a path (the shortest, 2½ hrs.) from La Bergue, 1¼ hr.'s drive on the road to Sixt.

d. On the S. shore of the lake, about 2 m. from Geneva, and a little to the l. of the high road to Thonon, is the *Campagne Diodati*, Lord Byron's residence in 1816, where he wrote 'Manfred,' and the third canto of 'Childe Harold.' Diodati, professor of theology, it will be remembered, was a friend and correspondent of Milton, who visited him here.

On the N. side, on the hill of Prégny, 2½ m. from Geneva, is the very commanding seat of Baron Rothschild, built with more magnificence than taste; fine *Views* from the grounds, to which admission is granted on Fridays from 2 to 6, by tickets to be obtained at the hotels.

e. Fernex, the residence of Voltaire, is situated within the French territory, about 5 m. N. of Geneva. On the way thither, near Grand Sacconnex, an eminence presents one of the best points of view of **Mont Blanc.**

Voltaire resided for nearly 20 years at Fernex, from 1759 to 1777. He may be said to be the founder of the village, which, before his time, consisted of but 6 or 8 hovels. He collected industrious colonists, introduced useful manufactures among them, and improved his estate, of about 900 acres, by draining, &c., besides building the *Château*, which still exists, but has been so much altered that few traces of the philosopher now remain. On the l. hand, as you enter the gates, he built the *Church*, originally inscribed with the words "Deo erexit Voltaire." The *Theatre*, in which his own tragedies were acted by amateurs, has been pulled down.

The situation of Fernex, is charming, in full view of the Alps and of Mont Blanc; but the windows of the house, excepting those of the Library, were turned directly away from the landscape. In the garden is a long berceau walk, closely arched over with clipped horn-beam—a verdant cloister, with gaps cut here and there, admitting a glimpse of the prospect. Here Voltaire used to walk up and down, and dictate to his secretary.

f. La Perte du Rhone, and the works of *La Compagnie Générale de Bellegarde*, at Bellegarde, on the French frontier, about 16 m., or 1 hr. by rly.

The train should be left at *Collonges Stat.*, and rejoined at Bellegarde, or *vice versâ*.

The carriage-road from Collonges to Bellegarde is very due. You enter

———" where the swift Rhone cleaves his way between
Heights which appear as lovers who have parted."

The Rhone valley was here blocked up by Cæsar, to prevent the emigration of the Helvetic nation, as described in his ' Commentaries.' This he effected by throwing up works, ramparts, ditches, and forts at suitable spots on the l. bank of the river, having previously destroyed the bridge at Geneva. He does not appear to have made a continuous wall—as the banks were so precipitous as to render this unnecessary; but to have cut ditches and thrown up earthworks only at points where a landing or passage was practicable.

The lofty Vouache on the side of Savoy, and the huge mass of the Jura chain, slope precipitously to the torrent of the Rhone. The road hangs midway in this prodigious passage; and the *Fort de l'Écluse*, which gives its name to the pass, protects the entrance of France. Infinite labour and expense have been used by the French government to strengthen this position since its destruction by the Austrians, 1814. Additional batteries have been hewn in the rock above the lower fortress, and these communicate with the guard-rooms below by a broad staircase, of more than 1000 steps, cut out of the solid mountain. Leave may sometimes be obtained from the governor to view the fortress; but at any rate the road passes through it, and enables the traveller to see something of its remarkable defences. From Collonges to

Bellegarde (Inns: Poste; Perte du Rhone) the road sweeps along the wild gorge through which the Rhone pours. At Bellegarde it crosses the narrow and rocky bed of the Valserine. The traveller will walk from the inn to the *Perte du Rhone* ($\frac{1}{4}$ of a mile); he will find plenty of squalid guides to show him the spot where the river, which he has accompanied from the clear cistern of its waters through the rough mountain pass, plunges at once beneath an accumulation of broken rocks which have fallen from above and covered its bed from side to side. The river disappears from view for 120 yds., but is now much diminished in volume. Nearly half of it, representing a force equal to 4000 horse-power, has been diverted, and is utilised by a company of Scotch capitalists, at a very large cost. The water is led by a canal and through a tunnel of 600 yds., cut in the solid rock, to 6 great waterwheels and 2 powerful hydraulic pumps, erected in the old bed of the Valserine torrent, and from this centre the motion is distributed by means of wire cables to the mills and factories of the company, situated on the plateau 250 ft. above the Rhone. The chief manufactures, and on a very large scale, are *paper*, made from the wood of the aspen and fir, and *phosphate* and *superphosphate* of *lime*, for manure, from a bed of fossil shells 4 ft. thick, occurring here in the cretaceous formation of the Jura, and so widely spread as to be practically inexhaustible. The *Malpertuis*, an abyss, somewhat similar to the Perte du Rhone, 1 m. from the Billiat Stat., should be seen, if possible.

g. Another pleasant excursion may be made to *Divonne*, where the river Versoix takes its rise in a pretty grotto at the foot of the Jura, and people go to the hotel "de la Truite" to eat a kind of pasty called Beignet de Divonne and the small delicate trout. M. Paul Vidart's great hydropathic establishment is here. The view from the terrace of the Château Divonne is very fine. The best road to go is by Coppet and Celigny, and to return by Fernex. The distance from Geneva to Divonne is 12 m.

Not far from Troinex, 4 m. S. of Geneva, a great curiosity called the *Pierre aux Dames*, or *Pierre aux Fées*, stood on a little hill between Troinex and Bossey, just over the French frontier. It is now to be seen in the Bastions close to the New University, and is a block of stone with rude carvings, in relief, of female figures about half the size of life. These are supposed to be Celtic. The stone is 10 ft. long, 5 wide, and 5 high. It is said to be granite, but is apparently limestone.

The *Pierres au Diable*, near Regnier, supposed druidical, 6 m. S.E. of Geneva, strew a large valley or plain, and, according to the legend, are fragments of a mountain dropped by the devil. Among them is a cromlech.

h. The *Dôle*, one of the highest points of the Jura range, rises 5505 ft. above the sea, and commands to perfection that wonderful view of the Lake and Alps which old travellers by the St.

Cergues road remember. The ascent is best made by sleeping at St. Cergues (Rte. 55). On the other side is the *Val de Dappes*, for the possession of which France and Switzerland disputed for some time.

i. The *Reculet*, a point of the Jura due W. of Geneva, is higher than the Dôle. Its ascent may be made in the following way: Drive to St. Genix, and sleep at Thoiry. Next day breakfast at the chalet of Narderan, and walk along the top of the chain, descending to Gex in time for omnibus to Geneva. Take provisions. The views are very fine.

Chamonix and the shores of Lake Leman may be visited by hurried tourists in 4 days from Geneva —thus, 1st, by early steamer to Lausanne or Vevey—by 2nd steamer on to Villeneuve—in the evening by the rly. to Martigny; 2nd, by the Tête Noire or Col de Balme to Chamonix (Rte. 141); 3rd, at Chamonix; 4th, back to Geneva (Rte. 138).

ROUTE 55.

GENEVA TO VILLENEUVE, BY LAUSANNE, VEVEY, AND CHILLON. LAKE OF GENEVA.—RAILWAY.

Geneva to	Eng. m.
Coppet	8
Rolle	20
Morges	29
Lausanne	37
Vevey	48
Villeneuve	56

The rly. as far as Versoix belongs to the Lyons and Geneva Co., beyond Versoix to the Western Rly. of Switzerland. At St. Maurice it falls into the Ligne d'Italie running from Bouveret to Brieg. From Brieg it is proposed to construct a railway to the Italian side. A company is formed for this undertaking, which will shortly be commenced. For those who are not in a violent hurry, a far more pleasant route is by

Steamboat.—*Steamers* leave Geneva and Villeneuve, at the two extremities, four times a day. They make the voyage from one end to the other in about 4½ hours, stopping to land and receive passengers at the towns and villages marked thus † on the N. shore. Other steamers between Geneva and the towns on the S. side of the lake. (Rte. 57.) With a return-ticket passengers have the option of going back by rail. Some steamers start from the pier on the rt. bank. Small steamers, called "Bateaux Mouches," run to the stations near the end of the lake, starting from corner of the Jardin Anglais. The traveller should ascertain from which side of the Rhone at Geneva his steamer will start.

The Lake of Geneva, called by the Romans Lacus Lemanus, has nearly the shape of a crescent, its horns being turned towards the S. It is the largest lake in Switzerland, being 56 m. long, measured close to its N. shore, and about 44 m. along its S. bank; it is 8 m. wide at the broadest part (between Evian and Ouchy), and its greatest depth, which is on a line between these villages, is 1230 ft. Its surface is about 1230 ft. above the level of the sea, but the height often varies in the year more than 50 inches, being usually lowest in the winter, between Jan. and April, and highest in Aug. and part of July and Sept., owing to the supplies then derived from the melting snows. Besides these periodical variations, the lake is subject to other more arbitrary changes of level, called *seiches*. This phenomenon consists of a sudden rise and fall of the water in particular parts of the lake, independently of the agency of the wind or of any other apparent cause. It is most common in the vicinity of Geneva. During these oscillations the waters sometimes rise from 5 inches to a foot, but on some rare occasions it has risen to 3 feet. The *seiche* never lasts longer than 25 minutes, and generally less. The cause of these *seiches* has not been explained with

certainty, but they are observed to occur most commonly when the clouds are heavy and low. The lake never freezes over entirely, but in severe winters the lower extremity is covered with ice. The sand and mud brought down by the Rhone and deposited around its mouth have caused considerable encroachments upon its upper extremity: even within the records of history Porte Valais stood on its margin, and its basin is reported to have originally extended upwards as far as Bex.

"Mon lac est le premier," are the words in which Voltaire has vaunted the beauties of the Lake of Geneva; and it must be confessed that, though it wants the stern sublimity of the Bay of Uri and the sunny softness of the Italian lakes, with their olive and citron groves, it has high claims to admiration. It also possesses great variety of scenery. The vine-covered slopes of Vaud contrast well with the abrupt, rocky precipices of Savoy, and the tree-laden festoons of vines around Thonon and Evian which give the landscape an Italian richness. Near Geneva the hills subside, admitting an exquisite view of Mont Blanc, whose snowy summit, though 60 m. distant, is often reflected in its waters.

At its E. or upper extremity the lake extends to the very base of the Alps, which by their close vicinity give its scenery a character of magnificence.

The boats on the lake are very picturesque, having lateen sails like the craft of the Mediterranean. The surface is generally calm, but not the dead calm of the mountain lakes; occasionally the *bise*, a cold N.E. wind, is very strong, and causes considerable motion in the steamers from Geneva until they get beyond Lausanne, and the S.W. wind is even stronger. These are the only winds which materially affect the lake.

Among the fish are the large trout and the Ombre Chevalier, both much appreciated, and the *Lotte*, the "Lota Commune," on which Rousseau's Julie makes her last repast, is described as "une espèce de barbeau, assez fade, peu cher, et commun."

Railway to Lausanne, 6 trains daily, in 1¾ to 2¼ hrs.

The railway embankment has been carried along the edge of the lake, thus in many places marring its beauty, and interrupting the view from the sloping banks and houses built on them.

The first part of the road lies among villas and pleasure-grounds not unlike English country-seats. Few spots in Europe present so many admirable sites for a dwelling as the shores of Lake Leman, in full view of Mont Blanc. At *Prégny* is Baron Adolf Rothschild's superb château. After a mile or two Mont Blanc is hid behind the intervening ridge of the Voirons, and does not reappear until near Nyon.

The parish of *Versoix*, through which the road passes, formerly belonged to France. The Duke de Choiseul, minister of Louis XV., irritated with some proceedings of the inhabitants of Geneva, proposed to raise a rival city at Versoix which should deprive Geneva of its trade. A pier was built, a grand Place laid down, streets running at right angles were marked out; but beyond this the plan was never carried into execution. Hence the verses of Voltaire :—

> " A Versoix nous avons des rues,
> Mais nous n'avons pas de maisons."

A little beyond Versoix (now an inconsiderable village) we pass out of the canton of Geneva into that of Vaud.

† *Coppet* (*Inns:* Croix Blanche ; H. et P. du Lac), remarkable for the *Château*, immediately behind it, but so placed as to command no view of the lake. It now belongs to the Duc de Broglie, son-in-law of Madame de Staël. It is a plain edifice, forming three sides of a square, the front towards the lake being flanked with a tower at each end. It was the residence of *Madame de Staël*, as well as of her father, the French finance minister *Necker*. There are portraits of her

by *David*, of her parents, M. and Mme. Necker, and a marble bust of M. Rocca, Madame de Staël's second husband. One room is pointed out as the study in which the authoress of 'Corinne' composed many of her works. Her inkstand and desk are still preserved. The grounds are traversed by shady walks ; and a clump of trees surrounded by a wall, in a field a little to the W. of the house, shrouds from view a sort of chapel in which Necker and his daughter are buried.

† *Nyon* (*Inns:* H. Beau Rivage; H. du Lac, close to the pier; Couronne ; Ange ; Grand Château de Prangins, 1 m. distant, good and comfortable), a town of 3650 Inhab., stands on a height ; but its suburbs, through which the carriage-road runs, extend to the lake. It was the Roman *Noviodunum*. From the Terrasse des Marroniers, near the old chateau, once the seat of the Bailli de Nyon, there is a very fine view. On a promontory is the château of *Prangins*. It belonged to Joseph Bonaparte, and he built *La Bergerie*, on a promontory, lately a residence of Jerome Napoleon. Ornamental pottery is made here.

[An excellent carriage-road ascends in zigzags to St. Cergues. There is an omnibus daily : carriage in 3 hrs., 12 fr. *St. Cergues* commands a beautiful view, and has several *Inns* and pensions. From it the *Dôle*, 5505 ft., one of the highest points of the Jura, can be easily ascended. Mules and guides at St. Cergues. The ascent requires about 3 hrs.

Excursions may be made from St. Cergues to *Morez* and *St. Claude*, by roads running through very fine scenery. The industry of the district is diamond-cutting, and the manufacture of sham precious stones.]

† *Rolle.* (*Inns:* Tête Noire ; Couronne ; Pension Knigge, good). 2000 Inhab. The hills around are covered with vineyards, and one of the best Vaudois wines is grown on the slope between Rolle and Aubonne, called La Côte.

On the opposite shore of the lake are the Gulf of Thonon, the valley of the

Dranse, and the snowy head of Mont Blanc peering over the mountains of the Chablais; further on, the rocks of Meillerie and the entrance of the Valais.

[A few miles above Rolle is *Aubonne* (*Inns:* Couronne; Lion d'Or), an ancient town of 1667 Inhab., with an Eastern-looking *Castle.* Byron says of it:—"The entrance and bridge something like that of Durham: it commands by far the fairest view of the lake of Geneva (and of Mont Blanc behind it); a grove on the height of very noble trees." Here Tavernier, the Eastern traveller, bought (or built) the château. The ch. contains the monument of the brave French *Admiral Duquesne,* the conqueror of De Ruyter—the chastiser of the Turkish and Algerine corsairs, whose services Louis XIV. refused to recompense, and whose body that monarch for a long time denied to his son,—exiled to Aubonne by the revocation of the Edict of Nantes, because Duquesne was a Protestant, and refused to adopt the king's religion. Aubonne is less than 3 m. distant from the lake. On the hills sloping down towards the lake called *La Côte,* between Aubonne and Nyon, grows the best Swiss wine, called *le Moulart.*

The *Signal de Bougy*—3 m. above Aubonne and 2730 ft. above the sea —is a celebrated point of view.]

† *Morges Stat.* (*Inns:* H. M. Blanc; H. du Port). At a distance of 1 hr. above this town of 4000 Inhab. rises the picturesque *Castle of Vufflens,* distinguished by its tall white square donjon and group of minor turrets, built of brick, with deep machicolations, probably in the 13th cent. It is said to have been founded by Queen Bertha in the 10th centy. Morges was the birthplace (1797) of *Fernan Caballero,* the nom de plume of Cecilia, daughter of the Spanish scholar Don Juan Nicholas Böhl de Faber. Above the town is the Arsenal of the Swiss Confederation. The carriage-road continues near the shore of the lake. The rly. turns inland to

Bussigny Junct. Stat. Here the lines from Yverdon (Rte. 49) and Berne join. Most of the trains from Geneva to Yverdon go on to Lausanne, and then back to Bussigny.

The distant view of Lausanne, seated on sloping hills and crowned by its cathedral and castle, is pleasing. The large building on the hill W. of the town, is the mad-house for the canton. Between Lausanne and the lake stands the village of

† *Ouchy,* which may be termed the port of Lausanne. (*Hotels:* Hôtel Beau Rivage, a splendid and good house, but dear; H. d'Angleterre, formerly Ancre—much improved, *Pension* 8 fr.; H. du Port.) Lord Byron wrote the 'Prisoner of Chillon' in the Ancre inn, in the short space of *two days,* during which he was detained by bad weather, June, 1816. The house was modernized, and all trace of Byron swept away, 1868.

Lausanne Stat., between Ouchy and Lausanne. An excellent table-d'hôte at the *Buffet,* 2½ fr. without wine. A rly. between Ouchy and Lausanne, worked by atmospheric pressure, is now open.

Omnibus to the Signal Hotel, on the hill between Lausanne and Vevey. Carriages are very dear at Lausanne, 2 fr. from the stat. to the H. Gibbon, scarcely 200 yds., but up a very steep hill.

LAUSANNE. *Hotels:* H. du Faucon, well kept in every respect, with moderate charges; H. Gibbon, fine position and garden; H. Richemont, same proprietor; Bellevue, quiet, reasonable; Belvedere; H. du Grand Pont, commercial. *2nd Class Inns:* H. de France; H. Mansfeld; H. des Messageries, all good. H. du Nord, commercial; Café Casino (excellent beer). Numerous Pensions.

Lausanne, capital of the Canton of Vaud, contains 30,000 Inhab., chiefly Protestant. The Pays de Vaud (Germ. Waadtland) belonged in early times to Burgundy; in the 13th cent. it became subject to the Dukes of Savoy; in 1536 it was conquered by the Bernese, and remained tributary to that republic until 1798, when it acquired its independence. In 1814 it became a member of the Swiss Confederation. The constitution was rendered more democratic by changes in 1830 and 1845. The language is French. The town, with its high roofs, castle, and cathedral, is itself picturesque, and very prettily situated on the lower slope of the *Mont Jorat*, which sinks gradually to the lake, intersected by ravines, giving it the form of distinct eminences. From this cause the old streets ranging over broken ground are a series of ups and downs, and many are very steep. A viaduct, called *Grand Pont*, or, from its builder, *Pont Pichard*, now spans the valley of the Flon, and renders the centre of the town and cathedral much more accessible than formerly. The town was much enlarged between 1870 and 1875, when the slope between the town and the rly. was covered by streets and houses.

Since 1874, the Supreme Federal Court of Justice has been placed at Lausanne, which is now the legal capital of Switzerland. Close to H. Gibbon is the

Church of St. François, with a good and conspicuous spire. The church is apsidal, and has tall windows with tracery in the heads.

The Castle and Cathedral are on an eminence in the old walled town, which is still called the Cité. Starting from H. Gibbon, and keeping to the rt. for a short distance, any of the streets to the l. will lead to

The Cathedral (ask for the key of the door, at the sexton's house, in the small square N. of the Cath., No. 5), a fine uniform example of Early Pointed, plain, but well-proportioned, 333 ft. long, 61 ft. high, founded A.D. 1000, but the existing building dates from 1275. It consists of a nave and 2 W. towers, of which only that to the l. is finished; transepts, each flanked by a low tower to the E., a central tower and spire, and a short apsidal choir. The spire was taken down in 1874. A new one has been erected in its place. The W. door, a fine specimen of Flamboyant, is a later addition erected between the buttresses of the W. towers. The *Porch of the Apostles*, to the S., is decorated with rich sculpture. The circular apse, at the eastern end, has round it a processional path forming a continuation of the aisles, and to the E. a small projecting chapel, which is a fragment of an earlier building in the Transition style. The Triforium Gallery is carried continuously along the nave, transept, and apse ; above it is a clerestory range of triple lancets.

Obs. the W. and S. portals, the rose-window in the transept, and portions of the fine carved stalls removed from the choir after a fire in 1823. The varied arrangement of the piers and vaulting-shafts in the nave is also interesting, and deserves attention.

Among the monuments are a mailed effigy of Otho Baron of Grandson (1399) ;—the tomb of Victor Amadeus VIII. (Voltaire's "Bizarre Amédée"), who was Duke of Savoy, Bishop of Geneva, and Pope under the title of Felix V. (1451), but resigned in succession all these dignities, preferring to end his days as a monk in the convent of Ripaille, near Thonon, on the opposite shore of the lake: it is much mutilated; of Bp. W. de Menthonex ;—of Harriet Stratford Canning, by Bartolini;—of the mother of the Prussian Minister von Stein. The Cathedral has been restored by M. Viollet-le-Duc.

There is a beautiful view from the *terrace* of the Cathedral, partially obstructed by the present prison, formerly the Bishop's palace.

Ascending again to the N., we reach the *Château*, or *Castle*, a picturesque, massive square tower with 4 turrets. It was originally the residence of the Bishops of Lausanne, but is now converted into public offices, and internally entirely modernised.

Passing out under the old archway of the Château to the N., you may either ascend to the *Signal*, which lies straight before you, or turn to the rt. and walk along the road at the side of the ravine of the *Flon*—a walk which shows the picturesque houses of Lausanne to advantage—and so return to the town. The large handsome building on the S. is the Hospital.

In the *College*, founded 1587, not far from the Cathedral, is a *Cantonal Museum*, in which are some objects of interest,—such as a collection of minerals from Bex and a model of the salt-mines there. It is not deficient in the other branches of natural history. A specimen of the *Silurus glanis*, one of the largest fresh-water fishes, came from the lake of Morat. Many *antiquities* discovered within the canton, at Aventicum, and Celtic remains from the Swiss lakes and the borders of the Lake Leman, also some relics of Napoleon, his Waterloo saddle, fowling-piece, &c., are preserved here. There is also a *Picture Gallery* (*Musée Arlaud*) in the Place de la Riponne, on the N. side of the Cathedral, containing modern and ancient paintings, works of *Calame, Diday, Gleyre,* &c. The fine sketch for Gleyre's well-known *Hercules and Omphale* is in a room on the ground floor.

The *Blind Asylum*, founded by the late Mr. Haldimand, an Englishman of Swiss descent, is admirably managed by M. Hirzel.

The house of Gibbon, in which he completed the 'History of the Decline and Fall of the Roman Empire,' is behind the church of St. François. Both it and the *garden* have been entirely changed. The wall of the Hôtel Gibbon occupies the site of his summer-house, and the *berceau* walk has been destroyed to make room for the garden of the hotel, but the terrace overlooking the lake, a lime and a few acacias, remain.

"It was on the day, or rather the night, of the 27th of June, 1787, between the hours of 11 and 12, that I wrote the last line of the last page in a summer-house in my garden. After laying down my pen, I took several turns in a berceau, or covered walk of acacias, which commands a prospect of the country, the lake, and the mountains. The air was temperate, the sky was serene, the silver orb of the moon was reflected from the waves, and all nature was silent." *Gibbon's Life.*

English Church Service in the new English chapel on the road to Ouchy: *Wesleyan S.* in the Rue Valentin.

The *Post-office* is in the Place St. François, opposite H. Gibbon. The Telegraph-office is down the hill. Theodore Roussy, 7, Rue de Bourg, has an excellent *Reading-room* well supplied with English papers, and a circulating library.

Railways to Geneva, Neuchâtel, and Bâle ; to Fribourg and Berne (Rte. 45), to Vevay, St. Maurice, and Brieg. The Stat. is below the town, on the road to Ouchy.

Steamboats touch at Ouchy, the port of Lausanne, on their way to either extremity of the lake, some of them crossing over to Evian and Vue Veesa.

Environs :—From Lausanne to the E. end of the lake the sloping hills are almost entirely covered with vines. The neighbourhood is famous for the number and beauty of the walks, particularly among the Jorat hills, to Belmont, &c. Here, and throughout the wine-growing districts bordering the lake, strangers must beware of the alleys between walls or high hedges, which abound in every direction. Appearing to lead up a hill, or to some favourable point of view, they are constantly closed at the end by a gate, with a notice against trespassers. The law is severely enforced against any one entering a vineyard without the owner's permission. Partial and pleasing glimpses of the lake are obtained from the *terraces* within the town, and from the fine boulevard of *Montbenon,* just W. of Hôtel Gibbon, on the old road to Geneva ; but far more extensive and beautiful prospects are presented from the heights above the town. The best spot for an extensive survey is a hill called the *Signal,* about 2000 ft. high, 3 m. distant by carriage-road. By a footpath beginning with a flight of stairs on the L, the distance may be shortened.

The Signal lies nearly N., directly behind the Château, and has a restaurant on the summit. Near it is the forest of Sauvabellin (Silva Belini), in which it is said the Druids once worshipped the god Bel, and thence its name. There are a great number of country-seats in the vicinity; that of *Vernant* is highly praised; its grounds have the character of an English park, with the Alps and the lake in addition. Mont Blanc is not visible from the Signal, but may be seen from the top of the Jorat, on the road to Berne, and from *Les Grandes Roches*, 1½ m. on that to Yverdon. A pleasant excursion is to go by rail to Chexbres; walk N. to the little *Lac de Bret* (picnic if so disposed); proceed W. to the ruin of the square *Watch-tower of Gourze* for the sunset; descend to Cully, and back by rail.

About 2 m. out of Lausanne, beyond the Calvaire, on the Berne road, is the *Cemetery of Pierre de Plain*. *John Philip Kemble*, the tragedian, is buried within it. His tomb is a plain flat slab, one of 9 or 10 in a row, all English graves. The house where he died is called Beau Site; the plantations were all laid out by himself.

A Celtic burial-ground has been discovered at Bel Air, near *Chéseaux*, 6 m. N.W. of Lausanne.

———

The Rly. to Vevey runs along the slope of the Jorat, here covered with vineyards industriously terraced high up the hills. It is generally 50 to 100 ft. above the lake, and affords fine views. Near Vevey, the valley of the Rhone appears in sight, overlooked by the snowy peaks of the Dent du Midi.

At Pully an inferior sort of coal, abounding in sulphur, is dug from a mine in the hill-side.

† 11 m. *Vevey Stat.*—Germ. Vivis—(*Inns*: Grand H. de Vevey, a magnificent hotel in extensive grounds on the lake outside the town, but near the station; fine view and healthy situation; Hôtel Monnet or Trois Couronnes, one of the best inns in Switzerland: charges not out of proportion with the comfort. From Oct. 15 to May 1 you may live here moderately *en pension*. Grand Hôtel du Lac, excellent, charming garden-terrace, and well-furnished house. These are all on the lake, first-class hotels. H. d'Angleterre; H. Pension du Château; H. Leman—2 very good houses with view of the lake. H. Mooser, above the town; Trois Rois; Croix Blanche; Poste; du Pont, close to the station; Faucon. Numerous *pensions* on the road along the shore of the lake. Place du Château, near the landing - place. One of the most beautifully situated and largest is the Pension Ketterer at the N. point of the bay of Clarens. Pension Cheminin, above the town, garden and fine view, well spoken of. There are many second - class pensions at 4½ to 5 fr.

There are 3 steamboat piers at Vevey. The porters have an extravagant tariff of charges for luggage.

[Between Lausanne and Vevey, is the excellent *Signal Hotel* on the top of the hill.]

Vevey, the Roman *Vibiscum*, is the second town in Canton Vaud, and has 7890 Inhab., chiefly Prot. It is principally distinguished for the exceeding beauty of its situation, at the mouth of the gorge of the Veveyse, on the margin of the Lake Leman, at a point directly opposite a range of mountains rising from the opposite shore. The writings of Rousseau have contributed not a little to its celebrity in this respect.

From the beautiful walk of the *Quai Sina*, from the shady *Promenade du Rivage*, or from the *Château d'Hauteville*, about 2 m. N.E. of Vevey, the eye surveys on the E. the mountains above Chillon, Villeneuve, and the gorge of the Rhone, the Alps of the Valais, and the Dent du Midi; and on the opposite shore the rocks of Meillerie, and the peaks of the Dent d'Oche. The pyramidal hill which seems to block the valley of the Rhone, is *Mont Catogne* (8461 ft.), near Martigny. Behind it is seen the snowy cupola of *Mont Velan*, overhanging the Grand St. Bernard. But the walks in the immediate neighbourhood are somewhat dull, as the whole country consists of vineyards, surrounded by stone walls.

In the *Ch. of St. Martin*, a little above the town, situated amidst trees and vineyards, and used only in summer (date 1438), *Ludlow* the regicide is buried, as well as *Broughton*, who read the sentence of death to Charles I. They died here in exile, a price having been set upon their heads; and repeated applications were made to the canton of Berne to deliver them up, which the government very properly refused to accede to. *Ludlow's house* was pulled down some years ago, and the site is now occupied by the H. du Lac; he placed over his doorway this inscription—" Omne solum forti patria." The tablet is removed to England. *Pleasant walks* and views from the gardens of Château de l'Aile, open to the public Mon. Thur. Fri., from 10 to 12. Rousseau's favourite inn, the Clef, is now a Café, on the Grande Place, and still distinguished by the sign of the Key.

There is a theatre at Vevey where, in winter, plays are acted and concerts given.

Eng. Ch. S. on Sundays in St. Clair. The *Russian Ch.* is worth a visit.

Physicians.—Dr. Muret; Dr. Perret; Dr. C. V. Guisan.

Benda's Library, next door to H. Monnet, has a large collection of photographs of the Alps, books, music, &c. The shops at Vevey are gay and good. Ormond et Cie. make the cigars so well known in Switzerland as *Vevey fins* and *Vevey longs*.

C. Prost, watch-maker and bijoutier, is in good repute here.

Excursions :—a, to the *Château of Hauteville*, 1½ m. N.E., fine view and pretty grounds; *b*, 2¼ m. still higher, the ancient *Castle of Blonay* (view from its terrace), which has belonged to the same family 700 years; *c*, ascent of the *Pleyaux* or Pleiades, 4213 ft., about 6 m., by the *Bains de l'Alliaz*, where is a cheap pension, chiefly patronized by Germans and Swiss; *d*, Clarens (see below); *e*, *Chillon*, a

morning drive. A pleasant path or char-road (first turning l. beyond La Tour) above the dusty highway, leads in 6½ m. to Montreux and Chillon. (The route may be varied by taking this upper road.)

f. To *Echallens* (9 m.) by a rly. on a metre gauge, running in part along the high-road.

Boats at 1 fr. the hour.

Omnibus from Vevey to Chexbres Stat. to meet the trains from Berne and Fribourg. Ascent in 1½ hr.

The *wines* of the neighbourhood, especially of the sunny district extending hence to Lausanne, and called *Lavaux*, enjoy a considerable reputation. The Romans are believed to have first planted the vine on these hills; and the discovery of a stone inscribed " Libero Patri Colliensi" proves that they had erected a temple to Father Bacchus at Collium, a little village now called Cully, on the margin of the lake, between Vevey and Lausanne.

A guild of high antiquity, called *l'Abbaye des Vignerons*, exists at Vevey to promote the cultivation of the vine; and for this purpose it despatches every spring and autumn " experts," to survey all the vineyards of the district, and upon their report it rewards the most skilful and industrious vinedressers with medals and pruning-hooks (serpes d'honneur) In accordance with ancient custom, which is possibly a relic of pagan superstition, this society celebrates once in 15 or 20 years a festival called *la Fête des Vignerons*. As many as 600 or 700 persons took part in the last festival, and a ballet-master of the French opera was employed to drill and instruct the rustics in dancing. The last anniversaries were in 1833, 1851, and 1865.

[The beautiful path from Vevey or Montreux over the *Col de Jaman*, and the road thence to Thun, in Rte. 42.]

¼ m. W. of Vevey is the hamlet of *La Tour de Peilz* with a pretty church-tower (with roadway under it) and castle built at the water-side in the 13th century. Attached to this château are 2 *round towers* of unknown antiquity, with high doorways and openings to the cardinal points. *Peilz* is Romande for *skins;* and according to the legend a Crusader, on his return from the Holy Land, finding his towers roofless, covered them with the skins of wild animals he had slain in the chase.

3½ m. *Clarens*, ¼ hr. by rail from Vevey (*Inns:* H. et P. des Crêtes, close to the stat.; H. Richelieu; H. Roy; Hotel Roth; P. Beausite; P. d'Ermitage; P. Moser; P. Verte Rive, cheap; H. and P. Lorius), sentimentally described by Rousseau in the 'Nouvelle Héloïse,' commands one of the finest views over the lake —the mountains of the Rhone valley and of the opposite shore, but was until lately a poor village, far less attractive than many of its neighbours, and it probably owed its celerity to a well-sounding name, which fitted it for the pages of a romance. It is now a clean handsome town, with large hotels. Twenty detached villas have lately been built in a sort of park, and are to be let furnished. The climate is mild, like that of the other villages at the E. end of the lake. Rousseau's admirers have puzzled themselves with endeavouring to identify the localities, though he has himself stated that they are "grossièrement altérés." The spot on which the beautiful "bosquet de Julie" is sought for is now a potato-field. Byron says that the trees were cut down by the monks of St. Bernard, and lavishes some unworthy and undeserved abuse upon those hospitable ecclesiastics; but he has forgotten to ask whether the bosquet really ever had any existence except in Rousseau's imagination. Byron, indeed, viewed the spot with a poet's eye, and the exquisite beauty of the surrounding scenery, which has been accurately described by Rousseau, called up all the poet's enthusiasm and inspiration.

In the ch.-yard of Clarens (fine view) is buried *Vinet*, the divine (d. 1847). In the same place is a monument by the sculptor Imhof.

Above the village the two Châteaux of Le Châtelard and Les Crêtes stand like watch-towers on two vine-clad hills.

E. of Clarens the shore is covered almost continuously with houses, many of which are Pensions. They change their names and reputations from year to year, and it is impossible to give a complete or satisfactory classified list. The accommodation in all is good, and the prices are kept down by competition. The attractions of the scenery and cheap living supply a constant succession of visitors. In midsummer the climate on the shores of the lake will be found mild and relaxing by those who come from the mountains, and at this season the high hill-sides of Glion or Les Avants will be found preferable. In autumn invalids are attracted by the "cure de raisin," a remedy of foreign doctors, or the "cure de petit lait." Of late years the winter climate of the head of the Lake of Geneva has been found to be suitable for consumptive patients (see p. 187). The first cluster of houses is Vernex-Montreux; the second, on the hill, under Mt. Cubli, Montreux; the third, on the shore, Montreux-Territet. Then come Veytaux-Chillon, l. of the road; the Castle of Chillon, and Villeneuve. There are said to be altogether at least 50 Pensions and Hotels between Vevey and Villeneuve.

N.E. of Clarens is *Mt. Cubli*, and N., further away, the *Pleïades*, fine points of view.

The sloping banks of the lake give place beyond Clarens to steep woods and precipices. The road passes round the retired bays at their feet.

† *Vernex-Montreux Stat. Inns:* H. du Cygne, a large first-class hotel, pension, 7 fr. H. de Montreux, close to the station; H. Suisse; H.-Pension Beau Séjour, H. National, first-class; P. Monney, P. Benet, P. Visinand, well managed (6 fr.) The village of *Montreux* is seated on an eminence (l.) above the road, at the mouth of a gorge descending from the Col de Jaman, and with its church, a little apart from its houses, is much prettier

in itself and in its situation than Clarens. The neighbourhood abounds in *Pensions* long established, and much frequented. Among the best are the Pension Vautier, in the village; below it, on the high-road and shore, the H. et P. Beau-rivage. *Eng. Church S.* A *Scotch Presbyterian Church* was opened in 1873. Benda's Library and Reading-room is open daily.

This part of the shore is sheltered from cold winds, and remarkable for its salubrity. "The statistical researches of Sir F. d'Ivernois have shown that Montreux is the place in the world where there is the smallest proportion of deaths and of imprudent marriages." Dr. Carrard, the leading physician at Montreux, speaks English.

Just beyond Montreux is *Montreux-Territet* (H. des Alpes, excellent; pension 8 fr. *Eng. Ch. S.*; H. Mt. Fleury; P. Mounod, good; H. d'Angleterre.

Among the numerous *excursions* (a list in the hotels) are:—to the *Col de Jaman* (Rte. 42) 2 hrs.; 1 hr. more to the lake at the foot of the Dent de Jaman; the *Rochers de Naye*, 4¼ hrs., visiting the *Tannaz à l'Ouraz* (Cave of the Wind); the *Castle of Chillon*, ¾ hr.

[1000 ft. or 2 m. by road above Montreux, on a commanding point of the mountain, under the Dent de Jaman, is the hamlet of *Glion.* (*Inns:* H. Victoria; H. Rigi Vaudois; splendid houses, with very fine view and gardens; H. des Alpes, small, but comfortable; *Eng. Ch. S.*)

The ascent can now be made by a funicular railway which climbs the steep hillside at a gradient of 3 in 5. The total ascent is 1000 feet.

At the foot of the Dent de Jaman, 2500 ft. above Montreux, is the village *Les Avants*, possessing a good hotel. It is reached from Clarens and Montreux by bad carriage-road in 2 hrs. Mule-path over Col de Jaman to Château d'Oex. About half a mile above Les Avants, a path turns to the left, and follows up the unfrequented valley of *Les Verrau.* From the *Col de Soladier*, which closes this valley, it is possible to turn to the left and ascend the *Folly*, a round grass top, fringed on every side with pines, and commanding a fine view, or to climb on the right the excessively steep slopes of the *Cap du Moine.* The latter point can also be reached by climbing directly for it from the valley, without going as far as the col; and the trouble of the climb will be well repaid. The *Dent de Lys*, still more to the west, and rather higher, can hardly be reached from this side, but can be easily ascended from Montbovon or Albeuve. It would be possible to ascend the Moleson from Les Avants by this Col de Soladier, and return, in a long day; but it would be advisable to take a guide. Finally, Les Avants is the best point from which to start to climb the *Rochers de Naye.* Parties are often made up at the hotel, to start about midnight, so as to see the sunrise over the Oberland. The view from the Rochers de Naye, of the Oberland, and a great part of the Mont Blanc range, is magnificent.]

Beyond Territet is † *Veytaux-Chillon Stat.* (H. et Pension Bonnivard; P. Masson, all good), and close to it the picturesque and renowned

Castle of Chillon, on an isolated rock, nearly surrounded by deep water, but within a stone's throw of the road, with which it communicates by a wooden bridge. It was built in 1238 by Amadeus IV. of Savoy, and was long used as a state prison, where, among other victims, many of the early reformers were immured. When Byron, in the 'Prisoner of Chillon,' described the sufferings of an imaginary captive, he was not acquainted with the story of the *real* prisoner, Bonnivard, prior of St. Victor, who, having rendered himself obnoxious to the Duke of Savoy by his exertions to free the Genevese from the Savoyard yoke, was seized by the Duke's emissaries, and secretly carried off to this castle. It has been commonly said that he was here immured for 6 long years in a dungeon, on a level with the surface of the lake; and they point out the ring by which he was attached to one of the pillars, and the stone floor at its base worn by his constant pacing to and fro, but there is reason to believe he was not treated with such severity. Byron afterwards wrote the sonnet on Bonnivard, from which the following lines are taken:—

' Chillon! thy prison is a holy place,
   And thy sad floor an altar; for 'twas trod
Until his very steps have left a trace
   Worn, as if the cold pavement were a sod,
By Bonnivard! May none those marks efface!
   For they appeal from tyranny to God."

At length, in 1536, the Swiss wrested the Pays de Vaud from Charles III. of Savoy. Chillon was the last place which held out for him; but an army of 7000 Bernese besieging it by land, while the galleys of the Genevese assaulted it by water, soon compelled it to surrender, and Bonnivard, with other captives, was set free. The changes which had occurred during the years of his imprisonment almost realised the legend of the Seven Sleepers. He had left Geneva a Roman Catholic state, and dependent on the Duke of Savoy; he found her free, and a republic, openly professing the Reformed faith.

The castle is now converted into a magazine for military stores; but the interior of the building is well preserved and the chapel particularly interesting. Strangers are shown the *potence*, a beam, black with age, to which the criminal was hung, and the hole in the wall through which his body was thrust into the lake, here some 500 ft. deep; the *Torture Chamber*, with a wooden pillar scored by the hot iron; the *Oubliette*, a frightful place; a trap-door, which shut out the light, and then a small spiral staircase of three steps, where the prisoner found no fourth step, and was precipitated to a depth of 80 feet upon large knives. The dungeon of Bonnivard is airy and spacious, consisting of two aisles, almost like the crypt of a church; its floor and one side are formed by the living rock, and it is lighted by several windows, through which the sun's light passes by reflection from the surface of the lake up to the roof, transmitting partly also the blue colour of the waters. Formerly it was subdivided into small cells by partition walls between the pillars. Byron's name, on one of the pillars, is a forgery: those of Shelley, Dickens, H. B. Stowe, &c., are genuine: but the name of Byron is far more lastingly associated with the spot.

It is by this castle that Rousseau has fixed the catastrophe of his Héloïse, in the rescue of one of her children by Julie from the water; the shock of which, and the illness produced by the immersion, are the cause of her death.

Between Chillon and Villeneuve, 10 minutes' walk from either, and a little above the lake, stands the *Hôtel Byron*, a large and well-managed hotel and pension. There are many delightful walks and rides in the neighbourhood.

The road to the hotel, from the Villeneuve Stat., crosses the rly. by a bridge, alongside which the rivulet Tinière is conveyed in an aqueduct. The thickness of the delta formed by this little stream, through which the rly. passes in a cutting, has attracted the notice of scientific observers. Not only has the entire delta been deposited by that rivulet, but it has also been equably deposited, as may be seen by the regularity exhibited in the rly. section.

† *Villeneuve Stat.* (*Inns:* H. de Ville, on the lake, H. Victoria, at the stat.) is an ancient walled town of 1480 Inhab. (*Pennilucus* of the Romans), situated under the *Rochers de Naye*, 6693 ft., at the E. extremity of the lake, where the road quits its borders to enter the valley of the Rhône. [The nearest rte. from the lake of Geneva to Château d'Oex is from Villeneuve by the *Col des Chaudes*, or *Col de la Tinière*, S. of the *Rochers de Naye*, which may be ascended (Rte. 42).]

About a mile from Villeneuve lies a small island, the *Ile de Paix*, one of three in the lake: it is thus mentioned by Byron in the 'Prisoner of Chillon:'—

"And then there was a little isle,
  Which in my very face did smile,
    The only one in view;
  A small green isle, it seem'd no more,
  Scarce broader than my dungeon-floor;
  But in it there were three tall trees,
  And o'er it blew the mountain-breeze,
  And by it there were waters flowing,
  And on it there were young flowers growing,
    Of gentle breath and hue."

The three trees still flourish there.

The valley of the Rhone opens with scenery of great grandeur, the mountains being varied and highly picturesque. The river flows through a flat alluvial deposit, but drainage and other improvements have redeemed it from the state of a barren and unwholesome morass. The encroachments of the land, even within the period of historical record, have been very great. Port Valais, *Portus Vallesiæ* of the Romans, in their time stood on the margin of the lake, but is now more than a mile and a half inland. The Rhone itself rushes along in summer burdened with mud, very unlike the torrent of azure and crystal which bursts out of the lake at Geneva. Upon this plain, at the mouth of the valley, Divico, the first Helvetian chief mentioned in history, defeated, B.C. 107, the Roman forces under Lucius Cassius, slaying their general and compelling his army to pass under the yoke.

The top of the mountain above *Yvorne* was thrown down by an earthquake, 1584. One of the best white wines of Switzerland now grows on the slope.

It is worth while to go out at night and see the process of catching trout in the torrents, affluents of the Rhône, by means of a lantern and spear.

The Winter Refuges on the Shores of Lake Leman.

Since 1840 medical men and invalids have discovered that the N. shores of the Lake of Geneva, from Vevey nearly to Villeneuve, including Clarens, Montreux Territet, Veytaux, &c., offer a sheltered region for winter and spring, which, owing to the complete protection afforded from N. and E. winds by a chain of mountains 3000 to 5000 ft. high, which hem in these sunny slopes, is peculiarly well suited for those labouring under chest complaints. The number of winter residents, one-half being English and Americans, who flock hither every year to profit by the mild climate, varies from 2000 to 3000. At the English Ch. service at Montreux or Vevey it is not uncommon to find congregations of 500. The winter is short and dry. On clear days the sun is very powerful, and its effect is increased by reflection from the lake. The nights, however, are *very cold,* so that the average winter temperature, December, January, and February, is as low as that of London. To accommodate this foreign colony, hotels and pensions almost without number have been provided, and the charges *en pension* are very moderate.

ROUTE 56.

VILLENEUVE TO BRIEG, BY MARTIGNY [GORGE OF THE TRIENT].—RAIL.

	Miles.
Villeneuve to	
Bex	15
St. Maurice	—
Martigny Stat.	26
Sion	44
Sierre	53¼
Visp	72
Brieg	73

This rly. opens direct communication from Paris by Lausanne to the foot of the Simplon.

Villeneuve, in Rte. 55. Thence the rly. ascends the valley of the Rhone, passing partly through fields, overshadowed by walnut-trees: the views up the ravines to the l. are fine.

Roche Stat. For the pass to Chateau d'Oex, see Rte. 42.

Aigle Stat. (*Inns:* H. and Pension Beau Site, by the stat., handsome and moderate, Mon Séjour; H. Victoria, and others. On an eminence outside the village is H. des Bains, an enormous hydropathic establishment and

Pension. Aigle, 1375 ft., 3400 Inhab.) consists of a quaint village with mediæval castle, now the prison. It is the ancient Aquileia, and is on the torrent Grande Eau. 2 m. S. are the black marble quarries of *St. Triphon,* and above Sepey the lovely Val des Ormonts. There is a road from Aigle by Sepey to Château d'Oex (Rte. 47).

Ollon St. Triphon Stat. Near this rises out of the marshes of the Rhône a square mediæval *tower,* 60 ft. high, entered by external stairs. It was probably a beacon or watch-tower. This is the stat. for Monthey and Champéry, but seems to have no carriages.

Bex Stat. (pronounced *Bay*). *Inns:* l'Union; Grand H. des Bains; Belle-vue, on the road to the stat. with beautiful view,—all three good. Grand Hôtel des Salines, about ¼ m. from the village, in its own grounds. These houses comprise pensions and establishments of baths, supplied with salt water from the salt-works. 4½ fr. a day for not less than a week. 3 fr. in winter for not less than a month—Pension des Étrangers; Pension Crochet sous Vends, recommended, moderate. Guides, horses, and carriages. 1-horse or 2-horse carr. to Aigle, 6 fr. 10 fr.; to Salines Devens, 5, 7; Frenière or Les Plans, 11, 16; Gryon, 12, 20; Champéry, 16, 26; Sepey, 14, 22; Hôtel des Diablerets, 33. At times the *mosquito* is very annoying.

'Bex et ses Environs par E. Rambert' is a useful local guide.

Bex, a town of 4000 Inhab., is beautifully situated at the mouth of the valley of the Avençon, in view of the Dent de Morcles and Dent du Midi, but is chiefly remarkable for its *Salt Mines* and *Salt Works,* which date from the 16th century. For many years they belonged to a merchant family of Augsburg named Zobel, but they are now the property of the canton. Down to 1823 the springs alone furnished the salt, and they were gradually failing, when M. Charpentier suggested the plan of driving shafts and galleries into the mountain. The result was the discovery of a large and rich vein of rock-salt, which has been traced 4000 ft. and for a height of 600 ft., varying in thickness from 2 to 50 ft.; and the annual produce is now augmented to 57,000 cwts., but it is procured at a much greater cost than at Schweizerhall near Bâle. Strangers commonly pay a visit to the mines, which are situated about 3 m. off in the valley of La Grionne. A carriage-road leads through beautiful scenery to the boiling-houses and evaporating-sheds at Les Devens. Hence you ascend on foot to the *mine,* which you enter with a guide. The salt is obtained either from the springs, six or seven of which, of various degrees of strength, burst forth in the interior, or from the rock-salt, which, after being extracted by the help of gunpowder, is broken into pieces, thrown into large reservoirs, called dessaloirs, and there dissolved. Each reservoir is usually filled with water 3 times. The 2 first solutions (lessivages) furnish a liquor with 25 or 26 per cent. of salt; the 3rd is much weaker, having only 5 or 6 per cent. The brine, either from the sources or from these reservoirs, containing above 20 per cent. of salt, is conveyed in pipes made of fir-wood to the boiling-house (maison de cuite); that which is less strong must be subjected to the process of graduation in the long buildings or sheds, open at the sides, which are passed at Bévieux and Devens. These evaporating-houses, or *maisons de graduation,* are filled to the roof with fagots of thorn-wood, over which the salt water, after being raised by pumps, is allowed to trickle drop by drop. The separation of the water in passing through colanders, and its exposure to the atmosphere as it falls, produce rapid evaporation while the gypsum dissolved in it adheres to the twigs, and crystallizes around them. The water is made to ascend and descend several times, becoming stronger each time, and at length is brought to the condition of saturated brine, fit for boiling. It will easily be perceived how much fuel is thus spared by not subjecting the weak solution to the fire at first.

The principal mines are those called *Les Fondemens* and *Le Bouillet;* the latter contains a gallery driven horizontally for 6636 ft., $7\frac{1}{2}$ ft. high and 5 ft. wide. At 400 ft. from its entrance is the round *reservoir,* 80 ft. in diameter and 10 ft. deep, excavated in the rock, without any support to its roof. In it the weak water is collected. A little farther on is another irregular reservoir, 7933 ft. in extent, supported by pillars, and destined to hold the stronger brine fit for the salt-pans without undergoing any intermediate process.

Many beautiful minerals are obtained from these salt-mines—such as very clear crystals of selenite, muriacite, anhydrite, &c.

The neighbourhood of Bex abounds in *pensions* and little mountain *Inns,* where fine scenery, pure air, and tolerable living are obtained at a very cheap rate. Montchalet, $1\frac{1}{2}$ m., on the way to the salt-works, Pension Meylan-Girod at *Frenière,* the Châlet Amiguet at *Chesière,* the house of Madame Rosen at *Ollon,* all deserve to be mentioned. At *Villard,* 2 hrs. above Bex, are comfortable *Inns* (H. Grand Moveran; Villard; Bellevue) and pensions, all commanding a noble view of the valley and adjacent peaks, and surrounded by sloping meadows and pinewoods, which afford charming and easy walks.

[Many interesting expeditions may be made. One of these, by the *Col de la Croix* (5 hrs.) to les Iles, and the H. des Diablerets, at the head of the Val des Ormonts (6 hrs.), passes *Grion* ($2\frac{1}{2}$ hrs.), where there is a rustic *Inn* (Croix Blanche), and near *Villard.* An excellent carriage-road leads to Grion.

Another interesting excursion of 10 hrs. is to the *Col de Chéville* (Rte. 58), at the foot of the Diablerets, through Grion, returning from Anzeindaz by a path (due S.) round the *Argentine,* by the chalets of La Varre, the Pont de Nant and Les Plans. *Les Plans,* a village below the Grand Moveran, in the deep valley between that mountain and the Argentine, is one of the most beautiful spots in the neighbourhood; by carriage-road from Bex, $2\frac{1}{2}$ hrs. It has a modest *Inn,* à la Mère Girod, and several pensions. For the mountaineer there are the Dent de Morcles and Grand Moveran. Christ at Les Plans is a good guide.

The *Dent de Morcles,* 9639 ft., commanding one of the finest views in the Alps, may be ascended in about 7 hrs. from Les Plans. 4 hrs. to the *Glacier de Martinet* (which in itself is worth an excursion); 2 hrs.' scramble up a couloir on the S. side, called the *Grandvire,* and 1 hr. more to the summit, the eastern of two wild crags or teeth. See also p. 190.

The *Grand Moveran,* 10,043 ft., is approached also from Les Plans, but at the chalets of Nant, the climber turns up the mountain and gains the ridge between the Grand and Petit Moveran. He descends on the other side and scales the summit from the E.

To the W. of Bex, beyond Monthey, lies the *Val d'Illiez,* with hotel and pension at *Champéry* below the Dent du Midi (Rte. 144).]

The Railway, leaving Bex, approaches the Rhone, and crossing it joins the Savoy Rly. from Bouveret (Rte. 57), near a spot where the valley is almost closed by a barrier of mountains.

> "Journeying upward by the Rhone,
> That there came down a torrent from the Alps,
> I entered where a key unlocks a kingdom:
> The mountains closing, and the road, the river
> Filling the narrow pass." *Rogers.*

The *Railway* has now to be added to these to complete the scene presented to the traveller at the old *Bridge of St. Maurice,* which spans the rapid river with one bold arch 70 ft. wide, leaning for support on the E. side upon the Dent de Morcles, and on the W. upon the Dent du Midi, whose bases are pushed so far forward as barely to leave room for the river.

The bridge, erroneously attributed to the Romans, is not older than the 15th century, but may possibly rest on Roman foundations. It unites the Canton Vaud with the Canton Valais; and a gate at one end, now removed, formerly served to close the passage: a circumstance alluded to in the lines of Rogers. Fortifications were erected by the Swiss in 1832 and 1847, above the road, to defend the pass.

The Railway is carried past the old bridge through a tunnel to

St. Maurice Junct. Stat., where the Vaudois line joins the Ligne d'Italie Rly., which is to connect Geneva with the Simplon pass by the S. side of the lake (see Rte. 57). Now open from Bouveret to Brieg. Passengers have to change carriages. St. Maurice is not a place to stop at, as there are far better inns at Bex.

N.B.—In taking tickets at Martigny or St. Maurice for Vevey, unless you specify "par Bex" you will be sent to Bouveret, and thence, "par le Lac," by steamer.

[Omnibus from the station to the *Baths of Lavey*, 1½ m., close to the Rhone, under the Dent de Morcles. These baths, built, 1836, over a sulphureous spring discovered in the river-bed, have been much improved. Spray baths, &c., have been introduced ; the fare is good, and the establishment superintended by an accomplished physician, Dr. Cossy. The water is said to be the hottest in Switzerland, 125° Fahr. at the source, and to owe its healing properties to free nitrogen.]

[Higher on the mountain-side, 10 min. above the village of Morcles, 3816 ft., is the *Hôtel-Pension Dailly*, comfortable, with a splendid view of Mt. Blanc. The Dent de Morcles can be ascended from this side.]

St. Maurice Stat. Passengers change carriages here. (*Inns:* H. Crisogono, good ; Des Alpes.) A town of 1650 Inhab., occupying the site of the Roman *Agaunum.* It owes its present name to the tradition that the Theban Legion under the command of St. Maurice, suffered martyrdom here by order of Maximian, A.D. 302, because they refused to serve against their fellow-Christians in Gaul.

The *Abbey*, the oldest Christian foundation among the Alps, established in the 4th century, endowed by Sigismund, King of Burgundy, was for many centuries one of the most celebrated of abbeys, and the town itself was the capital of one of the Burgundian kingdoms. In the *Treasury*, not shown without special permission, are preserved an agate cameo cup of antique Greek art, and a bottle or ampoule of Saracenic workmanship, presented by Charlemagne ; a crosier of gold, in the shape of a spire, the niches of it filled with figures an inch high, most elaborately worked ; a chalice, given by Bertha, Queen of Burgundy, 950 A.D. The *Ch.* was much damaged by fire in the 17th cent., and has been badly restored, but the tower is unaltered, and several Roman inscriptions are built into its walls.

On the face of the precipice opposite the station, high up on a ledge, is the little *Hermitage of Notre Dame de Sax* (of the rock), approached by a flight of 410 steps. It is worth a visit for the view. Lower down, on the road, is the *Chapel of Verolliaz*, said to be raised on the precise spot of the massacre of the Theban legion, and covered with rude frescoes.

Another curiosity is the *Grotte des Fées* in the limestone rocks above the bridge and château. It is the ancient channel of a stream which once flowed through the mountain, and in 700 yds. leads to a large cavern, in which there is a thundering fall of water, a small lake, and a boat.

Beyond St. Maurice the rly. traverses the scene of a catastrophe in 1835. In the autumn a violent storm of rain burst on the Dent du Midi, and brought down a torrent of mud near Evionnaz, which flowed down the valley for some distance, floating on its surface huge boulder-rocks, covering the high road for 900 ft., and overwhelming fields and orchards, and some few houses. No lives were lost, as the slow progress of the current allowed every one time to remove out of its way. The wretched hamlet Evionnaz occupies the site of an old town, *Epaunum*, destroyed by a similar mud-torrent in 563. The Rly. now skirting a precipice close above the Rhone, comes l. upon the very fine *Waterfall* of the *Salanfe.*

6½ m. *Vernayaz Stat.* (1530 ft.), about 1½ m. from the Falls, and 1 m. from the Trient. (*Inns:* *H. des Gorges du Trient, a handsome house close to the Trient; H. des Alpes.) Vernayaz is 3 m. from Martigny, and it is well worth while to stop there and see the Gorge and the Waterfall, and then walk or drive on to Martigny.

[*Waterfall of the Salanfe*, descends into the valley of the Rhone out of a narrow ravine (1½ m. walk rt. of the stat.), its source rising in the fissured sides of the Dent du Midi. The perpendicular descent of the stream is about 280 ft., but the final leap of the cascade not more than 120 ft. It is a fine object, both from its volume and height, visible from a considerable distance up and down. It is best seen on a sunny morning before 12 o'clock, when the iris hovers over it.

1 m. l. of the stat., another stream, the *Trient*, descending from the Tête Noire, issues out of a singular rent in the side of the valley called *Les Gorges du Trient.* At the entrance the Hôtel des Gorges, where tickets (1 fr.) may be taken admitting to a wooden gallery from which travellers can obtain a good view of the chasm, and of its depths worn smooth and hollow by the force of the water. By all means visit it. It may be compared with the Gorge of Pfäffers, being longer, but not so deep. The gallery extends ½ mile up the chasm, which leaves the mountain-side 5 or 6 m. further, but is inaccessible. The Gorge and the Fall may be seen in 2 or 3 hrs.

Carriages, guides, and horses can be had for the beautiful car-path to Chamonix by the valley of the Trient. From Vernayaz the path mounts in 52 zigzags through meadows and under chestnuts to *Salvan* (1 hr.) (H. and P. du Gorges; H. de Salvan). Near it are the *Gorges du Triège*, with bridge (100 ft. high) and a gallery like that of the Trient. *Finhaut* (2 hrs.) (P. du

Bel Oiseau; du Mt. Blanc) with most beautiful view on the l. of Val de Tête Noire, Glacier du Trient; on the rt. of Le Péron and Bel Oiseau; in front of the Buet and Aigs. Rouges. A little beyond the village, *Mont Blanc* is seen. From Finhaut to the junction with the road of the Tête Noire at *Châtelard* (H. Royal) in 1 hr. (see Rte. 141).

The *Dent du Midi* can be ascended from Vernayaz, by following the Salanfe to its source in the snow-fields, under the eastern face of the mountain. Up to Salvan the path is the same as for the Chamonix valley, it then diverges to the right through some beautiful woods. The upper course of the stream is a series of wild cataracts, in a deeply-cut bed. The last chalets, just under the tawny crags of the Dent du Midi, are situated in the midst of beautiful level pastures, through which the stream ripples quietly. Here a guide may be procured for the final ascent, if one has not been taken already at Vernayaz. The climb over the broken screes is excessively steep and hot; and it would be better policy to climb the mountain from Champéry, and descend upon Vernayaz.]

On the outskirts of Martigny, upon a commanding rock, rises the *castle* of *La Bâthiaz* (irreverently likened by the late Albert Smith to "an insolvent lighthouse") formerly a stronghold of the archbishops of Sion. The château was built by Peter of Savoy in the 13th cent., but the tower is one of the *Round towers* of Switzerland, of unknown age, and of such strength that it has survived the many attacks made upon the castle, both before and after the invention of gunpowder. Some soldiers of Napoleon's army broke the entrance into the ground chamber in 1800. The river Dranse passes out into the Rhone, between La Bâthiaz and

Martigny (Hotels: H. Clerc, excellent; H. du Mont Blanc, good and reasonable; H. de l'Aigle, at the station). *Eng. Church S.*

Martigny (*Octodurum* of the Romans) consists of two parts—the one situated on the rly., the other, Bourg de Martigny, more than a mile distant up the valley of the Dranse. Its position on the road of the Simplon, at the termination of those from the St. Bernard and Chamonix, renders it the constant resort of travellers. The landscape is imposing : a flat, open valley bordered by mountains of great boldness, but the place is plagued with mosquitos in summer. It is a small town of no prepossessing appearance, about 1600 ft. above the sea, placed near the spot where the Rhone receives the Dranse, a torrent by which Martigny itself and the village of Bourg de Martigny have been twice nearly destroyed, in 1545 and in 1818. Marks of the last inundation (Rte. 136) are still visible on the walls of many of the houses ; and the massive construction of the lower walls of the post-house is designed to protect it from the effects of similar catastrophes. The ch. has a large new organ, on which there are performances during the season. The *Bridge* is one of the finest specimens of the Swiss covered wooden bridges, with the arch above the roadway. The monks of St. Bernard have here their head-quarters in a *convent*, from which the members stationed on the Great St. Bernard are relieved at intervals. The monastery of the Great St. Bernard is a journey of 10 hours from hence. (Rte. 135.) From Martigny to the *Sallenche Waterfall* and *Gorge of the Trient*, near Vernayaz Stat. (3 m.), see above.

[The valley of Chamonix may be reached in 6 or 7 hours by the Col de Balme, or in about 5 hrs. by the Tête Noire (Rte. 141), now a carriage-road. The Forclaz, with a most beautiful view, is an easy walk of 2½ hrs.]

[From Martigny, or Sembranchier, in the valley of the Dranse, an easy and interesting excursion may be made to the summit of the *Pierre à Voir* (8124 ft.), a mountain in the range between the valley of the Rhone and the Val de Bagnes, 5½ hrs. to ride up, 3 hrs. down. The descent to

Saxon may be made in sledges (*traineaux*) which are kept for the purpose. Two persons sit in a sledge; a guide acts as horse and runs down with it over the grass. It is an amusing and perfectly safe way of making the descent. An *Inn* (closed) has been built near the summit. There is a good mule-path all the way. The panoramic view from the top is exceedingly grand and comprehensive. Guide, 8 fr.; mule, 8 fr. It can be ascended equally well, if not better, from Saxon les Bains or Chables (Rte. 136).]

At Martigny the Rhone makes an abrupt bend, forming nearly a right angle. For many miles above the town, the bottom of the valley through which it flows is a flat swamp, rendered desolate and unwholesome by the overflowings of the Rhone and its tributaries, which, not being carried off by a sufficient declivity in their beds, stagnate, and exhale an injurious malaria under the rays of a burning sun, and generate gnats not much inferior to mosquitos. Travellers do not suffer from the malaria, but the inhabitants of the valley are dreadfully afflicted with goître (§ 18), crétinism, and ague; and the appearance of decrepitude, deformity, and misery arrests the traveller's attention at every step. A tolerable wine, called Coquempin, is grown upon the hills; the low flats produce little except rushes, rank grass, and alders. The mountains which here bound the valley have a bare and desolate aspect.

Saxon les Bains Stat. (*Inns:* H. des Bains; H. des Valais; H. des Alpes, close to the stat., good and moderate), a watering-place at the foot of the Pierre à Voir. The Springs contain iodine and bromine.

Riddes Stat. S. the *Col de Verbier*, also called *Col d'Etablon*, to Chables in the Val de Bagnes. After crossing the Rhone the Railroad passes the footpath leading to the Diablerets and *Col de Chéville* (Rte. 58).

[Hence the *Haut de Cry* (9698 ft.), on the N. side of the valley, may be ascended. It was the scene of a deplorable accident on Feb. 28th, 1864. A Russian gentleman, M. Boissonet, and Mr. Gosset, with 4 guides, including Joseph Bennen, started for its ascent. The party had easily arrived at a point within 400 ft. of the summit, when the snow-field on which they were crossing diagonally gave way above them. The avalanche hurried downward, bearing the party with it. During the descent Mr. Gosset was once overwhelmed, then found himself again on the surface; lastly, when the motion ceased, after a descent of 1000 ft., he was again buried and was fast suffocating. The snow "regelated," to use the modern term, that is to say, compacted itself into ice (See *Introd.*, § 12) around him. His hands and wrists were fortunately disengaged. With failing powers he contrived to scratch away enough ice to admit air to his mouth. Three guides were happily uninjured, and they saw and released him; but M. Boissonet lay dead on one side, and poor Bennen on the other, both deep below the snow. Thus perished Bennen, one of the best of Swiss guides; the companion of Prof. Tyndall, and of many members of the Alpine Club, and the leader in numerous first ascents of Peaks and Passes.]

Ardon Stat., at the mouth of the Vale of the Lizerne. Here are ironworks.

Sion Stat.—Germ. *Sitten* — *Inns:* Poste, H. du Midi; good. It commands a fine view. There is a comfortable *pension* 2 min. walk from Sion, kept by Madame Muston (Protestant). Sion (Pop. 1871) has no less than three *Castles*, which give the town a picturesque and feudal aspect from a distance. Those who have time may ascend in 20 min. to the highest of the three, *Tourbillon*, seen on the l. in advancing from Martigny, built 1492, for many years the bishop's residence, but now a ruin. It commands a fine view; the high peak seen beyond Sierre is the Bietschhorn. The Dent Blanche above Evolena is also visible. The castle

called *Valeria*, standing on the southern rock, serves as a Catholic seminary. It contains the old ch. of St. Catherine, and some old frescoes. In the town below, is the *Old Cathedral*, a mixture of Romanesque and of Early Pointed architecture, which has, or had until very lately, escaped the hand of the restorer. Among the objects worth notice are a very perfect roodloft of the 13th cent. Close to it is the modern Bishop's Palace. The third castle, called *Majoria*, from the majors, or ancient governors of the Valais, its first occupants, was burnt in 1788 by a conflagration which destroyed the greater part of the town. In the *Jesuits' convent* is a collection illustrating the natural history of the Valais. It includes a lynx, killed near Sion.

La Tour de Force, a prison containing the condemned cells, and the Rue du Château, the place of execution, resembling the base of a tower, remind one of the past history of Sion. The latter is close to the rly., on the rt. going up the valley.

Sion contains 4900 Inhab., almost all Rom. Cath., and is the capital of the Valais (Latin Vallesia, Germ. Wallis)—one of the poorest cantons in Switzerland. It was formerly a flourishing country, as the ruins of the numerous castles and the remains of former splendour at Sion, Brieg, and Visp attest. Its bishops were, from the 10th century, also Counts of Wallis, holding directly from the emperor, and were engaged in frequent struggles with their neighbours the Counts of Savoy; and at the commencement of the 16th century Matthew Schinner, Bp. of Sion, was a powerful prince, whose alliance was courted by the sovereigns of Europe—principally, it is true, for the sake of procuring the services of the 40,000 Swiss men-at-arms he is said to have had at his disposal. The ancient limit of Wallis was a league below Sion, but Martigny and Val de Bagnes fell under the bishop's jurisdiction in 1475. Wallis proper was divided into

[*Switz.*] o

7 districts (zehnten), which send representatives to a "landrath" at Sion, presided over by a "landhauptmann," who was second only to the bishop. Val d'Hérémence and d'Hérens were outside this system, and had governors appointed by the "landrath," a fact of some interest in reference to the theory of their inhabitants belonging to a distinct and conquered race.

The *Hospital*, under the care of the Sœurs de Charité, contains many victims of goître and crétinism.

1 hr.'s walk from Sion is the curious *Hermitage of Longeborgne*, out out of the rock which overhangs the torrent.

[S. of Sion the Val d'Hérens stretches far into the main-chain of the Alps (Rte. 131), and enables the traveller to take a pleasanter road to Zermatt than that by the Rhone valley—by Evolena, 16 m. (post carriage daily), St. Luc, Grüben and St. Niklaus, a 4 days' ride. (Rtes. 129, 130.)

Mule-path to Bex, by the Col de Chéville (Rte. 58), and to Gsteig or Lenk (for Thun) by the Sanetsch or Rawyl passes (Rtes. 41, 39).]

St. Leonard Stat.

Granges Stat. The village, with a ruined castle, is seen beyond the broad bed of the Rhone.

Sierre Stat.—Germ. *Siders*—(*Inns:* Bellevue ; Poste, good).

Carriage to Vissoye, 10 fr. ; horse to Vissoye or St. Luc, 8 fr. A horse to Zermatt, by St. Luc and Grüben, 60 fr. To Lenk ; by the *Rawyl Pass*, 11 hrs., guide 12 fr.

Mt. Bonvin, or *Sex de Bonvin*, on the N. side of the valley, commands a view of Mt. Blanc. It is easily ascended.

[A steep path leads to the Baths of Leuk, turning out of the postroad before reaching the bridge over the Rhone. (Rte. 37.)]

[Opposite Sierre is the narrow opening of the *Val d'Anniviers* or *Einfisch Thal* (Rte. 130). By it is a pleasant route to Zermatt (Rte. 129).]

[The high-road, now little used, after crossing the Rhone, and winding for some distance through the *Pfyner Wald*, a wild, romantic district of pine-covered hillocks, formerly infested by brigands, passes, at the mouth of the gorge of the Dala, the picturesque town of Leuk (Rte. 37). To the rt., behind a sandy slope, is the gulf called *Illgraben*, and in the valley the hamlet of *Finge*, or

Pfyn (ad fines) on the boundary between the German language, which prevails above, as far as the source of the Rhône, and the French, which is spoken below.

The railroad continues along the base of the mountains on the rt. bank of the Rhone, traversing many cuttings and 2 tunnels, and passing along richly cultured slopes to

Salgesch Stat.

The Rhone and the Dala are both crossed before reaching

Leuk-Susten Stat. (H. de la Souste, good). Here travellers get out for Leukerbad and the Gemmi. Omnibus once a day to Leukerbad.

The line runs along the l. bank to *Turtman* (French *Tourtemagne*, called by the Romans *Turris Tamenica*, from a round tower, in which, according to tradition, much earlier inhabitants worshipped Bel or the Sun (?). A chapel to the Virgin now occupies the site).—(*Inns:* Soleil ; Lion, poor) 15 minutes' walk behind the inn is a *Cascade* of considerable volume, and a height of 150 ft. The neighbourhood is overspread with marshes and stagnant pools, and the road was frequently flooded by the swollen Rhone. This portion of the Rhone valley appears to have been devastated within the last two centuries : the tendency of the bed of the river being constantly to rise, owing to the quantity of detritus brought down with its waters. Advantage has been taken of the rly. embankment to make it serve for many miles, between Susten and Brieg, the purpose of a dyke. The Federal Government, have employed the best engineers in correcting the river drainage, so that there is good reason to hope that the valley may recover the prosperity described by old travellers. [The wild gorge behind the village leads up to a magnificent forest at the entrance of the Turtman Thal (Rte. 129), and by a bridle-path to the little inn at Zmeiden. Glacier-passes to the Eggischhorn, Lauterbrunnen, and Kandersteg, from the opposite valley of Lötschenthal, in which there is now a fair inn. (See Rte. 38.)]

The artificial channel of the Saltine is crossed just before

Visp or *Vispach Stat.* (2150 ft.) (Fr. *Viége*) (*Inns:* Poste ; Soleil, good and moderate; Restaurant de la Gare). Visp is hot and malarious. It is better not to sleep here.

A large village (2410 ft. above the sea), the starting-point for Zermatt & Saas (Rte. 126) finely situated at the entrance of the Visper-Thal, up which the Balferinhorn and its glaciers are finely seen. It was once the seat of numerous noble families, which have all disappeared, leaving only their houses, now inhabited by poor people, to attest the fact. There are 2 large churches, the upper one finely situated. The lower was formerly the ch. of the nobles, and ultimately became the property of the family of Blandrath, the last of them. An earthquake, which began on July 25, 1855, and recurred with diminished force at intervals during several months, left only 7 houses in Visp habitable, forcing the inhabitants to encamp. Nearly all the ceilings in the town fell, cracks in many of the houses are still to be seen. Visp was the centre of the earthquake, which was felt over an area of 300 miles N. and S., 250 E. and W.

The torrents which fall into the Valais are very dangerous neighbours. The bed of the river Visp is nearly 13 ft. above a part of the village, and the Saltine is nearly 11 ft. higher than Brieg. The miserable and poverty-stricken inhabitants are obliged to construct very considerable dykes to restrain them, but even these defences are liable to destruction every 2 or 3 years.

It is a pleasant walk over the mountains from Visp to the Simplon Hospice by the *Bistenen Pass* (2 low

cols) in about 6 hrs.; or an excursion (ladies can ride) may be made halfway to the grassy eminence called *Gebüden*, and small tarn above the Nanzer Thal. Hence there is a noble panorama, and fine view of the Oberland peaks and great Aletsch glacier. The path goes by *Visperterminen*, which has a curious pilgrimage shrine. Mule-path from this village to Stalden as well as Visp.

There is a glacier pass by the Baltschiederthal to the Lötschthal (See Rte. 38).

A little above Visp there is a bridge over the Rhone and a rough horse-path (a short cut) to the Bel Alp. Rt. the *Nanzer Thal*, a fine glen, running up to the Gamser Gletscher (see Rte. 121).

The ascent of the Simplon originally began at *Gliss*, and was 1 m. shorter than the road by Brieg. The large church of Gliss contains the monument, an elaborately carved triptych, of the knight Supersax, his wife, and 23 children; his castle above Naters is now a ruin. Behind the church is a *charnel-house*, filled with skulls—10,000 at a rough computation.

The railroad runs along the dam on the l. bank of the river to

Brieg Terminus (2260 ft.) (*Inns:* Couronne or Poste); H. d'Angleterre ; both good and reasonable), a town of 1200 Inhab., situated on a sunny slope 2460 ft. above the sea, by the side of the Saltine, and overlooking the course of the Rhone, which here makes a sharp bend. It is remarkable for the number of its large and towered mansions, built by local families enriched by the Italian trade. The most conspicuous buildings are the *Residence* of the noble family Stockalper, its 3 turrets crowned with large tin cupolas, and the *Jesuits College*. There is also an *Ursuline Convent.*

Situated at the junction of the roads from the Furca and the Simplon, and not far from the Rhone and Aletsch Glaciers and their inns, Brieg is a great resort of tourists. Diligences run twice daily over the Simplon and once to the Rhone Glacier and Furca. The cost of vetturino carriages varies according to the season and the demand. The Bel Alp may be reached on horseback in 4 hrs. (see Rte. 29).

The Simplon is described in Rte. 59.

ROUTE 57.

GENEVA TO MARTIGNY, BY THONON AND MEILLERIE, ALONG THE SOUTH SHORE OF THE LAKE OF GENEVA, RAILWAY.

Steamers twice a-day (touching at Belotte, Bellerive, Anière, Hermance, Thonon, Evian, on S. shore of lake), in 5 hrs. to Bouveret, where passengers take the rly. to Martigny. Postroad from Geneva to Bouveret, about 40 Eng. m.

A rly. branching from the Geneva-Lyons line at the frontier, and keeping within French territory, has been constructed to *Bouveret.* Its station at Annemasse will be connected with Geneva by a branch line (Rte. 152).

The description of the road is retained. The stations on the new railway are noted.

After quitting Geneva by the Quartier de Rive, a view opens out rt.; beyond the Salève rises the Môle, and the valley of the Arve is terminated by the Buet, by Mont Blanc and its glaciers. The shore of the lake is dotted over with villas of the Genevese. One of these, near the village of Cologny, the *Campagne Diodati,* is interesting as having been the residence of Lord Byron in 1816. He wrote here the 3rd canto of Childe Harold and the tragedy of Manfred.

Beyond the village of Corsier the Genevese territory is left, and we enter the ancient province of Chablais, now annexed to France, which extends along the lake as far as St. Gingolph. A monotonous plain is traversed in order to reach

11 m. *Douvaine.*

10 m. *Thonon Stat,* (*Inns:* H. de l'Europe, fair, adjoining the Terrace; Balances; Ville de Genève), an ancient town of 5500 Inhab., formerly capital of the Chablais.

[For the valleys of the Dranse, see Rte. 145.]

On quitting Thonon we pass on the left, between the road and the lake, *Ripaille.* Here is a fragment of the *monastery* for aged Military Knights (now a farmhouse), founded by Amadeus VIII. of Savoy, and in which, after the death of his wife, Mary of Burgundy, he passed five years as a hermit, with 6 chosen companions. Amadeus was called the Solomon of the age; he was a legislator and powerful prince, but abdicated, in turn, the dukedom of Savoy, and the Papacy into which he had been installed with the name of Felix V. He resided here after his second abdication, passing his time, not in the austere penance of an anchoret, but, according to the popular belief, in ease and dissipation. Hence the French proverb — "Faire Ripaille"— to enjoy a life of ease and luxury. It is, however, probable, that, even to the last, he had not abandoned the path of ambition, and that, far from being inactive, he was weaving political intrigues. He died in Geneva 1451, and was buried at Lausanne under a splendid tomb. Between Thonon and Rolle the lake is at its greatest width, about 7½ m.

A bridge of 24 arches carries the road over the Dranse, a torrent descending from the mountains of the Chablais, and occasionally augmented to a large volume by the melting snows.

3 m. *Amphion* (*Inns:* H. de Casino; H. des Bains d'Amphion, with garden on the lake, pension 8 fr.), an old town surrounded by a ruined wall, capital of the Pays de Gavot, with sulphureous baths.

3 m. *Evian Stat* (*Inns:* H. des Bains, good; H. d'Evian; H. Fonbonne, good 2nd-class hotel in an old château, table-d'hôte 3 fr. with wine; H. du Nord; Poste: in all, 6 hotels,

and 40 lodging-houses), a town of 3000 Inhab., much improved of late. On a height is the Bath-house, resorted to for its mineral waters. Dr. C. Depraz, resident physician, may be trusted. He served in the Crimea on our medical staff. The Dent d'Oche (7300 ft.) commands a fine view, and can be easily ascended.

Steamer to Lausanne. Omnibus to Amphion.

The *Rocks of Meillerie*, celebrated by Rousseau and Byron, were, under the orders of Napoleon, blasted to form a passage for the great road of the Simplon, which is here carried partly through them, partly on a terrace 30 or 40 feet above the lake. Previous to its construction, the little village of Meillerie was barely accessible, except by boats. About a mile off the shore, the lake attains its greatest depth, 1230 ft. Here Byron was nearly lost in a storm. Rousseau, in the Nouvelle Héloïse, has conducted St. Preux and Mme. Wolmar also to this port for shelter from a tempest. On the opposite shore is seen Clarens, and the castle of Chillon (Rte. 55).

10 m. *St. Gingolph Stat.* (*Inn:* Poste, an enormous building, once a convent, not good; Lion d'Or). Mosquitoes very troublesome all along the S. shore of the lake.

At St. Gingolph are some mineral springs flowing from amongst rocks in a picturesque spot. They were known to the Romans. The deep ravine of the Morge here divides Savoy from the Swiss territory. An ascent may be made to the *Dent d'Oche*, 7300 ft., in about 5 hrs.; to the *Grammont*, 7146 ft.; or to the *Cornettes de Bise*, 7999 ft., by ascending the banks of the Morge. The lower of the two points is much the more difficult. The Cornettes de Bise are best ascended from Vouvry in about 5½ hrs. The view of Mont Blanc, and of the lower ranges of Savoy, is magnificent. The Grammont is also most easily ascended from Vouvry.

2½ m. *Bouveret Stat.* (Restaurant at Stat.; *Inn:* La Tour) lies within the valley of the Rhone, a broad, flat, dreary swamp. *Avoid* sleeping, or even stopping here. The steamers land their passengers.

Port Valais, in the days of the Romans, stood on the waterside; all the ground between it and the lake, 1½ m., has been produced since the records of history, by the deposits of the river. At Port du Sex, where there is a bridge over the Rhone, leading to Villeneuve, the rocks on the rt. encroach so far as barely to leave a passage for the road. Advantage was taken of this in ancient times to construct a fort with loopholes for arrows, and embrasures for cannon, which effectually closed the entrance to the Valais, the only passage being over its drawbridge and through its gate. The plain is strewed with hillocks and débris of limestone, the remains of a landslip from the Grammont, A.D. 563, which fell down the ravine of Evouettes, all across the valley as far as Roche and Rennaz, burying a Roman station, and damming up the Rhone. It formed a temporary lake, which reached to the rocks of St. Tryphon, but at last burst its barrier near Port du Sex.

The canal of Stockalper, running nearly parallel with the road, was cut by a patriotic member of that ancient Brieg family about 1740 to drain this portion of the valley. At Vouvry is a good country *Inn*, H. Bonjéan.

6 m. *Vionnaz.* Above this village are some most remarkable boulders.

5 m. *Monthey Stat.* (*Inns:* Croix; indifferent; Cerf). [Behind this village is the Val d'Illiez, with its excellent hotel at Champéry, under the Dent du Midi. Good carriage-road. Mail cabriolet (3 passengers, every morning). (See Rte. 144.) In a lateral valley opening to the W. at Trois-torrents, 2 m. above Monthey, are the hotel and baths of *Morgin*, pension 4½ fr. a-day.] Carriage to Champéry, 10 fr.; riding-horse, 10 fr.; carr. to Morgin, 12 fr.; horse, 10 fr. Above Monthey, in a wood, 500 ft. above the Rhone, are the celebrated *Blocks*

of *Monthey*, supposed to have been deposited there by a glacier or by floating ice. They are chiefly of granite, and are being carried away for building. The largest must have weighed 8000 tons.

3 m. *St. Maurice Junct. Stat.* (Rte. 56). Buffet. Here the rly. from Geneva, by Lausanne and Vevey falls in. *Martigny* (Rte. 56).

ROUTE 58.

BEX TO SION, BY THE COL DE CHÉVILLE—DIABLERETS.

Bex.								H. M.
Gryon .	.	.	.	.	.	.	.	2 15
Soulalex	.	.	.	.	.	.	.	1 45
Anzeindaz	.	.	.	.	.	.	.	1 15
Col .	.	.	.	.	.	.	.	0 45
Derborenze	.	.	.	.	.	.	.	1 0
Bridge .	.	.	.	.	.	.	.	0 40
St. Bernard	.	.	.	.	.	.	.	1 30
Sion .	.	.	.	.	.	.	.	1 40
								10 50

This is a highly interesting pass, both from the geological phenomenon of its "Berg-fall," or mountain slip, and for the picturesqueness of the scenery on its W. side. The pass is, however, long, and it is advisable to sleep at Gryon, 2¼ hrs. from Bex (see Rte. 56); or, to start from Bex at daylight in a char. An excellent carriage-road has been made from Bex to Gryon, ascending the heights by numerous zigzags, some of which the pedestrian may cut off by the old mule-path. 1-horse carriage to Gryon 12 fr. The pedestrian will follow the stream of the Avençon for about a mile to Bévieux, where are some salt-works: the road then leaves the river, and, keeping rather to the N., begins to ascend the heights; part of the road is beautifully shaded by woods, and part is through vineyards and fields. The ascent is tedious by the road, steep, but beautiful, by the paths.

Gryon .(*Inn :* Pension Saussaz, homely), is prettily situated high on the slope of the mountain above the gorge of the Avençon. [There are charming paths by the Croix to (*r-mond Dessus*.] The situation is healthy. Side-saddles to be had; a mule to the col, 7 fr. There is little advantage in taking it beyond the col. Guide 12 fr. to Sion. After leaving Gryon, the rough road can be traversed by a char for 2 hrs., as far as Anzeindaz. The road is tolerably level, and about 1¼ hr. from Gryon crosses the stream to the l. bank, then goes through fine shady woods for about 20 min., and crossing the stream again reaches the chalets of *Soulalex*, beautifully situated in a green plain with spruce firs all round, and tremendous precipices above the firs. The road now keeps a little to the l., and rapidly ascends a narrow ravine to the chalets of *Anzeindaz*, which are situated on tolerably level ground. In one of these is a room with beds, and food may be obtained.

[The *Diablerets*, 10,666 ft., can be ascended in 4 hrs. from the chalets of Anzeindaz: guides at Gryon. The climb requires a steady head and a good guide. It is possible to pass over the mountain to the Sanetsch.]

From this a moderate ascent over the green pasture, rich in rare plants under the precipices of the Diablerets leads to

The *Col de Chéville* (6680 ft.). By ascending the mound on the rt. of the Col, a fine view is obtained of the great chain of the Alps to Monte Leone, and towards the S. of the bare peaks of the *Tête à Gros Jean* and *Grand Moveran*. The descent from the col turns at first to the rt., then to the l., and is very steep and rugged; there is no particular path, but it is not easy to miss the way. In about 30 min. the chalets of *Chéville*, and a little *Inn*, on a tolerably level space covered with rocky fragments, are reached. Keeping along the stream a short distance farther, and then bearing to the rt., a very steep descent through trees leads to the *Lac de Derborence*, and the chalets bearing the same name.

The valley here is nearly filled by

the wreck of the mountain which was once regarded by the peasantry as the vestibule of hell, and therefore named *Diablerets.* It is composed of limestone, in strata much deranged and steeply inclined. The lower beds are soft and shaly, and become disintegrated by the infiltration of water from the glaciers on the N.E. ; and thus the large masses lying above them are detached and hurled into the valley below, forming éboulements of the most tremendous kind. During the last century two catastrophes occurred, in 1714 and 1749. By the former, 15 human beings, 100 head of cattle, and 55 chalets were buried. The fall of 1749 arrested the course of the Lizerne, forming the little lake of Derborence.

The path keeps to the W. side of the lake, and traverses for more than an hour a wilderness of rubbish and fallen rocks. A little care is required to keep the track. The scene is one of the utmost desolation; overhead towers the ridge of the Diablerets, 10,666 ft. above the sea. Three of its five peaks have already fallen, and the two which remain threaten, sooner or later, to follow. The mountain is again rent with fissures, and scarcely an hour passes in which a slight noise is not heard or a fragment of stone does not fall. The accumulated débris is said to cover a space of 8 miles. The path winds round the mountain to the rt., and in about 35 min. from Derborenze crosses the Lizerne by a little bridge. There is no house near the spot; in fact there is none from Derborenze to Avent. After about 20 min. more of rocks and stunted firs the path begins to rise on the l. bank along the precipices which border the Lizerne. For the next 2 m. it is a mere ledge, sometimes cut out, sometimes built up, and overhanging sheer precipices of 1200 ft. Though there is no danger, the path is very narrow and far more formidable than that of the Gemmi. It now passes through some beautiful beech-woods, still upon a steep slope, and then reaches the little chapel of St. Bernard, whence

there is a view of the great chain of the Alps. Here the valley of the Lizerne is left; the path turns E. and descends rapidly to *Avent*, about 20 min. from St. Bernard, thence to *Conthey*, where is an *Inn*; and thence to the high road at the bridge of the Morge, about 2½ m. from Sion. A guide would show a pleasanter way through by-paths from Avent.

[There is a shorter rte. to the Valais by *not* crossing the bridge over the Lizerne, but by keeping on the rt. bank along a well-marked path, which, half-way down, develops into a char-road leading to *Ardon*. Thence by rly. to Sion or Martigny. This saves a full hour on foot.]

Route reversed. — Mules can be taken from Sion to the Col (a good 7 hrs.), and, if necessary, on to Gryon. The pedestrian should take the diligence or a char to the bridge over the Morge or to Vetroz. He will see his path as far as the chapel of St. Bernard plainly marked on the face of the mountain. When about 2 hrs. beyond the chapel he must look out for the bridge on the l. and cross the Lizerne. The path through the rocks is not very clear after this, and most travellers will be the better for a guide. Bearing round the mountain to the l., he will find the Derborence. Crossing the bridge above it, the ascent begins immediately behind the chalets, and is very steep for 15 min., then along a little valley for 20 min., then very steep and rugged to the Col, turning at last towards the rt. From the Col the path cannot be mistaken. Time actually occupied, exclusive of stoppages, ascending moderately, descending faster—

				H. M.
Bridge over Morge	.	.	.	0 40
St. Bernard	.	.	.	1 40
Bridge over Lizerne	.	.	.	1 45
Derborenze	.	.	.	1 0
Col de Chéville	.	.	.	1 20
Soulalex	.	.	.	1 0
Grion	.	.	.	1 15
Bex	.	.	.	1 30
				10 10

ROUTE 59.

PASSAGE OF THE SIMPLON. BRIEG TO
DOMO D'OSSOLA.

	Posts.	Eng. m.
Berisal	1 =	9
Simplon	1¼ =	12
Isella	1 =	9
Domo d'Ossola . .	1¼ =	11¼

Post-road: Brieg to Domo d'Ossola,
5 posts = 41¾ miles.

With post-horses the journey may
be accomplished easily in 1 day.
Villeneuve to Brieg, see Rte. 56.

Diligences daily to Domo, and thence
to Arona, whence the rly. is open to
Milan.

On foot the distance may be shortened, but it will require 12 hrs.' walking. In September the diligence does
not reach the finest part of the pass
till dark.

2-horse carr. Brieg to Baveno or
Stresa, 160 fr.; 3-horse carr., 240 fr.
Prices vary with the season. Travellers wishing to send luggage
into Italy by the diligence must con-
sign it at the Post-office on the evening before. The key must be sent
tied or fastened to each bag or box.

The construction of a route over
the Simplon was decided upon by Napoleon immediately after the battle of
Marengo, while the recollection of his
own difficult passage of the Alps by
the Great St. Bernard (at that time
one of the easiest Alpine passes) was
fresh in his memory. The plans and
surveys by which the direction of the
road was determined were made by
M. Céard, and a large portion of the
works was executed under the superintendence of that able engineer. It
was commenced on the Italian side in
1800, and on the Swiss in 1801. It
took 6 years to complete, though it
was barely passable in 1805, and more
than 30,000 men were employed on it
at one time. To give a notion of the
colossal nature of the undertaking, it
may be mentioned that the number of
bridges, great and small, constructed
for the passage of the road between
Brieg and Sesto, amounts to 613, in
addition to the far more vast and

costly constructions, such as terraces
of massive masonry miles in length;
of 10 galleries, either cut out of the
living rock or built of solid stone;
and of 20 houses of refuge to shelter
travellers, and lodge the labourers
employed in taking care of the road.
Its breadth is throughout at least
25 ft., in some places 30 ft., and the
slope nowhere exceeds 1 in 13.

Excepting the Cenis, this was the
first carriage-road carried across any
of the higher passes of the Alps. Its
cost averaged 5000*l.* a mile. In England the average cost of turnpike-
roads is 1000*l.* per mile. It was the
wonder of its day; but it has been
eclipsed by the triumphs of modern
engineering. The object of Napoleon in its formation was marked by
the question which, on two different
occasions, he first asked of the engineer sent to him to report progress
—"Le canon quand pourra-t-il passer
au Simplon?"

The pedestrian, ascending from
Brieg, may shorten his way to the
summit by at least 5 m. by following
the old horse-track, which mounts the
gorge of the Saltine, and entirely
avoids the détour to Berisal. The
path is steep, the scenery far less
interesting, and the way is, or was
a few years ago, not easy to find, as
the old path had in places been carried away. An unpractised pedestrian going without a guide might
easily get himself into difficulties.

The ascent of the Simplon begins
at *Brieg*. About ¼ mile above the
town the road leaves, on the rt., the
lofty covered bridge over the Saltine,
now little used, since most vehicles
make the détour by Brieg instead of
going direct to or from Gliss. The road
then makes a wide sweep, turning
away from the *Glisshorn*, the mountain which bounds the valley on the
rt., towards the *Klenenhorn*, on the opposite side, approaching a little hill
dotted with white chapels and crowned
by a calvary. It then again approaches
the gorge of the Saltine, skirting the
verge of a precipice, at the bottom
of which the torrent is seen at a vast
depth, forcing its way among black

and bristling slate-rocks.   At the upper end of the ravine, high above his head, the traveller may discern the glaciers under which the road is carried.   Looking back, he has a view of the valley of the Rhone, as far as Turtman, spread out at his feet; Brieg and Naters remain long in sight.   It is a constant pull against the collar from Brieg to the second refuge.   Here the road, carried for some distance nearly on a level, is compelled to bend round the valley of the *Ganter* until it can cross the torrent by another lofty bridge, called *Pont du Ganter*.   The upper end of this wild ravine is swept by avalanches almost every winter, the snow of which nearly fills it up.   This bridge is left uncovered, from the fear that the terrific gusts which accompany these falls might blow the arch away, were they met by the resistance of flat timber-work.   After crossing the bridge the road ascends by a zigzag to the third refuge, called

Berisal, or *Persal*, a post-station, with a good mountain *Inn* and Pension, consisting of 2 buildings connected by a gallery across the road. 2½ hours from Brieg: excellent fare and attention.

The first gallery which the road traverses is that of *Schalbet*, 95 ft. long—3920 ft. above Gliss.   Near this and hence to the summit, should the sky be clear, the traveller will have a glorious view of *the Bernese Alps*, which bound the Valais and form the rt.-hand wall of the valley of the Rhone.   The glittering white peaks of the Aletschhorn and Nesthorn, and the great Aletsch glacier, are magnificent objects in the landscape.

Fifth Refuge, called *Schalbet*.— " Here a picture of desolation surrounds the traveller.   The pine has no longer the scanty pittance of soil which it requires for nourishment; the hardy but beautiful Alpine flower ceases to embellish the sterile solitude; and the eye wanders over snow and glacier, fractured rock and roaring cataract, relieved only by that stupen-

dous monument of human labour, the *road itself*, winding along the edges of precipices, penetrating the primeval granite, striding over the furious torrent, and burrowing through dark and dripping grottoes beneath accumulated masses of ice and snow."—*Johnson.*

The portion of the road between the fifth refuge and the summit is the most dangerous of all, at the season when avalanches fall and tourmentes arise, on which account it is provided with 6 places of shelter, viz., 3 galleries, 2 refuges, and a hospice, within a distance of not more than 1¼ mile. The head of the gorge of Schalbet, a wild recess in the flanks of the Monte Leone, is filled with the Kaltwasser glacier, beneath which, along the edge of a yawning abyss, the road is necessarily conducted.   This field of ice in the heat of summer feeds 5 or 6 furious torrents, the sources of the Saltine, and in winter discharges avalanches into the gulf below.   To protect this portion of the road 3 galleries, called, from their vicinity to the glacier, *Glacier Galleries*, partly excavated, partly built of masonry strongly arched, have been constructed.   They serve in places as bridges and aqueducts at the same time, the torrents being conducted over and beneath them ; and the traveller is surprised to find his carriage suddenly driven in perfect safety underneath a considerable waterfall.   These galleries have been extended far beyond their original length, for greater security.   In the spring the avalanches slide over their roofs.

A few yards above the Sixth Refuge, is the highest point of the road, 6628 ft. above the sea.   About ½ a mile beyond it stands the

New Hospice, founded by Napoleon, but left unfinished until 1825, when it was purchased and completed by the monks of the Great St. Bernard.   It is a plain, solid edifice, containing several neat bed-rooms, a drawing-room with a piano, a refectory, a chapel, and about 30 beds for travellers of the common sort.   There is neither corn, nor hay, nor stabling for horses. but the house is comfortable, and warmed by a heating apparatus. It is occupied by 3 or 4 brothers of the community of the Great St. Bernard. Some of the celebrated dogs are kept here, but they are rarely employed on active service. The monks are happy to show the mansion to travellers, and to lodge and entertain them. Those who can afford it will always leave behind them remuneration at least equivalent to that which is paid at an inn. The establishment is similar to that on the Great St. Bernard, except that it is more limited in extent and funds. (See Rte. 135.)

[The ascent of *Monte Leone*, commanding a superb view, is made from here or the village of Simplon. For its height, 11,696 ft., it is an easy peak, and, with a guide and proper precautions, free from any danger. It is possible to descend by the Alpien Thal on to the Simplon road near Gondo, through most beautiful scenery.

Guides can be found at Simplon. Ignaz Dorsaz recommended.]

A large open valley of considerable extent, bounded by the snow-clad heights of the Fletschhorn and Monte Leone, and having the appearance of a drained lake, occupies the summit of the Simplon. It is a wild barren scene, though rhododendrons and coarse herbage grow. Below the road, on the rt., stands a small tower, which was the original Hospice. It was built by one of the Barons Stockalper. A gradual descent leads past the Seventh Refuge (ruined), in about 3 miles, to

Simplon — Ital. *Sempione;* Germ. *Simpeln*—(Inns: H. du Fletschhorn, good and best situated; H. de la Poste, tolerable). This village (4850 ft.) is an excellent halting-place for those who seek high Alpine air and pleasant excursions.

Above this village, but out of sight from it, towers the *Fletschhorn*, consisting of 2 peaks, N. the *Rossboden-*

horn, 13,084 ft., first ascended from the Simplon, by the Rossboden glacier, and S. the *Laquinhorn*, 13,176 ft., the two being separated by a deep gulf. S. of the Laquinhorn is the *Weissmies*, 13,225 ft., which can be ascended from Simplon in about 6 hrs.; the descent to Saas will take 4 or 5 hrs. more. [The passes over this range are described in Rte. 121.] The fine icefall of the Rossboden glacier may be visited in 4 hrs. A hut has been built at the Hohsaas for use in ascents in the Fletschhorn range.

[Opposite the old hospice a track ascends S. of E. to the *Bistenen Pass,* then crosses the Nanzer Thal to another low col, and descends upon Visperterminen. From this village mule-paths lead both to Stalden and Visp, a walk of 6 hrs. from Simplon. At the 2nd col is a small lake, and N. of it an eminence, easily reached in ¼ hr., commanding a fine view. On descending from this col avoid going to the rt.; the path is l. to some chalets.]

From Simplon the road descends by zigzags into the glen of the Diveria, in which it continues as far as Crevola. The road dives into the *Galerie d'Algaby*, and then, by a more gradual slope, enters the *Gorge of Gondo*, one of the grandest and most savage in the Alps, cut between precipices 2000 ft. in height.

The Diveria is here crossed by the wooden bridge of Ponte Alto, an approach to which has been formed by scarping the rock with gunpowder. Some way farther a projecting buttress seems to bar all further passage. It is perforated by a tunnel called *Gallery of Gondo*, 596 ft. in length; it was difficult and costly to make, on account of the extreme hardness of the rock. The miners were suspended by ropes until a lodgment was effected, to commence the side openings, which now serve to light the interior. Opposite one of them is seen the inscription "*Ære Italo,* MDCCCV. *Napoleon Imp.*"

Close to the very mouth of this remarkable gallery the roaring waterfall of the *Frassinone* leaps close to the road, which is carried over it on a beautiful bridge. The traveller should pause and look back after proceeding about 40 yards. The cliffs rise on both sides as straight as walls. A number of zigzags now lead to a bridge which was carried away by an avalanche during the dreadful storm which ruined a great part of the Simplon road in 1834.

Gondo (Gunz), the last village in the Valais, consists of a few miserable huts, grouped round a singular, tall building, 8 stories high, erected, like the tower at Simplon, by the old Brieg family Stockalper, in ancient days, for the refuge of travellers.

An hour's walk by the side of the torrent, which falls in a cascade down the rt.-hand wall of the valley, leads to the gold-mine of Zwischbergen. From the head of the glen there is a fine pass to Saas, easy for fair walkers (9 to 10 hrs). The summit commands a noble view over Italy, and of the Saasgrat.

The highroad enters Italy a short while before reaching the Piedmontese village of

Isella (*Inn;* H. de la Poste), one of the most beautiful points of the pass, where the Italian custom-house is situated. There is a pretty waterfall in a wood near the inn. Lumps of bottle-glass are sold here by the children, under the name of rock-crystal, to simple tourists.

Varzo. Here Val Cherasca opens l. [Through this beautiul valley several paths lead up to the cirque of the *Diveglia* Alp (3½ to 4 hrs.), whence foot-passes lead to the Simplon Hospice, the Binnen Thal or Premia (Rte. 61).]

Near the entrance of Val Cherasca a change comes over the scenery. The rich green of the chestnut mingles with the dark foliage of the fir. The last gallery is traversed near *Crevola.* The Diveria is crossed for the last time by a lofty bridge of 2 arches,

nearly 90 ft. high, at the spot where it issues into the broad Val d'Ossola.

The road here commands a glorious view of the lower valley and the opening of Val Formazza, out of which the Tosa flows from the pass of the 'Gries (Rte. 62). A road branches off here to Premia, on the way to that pass.

The traveller now finds himself in a different region and another climate: the balmy air, the trellised vines, the rich juicy stalks of the maize, the incessant chirp of the grasshoppers or tree-crickets, and, at night, the equally loud croakings of the frogs— the white villages, with their tall, square bell-towers, also white, not only scattered thickly along the valley, but perched on every little jutting platform on the hill-sides—all these proclaim the entrance to *Italy.*

Domo d'Ossola (*Inns:* H. de Ville or Ancienne Poste ; H. d'Espagne, both are fair ; H. Albisini, good, and has a museum arranged by the scientific landlord), an unimportant town, 2480 Inhab., with no interest, save that it is Italian—in every stone.

There is a curious *Calvary,* ½ an hour's walk S. of the town, worth a visit by those who do not intend to see Varallo, as well as for the view.

The ascent from this to the Hospice of the Simplon occupies 7 hrs.

Diligences twice daily over the Simplon and to Lago Maggiore.

Very interesting *Excursions* may be made from Domo :

a. Up the lovely *Val Anzasca* (Rte. 120), by Pié di Mulera, to Ponte Grande and Macugnaga.

b. To Lago Maggiore by the Val Vigezzo and Canobbio (Rte. 113).

c. To the Falls of the Tosa, 26 m. (Rte. 62).

d. Over the Antrona Pass to Saas, 13 hrs. (Rte. 121).

The route from Domo d'Ossola to Baveno and Lago Maggiore is described in Rte. 112.

ROUTE 61.

VIESCH TO PREMIA OR TOSA FALLS, BY THE BINNEN THAL.

There is no frequented pass over the range separating the Valais from Italy, between the Simplon (Rte. 59) and the Gries Pass (Rte. 62), a distance of above 30 m. This portion of the main chain has been little known to strangers, but the opening of Inns at Binn and the Alpe Diveglia is likely to lead to its being more frequented. The scenery on the Italian side of the chain is varied and romantic. The short valleys of *Blinnen* and *Rappen*, which fall into the upper valley of the Rhone near *Reckingen* and *Viesch*, are uninhabited, and uninteresting in point of scenery. The only considerable valley on this side is the *Binnen Thal*, which pours its torrent into the Rhone a little below Lax. About 3 hrs. above the mouth of the valley it divides into 2 branches : the main branch, mounting nearly due E., preserves its name ; the southern branch is called the *Lang Thal*, or *Heiligenkreuz Thal*, from the hamlet of *Heiligenkreuz*, where there is a chapel resorted to by pilgrims. A good mule-track leads through fine scenery to

Binn, 5013 ft. (H. Ofenhorn, well-situated, comfortable, guides), placed near the fork of the valley.

The view-point of the district is the *Bettlihorn*, 9775 ft., reached by a footpath in 5 hrs., descent possible to the second refuge on the Simplon road. This summit commands a splendid panorama of the Valais with the Pennine and Bernese Alps.

[1 hr. below Binn a track from Grengiols, lower down the Rhone valley, convenient for travellers going to Brieg, falls in.]

Both the branches above mentioned are formed by the union of smaller streams, each of them leading to a

pass over the chain. Five of these passes deserve to be mentioned.

a. The *Albrun Pass*, at the head of the Binnen Thal, is the easiest but the most circuitous for Crodo. By this pass there is a track, fit for horses, from Viesch to Crodo.

The summit, 7905 ft., between the *Ofenhorn* (E.), 10,728 ft., and the *Albrunhorn* (W.), 9515 ft., and about 7 hrs. from Viesch, is a table-land, wild and dreary. The track to the Val Devera and Crodo doubles back, and, having been hitherto nearly due E., now turns to the W. of S., descending over pastures on the l. bank of the Arbola to the lake of Codelago, and then by a most romantic descent, through rich scenery, reaches the high road a little below Premia.

b. There is a direct and easy route to the Falls of the Tosa, known to the hunters of the Binnen Thal. The traveller follows the stream (where the Albrun path leaves it on the left) up to the head of the glen, crossing the ridge S. of the Ofenhorn. The descent leads to the Lake of Lebendun, whence there is a direct descent to Pommat, or an easy route by the Nulfelgiu Pass to the Falls. The ground S. of the Ofenhorn is one of the few tracts in the central Alps still badly mapped.

[The mountaineer will prefer to cross over the top of the *Ofenhorn* (10,728 ft.), descending by the Hohsand glacier to the *Inn* at the Tosa Falls. The summit is reached in 6 to 7 hrs. from Binn. A good guide and rope are essential.]

c. The most direct, but a rough course from the Binnen Thal to Val Devera is by the *Col della Rossa*, 8120 ft. The path turns into a glen a little above *Imfeld*, and when the stream divides follows the W. branch to the little lake of Geisspfad, and then from its N. shore mounts to a wild level waste which forms the col. The descent is by steep rocks to the Devera Alp, where the track joins the route of the Albrun at the chalets of Ponte, at the head of the Val Devera.

d. A more interesting, but longer

and more fatiguing path, is that by the *Krieg Alp*, passing close to a remarkable tower of rock, conspicuous from the Eggischhorn, called the *Kriegalpstock*. The valley of Heiligenkreuz divides into three at the village of the same name; the rt. branch leading over the mountains to Berisal, the middle to the Ritter Pass, the l. to the Krieg Alp. This is followed up to the base of the Kriegalpstock. The path is not difficult, but ill marked, and might easily be missed without a guide. From the summit there is a steep descent, with rocks on either side, until the head of a gully or ravine is reached, *on the rt. side* of which the descent is not difficult. There is no passage to the l.

These routes meet at the chalets of *Ponte*, whence there is a paved mule - path down the *Val Devera*, fatiguing to the feet. The scenery is very beautiful. Before reaching *Croveo*, the first village, a stream is passed on the l., which descends from an upland glen, inhabited by a peculiar German-speaking community. Their village is called *Agaro*, or Ager. Passing through fine woods of chestnut and walnut, the path falls into the road of the Val Antigorio a little below Premia. About 2 m. farther is *Crodo* (see Rte. 62).

It is a long day's walk to reach Crodo from Viesch by any of these passes. By the Albrun the distance may be accomplished in 12 hrs.' steady walking; the route by the Krieg Alp requires 13 or 14 hrs.; that by the Col della Rossa may (it is said) be accomplished in 2 or 3 hrs. less time.

e. To the lovers of high Alpine scenery the most interesting pass out of the Binnen Thal is that of the *Ritter* or *Boccareccio Pass*, 8858 ft., reached from Heiligenkreuz by following the middle or S.W. branch of the valley, called the *Mätti Thal*. A little above the village this again divides into 2 short valleys, or rather ravines, of which the one leading l., or S., called the *Giebel Thal*, is followed up a steep but not difficult ascent.

When the traveller has reached what he had supposed to be the summit at the head of this valley, he finds himself at the lower extremity of an immense amphitheatre or cirque, about ¾ m. in diameter, bounded by nearly vertical walls of rock, whose strata lie in horizontal lines, like courses of masonry, to a height of 2000 ft., while rt. and l. rise the mountains of the *Hüllehorn* and *Helsenhorn*, more than 10,000 ft. This wall is scaled about the centre of the amphitheatre by a stiff scramble, and the true summit of the *Passo del Boccareccio* is finally attained. On advancing a short distance on the S. side, the traveller is astonished to find himself at the summit of another amphitheatre, still more colossal in its proportions—a nearly circular space, about 3 m. in diameter, W. of which are grouped the highest peaks of this portion of the chain—the *Hüllehorn*, *Bortelhorn* (10,482 ft.), *Furggenbaumhorn*, *Wasenhorn* (10,628) ft.); and, chief of them all, the *Monte Leone* (11,696 ft.). From the gaps between these peaks 5 glaciers descend, and here and there steep slopes of snow rest against the walls of the amphitheatre. It is by one of these snow-slopes that the descent is accomplished, for the rocks are too steep to be anywhere practicable. Several groups of chalets rest in the comparatively level space at the bottom of the *Cirque*. The chief of these, where there is a small chapel, is called San Giacomo. Higher up, at the *Alpe Diveglia*, a fair mountain *Inn* has been opened. If so disposed, the traveller may return into Switzerland by the glacier which descends into the amphitheatre from the N. side of the Monte Leone, over which the Simplon road is reached a short way below the Hospice, without encountering any serious difficulty. In the opposite, or due E. direction, there is a passage to the *Val Bondoler*, a wild, uninhabited glen, leading into the Val Devera, a few miles above Croveo. The easiest course, however, is to descend the valley through which the Cherasca torrent rushes down to intersect the road of the Simplon near Isella.

The passes above noticed deserve more attention than they have yet received. The Val Devera abounds in fine waterfalls and in picturesque points of view. The entire range is extremely interesting to the geologist.

ROUTE 62.

PASS OF THE GRIES:— ULRICHEN TO DOMO D'OSSOLA, BY THE VAL FORMAZZA (POMMAT), AND THE FALLS OF THE TOSA.

Ulrichen to
Falls of Tosa (bridle) . 6 hrs.
Andermatten . . . 1¼ „
Premia . . . . . 11 miles
Domo (carriage) . . . 15 „

This is a mule-pass, though, as the track crosses a glacier, it should not be undertaken without a guide by a solitary traveller, or by those unused to mountains. The traveller who follows it will be rewarded by scenes of much wildness, and of grandeur and beauty. Münster, 3 m. lower down the Rhone valley, has a better *Inn* than Ulrichen, and may be used as a starting-place.

11 hrs. from Ulrichen to Premia with mules, without halts. The Inn at the *Tosa Fall*, 6 hrs., is the best halting-place. In the Val Antigorio fair quarters are found at Premia and the Baths of Crodo.

From Ulrichen the path leads across the Rhone to the village Im Loch, where it enters the *Eginenthal*, a valley wooded below, but barren and uninteresting above. It crosses the stream of the Eginen near a pretty cascade 80 ft. high. A climb of about 2 hrs., first through larch-forest, then across a sterile, stony tract, and finally over a plain of green meadow, dotted with chalets, brings the traveller to the foot of the final ascent. Near this point a path, striking off l., leads by the Nüfenen (Rte. 63) to Airolo. Here vegetation ceases, snow appears in patches, and at last

the glacier blocks the way—a gently-sloping ice-field, descending some 4 m. from the *Blinnenhorn*, 10,932 ft., and the *Rothhorn*, crests on the frontier separating Switzerland from Italy. The path—marked by poles stuck upright in the ice—makes a short cut over an elbow of the glacier (S.S.W.), crossing it in about 20 min. to the col of the Gries, 8050 ft. above the sea. [It is possible for mountaineers to ascend hence the *Blinnenhorn*, returning by the Blinnenthal to the Rhone valley at Reckingen.]

The descent on the Italian side (as is usual among the Alps) is steeper than on the N. The upper part of the Piedmontese valley of Formazza, or Fruthwald, presents 4 distinct stages or platforms, separated by steps, or dips, from each other. The first is called *Bettelmatten;* the second *Morat* (morass), on which the miserable chalets of *Kehrbächi* (the highest winter habitations) are situated. The third is *Auf der Fruth*, with another hamlet, and a small chapel. Before reaching it, the traveller falls in with the river Toccia, or Tosa, which he follows to the Lago Maggiore. Beyond the hamlet the path crosses to the l. bank of the stream, and, descending the fourth declivity, arrives at the

FALLS OF THE TOSA, 5528 ft. (*Inn:* H. de la Cascade à la Frua, homely, but good), the approach to which has for some time been proclaimed by the roar of the water. It is one of the most remarkable cataracts among the Alps, spreading in its descent like a fan. Its characteristics are volume and elegance. It glides down a series of steps, and forms an uninterrupted mass of white foam for a length of perhaps 1000 ft., while the entire perpendicular descent is not much less than 500.

[Directly E. rises the *Basodine*, 10,748 ft., the loftiest summit of the chain separating the streams of the Tosa from those of the Maggia, and here dividing Switzerland from Italy. The ascent from the inn takes 4 to

5 hrs., and is free from difficulty. It is possible to descend to San Carlo, in Val Bavona, from the gap N. of the Basodine by the Cavergno Glacier, which affords fine ice-scenery, and through a glen abounding in water-falls; or, by a more direct route, from the top itself by the S. rocks of the peak and Val Antabbia (Rte. 113). The *Tainier Pass* crosses the ridge S. of the peak to Val Antabbia, and it is the most direct route to S. Carlo. It is a rough walk of 7 hrs.

From the head-waters of the Tosa is a pass, called the *Passo di S. Giacomo*, by which travellers from Domo d'Ossola or the Simplon to the St. Gothard may reach Airolo, by Hospital all' Acqua in the Val Bedretto. A mule-track, often faintly marked, leaves the Tosa just above the falls, and leads in about 4 hrs. to the poor inn at H. all' Acqua (Rte. 63). When free from clouds there is a fine view of the Gothard range from the col. Between the Tosa Fall and the top of this pass a track branches rt., at a tarn called the Fisch See, and leads by a fine rte. over the *Bocchetta di Val Maggia* (about 9000 ft.) to the head of the Val Bavona, which runs S. to the Val Maggia.

It is possible in the opposite direction to cross over the glaciers of the *Ofenhorn* to Binn.]

2 m. below the Falls is the village of *Fruthwald*, situated on the 4th pla-teau. Beyond it are *Gurflen* (Gro-vello), *Zumsteg* (Al Ponte) and *Pom-mat*, where a stream from the *Leben-dun Lake* falls in on the rt. Peter Sillig, of Fruthwald, is said to be a good guide. The inhabitants of the upper part of the valley, as far as Foppiano, are of German descent, speaking that language, and, accord-ing to tradition, are descendants of a colony from the Entlebuch. Owing to this intermixture of languages, almost all the villages have a German as well as Italian name. Half an hour below Pommat is

Andermatten, about 25 m. from Domo. Here is the principal church of the valley.

[A high pass, the *Forcolaccia*, crosses the mountains directly E. of Ander-matten to Val Bavona; and further S. the *Criner Furka*, 7631 ft., leads in 8 hrs.' walking through Val di Campo to Cevio and Bignasco, Rte. 113.]

The lower part of the vale of the Tosa abounds in exquisite scenery. The *Gorge of Foppiano* (Germ. Unter-Stalden), 5 m. below Andermatten, is particularly grand. Lower down it expands, and displays all the softer beauties of high cultivation, luxuriant vegetation, and thick population.

A *Car-road* begins below Ander-matten; 2½ hrs. from that place there is a fair *Inn*. At *Premia* (*Inn*, poor) a stream descending from the W. joins the Tosa, and the valley changes its name into Val Antigorio.

"The savage grandeur of the Val Formazza, down which the river takes its passage, and the delicious region through which it rolls in the Val Antigorio, cannot be painted in too glowing colours. In these high val-leys, fully exposed to the power of the summer sun, there is truly a 'blending of all beauties.' The vine, the fig, and the broad-leafed chest-nut, and other proofs of the luxuri-ance of the soil of Italy, present themselves everywhere to the eye, intermixed with the grey blocks rest-ing on the flanks and at the feet of the high granite ridge, out of whose recesses you have not as yet escaped. Instead of the weather-stained and simple habitation of the hardy Val-aisan, sheltered by the black belt of forest, upon which alone I had glanced yesterday, I now saw, on the southern declivity of the same range, the sub-stantial Italian structure, with its regular outline, and simple yet beau-tiful proportion, and the villa, the handsome church, or the stone cot-tage, surrounded by its girdle of vines—the vine not in its stiff and unpicturesque Swiss or Rhenish dress, but the true vine of Italy and of poetry, flinging its pliant and luxuriant branches over the rustic veranda, or twining its long garland from tree to tree."—*Latrobe.*

This charming valley is the chosen retreat of numerous retired citizens, such as bankers, jewellers, &c., who have built themselves villas in it. The mica-slate rocks occurring near Premia and San Michele are full of red garnets. There are several timber-slides from the high forests. The trees are floated down the Tosa, and thus conveyed to Milan. An excellent carriage-road has been carried up to Premia· from Domo d'Ossola, 4¼ hrs.' good walking.

[For passes between the Val Antigorio and Viesch in the Valais, see *Rte.* 61.]

At *Crodo* — Germ. *Crot* — (*Inn:* Leone d'Oro) is the Italian Custom-house. 2 m. below Crodo, 2¼ hrs.' walk below Premia, are the *Baths of Crodo*, a large and well-furnished house, opened 1848: charge en pension 5 fr. a-day, baths extra. The establishment is not very well managed, and passing travellers are charged unreasonably. The waters contain iron. A spring rises in· the gardens. Near this are gold-mines.· Carriages and horses may be hired.

Below Crodo the carriage - road crosses the river twice before it reaches San Marco, and then enters the *Simplon road*, at the lofty and beautiful bridge of Crevola, near the Cemetery, at the junction of the Vedro with the Tosa. (Rte. 59.)

3 m. farther on lies *Domo d'Ossola.* (Rte. 59.)

ROUTE 63.

PASS OF THE NÜFENEN, FROM OBERGESTELEN TO AIROLO.

9 hours = 23 Eng. m. This is neither a difficult nor a fine pass.

The way is tolerably clear, and by travellers accustomed to mountains might in fine weather be found without. a guide. It is a horsepath, ascending the vale of Eginen, as in Rte. 62, but, before reaching the Gries Glacier, turns to the l., and crosses the ridge of the

Nüfenen (pron. Nüfénen), 8009 ft. above the sea. This pass, unlike the Gries, has grass on its very top, which commands a fine view of the Oberland mountains. The summit is a plateau requiring 20 min. to cross, the highest part being on the Valaisan side. The path is marked by poles. There is at times a good deal of snow on the other side. The descent into the Val Bedretto is in places faintly marked, and scarcely distinguishable from tracks of cattle. On the S. slope one of the branches of the Ticino takes its rise. The path descends along its l. bank to the

Hospice all' Acqua, 5266 ft., homely. 3 hrs.' walk from Airolo. A path ascending rapidly through the rough pine-forest, crosses the valley from this S. into the Val Formazza to the Falls of the Tosa, 3½ hrs.' walk (see Rte. 62). A car-road leads from All' Acqua down the Val Bedretto, which, from its elevation, has but an inhospitable climate; long winters, and frosts not uncommonly in the height of summer, morning and evening. It is clothed with forests and pastures, from which its 612 inhabitants derive support in summer; while in winter the males migrate to Italy, to seek employment as servants. It is flanked on either side by glaciers, and is dreadfully exposed to avalanches (§ 14). The masses of fallen snow often remain unmelted on the margin of the Ticino till the end of September. At

Bedretto (small *Inn*), 4610 ft., the principal hamlet, the church-tower, which has been once swept away, along with the parsonage, is now protected by an angular buttress, directed toward the side from which the avalanches fall, so as to break and turn them away; 29 persons have, however, lately lost their lives here by a landslip. N.W. is seen the glacier of Pesciora, hanging on the flank of the *Pizzo Pesciora*, 10,246 ft., whose snow-clad heights contribute water to 3 seas—the Adriatic, Mediterranean, and North Sea. The valley leading to Airolo is very pleasing. In the lower part of it a scanty crop of rye is grown.

At *Ossasco* (*Inn*) steep tracks to Val Bavona and Val Lavizzara fall in

Airolo, in Rte. 34.

———

ROUTE 65.

ZÜRICH TO RORSCHACH, BY ST. GALL.—RAILWAY.

Zürich to		Eng. m.
Winterthur (Rte. 9) . .		16
Wyl		33¼
Flawyl		42¼
Winkeln		48¼
St. Gall		52
Rorschach		62½

3 trains daily, in about 4½ hrs. *Zürich* in 1 hr. to

Winterthur Junct. Stat., in Rte. 9. The railway runs through a series of thriving villages, and the scenery, though quiet, is pleasing. It here leaves the Romanshorn line and follows the valley of the Töss as far as Elgg, 7 m.; 6 m. farther it crosses the Murg and reaches

Wyl Junct. Stat., where a line branches rt. to Ebnat in the Toggenburg. *Wyl* (*Inns:* Adler, best; Löwe; Schönthal), has 2000 Inhab., several convents, much cotton-spinning, and a fine view of the Sentis. The rail next crosses the Thur river on

[*Switz.*]

a lattice-bridge 448 ft. long, and beyond

Flawyl Stat. (*Inn:* Rössli) the valley of the Glatt by a lattice-bridge of 3 arches, 380 ft. long and 120 ft. high.

Gossau Junct. Stat. Branch to Sulgen Stat., near Romanshorn.

Winkeln Junct. Stat. Branch to Herisau (Rte. 69), and *Urnäsch*, to be continued to Appenzell.

Brüggen Stat. 8 m. from St. Gall the valley of the Sitter is crossed by a wrought-*iron lattice Bridge*, of clever device, 560 ft. long, in 4 arches or spans. It is raised 175 ft. above the river, upon cast-iron piers resting on stone foundations. l. Lower down the stream is the *Krätzeren Brücke*, of 2 fine stone arches, erected 1810.

A long tunnel is then passed to *St. Gall Stat.* (St. Gallen).—*Inns:* Hecht, excellent; Hirsch; H. Stieger, both good. A convenient centre to make excursions from.

St. Gall, capital of the canton, and seat of a Rom. Cath. bishop, is situated in an elevated valley on the banks of a small stream called the Steinach, 2081 ft. above the sea. Pop. 22,000 (about 6000 Rom. Cath.). It is the centre of the cotton and linen trade of E. Switzerland, notably of *Swiss muslins.* It largely exports these goods, and has a market for them on Saturdays. Cotton-spinning and embroidery are also carried on. There are extensive bleacheries, and the neighbouring slopes are white with webs. The embroidered curtains and ladies' collars are very pretty and cheap.

The antique *walls* and the ditch, now converted into gardens, recall to mind the ancient history of St. Gall. In the early part of the 7th cent. St. Gallus, an Irish monk, left his monastery at Bangor on Belfast Lough, with St. Columbanus and other monks, to preach the Gospel on the Continent. When, after many

P

hardships, they reached the Lake of Constance, and were about to pass into Italy, St. Gallus, seized with illness, was obliged to be left behind. On his recovery he decided to proceed no further, but to devote himself to the conversion of the surrounding tribes, and settled on the banks of the Steinach, then a wilderness buried in primæval woods. He taught the wild people the arts of agriculture, as well as true religion. The humble cell which the missionary had founded became the nucleus of civilization: and fifty years after his death, when the fame of the miracles reported to have been wrought at his tomb, drew thousands of pilgrims to the spot, it was replaced by a magnificent edifice, founded under the auspices of Pepin l'Héristal. This *abbey* was one of the oldest ecclesiastical establishments in Germany. It became the asylum of learning during the dark ages, and was the most celebrated school in Europe between the 8th and 10th centuries. Here the classics of Rome and Greece were not only read but copied; and we owe to the labour of these obscure monks many of the most valuable which have been preserved to modern times in MSS.; among them Quintilian, Silius Italicus, Marcellinus, and part of Cicero. About the beginning of the 13th century St. Gall lost its reputation for learning, as its abbots exchanged a love of piety and knowledge for the pursuit of ambition. The desire of security first induced the abbot to surround his convent and the adjoining building with a wall and ditch, with 13 towers at intervals. This work was executed A.D. 954, and from that time may be dated the foundation of the town. He and his 100 monks of the Benedictine order thought it no disgrace to sally forth sword in hand and helmet on head, backed by their 200 serfs, in the hour of danger, when the convent was threatened by ungodly laymen. The donations of pilgrims from all parts of Europe soon augmented the revenues of the abbots. They became the most considerable territorial sovereigns in N. Switzerland. They were raised to the rank of princes of the empire, and were engaged in constant wars with their neighbours, and latterly entangled in perpetual feuds with their subjects at home. These bold burghers, who, in the first instance, owed their existence and prosperity to the convent, became, in the end restive under its rule. In the beginning of the 15th century Appenzell threw off the yoke of the abbot; at the Reformation St. Gall itself became independent of him; and in 1712 the ecclesiastical prince was obliged to place the convent under the protection of those very citizens whose ancestors had been his serfs. The French Revolution caused the secularization of the abbey, and the sequestration of its revenues followed in 1805. The last abbot, Pancratius Forster, died in 1829, a pensioner on the bounty of others, in the convent of Muri.

The *Abbey Church* (cathedral since 1846) of Italian architecture, was completely rebuilt 1766; it possesses, in the *Treasury* or Sacristy, some antique relics—the bell of the original hermitage, ch. plate, &c. Fine Organ.

The vast buildings of the *Monastery* date from the 17th and 18th centuries; and the part of it which formed the abbot's *Palace* (*Die Pfalz*) now serves as a R. Cath. Seminary for teachers. The *Convent Library* (open Mond. Wednes. and Satur. 9 to 12, and 2 to 4) (Stifts Bibliothek) contains over 1400 volumes of valuable MSS., such as numerous Latin classics, MSS. of the 10th and 11th centuries, Greek New Testament of the 10th century, Psalms of the 9th century, various ancient MSS. either from Ireland or transcribed by Irish monks; the Gospels of Sinlaam, bound in ivory tablets; Palimpsests, 4th century; also a MS. of the Niebelungen Lied, and many letters relating to the Reformation.

St. Laurent (Prot.), is a 12th-centy. ch., restored 1850-3. *St. Mangen* is said to be a ch. of the 9th cent.

The finest edifices are the *Cantonal School* or *Public Seminary*, on the road to Rorschach, and near it the *Museum*, which includes a small picture gallery, containing good works by native artists, and *Town Library*, and the *Orphan House*, outside the town, to the N.W.

At the *Casino Club* will be found an excellent *reading-room.*

Post-office near the Rly. Stat.

[The *Freudenberg*, 2871 ft., about 2 m., or half an hour's walk S.E., commands a panorama, including the lake of Constance and the mountains of St. Gall and Appenzell, with the Sentis at their head. A carriage-road leads up to the *Inn* on the top.

Excursion.—From St. Gall to Trogen, Gais, Appenzell, Weissbad, and back to St. Gall—a delightful day's drive (Rte. 68).]

The railway runs for full a mile through the suburbs of St. Gall; then down the side of a pretty and well wooded ravine to

Mörschwyl Stat. Thence it descends through green fields and orchards, with fine views over the lake, to

Rorschach, on the Lake of Constance : *Buffet* at the Stat. (*Inns :* Seehof, good, but rather dear; Hirsch, moderate ; Anker ; H. Bahnhof ; Post (Krone); Grüner Baum. On the lake, 2½ m. towards Arbon, is the Hotel of the Baths of Horn.)— This is a busy port and the Terminus of the railways to Zürich and Coire. [*Friedrichshafen*, the station for Ulm and Stuttgart; and *Lindau*, the stat. for Augsburg and Munich, on the opposite shore of the lake, are respectively reached in 40 min. and 1¼ hr. The steamers also touch at *Bregenz*, in the Austrian province of the Vorarlberg, the most direct way to Tyrol.] Rorschach, with 4368 Inhab., was once the principal corn-market in N. Switzerland, but is now superseded by Romanshorn. Much muslin is made. There are many ancient houses, with sculptured oriels in the picturesque street which stretches along the lake; and extensive *Swimming Baths* 5 min. below the town. The neighbouring vineyards produce *Markgräfler* wine.

On the slope, a little above Rorschach, is the large dilapidated building, called *Statthalterei*, or *Mariaberg*, a palace once of the proud abbots of St. Gall, now a government *School.* Its Gothic cloister, and vaulted refectory with bas-reliefs, deserve notice (date 1513). Fine view from the terrace. Above, perched on a projecting sandstone rock, is the desolate *Castle of St. Anna*, with its square keep; and ¾ hr. higher the *Rossbühel*, a hill which commands the whole lake. Another beautiful point of view is the *Weinachten Eck*, 4½ m. on the road to Heiden, particularly for the influx of the Rhine, and mountains above the town of Bregenz.

Railways to Constance and to Coire and Bregenz (Rte. 66), and to Heiden (Rte. 68). [It is a pleasant 3 days' walk (to Ragatz or Coire) through Heiden to the inn on the top of the Gäbris, thence to Weissbad : thence over Hoherkasten to the Rüthi rly. stat.]

ROUTE 66.

CONSTANCE TO RORSCHACH AND RAGATZ —THE BATHS OF PFÄFFERS.— RAILWAY.

The railway runs along the shores of the lake, commanding beautiful views of the mountains. The principal stations are

1 m. *Kreuzlingen* (Rte. 8).
2½ m. *Münsterlingen.*

9 m. *Romanshorn* (Rte. 10.)

5 m. *Arbon* (Rte. 8.)

2 m. *Horn* (here is a large Bathing Establishment.)

2½ m. *Rorschach*, Rte. 65.

After leaving Rorschach the rail skirts the foot of low hills green with vineyards. It passes *Wartegg*, a castle belonging to the ex-Duchess of Parma, and the ruins of the feudal castle *Wartensee*. *Weinburg*, on the height, is the seat of the Prince of Hohenzollern Sigmaringen. Fine view from his park, particularly from the *Steinerne Tisch*, or Stone Table, above the castle.

4½ m. *Rheineck Stat.* (*Inns:* Post; Ochs), a village of 1500 Inhab., with ruins of a *castle*, on the l. bank of the Rhine, about 4 m. above its mouth under vineclad hills. Diligence to Heiden. On the hills above is *Walzenhausen*, with a Kurhaus beautifully situated.

3½ m. *St. Margarethen Junct. Stat.*, a pretty village embowered in a grove of walnut and fruit trees. Here the line from Lindau comes in, crossing the Rhine by a long bridge. Rt., on the hills, is seen the village of Heiden (Rte. 65). The rail turns S. up the valley through a country rich in grain, especially maize, and abounding in orchards. The Rhine here is a wide, shallow, muddy, and unsteady stream, constantly changing its channel and overflowing its banks: it is not navigated except by wood-rafts.

8 m. *Altstädten Stat.* (*Inns:* Drei Könige or Post; Freihof; Splügen, at the stat.). The town is nearly a mile from the station. It is an old town, many houses on arcades. Its 7800 Inhab. are chiefly engaged in muslin-weaving and embroidery. [There is a road over the hill of *Stoss* to Gais, 6 m., Appenzell, 9 m., and Weissbad, 11½ m. Diligence through Gais to Appenzell. Another road, over the *Ruppen*, leads to Trogen, 9 m. There is also a footpath to Heiden, in 3 hrs. These

heights command a glorious view over the Alps of the Vorarlberg. The women of the lower Rheinthal are all diligently occupied in tambouring muslin; much of which goes to England.]

4 m. *Oberried Stat.* (*Inns:* Adler; Krone; Sonne). On the rt. is the ruinous old tower of Schloss Blatten. From Oberried to Feldkirch in Austria beyond the Rhine is 1¼ post.

[This is the best starting-point for the ascent of the Kamor, or of its precipitous neighbour the *Hoherkasten*, 5902 ft., which lies further S. The mountain-side is steep forest and then grass nearly to the top of Kamor (beware of holes in the limestone); the way then lies on a level along the flank of Kamor S. to Hoherkasten —the Appenzell Rigi—which has a neat little *Inn* on the top, with magnificent view of the Alps of Vorarlberg, Engadine, and Grisons. Between this peak and Kamor is the *Kamor Pass*, leading to the Baths of Weissbad. The ascent is about 3 hrs.]

3 m. *Rüthi Stat.* (2 humble *Inns*) under the *Kamor*, 5748 ft.

4 m. *Saletz Stat.*, for Sennwald (*Inn:* Krone). Down to the 17th century, this district belonged to the barons of Hohen Sax, many of whose castles, reduced to ruins by the Appenzellers, may be discerned upon the W. heights of the Rhine valley. One of this family, a Protestant, escaped with difficulty from the massacre of St. Bartholomew at Paris, and on his return home was murdered by his nephew. After this foul deed, it is the popular belief that the blessing of God was withdrawn from the race. In 1616 their vast domains were sold to Zürich, and soon afterwards the family became extinct. The body of the murdered man is still preserved in a coffin with a glass lid, dried like a mummy, under the church-tower of Sennwald. This circumstance, and the story connected with it, have given to the remains a reputation for sanctity; so that, though

a Protestant, the Catholics have stolen some of the limbs as relics, and once actually carried off the body across the Rhine; it was, however, speedily recovered.

1½ m. *Haag Stat.* From Sax the pass of the *Saxer Lücke* to Weissbad.

3 m. *Buchs Junct. Stat.* (*Inns:* Arlberg; Rössli; Sonne). Above it *Schloss Werdenberg*, seat of a noble family of that name, who played an important part in early Swiss history. It is in good preservation. A cross-road runs to Wildhaus, and a railway crosses the Rhine to Feldkirch in Austria.

3 m. *Sevelen* (*Inn:* Traube). Rt. the ruined castle of Wartau; l. beyond the Rhine, Vaduz, capital of the principality of Lichtenstein; and near the entrance of the Luziensteig pass Schloss Guttenberg. Behind it rises the grey head of the *Falkniss* with its chaplet of snow.

[The *Alvier* (7753 ft.) may be ascended hence in 4 to 5 hrs. by a good path. A solid house of refuge has been constructed near the top.]

7¼ m. *Sargans Junct. Stat.* (Buffet at the stat.; H. Thoma, close to it). The village is a mile off. Here the rail joins that from Wallenstadt and Zürich to Coire. (See Rtes. 13 and 81.)

4 m. **Ragatz Stat.** : Omnibus to the Baths ¾ m.: (*Hotels:* Quellen Hof, a magnificent Bathing Establishment, with terraced gardens; Hof Ragatz, originally the summer residence of the abbots; usually overcrowded. These houses are supplied with water from the hot springs of Pfäffers, conveyed hither in wooden pipes 12,500 ft. long. H. Tamīna, very good; 125 beds, from 2 fr.; good baths. Adjoining it is the *Dorf Bad.* These are all first-class. H. Schweizerhof, good and reasonable; H. Bahnhof, fair; Krone; Friedthal; Ochs; Bär). Furnished houses can be had.

Ragatz (2000 ft.) is a village of 1800 R. C. Inhab., at the mouth of the gorge through which the torrent Tamīna issues out to join the Rhine. It occupies a central position at the junction of the roads from Zurich, St. Gall, Feldkirch, and Coire, but thrives chiefly on visitors attracted by its excellent hotels, its beautiful scenery, mild climate, and abundant supply of the mineral waters of Pfäffers. The most conspicuous building is the Bathhouse and Hotel, called *Quellenhof*, a palace in extent and architecture, in the midst of gardens, well laid out, in which a band plays. It has an English chapel. The philosopher *Schelling* (died 1854) is buried in the Rom. Cath. Cemetery. His monument was erected by the King of Bavaria.

In full view of Ragatz rise the grand peaks and ridges of the Falkins, and in front the ruins of *Freudenberg Castle*, just W. of Ragatz, destroyed 1437 in the war between the confederates and Zürich.

The OLD BATHS OF PFÄFFERS, 2½ m. up the gorge of the Tamīna, *one of the most extraordinary spots in Switzerland.* Carriages wait at the station, and charge 8 fr. for 2 persons, 10 fr. for 3 or 4, there and back. Those who are able should walk; it is not possible to miss the way. The defile leading to it, a deep fissure in the mountain side, is romantic; the torrent forming waterfalls at every step.

The Old Baths are situated in two large piles of building, connected by a chapel, on a narrow ledge a few feet above the roaring Tamīna. They are so deeply sunken between the rocks that they may be said to be half-buried, and in the height of summer the sun shines upon them only from 10 to 2.

The hot springs of Pfäffers were, it is said, discovered by a hunter, about 1038, who, having entered into the abyss of the Tamīna, in the pursuit of game, remarked the column of vapour arising from them. They were certainly known in the 13th century, and were much frequented throughout the middle ages. For many years nothing was done to facilitate access to the source, hidden away at the bottom of a great gulf, and patients desirous of profiting by its healing virtues were let down from the cliffs above, by ropes, and, in order to reap as much benefit as possible, were accustomed to pass a week together, both day and night, in the bath, not only eating and drinking, but sleeping, under hot water, instead of blankets. The cause of the virtue of the water is not very evident, as a pint contains scarcely 3 grains of saline particles; it has a temperature of about 98° Fahrenheit. The patients at the old Baths are almost exclusively of the lower orders; those of the more opulent classes prefer living in hotels and lodging-houses in the sunny valley of the Rhine, to which the mineral waters are now conducted in pipes.

The situation of the old baths is both gloomy and monotonous, hemmed in between dripping walls of rock, and shaded by dank foliage, with only a narrow strip of sky overhead, and with small space or facilities for locomotion and exercise. To one fresh from the upper world, its meadows and sunshine, a visit to Pfäffers has all the effect of being at the bottom of a well or a mine, except for a few hours at midday. The atmosphere is kept at one regular temperature of chilliness by the perpetual draught brought down by the torrent; and the solitary and imprisoned ray which about noon, and for an hour or two afterwards, finds its way into these recesses, is insufficient to impart permanent warmth or cheerfulness.

Source of the hot spring.

A few yards above the old baths' the sides of the ravine of the Tamīna contract in an extraordinary manner, so as to approach within a few feet of each other; a little farther they even close over and cover up the river, which is seen issuing out of a cavern. The springs are reached through the bath-house, whence a bridge of planks leads to the entrance, which is closed by a door. The bridge is prolonged into the gorge, in the shape of a scaffolding or shelf, suspended by iron stanchions to the rocks, and partly laid in a niche cut out of the side. It is carried all along the chasm as far as the hot spring, and affords the only means of approach to it, as the sides of the rent are vertical, and there is not an inch of room between them and the torrent. Formerly the passage was along two, sometimes one plank, unprotected by railings; at present a platform, 4 feet wide, furnished with a hand-rail, renders the approach to the spring easy for the most timid, and perfectly free from risk. Each person pays 1 fr. for admittance. A few yards from the entrance, the passage is darkened by the overhanging rock. The sudden chill of an atmosphere never visited by the sun's rays, the rushing and roaring of the torrent, the threatening position of the rocks above, have a grand and striking effect. In parts it is almost dark, where the sides of the ravine one overlap another. The rocks in many places show marks of having been ground away, and scooped out by the rushing river, and by the stones brought down with it. For several hundred yards the river pursues an almost subterranean course. In some places the roots of the trees are seen dangling over-head. Had Virgil or Dante known the gorge of Pfäffers, they would certainly have conducted their heroes through it to the jaws of the infernal regions.

The shelf of planks extends 700 yards from the baths. At its extremity, at the bottom of a cavern rise the springs, of a temperature of about 100° Fahrenheit; the water is received into a reservoir nearly 15 feet deep, from which it is conducted in pipes. The first baths were miserable hovels, suspended, like swallows' nests, to the face of the rock : the only entrance was by the roof, and the sick were let down by ropes and pulleys. Marks of these structures are still to be seen. The springs generally cease to flow in winter; they are most copious when the snow has fallen in abundance, and continue from spring till autumn, after which their fountains are again sealed. The water has little taste or smell; it bears some resemblance, in its mineral contents, to that of Ems, and is used both for bathing and drinking.

After emerging from the gorge, the traveller may ascend the valley above it by excellent paths on the steep l. bank, and then keeping to the L., and descending a little, he will in about half a mile cross by a natural bridge beneath which the Tamīna, out of sight and hearing from above, forces its way past the hot springs. A kind of staircase (Steige) formed of trunks and roots of trees, on the rt. bank, leads to the carriage-road on an upper stage of the valley, which is covered with verdant pasture on one side, and with thick woods on the other. The two sides are separated by the gash and narrow gorge. This is, perhaps, the best point for obtaining a general view of the baths and the singular spot in which they are sunken. On looking over the precipice, you perceive, at the bottom of the ravine, at the depth of 300 feet, the roofs of the two large buildings. The upper valley, also, with its carpet of bright green, its woods, and limestone cliffs, the crags of the Calanda to the S., and the peak of the Falkniss on the opposite side of the Rhine, form a magnificent landscape.

It is a walk of 20 min. by the carriage-road, from the top of the Steige, and high above the Tamīna, to

Pfäffers (*Inns :* Taube ; Löwe). There is a more direct foot-path from the road below the Baths, crossing a fragile bridge, and ascending through the woods (1 hr.). In this village is the

Convent of Pfäffers, built 1665-97, in place of one destroyed by fire. It encloses a church, like all the convents of the Benedictine order. It is finely placed on a mountain-platform, commanding the valley of the Rhine, on one side backed by the Falkniss, on the other opening out towards the lake of Wallenstadt and the peaks of the Sieben Churfirsten. This monastery, founded 713, was suppressed, after an existence of 10 centuries, in 1838, by the government of St. Gall, in consequence of the finances of the convent becoming involved, and at the request of a majority of the brethren. The Government pensioned the abbot and monks, took possession of the convent and all that belonged to it, and have converted it into a lunatic asylum.

It once possessed a very extensive territory ; its abbots were princes; but the French, as usual, appropriated their revenues; and, at the termination of the French rule, but a small part of their property was restored to them, including the baths.

From Pfäffers the road, with a glorious view, descends in zigzags to Ragatz, passing the ruined *Castle of Wartenstein.* There is a short cut through the wood.

A pedestrian bound to Coire need not return to Ragatz after ascending the Steige, but may pass the convent and go by path to the Untere-Zoll-Brücke; or he may proceed to Reichenau by the *Kunkels* (see below, *c*).

The *Calanda,* or Calandaberg (9213 ft., the mountain on the rt. bank of the Tamīna, above the old baths) is a 5-hours' climb. Rough accommodation for the night may be obtained at the chalets called *Obern Maiensäss*, about 2 hrs. below the summit.

The *Piz Alun*, about 5000 ft., is another fine point of view, but quite easy to ascend, in 1½ hr. from Pfäffers village through St. Margarethen. It is the rocky crown of an almost precipitous descent to the Rhine, the highest crag being reached by a ladder. Many other *Excursions* may be made from Ragatz.

a. To *Luziensteig*, a fortified pass beyond the Rhine, 4½ m. between the Fläscherberg and the Falkniss. Carr.-road from Mayenfeld (or short cut from Ragatz Stat.) through beautiful woods to the small *Inn* on the top of the pass. Thence you may descend in 1 hr., through the fortified gateway, to *Balzers*, and to the ferry for Trübbach Stat. 30 min. The ascent of the *Fläscherberg* from Luziensteig is made by carriage-road reaching in succession the various forts, and the view from its top, and down the precipice which scarps one side of it, is striking.

b. To the *Piz Sol*, 9340 ft., the highest point of the *Grauehörner*. It is a long day's work.

c. By the *Kunkels Pass* to Reichenau. This pass is not very striking, but pretty, and a change from the Rhine valley. There is a carriage-road to Vadura, then char-road to Vättis, beyond that point a horse-path. A pedestrian can go by the old baths, and ascend the Steige to the road. It proceeds along the rt. bank of the Tamina, past many small slate-works, to the hamlet of Vadura. The valley is here tolerably wide and fertile ; soon afterwards it contracts and becomes walled in with precipices, pines growing on them wherever there is room. In about 2 hrs. from the Steige the valley turns rt. and opens out ; then comes *Vättis* (with a pretty little *Inn*, the Gemsli) opposite the entrance of the Calfeuser Thal. The path now lies over meadows, the precipices of the Calanda overhanging on the l. The numerous chalets of *Kunkels* are next reached, and then

the foot of the col, where the l. path must be taken ; and an ascent of 20 min., through clumps of beech and fir, leads to the head of the pass, 2½ hrs. from Vättis. There is not much view from the col itself. Keeping again l., the path plunges into the ravine of *Foppa*, and by a very steep descent Tamins is reached and then Reichenau (Rte. 87). Time, fair walking—

Ragatz.	hrs.	min.
Steige	1	0
Vättis	2	0
Col	2	0
Reichenau.	1	20
Total . . .	6	20

[Or reversed, by Pfäffers—

Reichenau	hrs.	min.
Col	1	40
Vättis	1	30
Pfäffers	2	0
Ragatz	0	35
Total . . .	5	45]

A French detachment crossed . this pass in 1799, and drove the Austrians out of Tamins.

d. The excursion up the *Calfeuser Thal* towards the glacier of Sardona the source of the Tamina, is seldom made, but the scenery is very grand. As far as Vättis the path is the same as that over the Kunkels. Thence a mule-path to *St. Martin*, where the *Ringelspitz*, 10,506 ft., rises l., the *Grauehörner* rt., and the *Scheibe*, 9587 ft., at the head of the valley. There is a pass to the Weisstannen Thal, on the N., and a difficult passage by the Sardona glacier to the Sernf Thal.

e. The *Scesaplana*. This is perhaps the most tempting excursion for an active pedestrian. He will do best to choose the route from Bludenz on the Austrian side for the ascent, returning by Seewis, an expedition of 2 days, sleeping at the hut at the Lunersee. (Rte. 94.)

f. Those who do not intend to cross

the Splügen into Italy, ought at any rate to visit the *Via Mala* and may return in a long day.]

ROUTE 67.

BREGENZ TO SARGANS (RLY.) OR MAYENFELD, BY VADUZ.

The direct route from Tyrol to north-eastern Switzerland is by the Vorarlberg Railway, which quits the valley of the Inn at Landeck, and enters the valley of the Rhine at Feldkirch. Pedestrians may reach Bregenz from Tyrol, or the Bavarian Alps, through the beautiful *valley of the Bregenzer Ach*, a mountain torrent which, after a course of about 35 m., falls into the Lake of Constance a little S.W. of Bregenz.

Railway, Bregenz to Buchs.

Bregenz Stat. (*Inns:* Oesterreichischer Hof; Bregenzer Hof; Schwarzer Adler, on the lake; Goldener Adler; Krone; Weisser Kreuz; Schweizerhof). The chief town of the Vorarlberg. (See HANDBOOK FOR SOUTHERN GERMANY.)

Feldkirch Junct. Stat., 21 m. (*Inns:* Englischer Hof, good; Lowe; Ochs), the frontier town of Austria, finely situated at the opening of the valley of the Ill, through which lies the road to Tyrol. Rly. to *Bludenz*, on the road to Landeck, Innsbruck.

The rail crosses the Rhine to join the rly. from Rorschach to Sargans at

Buchs Junct. Stat., Rte. 66.
[About 1 m. from the town the road

quits the Austrian territory to enter the principality of *Lichtenstein*, one of the smallest sovereign States in Europe, measuring about 12 m. in length by 3 or 4 in breadth. The Prince has very large possessions in Austria, and usually holds a high position at the Court of Vienna, not caring to exercise in person his rights of miniature royalty. He is, however, or was, a member of the Germanic Confederation, and contributed 55 men to the Federal army! The old road continues along the rt. bank of the Rhine, passing *Vaduz*, the capital of this minute State, below the mountain of the *Drei Schwestern.* About 5 m. farther *Balzers* (*Inn:* Post), formerly a post-station, at the foot of the heights, which are crowned by the fortress of *Luziensteig*, contested between the Swiss and Austrians in the 15th centy. and Thirty Years' War (1621-24), and in the war of the French Revolution. It was rebuilt 1830. To the rt. is *Schloss Guttenberg.* 4½ m. farther, over the beautiful *Luziensteig pass*, and about 18 m. from Feldkirch, is Mayenfeld Stat. Thence to Coire by rly. (Rte. 81).]

ROUTE 68.

RORSCHACH TO HEIDEN, GAIS, AND APPENZELL; WITH EXCURSIONS TO WEISSBAD, THE WILDKIRCHLEIN, AND THE HOCH SENTIS.

Canton Appenzell lies out of the beat of English travellers, completely surrounded by Canton St. Gall, and shut in on the S. by the Sentis Alps; on which side no great roads pass out of it. From the 13th to the 15th century the inhabitants of Appenzell were engaged in constant struggles with the powerful abbots of St. Gall, who were ever attempting to encroach on their liberties. In 1513 Appenzell joined the Swiss cantons as the 13th and last before 1798. The internal troubles caused by the Reformation resulted in the division of the canton, in 1597, into 2 districts, called *Rhoden*, independent of each other, but enjoying each only one vote at the diet. Nowhere else in Europe (except, perhaps in Canton Uri) have the primitive institutions of Teutonic democracy, on which our own Constitution is founded, survived in their original simplicity with so little interruption or alteration. The government, in both states, is a pure democracy: the General Assembly, or Landesgemeinde, is composed of every male born in the canton, and attendance at its annual meetings is enforced by a fine. Ausser Rhoden is very thickly peopled, having 4308 Inhab. to the Germ. sq. league, chiefly Protestants. They are almost exclusively engaged in manufactures of cotton, muslin, tambouring, &c. Inner Rhoden, on the contrary, with 1726 Inhab. to the sq. league, is a land of herdsmen, and Roman Catholic; and though manufactures have begun, it is not so prosperous as Ausser Rhoden.

There is a wonderful appearance of prosperity, of cleanliness and neatness in Ausser Rhoden, which is very pleasing. The hill-sides, green to their very top, are studded with the cheerful dwellings of the peasants. The villages of Trogen, Teufen, and Speicher are highly interesting, for, though the houses are of wood, they are tastily and comfortably built, and most of them have a well-tended garden. In fact many persons of ample fortune reside in these little towns, much of the Swiss muslin being made or embroidered here for St. Gall houses. Every cottage is filled with females assiduously busied in embroidery, and the extent of education, or rather of learning, is said to be extraordinary.

The Inner Rhoden is Catholic, and is not so prosperous, but the difference is now much less marked than formerly.

The Appenzellers are very fond of gymnastics; and a part of every holiday is devoted to wrestling. Hurling the stone is another favourite exercise. A mass of rock, varying in weight from half to a whole cwt., is poised on the shoulder, and then cast forward a distance of several feet. In 1805 a man of Urnäsch hurled a stone, weighing 184 lbs., 10 ft. The Appenzellers are also capital shots: rifle-matches are held in summer on almost every Sunday, and the cracking reports resound on all sides. The Appenzellers are much addicted to dancing and to assembling in public-houses, the number of which is astonishing. Being less overrun by strangers than other parts of Switzerland, the prices at inns are very much lower. For carriages however, they are higher, but the carriages and horses are, as a rule better.

Although the mountains of Appenzell are not of the first order of magnitude, there are few Alpine districts which will better reward the lover of pastoral scenery. For pedestrians arriving by the Lake of Constance, it offers the most direct and agreeable route for commencing a tour in the Alps. It is easily accessible by good carriage-roads from the E. and W.; and, though little frequented by English, is annually visited by large numbers of Germans and Swiss, who come chiefly for the *cure de petit lait*, or *molken-kur*, which is supposed to be very beneficial to health. This "cure" consists in drinking goats'-whey, here called *schotten*, which is brought in large quantities every morning, still warm, to the establishments. There can be little doubt that benefit is often derived, but it may be allowable to believe that the pure mountain air, healthful exercise, and regular life, have as large a share in the effect as the goats'-whey. The principal establishments of this kind are at Gais, Weissbad, Heiden, Gonten, and Urnäsch.

The mountains of Appenzell are

covered with *whortle-berries* so plentifully that 200 persons are engaged daily collecting them, and earn in 6 weeks, 8000 fr.

From Rorschach (Rte. 65), a rly. on the Rigi system runs up to Heiden, the gradient, however, never exceeding 1 in 11.

Soon after leaving Rorschach Stat., the train begins to ascend, and in less than 2 m. rises 650 ft. The views over the lake on the way are very fine. (Take seats on l.) At the top of this steep incline the line turns to the S., leaves the lake, and runs along the side of a well-wooded and deep ravine to *Schwendi Stat.* Heiden is now seen high up on the l. The rly. continues along the side of the ravine, then makes a sweep, and in something less than an hour from Rorschach, lands the passengers at

Heiden, 2644 ft. (*Inns:* Frei Hof und Schweizer Hof, both good ; Kuranstalt, comfortable). This village, of 3200 Inhab., consists entirely of large houses, in wide streets, each house standing alone, looking as if it had just been freshly painted. It is placed on the slope of the mountain overlooking the lake of Constance (1400 ft. below), with green fields and fir-woods around, above, and below. The village was burnt in 1838, and the inhabitants no doubt rebuilt it in wide streets, and with detached houses, in order to avoid a similar catastrophe. The aspect of the village is exceedingly cheerful. Many of the houses are pensions, or are let in lodgings ; but most of them are private houses, the inhabitants of which are engaged in weaving and embroidering muslin curtains. As far as the traveller can see, there is not a small or dilapidated house or a poor person in the place.

Heiden is much frequented during the summer for the whey-cure, and has a Kursaal and band. On Sundays the band plays chorales on the gallery running outside the high church tower.

[Excursions—

a. From the little *Chapel of St. Antony*, about 4 m. S., a beautiful view is gained, looking over the valley of the Rhine, and part of the Lake of Constance, and at the opposite ranges of the Vorarlberg and Lichtenstein mountains.

b. The top of the *Kaien* is 1¼ hr. from Heiden. By it Trogen may be reached on foot.]

There is an exceedingly beautiful drive (diligences daily) of about 7 m. to Trogen. The road rises steadily through green fields and woods, at the side of a ravine for about 3 m., when it reaches a pass with a fine view towards the Sentis. From this it is tolerably level to *Wald*, whence it descends by a series of zigzags to a fine bridge across a stream, then ascends again some 400 ft. to Trogen. The number of large and well-kept houses with muslin curtains in the windows is remarkable.

Trogen, 3000 ft. (*Inns:* Krone, fair; Rössli), the seat of the government of Appenzell (Ausser-Rhoden), with 2629 Inhab., a group of beautifully ornamented timber houses, each with its flower-garden. The Landsgemeinde meets here and at Hündwyl in alternate years.

From hence to Gais there is a carriage-road by *Bühler* (see below), making a considerable circuit ; but the more agreeable route is by carriage-road over the *Gäbris* (1¼ hr. up ; ½ hr. down to Gais), 4119 ft., with an *Inn* (clean and cheap), on the *Signalhöhe*, commanding a charming panorama—the Sentis and Alte Mann ; the Falkniss, Scesa Plana, and Ill Thal ; the lake of Constance, and distant Rigi and Pilatus. The

=5

finger-posts are very numerous on these hills, so that a pedestrian need rarely be at fault. A direct path from the inn to

Gais, 3000 ft. (*Inns:* Krone, with garden ; Ochs,—both good ; Hirsch, and many others). The bread is very white and good here. This little village of 2550 Protestant Inhab. and of neat timber cottages, mostly converted into lodging-houses by the peasants, their owners, irregularly scattered over lawn-like meadows, is situated in an open country, at an elevation of 3000 ft. above the sea. Its pure and bracing air, and *Cure of Goats'-Whey*, annually attract hither many hundred invalids from all parts of continental Europe ; and during the season, in July and August, the principal inns are generally full.

The chalet-built houses are particularly clean, trimly painted outside. The native songs of the cow-herds and dairy-maids of Appenzell are highly melodious; the music of the cows' bells is everywhere heard.

Gais lies in full view of the Sentis and its chain. For the road from Gais to Altstätten, see below.

[There is a diligence from St. Gall to Trogen in 1½ hr., and thence to Gais.]

Trogen to Appenzell, 12 m.
The carriage-road usually taken is round by Teufen. 1-horse carriage, 12 fr. The road is finely engineered, and, after an ascent and descent, it reaches

Teufen (*Inns:* Hecht, good ; Zur Linde ; H. des Alpes ; Bär). The inhabitants of this flourishing village of neat cottages are chiefly engaged in the manufacture and embroidery of muslin. N., on the *Schäfles Eck*, or *Fröhlichsegg*, is a much-frequented mountain *Inn*, with a fine view.

Here it leaves the road to St. Gall, and turns to the rt., descending through the usual green fields and woods to *Bühler*, another clean, handsome village. The road then goes up the side of a ravine, at the bottom of which are, in wet weather, a series of cascades. The road turns to the rt. just before reaching Gais (see above), and crossing to a pass from which is a fine view, descends to

Appenzell (2560 ft.) (*Inns:* Hecht, Löwe; both good). Though the chief place of Inner Rhoden, this is but a large village of 4300 R. Cath. Inhab, consisting of old wooden houses, with two convents, and a modern *Church* attached to a Gothic choir, painted with representations of banners and flags taken by the Appenzellers in the 15th cent. It derives its name from the country-seat of the Abbot of St. Gall (Abten-zelle, Abbatis Cella), which was anciently built here, when the country around was savage. It is now known for embroidery. It stands in a green and fertile valley.

The nearest stat. is Urnäsch (Rte 69). A rly. is in progress.

The *Landesgemeinde*, or Assembly of the canton, used to meet on a square, near a lime-tree, every year. In the Record Office, *Archiv*, are preserved a number of banners, taken by the Appenzellers of old— the flags of Constance, Winterthur, Feldkirch ; the Tyrolese free ensign, inscribed "Hundert Tausend Teufel," a trophy of Landeck, 1407 ; the Genoese banner of St. George ; and two captured from the Venetians. 1516, in the battle of Agnadel. About 2½ m. S.E. of Appenzell is

Weissbad, a pension, bathing, and goat's-whey-cure establishment, fairly well kept, and beautifully situated in a retired spot under the wooded *Kronberg*, at the foot of the Sentis. It has 202 bedrooms, but is frequently full. The nearest stat. in the Rheinthal is Altstädten, 2½ hrs.' drive by Gais.

Excursions.—*a.* To the *Alpensee*, 3

small lake under the Sentis, 1½ hr.'s walk : very pretty scene.

Three torrents, the Brühl (or Semtis)-bach E., the Schwendibach S., and the Weissbach W., issuing out of 3 valleys, unite at Weissbad, and form the river Sitter [see the relief-map or model of the district in the hotel].

b. Near the end of a precipice which walls in (N.) the middle valley, 1½ hr.'s walk or ride, is the singular chapel of the *Wildkirchlein.* It is best reached by the Weissbach valley (up the road rt. from the inn), of which a beautiful feature is the *Ohrli* (Little Ear), a pyramidal peak of the Sentis. In about 1½ m. the path ascends l. to the Bommenalp, which is in summer a perfect garden of wild flowers. The path divides at the foot of the cliffs, rt. to the Eben Alp, l. direct to Wild-kirchlein. The latter reaches in 20 min. the little *Inn* Zum Aescher, on a terrace under the precipice, and from this a narrow but well-railed ledge leads back along the cliff to a cavern, which is the chapel. A few paces farther is a second cavern, passing through the rock about 100 yds. to the Eben Alp. Within its mouth is the hermitage, now used as an *Inn* —Zum Wildkirchlein. It was built 1648 by an inhabitant of Appenzell, and dedicated to St. Michael, and on that saint's day mass is celebrated in the chapel. The *Ebenalp,* 5090 ft. above the sea, has also an *Inn* on the top. This is 20 min. walk from the cavern, and commands a more exten-sive and a different view, extending to the lake of Constance, and the Suabian hills. You can return direct from the Eben Alp to Weissbad, or cross the ridge, making a circuit back to the hermitage ; but the track down the cliff is awkward, and may at times be difficult.

c. The *Sentis,* the highest mountain in Appenzell, 8215 ft. above the sea. is ascended from Weissbad in 4 hrs. up, 3 down. The panorama is magnificent. About 1 m. beyond *Schwendi* (*Inn:* Fellenburg), where a

stream issues full-grown from the mountain-side, the path crosses the Schwendibach, and ascends l. in zigzags to an elevated pasture. It then runs high above the Alpensee along the face of precipices (a German was killed here in 1870) to the chalets of *Meglisalp* (2 hrs. 10 m. : dear *wirthschaft*). From this point the ascent (rt.) is over rough slopes, passing rt. the opening called *Wagenlücke.* It is steep by snow and rocks to the *Inn* (lately enlarged) under the summit, which is climbed by steps protected by a hand-rail.

d. To the *Hoherkasten,* the highest point of the *Kamor* range, a walk of about 2 hrs. From the top (an *Inn*) is a fine view over the Rhine valley and Alps of Vorarlberg and Grisons. Carr.-rd. to *Brüllisau* (1 hr.), where the path diverges l. up a green alp to a small *Inn.* Thence zigzags to the Kamor pass, just l. of the top of Hoherkasten. By going l. about a mile you can descend to Rüthi Stat., and it is possible to descend, by a steep path, to Sennwald stat.

e. By following up the Brühlbach from Brüllisau through a pretty gorge, a traveller looks down upon the beautiful *Semtisersee.* Higher up the valley an ascent l. leads to the *Saxer Lücke,* a pass to Sax in the Rheinthal, an ascent rt. by the *Fah-lensee* and *Krayalp Pass* to Wildhaus.

f. The Krayalp is on the E. side of the *Alte Mann* (7987 ft.), which can be ascended from this side ; on the W. side is the *Oberkellen Pass* (turn up l. at Meglisalp), 7 hrs. to Wildhaus. It is very steep on the S. side. There is another pass over the ridge nearer the Sentis.

Appenzell to Altstätten.

The first 3 m. of the road is the same as that to Trogen (see above).

The road then turns to the right, and soon reaches Gais (see above). It then rises gradually for about 2 m. with Stoss on the l.

The *Chapel of Stoss* is erected on the summit of the steep pass leading to the Rhein Thal, to commemorate the almost incredible victory gained by 400 men of Appenzell over 3000 Austrians on the 17th of June, 1405. The Archduke of Austria and the Abbot of St. Gall had hoped to take the Swiss by surprise with this preponderating force. But a handful of mountaineers, under Count Rudolph of Werdenberg, assembled in haste, gave them battle and defeated them, killing 900, and losing only 20 of their own party. The day is still kept by a service in the little chapel. The view from the Stoss over the valley of the Rhine, 2000 ft. below, and of the snowy mountains of Tyrol and Vorarlberg beyond, is of the highest beauty. A very steep descent leads by the side of a ravine and through woods and orchards with fine views over the valley of the Rhine, to

Altstätten Stat.   (Rte. 66.)

———

ROUTE 69.

ST. GALL TO APPENZELL [OR LICHTENSTEIG], BY HERISAU.

St. Gall.	Eng. m.
Waldstatt (Rly.)	12

The old road went through a very pretty country, crossing near Bruggen the gorge of the Sitter, by the Kräzeren Brücke, 590 ft. long, 85 ft. above the stream.

The rly. goes along the Winterthur line to Winkeln *Junct. Stat.* (Rte. 65). Thence a branch leads to

Herisau Stat. (*Inns:* Löwe, the best; Storch)—an industrious village of Ausser-Rhoden, contains 11,000 Inhab., stands 2334 ft. above the sea, and is situated on the Glatt, which turns the wheels of its numerous factories. It is a very singular place from its extraordinary irregularity of construction.

There are beautiful walks on the surrounding heights; two of them are topped by ruinous castles, the Rosenberg and Rosenburg, which, according to the story, were once connected together by a leathern bridge. The lower part of the *Church Tower*, in which the Archives are deposited, is the oldest building in the canton dating probably from the 7th century.

The articles chiefly manufactured here are muslins, cottons, and silk, the last a modern introduction : 10,200 persons are employed in Ausser-Rhoden in weaving muslins, and a very large number in embroidering them.

The *Hundswyler Tobel*, a very singular gorge or chasm, deep and wild, about 3½ m. from Herisau, deserves to be visited.

[About a mile N.E. of Herisau is the watering-place of *Heinrichsbad*. The *Badhaus* is an elegant establishment surrounded by pleasure-grounds, the creation of one Heinrich Steiger, a rich manufacturer. Two springs rising out of gravel, and impregnated with iron, carbonic acid, &c., are used for drinking and bathing. Goats'-whey and asses'-milk are also supplied. Accommodation in a cowhouse is provided for invalids suffering from diseases of the chest. The neighbourhood is exceedingly pretty.]

Waldstadt Terminus. Close by is the

Kuranstalt Hirsch, a large well-managed establishment with a beautiful view of the Sentis.

A diligence-road turns off to Schönengrund.

Hence through an undulating country to the frontier of Appenzell. St. Gall, is re-entered before arriving at

St. Peterzell. 3 m. beyond the ruined Castle of Neu-Toggenburg lies

Lichtensteig (Rte. 71).

[From Lichtensteig there is a very pretty drive to Uznach and the Lake of Zürich. The road goes up the steep ascent of the ridge of *Hümmelwald.* From its top a beautiful prospect expands to view; in front the Lake of Zürich, with the castle, town, and bridge of Rappersweil, in full relief on its margin; beyond the lake the pine-clad and snow-topped Alps of Schwyz and Glarus; on the E. the remarkable peaks of the Sieben Churfirsten, and N. the fertile vale of the Toggenburg (Rte. 71). The road divides on the opposite side of the hill rt. to *Rappersweil* (Rte. 13), L to

Uznach Stat. (Rte. 13).]

The railway continues to *Urnäsch Stat.,* 2713 ft. (H. Bahnhof; Krone), a large industrial village, its present terminus.

[Hence a path has been made to the *Sentis* (6 hrs.). 1½ hr. below the top, on the Thierweid, shelter is found in one of the S. Alpine Club huts.]

The road to Appenzell runs due E. past Gonten and Gontenbad, to Appenzell (Rte. 68). Diligence in 1½ hr. Railway in construction.

ROUTE 71.

WYL TO COIRE. THE TOGGENBURG.
70 Eng. m.

Wyl	Eng. m.
Ebnat	15
Wildhaus	17
Haag	7¼
Coire	31¼

Railway [*Toggenburger-Bahn*] from Wyl to Ebnat; 4 trains daily in 1½ hr.

This Rte. lies up the *valley of the Thur,* or *Toggenburg,* which extends nearly 40 m., from Wyl to the source of the river. It is a splendid specimen of a Swiss valley, very fertile in its lower portion; above Nesslau it is bounded by high mountains; N. by the Sentis, S. by the peaks of the Churfirsten. It was anciently governed by counts of its own. When their line became extinct, 1436, the district was claimed by Zürich, and a war ensued, in which the Swiss cantons for the first time fought with one another. It finally, in 1469, fell to the abbot of St. Gall, whose successors had continual disputes with the inhabitants, especially after the Reformation. In 1712 the abbots, after much fighting, were expelled, but restored in 1718. Since 1803, the Toggenburg has formed part of canton St. Gall. It is thickly peopled; its inhabitants manufacture muslin and cotton, and live surrounded by flowers in the very tidiest and prettiest of Swiss chalets.

The rly., after leaving *Wyl Stat.* (Rte. 65), continues in the valley of the Thur.

Lichtensteig Stat. (*Inns:* Krone; Rössli; both good), a town of 1500 Inhab. on the rt. bank of the Thur, in the ancient county of Toggenburg. A picturesque and handsome old *Place,* composed of lofty buildings with porticoes, forms the principal street. An iron bridge, 100 ft. above the river, leads to the rly. stat.

The valley of the Thur is studded with factories and with the country-seats of their proprietors.

Wattwyl Stat. (*Inns:* Rössli; Toggenburg), with 5300 Inhab., the largest and busiest village in the Toggenburg. About 1½ m. farther, stand the convent of Santa Maria der Engeln and the Castle of Yberg.

Ebnat Terminus (*Inns:* Krone, with dépendance, Rosenbühl, on a neighbouring hill; Sonne), terminus of the Toggenburg Rly., 2600 Inhab. Diligence daily to *Nesslau* and to *Haag* rly. stat., in the Rhine valley, 4¼ hrs.

Kappel, close to Ebnat, with 2300 Inhab., was rebuilt after a fire in 1854. In both villages are cotton-factories and dye-works. Rt., the valley of Stein, leading to the *Speer*, which may be ascended this way or from Nesslau in 4 hrs. Beyond Ebnat, near *Krummenau*, the road passes a natural bridge over the river, called the *Sprung* (or Leap).

rt., *Neu-St. Johann* (*Inn:* Schäfle), in a charming little valley.

Nesslau (*Inns:* Traube; Krone), a pretty village, where the Lauterbach flows into the valley from the Sentis. [*a*. Road up the Lauterbach about 5 m., passing *Rietbad*, 3 m., with sulphureous spring; then *path to Weissbad*; about 6 hrs. *b. Path to Wesen*: turn rt. at the Rössli inn; 3½ hrs. to the col, between the silvery precipices of the *Mattstock* and the *Speer*. ¼ hr. more to top of Speer, which is the farthest E. of several similar points: path down from a farmhouse E. of col. This is a beautiful walk.]

Through a defile to *Stein*.

Alt-St. Johann (*Inn:* Rössli), in a wild district. A little beyond it, at Unter-Wasser, the river Thur flows into the valley from its source between the *Sentis* and *Alte Mann*.

Upon the high ground dividing the valley of the Thur from that of the Rhine, stands the remote village of *Wildhaus* — (*Inn:* Hirsch, good),

3613 ft. above the sea, between the Schafberg and the peaks of the Churfirsten. *Lisighaus*, an adjoining hamlet, is remarkable as the birthplace of the Swiss reformer, *Ulrich Zwingli*. The house in which he first saw the light (Jan. 1, 1484) still exists. It is a humble cottage of wood; its walls formed of the stems of trees, its roof weighed down by stones to protect it from the wind. It has resisted the inroads of time for more than 350 years; and the beams and trunks which compose it are black with age. Zwingli's family were peasants; he quitted home when 10 years old, to go to school at Bâle.

[Wildhaus is about 8 hrs. from Weissbad, either by the *Krayalp Pass* just E. of the Alte Mann, or by the *Oberkellen Pass*, just W. of the same mountain. These passes are so steep on the S. side as to be rather difficult. The *Hinterruck Pass* to Wallenstadt requires a guide. The col lies a little E. of the *Scheibenstoll*, 7556 ft., the highest point of the Churfirsten.]

The road, surmounting the *Sommer Tobel*, descends by two sweeping zig-zags into the valley of the Rhine near Gams, and soon after reaches

Haag Stat. Thence by rly. to *Coire* (Rte. 66).

———

ROUTE 72.

WÄDENSWEIL TO EINSIEDELN — RAILWAY. EINSIEDELN TO SCHWYZ. MORGARTEN.

	Miles.
Wädensweil to Einsiedeln	9¼
Einsiedeln to Schwyz	13

The branch rly. to Einsiedeln leaves the main line from Zürich (Rte. 13) at Wädensweil (or Wädenschwyl, crosses a ridge into the valley of the Sihl, which it crosses near

Schindellegi Stat. (*Inn*: Hirsch). At *berbrücke Stat.* the line crosses the ber, and goes up the valley of the lpbach to

EINSIEDELN (French, *Notre Dame s Ermites*; Latin, *Monasterium remitarum*) 2900 ft. *Inns*: Pfau *Paon*); clean and good; Einsiedler of; Adler; the charges are raised ring the pilgrimage. There are in l 55 inns and 20 smaller houses, ostly designed for the reception of or pilgrims, and distinguished by a ngular variety of signs. The town as 8400 Inhab.

The Abbey of Einsiedeln rises high n an undulating plain 3000 ft. above ie sea, producing little but pasture. ; is partly sheltered by a range of ooded hills on the S.E.

The *Monastery* itself, an extensive uilding in the modern Italian style, imposing, not so much from its rchitecture as from its size and situaon in so remote and naked a solitude. he existing edifice dates from 1719, nd is the 6th or 7th raised on this spot nce the first foundation, the others aving been destroyed by fire. It ccupies a stately site upon the hillde, separated from the humbler uildings of the village by a wide quare.

The origin of the abbey is thus acunted for in the histories published der the authority of the monks :— the days of Charlemagne an anoret named Meinrad, of the noble ouse of Hohenzollern, repaired to is wilderness (then called the Finerwald) to end his days in solide and prayer, devoting himself to nd a little black image of the Virgin hich had been given to him by Ste. ildegarde, abbess of Zürich. This oly man was murdered by two robers in 861; but their foul deed, hich they had hoped would escape etection on a spot so remote from he haunts of men, was brought to ght by two pet ravens reared by leinrad, which pursued the mur-

derers with croaking cries, and flapping wings, over hill and dale, as far as Zürich, where their guilt was detected, and they suffered for it on the place now occupied by the Raven inn. The reputation of sanctity, which invested the spot where the saint had lived, increased so much after his death, that his cell was rebuilt, and a church founded by a community of Benedictine hermits (Einsiedler). The first abbot was Eberard, and it is affirmed by the monkish legend, and perpetuated in the bull of Pope Pius VIII., that when the Bishop of Constance was about to consecrate the church on the 14th of September, 948, he was aroused at midnight by the sounds of angelic minstrelsy, and was informed next day, by a voice from heaven, that there was no need to proceed with the sacred rite, as the church had been already consecrated by the powers of heaven, and by the presence of the Saviour. The Pope pronounced this a true miracle, and, in consideration, granted plenary indulgence to all pilgrims who should repair to the shrine of Our Lady of the Hermits, in the words inscribed upon the church, "Hic est plena remissio peccatorum a culpâ et a poenâ." The consequence has been that during 9 centuries the influx of pilgrims to the shrine and of wealth to the monastery has been almost uninterrupted. The pious benefactions increased the revenues and domains of the abbey to an enormous extent; it ranked second to St. Gall alone of all the monasteries in Switzerland. Its abbot became a prince of the holy Roman empire, with a seat in the Diet. He had his hereditary officers, his chamberlain, marshal, and cupbearer; and these posts were filled by personages of noble or princely rank.

The French revolutionary invaders of 1798 stripped Einsiedeln of its resources and treasures, and carried off the figure of the Virgin to Paris; but the monks, on abandoning the convent, transported with them into Tyrol a duplicate figure, which they assert to be the authentic original.

Notwithstanding these untoward circumstances, the abbey remains at the present day the richest in Switzerland, and the Black Virgin, whether an original or a copy, has lost none of her reputation. The average annual number of pilgrims who receive the sacrament in the church is 150,000. The great Festival is Sept. 14. Many of the pilgrims are deputies paid to do penance for wealthier sinners, who remain at home, and a pilgrimage thus performed by proxy is considered equally efficacious with one made in person.

The monastery contains about 100 Benedictine monks, including lay-brothers, novices, &c.

In the square in front stands a fountain with 14 jets, from all of which the pilgrims drink, as it is traditionally reported that our Saviour drank from one, but from which of them is not known.

In the centre of the conventual buildings stands, as is usual in Benedictine monasteries, the *Church*, which has been compared with that of St. John Lateran at Rome. The interior is somewhat gaudily ornamented with inferior paintings, marble and gilding. A few feet from the entrance stands the *Shrine* or *Chapel of the Virgin*, of black marble, with a grating in front, through which, by the glare of an ever-burning lamp, the spectator perceives the palladium of the temple, a little black figure of the Virgin and Child, attired in gold brocade, glittering with jewels, and bearing crowns of gold. The space in front is rarely free of worshippers, and commonly hundreds, nay, at times, thousands may be seen prostrate before it. The walls of this part of the church are covered with votive tablets, rude paintings in oil, which are chiefly representations of escapes from fire and water, all effected by the supposed miraculous interference of the image. In 1835, 250 new votive tablets were hung up, older ones being removed to make way for them.

In the *Chapel of the Magdalene*, a church of itself in size, on the l. of the choir, are 28 confessionals, over each of which is written the language in which confessions will be received in it, either German, Italian, French, or Romansch.

The *Treasury*, once so rich in church plate, was plundered by the French in 1798, and one splendid monstrance alone remains, but it is not readily shown. The monastery includes, besides the lodgings for the Abbot and the brethren, a handsome refectory, a kitchen, an hospital, a *library* containing 26,000 vols., a museum of fossils and minerals, a free school and boarding-school, the pupils of which are taught by the monks, and a large cellar running under the greater part of the edifice. During meals, passages of some approved author, such as Lingard's History of England, Cobbett's History of the Reformation, &c., are read aloud to the assembled brotherhood, and even at times portions of newspapers.

Zwingli, the reformer, was curate of Einsiedeln from 1516 to 1519. *Theophrastus Paracelsus* von Hohenheim was born here, or in the neighbourhood, in 1498.

[There is a rough but direct footpath to Schwyz, over the *Hacken Pass*, 4570 ft., a walk of 4½ hrs.; no guide needed. It lies up the valley of the Alpbach, to the hamlet of Alpthal; thence to an *Inn*, and the Col, which lies between the *Mythen* and *Hochstückli*. The latter, 5105 ft. above the sea, can be ascended in ½ hr. from the inn.]

The carriage-road to Schwyz (diligences daily) is by Biberbrücke; the footpath is shorter, crossing the Katzenstrick, a large tract of upland meadow, direct to Altmatt.

From Biberbrücke the road goes up the valley of the Biber to

Rothenthurm (*Inn:* Ochs, good), a vil.

lage of nearly 800 Inhab., the place of meeting of the general assembly of the Canton Schwyz, convened here every two years, in the open air, on the first Sunday in May. The Landammann is president, and every citizen above the age of 18 has a vote.

Rothenthurm receives its name from a Red Tower still standing and forming part of the defences of a long rampart, erected by the Schwyzers on their W. frontier, to ward off the inroads of their lordly and lawless neighbours. It extended as far as Art.

[About 2 m. W., on the confines of Canton Zug, is *Morgarten*. It is easily reached by a road turning to the rt. between Rothenthurm and Ecce Homo, and leading to the little chapel of St. James, on the borders of the lake of Egeri (Rte. 14).

MORGARTEN, memorable in the annals of the Swiss as the scene of their first struggle for independence, is the spot where the chivalry of Austria were worsted, and their leader, Duke Leopold, compelled to fly, 15th of November, 1315. Just where the ascent into the upland country of Schwyz commences, running up a narrow defile, the Austrians were met by the confederates, a mere handful of men, but of hardy frame and resolute spirit, posted on the ridge of the Sattel, near Haselmatt. The first bold charge of the Swiss, rushing on with swords and clubs, was aided by a discharge of rocks from the heights above, which quickly threw into confusion the ranks of heavy-armed knights. They attempted to fall back, but their evolutions were prevented by the infantry pressing on in their rear. Without room to manœuvre, or even to turn (for the naturally confined margin of the lake was at that time diminished by an unusual increase of its waters), the proud knights were totally at the mercy of their light-armed foes. Many, in order to escape the sword, perished by

plunging into the lake; the rush of the cavalry overwhelmed the infantry, and in a short time the whole army was thrown into panic and disorder. The Austrians lost the flower of their nobility, and Leopold with difficulty escaped. This astounding victory, the Marathon of Swiss history, was gained in 1½ hr., over a force of 20,000 well-armed men, by 1300 mountaineers, who now for the first time met an army in the field.

The appropriate memorial of their success erected by the Swiss was, according to custom, a *Chapel*, dedicated to St. James; and service is performed in it annually, on the anniversary of the fight.

The little village of *Biberegg*, on the opposite (E.) side of Rothenthurm, was the cradle of the family of *Reding*, one of the oldest and noblest in the canton, and whose name appears oftener with credit than any other. There is scarcely a battle in which they are not mentioned, and they have 45 times filled the office of landammann, the highest in the state. In 1798 Aloys Reding, a hero worthy of such an ancestry, led on the brave inhabitants of these mountains to oppose, in defence of their liberties and constitution, a far outnumbering force of French under General Schauenberg. The Swiss met the invaders in the valley of Rothenthurm, and drove them back as far as the lake of Egeri and the field of their ancient victory of Morgarten. This proved but a temporary gleam of success. Their victory had cost them so large a number of men, that they were unable to renew the contest; and an overwhelming force of French marching into the canton rendered all further resistance hopeless.]

From *Sattel* the new road traversing the flank of the Engelberg commands a fine view of the fall of the Rossberg (Rte. 18), lake of Lowerz, valley of Schwyz, and surrounding mountains. [The old road passes the chapel of Ecce Homo to *Steinen* (*Inns:* Rössli; Krone), the birthplace of *Werner Stauffacher*, reputed one of the three conspirators of the Grütli. A small *chapel*, adorned with rude frescoes of scenes from his life, and the battle of Morgarten, is dedicated to his memory. It was built in 1400. The *Bonehouse* is as old as 1111. A road has recently been made from Steinen to Arth.] The new road proceeds in a direct line, avoiding Steinen, to Schwyz.

Schwyz. (Rte. 18.)

[Travellers bound from Einsiedeln to the Rigi or Lucerne need not go to Schwyz. They may take the road from Sattel, and a little beyond Steinen turn to the rt. for Goldau (Rte. 18). There are diligences on both roads.]

ROUTE 73.

SCHWYZ TO GLARUS, BY MUOTTA, THE PRAGEL PASS, AND THE KLÖNTHAL.

	Stunden.		Eng. m.
Schwyz.			
Muotta	3	=	9
Summit of the Pragel	3½	=	10½
Richisau	1½	=	4½
Vorauen	1	=	3
Glarus	3	=	9
	12		36

These are the distances as reckoned in the country. Carriage - road in progress. A good walker will accomplish the distance in 10½ hrs. There being a carriage-road from Schwyz to Muotta, and from Richisau to Glarus, those who can walk 15 miles have no need of horses. Public carriage twice a day from Schwyz to Muotta. The road crosses the plain to *Ibach*, a scattered village

at the mouth of the Muotta Thal, which here assumes the character of a contracted gorge; higher up it opens out, and exhibits considerable capabilities for cultivation. The road ascends the L bank of the stream, traversing *Ober Schönenbach*, down to which point the Russians drove the French in their desperate attempt to force a way to the Russian army at Zürich, in 1799. The stone bridge (long since replaced by one of wood at a higher elevation), which carried the road over to the rt. bank, was taken and retaken many times; the mingled blood of the two nations crimsoned the stream which swept down their floating bodies.

Beyond *Ried* (Adler) there is another bridge, near which is the pretty waterfall of the *Gstübtbach*, and a third brings the traveller to

Muotta, or *Mutten* (a neat and cheap little *Inn*, Hirsch; Krone), the principal village of the valley, on the rt. bank of the stream. The parish contains 1885 Inhab. In the neighbourhood is the *Nunnery of St. Joseph*, a very ancient and primitive convent, founded 1280. The sisters are poor, and their mode of living homely; they make their own clothes and their own hay; the superior is called Frau Mutter. They receive visits from strangers without the intervention of a grating, and will even give a lodging to a respectable traveller. Whoever avails himself of this must remember that the convent is too poor to afford gratuitous hospitality. They speak no French.

[From Muotta a path leads by the *Kinzig Kulm* to Altdorf. It was by this path that Suwarrow brought his troops. Another pass leads by the *Bisi Thal* to the Baths of Stachelberg (Rte. 75). Both about 9 hrs.

On the night of Sept. 27th, 1799, the inhabitants of this remote and peaceful valley were surprised by the arrival of an army of an unknown nation and tongue, whose very name many of them had never heard, which came pouring down upon their cottages and green fields from the heights of the Kinzig Kulm, by paths and precipices usually resorted to only by a solitary shepherd. These were the 24,000 Russians under Suwarrow, whose march out of Italy is recounted in Rtes. 34, 75, and 80. Here the general first heard the news of the defeat of Korsakof and the main Russian army at Zürich. He at first gave no credence to the report, and would have hung the peasant who communicated it as a spy and traitor, but for the intercession of the lady mother of St. Joseph's nunnery. He was now beset on all sides; part of Lecourbe's division followed his rear, Molitor occupied the summit of the Muotta Thal, and Mortier and Massena blocked up its mouth. The bold attempt to cut his way out, through the forces of the latter general, was defeated, as already mentioned, chiefly by the unexpected arrival of a fresh reinforcement under Lecourbe in person, though with vast loss to the French. The veteran conqueror was compelled, for the first time in his career, to order a retreat, and to adopt the only alternative of crossing the Pragel into Glarus. The detachments of Molitor's advanced guard were quickly driven in before him, and the greater portion made prisoners. Suwarrow's rear-guard, however, encumbered with sick and wounded, was greatly harassed by Massena; but the republicans were again repulsed with loss, and driven back nearly to Schwyz. Suwarrow expected to be able to reach Zürich from Glarus, there to join and rally the broken forces of Korsakof; but Molitor, in person, warned of his approach, took possession of the position of Näfels, blocking up the outlet of the Linth Thal, as Massena had intercepted his passage down the Muotta Thal, and the Russian once more found his plans foiled and baffled. Fearing to be hemmed in on all sides, he gave his troops a few days of rest at Glarus, rendered absolutely indispensable by the fatigues

they had undergone, after which he once more took to the mountains, ascending the Sernf Thal (Rte. 80) and crossing the Panixer Pass to the Grisons.]

A little beyond the nunnery, at the end of the village, the view rt. into the Bisithal is beautiful.

The Pragel pass is exceedingly steep and stony on the Muotta side, and sometimes marshy, and is scarcely fit for horses, which moreover are not easily to be found at Muotta. There are no difficulties on the Glarus side.

From Muotta the path continues for about 25 min. among the fields and houses, then crosses the stream which descends from the Pragel, and immediately ascends its l. bank, very rocky and rugged for the first 2 hrs., after which and at the top there are large marshy or boggy patches with planks and stones laid across them. There is nothing striking in the scenery on this side.

The top of the Pragel (5062 ft.) is flat and viewless; there is a chalet where bread, wine, &c., can be procured, but it is abandoned in the first week of September.

The first part of the descent is gentle, but in about 20 min. the Klönthal opens, and the valley is partly blocked up by a huge barrier, which appears to be an ancient moraine; the path makes a détour to the left to avoid this obstacle, and then descends more rapidly through pines to

Richisau, where there is a homely Kuranstalt, kept by civil people.

The Klönthal, into which the traveller now descends, is exceedingly beautiful. On the rt. it is walled in by the *Glärnisch* rising in an abrupt and sheer precipice, and sharp edge of ice, and on the l. by the *Wiggis,* scarcely less abrupt. It is a charming walk or drive of less than an hour down hill, chiefly over green pastures, to

Vorauen (2800 ft.) (*Inns*: Kurhaus Vorauen, pension 6 fr.—baths excellent; H. Klönthal). A carriage can generally be obtained here for Glarus. There is a boat upon the

Klönsee, by means of which the walk may be shortened 2 m., and the scenery enjoyed to perfection. Deep in the recesses of the charming valley lies this lake, at the foot of the Glärnisch, whose vast grey cliffs descend at this point almost perpendicularly into the water. It is about 2 m. long, and surrounded by meadows of the most vivid green, covered until the end of autumn with flowers. The precipitous tracks along the side of the valley, by which some adventurous French pushed forward in pursuit of the Russians, are pointed out. Ebel justly called the Klönthal " une des vallées les plus gracieuses qu'il y ait dans les Alpes." Two Swiss have inscribed on a rock at the foot of the Glärnisch, by the side of a waterfall, an epitaph in memory of Solomon Gessner, the pastoral poet, author of the 'Death of Abel,' who used to repair hither from Zürich, and spend the summer in a châlet. Vorauen is a favourite excursion from Glarus, and a good starting-point for the ascent of the

Glärnisch. This mountain rises in precipices some 7000 ft. above the Klönsee, and for its height is remarkable for the amount of glacier lying on its crest. The summit of the ridge, of a horseshoe form, is crowned by three peaks, of which the loftiest, the *Hinter Glärnisch,* is on the W., 9584 ft. above the sea, and from the central mass a buttress, called the *Vrenelisgärtli,* projects E. towards Glarus. The way up lies for the first 2½ m. towards the Pragel pass, and then l. along a glen to a glacier descending S. The Swiss Alpine Club have built a hut 3¼ hrs. below the summit in the *Steinthäli.* This is ascended on the W. side to a point between the Mittel and Hinter Glärnisch, which are both accessible, but the latter, being the highest, is generally selected. As the Tödi and Clariden Alps rise close at hand, the view is very striking.

The traveller can descend from the glacier to the Dreckloch chalets, and thence by the Brach Alp and its lake to Stachelberg, 10 hrs. from Vorauen.

From Vorauen the excellent char-road follows the l. bank of the lake, and then begins to descend into the valley of Glarus. Keeping to the r. where two roads meet, the manufacturing village of *Riedern* is reached, from which the road, or a footpath on the rt. over the hill, leads to

Glarus (Rte. 74).

—

ROUTE 74.

WESEN TO GLARUS AND THE BATHS OF STACHELBERG—THE CLARIDEN GRAT PASS.

Railway from Wesen to Glarus and Linththal.

The canton of Glarus consists of one great Alpine valley, and of several tributaries branching from it, and penetrating deep into the mountains. The carriage-road terminates about 18 m. above Glarus at the Inn Zum Tödi under the cliffs of the Selbsanft. It is a truly Alpine district, abounding in very wild scenery.

Glarus was formerly subject to the Abbey of Säckingen, to the rights of which Austria succeeded. Glarus joined the Swiss cantons in 1352, and after the battle of Näfels gained par tially its independence ; and towards the end of the 14th centy. purchased the extinction of feudal rights, and finally made peace with Austria. The Reformation divided the canton and occasioned severe struggles and fighting. In 1798 the canton lost several dependencies. It contains 35,100 Inhab. (6900 Roman Catholics), all speaking German.

The railroad from Wesen crosses the Linth canal (Rte. 13), and enters the jaws of the valley of Glarus, flanked by precipices, and backed by the vast mass and snowy head of the Glärnisch.

Näfels Junct. Stat. (*Inns:* Hirsch; Schwert). [Here the direct rail from Zürich by the S. shore of the lake falls in.] A village of 2500 Inhab., in the gorge of the valley, and the chief place in the Rom. Cath. division of the canton. It is a Swiss *battle-field* of some celebrity. 11 simple stones, inscribed 1388, set up on the meadow of Reuti, hard by, mark the spot where, on the 9th of April of that year some 500 men of Glarus met a force of 12,000 Austrians, who, having taken Wesen by treachery, had burst into the canton and attacked a fortification extending across the valley at Näfels. The small body of Swiss, unable to hold this position, retired under their captain, Matthias am Bühl, to the heights above Reuti. Here they were joined by a few auxiliaries and some herdsmen from the neighbouring valleys, and when the Austrians had dispersed to plunder they rushed upon the enemy. They now not only checked the career of the foragers, but after 11 distinct charges, aided by volleys of stones and rocks discharged from precipices, which threw the Austrian cavalry into confusion, finally repulsed the invaders, who lost 2500 of their number.

The anniversary of the fight is still celebrated through the canton by an annual festival on the first Thursday in April. An engagement took place at Näfels, in 1799, between the Austrians and French.

A stream descends to Näfels from two mountain-lakes—the *Nieder See* (1 hr.), and *Ober See* (2 hrs.), and thence it is a delightful walk across the Wiggis to the little inn at Vorauen on the Pragel pass.

From *Mollis* (*Inn:* Bär), the village opposite Näfels, the river Linth is conducted into the lake of Wallenstadt by Escher's canal (see Rte. 13). In the churchyard of Mollis the heroes of Näfels are buried.

The valley of the Linth is subject to much danger and injury from the swelling of its torrents. The broad fringe of unsightly gravel visible on both sides of the Linth, the common drain of the district, will show what mischief that river occasions after storms of rain, and during the melting of the snows. The whole of the lower part of the valley is at times converted into a lake; and the little patches of ground, which have cost the peasant much hard labour and care to cultivate, are at once overwhelmed and ruined. The limestone mountains abound in caverns, which serve as reservoirs, and in the spring and early summer the rocks appear to stream from every pore.

Netstal Stat. The village (*Inns:* Schwert; Fridolin), with 2560 Inhab., is much exposed to avalanches. Rt. a carr.-road to Vorauen in the Klönthal, 9 m.

Glarus Stat. 1500 ft. (*Inns:* Glärner Hof, first-rate; at the stat.; Rabe; Sonne; Railway Restaurant). This little town (Pop. 5453), capital of the canton, is chiefly remarkable for its secluded situation at the base of the Glärnisch and Schilt, encompassed and shut in by the Alps. The inhabitants are distinguished by their industry and enterprise, which have converted Glarus into a place of manufacture, especially of cotton and printing of muslins.

They possess a *Club* (Casino), and a *Free School* for 700 children, erected by private subscription. The Gothic *church*, with 2 spires, is open to Protestant and Romanist alike. *Zwingli* was the pastor here, 1506 to 1546. The Linth is crossed by 2 bridges. A *cabinet of Nat. History* contains some of the fossil fish from the Plattenberg slate quarries in the Sernf Thal.

The *Burghügel*, an eminence surmounted by a chapel, commands the best view of the town, the green meadows around, and the arid limestone mountains ; the Glärnisch with three peaks, the highest 9584 ft., the Rautispitz, 7494 ft., and Kärpfstock, 9180 ft.

In 1861 Glarus was all but utterly destroyed by fire. At times the *Föhn* wind sweeps down the valley with the force of a furnace-blast. It is so much dreaded, that local laws have existed for generations, by which, on its setting in, every fire in the town, including those used for purposes of industry, must be extinguished. The very day before the fire occurred, the propriety of repealing these laws had been considered by the assembled inhabitants of the canton, and by an almost unanimous resolution it was resolved to maintain them. Then came the dreaded wind, and a spark, carried from one house to another, kindled a fire which was not extinguished till more than two-thirds of the town were laid in ashes. All the principal buildings were destroyed and 3000 people left houseless.

The name *Glarus* is a corruption of *Hilarius*, a saint to whom a shrine was built among these mountains at a very early period.

The *green cheese* called *Schabzieger* is peculiar to the canton. It owes its singular appearance, rank smell, and flavour, to an herb (Melilotus cærulea, blue melilot: Germ. Honigklee), which is partly cultivated in gardens within the canton, and partly imported from others. To fit it for use, it is dried, ground to powder, and, in that state,

mixed with the curds. The cheese is made of cows' milk. The curds are brought down from the high pastures in sacks, and, after having a due proportion of herb incorporated with them, are ground in a mill resembling that used for making cider. After being thoroughly kneaded for an hour or two the cheese is fit for pressing, and is ripe for use after a twelvemonth's keeping.

Beyond the Linth, in the village of Enneda, is the huge cotton-mill of Jeune and Co.

It is a pleasant 2½ hrs.' drive or walk from Glarus to *Obstalden* or Narexen, with a fine view over the whole lake of Wallenstadt and part of that of Zürich. A broad road leads thither from Mollis.

[Mountain paths from Glarus.

a. The *Pragel pass* (Rte. 73) by the Klönthal and Muottathal to Schwyz: the finest part of it is not more than 8 m. from Glarus, and may be reached in a carriage to Vorauen on the Klönsee.

b. Two mountain-paths lead to the Lake of Wallenstadt : one, by the *Kerenzenberg* over the W. shoulder of the *Mürtschenstock* (Rte. 13); the other, to *Murg*, passing under the E. side of the summit. The ascent of a peak of the Mürtschenstock may be combined with either of these excursions. A guide should be taken.

c. Two passes lead through the *Sernf Thal* to the valley of the Vorder Rhein :—

(1) The *Segnes Pass* (Rte. 79).
(2) The *Panixer Pass* (Rte. 80).

d. Three passes lead into Canton St. Gall, which is also reached through the Sernf Thal :—

(1) The *Flumser Pass*, diverging from the village of Engi, to the Flums stat. on the rly. between Wallenstadt and Sargans (Rte. 13).

(2) The *Rieseten Pass*, from Matt to Sargans (Rte. 79).

(3) The *Ramin* or *Foo Pass*, from Elm to Sargans, more difficult than the Rieseten, about 10 hrs.' walk.

The baths of Pfäffers may be reached by either of the last-mentioned passes, by crossing the ridge between the Weisstannen, and Calfeuser Thal.]

The main object with most travellers who visit Glarus is the scenery at the head of the Linththal, with the Tödi and its snowy satellites.

The railroad from Glarus to Linththal (12 m.; 1 hr.) crosses the Linth 6 times, and stops at 7 stations. The principal are *Mitlödi Stat.,*

Schwanden Stat. (Adler ; Bahn Restaurant; both good), a large manufacturing village with 2335 inhabitants, and Hätzingen.

Linththal Terminus (Rabe, good ; P. Tödi, recommended). ¼ mile distant are

The *Baths of Stachelberg* (2178 ft.), the best headquarters for the exploration of the beauties of the neighbourhood.

The hotel stands above the river, and directly under the woods of the *Braunwaldberg*, and its pleasure-grounds and windows command the mountains in which the Linth has its source. These present a singularly imposing appearance. On the l. rises the *Selbsanft*, a noble mass of rock shaped like a bell; on the rt. is the *Kammerstock*. Between the two are seen the snows of the *Glarner Tödi* (11,732 ft.) and Biferten glacier. E. opens the Durnach Thal, leading to the Richetli Pass, and l. of it is the *Saasberg.*

Stachelberg is in good repute as a watering-place, on account of the beauty of its situation, and the virtues of its concentrated alkaline sulphureous *spring.* The period of the "cure" is fixed at between 20 and 24 days.

Good guides are found here, with a tariff : Tödi, 40 fr.; Clariden Pass, 36 fr.; Sandgrat to Dissentis, 30 fr. Joachim and Salomon Zweifel, in Linththal; H. and P. Elmer, in Elm, recommended.

Walks.—Behind the hotel a stream descends in a cascade from a thickly-wooded cleft, and a path is carried up its side to the *source of the mineral spring.* Numerous footpaths have been made in the woods above the house, but from want of judicious thinning of the trees the views from them are limited.

Further to the rt. a horse-path ascends through forest to the pastures of the Braunwaldberg, whence the *Oberblegi See*, a tarn near the Glärnisch, may be visited, and descent made to Luchsingen.

The *Fatschbach* waterfall, at the foot of the ascent to the Urnerboden valley and Klausen pass, is 40 min. walk along the l. bank of the Linth.

The *Durnach Thal* can be reached in 20 min.

Excursions—The *Saasberg*, 6555 ft., and *Kammerstock*, 6975 ft., are both fine points of view and easy of access. The panoramas by G. Studer are engraved.

The *Pantenbrücke* and *Ober Sandalp* lie amidst the grand scenery at the head of the Linththal. By taking a carriage to H. Tödi the Pantenbrücke may be reached in 2 hrs., Unter Sandalp in 3 hrs., Ober Sandalp in 4¾ hrs. The following is the time walking :— 40 min. *Fatschbach Fall :* a bridge crosses the Linth to it. From the village of Linththal the ascent and descent, between meadows, of a long hill, formed of mountain débris from the l., bring the traveller to a wilder, narrower, and very beautiful part of the valley, where the graceful fall of the *Schreienbach* (35 min.), half mist, half water, comes floating, as it were, on the breeze it bears with it down a precipice. 10 min. farther is *H. Tödi* (good), with charming, romantic surroundings, its verdant little pastures being shut in by towering mountains, particularly by the wall of the Selbsanft, 9921 ft. Here the carriage-road ends, and the Linththal becomes a gorge. The path, crossing the stream, mounts steeply through a wood for 20 min.; passing in a recess a tablet on a boulder in memory of Hugo Wislicenus, Dr. Phil. at Zürich, lost when wandering alone on the Grünhorn, in 1866. 15 min. descent brings the traveller to the *Pantenbrücke*. This is a little bridge of stone, of which the arch is 20 ft. span and 140 ft. above the torrent, thrown across the chasm where it is narrowest and deepest. It is a wildly-secluded spot, hemmed in by forest and rock. An older bridge was swept away by an avalanche, 1852. On the opposite bank the path bears to the rt. through a beech-wood (another track goes up the mountain), descending to the Linth at the point where it is joined by the Limmern, 10 min. This torrent flows out of an amazing gorge—the *Limmerntobel*—quite inaccessible, cut 2000 ft. deep in the Selbsanft, which rises above it in precipices. The path crosses the Limmern on the level, and 10 min. beyond it the Linth, where the defile opens. Slopes of pasture and of slaty débris are now ascended beneath a mighty wall of rock, upwards of a mile in vertical height, when—the cliffs receding — a green basin is entered, 25 min. Here the snowy peaks of the Tödi and its neighbours rise in view. In 15 min. the Linth is recrossed to the chalets of the *Unter Sandalp* or *Unterstaffel*.

From this point, 4100 ft. above the sea, the views, though confined by the rocks which rise steeply around, are extremely striking. Nearly due S. is the magnificent, but rarely visited, Biferten glacier, enclosed by the precipices of the *Bifertenstock* and *Platalva* or *Hinter Selbsanft* on the E., and by the *Tödi* on the W. It sends down its torrent, the *Bifertenbach*, to join the main stream, here called the *Sandbach*, which is seen descending the precipitous rocks on the W. side of the valley in a magnificent cascade.

The rough pastures of the basin are now traversed for 25 min. to a solitary chalet at the foot of the ascent to the Biferten glacier. Turning from it rt. the path crosses the Bifertenbach, and in 10 min. reaches the *Ochsenblanke*, a series of zigzags leading up the slopes of the Ochsenstock. Near the top the path crosses the Sandbach in a profound chasm, and in a few minutes enters the basin (1 hr.) of the *Ober Sandalp*, or *Oberstaffel*. Another 10 min. brings the traveller to the chalets (excellent milk). The scene here presented is sternly alpine—a *cirque* of dark mountains of gneiss, rugged with peaks, and streaming with glaciers. The points rising through the ice from rt. to l. are the *Zutreibstock*, 8688 ft. *Geissbützistock, Vorder Spitzälpeli*, 9842 ft., and *Hinter Spitzälpeli*, 9596 ft. The Ober Sandalp chalets stand 6358 ft. above the sea, in the midst of bright green pastures, and their position is an admirable one for expeditions over the neighbouring heights, but they are comfortless quarters. For the ascent of the Tödi the hut built by the Swiss Alpine Club on the *Grünhorn*, 3 hrs. above the Lower Sand Alp, is a much better resting-place. A quick walker can return to Stachelberg from the Ober Sand Alp in 3½ hrs. The rte. back may be varied by ascending the *Beckistock*, 8491 ft.; then, passing over the shoulder of the *Gemsistock*, rejoining the path near the Pantenbrücke.

The *Tödi* is the giant of this portion of the chain of Alps, and its summit had been rarely ascended until 1863, when a comparatively easy rte. was discovered. The mountain consists of 3 peaks, which stand in triangular order, N. of the watershed dividing the valleys of the Linth and Rhine—the *Sandgipfel* (N.) the lowest, well seen from the Ober Sandalp—the *Glärner Tödi*, conspicuous from Stachelberg, and long considered the highest point,—and the *Piz Rusein*, the actual summit, S. of the Glärner Tödi, and 11,886 ft. above the sea. The *Klein Tödi*, on the W., is an outlying peak. The two principal points are connected by a snow-ridge, to which the natural road on the N. side is the *Biferten Glacier*. This was long thought impassable, and in some seasons, may be so. On the *Grünhorn* or *Bifertengrätli*, a point easily reached over pasturages, the Swiss Alp. Club has built a good hut. The glacier, when it can be passed, offers the best way, but its crevasses are sometimes formidable, and all the early climbers turned them by climbing a gulley called the *Schneerunse*, down which at certain times dash avalanches. It brings the traveller to the upper plateau, where his most serious difficulties are passed. In 1863 a safe and comparatively easy way was found on the S. of the mountain. The *Piz Rusein* is connected in that direction with the *Stockgron*, and the intervening ridge can be ascended in from 5 to 6 hrs. from the head of the Val Rusein, which runs up from a point in the Rhine valley, 2½ m. below Dissentis. From a gap in the ridge, called *Porta da Spescha*, in memory of the old monk who first explored the mountain (Rte. 82), the summit can be reached in about 1½ hr. A more direct route for a mountaineer descending to Dissentis, is by the Porta da Gliems. The Todi has also been climbed from the Sandgrat.

Pass of the *Sand Grat* to Disentis in Rte. 77.

The *Clariden Grat Pass* to the hotel in the Maderaner Thal can be accomplished in fine weather, and when the snow is favourable, in 10½ hrs. from Stachelberg, actual walking, or in 9 hrs. from H. Tödi. It is a long but very fine pass. In recent years the glaciers have ceased to present the difficulties encountered by early explorers. Above the Ober Sand Alp the traveller leaves to the l. the track of the Sandgrat, and climbs over broken ground and glacier slopes to the Claridengrat, a low ridge connecting the Tödi and Scheerhorn ranges. From the Col *Piz Rusein*, the chief peak of the Tödi and the *Porta da Spescha* are well seen. S.E. are the *Catscharauls* and the *Sand Grat*. The descent is down the l. bank of the Hufi glacier, a vast valley of crevassed ice, striking by its extent. The summit of the *Claridenstock* appears as a mere rock. Lower down some crevasses require caution. Soon after the ice has been quitted, on its l. bank the new hut of the S. A. Club is reached, and in 1 hr. more the inn in the *Maderaner Thal* (see Rte. 83). The views in the final descent are charming.

———

ROUTE 75.

MUOTTA (A) TO THE BATHS OF STACHELBERG, BY THE BISI THAL; (B) TO ALTDORF, BY THE KINZIG KULM.

The parallel valleys of the Muotta, which falls into the Lake of Lucerne near Brunnen, and the Schächen, which joins the Reuss near Altdorf, are separated by a rugged range of mountains, whose extremities are the Axenberg, impending over the Bay of Uri (Rte. 15), and the Schreienstock over Stachelberg. Two glens diverging to the southward from Muotta run up into this wild district. The eastern, called the Bisi Thal, leads to Stachelberg over the shoulder of the Schreienstock, while the western leads over the Kinzig Kulm to Spiringen, in the Schächen Thal, about 1½ hr. from Altdorf.

A. From Muotta to Stachelberg is a laborious walk of 9 or 10 hrs. A good horse-path leads up the *Bisi Thal* to the hamlet of Eigen; the scenery is wild and beautiful; the valley much narrower than the Muotta Thal, with overhanging precipices, and well wooded. In 2½ hours the traveller reaches

Eigen, a scattered hamlet. Beyond it the path is practicable only for the pedestrian, and requires a guide. After leaving the Bisi Thal the scenery is the most savage conceivable. The path, only traceable in many parts by the little piles of stones put up by the shepherds, climbs to a bare limestone "plateau," seamed in every direction by deep crevices like the crevasses of a glacier, but in places even more impassable. The descent to the Linththal is very steep, with fine views.

B. From Muotta to the *Kinzig Kulm* the track leaves the path to Eigen near the opening of the Bisi Thal, ascending nearly due S. "The ascent is continued obliquely up a steep broken slope, till the path arrives eventually upon the wooded edge of a chasm, in which the invisible stream, which issues from the high valley leading up to the pass, is heard descending in cataracts into the Muotta Thal. A track up the mountain side, on the right bank of this stream, is now pursued: and, after an hour's walking from Muotta, the abrupt ascent ceases, and the valley above is entered. Having passed through a wood, the path crosses the river for the first time by some châlets (1½ hour from Muotta). The river is recrossed after another quarter of an hour: a second forest is traversed. and a third bridge crossed (2½ hours from Muotta). The part of the valley below this bridge is narrow and picturesque, shut in on both sides by high white precipices. Over the E. range the sun did not appear, on the last day of July, till 8 o'clock. The rich green slopes N. of Muotta, speckled with chalets, and surmounted by vast cliffs, may be seen from favour-

able positions, through the opening of the valley. Beyond the third bridge, a wild open basin is found, out of which the track is seen ascending from the S.W. corner. At this corner the river is again crossed. 1½ hr. more are requisite before the summit of the pass is attained. Towards the summit, however, the track is faintly marked, the direction of ascent being towards the south, among little hillocks and hollows filled with snow. A short pole marks the crest of the Pass (6791 feet), which is gained in about 5 hrs. from Muotta.

"Great interest is attached to the Kinzig Kulm, in an historical point of view, as being the scene of Suwarrow's disastrous march from Altdorf in 1799. Having pounced down, as it were, upon the French from the heights of the St. Gothard, and driven them before him to Altdorf, he there found his progress barred by the lake of Lucerne, without a boat to cross it, his troops exhausted by fatigue and famine, and the country so completely drained by war as to be quite incapable of supporting them. The only alternative that remained to him, was to attempt to join the forces of the allies through the horrible defile of the Schächen; and to cross the rarely-trodden summits of the high Alps. The only passage up this valley was by a mere path; so that his army was obliged to advance in a single file, abandoning much of their artillery and baggage. Their march lasted 14 hours; and before the rear-guard had left Altdorf, the van had reached Muotta. Many of the Russians sank from fatigue by the wayside, and perished; others fell into the hands of the French, who hovered in their rear; the valley was strewn with dead bodies of men and horses, with arms and equipments. The remainder of this memorable march is described in Rte. 73.

The picturesque attractions of the Kinzig Kulm are of a high order, as the view which it commands is of great extent and magnificence. This view is rather improved by being seen from an eminence to the E., reached in 10 min. from the Col. "The descent into the Schächen Thal is long and steep, but the path is well traced, and the pole on the Kinzig Kulm, being seen for a long time, would help to guide the ascending pedestrian on this side, though it is useless for that purpose on the other. The path lies throughout down the pastures on the right bank of the stream, but generally at a considerable distance from it. The Schächen Thal is reached at a point a little below Spiringen, after a descent of 2½ hrs. From thence to Bürglen is a walk of ¾ of an hour, and another ½ hour brings the traveller to *Altdorf*."—*R.E.*

8 or 9 hrs.' walk from Muotta to Altdorf.

There is another pass called the *Kulm* (not Kinzig Kulm). Instead of leaving the Bisi Thal at Eigen, keep to it, and after passing a fine waterfall and some chalets, the *Kulm* is reached in about 6 hrs. from Muotta. From the col the view is very fine, and the descent very pleasant to *Unterschächen* (Rte. 76).

ROUTE 76.

STACHELBERG TO ALTDORF, BY THE KLAUSEN PASS.

Stachelberg.	H.	M.
Summit	5	0
Unterschächen . .	2	10
Spiringen . . .	1	0
Bürglen	1	30
Altdorf	0	20
	10	0

A walk of about 9 or 10 hrs. Carriage-road complete from Unter-

schächen to Altdorf, and projected throughout.

Charge for a horse from Stachelberg to the summit, 12 fr.; to Altdorf, 25 fr. The bridle-path is so well marked that guides may be dispensed with. It keeps along the l. bank of the Linth from the Baths, and turns out of the valley at the *Fätschbach* waterfall (40 min.) climbing 1½ hr. a steep alp to the long marshy vale of the Fätsch, or Urnerboden, which is bounded rt. by precipitous rocks, l. by steep pine-forest. 30 min. from the entrance the traveller passes a *wirthhaus* (Sonne), 30 min. farther, but l. of the path, on an old moraine, the hamlet of *Urnerboden* with rough *Inn* (H. Tell) and a chapel. [Hence the *Scheer Joch*, a glacier pass giving access to the upper region of the Hufi glacier, can be reached in 5 hrs.] 30 min. beyond this point, the pastures are left, and the ascent becomes rapid and rough, opening a noble view of the *Claridenstock*, 10,709 ft. In another 1¼ hr. the *Klausen pass* is gained. It is 6437 ft. above the sea, between the Clariden Alps on the S., and shattered limestone ridges on the N. The ridge is turf-clad, but much exposed to wind and weather. On the l. a wild slope, broken by crags and tiers of low precipices, and higher by glacier cliffs, rises to the Claridenstock. This mountain and its crown of ice are well seen from the path, but still better from an eminence to the N., which also commands the Gross Ruchen and Windgelle. On the top of the pass is a hut for shelter, and about 1 m. (20 min.) beyond it are the chalets of Balmwand. Here the path divides, leading l. by the rapid descent of the rocks of the *Balmwand*, or straight on along the higher level until it falls in with the track from the Kinzig Kulm, and descends upon Spiringen. This, though the longest, is said to be less fatiguing: it is probably also less beautiful.

The other and more frequented path

descends, by long and steep zigzags, into the *Schächen Thal*, passing in about 40 min. the grand and beautiful cascade of the *Stäubibach*. This torrent springs from its bed into the air with extreme fury, and is of such volume as to produce a thundering noise and clouds of spray. Close to the fall a very pretty chalet *Inn* was built in 1871. In about another hour the traveller reaches the beautifully situated village of

Unterschächen, 3350 ft., the first on the Uri side (*Inns*: H. et P. Clausen, good; Post, homely). The windows of the hotel look upon the ice-clad cliffs of the *Gross Ruchen*, 10,295 ft., at the head of the Brunni Thal, which opens opposite, and sends forth the main stream of the Schächen. The dark walls of the Ruchen rise more than 6000 ft. above this valley, which is well worth exploring. The *Ruchen Pass* leads to the hotel in the Maderaner Thal in 7 hrs.; the pass of the *Seeweli Joch*, on the N. side of the Gross Windgelle to Amsteg in about 8 hrs. The mountain on the l. bank of the torrent discharges dangerous avalanches in spring. At Unterschächen a carriage-road commences.

Spiringen, from which there is a steep zigzag descent. Flowers become abundant, and *clematis* covers the hedges. The *Uri Rothstock* is seen in front.

Bürglen 1½ hr. (*Inn*: Zum Wilhelm Tell), the traditional birthplace of Tell, at the mouth of the Schächen Thal. (Rte. 34.)

Altdorf (Rte. 34) in 20 min.

ROUTE 77.

STACHELBERG TO DISENTIS, BY THE SAND GRAT.

This pass has no difficulties for practised pedestrians, with a guide, though the usual precautions should be taken. An Englishman is said to have perished in a crevasse on the Sand Glacier in the last century, In favourable weather it is a passage of about 12 hrs. from Stachelberg to Disentis, but the time may be shortened 1½ hr. by sleeping at the Tödi inn.

The ascent from Disentis is not so long as that from Stachelberg.

The path to the Ober Sandalp, 4¾ hrs.' walk, has been described in Rte. 74. Beyond that point the track keeps near the stream, turning with the valley S. towards the Sand glacier, and near its foot ascending to some flowery slopes above the cliffs to the rt. The ice-fall is thus turned, and the glacier entered upon where it is smooth and of an easy gradient. For some way the track is identical with that to the Clariden Grat. Then bearing l. a steeper slope of snow is traversed to the *Col*, 9138 ft. above the sea, between the *Klein Tödi* 10,072 ft., and the *Catscharauls*, 10,049 ft. The view of the surrounding Alps is extremely fine. *The Tödi* is the most prominent object.

A steep but not difficult descent, partly over loose stones, leads to the Rusein Alp, the starting-point for ascents of the Tödi from its S. and easier side by the Porta da Gliems or da Spescha. The summit is reached in 6 to 7 hrs. A rough pass connects the Rusein Thal with the Maderaner Thal. The path then lies through the beautiful glen of the *Val Rusein*, chiefly among pine-trees overhung by rugged rocks. The path emerges on the road 2¼ m. below Disentis, close to the remarkable bridge over the *Rusciner Tobel*.

The time usually occupied in walking over this pass is as follows:—

	H.	M.
Stachelberg to H. Tödi . .	1	25
Ober Sandalp	3	20
Edge of Glacier	1	25
Sand Grat	1	5
Disentis	4	30

ROUTE 78.

STACHELBERG TO BRIGELS, OVER THE KISTENGRAT.

This is a singularly wild and striking pass, leading the traveller by a circuitous rte. to the head of that wonderful ravine which the Limmern-bach has cut in the sides of the Selbsanft and Ruchi. The col is 8281 ft. above the sea, and lies between the *Hausstock* (10,355 ft.), and the peaks of the *Tödi* group. A guide is necessary. " After crossing the Pantenbrücke (Rte. 74), which is nearly 2 hrs.' good walking from the baths of Stachelberg, the path turns rather sharply to the l., and ascends through pleasant woods and pastures for a time. 2½ hrs. from the Pantenbrücke, always rising, bring you to the secluded nook in which lie the chalets of the *Limmern Alp*, the highest belonging to the Linththal, 3 miserable hovels of loose stones, one a-piece for the cows, the goats, and the men. This little pasture is separated from the black precipitous face of the Selbsanft mountain by the *Limmerntobel*, the bottom of which the foot of man has never reached, and which can scarcely be seen from the edge. Here a man and 2 boys, with 3 or 4 cows and some goats, pass 3 months of the year, taking with them their supply of flour and bread. After quitting the Limmern Alp, there was no semblance of a path, and the snow, which in the middle of the previous day had been declared by the guide and peasantry to be impassable from its softness, had become early in the morning so hard and icy as to be nearly impassable in the steeper parts from its slipperiness. We passed close by the *Mütten See* (7786 ft.), leaving it on our left. It was then a mass of ice, no water being visible. In a different state of the snow a path is sometimes taken across a lower part of the mountain, leaving the Mütten See on the right, but it was too steep and slippery for us to attempt. We crossed a higher part of the mountain by aid of the solitary foot-tracks of some shepherd (made when the snow was softer, as the guide said, in search of some lost sheep), and which we luckily discovered just at the steepest part, where a slip would have carried one down over a precipice of unknown depth. The views of the distant Alps from the summit are very fine, and the descent into the valley of the Vorder Rhein, near Brigels, affords one continuous view of that valley from above Disentis, almost to its junction with the valley of the Hinter Rhein. Much depends on the season, the weather, and the state of the snow; but it is at least 9 hrs. from the baths of Stachelberg to Brigels (*Inn:* H. Kistenpass, fair). The village itself was nearly destroyed by fire some years since, and many of the houses are new. The chalet on the Limmern Alp is a little out of the way, and it would save time to carry refreshment and avoid it."

On the descent from the Col the traveller passes the *Frisal Thal*, an exceedingly fine glen, which runs W. to the *Brigelserhorn* or *Piz Tumbif*, S. of the Bifertenstock. There is a carriage-road down the mountain from Brigels through Waltensburg to Ilánz, a walk of 2½ hrs.

ROUTE 79.

GLARUS OR STACHELBERG TO REICHEN-
AU — RICHETLI   AND   SEGNES
PASSES.

As mentioned in Rte. 74, there are
two passes by which communication
is kept up between Glarus and the
valley of the Vorder Rhein in the
Grisons. They are both most easily
approached by the carriage-road which
has been carried for 14 miles up the
Sernf Thal as far as Elm, and is being
extended   across   the   Panixer   pass.
Pedestrians from Stachelberg will prefer the Richetli pass, which leads in
6½ or 7 hrs. from the Baths to Elm.

At *Schwanden Stat.* (Rte. 74) about
3 m. above Glarus the valley of the
Linth   divides   into   two   branches.
Out of the l. or E. branch issues the
Sernf: it is sometimes called Klein-
thal, to distinguish it from the larger
W. branch, or Linththal.   Diligence
to Elm twice a day.

About half-way to *Engi* (Sonne), rt.
there is rather a fine waterfall; and
¼ h. beyond it a noble view of the
Glärnisch.

At Engi the Sernf Thal is joined
by the Mühle Thal, by which there is
a pass in 7 hrs. to Murg on the Lake
of Wallenstadt.

Matt, with 2 poor *Inns*—Traube,
Adler — stands   on   the   rt.   bank   of
the Sernf, and   at   the   mouth   of
the minor vale of the Krauchthal,
up which runs a path to Mels or
Sargans, over the *Rieseten pass*, 8 hrs.
[To the bridge in the Krauchthal 1½
hr.; Rieseten chalets ½ hr., from
which the col is seen l. of two twin
knobs; *Col* (6644 ft.) 1 hr., between
the *Härten* (S.) and *Faulenstock* (N.).
Steep descent to Ober Seez Alp;
Weisstannen 2; Mels 3.]

The quarries in the Plattenberg, a
mountain of the grauwacke and clay-
slate, opposite Matt, furnish excellent
slates   for   roofing   or   for   writing.
Most of the schools in Switzerland
are supplied from them.   The slate
is known to geologists for the beautiful and perfect casts of fossil fish
in which it abounds.   The lower portion of the valley is unhealthy, as
may be learned from the occurrence
of goitre and crétinism (those afflicted
with the latter are here called Tölpel
—dolt, blockhead—§ 18); but the inhabitants of the upper extremity are
a fine and hardy race.

Elm (*Inns*, kept by Elmer, comfortable, and Zentner) 3215 ft. Heinrich and Peter Elmer are excellent
guides, and several glacier expeditions
can be made from here (Vorab, Hausstock, Sardona Pass, &c.).

This village has obtained a sad
celebrity from the great landslip, the
most disastrous in its results since
the fall of the Rossberg, which destroyed the lower hamlet on September,
11, 1881.   Seventy-nine houses were
destroyed, and 114 lives were lost;
the damage was estimated at 40,000*l.*
It was caused by an enormous mass
of slate-rock detaching itself from the
Tschingelberg and falling 4000 ft.
into the valley below.

[*Richetli Pass.*   The rte. from Stachelberg to Elm ascends the *Durnach
Thal*, and about 1 m. from the head
of that valley turns sharp up the
mountain l., or nearly due E., to the
col (7526 ft.).   The descent on the E.
side is for a few minutes very steep
to a wild flat basin, then steep again
but with a path, then easy but boggy
to the Sernf Thal.   A guide is
useful.   The col lies south of the
Kalkstöckli, which is S. of the *Kärpfstock*, 9180 ft., the highest point of
the *Freiberge*, or group of mountains
enclosed   by   the   Linth   and   Sernf
valleys.]

[From Elm the *Ramin Grat* or *Foo
Pass*, 6772 ft., leads to Sargans in 10
hrs., or Pfäffers in 12.   Ascent 4 hrs.
by a very rough path, impassable for
horses.   Fine view.   The descent into

the *Weisstannen Thal* is not easy to find without a guide. For Sargans that valley is followed to its lower extremity at *Mels*. For Pfäffers it is necessary to turn to the S.E. after passing the first chalet in the Weisstannen Thal, and to cross two ridges into the Calfeuser Thal.

There is also a direct glacier rte. from the top of the Segnes pass, by the Flimser Firn, Segnes and Sardona glaciers, to the *Calfeuser Thal.* This is a long and stiff day's work, but very varied and interesting. 11 hrs. to *Vättis* (an *Inn*), 2¼ hrs. from Ragatz.]

The *Segnes Pass* from Elm to Flims requires 6¾ hrs.' fair walking, but more the reverse way. The path crosses the Sernf just below Elm, into the Unterthal, and follows a cart-road to some slate-works, 20 min. It then ascends rt. into a gorge. This continues 40 min. to the stream which descends from the Segneshorn. Turning up it l., in 15 min. the traveller emerges upon pastures, exceedingly steep and pathless. Here avoid a track to the rt. and go straight up the slopes S.E. When the *Martinsloch*, a hole or natural tunnel through the mountain, is sighted the way cannot be missed, as the col lies just l. of it. High up, where the grass gives place to rock and stones, the track bears rt., and in 1 hr. 25 m. from the foot of the pastures to the rt. is the *Martinsloch*, through which on four days in the year— March 4 and 5, and September 14 and 15—the sun shines upon the village church of Elm. This orifice is nearly under the peak of the *Segneshorn* or *Piz Segnes*, which is 800 or 900 ft. above it, and 10,870 ft. above the sea. The rocks of the ridge form a wall, which at one place is weathered into a number of columns called the *Jungfrauen* (Maidens), and is broken down at the col. N.W. the snowy heights of the Kärpfstock, are well seen, and far away to the S. are the peaks of the Adula, and glacier of the Hinter Rhein below the Vogelberg and Piz Valrhein. On the S. side of

[*Switz.*]

the pass a steep slope of snow leads down to the *Flimser Firn*, a small nearly level glacier occupying a hollow in the mountain. This is crossed in ½ hr., and then descent made rt. to the bed of an ancient lake, 1 hr. 20 m. from col. The path follows the l. side, passing a fine waterfall, and at end of basin descends l. to the green Flimser alp 25 min., and down its slopes in 1 hr. 20 m. to Flims, 20 min. from the beautifully situated inn of the *Waldhaus*, and 2½ hrs.' walk from Ilánz.

ROUTE 80.

ELM TO ILÁNZ, BY THE PANIXER PASS.

From Elm (Rte. 79), the carriage-road is only carried up the valley for 2 miles. From Elm to Ilánz is a walk of 8 hrs.

[In going from Stachelberg by the Richetli pass, Elm is avoided, as the path to the Panixer is met at the foot of the Richetli, near the chalets of Wichlen, about 4 m. from Elm. But it would be a hard day's work to accomplish both passes, and there is no accommodation short of Panix, fully 10 hrs. from the Baths.]

An hour and a quarter from Elm brings the traveller in sight of the head of the W. branch of the Sernf Thal, and in front of the opening to the S., which leads to the Panixer pass. The ascent occupies 2½ hours, and for the last two the track is marked by poles. The scenery is desolate; the ground rises in stages, or, as it were, in steps, borne up by precipices. The first of these flats, gained in ¾ of an hour from the Sernf Thal, is the wild Jätzer Alp. Here are the last chalets.

R

The *col* (7907 ft.) commands a comprehensive view over the southern mountains of the Vorder Rhein, but is not otherwise remarkable.

The commencement of the descent is marked by poles, and turns W. towards a glacier fed by the snows of the Hausstock. The traveller is then left at the edge of a declivity to find his way down. It is necessary to turn S., and descend the loose, wet, and trackless slope, to gain a path which may be perceived far below on the mountain-pasturage. Before reaching this alp, the stream, just sprung in a considerable volume from its glacier, must be waded through. The track then lies for a time over the half-barren surface of the alp, which is raised on immense precipices above the valley of Panix. It then re-crosses the stream (which runs in a deep chasm hardly a yard in width), and ascends for some distance along the face of the precipices on the E., passing one place by a shelf cut out of the rock.

The traveller now reaches a wide green pasturage, and descends towards the S., turning by degrees, first E. and then N.E., so as to double round the head of the ravine. The rest of the way to the village of *Panix*, where there is a small country *Inn*, presents no difficulty, though some little embarrassment may be experienced in the woods. Panix is a long 2 hours from the col to which it gives name. It is here worth while to look back upon the pass. All approach seems so barred by precipices that to reach it might be considered impossible.

Below Panix there is a good path, running at a great elevation above the stream, and eventually leading to *Waltensburg*, whence a carriage-road, commanding the most beautiful views over the valley of the Rhine and opposite mountains, descends rapidly to Ilánz. From Panix to Ilánz (Rte. 82) is a walk of 2 hours.

Suwarrow, after the almost incredible march detailed in Rtes. 73, 75, remained like a stag at bay for three or four days at Glarus, engaged in constant skirmishes with the enemy. At length, finding it hopeless to oppose a force now so greatly superior in numbers to his own, he adopted the only alternative, of again leading his exhausted and diminished followers over the crest of the Alps. He broke up from his quarters on the 5th of October. The lateness of the season, the difficulties of the passage, and the vastly superior force pressing on his heels, rendered this a far more hazardous enterprise than that which he had previously accomplished. The miserable path up the valley would barely admit two men abreast: along this the army painfully wound its way in single file. The difficulty of the ascent was greatly increased by a fall of snow; but, as though the hardships of the road were not enough, the indefatigable French allowed the Russians no respite from their harassing assaults. Numbers lay down to perish on the snow; many, slipping on the fragments of slate, and along the rocks, polished by the frost, were hurled over the precipices, while the enemy's bullets were not slow in further thinning their ranks. After five days of toil, and four nights of little repose, since they were spent on the surface of the snow, Suwarrow crossed the ridge of Panix, and on the 10th of October gained the valley of the Rhine. Even on reaching the descent, many perished in attempting to cross the chasm of the Ramasca Alp. For months the birds and beasts of prey were gorged with their bodies, and the bones of many a warrior are still blanching in the ravines of the Jätzer. Thus terminated a march of 18 days' duration, perhaps the most extraordinary ever made by an army, incessantly engaged, fighting a battle almost every day, and obliged to traverse a country unknown, and completely destitute of resources. This remarkable retreat was accomplished with the loss of all the artillery, the greater part of the beasts of burden, and one-third of the men.

ROUTE 81.

RAGATZ TO COIRE — THE GRISONS — THE ROMANSCH LANGUAGE.

Soon after leaving Ragatz, the rly. crosses the Rhine by a covered wooden bridge, and passes out of Canton St. Gall into the Grisons, to

Mayenfeld Stat. (*Inns:* Rossli; Ochs), a little walled town nearly opposite to Ragatz, and about 12 m. from Coire, containing an ancient tower said to have been built in the 4th cent. by the Emperor Constantius. The valley of the Rhine has a grand appearance from this point. The *Falknis* is a conspicuous and striking object N.E. The Rhine alone is unpicturesque, from the width of its bed and the large space of unsightly gravel left bare in summer. Its bed is constantly rising, so as to threaten inundations; The railroad is carried along the rt. bank, crossing the *Lanquart,* an impetuous torrent, descending from the valley of Prätigau (Rte. 94). Above Meyenfeld, the H. Landhaus. The host is a good guide for the Scesaplana, &c.

Lanquart Stat. (*Inns:* Davoserhof; H. Lanquart). The Completer wine is grown near here. The towers of *Marschlins,* an ancient castle of the Salis family, are seen under the mountain to the E. [Diligences to Davos in 7 hrs. and to the Engadine by the Fluela, daily.]

Beyond this, the Convent of Pfäffers is visible from the road; the snowy heights of the *Calanda* rise on the opposite bank of the Rhine; and the ruins of feudal castles, perched upon knolls, overlooking the valley, give a picturesque character to the scene. One of the most conspicuous is *Haldenstein,* nearly opposite Coire, and N. of it are the ruins of *Lichtenstein,* ancient seat of that princely family.

Zizers Stat. (*Inn:* Krone), near which is Molinära, the country-seat of the Bishops of Coire.

From the valleys on each side proceed torrents, which have borne down the débris of the mountains, and have formed long hills, reaching to the Rhine. The height of these hills, next the mountains, must be several hundred feet. The post-road regularly ascends them, crosses the bed of the torrent at the top, and then descends

Coire Terminus—Germ. *Chur*; Romansch, *Cuera*—(*Inns:* Steinbock, a thoroughly good house; Weisses Kreuz, (Freieck); Lukmanier, near the rly. stat.; Stern (l'Etoile); Sonne—all good and moderate. Valtellina is the wine generally consumed in the Grisons, but *Completer,* grown near Maläns, is very good, and should be tried here.

Coire (2000 ft.), capital of the Grisons, the *Curia Rætorum* of the Romans, is an ancient walled town of 8900 Inhab. (2000 Rom. Cath.), about a mile from the Rhine, in a recess formed by the opening of the valley of the Plessur (Schanfigg Thal). In A.D. 452 it was already the seat of a bishopric, and its prelates became the most powerful temporal rulers in the neighbouring country. Its prosperity arises from the roads upon which it stands, which form the channel of communication from Italy into Switzerland and Western Germany. Through Coire pass the goods transported over the great Alpine roads of the Splügen and Bernardino. It is the place of meeting of the Council of the Grisons; a member of which claims the title of "Your Wisdom" ("Euer Weisheit").

The Protestant town was separated from the Catholic town by a wall with curious double gates, which each side closed at night.

It is a town of narrow streets, and high whitewashed houses. Entering it by the old gateway, close to the Steinbock, and turning sharp rt., you reach the parish ch., behind which a steep street leads to the clerical quarters, once walled in, and still entered by a lofty gateway. Within is a square, lined on one side by the *Bishop's Palace,* retaining no ancient features except 2 towers, which may date from the 10th centy. St. Lucius is said to have suffered martyrdom in that which contains the

Bishop's chapel, a room now destitute of all trace of antiquity. In front is the

Dom, or *Ch. of St. Lucius*, interesting for its architecture of early Pointed, but retaining traces of an earlier Romanesque Dom, of the fourth century. To it must be referred the rude statues of the Four Evangelists, Janus-like, in pairs, standing upon lions which flank the iron gate leading to the circular W. door. The oldest portions of the present building date from the 8th century. The choir is raised on steps, leaving open to the nave the crypt beneath, which rests on a single pier, the base a monster. There are singular old carvings (altar-piece or reredos) and paintings, and monuments of the noble Grison families, a sacraments-house with metal door, and two other fine shrines. Several of the chapels contain pictures attributed to *A. Dürer* and the younger *Holbein*, and there are also works of *Angelica Kauffmann*, painter and R.A., who was born at Coire, A.D. 1741. In the *sacristy* is preserved a treasure of mediæval art of great interest—church-plate, paintings, ivories, wood - carving, vestments of unusual beauty and excellence of embroidery.

Behind the Dom is the *Cantonal School* (formerly Episcopal), in which 350 Prot. and Rom. Cath. pupils are educated. The library is rich in Romansch literature.

The *Rosenhügel*, a public walk on the Julier road, ¼ m., commands a beautiful view of Coire; and the *Mittenberg*, N.E., to the top of which a path will take the traveller in 2 hrs., views up and down the valley of the Rhine. To the *mineral springs* of *Pasugg*, l. of the Julier road, and to the *Scalära Tobel*, a wild ravine opening on the Ragatz road, are walks of about 1½ hr. The *Calanda*, 9213 ft., can be more easily ascended from Coire than from Pfäffers.

Diligences every day to Chiavenna by the Splügen, in 12½ hrs. (Rte. 87); to Bellinzona, by the Bernardino, in 17 hrs. (Rte. 91); to Hospenthal by the Oberalp (Rte. 82), or Biasca by the

Lucmanier (Rte. 85); to Samåden (daily) in 12 hrs., by Tiefenkasten, over the Julier Pass (see Rte. 92). 1-horse carriage to Thusis, 15 fr.; 2-horse carriage, 30. An alternative rte. to Tiefenkasten is by Thusis and the Schyn pass. Two horses to Chiavenna, 135 fr.; Bellinzona, 180 fr.; Hospenthal, 135 fr.; St. Moritz, 130 fr.

The Romansch Language.

The *Romansch* (properly the *Ræto-Romansch*) language is one of those which, in the course of the middle ages, took their rise from the common or Rustic Latin (Lingua Romana rustica), spoken in different parts of the Roman empire in Europe. The Provençal of the S. of France is another, and the Wallachian (Romouni) is a third of these tongues still existing. The Ræto-Romansch was at one time spoken all through the Roman province of *Rætia*, which included the modern countries of the Grisons, the Tyrol, and the adjacent districts of Switzerland and S. Germany, where many Romansch proper names of places still remain, though the inhabitants speak German. Besides a considerable mixture of pure German, the Ræto-Romansch contains several hundred words, relating to Alpine life and occupations, derived from the aboriginal Alpine tribes, whom Livy asserts to have been related to the Etruscans.

The population of the Grisons, in 1880, amounted to 93,864, of whom about 42,000 speak Romansch, 36,000 German, and 12,000 Italian (in the S. districts of Misocco, Bregaglia, and Poschiavo). As regards grammatical differences, the Romansch of the Grisons is divided into three principal dialects, which prevail in—1. The Upper Engadine; 2. Lower Engadine; 3. The Oberland, or upper valley of the Vorder-Rhein.

The literature of the Ræto-Romansch language dates back to the latter half of the fifteenth century, beginning with popular songs relating to warlike exploits, succeeded in 15..

an epic poem by Johannes Travers, hief actor in the events he describes. e first printed book was the transion of the New Testament into the lect of the Upper Engadine by chem Bifrun, a lawyer of Samâden. was published 1560, and had great luence in the extensive spread of Reformation through the whole tian valley of the Inn. It was lowed by other translations of the ole Bible, by books of prayer, catesms, &c., throughout the Romansch isons; and the example set by the otestants was quickly followed by Roman Catholics.

Most of the inhabitants of the isons are bilinguals, who, if they ak Romansch, speak Italian or rman likewise. There are three mansch newspapers published at ire and Disentis in the dialects of Lower Engadine and Oberbund.

The traveller in the Grisons may reminded that the Romansch names places, of two syllables, generally ve the accent on the last syllable, Ardéz, Cernéz, Lavín, Mascín, Ratz, Sargáns, and that the Romansch mes of many places differ materially m the German: e.g., Disentis, Rom. uster; Brigels, Rom. Breil; Walnsburg, Rom. Vuorz la foppa; Ems, m. Domat.

History and Government of the Graunden or Grisons.—For nearly two nturies after the first Swiss union, at part of the country of Rhætia w called Graübunden groaned unr the tyranny of almost numberless tty lords, who, though they possed but a few acres of land, or en no more than the number of uare feet on which their castle stood, t assumed the rights of independent vereignty, waging perpetual petty ar with their neighbours—oppressg their own subjects, and pillaging l travellers — the ancient form of vying duties and customs. The best tion of the state of society which exted during this period of the Faustcht (club law), may be formed from e number of feudal ruins which ud not only the main valleys of

the Rhine, but even the lateral valleys and gorges of the Rhætian Alps. At last a day of retribution came. The peasants rose in revolt and threw off the yoke of the nobles—with less violence than might have been expected, chiefly because the great ecclesiastical potentates, the Bishop of Coire, the Abbots of St. Gall and Dissentis, and some of the more influential barons, sided with the peasants, directing, instead of opposing, the popular feeling.

The result of this was the Grison Confederacy (about 1471), quite distinct from the Swiss Confederacy, composed of *Three Leagues* (Bünden)—the Upper, or Grey League (Ober, or Graue Bund), 1424 (named from the simple grey home-spun coats of those by whom it was formed); the League of God's House (Ca Dè in Romansch, in Germ. Gotteshaus Bund), so called from the church of Coire, the head and capital of this league, 1396; and the League of the Ten Jurisdictions (Zehn-Gerichte), of which Davos is chief town (1436).

The government produced by this revolution presented a remarkable example of the sovereignty of the people and of universal suffrage. Not only every valley, but in some cases every parish, or even hamlet in a valley, became an independent commonwealth, with a government of its own, with peculiar local administrative rights and privileges. Sometimes one of these free states, sometimes several together, formed a commune or schnitze, literally slice (gemeinde or gericht); each commune had its own general assembly, in which every citizen of the age of 18, sometimes younger, had a vote, and by which the magistrates and authorities, down to the parson and schoolmaster, were elected. With such a complication of machinery, it is difficult to understand how any government could have been carried on. Two great families, those of Planta and De Salis, in the end, long monopolised the chief influence, as well as the patronage and offices of the federal government.

Towards the end of the 15th centy.

the Grisons concluded a permanent alliance with the Swiss. The liberty of the Grisons was established against the House of Austria by the battle of the Malser-heide, A.D. 1499. In 1512 the Grisons conquered Chiavenna and the Valtellina, over which they retained the paramount authority until 1798. In 1803 the Grisons became a Swiss canton by Napoleon's Act of Mediation.

A new local and administrative organization was introduced in June, 1851. According to this, the old historic names and divisions are abolished, and the canton is portioned out into 14 districts, 39 circles, and 205 communes or parishes.

———

ROUTE 82.

COIRE, UP THE VALLEY OF THE VORDER RHEIN, TO DISENTIS, AND ACROSS THE OBERALP TO ANDERMATT.

Coire.	Eng. m.
Reichenau	6
Ilánz	14
Trons	12
Disentis	7½
Andermatt	20

Carriage-road to Andermatt. Diligence in 9 hrs. to Disentis, 13 to Andermatt, stopping to dine at Trons. 1-horse carriage to Reichenau, 6 fr.; 2-horse carriage to Ilánz, 45; to Disentis, 80; to Andermatt or Hospenthal, 135. Good *Inns* at Waldhaus, Ilánz, Trons, Disentis and Sedrun. This road was made in 1865, in continuation of the road across the Furca to Brieg, thus giving carriage communication between the valley of the Rhine and the valley of the Rhone.

As far as Disentis the scenery is varied and beautiful; in parts very fine. Thence to Andermatt the road is chiefly over open Alpine pastures. The number of small castles on heights is remarkable; it is as much the castellated Rhine here as below Mayence. From Coire to

6 m. *Reichenau* (*Inn :* Adler), see Rte. 87. Here the Splügen and Bernardin road diverges up the valley of the *Hinter Rhein,* at the entrance of which is the castle of Rhäzuns.

The road to Andermatt follows the valley of the *Vorder Rhein.*

The carriage-road strikes up the side of the hills through the village of *Tamins* directly over Reichenau. Here the traveller enjoys a beautiful view of both valleys of the Rhine. The river runs between cliffs, and the road, leaving the Rhine, twists and rises on the mountains through *Trins* (*Inn :* Calanda), with ruins of *Hohentrins,* a castle said to have been built by Pepin d'Heristal, and *Mulins,* passing l. the *Flimser See,* to

7 m. *Flims* — Rom. *Flem* — (*Inn :* Post — fair), a village under the precipices of the *Flimserstein,* 3616 l. above the sea, named, from the number of sources around it, *a flumina.* [Rt. the path to Elm, by the Segnes pass (Rte. 79), 7 hrs., guide 10 fr. The *Segneshörner* are seen above the Laaxer Alp.] In the castle is some curious wood-carving. Just beyond Flims, at Waldhäusen, is the

H. and P. Waldhaus, a *Luft* and *Molken Cur,* with 60 beds, and the *H. and P. Segnes,* on the verge of a great pine-forest called *Mutta Wald.* The road passes through this wood, with the *Laaxer See* in a deep hollow l. (it contains a warm spring); then close to the grand ravine of the *Laaxer Tobel* to

Laax (*Inns :* Adler; Kreuz). Here are two old châteaux, formerly of the Counts of Toggenburg (L.) and Counts Von Mont (rt.) From this village the road descends a hill of 3 m. with fine view of *Piz Riein, Piz Fez,* and *Piz Mundaun,* passing *Löwenberg* (rt.), once a castle of the bishops of Coire.

7 m. *Ilánz* (2250 ft.)—in Romansch, Glion—(*Inns :* Oberalp, good; Lucmanier). Ilánz was the capital of the Graue Bund, and is beautiful situated astride the Rhine at the entrance of

the Lugnetz Thal, and in full view of *Piz Tumbif* (or *Brigelserhorn*), above Trons. Its 668 Inhab. speak Romansch, and this dialect prevails in a large portion of the valley, while German is spoken in the mountain villages. Many fine old houses, in a state of dilapidation, prove that Ilánz was once the abode of noble families.

[*Walks*—to *Fellers*, ¾ hr.: thence to *Crap St. John*, 1 good hr.—to *Ladir* and *Ruschein*, on the mountain side N. Beautiful views.

Piz Mundaun (6562 ft.) commands a fine panoramic view. The top is easily reached in 3 hrs., and the *Inn* on the alp in 2. Horse, 8 fr., guide, 5 fr.; with descent to Trons (4¾ hrs.) 10 fr. To the *Frauenthor*, 1 hr. (Rte. 86).

By the Lugnetz Thal and *Valserberg pass* to Splügen in Rte. 89. By the same valley there is a pass to *Olivone*, in Val Blegno (Rte. 86). The *Panixer* pass to Elm from Waltensburg (Rte. 80). The *Kistengrat* to Stachelberg from Brigels (Rte. 78). To *Thusis* or Splügen a day's walk of 10 or 11 hrs. by the rt. bank of the Rhine and the Savien Thal (Rte. 90).]

From Ilánz, those on foot can take a path over the mountains, under Piz Mundaun, through a district called *Obersaxen*, to Trons; but it is not easy to find the way, and there are ravines or *graben* to cross. Proceeding by road:—

The Rhine is crossed to *Tavanasa* (Kreuz), and the road runs under wooded precipices to

10 m. *Trons* or *Truns*—Rom., *Tron* —(*Inns* : Krone; Tödi; both good: the diligence from Coire stops to dine here), a village in a singularly beautiful situation under *Piz Tumbif*. Its 800 Inhab. are Rom. Cath., and speak Romansch. Abandoned iron-works in the vicinity. Trons is chiefly remarkable, however, as the cradle of liberty among the Rhætian Alps. Beneath the shade of a neighbouring forest the peasants met at the beginning of the 15th century, to concert plans for liberating themselves and their children from the oppression of their feudal lords, three or four of whose castles, now in ruins, may be seen frowning from the neighbouring crags.

At the entrance of the village, on the side of Ilánz, stood, till 1870, the decayed but venerated fragment of a *sycamore*, beneath whose once-spreading branches the deputies of the peasants met the nobles who were favourable to their cause, in March, 1424, and took the oath of fidelity to one another, and to their free constitution then established. According to tradition this remarkable oath was administered by the Abbot of Disentis. The confederates swore "to be and to continue good and true friends ; to hold together in war and in peace ; to maintain each man his own rights by law, and not by the strong hand; to withstand all lawless violence; and to punish the unruly who will not obey the sentence of the law." Such was the origin of the GREY LEAGUE, *Graue Bund,* so called from the grey beards or the grey homespun garb of the venerable assembly. Close to the sycamore-tree stands the little *Chapel of St. Anna,* the portico adorned with Bible texts, "In libertatem vocati estis;" "Ubi Spiritus Domini, ibi Libertas;" "In te speraverunt Patres;" &c., and with two fresco paintings. One represents the first formation of the League, the principal figures being the Abbot of Disentis, in the robes of his order; the Count of Sax, with a white flowing beard; and the lord of Rhäzüns. The other picture shows the renewal of the oath in 1778: the deputies here appear with starched frills, and hair powdered and frizzled; in silk stockings and with walking-sticks.

View from the ch. of St. Maria above the village.

[From Trons the *Piz Urlaun* (11,063 ft.), S. of the Tödi, and the third of that group in height, was ascended as early as 1793 by Placidus à Spescha. The rte. lies up the centre of the Pantaiglas glacier (which in itself is worth visiting), by the E. face of the S. arête, and then by that arête to the top. It has been recently climbed in about 6 hrs.

Piz Tumbif.—The lowest of the 3 peaks can be ascended without much difficulty. Carriage to the foot of the hill to Brigels, ½ hr.; thence walk to Waltensburg, 1 hr.; Brigels, 1 hr.; foot of peak, 3 hrs.; up steep glacier to saddle, about 1½ hr.; along the ridge to the point, about 20 min. The 2nd peak has one *mauvais pas.* The highest point, 10,555 ft., can be reached only by a long and very difficult arête.]

The inhabitants of the upper part of the valley, about Disentis, are Roman Catholics. The mountains which bound it change from lime-stone to primitive rock, and give a different character to its scenery. The road is bold.

Opposite *Somvix* (*Inn:* Post) (Rom. *Sumvigl*; Lat. *Summus-vicus*), abound-ing in cherry-trees, is the opening of *Val Somvix,* wild and savage, and well worth exploring. [About 1 hr. up the valley is *Teniger Bad,* where rude baths are found, and in about another hour *Val Lavaz,* with the *Lavaz Joch* at its head. This is a very interesting pass (8232 ft.), leading to the Luk-manier road at Curaglia, and com-manding a splendid view of the Me-delser glacier. At the upper end of the Val Somvix are the passes of the *Greina* to Olivone, and the *Disrut* to Val Lugnetz and Ilánz (Rte. 86).] Somvix ch.-tower is lofty and pictu-resque. There are paintings on the ch.-yard porch, and devices on some of the houses. Nearer Disentis is a dark, steep forest, with alpine cedar, and here a wooden bridge, 160 ft. above the stream, and 210 ft. long, carries the road over the grand *Ruseiner Tobel.*

7½ m. *Disentis* (3800 ft.) (*Inns:* H. and P. Disentiser Hof, Baths; Con-drau Zur Krone; Condrau Zur Post; Berther or Adler—all good. E. C. S.

The *Benedictine Abbey* of Disentis (Rom. Mustèr; Lat. Monasterium), one of the oldest ecclesiastical establish-ments in Switzerland, founded in 614, it is said, by the Scotch monk Siegbert,

a companion of St. Gall, was the nucleus of early civilization in this wild and remote country It stands on a terrace, about 3800 ft. above the sea, with a village clustered round its base, and at the junction of the two Alpine torrents which unite in forming the Vorder-Rhein. It is protected by a forest from falling avalanches, but has twice been burned in modern times; first in 1799, when the French destroyed it, together with the library formed in the 7th and 8th centuries, and again in 1846. It was rebuilt, and is now in part used as a school for the canton, and has an imposing appear-ance, from its size and position, tower-ing above the humble village, as its rich and powerful abbots, in the middle ages, lorded it over their vas-sals. They were, at one time, allies of the House of Habsburg, and the abbot and his banner occupied the van at the battle of Morgarten. At a later period, however, 1424, Abbot Peter of Pontaningen was one of the founders of Grison liberty, who met under the sycamore at Trons. Placidus à Spescha, the first explorer of the neighbouring mountains, was long an inmate of the monastery.

A newspaper is published here in the Romansch dialect.

View up the Lukmanier pass of *Piz Scopi;* further l. is *Piz Cristallina. Piz Muraun,* 9511 ft., opposite the Ruseiner Tobel, may be ascended, and commands a fine view. You can ride halfway. Good guides are to be heard of at the principal inns.

[The carriage road over the *Luk-manier* runs up the Medelser Thal by the hospice of Santa Maria, to Biasca (Rte. 85); from Santa Maria is a path over the *Uomo Pass* and down the Val Piora to Airolo, 10½ hrs. (Rte. 84); another, by Val Rusein and the *San Grat,* to the Baths of Stachelberg (Rte. 77). The *Brunni Pass,* to the head of the Maderaner Thal (an Inn); and the *Kreuzli Pass* to Amsteg, 10 hrs.' good walking (Rte. 83).]

At Disentis the Medels (or Middle) Rhein, joins the Vorder Rhein.

The road from Disentis to the Oberalp leaves the Medelser Thal c the l., and ascends the vale of Tavétsch by the l. bank of the Vorder Rhein, now reduced in breadth and volume to a mountain-torrent.

5 *Sedrùn* (4600 ft.) (*Inn*: Krone, good), the chief place in the upper valley. Rt. Val Strim leading to the Kreuzli pass.

2 *Rueras*—Rom. *St. Giacomo*—(*Inn*: Oberalp). On a hill nearly surrounded by the Rhine stand the ruins of the *Castle of Pultmenga* or *Pontaningen.* [From this point a path, now disused, called the *summer path*, diverges to the rt., crossing a shoulder of the Crispalt to the *Passo da Tiarms*, 7061 ft.]

Above Rueras a narrow gorge opens on the valley, which is here dreadfully exposed to avalanches. In 1808 one fell from the Culmatsch upon the village of Selva, and killed 42 human beings and 237 head of cattle. The carriage-road is carried through

Tschamut, or *Chiamut* (5400 ft.) (*Inn*: Rheinquelle, good), the last village in the Tavétsch-provided with a church. The valley of Tavétsch is the cradle of the Vorder Rhein: it is supplied from 3 branches, having their sources in the mountains which wall in its upper extremity; the *Crispalt*, N.; the *Six Madun* (Cima di Badus), and the *Cornäre*, S.; the *Berglistock* and *Schneehuhner*, N.W. The S. branch, which is considered the true source, is the outflow from two small lakes, the *L. de Siarra*, and the *L. Toma* (about 2 hrs.' walk), the latter 7690 ft. above the sea, on the N. flank of the Sixmadun. At Tschamut one of the branches is crossed, after which, adieu to the Rhine.

The carriage-road, adopting a line more safe from avalanches than the old winter path, ascends the Val Surpalix by ten sweeping zigzags, and, crossing the boundary of Canton Uri, reaches

The Oberalp Pass, 6703 ft. above the sea. On the opposite declivity, a small lake, famed for its trout, lies at the foot of the traveller. This is the *Oberalp See*, one of the head-waters of the Reuss: it is beset with bogs, and was the scene of a struggle between the French and Austrians in 1799. The road skirts the N. shore. A capacious *Hotel* (Oberalp) has been built on its margin. The vale of Urseren, with Hospenthal in the distance, and the inn on the Furca, now open to view, and a long descent by well-drawn zigzags, which may be much abridged by the pedestrian, first through a naked valley of pastures, and then down a broken declivity, brings the traveller to

Andermatt, on the St. Gothard (Rte. 34).

ROUTE 83.

THE MADERANER THAL—KREUZLI PASS TO DISENTIS.

The *Maderaner Thal*, though a singularly picturesque Alpine valley, was comparatively neglected until a good mountain hotel and pension was opened 3½ hrs. by bridle-path from Amsteg, in the centre of the finest scenery. The valley terminates E. in the *Hüfi glacier*, and a snow-field of enormous extent, of which the summit, called *Clariden Grat*, connects the Catscharauls on the S. with the Claridenstock on the N. The sides of the valley, descending from these heights, are formed on the N. by the Scheerhorn, Klein Ruchen, Gr. Ruchen, Gr. Windgelle, and Kl. Windgelle; on the S. by the Düssistock, Oberalpstock, and Bristenstock. A steep ascent from Amsteg of 15 or 20 min., through the forest, lands the traveller abruptly on the first and most beautiful stage of the Maderaner Thal, where the valley is not only charming in its scenery but richly fertile—quite a bower of fruit and walnut trees and flowers. At the entrance stands the little chapel of St. Antony, and further on the hamlet of *Bristen*; its chalets perched on broken ground, above a rocky dell, where, in the din and spray of the roaring *Kärstelenbach*, a little bridge is crossed. This is one of the prettiest spots in the valley, [From the chapel a level path, commanding fine views, bears round the base of the Bristenstock to the St. Gothard road, at the second bridge above Amsteg; a most useful short cut for pedestrians ascending the Reussthal.] Further on, the Kreuzli rte. diverges rt. up a lateral glen, and l. a path climbs to the pastures below the Windgelle, where there is a small lake, the beautiful *Golzern See*, 2 hrs. from Amsteg. Higher up, between the Windgelles, one of those curious limestone plateaux, locally called *schratten,* rent by deep fissures. [From the S.E. corner of the Golzern See is a steep path direct into the Maderaner Thal.] From this point of the path the cliffs on the l. conceal the Windgelle, but on the rt. the mountains rise in precipices and gloomy peaks. A long and rapid ascent by the side of a gorge, through which the torrent thunders and falls, leads to a higher region of forest. The path is very beautiful, and shortly opens a view of the inn on a distant knoll deep in the woods. The stream is crossed for the last time near the chalets of *Stössi,* and mounting among the pines, by the chalets of *Waldibalm,* the path reaches the comfortable hotel

Zum Schweizerischen Alpen Club, with a beautiful view down the valley. This is a convenient starting-point for the Clariden Grat, and other high passes and ascents. It is much used by the Swiss as a *pension.* There are walks and seats in the wood, and a path in 1 hr. to the Hüfi glacier, remarkable for the purity of its ice and the grandeur of its ice-fall (not seen from the path). The scenery is magnificently alpine, and there are many waterfalls. A hut has been built near the Hüfi Glacier, 2½ hrs. above the Hotel, by the Swiss Alpine Club, but mountaineers of moderate activity will find the inn a sufficiently high starting-point. A good walker can reach Amsteg from the inn in 2½ hrs. A longer way of returning is by the *Golzern See,* by path towards the Hüfi glacier, and ascent l. to the Gnof Alp, then along the Staffel Alp, pass-

ing high above the hotel. There is a rough way up the precipice below Waldibalm.

Among numerous expeditions to be made by mountaineers with guides from this inn are the following:—

Ascents of the *Scheerhorn,* 10,814 ft., *Oberalpstock,* 10,925 ft., *Dussistock,* 10,712 ft., *Gross Ruchen,* 10,295 ft., *Grosse Windgelle,* 10,462 ft., and *Klein Windgelle,* 9846 ft.

Brunni Pass to Disentis, crossing the Brunni glacier; 10 hrs.; guide 20 fr. From the pass the Ober Alpstock can be climbed in 2 hrs.

Scheer Joch, 9269 ft., to Urnerboden on the Klausen Pass, crossing the ridge between the *Scheerhorn* and the *Kammlistock* 10,609 ft.

Ruchen Joch, 8760 ft., to Unterschächen on the Klausen pass in 8 hrs. It lies between the Gross and Klein Ruchen. Ascent at first on steep slopes above the Hüfi. gl. Descent on slaty *débris,* whence another name for the pass — *Ruchen-Kehle,* Shales of the Ruchen.

The *Clariden Grat* to the Baths of Stachelberg (Rte. 74).

The *Kreuzli Pass,* from Amsteg to Disentis, in 10 or 11 hrs., is easy to the pedestrian, but not practicable for horses. It is a fine pass. About 1 hr. from Amsteg, and a little beyond Bristen, the path, crossing the Kästelenbach, and then the stream from the Etzli Thal, below a cascade, mounts to that valley by a considerable ascent. The first bridge over its stream, above the fall, is not crossed, but the three following are. The scenery of the rugged forest is truly alpine. On the W. rises the Bristenstock, on the E. the Oberalpstock and Weitenalpstock. Passing a narrow defile the traveller emerges into a wild barren valley, at the chalets of *Etzliboden,* where the third bridge is crossed (about 2 hrs. from Amsteg), the last trees are passed, and the path mounts continually for nearly 2 hrs. along the W. flank of a naked desolate mountain. It skirts on its way, in the bed of the stream, the remains of an immense avalanche which fell 1849—a mass of rocks, probably half a mile long.　Beside it stands a cross.　After a steep ascent, the traveller enters a small marshy basin, where the valley changes its direction from S. to W. At this point the rte. to the Kreuzli turns to the l., passing the stream by a bridge, and ascending the eastern mountains.　The track is not here perceptible, but it soon reappears.

[It is well worth while to follow the valley for about ½ a mile above the basin just mentioned, instead of immediately leaving it for the pass. The river is pursued towards the W., till it is lost in a short defile beneath the snow with which the bed is choked.　Gigantic blocks, heaped one above another, form one side of this cleft.　The snow affords good walking, and the defile gives admittance into a large hollow of the most savage character.　It is utterly sterile, and a mere receptacle for fallen rocks and snow.　The glaciers of the *Piz Giuf* and *Mutsch* sweep down upon it; craggy mountains of the boldest elevation girdle it in; their splintered summits rise on all sides.　To visit this spot would not increase the day's walk by much more than half an hour.]

The track to the Kreuzli continues to ascend E. up an uneven slope, until it reaches the opening of a high, short valley, by pursuing which the summit is to be gained.　From this point there is an unexpected view of the bay of Uri. The last ascent is rough, the ground being covered with loose blocks, alternating with patches of snow. The track only appears at intervals, generally upon the snow; but the course of the little valley is in itself a guide.　The crest of the pass, marked by a pole, is reached in 5 hrs. direct from Amsteg, or 6¼, allowing halts to enjoy the view, and has an elevation of 7710 feet above the sea.

The views from the Kreuzli are on both sides extremely savage, but particularly those to the N.—of the *Weitenalpstock*, a neighbour and rival of the Oberalpstock.

It is a rough descent into the *Val Strim* down a steep declivity, broken by jutting crags, between which is an occasional goat-track.　Neither is the path down the valley—when its bed is attained, and the ice-cold river, just sprung from its glaciers, crossed—anything like a good path.　It requires two long and rather fatiguing hours from the summit to reach the village of Sedrûn or Tavétsch in the valley of the Vorder Rhein.　The valley of Strim is uninhabited, and its nakedness not relieved by a single tree, not even a stunted fir.　(See Rte. 82.)

———

ROUTE 84.

DISENTIS TO AIROLO, BY THE UOMO PASS. (11 hrs.)

"As far as the hospice of Santa Maria, the way to this pass is the same as that to the Lukmanier (Rte. 85).　At Sta. Maria the barren little valley of Termine opens S.W. and leads to the *Uomo Pass.*　The path mounts the rt. bank of the stream which waters this valley.　There is no difficulty, but the ascent is rough, rapid and continuous.　The summit of the pass (7257 ft.) is reached easily in an hour and a half from Santa Maria.　The ground is flat and boggy, and not adapted for a path : it is accordingly traced along a gentle slope in the S. edge of the marsh, where there are one or two rude chalets.

"The descent is scarcely begun before a commanding view of the knot of the St. Gothard Alps opens out in front. The track lies down the pastures, or alp of Piora, which produce a cheese of considerable repute in the canton.　The declivity is at first rapid, but soon reaches a little plain and *Lake of Cadagno*, and then the *Lake of Ritom*, one of the largest high Alpine tarns, 6000 ft.　Here a large new Inn, (Hôtel Piora) has been opened.

"The descent from the lake is abrupt and long, the river forming in quick succession three very fine falls.

"After passing the third fall, the path is fairly out of the Val Piora, and on the flanks of the Val Leventina, having been throughout, during the descent on the rt. bank of the stream, which it now abandons. The rest of the way is very interesting. The Val Leventina and the St. Gothard road lie far below the traveller, whose course is high on the slopes of the mountain to the village of Madrano. Here the Val Canaria breaks the side of the chain : the path descends, crosses the stream of that valley, and falls into the St. Gothard road a little below Airolo."

ROUTE 85.

PASS OF THE LUKMANIER—DISENTIS TO OLIVONE IN THE VAL BLEGNO.

	Miles.
Olivone	24
Biasca	14

A diligence daily in summer.

A carriage-road has been made over this pass, passing through 12 tunnels before reaching Curaglia. In the execution of these works rich deposits of crystals have been found. Though known to the Romans, and frequented in the middle ages, the old pass has been little used in modern times, particularly since the completion of the road over the Bernardino. Lately it has acquired notoriety from the facilities it offers for the construction of a rly. through the Alps. A succession of comparatively level valleys lead on either side to the summit, which could be pierced by a tunnel of 15 m., to enter the mountain at Perdatsch and emerge at Campo in Val Blegno. The question of the superior advantages of this line or of one over the St. Gothard had been debated for many years, before, in 1869, it was decided in favour of the latter, when Switzerland, Italy and Germany entered into an agreement to construct the line over the St. Gothard.

The *Medelser Thal*, up which this route lies as far as Sta. Maria, runs in a direction nearly S. from Disentis, and is traversed through its whole length by the Mittel Rhein. The entrance is a rocky wooded gorge, called Conflons, because the Vorder and Mittel Rhein unite below it. An ancient track, no longer passable, and the new carriage-road pass through this defile, in which the Rhine forms two cascades.

The scenery of this portion of the road rivals that of the Via Mala.

Curaglia is a village on the rt. bank of the M. Rhein, placed just above the influx of the torrent from the Medelser glacier, a very extensive icefield spread around the peaks of the *Piz Medel* and *Piz Cristallina*, and best reached from the hamlet of Fuorns. A little further the river is crossed to *Platta* (new Inn), the principal place in the valley. In 1 hr. more, passing the hamlet *St. Rocco*, a spot is reached, whence looking back, the view of the Tödi is superb. The traveller then passes *Fuorns* and *Acla* to *Perdatsch* at the opening of the savage Val Cristallina, which runs in a S.E. direction, and sends forth one branch of the Mittel Rhein. It is celebrated for its rock-crystals, of which the shrine of San Carlo Borromeo, in the Duomo of Milan, is made. [It divides into two branches, *V. Casaccia* running S., *V. Ufiern* (Rom. for *Inferno*) E., and by the latter is a pass of 7887 ft. to Olivone. The highest peaks of the Medelser Gebirge are all easy of access to climbers with guides and rope.] Below Perdatsch the Mittel Rhein plunges, in a fall of 100 ft., into a deep gulf. The ascent now becomes more rapid, and the scenery wilder and finer. The little *hospices* of *St. Gion* and *St. Gall*, each with its warning bell, are passed, and in about 5 hrs. from Disentis, Sta. Maria is reached. Here four streams unite to form the Mittel Rhein, the principal affluent flowing from the W., by the Val Cadlimo, from a small lake at the foot of the Monte Scuro.

Sta. Maria, at a height of 5925 ft., is a hospice kept up for the benefit of travellers, and, though very wretched in appearance, it provides tolerable accommodation for man and horse.

S.W. of it is the Val Termine leading to the *Uomo Pass* (Rte. 84); and E. the *Scopi*, which may be ascended in 5 hrs. In a southerly direction a walk of half an hour brings the traveller to the pass of the

Lukmanier (in Latin, *Mons Lucumonius;* in Romansch, *Lukmajn*, or *Culm Sta. Maria*), 6289 ft. above the sea, the lowest passage through the main chain between the Mt. Genèvre and Maloja, by which, it is said, Pepin with his army passed A.D. 754, on his invasion of Italy. Poles mark the direction of the road across the col, and a cross on the summit the boundary of the Grisons and Canton Tessin. Hence the road to Olivone and the Val Blegno descends Val Casaccia to the hospice of

Casaccia; and, a few miles lower, to that of

Camperio, both founded, it is said, by San Carlo Borromeo, for the reception of travellers.

The first glimpse of the tower and plain of

Olivone, 2927 ft. (H. Olivone, fair), the highest village in Val Blegno, from the wooded steeps of the Lukmanier, is very striking, the descent to it beautiful, and the village itself one of the most charming spots in the Alps. Olivone is a good starting-point for excursions in the Rheinwald and Medelser groups.

[Besides the Lukmanier, the Disrut and Greina Passes lead N. to the Vorderrheinthal, and the Scaradra Pass W. to the extreme head of the Lugnetz Thal. The Rheinwaldhorn (see Rte. 91) is accessible through Val Carassina.]

The *Val Blegno* (Germ. *Polenzer Thal*) is traversed by the Brenno, which enters it from a narrow cleft in the mountain. All the valley is very beautiful.

From Olivone to Biasca, a distance of 14 m.

Many of the chocolate-sellers and chestnut-roasters, who swarm in the streets of the cities of Italy, come from Val Blegno.

At *Acqua Rossa* (1758 ft.) is a large Bathing Establishment and Hotel, a

centre for beautiful walks and excursions. The resident physician has written an interesting guide to the locality.

At *Malvaglia* (H. de l' Etoile), 10 m., a glen opens on the rt. leading to the heart of the Rheinwald group. Glacier passes can be effected from it to the source of the Rhine and San Bernardino.

Biasca Stat. (Rte. 34), on the St. Gothard railroad, 3 hrs.' drive from Olivone (4 the other way).

ROUTE 86.

A. ILANZ TO OLIVONE BY THE DISRUT PASS. B. TRONS TO OLIVONE BY THE GREINA PASS.

Car-road to Vrin. This route (12 hrs.) leads S. from Ilanz high up along the flank of the *Piz Mundaun*, on the W. side of the *Lugnetz Thal*, a beautiful valley, contracted at its opening into a mere defile. In about 1 hr., or half-way to *Combels*, the traveller passes the *Frauenthor*, an ancient gateway, which was successfully defended by the women of the valley against the Count de Montfort, when the men were fighting on the heights above it. To commemorate their prowess the women have the privilege of sitting on the rt. side of the church. On the opposite side of the valley are the Rieiner Tobel, *Piz Fez* and *Piz Riein*. [Beyond the forest, about ½ m. short of Combels, a road diverges l. downhill to *Peiden* (humble *Inn*). Below this village, at the mouth of a wild gorge, is the *Badhaus of Peiden*. Its mineral spring was injured by a flood in 1868, but has been reopened.] About 2 m. above Combels the valley divides; the S. branch, or St. Peters Thal, leading to the pass of the *Valserberg* (Rte. 89).

The rte. to the Disrut, after leaving *Combels*, passes *Villa*, chief place in the Lugnetz Thal, with a fair *Inn* and curious old houses, and runs over an elevated and extensive tract of open fields, to *Lumbrein* (*Inn*), where the scenery is beautiful, with *Piz Regina* l. The path then reaches a point, where the Lugnetz Thal loses its name, and is continued on the rt. by the deep gorge of Val Cavel, on the l. by the Vrin Thal. Beyond this ravine is the village of *Vrin* (5 hrs. from Ilánz). 4789 ft. (*Inn:* Casanova's.) Good guides.

[Here the *Val Vanescha* opens S., offering to good walkers a preferable route to Olivone by the Vanescha Alp and *Luzzone Pass*, 8½ hrs. The ascent of *Piz Terri* (10,338 ft.), first climbed by Placidus à Spescha, offers a sharp scramble and a fine view.]

On leaving Vrin the path keeps the left bank and crosses the river, which it recrosses almost directly to the rt., the valley branching again. The last hamlet is *Buzatsch* (1½ hr. from Vrin), from which there is an ascent of nearly 2 hrs. For the first hour there is a track; the rest of the way may be called pathless, and in unsettled weather will not easily be found without a guide. The final climb is up a shallow gully partly filled with snow, partly with loose débris. The head of this gully is the

Disrut (or *Diesrut*) *Pass*, 7953 ft., 8½ hrs. from Ilanz. The view of rugged mountains is striking.

The descent on the other side is to the plain of the *Val Greina*, the head of the V. Somvix, and the traveller must be cautious not to bear away to the rt., or he will return to the Rhine valley. His course is about S.W. to the Greina Pass. The descent from the Disrut is steep and rough, but after a short ½ hr. of scrambling and slipping down a crumbling declivity and a bed of snow, the highest part of the plain is reached. To the W. the great Gallinario glacier is seen.

B. *Trons to Olivone by the Greina Pass.*

At Surrhein, 1½ hr.'s walk from Trons, the Somvixthal opens l. It is a wild and picturesque glen. 1 hr. from Surrhein, in an opening, stands Tenniger Bad, interesting as a specimen of a primitive Swiss bathhouse. The baths are wooden troughs fitted side by side, so that alternate patients lie the same way. A steep ascent leads to the Rhun Alp, ¾ hr., where there is a Swiss Alpine Club hut, for excursions in the Medelser Gebirge; key at Tenniger Bad.

[Hence the *Lavazjoch*, an interesting pass skirting the N. side of the Medelser Gebirge, and affording excellent views of their glaciers, leads in 4½ hrs. to the Medelser Thal.]

The path to the Greina ascends steeply under Piz Vioz to the long level plain which here forms the summit of the Alps.

The ascent to the ridge of the *Greina* (7743 ft.) is all but nominal. The descent on the other side into the *Val Camadra*, the highest part of the *Val Blegno*, is rough. After crossing a wet stony flat, it is requisite to ascend the right of the two spurs into which the broken ridge is split, and then to make a very steep descent among stones and blocks into the valley, which is gained in about half an hour after leaving the summit. The head of the Val Camadra is partially occupied by a bed of snow, and overhung on the W. by the Camadra glacier, a portion of the field of ice to which the Medelser glacier belongs. Over this lies a pass to the Medelser Thal.

Val Luzzon, which opens from the E., leads to the Scaradra Pass (see Rte. 89).

The descent to *Olivone* will occupy fully 3 hrs. It is advisable to reach Olivone by daylight, as there is a ravine below Ghirone, where the path skirts the edge of unguarded precipices.

ROUTE 87.

COIRE TO CHIAVENNA—THE VIA MALA —PASS OF THE SPLÜGEN.

Coire.	Eng. m.
Reichenau.	6
Thusis.	11
Andeer	8
Splügen	8½
Campodolcino.	16½
Chiavenna.	7½

2-horse carr. to Thusis, 30 fr.; to

Splügen, 65; to Chiavenna, 135; to Colico, 160.

In posting, an extra horse must be taken from Thusis or Chiavenna to the summit.

Diligences twice daily in summer from Coire to Lake of Como and (rail to) Milan, reaching Splügen in 7¼ hrs., Chiavenna in 12¼. Rail thence to Colico. About 7 hrs.' posting from Coire to Splügen, about 4½ hrs. from Splügen to Coire. The best hotels on the pass are at Thusis (first-rate) and Splügen.

Steamers run from Colico to Como and Lecco, and this part of the journey is most pleasantly made by water.

From *Coire* (1960 ft.) (Rte. 81) to *Ems*, a Rom. Cath. and Romansch village of 1400 Inhab., there is not much deserving notice. On the rt. is the *Calanda* range; and on the same side the village of *Felsberg*, partly buried by a slip from threatening rocks above it.

The road is nearly level, and crosses the Hinter Rhein by an iron bridge close to its junction with the Vorder Rhein, at the entrance of

6 m. *Reichenau* (1940 ft.) (*Inn:* Adler, once a convent, adjoining M. Planta's garden), a group of houses at the junction of the two Rhines, which run full tilt against each other.

The *Château*, a seat of the Plantas, was at the end of the last cent. converted into a school by the burgomaster Tscharner. In 1793 a young man calling himself Chabot arrived here on foot, with a stick in his hand and a bundle on his back. He presented a letter of introduction to M. Jost, the head master, in consequence of which he was appointed usher; and for 8 months gave lessons in French, mathematics, and history. This forlorn stranger was no other than Louis Philippe, then Duc de Chartres, who had been forced, by the march of the French, to quit Bremgarten, and seek concealment here in the performance of the humble duties of a schoolmaster. His secret was known only to M. Jost. His cheerful room is still shown. The house contains pictures by Winterhalter, and other memorials of the Orleans Family. [Rt. *Kunkels Pass* to Ragatz (Rte. 66, c).] Fine specimens of the Golden Eagle (*Steinadler*) in the inn, 2 birds which fell fighting on the top of a diligence, and were killed by the guard.

At Reichenau the road to Disentis is carried first over the Vorder Rhein above the point of junction by a covered wooden bridge of one fine arch. The more abundant waters of the Hinter Rhein, stained by the Nolla torrent at Thusis, are nearly black; while those of the Vorder Rhein, bearing the silt of glaciers, are grey.

The junction is best seen from M. Planta's garden.

Our road now leaves the valley of the Vorder Rhein (Rte. 82) on the l., and follows the Hinter Rhein.

After an ascent from Reichenau, the road of the Splügen runs over an open country, with view back on the Flimserstein, Ringelspitz and Calanda, by *Bonaduz* (*Inn:* Post) and *Rhäzüns*, where l., on the rocky bank of the Hinter Rhein, rises the *Castle of Rhäzüns* (Rætia ima), and near it the little *Ch. of St. George*, interesting for its mediæval frescoes. The section on the Rhine valley, next traversed by the road, 7 m. in length, extending to Thusis, is called the valley of *Domleschg* (Vallis Tomiliasca), bounded W. by the pastures of the *Heinzenberg*, a range green and smiling on this side, but precipitous and savage towards the Savien Thal. To the E. is the *Stätzerhorn*.

This part of the Rheinthal is particularly remarkable for the number of *castles* (21) on either side of the river, mostly in ruins. They contribute not a little to the charms of the landscape, and serve at the same time as monuments of a revolution by which the power of a feudal aristocracy was broken, and their strongholds burnt by the peasants whom they had long oppressed.

Another peculiarity of this district is the intermixture of language and religion. There are scarcely two adjoining parishes, or even hamlets, speaking the same tongue and professing the same faith. Thus at Coire German is the language, and Protestant the religion of the majority; at Ems, the first village on the road, Romansch (Rte. 81) is spoken. Tamins and Reichenau are Rom. Cath. and German; Bonaduz, divided from them by the Rhine, is Rom. Cath., and speaks Romansch. Rhäzüns and Katzis are two Roman Catholic villages; but in the first the language is German, in the second Romansch. The inhabitants of the Heinzenberg and Thusis are Protestant and German; of Zillis, and throughout the valley of Schams, Protestant and Romansch. Splügen and Hinterrhein form the boundary at once of the Romansch language and Protestant religion.

At the entrance of the Domleschg, on the opposite side of the river, are the chalybeate baths of *Rothenbrunn*, and, crowning a cliff, the ancient castle of the Counts of Travers—*Ortenstein*, one of the finest in the valley: it has been restored, and now belongs to the Juvalta family. Near *Katzis* a beautiful view opens out S.E. up the Schyn pass through which the Albula descends to join the Rhine. The Rhine valley here shows the ravages produced by the torrent *Nolla*, which, rising on Piz Beverin, W. of our route, joins the Rhine at Thusis, nearly at right angles. It at all times pollutes the river, and is subject to very sudden swells after rain, when it rushes down, tearing up rocks and carrying along with it a vast quantity of black mud and gravel. Its unruly waters are now restrained by dykes constructed along the banks of the Rhine.

16 m. *Thusis* (2450 ft.) (*Inns:* H. and Pens. Via Mala, with garden, comfortable, facing the Via Mala, a pleasant resting-place; Post; Rhætia), a village of 1000 Inhab., finely situated on a terrace at the mouth of the Via Mala, and opening of the Schyn pass.

Dr. Buol, a good homœopathic physician, resides here.

Thusis was almost entirely destroyed by fire in 1845. There are delightful *walks* to the ruins of *Hohen Rhätien*, on the height above the entrance of the Via Mala; to the castles of *Ober Tagstein* and *Nieder Tagstein*, on the l. bank of the Rhine; the gorge of the *Nolla;* the old mule-road of the Splügen, to Rongella (up the opening rt. of Via Mala), returning by Via Mala.

Longer *excursions* can be made to the *Stätzerhorn* (Rte. 92), a splendid point of view E. of the Coire road; by Sils and the ruins of Campi to the *Schyn Gorge*, as far as Solisbrücke (Rte. 93). *Diligence* daily to Tiefenkasten, to Platz, in the *Savien Thal*, by the *Stege* pass under Piz Beverin, 5 hrs., to the top of *Piz Beverin*, 9842 ft.

Just beyond Thusis the muddy Nolla, flowing from the Piz Beverin, through a waste of débris, is crossed by a handsome bridge. Here is the *Rosenbühl* (a brewery, with rock cellars), a good point of view.

The valley seems closed by mountains, so narrow is the opening of the chasm which gives a passage to the river and the road. The E. side of this portal was guarded by the now ruinous castle of *Hohen Rhätien*, or *Hoch Realt* (Rætia Alta), standing in the fork between the Albula and the Rhine, and from its lofty platform, 400 ft. high, looking down upon both valleys. It is accessible by a path from the village of Sils, but is almost encircled by the sheer precipice which falls to the Rhine. These mouldering ruins *traditionally* owe their origin to Rhætus, chief of the Etruscans, who, it is related, driven out of Italy by the Gauls, here established his stronghold B.C. 287, and transplanted into the Alps the people and language of Etruria. The roofless chapel of St. Johann, standing beside the ruins of the castle, is stated to have been the earliest, and for a long time the only Christian temple in the valley, where heathenism prevailed to a comparatively late period. The group of ruins consists of this chapel and 3 old towers (with herring-bone work), ¾ hr. from Thusis. The path goes up further, to an alp above the Via Mala cliffs, a beautiful spot, with view of Piz Beverin, and of the Ringelspitz and Calanda, down the Domleschg valley.

The VIA MALA, extending 3½ miles, is one of the most celebrated defiles in Switzerland. The precipices rise in some places 1600 ft., and for a short distance are scarcely more than 10 yards apart. Its ascent begins ¼ m. beyond Thusis, and to see the defile well a traveller should quit his carriage and *walk* to the 2nd bridge.

At the mouth of the defile, the cliffs afforded in their natural state not an inch of space along which a goat could clamber; and, in ancient times, this part of the chasm was deemed inaccessible. The peasants gave it the name of the Lost Gulf (Trou perdu, Verlorenes Loch); and, when they wanted to go from Thusis to the higher valley of Schams, they ascended the vale of the Nolla for some distance, passed over the shoulder of Piz Beverin, and descended at Zillis. A second road, formed in 1470, crossed the mountains as before, but dipped down, from the chalets of Rongella, into the depths of the Via Mala, near the first bridge. This inconvenient path, after being used for more than 300 years, was superseded by the present magnificent highway constructed in 1822 by the engineer Pocobelli. Avoiding the détour, he at once plunged into the defile, and pierced the buttress by the gallery or tunnel of the

Verlorenes Loch, 216 ft. long. The view from it, looking back through the vista of black rock, and the fringe of firs, upon the ruined tower of Realt and the sun-lit valley of Domleschg, is singularly beautiful. The grooves of the boring-rod indicate the labour of constructing this part of the road. It was literally forcing a pas-

sage through the bowels of the earth; and the whole width of the carriage-way has been gained by blasting a notch, as it were, in the side of the mountain. For more than 1000 ft. the road is carried along beneath a canopy, thus artificially hollowed out. It is protected by a parapet, below which, at a very considerable depth, the contracted Rhine frets the foot of the precipice. A little higher up, the gorge widens into a small circular basin, in the midst of which stands the Post Office of *Rongella;* but it soon closes again, and the pass attains the height of its grandeur beyond the first of the 3 bridges, by means of which the road is conveyed from side to side.

The *Middle Bridge,* a most striking object, from its graceful proportions, is approached by a second gallery, protected by a wooden roof to ward off falling stones. Here, the precipices on one side actually overhang those on the other, the direction of the chasm being oblique: towards the N. there appears no outlet. The Rhine, reduced to a thread of water, is barely visible, foaming in the depths below. In one place it is entirely lost to view —jammed in, as it were, between the rocks, here so slightly separated, that small blocks and trunks of fir-trees, falling from above, have been caught in the chink, and remain suspended above the water. The ordinary height of the bridge above the river is 250 ft.; and the water, as mentioned above, is in one place invisible at ordinary times, yet during the inundation of 1834 it rose to within a few feet of the bridge.

For a short way further, the road is little more than a shelf hewn out of the precipice, but the defile rapidly widens, and at the 3rd, or upper bridge, a fine structure — replacing one swept off in 1834 — it emerges into the open valley of *Schams* (Sexamniensis, from 6 brooks, which fall into the Rhine from its sides). Its green meadows have a pleasing effect when contrasted with the gloomy scene behind, but suffered much from the inundation of 1834, which converted the valley into a lake, destroyed a great part of the road, and rendered a new line neces-sary. The inhabitants are Protestant and speak Romansch.

The valley is bordered by high terraces, which have been cut by water, and show that the valley was once filled by a lake whose waters were dammed by a barrier of rocks until the passage of the Via Mala was worn, and the lake was thereby drained off.

Zillis (*Inn:* Kreuz), with old and curious fresco paintings in the ch. Beyond it, on the rt., are villages on the mountain slopes, along which ran the Roman road, and above them *Piz Beverin*. About 1 m. short of Andeer an inscription on a bridge (*Inn:* Ochs) commemorates the completion of the great highways over the Splügen and Bernardino :— " *Jam via patet hostibus et amicis. Cavete, Rhæti! Simplicitas morum et Unio servabunt avitam libertatem.*" Rt. is a tempting view of the glen of the Fundogn, of the *Grauhorn*, and other peaks of *dolomite*, between Andeer and the head of the Savien Thal. On the same side, perched on a hill, is the picturesque tower of *Castellatsch*. The *Surrettahorn* terminates the vista of the Schams valley S.W. Looking back, the *Stätzerhorn* is seen beyond the Via Mala.

23½ m. *Andeer—Inn :* (3200 ft.) H. Fravi; good. The source of the *mineral spring* at Pigneu, which supplies the *Baths* here, was destroyed by a flood in 1869. This is the chief village in Schams, and has 580 Inhab., who, like their neighbours, are Protestants, and speak Romansch. Over the doors of many of the cottages are quaint verses and mottoes in that language.

[The ascent of *Piz Beverin*, 9843 ft., is made from Andeer in about 6 hrs. It is not difficult, and the view is mag-nificent. The ascent begins at Zillis. Guide from Andeer 5 fr.; horse, 9 fr.; chaise-à-porteurs, 6½ fr. a man.]

The ruined castles visible in the valley of Schams have an historical interest, from being monuments of the dawn of Grison liberty. In the middle of the fifteenth century they served as the residences of bailiffs, zwingherrn, or landvogts, depen-dants of the Counts of Vatz or of the Bishop of Coire, whose exac-tions at last roused the peasants to arms, and the castles were stormed and burnt 1451. One of the first that fell was *Bärenburg*, which is passed on the l. after quitting Andeer.

About 2 m. above Andeer, on an ascent, where the mountains are again closing on the traveller, is the open-ing of the Averser Thal (Rte. 88), a convenient route for pedestrians pro-ceeding to the Engadine, who wish to take the Via Mala on their way.

Passing the mouth of this valley, the road mounts by zigzags into the gorge of the *Roffla*, which closes the S. end of the oval vale of Schams, as the Via Mala does the N. The Rhine here descends in the cataract of the Roffla. It does not rank as a first-rate waterfall, but the scenery is picturesque—the valley being thickly wooded.

In about 3 m. the gorge terminates in a narrow passage and archway of rock, which once apparently dammed in the waters of the Rheinwald Thal, as the scoopings of a torrent are beautifully seen 30 ft. overhead. Here opens a pastoral vale, extending to the sources of the Hinter-Rhein. Rt. is the village of *Sufers*. Some 3 m. more, through pine-forest, brings the traveller to

32½ m. *Splügen*—Ital. *Spluga*, Rom. *Speleuga* (*Inn:* Bodenhaus, very good: *pension* 8 fr., with wine). This little village, but chief place of the Rhein-wald, is situated at the point of separation of the two Alpine passes of the Splügen and Bernardino, at a height of 4757 ft. above the sea. It suffered severely from the flood of 1834, which swept away more than a dozen houses. The covered bridge over the Rhine escaped, but has since been replaced by an iron girder bridge.

Splügen anciently belonged to the lords of Sax, on the S. slope of the Bernardino, but it afterwards joined the Grey League.

Above the village, in the bed of the

stream from the Löchliberg, is an ancient hermitage, and in the ch.-yd. are curious monuments to the Georgiis. The prominent mountains are the *Guggernüll* and *Einshorn*, 9649 ft., l. of the valley, and over Splügen the dolomite *Kalkberg.* Behind the Guggernüll is the *Tambohorn*, 10,748 ft., but it is not seen from the village.

Walk—¼ hr. E. of the ch. to the *castle* ruins; then through forest to Sufers by the old Splügen mule-path, supposed to have been a Roman road.

[*Excursions*—*a.* To 3 *lakes*, full of trout, under the Surettahörner. Turn up l. just beyond the Rhine bridge. 2 hrs. up S.E., glorious view. *b.* Ascent of *Guggernüll*, with view of Tambohorn. *c.* Ascent of *Tambohorn*, 4½ hrs. up. The rocks at the top are steep and require care. Guide 14 fr. *d.* Ascent of *Surettahorn*, 9971 ft.

Diligence twice daily to Chiavenna in 5 hrs.

Löchliberg Pass, down the *Savien Thal* to Coire (Rte. 90; *Valserberg Pass*, down *St. Peters Thal* to Ilánz (Rte. 89).]

At Splügen properly commences the pass of the Splügen. It is very ancient, having been known to the Romans; but until modern improvements it was one of the most difficult, and sometimes dangerous, of the frequented passes. The road was completed by the Austrian Government in 1823, to compete with the newer Swiss road over the Bernardino, which diverges at Splügen. The engineer was the Chevalier Donegani. The *time walking* is given as far as the Madesimo fall.

The Splügen road crosses the Rhine, and ascending some zigzags enters through a short tunnel (25 min.) the valley of the Oberhausen-bach, a small torrent which joins the Rhine at Splügen. This it follows by a gentle ascent, and an entirely new line, the old one having been demolished by the tempest of 1834, when road and bridges were carried away, and piles of broken rocks spread over it. In 50 min. from the tunnel, one on foot will reach the main series of zigzags leading up the final steep. An *osteria* stands near the top, and at one point the peak of the *Tambohorn* is seen rt. Above the zigzags is a covered gallery of 369 paces (25 min.), and beyond it (10 min.) the

6¾ m. *Summit of the Pass*, 6945 ft. above the sea, between the *Tambohorn* and *Surettahorn.* Along this narrow ridge, which is 4¾ m. (1¾ hr.'s walk) from Splügen, and more than 2000 ft. above it, runs the boundary line of Switzerland and Italy. Immediately after surmounting it the road begins to descend, passing the first cantonnièra, or house of refuge; and, lower down, a series of tourniquets to the *Osteria Mte. Splügen* and

Italian Custom-house (25 min.)—a melancholy group of buildings where luggage is searched. The custom-house stands at one end of an oval basin, surrounded by mountain peaks, a scene of extreme desolation; not a shrub of any kind grows, and the snow often reaches the windows of the first story of the houses. To the N. E. is the *Surettahorn.* At the further end of this basin, where the road crosses the stream, the old bridle-path descended to the rt. direct to Isola, through the defile of the *Cardenello*, a very perilous valley, from its constant exposure to avalanches.

The French army of Marshal Macdonald, who crossed the Splügen between the 27th November and 4th December, 1800, long before the new road was begun, in the face of snow and storm, lost nearly 100 men, and as many horses, chiefly in the passage of the Cardenello. His columns were literally cut through by the falling avalanches, and man and beast swept away to certain destruction. The carriage-road avoids this gorge altogether, proceeding at a high level along the mountain side. From the Cantonnièra della Stuetta (35 min.) there is a grand view to the rt.—the finest on the pass—of the *glacier of Curciusa*, and the peaks *Pizzo Terre*, *Cima di Balnisio*, and others, towering to the sky beyond the deep valley. 20 min., a gallery of 244 paces, then zigzag descent to Cantonnièra di Teggiate (10 min.) Two galleries follow, of 221 and 567 paces.

These galleries, the longest on any Alpine road, are constructed of the most solid masonry, arched, with roofs sloping outwards, to turn aside the snow, supported on pillars, and lighted by low windows like the embrasures of a battery. They protect this portion of the road from avalanches. From the entrance of the second gallery there is a most striking view down upon the roofs of Isola, and the long line of zigzags, which led to that village, abandoned since 1838. At *Pianazzo* this old road is left for the new one, which is shorter by 3 m., and was rendered necessary by the injury done by the storm of 1834, and also by the danger to which the route between Isola and the cascade of the Madesimo was exposed from avalanches, which fall regularly into the glen of the Liro, below Pianazzo, In 1835, 5 peasants and 8 horses were overwhelmed by the snow in this glen as they were returning from conducting the diligence on a sledge over the mountain.

There is a fair *Inn* at Isola.

Pianazzo stands at the same height above the sea as the bridge over the Rhine at Splügen. The road, after passing through it, crosses the little stream of the *Madesimo*, within a few yards of the verge of the precipice, over which it throws itself in a beautiful fall, 800 ft. high. The view, looking down the fall from a little terrace (which everyone should visit) is very fine. [From near the bridge, a track ascends the stream to the *Passo di Madesimo*, a mule-pass to Canicul in the Averser Thal. From Pianazzo the walk back to Splügen is 3¼ hrs., 2 hrs. to the col.] The road now passes through a tunnel and covered gallery, and then descends to the bottom of the valley by numerous zigzags. From the corners fine glimpses of the fall are obtained.

17 m. *Campo Dolcino* (3550 ft.), which,

in spite of its sweet-sounding Italian name, is but a poor village (Post, excellent), on a small grassy plain, on the borders of the *Liro*.

A further improvement has been made in the continuation of the road, which, on quitting the plain, threads the gorge of *San Giacomo*; an inscription commemorates its completion by Carlo Donegani, in the reign of the Emperor Francis II. The vale of the Liro presents a desolate aspect, from the fallen rocks, which fill the lower part of it. They are composed of a species of white gneiss, exceedingly brittle, and which, after exposure to the weather, assumes a red colour. It must have been a difficult task to carry a road through such a wilderness; and it is accordingly in many places narrow, the turnings sharp, and the terraces too short. The desolation of the scene would be greater were it not for the chestnut-trees. The tall white campanile of the church of Madonna di Gallivaggio, with these woods and precipices, forms an agreeable picture. Near it, at the village San Giacomo, the Liro is spanned by a new and bold bridge.

A mile or two farther, the valley opens and Chiavenna appears in view, a picturesque town, under an Italian sun.

25 m. *Chiavenna* (1050 ft.)—Germ. *Clefen*, Clavena of the ancients—(*Inn:* H. Conradi, good), a town of 3800 Inhab., is charmingly situated below steep wooded mountains of singular beauty, at the junction of the valley of S. Giacomo with that of the Maira, called Val Bregaglia. It benefits from its position at the junction of the Splügen and Maloja roads, is celebrated for its *beer*, the best in N. Italy, and maintains several spinning-mills for silk and cotton. An ingenious manufacturer named Vanossi at one time wove here a fire-proof cloth of asbestos,—a mineral which abounds in the neighbouring mountains. As in Sion and other towns, there are many remains of former wealth and splendour. Opposite the Conradi inn, at

the foot of a curiously coloured rock, is a large ruined *Palazzo* begun by the Grisons family De Salis, but never completed, in consequence of Chiavenna being annexed to Italy by Napoleon, 1797 : strangers are admitted to enjoy the fine *view* from the castle-hill called Il Paradiso. The castle was made a strong fortress by the Visconti of Milan, and was demolished by the men of Graubünden in 1622. The *Ch. of S. Lorenzo* has a tall campanile standing within a square enclosure, surrounded by a cloister. On one side are two bone-houses, filled with skulls arranged in patterns, and, adjoining them, in the octagonal *Baptistery*, an ancient stone font, with rude bas-reliefs. Behind the church there is an avenue; a lane runs out of it southwards, from which a pleasant winding footpath leads up the hill-side. The citizens keep their Valtellina wine in grottoes, which form excellent cool cellars and are called Ventorali.

Chiavenna belonged to the Dukes of Milan down to the 16th century, when the Grisons became possessed of it, with the Valtellina and Bormio. Napoleon added it to Italy, and the Congress of Vienna transferred it to Austria. In 1859 it became Italian.

[About 3 m. up the *Val Bregaglia*, near Pleurs, memorable for the fate of its inhabitants, who were buried by the fall of a mountain (Rte. 98), is a peculiar manufacture of a coarse ware for culinary purposes, made out of potstone (lapis ollaris). This stone is easily cut, or turned in a lathe, and endures heat. Pliny calls it lapis Comensis, from its being exported from the lake of Como.

The description of the road up the beautiful Val Bregaglia, and over the pass of the Maloja, is given in Rte. 98. Visitors to Chiavenna should drive a short way to get an idea of the valley, which, with its dark purple rocks and chestnut woods, is finer than the descent from the Splügen. Very good hotels are now open at Promontogno and Soglio, in charming situations.]

Near *Gordona*, S.W. of Chiavenna,

is a waterfall worth notice. At the distance of $\frac{1}{2}$ hr. from the town on the Colico road, the river on the rt. must be crossed. A walk of $\frac{1}{2}$ hr. leads thence to the Fall.

The diligences from Chiavenna to Coire, in $13\frac{1}{2}$ hrs., pass at a very early or late hour. A voiturier to Coire charges 135 fr., sleeping the first night at Andeer. A bargain should be made that he should change horses at Campo Dolcino, and so go at a better pace and avoid waiting 2 hrs. at that village. For the railway from Chiavenna to Colico and the Lake of Como, see Rte. 116, and for the road to St. Moritz, see Rte. 98.

ROUTE 88.

ANDEER TO CASACCIA, BY THE AVERSER THAL, FORCELLINA AND SEPTIMER PASSES.

11 hrs.' steady walking: take provisions. A carriage-road is projected from Andeer to Bivio (Stalla) on the Julier pass.

This is a good route for pedestrians who wish to see the Via Mala on their way to the Engadine, but it is little known and unfrequented. $1\frac{1}{2}$ m. above Andeer a considerable torrent joins the Hinter Rhein from the S.E. It is called the *Averser Rhein*, and the valley through which it flows the *Ferrera Thal*. The lower portion is one of the finest of the northern defiles of the Alps. Close to the opening there is a waterfall. The path is carried through a narrow thickly-wooded gorge, and passing some marble-quarries reaches

Canicül (a rough *Inn*), under the precipices of the *Piz Starlera*, 10,000 ft., and about 3 hrs. from Andeer; W. of it is the *Surettahorn*, 9971 ft., and S.W. the Val Emet, and *Passo di Madesimo* leading to the Splügen road; $2\frac{1}{2}$ hrs. farther, ascending by a tolerable path, the traveller, after passing Crot and the entrance to the *Madriser Thal*, through which passes lead to Promontogno and Castasegna in Val

Bregaglia, reaches the chief village of the valley,

Cresta—with a rougher *Inn;* both here and at Canicül the curé receives hospitably the few strangers who pass. Of course, on leaving, a present should be made to the housekeeper.

Cresta is one of the highest villages in the Alps, being 6380 ft. above the sea. The last straggling pine-trees are seen around it. The valley now opens into a wide expanse of Alpine pasture, reaching nearly to the summits of the mountains; and in about 4 m. leads to a group of chalets called *Juf,* said to be the highest hamlet in Europe, 6905 ft. above the sea. Many passes diverge from it:— one N., crossing the mountains between the *Fopperhorn* and *Piz Scalotta* to the Val Faller and Molins, on the Julier pass; another E., called the *Stallerberg* (8478 ft.), an easy pass to Bivio on the road of the Julier (Rte. 92)—the summit may be reached in 2½ hrs. from Cresta: Bivio in 2 hrs. from the summit—and a third

The pass of the *Forcellina* or *Furkel,* at the head of the Averser Thal, over which lies the route to Casaccia. The ascent presents no difficulty; but as there is little to point out the true direction, which lies S.E., on the N. bank of the stream, a guide is required. The summit (8770 ft.) —about 2½ hrs. from Cresta—commands a wide view over a wilderness of peaks. The descent on the E. lies down a slope of snow scarcely steep enough for a glissade, and then over rocks until the paved track of the Septimer is reached close to the summit of that pass, where once stood a small hospice, or place of refuge, now in ruins.

The *Septimer Pass,* an old Roman road, and in the Middle Ages one of the most frequented routes into Italy, now an indifferent but well traced bridle-path, in parts displaying the old paved Roman track, leads from

Bivio to Casaccia, 4 or 4½ hours' walk. The S. side is much more steep and stony than the other. The summit is 7582 ft. above the sea, and in the view the Piz Muretto and Monte del Oro beyond Casaccia are conspicuous features. Though impracticable for any kind of vehicle, this was once a frequented highway between Italy and Switzerland until the formation of the carriage-road over the Splügen, which is a lower pass, and 10 m. shorter.

In about 2 hrs. from the Forcellina the traveller reaches the little village of *Casaccia* (Rte. 98). This pass, though it offers no difficulty to the mountaineer, is rather a hard day's work.

ROUTE 89.

NÜFENEN TO ILANZ, BY THE PASS OF THE VALSERBERG AND ST. PETERS THAL.

Nüfenen to						Hrs.	Min.
Pass	.	.	.	.	.	2	30
Platz (Vals)	.	.	.	.	2	40
Haspel	.	.	.	.	.	1	0
Peiden	.	.	.	.	.	2	0
Frauenthor	.	.	.	.	0	55
Ilanz	.	.	.	.	.	0	55
						—	—
						10	0

A new carriage-road. The above is the time easy walking. Carriage-road from Vals to Ilanz. The most notable points of the pass are the view W. on descending to Platz, the gorge between Haspel and St. Martin, and the scenery in the forest below Peiden.

Just beyond Nüfenen (see Rte. 91) the footpath to the Valserberg branches off rt. by the side of a little stream, reaches in a few minutes the base of the cliffs rising N. of the valley, and continues to ascend along it. These cliffs extend to the pass, and are an excellent guide. A wooded spur separates the hollow looking towards Nüfenen from that leading down to Hinterrhein. After an ascent of less than an hour, this spur is crossed nearly at its point of divergence from the chain, and just above the wood which clothes its lower part. The high pastures overlooking Hinterrhein are now reached, and the path from that village falls in. There is a good view from this point of the zigzags of the Bernardino, of the *Marscholhorn*, S.W., *Piz Tambo*, S., the *Kirchalphorn* and Fanella glacier, W.

The last ascent to the Valserberg is rather steep, but marked by piles of stones. The Col is a narrow gap (8225 ft.), commanding N. a wild and barren mountain country, in which the rocks of the *Breitengrat*, between St. Peters Thal and the Vrin Thal, are conspicuous.

For nearly an hour from the summit the way is marked by poles, and lies high above the Peilerbach, which flows on the l. from the Fanella gl. The descent is steep to the highest chalets (1 hr. 5 min. from Col), where a stream from the *Bärenhorn* on the rt. is crossed. The path then goes along its rt. bank [left of the main stream] to another steep descent, whence there is a view W. over a noble pine-forest to the remarkable pyramid of the *Zavreilahorn*. Below lies

St. Peters Platz (or *Vals*, more properly, name of the district), 3870 ft. (*Inns* : Piz Albin and Piz Aul, both homely.) Good guides. This village lies deep in a mountain basin, on the Valser-Rhein, or Glenner, protected by a dyke from a smaller but dangerous stream from the *Weissensteinhorn* (E).

St. Peters Thal, which is here entered, joins the main valley of Lugnetz at Furth ; and some miles further W. the Lugnetz Thal branches into the smaller valleys of Vrin and Cavel. In St. Peters Thal the language is German, as well as in the Rheinwald and Savien Thal. In the districts of Lugnetz and Vrin, Romansch is spoken.

[The scenery of St. Peters Thal above Platz is very fine, the valley terminating among the glaciers of the Rheinwald group. A path formed of large slabs leads, in 3 hrs., by a considerable ascent and descent, through magnificent pine-forests above a formidably deep gorge, to the hamlet of *Zavreila*, at the foot of the pyramidal *Zavreilahorn*. The long green basin of Zavreila is of the finest turf, bounded rt. by black precipices, l. by a bushy slope, with Pinus cembra and rocks. At the village the valley branches. The rt. branch leads to the Lenta glacier and *Rheinwaldhorn*, with passes over the glacier to Olivone and Hinterrhein, and another pass the *Scaradra* to the Val Blegno, a little above Olivone, mounting W. from the chalets of Lampertsch. The *Rheinwaldhorn* is easily attained from this side. The l. branch runs to the Kanal glacier and *Guferhorn*, and to the Zapportgrat Pass to Hinterrhein. All these are glacier excursions, but free from serious difficulties.

From Platz also are the *Frunt pass* and *Lies pass* to Vrin, each about 5 hrs., and commanding a superb view of the Adula mountains ; and the *Tomil-Alp Pass* to Savien Platz. The *Weissenstein*, l. of the last, is another fine point of view. All 3 passes are quite easy.]

The little basin of Platz was sadly devastated by the torrent in 1868. The St. Peters Thal below Platz is one of the finest in the Grisons. ¼ m. below the village the road enters a wooded gorge, and becomes extremely romantic. It passes under an ancient chapel, and lower down by a natural pillar called the *Valserstein*. Crossing the stream, the path is with difficulty carried along the broken declivity. The ravine opens at the chalets of *Haspel* and *Lungenei*, finely placed on green slopes. A second and most remarkable gorge succeeds. The path is forced to ascend, and winds in and out, on the verge of fearful precipices, until a little oratory by its side marks the close of the long defile (6 m.). The fertile valley of Lugnetz opens out, and the traveller descends through *St. Martin* to

Furth (*Inns*, poor ; Post; Piz Mundaun), opposite *Ober-Kastels*, but separated from it by a chasm. Hence one path goes along the rt. bank to *Peiden Bad*, recently restored, and up by char-road to Peiden; another, crossing the chasm, to *Combels*. Above Peiden the roads unite, soon enter the forest, and descend through the *Frauenthor* (Rte. 86) to *Ilanz*. This valley is remarkable for the wild rifts—called *graben* or *tobel*—in which the streams run.

ROUTE 90.

REICHENAU OR ILANZ TO SPLÜGEN, BY
THE SAVIEN THAL AND PASS OF THE
LÖCHLIBERG.

11 hrs. A good road runs through *Bonaduz*, to the German Protestant village *Versam* (6 m.), where the fearful gulf of the *Versamer Tobel* is crossed by a remarkable wooden bridge, with a span of 200 ft. (probably the widest wooden bridge on this principle existing), and 232 ft. above the torrent Savien. The same spot may be reached from Ilánz (8½ m.) by a charming country road. Here a road turns S. up the wild valley of the Savien or Rabiusa, a remarkable ravine, of which the W. side only is cultivated and inhabited by a Protestant population of about 1000 souls, Germans, who were settled here in the days of the Hohenstaufen Emperors. The almost uninhabited E. side is in places formed by precipices of the *Heinzenberg*. The road is carried up the l. or W. bank of the Rabiusa, by the hamlets of Acla, leaving Tenna high on the rt., Neukirch, (here the road stops, 1885) and *Platz*, where the Rathhaus *Inn* is ill-provided.

[A path strikes off hence over the col called *Stege* across a shoulder of the *Piz Beverin* (9843 ft.) to Thusis, 4 hrs. The beginning of the ascent is very steep, but afterwards the way lies over grass. The summit of the pass is about 6000 ft., and is reached in 1½ hr. from Platz. It commands a fine view over the Grisons Alps. The descent to Thusis traverses the remarkable plateau of the Heinzenberg, an open plain rising by degrees above the valley of Domleschg.]

From Platz the direct way to Splügen continues over the meadows of the Camana Alp to *Thalkirch* (2 hrs.), the oldest and highest church in the district. Here begins the ascent of the *Löchliberg Pass*, 8169 ft. above the sea, and about 2 hrs. from Thalkirch. A fine waterfall is seen left. The pass lies between the *Löchliberg* (E.), a grand head of rock, crowned by dolomite towers, 9990 ft., and the *Bärenhorn* (W.) 9620 ft., which is easily reached, and commands a fine view. The ascent is easy. On the other side the path is well marked, down mossy ground, opposite slate mountains covered with débris, and soon reaches a valley running direct to *Splügen* (see Rte. 87). At a chalet about half-way there is a beautiful view of the *Tambohorn* and *Suretta-hörner*.

It is a walk of about 25 m. from Versam to Splügen.

ROUTE 91.

PASS OF THE S. BERNARDINO —SPLÜGEN
TO BELLINZONA.

	Eng. m.
Splügen	
Hinterrhein	6¾
San Bernardino	12¼
Mesocco	9
Cama	10¼
Bellinzona	11¼
Total	50¼

Diligence from Coire to Bellinzona, 16½ hrs.; Splügen to Bellinzona, 8½ hrs. 2-horse carr. from Coire to Bellinzona, 180 fr.

1-horse carriage from Splügen to Hinterrhein, 8 fr.; 2-horse carriage to Bellinzona, 115 fr.

In posting from Coire by the Splügen to Chiavenna the same carriage may be taken all the way, but on the Bernardino the carriage is changed at each stage between Splügen and Bellinzona.

The road over the Bernardino was constructed in 1822, under the direction of the engineer Pocobelli, at the joint expense of the Sardinian and Grison governments. About 6-7ths of the sum required were advanced by the King of Sardinia, who duly appreciated the advantages to be derived from a highway which should connect, by a direct line, the port of Genoa and Turin with Switzerland and W. Germany.

As far as Splügen (Rte. 87) the road is the same as that over the Splügen pass. At Splügen the San Bernardino road, leaving the bridge of Splügen (4757 ft.) on the l., advances up the valley of the Hinter Rhein, below the *Guggernüll*, and then the *Einshorn*, l., and with the *Kirchalphorn* and Fanella glacier in front.

Nüfenen (Inn: Post), a cheerful village, opposite the opening of the Areue Thal, a valley with grand alpine scenery, between the *Tambohorn*, l., 10,748 ft., and the *Einshorn*, rt.

The pass of the Valserberg leads hence to Ilanz (Rte. 89).

Hinterrhein (Inn: Post, rough), the highest village in the valley, 5328 ft. above the sea. Glacier guides are found here.

[An excursion to the *source of the Rhine* will take 7 or 8 hours going and returning, exclusive of stoppages. The source lies about 7 miles higher up the valley, ½ of which distance, or ½ late in the summer, can be performed on horseback, the rest on foot; the walk is rough and fatiguing, over débris and stones, and a guide is necessary to show the way. The scenery is savage. The river takes its rise at the extremity of a frost-bound valley, from beneath the *Rheinwald glacier*, and at the base of the highest peaks of the Adula Gebirge. The traveller leaves the high road ½ m. above Hinterrhein, following the S. bank of the river, or rather of its broad bed of stones. The track has been recently improved. A bridge leads to the Zapport Alp on the opposite bank.

Half an hour more (3½ hrs. from Hinterrhein) brings the traveller to a spot whence he looks down on the fountain-head at the foot of the glacier, where a grey torrent, "Rheni luteum caput," bursts out from the ice, and plunges into a dark gorge known as Hölle (Hell). Here the Swiss Alpine Club has erected a hut for the convenience of travellers who sleep here before attempting the ascent of the loftiest peaks of the Adula group. There is another point of view directly under the Vogelberg —a small green spot, surrounded on all sides by snow and ice, and called ironically "Paradies" (Paradise). Directly above it a rocky rib runs upward to the Vogelberg, and divides the great Zapport glacier on the E. from that of Rheinwald on the W. The *Piz Valrhein* or *Rheinwaldhorn*, 11,148 ft.; the *Guferhorn*, 11,132 ft., and the *Vogelberg*, 10,564 ft., can be climbed from the hut. The Rheinwaldhorn was first climbed in 1789 by Pater Placidus à Spescha. It has since been reached from every quarter (Rte. 89). The easiest route is from the saddle to the N.E. of the peak, which forms a pass to the Lenta Glacier. There is little difficulty in descending the W. face of the mountain to Olivone through Val Malvaglia, and ways have been found by which active mountain-climbers can cross the glaciers into any of the valleys which radiate from them. The rival peak of the Gufer-horn is fairly easy of access from the *Zapportgrat*, a glacier pass on its E. side which leads over by the Kanal-thal to Vals (Rte. 89).]

The road over the Bernardino bids adieu to the Rhine, crossing it by a stone bridge, after which it breasts the mountain by sixteen zigzags; many of the turnings are very abrupt

A striking view opens out over the head of the Rhine valley and the glaciers of the Adula. On the rt. of the road rises the *Marscholhorn* or Piz Moesola, 9521 ft.; on the l. the black peak of the *Schwarzhorn*.

This passage over the Alps is said to have been known to the Romans: it was called the Vogelberg down to the beginning of the fifteenth century, when a pious missionary, Bernardino of Sienna, preached the Gospel through these remote Alpine valleys, and a chapel dedicated to him, on the S. side of the mountain, gave rise to the name which it still retains. It was traversed, in March, 1799, by the French army of Lecourbe, at a season when winter still reigns on these elevations, and before the mountain possessed any other road than a miserable mule-path.

The summit of the pass, 6770 ft. above the sea, and 1400 ft. above the village of Hinterrhein, is partly occupied by a lake called *Lago Moesola*, the source of the Moesa, along whose margin the road runs. At this point a very substantial but homely *Inn*, or house of refuge, has been erected. The head of this pass is grander and less dreary than the heads of some of the other great road passes.

A little way down the S. slope the Moesa is crossed by a handsome bridge of a single arch, 110 ft. above the river, named after Victor Emanuel I., who contributed so largely to the construction of this road. The carriage-way is here covered for some distance with a substantial roof, supported on solid buttresses, to protect it from avalanches and whirlwinds of snow, to which this gully is much exposed at times. A few strag-gling and stunted pines here make their appearance; a little lower down, trees 40 or 50 ft. high may be seen clinging to the rock, with barely 2 ft. depth of soil beneath them; their roots scarcely strike downwards at all, but spread far and wide in a horizontal direction, so that when a tree is thrown down by the wind, roots and soil are peeled off at once, and nothing but bare rock remains. The S. face of the mountain is as usual more abrupt than the N.; but the road is skilfully carried down it, and so gradually, that a driver, accustomed to it, trots quickly the whole way. The traveller sees the path beneath his feet, extending like an uncoiled rope, and as he moves backwards and forwards, following its turns, he appears to hover over the valley, and might fancy himself fastened to the end of a pendulum, and balanced in mid-air. The passage of the mountain from Hinterrhein is effected in about 3½ hrs. to

San Bernardino (5340 ft.) (*Inns*: H. Brocco, large and good; H. Bellevue; H. Ravizza; H. Minghetti, a village and watering-place, the first in the valley of Mesocco, consisting of a few houses planted half-way down the descent on a small plain or ledge, in a romantic situation. There is a chalybeate spring with *Baths*, having a temperature of about 40° Fahr. It is one of the highest mineral sources among the Alps, and annually attracts a considerable number of patients, for whom large hotels and pensions have been built. The situation is very fine, and the village serves as excellent head-quarters for a mountaineer wishing to explore the neighbouring ranges.

About 2 m. beyond S. Bernardino the traveller plunges by a series of curious and complicated zigzags into the lower valley of *Mesocco* (in Germ. Masox- or Misoxthal; Ital. Val Mesolcina), which is celebrated for its beauty. Near the road are two fine falls of the Moesa.

At *S. Giacomo* are quarries of gypsum, and another fall of the Moesa. It is a continual descent as far as Mesocco and the Ponte di Soazza, which is only a few hundred feet higher than Coire, in the valley of the Rhine. This will give some idea of the abruptness of the southern side of the Alps contrasted with the northern.

Mesocco (2560 ft.) (*Inn:* H. Posta), a village of 900 Inhab., called also Cremeo. See the views from its churchyard and old castle.

In the neighbourhood of Mesocco the luxuriant growth of the chestnut and walnut, the abundant crops of maize, the presence of the vine and the mulberry, which succeed each other within the space of a few miles, remind the traveller that he is on the S. side of the Alps; and he soon becomes otherwise aware of this change by the altered language, the laziness and dirt of the inhabitants, and their miserable habitations. The situation of Mesocco is charming. A little way below it, in the middle of the valley, rises the ruined *Castle of Mesocco*, with 4 turrets, a feudal seat of the powerful lords of Masox, sold by them, 1482, to the Milanese general Trivulzio, taken and destroyed by the Graubünden in 1526. The valley is bounded by precipices, over which dash a number of waterfalls, assuming the shape of that which in Scotland is called the Mare's Tail. The castle knoll seems formed to command the passage up and down.

[From *Soazza* a very steep path, not practicable for horses, ascends the E. side of the valley, and leads to Chiavenna in 8 hrs. by the *Forcola Pass*.]

The valley of Mesocco was laid waste by a fearful thunderstorm and inundation in August, 1834, which overwhelmed the land in many places with torrents of rocks, and left behind beds of gravel and alluvium, in places 90 ft. high, thus condemning it to sterility. 50 houses, 200 chalets, and many bridges were swept away. An inscription has been attached to a huge mass, stating that it and others descended from the Forcola.

Below *Soazza*, on the rt., the graceful *Cascade of Buffalora* precipitates itself from the top of a rock.

Lostallo (*Inn:* Posta, tolerable). The general legislative assemblies of the men of the valley are held here.

2½ m. farther is the post station at *Cama*, where figs and mulberries begin to appear.

Leggia.

At *Grono* (H. Calancasca, good; the landlord knows the neighbouring mountains), the Val Calanca opens from the W. [A good road leads up the picturesque *Val Calanca* to *Rossa*, where there is a small *Inn*. From this there are the *Giumella Pass* (7000 ft.) to the Val Blegno, and the *Passetti Pass* to San Bernardino, besides glacier passes to the Rhine source. The inhabitants of Val Calanca are chiefly glaziers, and leave the valley to work in Italy, France, &c.]

Roveredo (970 ft.) (*Inns:* Angelo; Croce Bianca, tolerable), a village containing nearly 1000 Inhab., with the ruined castle of Trivulzio in its vicinity. The Prior of Roveredo and 11 old women were burnt for practising witchcraft, by San Carlo Borromeo, in 1583, at his first visitation of the diocese. The rivers hereabouts are used to float down the timber cut in the forests of the higher transverse valleys.

S. Vittore is the last village in the Canton Grisons: below it we enter Canton Tessin and the Val Riviera, and the road joins that descending from the St. Gothard (Rte. 34). The entire valley of the Mesocco, is one of the most beautiful in the Alps. Passing the battle-field of Arbedo, we reach Bellinzona Stat. (Rte. 34), whence Rly. to Locarno (Rte. 112), or Lugano.

ROUTE 92.

PASS OF THE JULIER.   COIRE TO ST. MORITZ.

Coire.	Eng. m.
Churwalden	6¼
Tiefenkasten	11¼
Tinzen	6¼
Molins	4¼
Bivio [Stalla]	6
Silvaplana	9¼
St. Moritz	3¼
	—
	48¼

The traveller from Coire to the Engadine may go by the Albula or by the Julier. There are 2 roads to the Julier, which meet at Tiefenkasten: the one by the Valbella pass, 21 m.; the other by Thusis and the Schyn pass (Rte. 93), 29 m. From Tiefenkasten he has again the choice between the Julier and Albula.

The carriage-road of the Valbella and Julier, is traversed daily in summer by a *diligence* to Samâden, in 13 hrs. (in 11 from Samâden to Coire). The road is open all the winter, when the journey is performed more quickly in a sledge. Carriage by *extrapost* in 11 hrs., at 128 fr., or by *voiturier*, 2 horses, one night on the road, 130 fr. By Thusis and Schyn Pass, 5 fr. more for each horse. The daily mail over the Julier goes by Thusis and the Schyn.

The scenery of this route is, as a whole, dull. The road, however, is excellent, and to St. Moritz more direct than the Albula, by which the traveller can return. Leaving Coire he ascends rapidly along the course of the Rabiosa. l. is the opening of the Schanfigg-Thal (Rte. 95). Passing *Malix* (where, l. of the road, is the ruined castle *Strassberg*), the traveller reaches

Churwalden 4068 ft. (*Inns:* H. Gengel ; Krone ; both good), and about 2 m. beyond it

Parpan (*Inns:* Kurhaus Parpan ; H. Stätzerhorn), a bleak village, with the old mansion of the Buol family. The *Stätzerhorn*, 8458 ft., a fine point of view to the W. (an *Inn*), can be ascended by a good bridle-path in

3 hrs. A short way beyond Parpan is the summit of the pass, 5089 ft. above the sea, miscalled *Valbella*, as it is a desolate plateau, connecting the *Stätzerhorn* with the *Weisshorn*, 9111 ft., *Rothhorn*, 9406 ft., and *Lenzerhorn*, 9544 ft., on the E. The road now descends by the *Vatzer See*, encircled by forest, and along the *Heide*, a heathy tract, where a road branches rt. to *Obervatz*, known for its time-honoured stone *Gallows*, and to the *Schyn Pass* (Rte. 93). On the l. is the *Lenzerhorn*.

Lenz (Lonsch) (*Inn:* Krone ; a fair dining-place). [Here the direct road to Davos and to the Albula diverges l. by Brienz (Rte. 94, B.)] To the S.E. are seen the *Tinzenhorn* and *Piz St. Michel*, peaks of the magnesian limestone called dolomite, after the French geologist, M. Dolomieu, between the Julier and Albula passes. Beyond Lenz, the Romansch tongue (Rte. 81) is almost exclusively spoken; German is rarely understood, except at the inns.

The Julier road descends in numerous curves to the river *Albula*, which enters the Rhine through the remarkable Schyn defile near Thusis.

Tiefenkasten—Rom. *Chasté* = castle —(*Inns:* H. Julier; H. Albula ; both good), a village, situated, as its name implies, in a deep hollow (Tiefe, abyss), at the entrance of the Schyn pass, and of the *Oberhalbstein*, a valley running S. to the foot of the Julier and Septimer.

The road on the l. goes to Alvencu Bad and the *Albula Pass* (Rte. 93); that on the rt. to Thusis by the Schyn defile (Rte. 93).

The Julier road ascends at once, and steeply for a good hour, up the side of a grand wooded ravine, and for some distance along the edge of a precipice, called *Stein*. At the upper end it opens into the valley named from its position *above* (oberhalb) the *Stein*. It is a string of ancient lake-basins and gorges, scattered over with villages and a few ruined castles. Passing Conters and Schweiningen (*Inns*) the road reaches

Tinzen (*Inn:* Post).

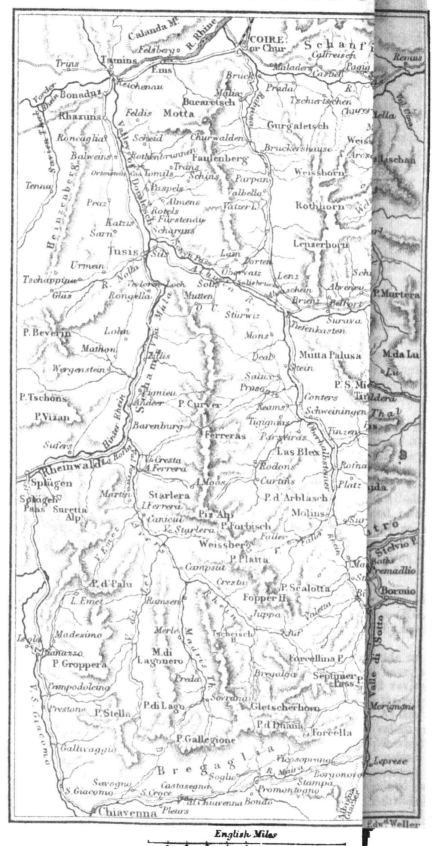

English Miles

[Here the *Val d' Err* leads into the heart of the range separating the Albula and Julier. Fine and easy passes lead in 4 to 5 hrs. between the three Dolomite peaks of the Piz St. Michel, Tinzenhorn, and Piz d'Aela to Bergün and Alveneu, and a glacier pass to Val Bevers and Samâden.]

Rt. is *Piz Curver*, 9761 ft. Another ascent through a wooded rift lands the traveller at *Roffna*, whence there is a long straight road to the beautiful defile which leads to Molins. In this the gradient is easy, through pine-woods and lawns of soft turf; the stream is of exquisite transparency.

Molins, Mühlen, 4811 ft. (*Inn*, Löwe, good; here the diligence dines), romantically situated, in a little amphitheatre, amidst the finest scenery of the Oberhalbstein. E. are the granite peaks of *Piz d'Err*—of. which the highest (the N.) is 11,139 ft.

[A fine and easy glacier pass may be made by ascending one of them, and descending into the Bevers Thal. Samâden may be reached thus in 8 hrs. It is possible to cross the ridge at a lower point, if the weather is not fine enough to promise a view. Further to the rt. is the *Cima da Flix*, 10,945 ft., and between it and Piz d'Err a glacier.]

S.W. is the *Piz Platta*, 11,109 ft., separating the branches of the Val da Faller, through which foot-passes lead to the Aversthal. Above Molins, the road passes the picturesque tower of the *Castle of Splüdatsch* on a wooded height, and near the next village, *Marmorera*, or Marmels, the ruins of 2 other castles.

Bivio or *Stalla*, 5827 ft. (*Inn*, fair), a poor village at the branching of the Julier and Septimer passes (Bivium). It is placed in a secluded basin, shut in by high mountains, in a climate so severe that all vegetation is stunted. Not a tree grows, and the people are reduced to burn sheep-dung for fuel. Potatoes rarely ripen at this height.

It takes about 2 hrs. to ascend from Bivio to the *Summit of the Julier Pass*, 7503 ft. (*Inn:* Berghaus), the road being remarkably safe from avalanches, the scenery wild, but monotonous. Rt. is the bold crag of *Piz Langref*, further rt. *Piz Lungen*, 10,400 ft. On the top, the road passes between two rude pillars of a bluish-grey schist, called *Julius's Columns*, which some suppose to be remains of a Celtic temple to the Sun or *Jul*, and others marks on the Roman military road carried by Augustus from Chiavenna over the Maloja and Julier. They are about 4 ft. high, and destitute of inscription. Roman coins have been found near them. Rt. is a small tarn below the cliffs of *Piz Pulaschin;* l. *Piz Julier* or *Piz Munteratsch;* lower down, *Piz d'Albana*. Between June and August large flocks of Bergamasque sheep are often seen on these pastures, attended by wild-looking shepherds from the Val Brembana.

The descent into the Engadine commands a magnificent view down into the deep-sunk valley of the Inn and upon the pine-girt lake of Silvaplana, backed by *Piz Corvatsch, Piz Surlei,* and *Piz Rosatsch*. Above the nearer ridge rise the snowy crests of the highest peaks of the Bernina range.

Two or three long zigzags bring the traveller down upon Silvaplana (Rte. 99).

ROUTE 93.

COIRE TO SAMÂDEN — PASS OF THE SCHYN AND ALBULA.

	Miles.
Coire by Lenz to	
Alveneu Bad	21
Coire by Thusis and the Schyn to	
Alveneu Bad	30
Filisur	3
Bellaluna	2¼
Bergün	3
Weissenstein Inn	5¼
Summit of Pass	3
Ponte	6
Samâden	3¼

Two-horse carriage, stopping one night, 120 fr. By Thusis and the Schyn pass 5 fr. more for each horse. This is a finer route than that by the Julier pass. It is 8 hrs.' moderate walking from Alveneu Bad to Samâden. Diligence daily from Coire in

12½ hrs., halting at Bergün (7½ hrs.) to dine.   The road as far as

Lenz, is identical with the preceding route. At Lenz the road to the Albula Pass turns round the shoulder of the mountain to the E., leaving Tiefen-kasten on the rt.; and passing the village of (1 hr.) *Brienz*, and on the l. the castle of *Belfort*, perched on an almost in accessible rock, descends to the

Baths of Alveneu, a large and good hotel. Adjoining the house the sulphur spring bubbles up through long waving weeds.

The *Schyn Pass*. A longer but far more picturesque route from Coire to Tiefenkasten and Alveneu Bad, is by Thusis and the Schyn road.

Opposite Thusis the Albula river enters the Rhine from S.E., through the *Schyn* (or *Schein*) *Pass*. It is on a larger scale than the Via Mala, but is seen from a different point of view, the road being carried mid-way along the upper cliffs instead of below them, in the ravine of the torrent. Thusis to Tiefenkasten, about 10 m., takes about 2 hrs.' driving—ascent most part of the way.

Crossing the Rhine, the road runs to *Sils*, where the ascent begins. Soon the ruins of *Campi Castle* are seen l., close to orchards and lawns, but on the edge of a wild cliff overhanging the river. Threading the forest of firs the road pene-trates buttresses by tunnels, winds on precipices, and gives good views into the depths. It scarcely descends to reach the *Solisbrücke*, where the ra-vine terminates, but the bridge spans a chasm at a height of more than 400 ft. above the rushing waters of the Albula. The road now ascends between green knolls and slopes, in-terspersed with pines, to *Alvaschein*, from which it is downhill, with view of the wooded sides of *Piz S. Michel* (S.E.), and the bare yellow cone of the *Lenzerhorn* (N.E.) to Tiefenkas-ten. The old bridle-path runs on the other bank of the Albula, high up to the N., through Scharans to Alvaschein.

[On the mountain opposite Alveneu is a waterfall, by the side of which a series of ladders lead up to a wild valley, between the Tinzenhorn and Piz St. Michel, and to the pass of the *Tinzenthor*, a narrow cleft in a steep dolomite ridge, elsewhere impass-able, by which Tinzen on the Julier road may be reached—a walk of 6 hrs. The singular and inaccessible-look-ing peak of the *Tinzenhorn*, 10,276 ft., the "Little Matterhorn," conspicuous from Davos, is without serious difficulty ascended by the rocky face above the Tinzen Thor. *Piz St. Michel*, 10,371 ft., can be ascended in 5 hours from the hotel.]

The village of *Alveneu* lies l., about 2 m. up-hill, and the road to Davos mounts towards it. Crossing the mouth of the Davos Thal and the Landwasser running out of its gorges, the Bergün road bends S. with the Albula, ascending to

Filisur, a large white picturesque village (H. Schönthal). N. are the ruins of *Schloss Greifenstein*. About 2 m. above Filisur are the abandoned iron-works of *Bellaluna*, with an *Inn*. The valley is densely wooded. Here the ascent begins, with grand moun-tain slopes to the rt. In 1½ m. the road enters a narrow ravine flanked by the cliff called *Bergüner-Stein*, and for more than 1000 ft. is hewn, or blasted, out of the face of the rock, the Albula roaring at a depth of 500 or 600 ft. Beyond this gorge, in a beautiful basin, under the spurs of the dolomite peak, Piz d'Aela, lies

Bergün — Rom. *Bergogn* — 4557 ft. (*Inns*: Piz d'Aela, good quarters; Kreuz ; Sonne), a village of about 600 Inhab., chiefly Protestants, speaking Romansch. The houses, brilliant in paint and whitewash, are of a superior class, indicating the comparative wealth of the population, many of whom are muleteers or carters by profession, who established themselves here when this route was more fre-quented. The church is remarkable. Bergün is beautifully situated among the mountains at the opening of Val Tuors, which leads by the *Eschia pass* to Zutz, over the extensive gla-cier of Porchabella under *Piz Kesch*,

11,211 ft. Other passes lead to Davos by the Sertig Thal and to Va Sulsanna. S.W. is the dolomitic peak of *Piz d'Aela*, 10,893 ft. A Club hut has been built 2½ hrs. above the village, to facilitate the ascent of this peak and its neighbours, the Tinzen-horn and Piz St. Michel, all rough rock climbs. Good walkers will not need to use it.

A steep ascent, passing a waterfall and small lake leads to the

Gasthaus Weissenstein (fair) under *Piz Giumels*, of which the white gypsum rocks are supposed to have given name to this place, and the pass. There was a lake by the inn, which burst its bounds in 1859. [From this point an active mountaineer can cross the ridge S. and descend by the Val Bevers to Samáden.] The ascent now becomes very rapid; the road takes a wide sweep to the rt. A shorter footpath, exposed to ava-lanches, climbs l. along the N. side of the former lake, where traces of the Roman road have been discovered. At the top of the hill the traveller enters the savage hollow called *Teufelsthal*, filled with broken rocks, hurled from the heights along with the snow, which renders this part of the pass dangerous in spring. Here, for above 2 m., the road runs nearly on a level, along as wild a drift-way as can be imagined. Its highest point forms the

Pass of the Albula, 7589 ft. above the sea. It is a scene of complete deso-lation. N. rise the limestone cliffs of *Piz Uertsch*, or *Piz Albula*, 10,738 ft., S. the granite buttresses of *Piz Giumels*, 9623 ft., a point in a ridge running up to Piz d'Err.

The descent into the Ober Engadin is in spring also exposed to avalanches. It is 1½ hr.'s walk from the summit, with view of *Piz Mezzem*, to

Ponte or *Punt* (*Inns*: Albula; Krone, improved), at the foot of the pass. A straight road ascends to *Samáden* (Rte. 99).

ROUTE 94.

A. COIRE OR RAGATZ TO DAVOS-PLATZ, BY THE PRÄTIGAU. B. DAVOS TO LENZ BY THE LANDWASSER THAL.

Lanquart Stat.	Stunden.	Eng. m.
Küblis	5¼	16¼
Klosters	2½	7¾
Davos-Platz	3¼	10

The ascent of the Prätigau begins from the Lanquart Stat., on the Coire Rly. Two *Diligences* daily in summer, one in winter from Lan-quart through Klosters to Davos in 7½ hrs.

The entrance of the Prätigau is through the gorge of *Klus*, giving passage to the furious torrent *Lan-quart*, and once commanded by the castle *Fragstein*, of which ruins are still visible; a wall, extending to the river, once closed the passage. The valley, 20 m. long, shut in by high mountains, is rich in pasture, and famed for its large cattle. It contains a population of about 10,000, who speak German, though Romansch was the language to the 16th cent., and the names of places are still Romansch. On the N. the *Rhœtikon* chain separates the Prätigau from the Vorarlberg and from the valley of Montafun. Its most remarkable sum-mits are the *Falkniss*, overlooking the Rhine, and the *Scesa Plana*, the highest of the range. This chain is a spur of the mountain range N. of the Inn, which forms the watershed between the North Sea and Euxine, as the Bernina separates the waters flowing to the Euxine and Adriatic. Several passes lead N. into the Vorarlberg (see Rte. 97).

[A branch road leads up to *Seewis* (3000 ft.) (H. P. Scesaplana, Kurhaus, both fair), a village in a high sunny and mild situation on the slopes left, much frequented by Swiss. The ascent of the *Scesa Plana* (9738 ft.) is generally made from Bludenz on the N.E. side, the traveller sleep-ing at a Club hut by the *Lüner See*

E. of the peak ; but it can also be effected from here (Rte. 97).]

The road ascends the rt. bank of the Lanquart to *Schiersch* (*Inn:* Krone), and then crosses to the l. bank, passing *Jenatz* (Heims' *Inn*). ¼ hr. further is *Fideriser Au.* The village of Fideris stands on a height 2 m. off the road, and is not visible from it.

[A very bad road leads to the *Baths of Fideris*, 2 m. S. of the village, in a wild and romantic gorge, 3465 ft. above the sea. The waters, considered efficacious in chest complaints and intermittent fevers, are alkaline, and the strongest of their class in Switzerland, resembling seltzer-water. The two *Bath-houses* can lodge more than 200 persons. The accommodation is second-rate, although the baths are often crowded; the table-d'hôte is well supplied.]

Opposite Fideris rises the ruin of *Castels*, which was stormed and taken, in 1622, by the peasants, armed with sticks alone. It was held at the time for the Emperor Ferdinand, who wanted to make himself master of the Grisons, and extinguish the Protestant religion. A path leads S. in 3½ hrs. into the Schanfigg Thal.

Above Fideriser Au the road up the rt. bank traverses a romantic defile, wooded and rocky, and through the picturesque village of *Küblis* (*Inn:* Krone). Instead of following the old road, it is pleasanter, though not shorter, to take the new road by the village of *Serneus* and the *Baths of Serneus* (*Inn*), frequented by natives, where very fair accommodation may be had. At the Post stat., *Mezza Selva*, opposite the baths is a good *Inn*, picturesquely situated, with a noble view towards the Silvretta Ferner, a good half-way house to Davos. About 3 m. farther is *Klosters* (*Inns:* H. and P. Brosi, good ; H. Vereina, good ; H. Silvretta, fair; Pension Florin), a scattered village of 4 hamlets, named after a suppressed Convent, on the rt. bank of the Lanquart, about 4000 ft. above the sea. It is to be recommended as a halting-place to travellers anxious to enjoy the fine scenery of the Silvretta group, or to invalids, who may here acclimatize themselves before proceeding to the still more alpine air of Davos.

[From the village the ice-fields of the Silvretta Ferner are seen closing the valley. A road has been made as far as the Sardasca Alp (2 hrs.). 1½ hr. further is a *hut* of the Swiss Alp. C. on the bank of the glacier. It may be made the object of a pleasant excursion from Klosters. Above the Sardasca Alp a steep ascent leads to the hut, 300 yds. from the ice. The head of the Prätigau is closed by two glaciers, the broad Silvretta glacier, and the lower and narrower Winterthäli of the Federal map. Over the Silvretta Glacier lies the easy glacier pass leading to Val Tuoi, and so to the Engadine in 6 or 7 hrs.

From the head of the Winterthäli, or Verstankla Glacier, it is possible to descend into Val Lavinuoz, and thus reach Lavin in 4½ hrs. from the hut. Piz Linard is a noble object during the descent. The bold peaks which crown the Silvretta Ferner have been conquered by Swiss climbers. Piz Buin, a snowy eminence, is the easiest of access, and is frequently ascended from the Club hut in 4 to 5 hrs.

The S. branch of the valley leads by the *Vereina pass*, 8133 ft., direct to Süs in 8 hrs.' good walking.]

Good glacier guides are found at Klosters.

A char may be hired for 8 fr. to Davos Platz, 2 hrs.' drive, 3 hrs.' walk.

In winter it is a favourite amusement to run down toboggans from a point a little below Wolfgang to Klosters, and races are held annually on this course.

The road to Davos, leaving the valley, turns nearly S., and after a long ascent, mounting in zigzags, passing rt. the *Schwarz See*, crosses a low watershed at a point known as *Wolfgang* (5340 ft.) (H. Davos Kulm), and, descending, passes l. a larger lake, the *Davoser See*.

At *Davos-Dörfli* (*Inns:* Kurhaus Davos-Dörfli ; Fluela ; H. Bellevue) e valley of the Fluela (Rte. 96) reached.

Davos am Platz, 5105 ft. above ie sea—Rom. *Tavoise*, behind—(*Inns:* L. Buol, H. Belvedere, H. Victoria, xcellent; H. d'Angleterre, equally ood; Kurhaus Davos, with 3 villas; ätia, all good; Schweizerhof and ur Post;—H. zum Strela, very fair vhey cure); P. Waldhaus; Rathaus, renewed. The pension price t Davos averages 6 to 10 fr. a ay, including rooms. An English hurch.)

Since the influx of foreign visitors as become a steady source of profit > the place, several good shops have een opened, where almost every ecessary article can be procured; aths have been cut in the woods bove the village, which are kept pen through the winter; a fair band lays in turn at the principal hotels: weekly newspaper, in German and nglish, is issued; a skating-rink has een established; and the Canadian musement of tobogganing is prac sed to the great satisfaction of the ardier invalids. . In September good 'out-fishing is added to the amuse ients of the place. A good school as recently been established by Dr. erthes, gymnasial director, intended pecially for delicate boys.

The Rathhaus is decorated with the eads of more than 30 wolves slain t the neighbourhood. A wolf-net volf-garn) is still hung up here.

Besides the wolves' heads, bears ιay sometimes be seen at the Rath aus. They are mostly shot near ernetz in the Engadine, and brought > Davos by the huntsmen to claim ie reward of 100 frs. a head offered ιr bears in the Grisons. Three heads f bears were brought in in the winter f 1878-79.

Within the building is an old Room f Assembly, called *die grosse Stube*, 'ith fine pieces of 16th-century glass, ontaining hunting-scenes, coats of rms, private marks of the Buol ιmily, &c. Davos was the capital f the Zehngerichte in the days when ie 3 leagues of the Graubünden

[*Switz.*]

formed an independent state, and at that time the great room served as the parliament hall of a sovereign peasant state.

Davos is the name of a remote mountain district, lying at an average height of 5000 ft. above the sea, sur rounded by mountains of moderate elevation which do not impend closely over its wide sunny meadows and frag rant fir-forests. The scenery, to those accustomed to the Bernese or Pen nine Alps, seems tame; but the position of these villages, protected by intervening chains from the influence of the moist air currents rising from Italy, which affect the Engadine, pro cures them a winter climate unrivalled in the Alps for dryness, stillness, brightness, and equable temperature. It is to German physicians that the discovery of its advantages as a *winter* resort for patients with delicate lungs is due, and it is by Germans that the hotels are chiefly filled. But English doctors now frequently send patients here for the winter; and the comforts which invalids of this description re quire are generally obtainable. In the winter of 1878-9 there were 200 English residents. In addition to the hotels, private villas can be hired, and the valley is becoming a Swiss or Arctic Mentone.

The climate of Davos in the case of consumption seems specially adapted to what is known as pneumonic phthisis, and to diseased conditions of the lung, where after chronic in filtration cavities have been formed. In merely incipient stages of the malady its influence is decidedly favourable. Young people and chil dren thrive wonderfully; and those whose appetites and digestion are languid, speedily acquire the power of nutrition. The general stimulus of a pure and bracing air, the advan tage of remaining for hours together in the open without taking cold, and the improved faculty of muscular exercise without fatigue, seem to be the secrets of a cure in which Nature is left almost wholly to herself.

Excursions.—There are many ex cursions from Davos. The road of

T

the Fluela Pass and the car-road up
the Dischmathal to Durrenboden
afford drives. From Durrenboden travellers may visit the Scaletta Glacier
and, if good walkers and provided
with rope and guides, climb *Piz
Vadret* (N. peak difficult, S. easy) or
cross the *Valloria Pass* (see Rte. 99) or
the *Grialetsch Pass*, both easy glacier
routes leading to the Engadine. More
picturesque is the *Sertigthal*, a charming Alpine valley, opening opposite
Frauenkirch. At Sertig Dörfli, 2½
hrs. from am Platz, there is a homely
Inn. Hence 2 foot-passes lead in 4
or 5 hrs. to Bergün. For fair
walkers the *Schwarzhorn* (10,338 ft.),
a peak in the chain dividing the
valleys of Fluela and Dischma, is
an indispensable expedition. It is
a magnificent point of view, commanding a panorama to most tastes
preferable to that from Piz Languard.
It can be ascended from either valley,
so that a traveller may go by the one
and return by the other. The best
starting-point is the Flüela Hospiz,
from which 2½ hrs. are required.

B. DAVOS TO LENZ, BY THE LAND-WASSER THAL.

Davos Platz to	Miles.
Lenz	22
Lenz to Coire	14

The Davos Thal, below Platz, retains its pastoral character for 7 m.,
but lower down it is much contracted
and romantic in its scenery. At
Schmelzboden there were formerly
zinc, lead, and silver works. By
this route travellers reach Davos from
Coire in 7 hrs. Diligence daily.
In summer there is a service twice a
day through Thusis from Coire.

The new carriage-road through the
Landwasser Thal was made in 1873,
at a cost of 24,000l. The road passes
3 m. *Frauenkirch*, at the entrance
of the Sertig Thal: 2 m. *Spina Bad*
(hotel enlarged), below the *Rinner-
horn* (E.): ¾ m. *Glaris*: 2¼ m. *Schmelzboden.*

After leaving Schmelzboden, the
road plunges into the deep and narrow
gorge of the Züge, so called because

it is swept on both sides by avalanches, whose ruins even in midsummer cool the air among the
rifted and impending precipices.
Still following the course of the
Landwasser, and passing through five
galleries cut in the rock, the road
reaches a point called the Bärentritt,
or Känzli, whence there is a wild
prospect over forest, crag, waterfall,
and distant mountains, and down
into the desolate, thickly - wooded
chasm of Leidboden. From the Bärentritt the ascent begins to Wiesen,
winding through forests of larch and
spruce, very tall and slender, with
eminently picturesque outlooks to the
high-perched huts of Jennisberg on
the one hand, and on the other to the
Valbellahorn, while a noble panorama of the peaks that dominate the
Albula and Julier Passes, gradually
unfolds to south and west. For
variety and grandeur this road, especially in the winter, surpasses its
continuation, the Schyn-Strasse, and
may even compete with the famous
Via Mala. Here, too, the sudden passage from a narrow rock-hemmed
gorge to the sunny terrace of grass
meadows, whence Wiesen sweeps the
range crowned by the Piz d'Aela, Tinzenhorn, and Piz St. Michel, and the
distant mountains that divide the Julier
from the region of the Splügen, affords
a scenic change which is in its way unrivalled.—*J. A. S.*

Wiesen (H. Palmy, good ; Hôtel
and Pension Bellevue), beautifully
situated, 4800 ft. The hotels are
kept open all the year ; a doctor
resides in the Bellevue. This village
will probably become a rival to Davos,
over which, as a health resort, it has
some advantages. It has more sun, no
valley wind, and no moisture from
damp meadows. On the other hand,
the *Föhn* is more felt. Dr. Weber of
Alvenen Bad, attends patients here.
[The *Sandhubel*, a neighbouring summit, can be ascended on horseback
in 3 hrs., and commands an extensive panorama. A path crosses the
stream direct to Filisur, on the Albula
road, 4 m.] Beyond Wiesen the *Tei-
tobel* is passed to 3 m. *Schmitton*, with

paintings on the houses. The terrace-like road commands a continually fine and shifting view of the ranges between the Albula, the Julier, and the Engadine. 1½ m. *Alveneu*, ¾ m. above *Alveneu Bad.* Beyond Alveneu the road divides. One branch leads by Bad Alveneu to Tiefen Kasten; the other, passing the picturesque ruins of Belfort and Brienz, leads to Lenz (Rte. 92).

ROUTE 95.

COIRE TO DAVOS-PLATZ, BY THE STRELA PASS.

Carriage-road as far as Langwies, 14 m.; beyond, mule-path.

The Schanfigg Thal is a peculiar valley. There are no villages in its bed : all are on the mountain sides. From Maladers to Langwies, the road can scarcely ever be less than 1000 ft. above the Plessur river. It passes, on its way, through several villages, occupying the tops of spurs or promontories projecting from the northern mountains, and divided from one another by lateral ravines, which have to be dipped into and doubled round. To the S. of the river, and also on the W., where the Julier road runs, the country is of a similar character.

From the Ch. of St. Lucius at Coire it is a continuous, and soon steep, ascent to the fertile Schanfigg Thal at

Maladers. Thence to *Calfreisen*, with an ancient tower. The Castelertobel is crossed on a lofty arch. Then *St. Peter*, with a waterfall and water-mill.

Peist (Inn). Langwies (H. and P. Strela, new house; bei P. Jäger; both homely, but good), where the Aroser-wasser descends from the S., flowing 8 m. from the *Welsch Tobel*, through a remote mountain district. Here the pass begins. The valley contracts, and an ascent is made up a pretty pasture belted by forest. Rt. are the rocky heights of the *Weissfluh* and *Küpfenfluh.* Beyond the last

group of chalets the stream is crossed, and a stiff climb to the rt., of ½ hr., brings the traveller to the

2.20 *Strela Pass* (7799 ft.) between the *Schiahorn* (easily reached in 1 hr., good view) and *Küpfenfluh.* The view S. is best seen after a short descent, and comprises all the summits of the chain towards the Engadine, from the valley of the Albula to the Tyrolese frontier.

The descent is steep but short (1 hr.) to Davos am Platz.

ROUTE 96.

DAVOS TO SÜS AND TARASP IN LOWER ENGADINE, BY THE FLUELA PASS.

A carriage-road of 20 m., kept open through the winter. Two *diligences* daily from Lanquart stat. to Tarasp in 14 hrs. by the Prätigau (Rte. 98), and this pass.

The Fluela Thal leading to this pass is entered at *Davos Dörfli*, about a mile above *Davos am Platz.* The ascent is easy throughout; there is little remarkable in the scenery, which is of a wild and dreary nature. There is a rude *Inn*, called Tschuggen, about 2 hrs. from Davos, and just half-way to the pass. The summit (7891 ft.) is a small plain occupied by pools of the *Schotten See* (*Hospiz Inn*, fair). To the E. rises the *Fluela Weisshorn*, to the W. the *Schwarzhorn*, which is easily ascended from this side (Rte. 94).

After a gradual descent for a time towards the S., a wild barren valley is seen running E. The road passes along the mountain side above this valley, into which it descends by degrees. Rt. appears the glacier of Grialetsch, surmounted by the Piz Vadred (10,610 ft.)

[At Pra, about an hour from Süs the Val Fless opens, up which a rough path leads over the *Vereina* pass (8300 ft.) to Klosters (Rte. 94), about 9 hrs.]

Süs (2 *Inns*) is a good 2½ hours' walk from the top of the Fluela. (See Rte. 99.)

5 hrs. in carriage, 6 hrs. by short cuts on foot, are required to reach Süs from Davos. 2 hrs. from Süs will take the traveller to the Baths of Tarasp (Rtc. 99).

ROUTE 97.

PASSES OF THE RHÄTIKON — VORARL-BERG TO THE PRÄTIGAU.

The *Cavell Joch* is a fine pass of 9 or 10 hrs. *Guides* may be found at Brand.

Leaving *Bludenz* (*Inn:* Post, see HANDBOOK FOR SOUTH GERMANY), and crossing the stream, a shady road leads to the village of *Bürs*, where there is a gorge worth visiting even by those not bound mountainwards. Bearing to the rt., the ascent commences by zigzags through a pretty forest, the village of *Bürseberg* soon appearing on the rt. It is a constant ascent, commanding views of the gorge of the Alvierbach, the mountains of Vorarlberg, and the glaciers of the Scesa Plana, all the way to

2½ hrs. *Brand* (decent little *Inn*). A little above Brand the stream is crossed and some chalets reached, beyond which the ascent is rougher, the path taking an abrupt turn to the l.: the valley is blocked at the upper end by a vast wall of rock 1000 ft. high, extending from the Scesa Plana to the precipices of the Zimbaspitz. The path crosses the stream several times until close to the foot of the wall, when it finally passes it to a steep slope of débris, fallen from the Scesa Plana on the rt. Up this the ascent lies, and it is a very stiff climb of fully 1 hr. to the top of the rocky wall, on reaching which the traveller beholds a curious scene. Occupying, as it were, a sort of crater, and enclosed on *all* sides by crags and precipices, a lake is discovered some 150 ft. below the path on the other side of the wall. It is called the

1½ hr. *Lüner See*, and is about a mile in circumf.; its waters are carried off by 2 subterranean outlets through the rocky barrier which rises above it from 50 to 200 ft. Fine view to the N. A hut has been fitted up for the accommodation of travellers, near the Lüner See, by the German Alp. Club.

[From this point the *Scesa Plana* may be ascended in 4 hrs., view extremely grand, over Suabia, Rhine valley, Lakes of Zürich and Wallenstadt, Alps of Appenzell, Bern, Tyrol, to Örteler. Should this ascent be combined with the pass, it would be advisable to sleep at Brand the previous night.]

Path continues round the lake till the opposite side is reached; then ascent continues, keeping to the n. until the pass (7562 ft.) is reached from which splendid view over the Grison and Glarus Alps (6 full hrs. of constant ascent from Bludenz).

Descent at first steep grass, then hopeless bog, until reaching chalets in 1 hr. From this point the path is peculiar. Instead of following the course of the stream (down which, however, it is possible but not easy to force a way), it strikes to the n. *ascending* and keeping close to the Scesa Plana, in order to avoid several torrents descending from that mountain. Path bad, boggy, and confusing, but after a while the true descent is observed on the *opposite* side of the *last* torrent, which is reached in 1 hr. from the chalets; crossing stream by a bridge, a very bad road (in course of improvement) leads, in 1 hr., to

Seewis, in Prätigau (*Inn:* Scesa Plana), Rte. 94.

The *Schweizerthor* is another fine pass. It leads from Vandans to Schiersch. The path is up the Rells Thal, and S. from the head of it to the col, 7120 ft.; one of the wildest scenes imaginable, between the precipices of the *Kirchelispitz*, W. and those of the *Drusenfluh*, E. The descent winds about to avoid the deep gullies, and is steep and lonely as far as Schuders, whence it is easy to Schiersch.

The *Drusenthor* is the easiest of the passes from the Vorarlberg, sometimes crossed by horses. It leads from Schruns to Schiersch.

The *St. Antonier Thal*, a picturesque side-glen of the Prätigau, opening at Kublis, leads to 3 passes, but they are too little in the track of English travellers to call for notice here.

From Klosters two passes, the *Schlappiner Joch* and *Garneira Joch*, lead in 8 hrs. to St. Gallenkirch and Gaschurn respectively. The latter is the easier pass. The highest pass in this range is the *Sardasca Pass*, connecting the alps above Klosters with Pattenen.

ROUTE 98.

CHIAVENNA, BY VAL BREGAGLIA, TO THE UPPER ENGADINE.

Chiavenna to						Miles.
Castasegna	.	.	.	.	.	6
Promontogno	.	.	.	.	.	2
Vico Soprano	.	.	.	.	.	3¼
Casaccia	.	.	.	.	.	4¼
Top of Maloja Pass	.	.	.		.	3

Diligence daily from Chiavenna to Maloja in 6 hrs. The reverse way in 3 hrs.

Since the opening of the St. Gothard Railway this has become a favourite approach to the Engadine. Como is reached as easily as Coire. The voyage up the lake, the short railway to Chiavenna, and the comparatively short drive up the beautiful Val Bregaglia are substituted for the somewhat tedious drive over the Julier.

The road ascends by the rt. bank of the Maira, in face of a pretty cascade formed by the Acqua Fraggia descending from a little mountain lake. About 3 m. above Chiavenna it passes, on the opposite side of the river, the grave of *Pleurs* or *Piuro*, buried, with its 2430 Inhab., by the fall of Monte Conto, on the night of the 4th of Sept. 1618. It was a handsome and thriving town. It now lies beneath a heap of rocks and rubbish, 60 ft. deep. Every soul within it perished, and the long-continued excavations of all the labourers that could be collected failed in rescuing anything alive or dead. The traces of the catastrophe are now nearly obliterated, the spot is grown over with a wood of chestnuts, and a village of the same name occupies an adjoining site. The inhabitants had received many warnings, which were unfortunately disregarded. For ten years large crevices had existed on the mountain; and heavy rains preceded the catastrophe. Masses of rock fell the day before the event, the rents widened, and shepherds observed their cattle fly from the spot with marks of extreme terror.

The *Val Bregaglia* (Præ-Gallia ?)—Germ. *Bergeller Thal*,—shut in by high mountains, is one of the most fertile and beautiful valleys in the Italian Alps. Many of its inhabitants emigrate, and adopt the business of chimneysweeper.

After passing through *Santa Croce* and *Villa di Chiavenna*, each embosomed in chestnut woods, the road reaches the Swiss frontier at

Castasegna (*Inn* : Schumacher's Restaurant), 2362 ft. Above this the white mulberry no longer flourishes, and this is therefore the limit of the culture of the silkworm. About 2 m. within the frontier, to the rt. at

Promontogno, 2687 ft. (*Inn*, Bergellerhof, large, comfortable), a rock promontory stretches across the valley, forming a barrier through which the carriage road is tunnelled. It is a scene of extreme beauty, and the vegetation is of the utmost luxuriance. On a height above is the *Castle of Bondo*, belonging to that branch of the Salis family which is settled in England. The ruin of *Castelmuro*, on the hill above Promontogno, is conspicuous by its donjon, from which two walls, 15 ft. high and 10 thick, descend into the gorge to the riverside. The castle formed the key of the valley. Its name is derived from the Roman station *Ad murum*.

[From Promontogno a road ascends in zig-zags to *Soglio*, a very picturesque village, 3569 ft. above the sea, well protected from cold winds. (*Inn*, H. and P. Giovanoli, an old palace of the Salis Soglio family, good.)]

Promontogno stands close to the

opening of *Val Bondasca*, a most romantic glen, terminated by the Bondasca Glacier, over which lie 2 steep and somewhat difficult glacier passes to Val Masino — the *Passo di Bondo*, the W. col, leading to the W. branch of the Italian valley and the Baths of Masino, the *P. di Ferro* to the E. branch. The head of the V. Bondasca, encircled by magnificent granite pinnacles, is well worth a visit. Those who do not wish to cross from it into Italy will find an easier pass leading to the Albigna Glacier (see *post*), a most beautiful excursion of 8 or 9 hrs. The names of the summits between the Bregaglia and the Val Masino were wrongly given in the Swiss Federal Atlas. The C. del Largo of early explorers is now *C. di Castello*, the Punta Trubinesca *Piz Cengalo*, the C. di Tschingel *Piz Badile*. The two last-named peaks are conspicuous from St. Moritz and many points in the Engadine. A steep but easy pass, practicable for horses, leads into the Avers Thal.]

The chestnut here gives place to the pine ; the road enters an open and pastoral reach of the valley.

Stampa is the next village; then *Borgonuovo*, beyond which the road runs through a waste of rocks swept from the mountain gorges by a flood in 1870. l. is the *Pizzo della Duana*, 10,280 ft.

Vico Soprano (Vespran) (*Inn:* Krone or Post, improved), a German village of 504 Inhab., 3566 ft. above the sea. It is the chief place in Val Bregaglia, which is throughout Protestant.

[The *Zocca Pass* leads to Val Masino and to Morbegno in the Valtellina. This easy glacier pass is not often traversed, but is very grand. It turns S. from the high road, a little above V. Soprano, and soon crosses to the l. bank of the Albigna torrent, which descends in one of the finest waterfalls in the Alps. After a long and steep ascent, the path reaches the level of the Albigna glacier, which is easy and usually free from crevasses, to the col, 8957 ft. A steep descent leads to the Rasica Alp, at the E. head of Val Masino, about

2 hrs. from the beautifully situated *Baths of Masino*, in the W. branch of the valley. Down the wild and striking Val Masino there is a good road to Morbegno (Rte. 101).]

The road now zigzags through forest (old path shorter) to a high level, near the end of which, just under the Maloja, lies

Casaccia (*Inn:* Hotel Stampa), hamlet at the junction of the Septimer and Forcellina passes (see Rte. descending from Val Forno 479?. At this place begins the final ascent and the road, leaving a ruined *Ch. of Gaudenzio* l., winds towards the steep and wooded crescent of the Maloja ridge.

The upper part of the valley walled in by precipices, up one of which the road climbs by a series of terraces, and at one of the angles half-way up, a path turns aside to the *Fall of the Ordlegna*, which is worth seeing (5 min. there and back). The conductor of the diligence will take you there by a short path up the zigzags, and you can catch the diligence at the top.

Maloja Pass (5942 ft.) About three quarters of a mile further is (*Kurhaus Maloja*, an enormous establishment built by a Belgian company, which offers visitors the most varied attractions — pigeon-shooting, &c. E.C. H. Chalet ; Malojakulm). The Belgian company have built chalets in the neighbourhood which are let for the season, and the formerly deserted wind-swept pasturage has completely lost its native character.

Unlike most alpine passes, the summit of the Maloja is a grass bank only a few feet higher than the lake of Sils. The traveller who has climbed the steep ascent out of the narrow head of Val Bregaglia, finds himself suddenly introduced to the very different landscape of the Upper Engadine.

For excursions from Maloja and the road to *St. Moritz*, see Rte. 99.

ROUTE 99.

THE ENGADINE. MALOJA TO NAUDERS
AND THE PASS OF FINSTERMÜNZ.

Maloja.						Eng. m.
Sils .	.	.	.	.	.	4½
St. Moritz.	.	.	.	.	.	7½
Samáden .	.	.	.	.	.	3
Scanfs .	.	.	.	.	.	12
Zernetz .	.	.	.	.	.	7½
Tarasp-Bad	.	.	.	.	.	18
Martinsbrück	.	.	.	.	.	15
Nauders .	.	.	.	.	.	4½
Finstermünz .	.	.	.	.	.	2½

Diligences from Chiavenna to Samáden: and from Samáden to Nauders
in 9½ hrs. A good carriage-road,
made by the Swiss Government
1860–66. From Maloja to Landeck
two days' drive, stopping at Tarasp
Baths.

The Engadine (Rom. *Engiadina*), or
Valley of the Inn, is nearly 60 miles
long, and is one of the highest inhabited valleys among the Alps, varying between 5897 ft. above the sea, at
Sils, and 3343 ft. at Martinsbruck. It
is naturally divided into two districts
—the *Ober Engadin* extending from
the Maloja to near Zernetz, and
the *Unter Engadin* thence to the
frontier of Tyrol. There is no other
valley among the Alps where so
many and such populous villages are
to be found at so great an elevation. It has at least 20 important tributary valleys. Owing to its height,
and the barrier of glaciers which
separates it from Italy, the Ober
Engadin possesses a severe climate.
In May 1799 the French artillery
crossed the lakes on the ice. It may
be regarded as one great meadow
from end to end. The hay is cut in
the middle of July, and the cattle,
which are the wealth of the people,
feed on the grass until the snow
descends. The Unter Engadin is
nearly one continuous defile, down
which the road descends rapidly, at
times on a level with the Inn, at
others high up on the edge of precipices. There is very little level
ground, and the lower slopes are
covered with forest. The Engadine is
one of the most opulent valleys

among the Alps; but the source of
its wealth must be sought for in another theatre. The sons of the valley,
for the most part, quit home at an
early age, scatter themselves over the
Continent, and are to be found in most
of the capitals working as pastrycooks,
confectioners, distillers of liqueurs,
clerks in warehouses, keepers of cafés,
and sellers of chocolate. Many of
them thus acquire independence, and
become millionnaires in florins, with
which they return to end their days
in their native valley. They display
their wealth especially in the architecture of their houses, which are distinguished by their large dimensions and
solidity, by their decorations of whitewash, gilding, frescoes, escutcheons,
and elaborate wrought-iron *grilles* and
gates. One reason for their large size
is that they often comprise, under the
same roof, barn, stable, and cowshed.
Owing to the severity of the climate
the cattle must be kept indoors during
the 7 or 8 months of winter. Poverty
is rare, beggary almost unknown; and
the people, who are—except at the
village of Tarasp—Protestants, are
creditably distinguished for their mo-
rality. Their pastors are held in great
respect, but their pay is miserable.

The language is *Romansch* (see
Rte. 81), but German is taught
in the schools; among the returned emigrants, in almost every
village, may be found individuals
speaking French, Italian, or even
English. The wine of the Valtellina may be had good and cheap.
Iva, the liqueur of the country, is
flavoured with the alpine plant *Achillea
moschata*, a species of milfoil. The
valley contains 10,600 Inhab.

Most of the higher sheep-pastures
of the Engadine are let out every
summer to Bergamasque shepherds,
from the valleys Seriana and Brembana,—a wild set of men, but hardy and
honest, clad in homespun brown and
white blankets, and feeding frugally
on polenta of maize-meal, and a little
cheese. They arrive about the beginning of July, with their flocks lean and
meagre, after their long march, performed generally in the cool of the

night. After a solitary sojourn of nearly 3 months, spending often the night as well as the day in the open air, they return home with fattened flocks and long fleeces, which are sold to the wool manufacturers of Bergamo.

Since 1852, when the influx of travellers began to increase, great improvements have taken place in the accommodation. Many new inns have been built throughout the Engadine, and the villages have for the most part entirely lost their characteristic aspect of homely, unpretentious comfort.

Maloja (See Rte. 98).

[This is the starting-place for several excursions and glacier expeditions, On the *Monte Lunghino* (9120 ft.), between the passes of the Septimer, Julier, and Maloja, are the sources of the Maira, the Oberhalbstein Rhein, and the Inn, which respectively flow into the Adriatic, the North Sea, and the Black Sea. A small lake on the E. side of the peak, 2 hrs. from the hotel, is the *Source of the Inn*. The view from Monte Lunghino (on the ridge right of the peak), is very fine.

In the opposite direction a visit to the tarn known as the *Lago di Cavloccio*, may be combined with the Forno glacier. This long ice-stream exhibits all the phenomena of more famous glaciers, except tourists, out of whose beat it still lies. There is often a fine ice-cave at its extremity, and the cirque at its head between the fine peaks of the *Cima di Castello*, 11,160 ft., *Monte Sissone* and the *Cima del Rosso* (all of which can be ascended from it), is a very striking scene (3 hrs.' walk from Maloja). A pass known to the shepherds connects the lower part of the Forno glacier with the chalets at the foot of the Albigna glacier, a fine walk. An active pedestrian might, in place of descending, cross a second pass to Val Bondasca, thus obtaining a complete view of the very grand scenery of this granite chain.

A fine and not difficult glacier pass, *Passo di Sissone*, leads to Val Masino. On the l. from the foot of the Forno glacier, a path ascends to the Muretto pass (Rte. 100).

From Maloja travellers may visit the smooth monotonous *Val Fedoz*, closed by a glacier, and continue along the S. shore of the Lake of Sils by a charming path to Sils Maria, or turn rt. into the Fexthal. From the head of Val Fedoz is a glacier pass to Val Malenco. There is a steep grass-pass into the Fexthal. The ascent of the *Piz della Margna* (10,257 ft.), the bold summit perpetually in sight from the Ober Engadin, is also made from here in 4 hrs. It commands a noble view.]

Leaving Maloja the high road down the Engadine descends a few feet, but the peculiarity of this pass is that on one side there is little descent; in fact, the fall to the lake of St. Moritz, or in 12 m., is only 140 ft. and the village of St. Moritz stands higher than the top of the pass. The traveller soon encounters the infant *Inn* (in Romansch *Oen* or *Ent*), which hastens to pour itself into the *Lake of Sils*, 5887 ft. above the sea, and 3½ m. long, extending as far as Sils. Below the lake a road on rt. leads through *Sils* (*Inn:* Badrutt's H. de la Grande Vue, sometimes let as a villa) to

Sils Maria (*Inns:* Edelweiss, comfortable; Alpenrose, good), the prettiest village in the Engadine. It is situated on a beautiful sheltered meadow under *Piz Corvatsch*, at the mouth of Val Fex, and opposite the rocky peaks of *Piz Lungen*.

[The foot of the Fex glacier is 5½ m. or 2 hrs. from Sils Maria, and is well worth visiting: grand glacier view, with the peaks (from l. to rt.) of *il Chapütchin*, *Piz Tremoggia*, *la Chapütscha*, and *Piz Güz*. Char-road to Curtins (3 m.), whence, the *Fuorcla Fex*, a steep foot-pass leads l. between the Chapütschin and Piz Corvatsch to the Roseg Glacier, and thence to Pontresina. The *Fex Glacier* or *Chapütscha* Pass leads over to Chiesa in Val Malenco. It is an easy glacier pass of 8 hrs., and is often crossed in summer by parties of haymakers coming from the S. valleys. Guide and rope requisite.]

The lake of Sils is succeeded by those of Silvaplana and Campfèr. About 1 hr. brings a carriage to

Silvaplana (H. de la Poste, or Riv' Alta, good; Wilden Mann, cheap; H. Corvatsch; Haus Rizzi), situated on meadows, between 2 lakes, feeders and reservoirs of the river Inn, and in close proximity to fine larch and *Pinus cembra* woods, 5960 ft. above the sea, and 3¼ m. from St. Moritz.

[*Excursions* to the *Inn* in the Roseg-thal (5 hrs.) and Pontresina by the *Fuorcla da Surlei*, 9042 ft. The path ascends S. from the chalets of Surlei towards a glacier on the flank of Piz Corvatsch. Near the foot of the ice it turns l., up rocks to the pass from which the peaks of the Bernina chain and the Roseg glacier are finely seen.

From the pass, *Piz Corvatsch* may be reached in 2 to 2½ hrs. over easy snowslopes; rope and guide necessary.]

Surlei, half-ruined by floods, in 1795, 1 m. distant, on the other side of the lake, commands a distant view of the Bregaglia mountains. There is a beautiful walk from it through the forest to St. Moritz Kurhaus.

Piz Julier, a steep rock peak N. of the Engadine, conspicuous in the view from Pontresina, may be climbed. It was a stiff scramble, but the way has recently been made easy.

From Silvaplana the road skirts the *Campfèr Lake* to

Campfèr (*Inns*: H. Julier; H. d'Angleterre, both good). Fine view of the Campfèr Lake, backed by *Piz della Marqna*. Here two roads branch, one running direct along the mountain side to St. Moritz, the other to the Kurhaus, dipping to the rt. into a prettily wooded gorge. Campfèr is about the same distance as St. Moritz Dorf from the Bad, and an omnibus runs to and fro.

St. Moritz, Bad * on the rt. bank of the river, just above its influx into the green lake of St. Moritz, 5804 ft. above the sea. This establishment,

---

* 'A Season at St. Moritz' (Longmans) by Dr. Burney Yeo, of King's Coll. Hosp., gives a full and interesting account of the medical aspects of St. Moritz.

---

of 80 baths and an hotel which can accommodate 300 persons, was built in 1836. It has recently been greatly enlarged. Near are the H. Victoria du Lac, Hof St. Moritz, and Bellevue. A covered hall, for exercise in wet weather, leads to the 2 springs—the St. Maurice and Paracelsus. The former, the *Old Source*, there is reason to believe, was used by the Romans, and the waters were visited and highly praised by Paracelsus in 1539, by Conrad Gesner and Wettstein. They fell into disuse at the close of the last century, but are now, together with the fine mountain air, considered a remedy for many maladies. The water is chalybeate, sparkling with free carbonic acid, and containing, besides the small quantity of iron, carbonates of lime, magnesia and soda, and sulphate of soda. It is used internally and for baths. As an internal remedy it is tonic and refreshing. Its defect is the large amount of lime in solution, which makes it constipating, and unfits it for congestion of the liver, for which it has been erroneously recommended. For bathing, the water is heated, and owes its virtues to the pungent effects of the free carbonic acid on the skin. The baths are of wood, unless you pay 5 fr. extra for one of marble. Dr. A. Biermann is the physician of the establishment, and speaks English fluently; Dr. Veraguth and Dr. Berry, Surgeon of Division in the Federal army, practitioners at St. Moritz. Early hours are kept, a band playing during the season from 7 to 9 A.M.

The Kurhaus is situated on flat land, at the foot of *Piz Rosatsch*. It has little view, but many pretty walks: one through the woods towards Surlei; another along the side of St. Moritz lake to the *Meierei* (farm), and thence to Pontresina, 4 m.; another of ¾ hr. to a point of view on the slope of Piz Rosatsch.

The Kurhaus hotel is very comfortable: *pension* 10 fr. 25 c. The season begins on the 15th of June and ends on the 15th of September, but in ordinary years some of the finest weather occurs later. During the season the thermometer may sink for 3 or 4 days to 40° Fahr., but the average in the daytime is 57°, and for the first half of October, often in brilliant weather, 52°, and at no time of the year is snow impossible. The winters are severe, but sunny. In 1869 the St. Moritz *Skating Club* (mainly English) commenced their pastime on the 25th of Oct., and enjoyed it until the end of March. On the 24th of Jan. the minimum thermometer registered —13°, and the ice on the lake was 3 ft. thick.

On leaving the Baths the road recrosses the river, and leads up a long mile and a quarter to the village of

St. Moritz Dorf (*Hotels:* Engadiner Kulm, on the ridge at the upper end of the village, very large house, *pension* 9 fr., frequented by English; H. Caspar Badruth (both open all the year). There are many smaller houses in the village and between it and the baths, and the number increases yearly. Among these may be mentioned H. and P. Suisse; H. Belvedere; H. Post; H. Wettstein; H. Gartmann; H. Veraguth, civil landlord, fair cooking, *pension* 7 fr. There are numerous pensions).

St. Moritz, with 500 Inhab., is pleasantly situated, with a S. aspect, on the slope of the mountain, 6100 ft. above the sea. Woods of larch and cembra close picturesquely round it; below, at a depth of 300 feet, is seen the little lake; E. the eye ranges down the Engadine as far as Zernetz, and westward to the peaks beyond the Maloja pass. The landscape, without the grandeur of Central Switzerland or the romantic beauty of the Italian Alps, has a bright and pleasing aspect.

The village is large, and a pleasanter, drier, and generally warmer place of residence than the Kurhaus, though exposed at times to the full force of the bitter winds which sweep along the trough of the Engadine. There is good *trout fishing* in the streams and in the lake. The spinning minnow is a good bait. A *bank* is open at St. Moritz all the year, and

there are several well-provided shops open in summer.

Drs. Holland and Berry (all the year); Dr. Drummond (in summer); Mr. Schaffner, American dentist (in summer).

English and *Roman Catholic Churches* have been built. The E. Ch. is halfway between the Baths and village. In winter E. C. S. in the Kulm Hotel.

Carriages.—1 horse, for the day, 15 fr.; 2 horses, 30 fr.; to Pontresina, 7 to 8 fr.; Bernina Pass, 15, 30; Sils Maria, 8, 16; Maloja, 10 to 12, 20. There is a printed *Tarif*.

An Electric Railway to Pontresina is projected.

Guides.—6 to 8 fr. the day; return, 6 fr. *See* Tarif.

There are many pleasant *walks*:— down the meadows to the gorge and *fall of the Inn*, below the lake; to the Alp *Laret*, 1½ hr. N.E.; to the *Piz St. Gian*, ½ hr. or the *Alpina* restaurant, from which fine views are gained over the upper part of the Inn valley.

Longer *Excursions* are (*a*) to Sils Maria and the Fex Thal; (*b*) *Piz Nair* 10,040 ft., 3 hrs.' ascent. View of the Bernina chain as beautiful as from Piz Languard. (*c*) Up the *Suvretta* valley, over a pass past the little lake (8590 ft.) under Piz Nair, and down the North Suvretta valley, and the valley of Bevers, to Bevers (7 hrs.). Back by road to St. Moritz (see also p. 269). (*d*) *Piz Ot* (see Samåden). (*e*) *Pontresina* (Rte. 100). This is a pleasant walk of about 4 m. From the Kurhaus the new path is along the S. shore of the little lake. From the village the path crosses the stream just below the lake, near the waterfall, and then keeps near the shore of the lake to the Meierei mentioned above, where the two paths meet. The path then bears rather to the l., past the little Statzer See, and then turns to the rt., but going round the foot of the *Rosatch*. Beware of taking one of the paths going up into the wood. Keeping to the rt., Pontresina will soon be seen. The path crosses a foot-bridge below the village. Ascents of *Piz Rosatsch*, 9827 ft., *Piz Surlei*, 10,456 ft., or *Piz Corvatsch*, 11,345 ft.,—all easy for good walkers with a guide.

The road after leaving St. Moritz winds down a wooded zigzag, with charming peeps of the snowy mountain tops, and of the Inn, gently flowing through meadows, to the cheerful hamlets of *Cresta* and *Celerina*—Rom. *Schlaringa*—(*Inn*: H. Murail), where a cross road diverges to Pontresina. Here the valley broadens out to a plain about 1½ m. across, and this continues to be its character as far as Cinuschel, 12 m. lower down. 1½ m. of rather marshy country brings the traveller to

Samâden (5600 ft.) (Rom. *Samedan*), the principal and wealthiest village in the Upper Engadine, with 700 Inhab., shops and lodging-houses. (*Hotels*: H. Bernina, well kept, moderate, open all year. Kurhaus Samâden or Engadinerhof; H. des Alpes; Krone; Innthal, small.)

Eng. Ch. S. in the English chapel. a picturesque edifice designed by Mr. Ernest George, architect, of London.

Here is a curious mansion of the Salis family, now owned by Mons. A. de Planta. These are both old and noted Engadine families. The Salis no longer reside in the valley, but the Plantas do, and are possessed of considerable property and influence. Both families have branches in England. A bear's paw (Planta), of frequent occurrence on buildings, is the crest of that family. Samâden is situated on rising ground under Piz Padella, but opposite a marshy plain through which the river flows in a straight line between artificial banks. Its position is central and convenient, but unpicturesque. Guides, horses, and carriages in abundance. Samâden is 11 hrs. from Coire, 6 from Chiavenna, and 14 from Tirano.

Charges.—Horse to Piz Ot, 9 fr.; Muottas Murail, 8 fr. *Carriage*, 1-horse, to St. Moritz Baths, 5 fr.; Silvaplana, 6; Sils, 8; Maloja, 12; Pontresina, 3.50; Morteratsch Glacier, 7; Bernina Pass, 12; Ponte, 4. For 2 horses the charge is about double: to Coire by the Albula, 120 fr., by the Julier, 130; Chiavenna, 60; Le Prese, 55; Bormio,

130; Tarasp, 55; Davos by the Fluela, 70.

Guide to Piz Ot, 7 fr.; Piz Padella, 5; Muottas Murail, 4; Piz Languard, 8.

[*Excursions.* — (*a*) *Ascent of the Muottas Murail* to the S.E. (8273 ft.), in 2½ hrs. (Rte. 100). (*b*) *Ascent of Piz Ot*, to the N.N.E. (10,660 ft.), in 3¼ hrs. by a good path, but steeper than that of the Piz Languard (Rte. 100); the view is in some respects finer, including the crest of the Monte della Disgrazia, and showing the Bernina group under a more imposing aspect. Horses may be taken half-way, as far as a fountain of delicious water that issues from under a block of granite. A guide is requisite except for experienced travellers. (*c*) The *Bevers Thal* (see below). The old *Church of St. Peter*, N.W., and 300 ft. above the village, contains the tombs of the Salis, Planta, and other Engadine families.]

Diligence to Coire daily. Opposite Samâden is the valley of Pontresina with the road to the Bernina Pass (Rte. 100).

After leaving Samâden, the high road is dull as far as Zernetz. The first village is *Bevers*.

[Hence excursion up the *Bevers Thal*, the most picturesque of the northern glens of the Engadine. Botany interesting: good char-road for some distance up, 6 hrs. going and returning. There are glacier passes from it to the Albula and Julier roads (Rte. 92), and a rough horse-path over a low ridge to St. Moritz, an excursion of 7 or 8 hrs. of which 3–4 on foot or horse.]

4¼ m. *Ponte* (*Inns*: Albula; Krone, both good and moderate), where the Albula road falls into the valley (Rte. 93). Rt. is *Piz Mezzem*, 9728 ft. The possession of the bridge which gives name to this village was desperately disputed by the French and Austrians on the 9th March, 1799. They fought for 6 hrs. in the snow, which in some places was 5 ft. deep. Opposite Ponte is *Campovasto*, or *Camogask*, at the mouth of Val Chiamuera, leading by the *Fuorcla Pass* to the Val da Fain, and by its W. branch, Val Lavirun, by the *Lavirun Pass* to Val Livigno.

¼ m. *Madulein* (*Inn:* Guardaval), and over it the ruined Castle of *Guardaval*, built 1251 by Bp. Volkard of Coire, to guard his estates. The story of its capture by Adam of Camogask is a myth. [N. is Val d'Eschia, and at its head the easy glacier *Eschia Pass* to Bergün by Val Tuors. From the pass, *Piz Kesch*, 11,211 ft., the highest peak in the chain N. of the Engadine can be ascended by fair climbers.]

2¼ m. *Zutz* (*Inns:* H. Concordia, large, good ; Schweizerbund, good ; P. Poult. 5617 ft.) A tower remains of the Stammhaus, or original castle of the Planta family, who, as far back as 1139, held the Engadine in fief. The climate here first becomes milder, Zutz being sheltered from the blasts descending from the Maloja, and on the N. by *Piz Griatschouls* (9754 ft.). The village is consequently gaining in reputation as a winter resort for patients.

1½ m. *Scanfs* (*Inns:* Traube ; Steinbock ; Stern, all poor). Pop. 500. (Val Casanna opens, see Rte. 102.)

1½ m. *Capella.*

[Here the path across the *Scaletta* pass to Davos turns off. There is char-road up the *Sulsanna Thal*, as far as Sulsanna, and thence, bridle-path over the *Scaletta Pass*, 8613 ft. The summit of the pass is a wild plateau, between the *Piz Vadret*, 10,610 ft., and Scaletta glacier rt., and the *Bockenhorn*, 10,038 ft. l.; the actual top being marked by a hut for shelter. There is not much view from the col, but the valleys on both sides are pleasing. The descent lies down the Dischma Thal. From Dürrenboden in the Dischma Thal there is a char-road which falls into the high road about a quarter of a mile above Davos. From Capella to Davos is about 8 hrs. Guide not wanted. Good walkers, with a rope, may avoid the dull part of the pass and obtain a magnificent view by crossing the glacier of Piz Vadret (*Valloria Pass*). The S. peak of *Piz Vadret* is easily climbed; the N. is difficult.

In 1322 a troop under the Count of Montfort were pursued with great slaughter over the Scaletta Pass. They had crossed the mountains on a raid from the Engadine to Davos, but were met and defeated at Kriegsmatten in the Dischma Thal. Relics of this fight have been found in recent times.

The *Sertig Pass* also leads from the valley of Sulsanna to Davos in about 9 hrs. On the Fontana Alp, at the head of the valley, this path diverges l. from that to the Scaletta, following the l. bank of the stream. From the col, 9062 ft., are seen the Piz Kesch and Porchabella glacier. From Dörfli there is a char-road.]

Cinuschel is the last village of Ober Engadin. The Inn valley here narrows, and the road enters a pineforest. Near Brail the road crosses a stream from the N. by a new stone bridge — *Punt Auta* (Ponte Alto), which marks the division between Upper and Lower Engadine. High up on the l. may be seen the old Punt Auta of wood, by which the old road spanned the ravine. 2 m. lower down our road crosses the Inn by a wooden covered bridge. The pointed Piz Linard first comes in sight a short way before entering the expanded basin, covered with crops of barley, in which lies

7½ m. *Zernetz* (Bär, good), at the junction of the Spöl with the Inn.

This large village, 4912 ft. above the sea, was destroyed by fire in 1872, except the church, which stands detached.

[An *excursion* may be made to *Val Cluoza*, just within the opening of the Val Fuorn. Densely covered below with primeval forest, the haunt of the bear, it branches into 2 desolate glens, aptly called *Valley of Rocks* and *Valley of the Devil* (del Sasso : del Diavel). The latter (to the l.), with huge and strangely-coloured dolomitic cliffs, is perhaps the wilder and more striking. There is a fine pass at its head to Val Fiera and Livigno (7–9 hrs.' walking).

Up the valley of Fuorn runs a carriage-road by the *Ofener* or *Buffalora Pass* to Sta. Maria in the Münster Thal—7 hrs'. walking (6 hrs'. drive to

Mals). In its ascent from Zernetz the road rises high above the ravine of the Spöl. The Ofen branch enters a pine-clad valley with one solitary house—the humble but hospitable *Ofen Wirthshaus.* This is 2¼ hrs. from the *Ofener Pass,* 7070 ft. The Münster Thal is reached at Cierfs in 1½ hr., and 2 hrs. more bring you to *Santa Maria.* By keeping to the rt. branch of the stream in ascending from Zernetz, the Val Livigno is entered, and from the head of this Italian valley you may return to Switzerland, either by a pass to the S. which takes you into the Bernina road at Pisciadella, or by one W. into the Val da Fain, leading to the Bernina Houses, or by the Casanna Pass (Rte. 102).]

On quitting Zernetz the road crosses the Inn on an iron bridge and traverses a picturesque wooded defile. The vista is closed by the snowy Piz Linard.

3¾ m. *Süs* (*Inns:* Schweizerhof; Rhætia—both fair; Fluela), a dirty village, surmounted by a castle, of which the foundations may be Roman. [Here is the junction of the road from Davos by the *Fluela Pass* (Rte. 96, diligence daily), and the footpath by the *Vereina Pass* from Klosters (Rte. 94). The latter, 8133 ft., and badly marked, requires a guide.]

1¾ m. *Lavin* (*Inns:* H. Linard; Steinbock), a village rebuilt after a fire in 1869.

[N. rises the pyramidal *Piz Linard,* 11,208 ft., the highest of the Silvretta Alps, and of the entire range N. of the Engadine, excepting Piz Kesch, which is 3 ft. higher. It therefore commands an uninterrupted view, and the path has been so improved by the Swiss Alp. Club that it presents no unusual difficulties. The mountain stands between the parallel valleys of Sagliains and Lavinuoz. The course from Lavin is by the latter, and by a side glen called Glims, to the foot of the S. arête, the only point from which the peak is easily accessible. The summit is a narrow ridge terminating N., at the highest point in a precipice. The ascent is made from

either Süs or Lavin, but it is necessary either to start at 3 A.M., or to sleep in a hut halfway up the mountain. Planta, of Süs, is a good guide.

Under Piz Linard opens the narrow glen of *Val Lavinuoz;* a good path leads to the glacier. Competent icemen will find no difficulty in turning its icefall, and thus reaching the upper level of the Silvretta glaciers and the passes leading to Klosters. These, however, are generally approached through *Val Tuoi,* which affords an easier route.]

From *Piz Miezdi* (9593 ft.), S. of Lavin, an ascent of 4 hrs., the Silvretta Ferner and long vista of the Engadine are well seen. The names *Lavin, Zutz,* and *Ardetz,* are said to be Romansch corruptions of the Latin Lavinium, Tutium, and Ardea.

Beyond Lavin the mountains slope to a precipitous chasm, which forms the bed of the Inn, and the villages are often perched on steep heights, as in the case of

Guarda (*Inns:* Sonne; Silvretta, fair; good guides). Here *Val Tuoi* opens with fine glacier passes to the Prätigau and Montafun. *Piz Buin,* one of the highest of the Silvretta Ferner can be climbed in 6 hrs.

5¼ m. *Ardetz* (*Inns:* Sonne; Kreuze; Krone), situated high above the river, but commanded by a castle called Steinsberg, rising above it on precipitous rocks. N. is *Piz Cotschen,* 10,925 ft., a grand point of view. A steep descent under threatening cliffs brings the road again to the level of the Inn. The scene is very striking.

[Near Ardetz, *Val Tasna,* one of the most imposing glens of the Silvretta group, opens N. It leads to the *Futschöl Pass,* a fine glacier pass by which the traveller attains Galthür, the highest village in the Austrian Paznaunthal. On his rt. in descending is the noble peak of the *Fluchthorn* (11,142 ft.), a difficult ascent. This chain and the valleys on its N. are too little visited by English travellers.]

5¼ m. *Tarasp-Bad* (4182 ft.) (*Bathhouse and Hotel*), one of the largest establishments in Switzerland, built by a company at a cost of 60,000*l.*; 200 rooms, 300 beds, 70 baths. The *Mineral Springs*—2 saline-alkaline, resembling those of Kissingen and Vichy; 2 acidulous-chalybeate (tonic), nearly identical with those of St. Moritz. The *Climate* is alpine and bracing, but mitigated, and the air not so dry or rare as in the Upper Engadine. *Eng. Ch. S. Resident physician.* The Kurhaus lies between the road and river, at the bottom of a deep trench, in a situation with little view and few charms for lovers of the picturesque. To most English tastes the villages of *Schuls* and *Vulpera*, placed respectively at the same height on the N. and S. slopes of the valley, offer preferable residences. In selecting between them it should be borne in mind that the N. hillsides are bare and dull, but command fine views, while S. of the Inn, at a height of 500 to 1500 ft. above its channel, stretch a series of wooded terraces, affording shady and picturesque walks which can be extended into the wild glens of the dolomitic range. At Schuls, therefore, the traveller finds a fine view and a dull neighbourhood; at Vulpera, charming near walks, but a somewhat dreary prospect of the opposite N. chain.

S. of the Inn, 500 ft. above the river, stands

Vulpera (*Inns :* Bellevue ; Vulpera, both good ; Alpenrose : *Pensions :* Karl, Steiner, Tell). On the same side of the valley lies

Fontana, the largest of the hamlets forming the commune of *Tarasp*, 4596 ft. above the sea (H. Tarasp, new). It is situated below the ruins of *Tarasp Castle*, formerly residence of the Austrian Bailiffs, and now the property of M. A. de Planta. It was rebuilt after 1625 when it was destroyed by lightning. There is a pleasant path to Ardetz by the rt. bank of the Inn.

The neighbourhood is distinguished for the number and potency of its mineral springs, rising on a line of fault between the gneiss and mica-slate for a distance of 3 m., and not far from them, in places, issue *Mofettes*,

or jets of carbonic acid gas, destructive to insects, mice, or birds that approach them ; one, which strangers generally visit, is about 15 min. walk from Schuls, near the old road to Fettan.

1½ m. beyond *Tarasp-Bad*, on the high road looking S. is

Schuls—Rom. *Schuol* — (*Inns :* in Ober-Schuls, Belvedere, very good ; H. Post ; H. and P. Schuls ; Piz Chiampatsch, all good) the most populous place in the Engadine, containing 900 Inhab., and grandly situated. Below the old ch., 2 bridges over the Inn and the Clemgia lead to Tarasp.

Physician : J. Pernisch, M.D., Wurzburg, speaks English, attends Tarasp Kaths.

[These villages or *Tarasp-Bad* may be used by the traveller as a centre from which numerous ascents and passes can be made.

Walks. a. Take the river-path to the castle and return by *Vulpera*. b. N. over the *Fettan Alp* to Val Tasna, and return by the ruined castle of Steinsberg at Ardetz. c. Walk or drive down the valley to *Sins*, perhaps the neatest village in the Engadine, with old frescoes on the walls of the houses and a fine view. Return by Weisshaus. d. To the plateau of *St. Jon*, on the rt. bank of the river,—a lawn of mossy turf, with an old ruin, the whole surrounded by forest.

Excursions. a. N. of Schuls is Val Clozza, running up to the *Minschun*, 10,076 ft., and *Piz Chiampatsch*, 9580 ft. The latter, which rises N.E. of the valley, may be ascended in about 4 hrs., and commands an excellent view of the Lower Engadine, and of the glaciers of the Silvretta Alps, and Orteler country. Ladies can ride to within ½ hr. of the top, and the path above is easy and safe.

b. On the S., the Münster Thal may be reached by *Val Scarl*, a narrow and savage valley, in the woods of which bears are still found ; the distance to Sta. Maria being about the same as that by the Buffalora Pass. There is a very rough car-road for some distance.

c. Just E. of Val Scarl the *Val Lis-*

channa offers a wild rte. to the extensive Lischanna glacier and *Piz Lischanna*, a dolomite peak. A hut has been erected near the glacier. Descent can be made by *Piz Cornet* into Val Scesvenna, returning by the Scarl Thal.

d. Piz Pisoc (10,427 ft.), with snowy crest, which fronts the Kurhaus, requires a good guide. It has been ascended in 4½ hrs. from *Tarasp-bad* by Val Zuort. The lower cliffs are surmounted by means of a snow-filled couloir. The general steepness and intricacy of the rte. are the difficulties.

e. The *tour of Piz Pisoc* is made by Val Scarl, Val Minger, and Val Plafna. 6 to 8 hrs. through very wild scenery.

f. The pine-woods of the *Val d'Assa*, below Remüs, enclose a beautiful waterfall, and 5 m. up the valley, in a deep cavern, is the *Fontana Christaina*, an intermittent spring, flowing at 9 A.M., at noon, and towards evening.]

Beyond Schuls the road runs through beautiful scenery, to

6 m. *Remüs* (burnt in 1880) where a stone bridge, replacing the old wooden *Punt Piedra*, crosses the Wraunka Tobel. Above it is the ruined *castle* Tschanuff, burnt by the Austrians in 1475; N. rises the *Muttler* (10,827 ft.), commanding a noble view. Near Remüs two glens join the Inn valley. S. *Val d'Uina*, a wild recess leading to passes to Scarl or Mals. The road crosses the Wraunka Tobel, a deep gorge N. of *Val Sinestra*, leading by the Fimberjoch to Ischgl in the Paznaunthal.

The valley of the Inn is magnificent on approaching

7½ m. *Martinsbrück* — Rom. *Punt Martina* — (*Inn :* H. Demoth), the last place in the Engadine. A footpath follows the l. bank of the river into the *gorge of Finstermünz*, which well deserves to be visited either on foot or by carriage, driving round by Nauders, by all who do not intend to traverse it on the way to Innsbruck. The road ascends a wooded eminence, the boundary between **Switzerland** and Tyrol, and enters

the *Austrian Frontier* a short distance from Nauders.

[From Martinsbrück, an interesting excursion may be made to the *Samnaunthal*. The mouth of this remote valley belongs to Austria, but its upper hamlets, holding a population of some 300 souls, are Swiss. During half the year they are cut off from all access to their countrymen, except through Austrian territory. The entrance to the basin in which *Compatsch* (a homely *Inn*) lies is through a picturesque defile. Two passes, easy in summer, communicate with the Lower Engadine, near Remüs.]

4¼ m. *Nauders* (*Inn:* Post, tolerable); a village splendidly placed, where the valley opens wide enough for beauty, at the meeting of the glen which leads to the low carriage-pass into the Vintschgau with the trough of the Inn. At a distance of about 15 m. the great Orteler Spitz fills up the end of the valley "like a tall pale mountain phantom." (See HANDBOOK FOR SOUTH GERMANY.)

ROUTE 100.

SAMÂDEN TO PONTRESINA, TOURS OF PIZ BERNINA.

	Eng. m.
Samâden.	
Pontresina	3

The *Bernina Alps* separate the valleys of the Engadine and Bregaglia from the Valtellina, running from the head of the Lake of Como, E.N.E., to the low Foscagno Pass, which connects Livigno and Bormio. They are naturally divided into three subgroups by the Muretto and Bernina Passes. The *Monte della Disgrazia*, 12,074 ft., is the highest of the W. division, which contains the second in length of the glaciers, the Ghº di Forno. In the central and most important group, *Piz Bernina* attains 13,294 ft., *Piz Zupo*, 13,120 ft., and there are five peaks above 12,000, and many above 11,000 ft. The highest summit

E. of the Bernina Pass is the *Cima di Piazza*, 11,713 ft.

From *Samåden* (Rte. 99) the road over the Bernina Pass ascends by the rt. bank of the Flatzbach. There are fine fir-forests in this valley 7000 ft. above the sea, mostly consisting of the *Pinus cembra*.

[There is a footpath from St. Moritz to Pontresina, which crosses the Inn between the lake and waterfall, and leads by the Statzer See and through a wood.]

Pontresina (*Inns :* H. Roseg, a large house at the entrance of the village, good, fine view ; H. Saratz, good ; H. Languard ; H. Enderlin ; H. Pontresina and Bellavista; Krone, Weisses Kreuz, all good, in the village ; Steinbock, in the upper village, homely; there are several good lodging-houses. The Krone and H. Enderlin are open all the year. Skating-rink in winter. *Eng. Ch. S.*

Pontresina, 5915 ft. above the level of the sea, with 400 Inhab., stretches along a high bank above the Flatzbach, opposite the entrance of the beautiful Roseg valley. It is most fortunately placed, surrounded by magnificent glacier scenery. The inhabitants have had the wisdom to lay out many roads and walks, accessible to ladies and children, who may climb the neighbouring heights by easy zigzags, or visit the gorge and cascade of the Flatzbad. The tariff for carriages is high. 1-horse carriage for 2 persons —to Samåden 4·50 c., St. Moritz 7, Maloja 16, Bernina Houses 6, Poschiavo 35, Le Prese 35. For glacier expeditions Pontresina is admirably placed. *See* printed Tariff. Hans Grass is President of the Guides Society, and by far the best man. As a body, the Pontresina men are inferior in skill and manners to the best guides of the Bernese Oberland, and, unless they have changed their practice recently, are apt to be careless in the use of the rope. Enderlin, host of the Kreuz, a collector and vendor of botanical specimens. Flüry is a fair photographer.

Excursions.— a. Muottas Murail. —

This is a short walk or ride of 1½ to 2 hrs. to a brow on the hill above the junction of the Inn and the Flatzbach. It commands one of the best general views of the neighbouring valleys and the mountains.

b. Piz Langard (Lungo Guardo), 10,715 ft., is far more easily reached than most points of equal height, and the panorama is most extensive, though less striking than some others in the neighbourhood. It not only includes the whole of eastern Switzerland and part of Tyrol, but in clear weather extends westwards to Monte Rosa and Monte Viso. Horses (9 fr.) may be taken 2-3rds of the way. A guide is scarcely necessary. The ascent occupies 2½ to 4 hrs. according to the pace. The path leaves the high road to the Bernina, at the upper village, and then strikes up through rocks and into a forest. Above the forest the path lies along a valley which runs up towards *P. Albris.* Piz Languard rises in a steep-sided cone, and has to be climbed by a zigzag path. The return may be varied by crossing a snow pass to Val da Fain and the Bernina Houses (about 6 hrs.). The stony valley is ascended to the glacier under P. Albris: up the ice for a short way, and then over the ridge l. On the other side bear rt. along the bottom to *La Pischa,* a waterfall down the crags overhanging the V. da Fain (rich in rare plants).

c. The *Roseg Glacier* is reached through the beautiful *Val Roseg.* There is a char-road to within a mile of the glacier, where a small *Inn* has been built 2½ hrs'. walk from Pontresina. The glacier itself is for a long distance safe and easy, though the getting on to it often requires some care, and ladies may spend an agreeable day in exploring its beauties, or in enjoying the magnificent view from its l. (N.W.) bank. It is a more fatiguing excursion to an alp called Agagliouls (middle point), separating the two glacier streams of Roseg and Tschierva. A guide (10 fr.) is necessary. A circle of snowy peaks surrounds this Alp ; the Tschierva, Morteratsch, Bernina, Roseg, Sella,

Chapütschin, and Corvatsch. Travellers now prefer to reach a point high on the l. bank of the glacier, where a hut has been erected by the Swiss Alpine Club at a spot known as Mortel. Splendid specimens of the Arolla pine (*P. Cembra*) grow in the forests of Val Roseg, especially on the north-western mountain slopes over the glacier, some 7000 ft. above the level of the sea.

[From the inn a path slants W. up the mountain towards the *Fuorcla da Surlei*, a pass of 5 hrs., to Silvaplana, with magnificent view. It is perfectly easy. From the Fuorcla *Piz Corvatsch* can be ascended over an easy glacier (guide and rope necessary). A steep pass, the Fex Fuorcla, leads W. of Piz Corvatsch to the Fex valley in 8½ hrs.]

d. The Morteratsch Glacier, with its tributary the *Pers Glacier*, extends for 6 miles from its sources under Piz Bernina and Piz Zupo. A favourite excursion is to an island of rock—" the Jardin " of this district—called *Isla Pers*, 8169 ft., above the junction of the Pers with the Morteratsch glacier. The glacier is about 4 m. from Pontresina, along the high road to the Bernina Pass, but there is a footpath through woods and meadows running by the l. bank of the river. Drive (40 min.) or walk to the *fall of the* Bernina stream on the east side of the valley, a short distance below the foot of the glacier. Or walk over the second bridge from Pontresina and along the W. side of the valley. A good restaurant at the head of the valley. Then up (¼ hr.) to the right through forest to the gl.-side. Thence along the gl., the E. lateral moraine, and gl. again, to the junction of the two glaciers. On the l. bank of the Morteratsch Glacier, under Piz Morteratsch, at a spot called Boval, a substantial hut has been built for the use of mountaineers. A rocky slope has to be climbed to the Isla. From this point the *tour of the Diavolezza* is continued, by crossing obliquely the Pers Glacier and then making a rough ascent over rock to the *Diavolezza Pass*, 9670 ft. The views are most magnificent. The descent is by

a steep snow-slope to a hollow containing a lovely blue lake, into which ice is precipitated from an overhanging glacier. The track then bears to the l. and descends to the Bernina Houses (where the carriage may be sent). This tour is often made in 6½ hrs. from the Bernina fall to the Bernina Houses, but is easier and finer the reverse way. Guides necessary.

e. The Black and White lakes at the head of the Bernina pass, the Bernina fall, and Morteratsch gl., may be visited in 1 day's drive; or from the *Bernina Hospice* the traveller may walk to the *Grüm Alp* (a restaurant) for a wonderful view of the Palü glacier, and towards Italy.

From the Sassal Masone rt. of the Grüm Alp, and about the same time from the Hospice, the view is still finer.

Mountaineers will find plenty of occupation around Pontresina. The range which runs S. from the village rises from *Piz Chalchang* through *Piz Tschierva* and *Piz Morteratsch* to the *Piz Bernina*. W. of this monarch of the chain are *Piz Roseg, La Sella*, and other peaks; E. the crags of the *Crast' Agüzza, Piz Zupo, Piz Palü* and *Piz Cambrena*.

Piz Bernina (13,294 ft.) was first climbed in 1850 by Herr Coaz of Coire, who, leaving the Bernina Houses at 6 A.M., reached the top in 12 hrs., and returned by moonlight. Messrs. Hardy and Kennedy share the honour of having shown the way to their countrymen in 1861. Starting at midnight from the Boval hut, they mounted the rocks between the Pers and Morteratsch glaciers, to the upper slopes, which they traversed to the foot of the Crast' Agüzza. Of late years a shorter rte. has been followed by the centre of the ice-fall and the long N.E. ridge. This route is liable to be rendered impossible by changes in the ice, and is sometimes exposed to the fall of séracs. The route taken up the final peak varies according to the state of the snow. In some years it is attained with little difficulty by the N.E. ridge ; in others the ascent of the face requires care and steadiness in *all* the climbers.

The *Piz Zupo*, 13,120 ft., is approached like Piz Bernina by the Morteratsch icefall. The final ascent by the W. ridge is alone difficult. The rocky tooth of the Crast' Agüzza is a stiff rock-climb.

Piz Palü, 12,835 ft., is ascended by the Pers Glacier, and a steep snow-wall, and is difficult. It is preferable to pass over the triple crest from the Bella Vista Pass and descend by the Pers Glacier. This crest is often a cornice, and must not be too closely approached.

Piz Morteratsch, 12,316 ft., can be ascended in 8 or 9 hrs. from Pontresina on the W., by way of the Roseg glacier, and is not difficult. On the E. the mountain is exceedingly steep. It was here, in 1864, that Prof. Tyndall, with two friends and the guides Jenni and Walther, were carried down on an avalanche, and narrowly escaped with their lives. Danger may be avoided by keeping to the rocks to the left of the ice-slope.

Piz Roseg. The highest peak (12,936 ft.) is accessible by a very narrow arête, which connects it with a lower summit on the N. The latter is climbed from near the Sella Pass by steep snow and rocks (4 hrs.) The passage of the arête is a more formidable undertaking, and was effected in 1863 for the first time, by Messrs. Moore and Walker with Jakob Anderegg.

Comparatively easy snow peaks, suitable for unpractised climbers, are *Piz Corvatsch, Piz Tschierva,* and *Piz Chapütschin.* Good guides necessary.

The following are the principal glacier passes—

1. From *Val Roseg* :—

a. The *Fex Fuorcla* from the Roseg glacier *Inn* to Sils Maria by a pass between the *Chapütschin* (11,132 ft.), and *Piz Corvatsch* (11,345 ft.), and down the Fex valley, 8½ hrs.: easy.

b. The *Chapütschin Pass,* E. of Piz Chapütschin, little used. A difficult descent over steep rocks leads to the

névé of the Fex glacier, whence the traveller may turn rt. to Sils Maria, or l. to Val Malenco.

c. The *Sella Pass* (see *post*).

d. The *Tschierva Sattel.* The passage of the rocky curtain connecting Piz Bernina and Piz Roseg, is a *tour de force* attractive only from its extreme difficulty. It leads to the Scerscen Glacier.

e. The Fuorcla Prievlusa between Piz Bernina and Piz Morteratsch leading to Boval is also difficult.

2. From the *Morteratsch Glacier—*

a. Crast' Agüzza Sattel. This is a very fine but difficult pass, the descent on the S. side lies over steep rock to the Scerscen glacier. It is best taken from the S., and may be used in combination with the Sella Pass in making the tour of Piz Bernina in a single day from Pontresina.

b. The *Zupo* and *Bellavista Passes.* These two high glacier passes lead respectively W. and E. of the peaks of the Bella Vista to the Upper Fellaria glacier. The latter is the easier.

It is also possible to pass from the Pers Glacier to the Fellaria glacier, over Piz Palü.

TOUR OF PIZ BERNINA.

The lower passes, the Muretto and Canciano.—A very small proportion of the visitors to the Engadine undertake this tour. Yet those who have not seen Monte della Disgrazia from the crest, or better still from the S. slopes, of the Bernina chain, have missed the finest view in eastern Switzerland. The natives of the Engadine, however, naturally do nothing to encourage their guests to wander out of it; and the people of Val Malenco have only lately shown any enterprise in preparing for tourists. The chief obstacle to the tour of Piz Bernina becoming as popular as that of Mt. Blanc or Monte Rosa, is the bad state of the Muretto path, which was formerly much used for commercial purposes, and might well again be made practicable for animals. At present it is necessary for the traveller to walk at least as far as Chiareggio, and to obtain horses there would be a matter requiring careful previous arrangement. Until the Muretto is used by horses, many will prefer the easy glacier pass over the Fex Glacier, a sort of St. Théodule (Rte. 99).

The *Muretto Pass*, Maloja to Chiesa, 8 hrs. An hour from the Hotel the foot of the great Forno Glacier (Rte. 99) is passed on the rt. An ascent over rocks and beds of snow leads (1½ hr.) to the pass (8616 ft.), a dreary scene. A short descent brings into sight the superb mass of the Monte della Disgrazia streaming with glaciers, a view justly compared to that of Monte Rosa from the Moro. Beautiful views of the neighbouring ranges are before the eyes during the whole descent to Chiareggio (wretched *Inn*), where the ruins of long disused stables and storehouses show the former importance of the pass.

[The *Passo di Mello*, a fine and not difficult glacier pass, leads to S. Martino in Val Masino, in 10 hrs. The *Disgrazia* has been ascended from Chiareggio, but is better attacked from the **W.**]

A somewhat monotonous track leads in 3 hrs. through pine-forests, and then along bare slopes to *Chiesa* (3480 ft.), in a beautiful situation at the junction of two valleys (Albergo Olivo, fair). Guides may be found here for the ascent of *Monte della Disgrazia*. The excursion to the *Lago di Palü* and *Monte Nero* (Rte. 101) is easy and well worth making (7 hrs.). There is a fine but long glacier route by Val di Torre to Val Masino, passing over the shoulders of Monte della Disgrazia. Carriage-road to Sondrio (Rte. 101).

Passo di Canciano. Chiesa to Poschiavo, or Le Prese; horse-track, 7½ to 8 hrs.; guide desirable, owing to the intricacy of the path. *It is described below in the reverse direction.*

"Poschiavo to Pass 4 hrs.; 4 down to Chiesa. The descent to Lanzada is intricate, through deep and broken valleys. [Ascending from Lanzada, wrong turnings may easily be taken.] From the Bernina road, very steep to the two chapels of *Selva* (1 hr. 20 m.). Then level for 25 min., with waterfalls rt. and l. Then rt., steep forest, in 25 min. to a chalet, where the path turns l. Passing in 10 min. another chalet, it circles l., then mounts rt. into the final glen, bearing N.W. l. are curious rocks under Piz Canciano, one like a tower. Stream is crossed to a third chalet on l. bank, (35 min.). Thence ascent of valley keeping to the rt. The col (1 hr.) is a notch just under, and E. of the glacier of *Piz Canciano*. Grand view of the Fellaria glacier and Piz Zupo. Descend rt. bank of Poschiavino, with *Mte. Spondacia* l., to some huts under savage rocks (1 hr.). Here cross the stream, and down steep path of stone, amid rounded and polished rocks, and *rocs perchés*, to Val Campo Moro (35 min.).

"Opposite is *Mte. Sasso Moro*, rt. the ice-fall of the Fellaria gl. Crossing the torrent, the path leads to a basin with cluster of chalets (15 min.). Beyond it a gorge, and descent, wonderful in its scenery, to another secluded basin and group of chalets, where Val Lanterna joins on the rt. Thence, over a low gap, and down a very steep gully to the narrow but fertile valley of Lanzada, with villages and grand view of the *Disgrazia*. Lanzada (2.15), with very rough *Inn*. Thence about 2 m. to *Chiesa*."

From the Canciano Pass the mountaineer may in 2½ hrs. reach the *Piz Scalino* (10,925 ft.), an outstanding summit commanding a glorious panorama. A direct descent to Lanzada by the Prabello Alp may be found.

Another somewhat longer route is by the *Rovana Pass*, crossing the crest N. of the Canciano, and at the foot of the *Piz Verona* (11,352 ft.), which is easy of access from this side.

From Poschiavo the traveller may return to the Engadine by the Bernina Pass (Rte. 101).

HIGH-LEVEL TOUR OF PIZ BERNINA.

This is a long glacier expedition, leading through magnificent snow scenery, and free from danger in fine weather, if the rope is properly used (which it is not always by Pontresina guides).

Before the glaciers were so well known, it was customary to pass a night at the *Fellaria* chalets, thus adding at least 4 hrs. to the expedition, but dividing it into two days. Those who wish to break the expedition may now do so at the Club-hut built by the Italian Alpine Club on the rocks between the Scerscen and Fellaria Glaciers, which is sometimes used for the ascent of Piz Bernina from the side by the Crast 'Aguzza Sattel. It is necessary to sleep either at the *Inn* in the Roseg Thal, or at the Bernina Hospice.

From the latter the *Cambrena Sattel*, a gap in the ridge S.E. of Piz Cambrena is reached in 2½ hrs. From here the traveller attains by the upper slopes of the Palü Glacier, the névé basin from which it and the Fellaria Glacier alike descend. Leaving on his rt. the gaps known as the Bellavista and Zupo Passes, he descends to the lower plateau of the Fellaria Glacier. This is connected by a snowy terrace (*Club-hut*) with the magnificent cirque of the Scerscen Glacier, overhung by the ruddy crags of Piz Bernina and Piz Roseg. On the l. the Disgrazia and the Lombard Alps are fine objects. On the rt. the steep rocks leading to the *Crast' Agüzza Sattel* are passed, and beyond the base of Piz Roseg a gentle ascent up a slope full of concealed crevasses leads to the *Sella Pass*, a broad gap affording easy access to the head of the Roseg Glacier, the descent of which (3 hrs.) seldom presents any serious difficulties. It is useless to give exact times for an expedition in which all depends on the firmness of the snow. Under the most favourable conditions, 11 hrs.' walking must be allowed from the Bernina Hospice to the Inn in the Roseg Thal.

Either from the Fellaria or the Scerscen Glacier, it is possible to descend into Val Malenco.

ROUTE 101.

PONTRESINA TO COLICO, BY THE BERNINA PASS AND THE VALTELLINA. VAL MALENCO. VAL MASINO.

	Miles.
Bernina Häuser	6
Poschiavo	15
Le Prese	3
Tirano	8
Sondrio	16½
Morbegno	16
Colico	11
	75½

Two *diligences* daily to Tirano, in 7½ hrs. Opposite the Morteratsch Glacier (see Rte. 96), the road begins to ascend beside the waterfall, commanding a superb view of the highest summits of the Bernina.

6 m. from Pontresina is the cluster of buildings known as the *Bernina Houses* (6723 ft.). [On the l. is the opening of the *Val da Fain*, a favourite resort of botanists, through which a path leads over the *Stretta Pass* (8150 ft.) to the Val Livigno, on the way to Zernetz, or to Bormio by San Antonio (*Inn*), Trepalle, and the Foscagno Pass (Rte. 102).]

From this the road ascends gradually over a somewhat dreary waste, passing on the l. Val Minor, with view of Mt. Pers and the gl. of Cambrena.

On rt. lies the *Black Lake*, fed by springs and sending its waters into the Black Sea, separated only by a low bank from the *White Lake*, receiving the drainage of the Cambrena Glacier and discharging into the Adriatic. The road mounts round the head of a small ravine to

4½ m. The *Bernina Hospice*, 7600 ft. An excellent *Inn*, resorted to by travellers for whom the air of the Engadine is not sufficiently bracing.

[*Excursion* to the *Grüm Alp*, 1½ hr. distant by a path, at first descending to and skirting the lake, and afterwards winding round the hills. This is a grand point of view of the icefall of the Palü Glacier. From the alp (restaurant), Poschiavo and its valley are seen far below. The old horse track, the shortest from Pontresina to Poschiavo, descends in 2 hrs. through very fine scenery. The steep descent is divided by the beautiful level pasturage of Cavaglia. Below this the torrent plunges into a romantic gorge.]

Close to the Hospice is a tarn, *Lago della Crocetta,* and 5 min. above it the bleak

Bernina Pass, 7658 ft., between the *Cima di Carten* and *Piz Cambrena.* Directly rt. a ridge called *Pizzo Campaccio* divides the head of the southern valley into Val Agone and Val di Pila, the road descending the one, the waters of Lago Bianco the other. [Up the Val Agone a road, said to be practicable for chars, leads over the *Forcola Pass* to Livigno in about 5 hrs.] The descent of the Bernina-road, in places protected by galleries, is steep to

4¾ m. *La Rösa* (a poor mountain *Inn*), whence it passes by the opening of Val di Campo.

[To *Bormio* by the *Passo di Val Viola* 8 to 9 hrs. Leave the high road l. below La Rösa (if ascending it below Pisciadella), and ascend the Val di Campo, which leads to the Val Viola, a continuation of it at a higher level. Near the head of Val di Campo the path branches (l. up the Val Mera to *Livigno* by a pass of 8776 ft., W. of the 3-peaked *Corno di Campo*): our route is straight on, and over the l. of the head of the Val di Campo, passing rt. the charming little *Lago Saosco,* encircled by rocks and forest, and the grand precipice of the *Corno.* There is no inn between La Rösa and the Baths of Bormio. About 3 hrs. down the Val Viola the traveller meets the track descending from the Foscagno Pass (Rte. 102), and at Isolaccia, 6 m. from Bormio, a rough car-road.]

On the l. are seen the precipitous peaks of the Pizzo di Teo and Pizzo di Sena.

Pisciadella, the first hamlet near the mouth of Val di Campo. Hence the descent is rapid and picturesque to

San Carlo, where the old horse-path falls in ; 1 m. further is

9 m. *Poschiavo* (*Inns :* Croce Bianca, or Posta, a curious old house, good and reasonable ; H. Albrici), a town of 2000 Inhab., built in the Italian fashion. It is the principal place in the valley, and mainly supported by the traffic of goods. Rom. Cath. Ch., date 1494. Above it, on a height, are the ruins of the castle of Olgiati.

Nearly one-third of the inhabitants of this populous valley are Protestants ; but owing to the jealousy of the Roman Catholics, their church is almost a fortress, and capable of defence against attacks. The language is a corrupt Italian.

[*Excursion* to the *Pizzo Sassalbo,* 9377 ft., E., an ascent of about 5 hrs., noble view. For the Canciano and Rovana passes, Piz Verona and Piz Scalino, see Rte. 100.]

3 m. *Le Prese,* 3215 ft. above the sea, at the N. end of the little lake of Poschiavo, famed for its large trout. Le Prese is frequented for its charming situation, sunny climate, and sulphureous waters. The *hotel* is comfortable, with excellent table-d'hôte: *pension,* 7½ to 8 fr., and the *Bathing establishment* is well managed. With the exception of the road skirting the lake there are not many *near* walks. Excursions to the pilgrimage *Church of S. Romerio,* from the S. end of the lake. The climate is cool and pleasant. Boats and trout-fishing. 1-horse carriage to Tirano, 10 fr.

3¾ m. *Brusio* (*Inn:* Posta), with 1146 Prot. and R. C. Inhab. On quitting the lake, the torrent Poschiavino passes through a very narrow defile. It is a raging torrent, and, as it approaches the Adda, is restrained by stone dykes, but even these have proved insufficient to protect its banks. Passing *Campaccio,* the Italian custom-house at *Campo Cologno,* and the frontier at *Plattamala,* where the ruinous fort is worth a visit, the road enters the Valtelline at

3½ m. *Madonna di Tirano* (*Inn:* S. Michele, better than those at Tirano), a village known for its picturesque church, which for upwards of 3 centuries has been the resort of pilgrims. An avenue of poplars leads to

¾ m. *Tirano* (1500 ft.) (*Inns:* Italia ; Porta Vecchia), on the road from the Stelvio to the Lake of Como, 6000 Inhabitants.

The traveller going towards the Lake here enters the *Val Tellina*, long subject to Canton Graubünden, but since 1797 part of Lombardy.

This is one of the largest and most fertile of the southern Alpine valleys. Its beauty, however, is rarely appreciated by those who roll along the interminable stretches of the hot and dusty high road.

At Tresenda the *Aprica* road branches off on the l. to Edolo. 12 m. further the traveller reaches

Sondrio, Stat., a town with many imposing buildings (*Inns:* Posta, comfortable, grape-cure may be taken here; Maddalena), 6500 Inhabitants.

The twin rock-peaks seen at the head of Val Malenco are those so conspicuous as snow cones at the head of the Rosegthal in the view from Pontresina. There is a fine view from the castle. On the further side of the Adda is a church built A.D. 537. The town has suffered much from inundations of the Malero torrent, descending from the S. glaciers of the Bernina. It is now restrained by a deep artificial channel.

[A good road leads to *Chiesa* in Val Malenco, 3 hrs.' drive through very beautiful scenery. The Inns at Chiesa have been improved (Albergo Olivo, best). Guides are found here, and it is the best head-quarters on the S. side of the Bernina, though too far from the glaciers to be convenient for high mountain excursions. The traveller who does not propose to cross the Muretto or Canciano Pass (see Rte. 100) should ascend to the charming Lago di Palü and the ridge of Monte Nero, commanding a noble view of the peaks of the Bernina and the *Monte della Disgrazia*. The latter summit can be reached by sleeping in Val Torre, but is more generally attacked from the Club-hut in Val Sasso Bisolo (see below). Passes also lead from Sondrio to the Bergamasque valleys.]

A *Railway* descends the valley from Sondrio to Colico on the Lake of Como, 25½ miles.

Stat. Ardenno Masino, 10 miles.

[A good road leads up Val Masino to the Baths of Masino, which have long been a place of resort to North Italians. A steep ascent of 11 m., through scenery continually growing in savage wildness, leads to San Martino at the fork of the valleys. Shortly below the junction the remains of a "berg-fall" are passed. One of the blocks has been since the 17th cent. reckoned the largest of its kind in the Alps. This "lapis colosseus," as an old author calls it, measures 250 ft. in length, 120 in breadth, and 140 in height. The *Val dei Bagni*, the western and shorter of the two glens, is some 2 m. in length. In a deep basin at its head, surrounded by wooded cliffs, lie the *Baths* (3750 ft.). The accommodation is fair, and the food excellent; prices high. No glacier guides.

The pedestrian may cross rough passes to *Val Codera*, a fine glen, and Colico ; or by two passes to Castasegna. The mountaineer may, by fine but difficult passes, reach the Bondasca Glacier and Promontogno, in Val Bregaglia, or may ascend the highest of the bold granite peaks which rise N. of the Baths.

The *Piz Cengalo* (formerly known as the *Punta Trubinesca*, 11,106 ft.), despite its formidable appearance, is easy of access to moderate climbers by its N.W. ridge in 5-6 hrs., and commands a very singular and beautiful view extending over the whole Upper Engadine, the greater part of the Bregaglia, and a large portion of the Lake of Como, seen perhaps from no other summit of similar elevation. It is the highest of the two rocky peaks seen in the distance from St. Moritz.

The eastern branch of Val Masino leads from San Martino to 3 glacier passes; (1) the *Zocca*, leading to Vico Soprano (see Rte. 98) ; (2) the *Sissone Pass* to Maloja, about 11 hrs. ; and (3) the *Passo di Mello* to Chiareggio in Val Malenco. From this glen, or from the Club-hut in Val Sasso Bisolo, a glen which joins Val Malenco lower down, the noble peak of the *Disgrazia* may be reached.

The ascent of the ridge of the mountain is sometimes difficult, and always requires good guides. The view is one of the finest in the Alps.

For further information, see Freshfield's 'Italian Alps.']

5 m. *Morbegno Stat.* (*Inn:* Post, good),with a fine church.

Passes lead hence to Val Brembana.

The rail runs between finely-shaped ranges, Monte Spluga N., Monte Legnone S., until it enters the marshes of the Adda and reaches *Colico Terminus*, 10 miles (see Rte. 116).

ROUTE 102.

ZUTZ TO THE BATHS OF BORMIO, BY LIVIGNO, THE CASANNA AND FOSCAGNO PASSES.

The remote valley of Livigno is watered by the Spöl, a tributary of the Inn, and belongs geographically to Switzerland. The stream, however, forces its way out to Zernetz through a deep and difficult gorge, while very low and easy passes connect its head-waters with Bormio. The upper valley has consequently shared the political fortunes of the Val Tellina, and is now—with the exception of some pasturages near the Splügen pass—the only territory N. of the Alps forming part of the Italian kingdom.

The easiest ways to Livigno from the Engadine are by the Stretta (Rte. 101) or Casanna pass. The latter (8332 ft.) is a good horse-track, leaving the high road near Scanfs, from which the *Inn* at San Antonio is reached in 6 to 7 hrs. The ascent lies through a finely wooded glen, and from the pass the Orteler group is well seen. In 1635 the Duc de Rohan, the Huguenot leader, led an army across the Casanna pass, with which he fell on and defeated the Austrians in the Val Tellina. The descent lies through the green pasturages of Val Canaria.

[The pedestrian who does not object to a rough and pathless walk may see some very wild scenery by following to its head *Val Trupchum*, a densely wooded valley branching l. from Val Casanna. The ridge under Piz Fiera is climbed, and a descent found into Val Fiera, through wonderful dolomite scenery, between lemon-coloured cliffs crowned by red and grey pinnacles.]

Val Livigno is a secluded pastoral basin, 6200 ft. above the sea. The broad green valley, sown with rich brown chalets and framed in pine-woods, broken here and there by a glimpse of snowy peaks, presents an unusual and pleasing landscape. Near *San Antonio* there is a clean but homely *Inn*.

[A path follows the gorge of the Spöl to the Ofenhaus, 4 hrs. To Zernetz there is a fine route by the *Passo del Diavel* in 8 hrs.; to the Bernina road easy horse-tracks, leading to the Bernina Houses, or La Rosa, in 4 or 5 hrs. Gaps between snowy peaks of 10,000 to 11,000 ft., practicable for mountaineers, lead to the chalets at the head of Val Viola, on the path from La Rösa to Bormio.]

The traveller bound for Bormio ascends in 1 hr. to *Trepalle* (6850 ft.), one of the highest hamlets in the Alps. A short ascent leads to the *Foscagno Pass*, whence there is a rough car-track to Bormio (3 hrs.), joining that of Val di Dentro, at Semogo. The *Cima di Piazza* (11,713 ft.), the highest summit between the Bernina and Orteler Groups, rises opposite, and is a magnificent object.

In 4½ hrs. from Livigno an active walker will reach the great Stelvio road and

The *Baths of Bormio*—Hotel and pension, very good. Baths of various kinds, and at any temperature. Dr. Fideli speaks English. The village of Bormio is old and curious. Its church of Combo contains frescoes of considerable merit, particularly of the 4 Evangelists, on the roof of the choir, painted apparently by some pupil of Romanino of Brescia. A local school of painters seems to have flourished in this valley. Several churches have curious frescoes of the 15th century, and some are very picturesque. See HANDBOOK FOR S. GERMANY.

INDEX TO SWITZERLAND.

Routes marked with an *asterisk* are *reversed*.

LONDON:
PRINTED BY WILLIAM CLOWES AND SONS, LIMITED,
STAMFORD STREET AND CHARING CROSS.

MURRAY'S ENGLISH HANDBOOKS.

HANDBOOK—LONDON AS IT IS. Maps and Plans. 16mo. 3s. 6d.

HANDBOOK—ENVIRONS OF LONDON—Including 20 miles round the Metropolis. Two volumes. Post 8vo. 21s.

HANDBOOK—ENGLAND AND WALES. Arranged alphabetically. 16s. One Volume. Post 8vo.

HANDBOOK—EASTERN COUNTIES—Chelmsford, Harwich, Colchester, Maldon, Cambridge, Ely, Newmarket, Bury St. Edmunds, Ipswich, Woodbridge, Felixstowe, Lowestoft, Norwich, Yarmouth, Cromer, &c. Maps and Plans. Post 8vo. 12s.

HANDBOOK—KENT—Canterbury, Dover, Ramsgate, Rochester, Chatham. Map and Plans. Post 8vo. 7s. 6d.

HANDBOOK—SUSSEX—Brighton, Chichester, Worthing, Hastings, Lewes, Arundel. Map and Plan. Post 8vo. 6s.

HANDBOOK—SURREY AND HANTS—Kingston, Croydon, Reigate, Guildford, Dorking, Boxhill, Winchester, Southampton, New Forest, Portsmouth, and The Isle of Wight. Map and Plans. Post 8vo.

HANDBOOK—BERKS, BUCKS, AND OXON.—Windsor, Eton, Reading, Aylesbury, Henley, Oxford, Blenheim, and The Thames. Map and Plan. Post 8vo. 7s.

HANDBOOK—WILTS, DORSET, AND SOMERSET—Salisbury, Chippenham, Weymouth, Sherborne, Wells, Bath, Bristol, Taunton, &c. Map and Plan. Post 8vo. 10s.

HANDBOOK—DEVON—Exeter, Ilfracombe, Linton, Sidmouth, Dawlish, Teignmouth, Plymouth, Devonport, Torquay. Maps and Plans. Post 8vo. 7s. 6d.

HANDBOOK—CORNWALL—Launceston, Penzance, Falmouth, The Lizard, Land's End, &c. Maps and Plans. Post 8vo. 6s.

HANDBOOK—GLOUCESTER, HEREFORD, AND WORCESTER—Cirencester, Cheltenham, Stroud, Tewkesbury, Leominster, Ross, Kidderminster, Dudley, Bromsgrove, Evesham. Map and Plans. Post 8vo. 6s.

HANDBOOK—NORTH WALES—Llangollen, Bangor, Carnarvon, Beaumaris, Snowdon, Llanberis, Dolgelly, Cader Idris, Conway, Aberystwith, &c. Map. Post 8vo. 7s.

HANDBOOK—SOUTH WALES—Monmouth, Llandaff, Merthyr, Vale of Neath, Pembroke, Carmarthen, Tenby, Swansea, and The Wye, &c. Map. Post 8vo. 7s.

HANDBOOK—NORTHAMPTONSHIRE AND RUTLAND—Northampton, Peterborough, Towcester, Daventry, Market Harborough, Kettering, Wellingborough, Thrapston, Stamford, Uppingham, Oakham, &c. Post 8vo. 7s. 6d.

HANDBOOK—DERBY, NOTTS, LEICESTER, & STAFFORD—Matlock, Bakewell, Chatsworth, The Peak, Buxton, Hardwick, Dovedale, Ashborne, Southwell, Mansfield, Retford, Burton, Belvoir, Melton Mowbray, Wolverhampton, Lichfield, Walsall, Tamworth. Map. Post 8vo.

HANDBOOK—SHROPSHIRE AND CHESHIRE—Shrewsbury, Ludlow, Bridgnorth, Oswestry, Chester, Crewe, Alderley, Stockport, Birkenhead. Maps and Plans. Post 8vo. 6s.

March, 1878.

[Continued.

CPSIA information can be obtained at www.ICGtesting.com
Printed in the USA
BVOW09s1424150714

359257BV00018B/507/P